MY COLUMBIA

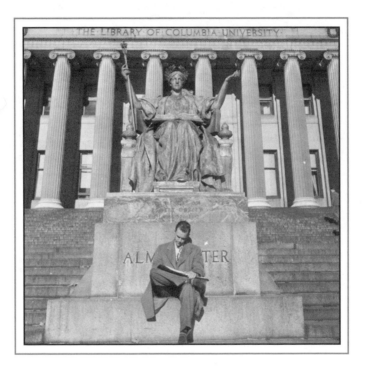

MY COLUMBIA

Reminiscences of University Life

Edited by Ashbel Green

A Columbia University Publication

A Columbia University Publication

Series editor: Jerry Kisslinger, Columbia University

Series creative director: Sandy Kaufman, Columbia University

Design: Office of University Publications

A complete CIP record is available from the Library of Congress

Printed in the United States of America.

ISBN 0231-13486-X

c 10 9 8 7 6 5 4 3 2 1

p 10 9 8 7 6 5 4 3 2 1

Every effort has been made by the publisher to clear the required
permissions for the selections in this collection. Please contact the
publisher for any necessary corrections which will be made at the next opportunity.

Contents

Introduction

O f the hundreds of thousands of students who have attended Columbia University in the 250 years of its existence, not a few have written about their experiences at the institution in their autobiographical memoirs. The idea behind this book was that many remarkable writers who have attended or taught at or administered Columbia would have interesting points of view about what they encountered in their years on Morningside Heights—and before.

Other books have described life at Oxford, Harvard, and Yale, but these tended to consist of commissioned articles. The choices that have been made for this volume are part of the authors' lives; thus the Columbia experience comes out of the context of those lives.

In truth, there was so much available that, to keep *My Columbia* to a feasible length, a great number of excerpts could not be published in this volume. I have read through more than 100 books by Columbia authors and have regretfully been unable to use many worthy pieces.

I hope that what is offered here is representative of the schools that make up the university, but most items were written by men and women of Columbia and Barnard Colleges. Also included are reminiscences of those involved with the schools of law, medicine, architecture, business, journalism, and Teachers College, as well as the graduate faculties. The reader will note that there is nothing subsequent to the early 1970s—we will have to wait for the memoirs of the past three decades to catch up to that period.

Not all enjoyed their time at Columbia, as a few of these recollections make plain. But the notion is that what the university provided these men and women had a substantial impact on the shaping of their lives. It may go too far to call these experiences unique, but I hope they will be regarded as thoughtful and thought-provoking.

Beyond remembrances, I have chosen some poetry and excerpts from novels and, in one instance, a series of letters between an undergraduate and her mentor. Some of the phrases may seem incorrect, but I have essentially left the texts as they were originally printed.

My Columbia is not designed to be an exercise in nostalgia, but rather a celebration of an extraordinary institution whose future looks to be as rich as its past. "A university," Benjamin Disraeli once said before the House of Commons, "should be a place of light, of liberty, and of learning." These selections are meant to go beyond those noble goals, to show how students and teachers felt about a definitive time in their lives.

Ashbel Green

MY COLUMBIA

George Templeton Strong

George Templeton Strong was a New York attorney and Trustee of Columbia College. While a college sophomore, he began a daily diary that he would keep for 38 years. Eventually running to 2,250 pages, it offers valuable insights into nineteenth-century New York life. The Diary of George Templeton Strong—*co-edited in 1952 by Columbia historian Allan Nevins—is excerpted here. The comments in darker type are by Professor Nevins.*

Strong's diary begins the day he returned for his second year as a member of the class of 1838 at Columbia College. For the next three years college was all-important, and beginning with brief jottings he developed into so eager a diarist that he left one of the most extensive, honest, and amusing records ever written by an undergraduate.

Columbia, beginning its eighty-first year in 1835, was situated in the residential section of New York on College Green, a quiet two-block fenced area shaded with sycamores and bounded by Murray and Barclay Streets, College Place (West Broadway) and Church Street. Park Place led eastward one block to "The Park," now City Hall Park. The college edifice, a long, narrow building facing south, three and a half stories in height and surmounted by a small astronomical observatory, had been built in 1756–60. King's College and its student body, never numbering over thirty, had been housed in it; the Revolution halted instruction, and during the British occupation the building was used as a military hospital. The college, revived and renamed Columbia after the war, had enlarged the structure to provide residences for the faculty, but for more than a century, beginning about 1800, furnished no dormitory accommodations for students, a fact which largely restricted enrollment to residents of New York City.

Although King's College had graduated men who played important parts in the Revolution and the establishment of the new republic, the school had been preponderantly Anglican, and therefore Tory. After the war the people to whom it would have looked for support had had their property expropriated and were in exile in Canada and England. Although President Washington had given his blessing to Columbia by attending the commencement of 1789 a few days after his inauguration, and the new corporation included Hamilton and other Revolutionary patriots, the new wealthy and ruling classes of New York did not show any haste in coming to its support, and for well over half a century Columbia remained relatively poor. The student body, homogeneous during this period, was drawn largely from the homes of the wealthier professional and commercial citizens.

The faculty in Strong's time consisted of five men of marked individuality who taught a fixed course of study heavily weighted with the classical disciplines: William Alexander Duer, president, who lectured to seniors on constitutional jurisprudence, and Professors Charles Anthon, James Renwick, Henry James Anderson, and John McVickar. Various other men held the title of professor in Columbia College in these years, but their position was actually that of privat-dozent; they were principally employed elsewhere and were available to students for instruction in subjects outside the regular curriculum at extra fees. We need not accept all Strong's adolescent judgments of the stern gentlemen composing the faculty; in later years he revised many of these estimates himself.

Matriculation was conducted by the president himself; each student signed his name in the order of his scholastic rank in a large folio volume, promising to abide by the statutes of the college. At the beginning of the term in 1835, President Duer admitted one hundred students: twenty-two Seniors, twenty-three Juniors, twenty-nine Sophomores, and twenty-six Freshmen. The annual tuition fee was $90.

October 5, MONDAY. 108 Greenwich Street, New York. Went to college at half-past seven and had the pleasure of remaining there *solus* till half-past nine. Matriculated for the Sophomore year, and had the most atrocious pen to write my name with that mortal ever beheld. *Afternoon,* cloudy again, and rainy tomorrow, I suppose. Purchased some jars for an electrical battery.

October 6. As I anticipated, raining most diabolically. How on earth we shall get to the church I can't imagine, for it blows and rains tremendously, and no signs of clearing, either. I suppose we shall have to go in funereal style—in carriages—and the faculty in a hearse.

Afternoon. We went in omnibuses. In spite of the weather, the church was very crowded and very hot. The speaking was better than usual, far better than at the [New York] University last July. The music was capital. I took the first classical medal. Got home at half-past three.

Columbia at this time held its commencement at the beginning of the academic year. The exercises described above were in St. John's Chapel on Varick Street, and twenty-three were graduated. Top man was Orlando Harriman, Jr., afterwards an Episcopal clergyman and the father of Edward Henry Harriman (1848–1900), railroad executive, whose great estate, Arden, at Harriman, New York, was given to Columbia in 1950. The best-remembered graduate of 1835 was the literary scholar, Evert Augustus Duyckinck.

October 10, SATURDAY. Went to college and entered the library and took out a book, as the statutes allow. Came home and struck off for Staten Island; went on top of the pavilion and was back by half-past one. *Afternoon*—fixed jars for battery.

October 12. Taking notes with Renwick. His room puts one in mind of Virgil's vision of Tartarus, and it smells like everything horrible.

October 13. Recited Aristophanes for the first time; very amusing when read as it ought to be. Purchased an electrometer for my machine.

October 14. Recited Plautus this morning for the first time. My Delphini edition helps me along gloriously and the variorum notes are well worth examining.

October 16. Geographical lecture with Anthon. Renwick gave us a lecture today in a voice like the wheezings of a broken-winded bellows.

October 17, SATURDAY. Out all the morning. Made a good haul in the numismatological line. *Afternoon*—coated the rest of the jars. I suppose, though, that this battery is destined to turn out like the generality of my other attempts, and that is, not amounting to much. My electrical machine is out of order too, so I don't see how I am to charge the battery if I should finish it.

October 21. . . . An idea has entered into my mind, viz., to make a plate electrical machine, for my own is as much out of health as ever. Plate glass is most atrociously dear, though. Looking at my *Scriptores Græci Minores* which arrived yesterday; beautifully printed, but Gaisford might have raised a little more commentary while he was about it.

October 27, Afternoon. Went out after a turner to make the frame of my machine—31 Greene Street up an alley five feet high and one broad— and of a most unchristianlike dirtiness; the man has an unpronounceable

Dutch name which I forget. They have just come from Germany and can neither speak English nor understand it decently. As to the frame, if it gets done at all, I fancy it will be fit for nothing but firewood, for I couldn't get the man to understand me, though I preached for half an hour.

October 29. Made a cruise up to Greene Street. Frame "ees noot fee-neeshed yet, sare." McVickar in the course of his lectures said that he had a work bearing the date 1473, the oldest in the country. *Quære de hoc:* I have one of 1470.

November 3, TUESDAY. The frame of my machine finished at last; answers pretty well. We have been recording all this week. Tomorrow Herodotus.

November 5, THURSDAY. Went to college; got there at half-past eight. At about quarter of nine, nearly all the Freshmen and Sophomores being assembled, a party of the former posted themselves near the chapel gallery door and commenced a racket: two benches kicked downstairs, hats, books, shot and slates with a variety of missiles flying in every direction. Enter the worthy Mr. Dugan, with his usual "less noise, gentlemen," but in two minutes more the hubbub was recommenced in a sort of treble note that sounded like the yells of a strangled cat. Thirty boys (young gentlemen, I mean) with vigorous lungs, screaming in chorus, is no joke, and when some of the Sophomores joined, the noise was "prodi-gi-ous." Re-enter Dugan, and exit again with the same effect as before; then comes a noise of something advancing upstairs like distant thunder, and the Praeses himself makes his appearance, like a porpoise in a gale of wind. "All attend me in my room, if you please, gentlemen"—and exit the Prex leaving all of us, and especially the Freshmen, in a state of considerable bother. In two minutes, behold us all comfortably seated in the President's room, which has at least one advantage over the outside of the chapel door, and that is a good fire. Then comes a preachment from the Prex which I shall not take the trouble of writing down, but as the essence of a letter usually lies in the postscript, so the substance of his speech lay in the end thereof, which was as follows: "I shall therefore expect to see you all before the Board tomorrow morning at ten." Very agreeable prospect this. However, the Prex said that there were some amongst us that he couldn't, wouldn't, shouldn't and didn't suspect of being such spooneys as to make a noise for nothing at all, but still he wanted to investigate the matter and so we must come. I was certainly quiet enough at the time and I guess I can prove it. I suppose a majority of the others will scrape off by lying; it's human nature. I thought that I should be in a predicament, while in the Prex's room, if he attempted to decimate us, for I found that as we sat I was precisely the tenth from the end. It's an unpleasant business altogether, for though I don't see what they can prove against me or what they can accuse me of, unless of having been in the second story when some fools were making a noise in the third, I suppose I shall get into a scrape; it's just my luck.

November 7, SATURDAY. Went to college, and after trotting up there in the rain and hearing some absurd attempts at speechification in the chapel, went downstairs, and after a while we were summoned into the Sanctum Sanctorum. Present besides the Praeses, Anthon, Renwick, McVickar and Anderson. Roll called—there being forty-five of us—then the venerable Prex proceeded to make a speech at us in which he told the learned Board what naughty boys some of us had been, and then asked us separately whether we had any hand in it, to which question about half, and myself, of course, among the number said No, and the other half made some very wry faces and said Yes. Then the Praeses wiped his spectacles and blew his nose and told us that he shouldn't say anything more about it and we might be off, concluding with "I presume, gentlemen, that you are satisfied?" addressed to the Honorable Board, to which weighty question McVickar replied "Yessar," Renwick gave his head a jerk sideways, Anthon gave his ineffable skull a movement of six inches from the perpendicular, and Anderson, who had nearly fallen asleep during the Prex's harangue, replied by an inarticulate grunt. We cleared out as fast as possible and went down into Renwick's room to see some experiments on combustion with chlorate of potassium, in oxygen, chlorine, etc. We had not oxygen enough, so Douglass and myself stayed to make some. Remained there till two o'clock and then came off. *Afternoon.* Went to college again. Got there before Douglass, and burned my fingers with some phosphorus like a fool and stained my clothes with sulphuric acid like a spooney. Got home at six.

November 21, SATURDAY. Was voted in unanimously last night at the Philolexian. Walked up after college with John Hone and made a splendid haul of antique coins in exchange for minerals, thirty specimens, including one of the Ptolemies. On my way home encountered Chittenden, brought him home, and fired off some more of the phosphuret of lime, thereby scenting the house from top to bottom. At college Spear engaged to come down this afternoon, and as he invited himself, I thought it only fair to direct him to *180 Greenwich.* He found the place notwithstanding, and when he came I saluted him with the remainder of my phosphuret of lime, thereby increasing the stench to infinity, so that when my honored parents entered the house they were nearly knocked down backwards.

November 25. The glorious Evacuation Day, glorious in one point, at least, and that is that it allows us to kick up our heels all day at our leisure.

Douglass came down in the course of the morning and we posted up to college together to try some chemicals. The laboratory was locked up, so we got in the window and spent three hours there making musses and stenches without number.

November 26. Exactly a year ago today that I commenced my gymnastic operations. This is first-rate weather for exercising. I wish the establishment was downtown.

November 27. FRIDAY. At about six it began to snow and I took up my march for the Philolexian. I found nobody there, everything dark and locked up, and I was anticipating a comfortable sojourn in the snow for an hour or so, when Dugan's little imp came to light the fire and dust the room, and it was soon quite respectable. They soon collected and at about seven the meeting was called to order by the worthy Mr. [Russell] Trevett, the vice-president, the president himself being absent. Then I made myself scarce, and was summoned into the room again soon after to witness the sublime ceremony of initiation into the occult mysteries of Philolexianity. I thought I should have had the impoliteness to laugh in the face of the august officers while the "ceremony" was going on ... and no wonder, the vice-president staring in my face like a bullfrog in spectacles and Mr. Secretary fumbling about for a pen, and at last finding one that wrote like a poker. Then began the other matters; the subject for debate was: "Are literary reviews advantageous to literature?"—decided affirmatively. The debate was a very good one and the *Observer* was read; a composition (absurd) followed, and then a miscellaneous discussion.

Few American colleges of the nineteenth century were without a fair of literary societies with Greek names. Columbia's, called Philolexian and Pei-thologian (established in 1802 and 1806 respectively), had meeting rooms in the college building, and each boasted a library of some two thousand volumes of current fiction and belles-lettres, fields entirely unrepresented in the college library. *The Philolexian Observer* was a manuscript magazine read at meetings. Strong wrote for it constantly, frequently making use of articles in the obscure journals and books to which his insatiable reading led him. He was an enthusiastic member of the society, and rarely missed a meeting.

December 4, FRIDAY. Anthon has been highly savage all week, but today he was absolutely ferocious; the geographical lecture was highly edifying. *Evening.* Went off to the society in company with Papa, who was condemned to be vice-president of the Webster meeting. As it rained, our meeting was rather thin. The debate was rather dry. "Ought this country to aid Texas?"—decided in the negative. Afterwards some young scamps thought proper to vote in Mr. Satan as president of the anniversary committee. Rejected on the ground that he did not belong to the society. *Quære de hoc:* I am inclined to judge that he does.

December 10, THANKSGIVING DAY. Went to church; after church went up to the Bowery to see the "splendid collection of wild Hanimals" which arrived there. I do not think that it is quite as well attended as it was last year. Otherwise it is precisely the same old thing over again.

December 12. Diabolical weather, snowing and rainy. Woke up as stupid as possible. Rode to college and began arranging for the experiments. Renwick came in soon after. The experiments began as soon as the class came. All that we did was to make some most atrocious stenches with olefiant gas and phosphoretted hydrogen. A carriage was sent for me about one, and I came home. *Evening.* Sufficient for the day is the evil thereof, and on this principle I did not look at a lesson as I felt too stupid for studying. Took up the *Mysteries of Udolpho* instead and fell asleep in the midst of winding passages, unearthly sounds, ghosts, devils, distressed maidens and tyrannical ruffians—no great compliment to Mrs. Radcliffe's powers to entertain.

December 16. Went to college and bargained with [Richard Henry] Douglass for a gold Arabic coin of his. *Evening.* At about nine o'clock there was an alarm of fire. Papa went to bed notwithstanding it looked near the office. The fire is evidently an extensive one and shines splendidly on the shipping and houses in the rear. Mr. [Rensselaer] Havens has just come to call Papa up, as the office is in danger. It is a tremendous fire, by his account. They have just left. *Eleven o'clock.* Mr. Lambert has just come in. He thinks the office out of danger, but the fire is still raging in Exchange, Pearl, Front Streets, etc. It is very cold—mercury at zero—and by his account the fire is yet unchecked. *Twelve o'clock.* The fire as we can see from the front windows is still raging, and Papa has not returned. I would give a good deal to be there. I shall turn in, notwithstanding, as my anxiety for the office cannot prevent me from feeling very sleepy.

December 17. Very bad news. Papa came in this morning at five and his return woke me up. The Exchange, the office, everything in that quarter is going, and by his account we are in some danger, as the fire is unchecked. I went to college at eight. The smoke is hanging over all that part of the city, and from what I could learn, the fire is unchecked. At half-past eleven I left the college and walked down with Douglass, whose father's store is burnt. Such a scene of confusion I never witnessed. The fire is still raging in South Street. Papa has got a new office at 12 Wall Street. Brought Douglass home with me. *Afternoon.* Went up to the region of the fire, which is not yet got under. It presents a splendid spectacle.

December 18. Everybody is talking of the fire, which is now got quite under. The citizens have turned out as patrols. The loss is estimated at thirty million dollars. Went to the society in the evening.

Strong's account of the Great Fire of 1835 is somewhat disappointing in the light of his later interest in such spectacles. He soon became an enthusiastic fire-goer and in time developed a real connoisseurship, disdaining mean and uninteresting fires and taking a great interest in the really spectacular ones, of which he wrote as careful a review as he would of a stage performance. In common with most enthusiasts, he was usually on the side of the fire, but when the big store directly at the rear of his home burned on the night of May 30, 1837, he worked valiantly, and wrote a fine tribute to the firemen.

December 22. A considerable number of the students missing, having taken the holidays into their own hands. After the third hour, I asked McVickar, the "extempore Prex," to let the upper classes have the use of the chapel for a class meeting (to draw up a petition and have a little sport). He enquired "What was the object?" and then observed that "we might have it, but that he could grant nothing contrary to the letter of the statutes." It seems that he gave different directions to Cerberus, for after the fourth hour when we went upstairs we found ourselves locked out, and a row ensued. Mr. Dugan in vain endeavored to keep the peace and the rebels were only dispersed by the appearance of McVickar himself, who was coming in a great hurry, looking like a turkey cock in a gale of wind. He was evidently resolved to inflict a speech upon us, but on reaching the scene of action he found that all had vanished and that he had nothing but Dugan and Dugan's black dog on whom to expend his oratory, quite a disappointment.

December 23. Went to college. On entering the chapel we found Mack's audience to consist of *no* Seniors, two Juniors, five Sophomores and thirteen Freshmen. He waited as long as he decently could in hopes of a fresh supply, but in vain, until in the midst of the prayer three Sophomores walked in one after another, each accompanying his entrance with a tremendous slam of the door. No objection was made; he was glad enough to get an audience on any terms. Went into Anthon's room. He looked round the room—evidently in a considerable degree of wonder— "No more students in the chapel, Mr. Strong?" "No, sir," said I. "Well, gentlemen," was the reply, "of course, as a professor I can't give you such a piece of advice—altogether contrary to my principles—but nevertheless, if I was in your place, 1 rather think I should vanish out of the back door." We took his advice, of course.

Michael Pupin

1883 COLUMBIA COLLEGE

The physicist Michael Pupin taught at Columbia from 1889 to 1935. A prolific inventor, he was awarded 34 patents between 1894 and 1923. A Serbian immigrant from Austria-Hungary, Pupin studied X-ray radiation for a time before turning his attention to electromagnetics. He pioneered innovations that extended the range of long-distance telephone communication and allowed the transmission of multiple messages over the same circuit. Pupin was a founding member of the National Research Council, formed at the behest of President Woodrow Wilson. His autobiography, From Immigrant to Inventor, *won the 1924 Pulitzer Prize and is the source of this selection.*

The Columbia boat-race victory at Henley occurred in 1878. By that time I had already with the assistance of Bilharz finished a considerable portion of my Greek and Latin preparation for Princeton—or, as I called it, for "Nassau Hall." My change of allegiance from Princeton to Columbia was gradual.

Columbia College was located at that time on the block between Madison and Park Avenues and between Forty-ninth and Fiftieth Streets in New York City. One of its proposed new buildings was, according to report, to be called Hamilton Hall, in honor of Alexander Hamilton. When I learned this I looked up the history of Alexander Hamilton. One can imagine how thrilled I was when I found that Hamilton left the junior class at Columbia College and joined Washington's armies as captain when he was barely nineteen, and at twenty was lieutenant-colonel and Washington's aide-de-camp! What an appeal to a young imagination! Few things ever thrilled me as much as the life of Alexander Hamilton. Every American youth preparing for college should read the history of Hamilton's life.

One cannot look up the history of Hamilton's life without running across the name of another great Columbia man, John Jay, first Secretary of Foreign Affairs, appointed by Congress, and the first Chief Justice of the United States, appointed by Washington, and a stanch backer of brilliant Hamilton. Chancellor Livingston, another great Columbia man, administered the first constitutional oath of office to Washington; he also completed the purchase of Louisiana from France. The more I studied the history of Hamilton's time the more I saw what tremendous influence Columbia's alumni exerted at that time. Cortlandt Street being near Trinity Church, I walked there to look at the Hamilton monument in the Trinity churchyard. This monument was the first suggestion to me of a bond of union between Trinity Church and Columbia College. Before long I found many other bonds of union between these two great institutions.

Every time I passed Columbia College in my long walks up-town and looked at the rising structure of Hamilton Hall, I thought of these three great Columbia men. What student of Hamilton's life could have looked at Hamilton Hall on Madison Avenue without being reminded of the magnificent intellectual efforts which two young patriots, Hamilton and Madison, made in the defense of the federalist form of the new American Republic? It happened thus that my memory of Nassau Hall at Princeton gradually faded, although it never vanished. The famous boat-race victory of a Columbia crew at Henley would not alone have produced this effect. It was produced by three great New York men of the Revolutionary period who were alumni of "Columbia College in the City of New York." Columbia had at that time a school of mines and engineering, separate from the college. I was much better prepared for it than for Columbia College, thanks to the evening lectures at Cooper Union, and to my natural inclination to scientific studies, but I imagined that the spirit of Hamilton, Jay, and Livingston hovered about the academic buildings of Columbia College only

☼ ☼ ☼

As the time went on I saw that entrance into Columbia College was within easy reach so far as my studies were concerned. But here again the old question arose which I first asked myself three years before, when the train, taking me from Nassau Hall to the Bowery, was approaching New York. "Social unpreparedness" stared me in the face. I could not define it, but I felt its existence. I shall try to describe it. Columbia College, a daughter of great Trinity Church, an alma mater of men like Hamilton, Jay, Livingston, and of many other gentlemen and scholars who guided the destiny of these great United States—can that great American institution, I asked myself, afford to enroll a raw Serbian immigrant among its students; train me, an uncouth employee of a cracker factory, to become one of its alumni? I thought of the first sentence in the Declaration of Independence, but it did not persuade me that I was an equal of the American boy who was prepared to meet all the requirements necessary for entrance into Columbia College, because I was convinced that in addition to entrance examinations there were other requirements for which no prescribed examinations existed. The college of Hamilton and of Jay expected certain other things which I knew I did not have and could not get from books. A jump from the Cortlandt Street factory to Columbia College, from Jim and Bilharz to patriarchal President Barnard and the famous professors at Columbia, appeared to me like a jump over Columbia's great and venerable traditions. Old Lukanitch and his family and their American friends helped me much to start building a bridge over this big gap, but the more I associated with these people, who lived around humble Prince Street, not far from the Bowery, the more I saw my shortcomings in what I called, for want of a better name, "social preparedness." "How shall I feel," I asked myself, "when I begin to associate with boys whose parents live on Madison and Fifth Avenues, and whose ancestors were friends of Hamilton and of Jay?" Their traditions, I was sure, gave them an equipment which I did not have, unless my Serbian traditions proved to be similar to their American traditions. My native village attached great importance to traditions, and I knew how much the peasants of Idvor would resent it if a stranger not in tune with their traditions attempted to settle in their historic village.

* * *

Several incidents in my college career bear upon the interesting feature of athletics in American college life, and I shall describe them later even at the risk of appearing egotistical. This feature is characteristically American and is quite unknown on the continent of Europe.

Eight hours each day I devoted to study: three in the morning to Greek, three in the afternoon to Latin, and two in the evening to other studies. It was a most profitable summer outing of over three months, and it cost me only thirty dollars; the rest was paid in sawing and splitting of kindling-wood. Whenever I read now about the Kaiser's activities at Doorn, I think of my summer activities in 1879, and I wonder who in the world suggested my scheme to William Hohenzollern!

During the last week of September of that year I presented myself at Columbia for entrance examinations. They were oral, and were conducted by the professors themselves and not by junior instructors. The first two books of the Iliad, excepting the catalogue of ships, and four orations of Cicero, I knew by heart. My leisure time at my Passaic River "villa" had permitted me these pleasant mental gymnastics; I wanted to show off before Bilharz with my Greek and Latin quotations; to say nothing of the wonderful mental exhilaration which a young student gets from reading aloud and memorizing the words of Homer and of Cicero. The professors were greatly surprised and asked me why I had taken so much trouble. I told them that it was no trouble, because Serbs delight in memorizing beautiful lines. The Serbs of Montenegro, for instance, know by heart most of the lines which their great poet Nyegosh ever wrote, and particularly his great epic "The Mountain Glory." I told them also of illiterate Baba Batikin, the minstrel of my native village, who knew most of the old Serbian ballads by heart. Besides, I assured the professors, I wanted to do in Greek and Latin as well as I possibly could, so as to gain free tuition. For the other studies I was not afraid, I told them, and they assured me that my chances for free tuition were certainly good. The other examinations gave me no trouble, thanks to my training with Bilharz and with the lecturers in the evening classes at Cooper Union. A note from the Registrar's office informed me a few days later that I was enrolled as a student in Columbia College with freedom from all tuition fees. There was no person in the United States on that glorious day happier than I!

The college atmosphere which I found at Columbia at that time gave me a new sensation. I did not understand it at first and misinterpreted many things. The few days preceding the opening of the college sessions I spent chasing around for a boarding-house, while my classmates were hanging around the college buildings, making arrangements to join this or that fraternity, and also solidifying the line of defense of the freshmen against the hostile sophomores. There was a lively process of organization going on under the leadership of groups of boys who came from the same preparatory schools. These groups led and the others were expected to follow without a murmur. Insubordination or even indifference was condemned as lack of college spirit. This spirit was necessary among the freshmen particularly, because, as I was informed later, there was a great common danger—the sophomores! I saw some of this feverish activity going on, but did not understand its meaning and hence remained outside of it, as if I were a stranger and not a member of the freshman class, which I heard described, by the freshmen themselves, as the best freshman class in the history of Columbia. The sophomores denied this in a most provoking manner; hence the hostility. Nobody paid any attention to me; nobody knew me, because I did not come from any of the preparatory schools which prepared boys for Columbia. One day I saw on the campus two huge waves of lively youngsters beating against each other just like inrolling waves of the sea lifting on their backs the returning waves which had been reflected from the cliffs of the shore. The freshmen were defending a cane against fierce attacks of the sophomores. It was the historic Columbia cane rush, I was told by Michael, the college janitor, who stood alongside of me as I looked on. It was not a real fight resulting in broken noses or blackened eyes, but just a most vigorous push-and-pull contest, the sophomores trying to take possession of a cane which a strong freshman, surrounded by a stalwart body-guard of freshmen, was holding and guarding just as a guard of fanatic monks would defend the sacred relics of a great saint. This freshmen group was the centre of the scrimmage and it stood there like a high rock in the midst of an angry sea. Coats and shirts were torn off the backs of the brave fighters, some attacking and others defending the central group, but not a single ugly swear-word was heard nor did I see a single sign of intentional bloodshed. Members of the junior and senior classes watched as umpires. Michael, the janitor, who knew everybody on the college campus as a shepherd knows his sheep, was not quite certain about my identity. He asked me whether I was a freshman, and when I said "yes," he asked me why in the world I was not in the rush, defending the freshmen body-guard. He looked so anxious and worried that I felt sure of being guilty of some serious offense against old Columbia traditions. I immediately took off my coat and stiff shirt and plunged into the surging waves of sophomores and freshmen and had almost reached the central body-guard of freshmen, eager to join in its defense, when a sophomore, named Frank Henry, grabbed me and pulled me back, telling me that I had no business to cross the line of umpires at that late moment. I did not know the rules of the game and shoved him aside and we clinched. He was the strongest man in Columbia College, as I learned later, but my kindling-wood operations on the banks of the Passaic River had made me a stiff opponent. We wrestled and wrestled and would have wrestled till sunset like Prince Marco and the Arab Moussa Kessedjia in the old Serbian ballads, if the umpires had not proclaimed the cane rush a draw. The main show being over, the side show which Henry and I were keeping up had no further useful purpose to serve, and we stopped and shook hands. He was glad to stop, he admitted, and so was I, but he told my classmates that "if that terrible Turk had been selected a member of the freshmen body-guard the result of the cane rush might have been different." I told him that I was a Serb, and not a Turk, and he apologized, saying that he could never draw very fine distinctions between the various races in the Balkans. "But, whatever race you are," said he, "you will be a good fellow if you will learn to *play the game.*" Splendid advice from a college boy! *"Play the game,"* what a wonderful phrase! I studied it long, and the more I thought about it the more I was convinced that one aspect of the history of this country with all its traditions is summed up in these three words. No foreigner can understand this country who does not know the full meaning of this phrase, which I first heard from a Columbia College youngster. No foreign language can so translate the phrase as to reproduce its brevity and at the same time convey its full meaning. But, when I heard it, I thought of the bootblacks and newsboys who, five years previously, had acted as umpires when I defended my right to wear a red fez. To "play the game" according to the best traditions of the land which offered me all of its opportunities was always my idea of Americanization. But how many immigrants to this land can be made to understand this?

Some little time after this incident I was approached by the captain of the freshman crew, who asked me to join his crew. I remembered young Lukanitch's opinion about oarsmanship at Columbia, and I was sorely tempted. But, unfortunately, I had only three hundred and eleven dollars when I started my college career, and I knew that if I was to retain my free tuition by high standing in scholarship and also earn further money for my living expenses I should have no time for other activities. "Study, work for a living, no participation in college activities outside of the recitation-room! Do you call that college training?" asked the captain of the freshman crew, looking perfectly surprised at my story, which, being the son of wealthy parents, he did not understand. I admitted that it was not, in the full sense of the word, but that I was not in a position to avail myself of all the opportunities which Columbia offered me, and that, in fact, I had already obtained a great deal more than an immigrant could reasonably have expected. I touched his sympathetic chord, and I felt that I had made a new friend. The result of this interview was that my classmates refrained from asking me to join any of the college activities for fear that my inability to comply with their request might make me feel badly. I had their sympathy, but I missed their fellowship, and therefore I missed in my freshman year much of that splendid training outside of the classroom which an American college offers to its students.

At the end of the freshman year I gained two prizes of one hundred dollars each, one in Greek and the other in mathematics. They were won in stiff competitive examinations and meant a considerable scholastic success, but, nevertheless, they excited little interest among my classmates. Results of examinations were considered a personal matter of the individual student himself and not of his fellow classmen. The prizes were practically the only money upon which I could rely to help carry me through my second year. The estimated budget for that year, however, was not fully provided for, and I looked for a job for the long summer vacation. I did not want a job in the city. My kindling-wood activity of the preceding summer suited me better, and after some consultation with my friend Christopher, the kindling-wood peddler of Rutherford Park, I decided to accept a job on a contract of his to mow hay during that summer in the various sections of the Hackensack lowlands. No Columbia athlete ever had a better opportunity to develop his back and biceps than I had during that summer. I made good use of it, and earned seventy-five dollars net.

When my sophomore year began I awaited the cane rush which, according to old Columbia custom, took place between the sophomores and the freshmen at the beginning of each academic year, and I was prepared for it; I knew also what it meant to "play the game." This time my class had to do the attacking and I helped with a vengeance. The muscles which had been hardened in the Hackensack meadows proved most effective and the result was that shortly I had the freshmen's cane on the ground, and was lying flat over it, covering it with my chest. The pressure of a score of freshmen and sophomores piled up on top of me threatened to squeeze the cane through my chest bone, which already, I imagined, was pressing against my lungs, my difficult breathing leading me to think that my last hour had come. Fortunately, the umpires cleared away the lively heap of struggling boys on top of me, and I breathed freely again. Some freshmen were found stretched alongside of me with their hands holding on to the stick. An equal number of sophomores held on, and, consequently, the umpires declared the rush a draw. Nobody was anxious to have another rush, and it was proposed by the freshmen to settle the question of class superiority by a wrestling-match, two best out of three falls, catch as catch can. They had a big fellow who had some fame as a wrestler of great strength, and they issued a defiant challenge to the sophomores. My classmates held a meeting in order to pick a match for the freshman giant, but nobody seemed to be quite up to the job. Finally I volunteered, declaring that I was not afraid to tackle the freshman giant. "Do you expect to down him with Greek verses and mathematical formulae?" shouted some of my classmates, who had grave doubts about the muscle and the wrestling ability of a fellow who had won Greek and mathematical prizes. They knew nothing about my strenuous mowing in the Hackensack meadows during three long months of that summer. The captain of the class crew approached me, felt my biceps, my chest, and my back, and shouted, "All right!" The wrestling-match came off, and the freshman giant had no show with a boy who had learned the art of wrestling on the pasture-lands of Idvor, and had held his own against experienced mowers in the Hackensack meadows. The victory was quick and complete, and my classmates carried me in triumph to Fritz's saloon, not far from the college, where many a toast was drunk to "Michael the Serbian." From that day on my classmates called me by my first name and took me up as if I had been a distinguished descendant of Alexander Hamilton himself. My scholastic victory in Greek and mathematics meant nothing to my classmates, because it was a purely personal matter, but my athletic victory meant everything, because it was a victory of my whole class. Had I won my scholastic victory in competition with a representative from another college, then the matter would have had an entirely different aspect. *Esprit de corps* is one of those splendid things which American college life cultivates, and I had the good fortune to reap many benefits from it. He who pays no attention to this *esprit de corps* in an American college runs the risk of being dubbed a "greasy grind."

The sophomore year opened auspiciously. Eight of my classmates formed a class, the Octagon, and invited me to coach them in Greek and in mathematics, twice a week. The captain of the class crew was a member of it. I suspected that he remembered my reasons for refusing to join the freshman crew and wanted to help. The Octagon class was a great help in more ways than one. I gave instruction in wrestling also to several classmates, in exchange for instruction in boxing. This was my physical exercise, and it was a strenuous one. Devereux Emmet, a descendant of the great Irish patriot, was one of these exchange instructors; he could stand any amount of punishment in our boxing bouts, which impressed upon my mind the truth of the saying that "blood will tell." Before the sophomore year was over my classmates acknowledged me not only a champion in Greek and in mathematics, but also a champion in wrestling and boxing. The combination was somewhat unusual and legends began to be spun about it, but they did not turn my head, nor lull me to sleep, not even when they led to my election as class president for the junior year. This was indeed a great compliment, for, because of the junior promenade, the dance given annually by the junior class, it was customary to elect for that year a class president who was socially very prominent. A distinguished classmate, a descendant of three great American names, and a shining light in New York's younger social set, was my chief opponent and I begged to withdraw in his favor; a descendant of Hamilton inspired awe. But my opponent would not listen to it. He was a member of the most select fraternity and not at all unpopular, but many of my classmates objected to him, although he was the grandson of a still living former Secretary of State and chairman of the board of trustees of Columbia College. They thought that he paid too much attention to the fashion-plates of London, and dressed too fashionably. There were other Columbia boys at that time who, I thought, dressed just as fashionably, and yet they were very popular; but they were fine athletes, whereas my opponent was believed to rely too much upon the history of his long name and upon his splendid appearance. He certainly was a fine example of classical repose; his classmates, however, admired action. He was like a young Alcibiades in breeding, looks, and pose, but not in action.

Some of the old American colleges have been accused from time to time of encouraging snobbery and a sprit of aristocracy which is not in harmony with American ideas of democracy. My personal experience as a student at Columbia gives competency to my opinion upon that subject. Snobs will be found in every country and clime, but there were fewer snobs at Columbia in those days than in many other much less exalted places, although

Columbia at that time was accused of being a nest of dudes and snobs. This was one of the arguments advanced by those friends of mine at the Adelphi Academy who tried to persuade me to go to Princeton or Yale. The spirit of aristocracy was there, but it was an aristocracy of the same kind as existed in my native peasant village. It was a spirit of unconscious reverence for the best American traditions. I say "unconscious," and by that I mean absence of noisy chauvinism and of that racial intolerance by which the Teutonism of Austria and the Magyarism of Hungary had driven me away from Prague and from Panchevo. A name with a fine American tradition back of it attracted much attention, but it was only a letter of recommendation. He who was found wanting in his make-up and in his conduct when weighed by the best Columbia College traditions—and they were a part of American traditions— had a lonely time during his college career, in spite of his illustrious name or his family's great wealth. Foreign-born students, like Cubans and South Americans, met with a respectful indifference so long as they remained for- eigners. Needless to say, many of them adopted rapidly the attractive ways of the Columbia boys. But nobody would have resented it, or even paid any attention to it, if they had retained their foreign ways. A hopeless fellow became a member of that very small class of students known at that time as "muckers." They complained bitterly of snobbery and of aristocracy. I do not believe that either the spirit of plutocracy, or of socialism and communism, or of any other un-American current of thought could ever start from an American college like Columbia of those days, and bore its way into American life. That type of aristocracy which made the American college immune from contagion by un-American influence existed; it was very exact- ing, and it was much encouraged. But when American college boys, accused of bowing to the spirit of aristocracy, have among them a Hamilton, a Livingston, a DeWitt, and several descendants of Jay, and yet elect for class president the penniless son of a Serbian peasant village, because they admire his mental and physical efforts to learn and to comply with Columbia's tra- ditions, one can rest assured that the spirit of American democracy was very much alive in those college boys.

✿ ✿ ✿

In my preceding account of my preparations for college and of my life in college there is much which sounds like a glorification of muscle and of the fighting spirit. I feel almost like apologizing for it, but do I really owe an apology? My whole life up to this point of my story was steered by condi- tions which demanded muscle and the fighting spirit. To pass six weeks dur- ing each one of several summers as herdsman's assistant in company with twelve other lively Serb youngsters as fellow assistants, meant violent com- petitions in wrestling, swimming, herdsman's hockey, and other strenuous games for hours and hours each day, and one's position in this lively community depended entirely upon muscle and the fighting spirit. Magyarism in Panchevo and Teutonism in Prague produced a reaction which appealed to muscle and to the fighting spirit, which finally drove me to the land of Lincoln. Muscle and the fighting spirit of the bootblacks and newsboys on Broadway met me on the very first day when I ventured to pass beyond the narrow confines of Castle Garden, in order to catch my first glimpse of the great American metropolis. No sooner had I finished serving my apprenticeship as greenhorn, and advanced to a higher civic level, than I encountered again muscle and the fighting spirit of the college boys. In the beginning of my college career I found very little difference between the pasture-lands of my native village and the campus of the American college. The spirit of playfulness and the ferment of life in the hearts of youth were the same in both, and were manifested in the same way, namely, in athletics which encourage a glorification of muscle and of the fighting spirit. This was most fortunate for me, because it offered me a wide avenue by which I could enter with perfect ease into that wonderful activity called college life. Other avenues existed, but to a Serbian youth who but a few years before had been a herdsman's assistant these other avenues were practically closed. I have described the avenue which was open to me, but with no intention to indulge in an egotistical glorification of that avenue.

* * *

Many of my fellow students were, just like myself, very fond of athletics and of other activities outside of the college curriculum, and yet we were enthusiastic students of Greek literature, of history and economics, of constitutional history of the United States, and of English literature. But here was the secret: Professor Merriam was a wonderful expounder of the great achievements of Greek civilization; Professor Monroe Smith made every one of us feel that history was an indispensable part of our daily life; Professor Richmond Mayo-Smith made us believe that political economy was one of the most important subjects in the world; and Professor Burgess' lectures on the Constitutional History of the United States made us all imagine that we understood the spirit of 1776 just as well as Hamilton did. These professors were the great scholars of Columbia College when I was a student there, and they had most attractive personalities too. The personality of the professors, like that of the famous Van Amringe, and their learning, like that of the venerable President Barnard, were the best safeguards for students who showed a tendency to devote themselves too much to the worship of muscle and the fighting spirit, and of activities outside of the college curriculum. Fill your professorial chairs in colleges with men of broad learning, and of commanding personality, and do not worry about the alleged evil influences of athletics, and of other college activities outside of the recitation-room. That was the recommendation of trustee Rutherfurd forty years ago; to-day I add: the college needs great professors just as much as the various research departments of a university need them; perhaps even more.

Literary societies, college journalism, glee-club practice, and exercises in the dramatic art consumed, when I was a college student, just as much of the college student's time as athletics did. They and athletics constituted the outside college activities. The recitation-room brought the student into touch with the personalities of the professors; college activities outside of the recitation-room, whether they were athletics or anything else, brought the student into touch with the personalities of his fellow students. Each one of these influences had, according to the experiences of my college life, its own great value, and contributed its distinct share to what is usually called the character-forming of the college student, but what Rutherfurd, the Columbia College trustee, called training in the principles of conduct becoming an American who is loyal to the best traditions of his country. Neither one nor the other influence can be weakened without crippling seriously that great object which trustee Rutherfurd called "the historical mission of the American college."

Annie Nathan Meyer

Author of fiction, plays, and memoirs, Annie Nathan Meyer enrolled for a time in Columbia's Collegiate Course for Women and became an ardent advocate for women's education. She was instrumental in the founding of Barnard College in 1889 and served as a Barnard Trustee for the remainder of her life. Excerpted here is her 1935 account of the College's early years, Barnard Beginnings.

The Columbia Library building, at Forty-Ninth Street and Madison Avenue, had been completed only two years before at a cost of four hundred thousand dollars. Plenty of books were hidden away in ugly stacks, but there were many thousands of handsomely bound volumes on the open shelves which ran about the high walls in two tiers. A platform with a decorative iron rail around it gave access to the upper one, from which one could look down on the readers at the tables with their green-shaded lamps, up at the lovely vaulted ceiling of carved oak, and at the stained-glass windows which added to the general ecclesiastical effect. These magnificent volumes, mostly bound in full levant and exquisitely tooled, were the gift of Stephen Whitney Phoenix, of the Class of 1859, and formed what was known as the Phoenix Library.

Whatever inadequacies there were in the Collegiate Course for Women seemed more than made up for in the opportunity of browsing here.

After all, for all our theories, experiments, discussions, and what not concerning the best methods of education, can anything be much better than being turned loose among good books?

In this I did not agree with Elizabeth Barrett Browning:

> 'Sublimest danger, over which none weeps,
> When any young wayfaring soul goes forth
> Alone, unconscious of the perilous road,
>
> . . . . . .
>
> To thrust his own way, he an alien through
> The world of books.'

And yet I—and all my girl friends of the period—adored her. As I sat, a year or so ago, among the audience of the play, *The Barretts of Wimpole Street,* the ignorance of the present generation concerning the original of Miss Cornell's impersonation seemed incredible to one who as a girl had reveled in the romance of her life and eagerly learned whole passages of her poetry by heart. How underscored and dog-eared was that magic scene where Aurora proposes to her beloved:

> 'But I love you, sir;
> And when a woman says she loves a man,
> The man must hear her though he love her not.'

Elizabeth Barrett Browning was bracketed in our affections with the author of *Jane Eyre.* From each we derived the same virginal thrill.

A library, especially a college library, may be a place of ghosts and shadows. Or it may be a place overflowing with dynamic energy, as up and doing as a modern business office. Before the coming of Melvil Dewey as Librarian of Columbia College in 1883, the College Library had not gathered together a number of small departmental libraries scattered among the various departments. By the time I had begun to study at Columbia, the new Library had just begun to function in the new building, which the local press of the day called "the most beautiful Library Building in the world."

Suddenly the place becomes alive. It is full of a driving force. It becomes something more than a place for study and contemplation. Something has happened, too, to each and every one of the attendants. Briskness, alertness, service, become the order of the day. The Library becomes a school for the training of librarians.

The Reading Room, the catalogues, the books on the open shelves and, equally, those that are hidden away in the great stacks, exist for the reader, to smooth his way, to make pleasant and profitable the path of the inquiring scholar. The entire resources of the Library are marshaled.

Returning to visit the Library after I had discontinued taking the Collegiate Course, I was deeply impressed by the vivid personality of the new Librarian.

Melvil Dewey was a tall, loosely jointed man, built on generous lines. His voice was as big and hearty as his huge body. From the very first one sensed a bigness that was not merely structural. Here were vision and idealism, with plenty of purposeful punch to put them over! Although Dewey's immediate prepossession was the establishing of the Library as a living force in education, and the training of librarians imbued with this ideal, there was room in his mind, as he soon proved, for other enthusiasms.

Dewey was a graduate of Amherst and had been its Librarian for three years before leaving to take the position at Columbia. He had founded the American Library Association and the *Library Journal,* which became the official organ of all libraries of the United States and Great Britain; and was, moreover, the founder of the Library Bureau and of the New York Library Club.

Once installed in this new position, he promptly started the *Quarterly Magazine of Library Notes,* and founded the Columbia College School of Library Economy. Besides all this, he managed to incorporate the Children's Library Association, which, in a praiseworthy attempt to root out the growing love of the untutored child for trashy literature, undertook to supply the poor children of New York with good books and illustrated papers. And, on the side, being an extremely active member of the American Meteorological Society, and its Secretary, he originated the system of Standard Time.

What more natural than that such a man should pause for a few moments to initiate the movement that was to lead to the founding of New York's first, and for many years, its only, woman's college! One day, during a conversation with Mr. Dewey, I told him how utterly futile I considered the much-boasted-of Collegiate Course for Women and how greatly a real collegiate training for them seemed to me to be needed in the city. It was as if a lighted match had been thrown upon a ready-built bonfire. His enthusiasm was contagious. Of course there should be a college for women in New York; there must be! We must obtain one! He agreed with me that the present scheme was utterly absurd. Obviously, if women could get from a few examinations all that men got from daily intercourse with Faculty and with students, and from hundreds of lectures, and work in the laboratories, then either women were miraculously gifted or else—and this was an alternative pretty serious to contemplate—all the millions and millions at the moment locked up in college endowments, in laboratories and lecture halls, were just so much sheer waste!

To all of this I wholeheartedly agreed. But what was to be done about it? What could I do about it?

Why, start a college for women myself. That was all.

I to start a college—a young woman of twenty, not even a graduate of a college myself, not even the graduate of a school! The wife of a physician comfortably enough off, but certainly not possessing any fortune, not rich even according to the modest standards of the day, how was I to get the wherewithal to make even the first tiny beginnings? And, serious obstacle, although both of my parents had at one period entered actively into New York society, at the time of which I write I possessed practically no important social connections at all, knew none of the people who would inevitably have to be the ones to launch such a movement. I even knew few, if any, of the men and women who were interested in the problems of education. Yet to start a college for women in New York! It might well be thought a preposterous and ridiculous idea! And yet to me, while it was certainly startling and challenging, it wasn't ridiculous. I was tremendously eager to accomplish something worth while, to meet some great test. The fact that the job was bristling with difficulties—some of them seemingly insurmountable—made it all the more thrilling to undertake, all the more worth while.

When, a few months later, I called upon old Mrs. Wendell, the mother of the distinguished Harvard Professor, she had actually wept (so she afterward confided to me) thinking of "that sweet young girl wasting her life in the impossible attempt to found a woman's college connected with Columbia." She was certain that the slender, frail-looking bride, who tipped the scales at less than a hundred pounds, had no conception of the struggle that lay before her or of the discouraging failures of the past.

It was nearly thirty years after this that one day glancing at my daughter, who had by then reached the age at which I was when I was working to start the College, the whole thing seemed fantastic. Not only would it be difficult to make anyone else believe it, but could I believe it myself!

"You little shrimp," I called out, "do you mean to tell me that I looked as absurdly young as you when I was calling on all those dignitaries!"

As a matter of fact, she must have looked far more mature, for she weighed at least twenty pounds more than I did at her age.

* * *

I now set myself to accomplish five tasks:

First, to acquaint myself thoroughly with the entire national situation. What colleges in the United States were open to women? Where were they located and how long had they been in existence? Also were these coeducational, "Annexes," or separate colleges for women? I was so naive and misinformed as to be greatly surprised when Mr. Arthur Gilman, Secretary of the Harvard Annex, wrote me that so far as he knew no college in the country was self-supporting.

Second, to get in touch personally with every man and woman in the neighborhood of New York who might possibly support the movement to establish a college for women, whether this support were to be financial or solely advisory, or even if it meant mere social approval.

Third, to strengthen public opinion in favor of the higher education of women, by every method possible, not alone through personal talks, but by means of interviews and letters in the daily papers, as well as editorials inspired or written by myself. With this objective I arranged for the publication of carefully prepared articles by well-known educators, physicians, the Bishop of New York, and other persons of influence, each one aimed to break down one or another of the various prejudices which I found had gathered about this question of the collegiate education of women.

Fourth, to win over, both individually and as a body, the Trustees of Columbia College to a plan for the establishment of a college for women, affiliated with Columbia College.

Fifth, to build up a body of men and women who would command the confidence of the public and would undertake to direct this college.

In the accomplishment of the fourth task, I was soon to interview every member of the Columbia Board. Not one escaped.

The interest of President Barnard in the education of women would, of course, be taken for granted, as he had for years made his advocacy known. But I knew enough of the politics of the situation to realize that to most of the Trustees the backing of President Barnard would have little weight, might indeed be a detriment. For it was said that, in spite of his logic and eloquence, his strong views in favor of coeducation, vehemently and constantly expressed, had wearied most of these conservative men, and had even estranged some of them. Indeed, it was advantageous to my plan for an affiliated college that President Barnard had never cared for this idea, but had always insisted on coeducation or nothing.

Even though some powerful men in the Church had approved of the higher education of women, notably among them the gracious Rector of Grace Church who was to become Bishop of New York, another influential dignitary in the same diocese not only disapproved, but gave voice to his disapproval in no uncertain language. "I shall oppose it to the end!" announced Dr. Morgan Dix, the Rector of Trinity, who was also a Trustee of the College.

For this stand Dr. Dix had been subjected to many attacks. The editor of the *Home Journal* waxed bitterly ironic: "There is one arithmetic for the boy and another for the girl. The exact sciences are for men; they are bad for women because of their tendency to enlarge the mind and furnish a lodgment for ideas. An enlarged mind is a deformity in the feminine organization, and ideas are as superfluous in a woman as they would be in a bottle of Lubin's extract. They are more than superfluous, they render the possessor uncomfortable to men as lords of creation. They nip the bud of man's egotism, they cut the flower of his self-love, they damage the stalk of his conceit. They cause, moreover, the preacher says, cold shivers to run down his magnanimous back. Now the chief object of the Almighty in the creation of women being to please men—particularly those who are a little narrow in the upper story—it follows that this petition for opening Columbia College lectures, and indeed the whole movement for what is called the higher education of women, but which is really higher disagreeableness, is a wrong, a monstrous wrong, a high-heeled rebellion against the order of the universe."

Later the press did its best to make of Dr. Morgan Dix an inconsistent man, and, moreover, a thwarted man. "In spite of his positive assertion," chortled one paper, "in less than a year Dr. Dix was the chairman of a committee that recommended a special course for women, so as to give to such women as desire a college education the advantages of examinations by the college authorities."

The truth was that, far from being thwarted, Dr. Dix had actually gained his point. For in his Diaries, and certainly in his work as Chairman of the Select Committee, Dr. Dix does not appear as an enemy of women's education *per se,* but rather as a vigorous and determined opponent of their education with men, or as *if they were men.* This is a subject on which we of today might well seek further enlightenment.

Small wonder that this all bred confusion, for, as I soon pointed out in articles and speeches, the rallying cry of the band of enthusiasts who had thus far carried on the battle amounted in spirit, if not in actual words, to "Coeducation or No Education!" It was perfectly true that of these enthusiasts Dr. Morgan Dix was their most cogent and eloquent opponent.

❊   ❊   ❊

What was implied by this goal of an affiliated college? The course that was established for women students expressly provided that no woman should attend any of the lectures that were given to the men, thus avoiding the complications of a mixing of the sexes in the classrooms. While the authorities at Columbia at first decided to reward the women students only with certificates, it was only a few months before the truly revolutionary resolution was made to confer upon them the academic degrees of Bachelor of Arts, Master of Arts, and even Doctor of Philosophy.

I call it revolutionary, for it was a complete and thrilling acceptance of the principle of equal pay for equal work, a principle which half a century later has by no means come into universal acceptance. Columbia, it should always be remembered, was the first of the men's colleges to offer its higher degrees to properly qualified women graduates of other colleges. Many years later, Yale did this, but without offering any opportunities to undergraduates.

There was tremendous enthusiasm when, in 1886, Miss Winifred Edgerton, a graduate of Wellesley College of the Class of 1883, was the first woman recipient of the Doctorate from Columbia College.

While the announcement of the opening of Columbia's Course was received with much acclaim, it was inevitable that, when the precise nature of this largess was understood, much dissatisfaction should also be aroused. I cannot refrain from quoting the witty commentary made several years later by Barnard's first Dean, Emily James Smith: "The Trustees of Columbia College said in effect, 'We are not prepared to educate girls; if, however, they can contrive to educate themselves, we will certify the fact.'"

Passing examinations without instruction might very well be compared to making bricks without straw. Therefore, a dozen years after the presentation of the Sorosis Memorial, and six years after the meeting at the Union League Club, when another attempt was made to gain the advantages of Columbia for women, it was determined that straw in plenty and of an excellent grade should be provided the brickmakers.

It must be kept in mind that all the other attempts had been attempts to establish coeducation at Columbia. It was generally assumed that the simplest way to throw open to women the advantages of Columbia College was to have women in the classes side by side with the men. It was so simple that President Barnard, although advocating what is now known by the term, became impatient over the insistence upon a special word to describe it. He protests: "By whom this word, coeducation, was invented I do not know. It is an odious word and I presume the design of the inventor may have been to prejudice the cause we advocate, by making it seem to be our chief object . . . while it is purely incidental and unimportant. We might with the same propriety apply the term, coeducation, to the teaching of the Sunday Schools. . . . We might as well characterize Churches as coeducational institutions. . . . When I demand for women admission to our colleges, I am demanding for them education, and not the privilege of being educated with men. . . . I have never used the word, coeducation, and I never shall use it."

This new movement, *of which Barnard College was the direct outgrowth,* was initiated by "Certain Friends of the Higher Education of women," and had for its objective "the opening and establishment of a college for women to be affiliated with Columbia College." It never attempted nor desired to establish coeducation, and in so much it differed essentially from any movement which preceded it.

The Trustees of Columbia having seen fit to offer degrees to women without any means of instruction, these new believers in the higher education of women now came forward to offer to provide, for the attainment of these degrees, buildings, equipment, and instruction. Of the older institution, it might be said they craved only its blessing.

The Chairman of the Academic Committee of Barnard College, in her Report for 1891, declared that: "The most fortunate thing in the history of this College is that no one seems to have practically perceived the full significance of this clause. Anybody in the City of New York was at perfect liberty to found an annex to Columbia without asking for permission. Fortunately, the permission was asked and granted; fortunately, both parties to the contract were made so responsible that a failure or a blunder on either side was a disgrace to both."

There is truth in this, but not the whole truth. It most certainly did occur to the early workers for the College that permission was implied in the context of the Circular of Information published by the authorities of Columbia. But one has only to read the Memorial that was presented at this time to realize that it had also occurred to them at the same time that it would be none too easy, under any circumstances, to raise the money for the scheme, and without the public approval of Columbia College, it would be practically impossible.

I realized that the situation that existed in New York was exactly the opposite from that which confronted the people of Boston. Harvard had refused to grant to women the recognition of its degree, notwithstanding the fact that for some eight years women had been receiving excellent instruction from members of its own august Faculty in the subjects which were prescribed for Harvard students. The Harvard "Annex," as it was called, had been brought into existence in order to secure for women the advantages of the lectures and instruction which were given for men at Harvard. But the sole recognition which the conservative old institution conferred upon the "Annex" was to permit its President to sign the certificates issued by the Society for the Collegiate Instruction of Women.

This certificate read: "We hereby certify that under the supervision of this Society——has pursued a course of study equivalent in amount and quality to that for which the degree of Bachelor of Arts is conferred in Harvard College, and has passed in a satisfactory manner examinations on that course, corresponding to the College examinations. In testimony thereof we have caused these presents to be signed by our President and Secretary and by the Chairman of the Academic Board this day of——in the year of our Lord, one thousand eight hundred and——"

As I wrote in an article which appeared in the *Nation* of January 28, 1888: "In Cambridge, Massachusetts, they have an Annex and are praying for certain conditions that will insure its permanent existence and success. In New York we have the conditions that would bring permanent existence and success, but we have no Annex."

This article has been called the first broadside in the campaign for the founding of Barnard College. A copy of it now lies in the cornerstone of Barnard's first building on its present site. It closed with the appeal to "begin at once to organize an association for the collegiate instruction of women by Professors and other Instructors of Columbia College."

It was hoped that enough money could be raised to secure some rooms in the neighborhood of Columbia College where certain members of the Columbia Faculty could repeat to women the lectures which they gave to their men students. Not alone was it necessary to secure instruction for the women, but, obviously, since it was to be crowned by the degrees of Columbia College, the instruction must command the confidence of the Columbia authorities. The simplest and surest way to secure this confidence, and also the confidence of the public, was to engage the services of those upon whom Columbia had already set the seal of its approval—in other words, the members of its own Faculty.

It was not so difficult to persuade the professors to give additional instruction at an affiliated college as might have been expected. To begin with, many of the heads of departments thought it a shame to refuse admission to women, and not alone gladly offered to teach the women students, but offered to teach them, if necessary, without further compensation. Moreover, since the younger members of the staff were neither so busy nor so well paid as today, it had been their custom for some years to add to their income by lecturing in one fashionable school or another. Indeed, the schools vied with one another in giving publicity to the fact that some distinguished Columbia professor gave instruction to their fortunate young ladies.

It is true that while the men and women who started Barnard College never asked Colombia to grant coeducation, nevertheless, almost all of them would have subscribed to President Barnard's dictum: "The establishment of an annex is desirable only if considered as a step toward what I think must come sooner or later, and that is the opening of the College proper to both sexes equally." But I had never looked upon the affiliated college as a mere sop to be thrown over as soon as something better could be wrested from Columbia.

In an article which I wrote for the *Evening Post* in 1891, I took exception to some of the statements made by Mrs. Alice Freeman Palmer in the September *Forum* of that year. I was duly grateful for her suave acceptance of the fact that "the affiliated college is one of the three tolerably clear, consistent, and accredited types of education." This, coming from the former President of Wellesley College, was a concession, but I objected strongly to her remark that the Harvard Annex was typical of what might be accomplished by the affiliated college. Mrs. Palmer denied that Barnard could be deemed a true Annex because all of her teaching was not by the teaching force of Columbia. Before proving the distinguished lady in the wrong, with entire good humor I quoted from "The Nightingale," a poem by my cousin Emma Lazarus.

> 'No bird is this; it soars beyond my line.
> Were it a bird, 'twould answer to my law.'

I recall with what satisfaction I assured Mrs. Palmer that, although all of Barnard's teaching force did not necessarily teach at Columbia, Columbia "assumed all responsibility for the instruction given at Barnard, not alone, as was commonly supposed, by merely conferring its degree upon Barnard graduates, but by passing officially upon all appointments made by Barnard College." Furthermore, all examinations were conducted by Columbia. Since the friends of Barnard naturally stressed the fact that it was then the only Annex whose graduates won the degree of the parent college, Mrs. Palmer protested with some acerbity that we displayed an unholy worship of the degree. In my *Evening Post* article I rejoined that "the degree ought to mean precisely as much to a woman as to a man."

At that period there were many of those defiant coeducationalists who "despised all Annexes," who approved of no half measures. It may be said that these would have cheerfully let women wait until doomsday for college education rather than accept one iota less than the admission of women to all classes of the men's colleges. As a significant protagonist of that attitude, I well recall a disdainful woman from the West who arose at a meeting of the International Council of Women and, while I listened in amusement, scornfully declared : "I want to say here tonight that those bright, enthusiastic, large-brained, and big-hearted young women of the West, those young women who have in their eyes the distant horizons of their prairie homes, will have nothing to do with Annexes."

However, three years later, in 1891, in an article in the *New York Evening Post*, after quoting the words of this fire-eater, I was able to write complacently: "There seems to be a great step forward from this scornful utterance to the statement in Mrs. Alice Freeman Palmer's 'Review of the Higher Education of Women' in the September *Forum,* that 'The affiliated college is one of the three tolerably clear, consistent, and accredited types of education.'"

I confess to a pride in having defended the affiliated college at a time when it was neither popular nor understood. To me nothing in the education of women mattered so much as the creation of right standards, and this was effected by the establishment of the affiliated college. My faith was surely justified, for in 1891 I was happy to proclaim (to the Council of Women in Washington) as an established fact: "Barnard College *is* Columbia."

In the archives of Barnard College, I recently came across a piece of writing bearing on this. It is in the handwriting of the then Chairman of the Academic Committee, with whom I remember to have collaborated in its preparation: "Barnard College was founded in the belief that an annex whose parent college guarded the dignity of its degree . . . would not be the transition between the separate college and the coeducational college, but the solution of the problem."

James Earl Russell

James Earl Russell joined the faculty of Teachers College in 1897 and became its dean in January of the following year; he would hold the position until 1937. Under his leadership, Teachers College developed numerous new programs of study, welcoming men and woman alike, and increased enrollment from less than 200 to more than 5,000. His 1937 book, Founding Teachers College, *is excerpted here.*

The two streams of influence that joined in Teachers College, so aptly pictured by Doctor Hervey, did not placidly pursue their courses during his term as President from 1891 to 1897. The waters were troubled by the reluctance of the philanthropists to give precedence to educational leadership. A Lady Principal shared the administration with the President and, I suspect, she stood closer to the sources of financial support than the President himself. Whatever the cause, the resignation of the President and two professors of psychology and methods of teaching as of July 1, 1897, and the death of the Lady Principal later in the summer, cleared the way for a new deal.

My invitation to join the faculty came from my old friend and teacher, Doctor Wheeler, who had tentatively accepted the presidency. He wrote me that as he was not familiar with the technical training of teachers he wanted me to head that department. I had visited the College at "Number 9" some ten years before and was not greatly impressed with what I saw, but I concluded if it had become good enough for Wheeler it was good enough for me. Accordingly I resigned a post in which I was happy and which gave me a free field for whatever ability I had, for a leap in the dark which I was soon to regret as positively as later on I was to rejoice in the opportunity it gave me.

As soon as I could be honorably released I came on to New York. Miss Dodge met me at the front door of Teachers College. She presented me at once to Doctor William T. Harris who had paved the way for my work abroad by both personal and official introductions and to whom I had paid obeisance for many years as the acknowledged leader of educational thought in America. He was about to give the final lecture in a course for which he had been engaged to fill in the gap before my arrival. Indeed, I was glad it was his last appearance, because I should have been terrified if he had ventured to attend my initial performance.

At the first opportunity Miss Dodge told me that Doctor Wheeler had decided not to accept the presidency. This was a body blow. My one objective in accepting the professorship was that I might be associated with the man who had inspired me to become a teacher. Now that I was stranded with all bridges burnt behind me I began to survey the situation. Here was a private normal school with sixty-nine regular students of junior-college grade and a demonstration school of some four hundred pupils. And what, with my ignorance of high finance, was an insuperable obstacle, an annual deficit in current expenses of $80,000—an amount well-nigh sufficient to run the University of Colorado. Coming from the West, where the emphasis was all upon publicly supported schools from the lowest grades to the university, I could see no place for such an institution.

My dream was of a professional school of university rank. Consequently a few days later when Miss Dodge brought Mr. Macy to call on me, our conversation turned on the type of man needed for the presidency. They had under consideration an eminent professor of Latin in an eastern college and the superintendent of schools of Toronto, Canada. Neither of these men fitted into my conception of a professional school. So I suggested that our proximity to Columbia University, which was just settling its new plant across the street, might lead to an affiliation of advantage to both parties.

I was not aware that President Barnard had reported again and again to his Trustees in the 80's the want of attention in Columbia College to what he declared was its own most important business, viz., the study of education as a science. His exposition, supported by incisive argument and a wealth of illustration, fell on deaf ears and was buried without decent consideration in the archives of the Board. Nor did I know then that as recently as 1891, the Trustees of Teachers College, grown weary, I fancy, with carrying the incubus imposed by its educational Frankenstein, had offered to turn the institution over to the University, only to have the proposal rejected by the University Council on the grounds that "there is no such subject as

Education and moreover it would bring into the University women who are not wanted."

In ignorance, therefore, of the accumulated opposition, not to say hostility, in the University of twenty years' standing, I had the temerity to propose that a president of Teachers College could be dispensed with if the institution were made a professional school in the University system. Asked to put the plan in writing, I did so overnight; it was copied by our one lone stenographer and sent on to Miss Dodge. Nothing further was asked of me for about two weeks until the third Thursday of November when I was called from class late in the afternoon, to meet at the foot of the stairs at the main entrance, Spencer Trask, Chairman of the Teachers College Trustees, and President Low of the University.

Mr. Trask handed me a written document saying that the Trustees were in session and ready to adopt my plan of affiliation with the University but that President Low had stipulated I should be Dean. One glance at the paper in my hand showed plainly enough that instead of becoming a professional school on a par with the others, we were to be the stepchild of the University department of Philosophy and Education. My reply was that the plan was not mine and that I was not qualified to be dean. My ambition was to teach, not to spend time in administrative work.

Mr. Low was a great harmonizer. As for the deanship, he said, that was a temporary arrangement until a suitable person could be found, and as for the agreement then proposed it was the only one that the University was willing to accept. He assured me, however, he had no doubt that all I wanted could be had in good time. Fearful of what might happen if an academician were to become president I forced myself to say that in the emergency I would do what I could, provided I might resume my teaching the following year.

Thereupon the Trustees adopted the plan as revised by the University and elected me Dean for the current year. Despite two formal resignations within the ensuing twelve months I was unable to extricate myself for fully thirty years from the web in which I had so trustingly enmeshed myself.

The agreement set as the price of adoption into the University family, the surrender of all control over courses leading to a degree. In effect we were officially restricted to the management of the Horace Mann School and to such offering as we cared to make for special and technical students who were not qualified for admission under some University faculty.

Another important article of the agreement was that "the University is and shall be under no implied obligation, responsibility, or liability of any kind whatsoever for the maintenance, support, direction, or management of Teachers College, or for the disbursement of the income thereof." In other words, our children might have the University name but we were required to feed and clothe them. We soon found a way, however, of asserting our paternity by making candidacy for a Teachers College diploma, a concession made to our professional interests, prerequisite to candidacy for a degree. Two years later we were granted control of an undergraduate curriculum leading to the degree of Bachelor of Science, but it was eighteen years before we attained the status of a sovereign state in a federal union.

In surveying this early history, humiliating as it sometimes was, I realize that it was too much to expect that a university, itself barely emerged from a conventional college, would accept on faith a new type of professional education for which neither the financial support nor a competent staff was in sight. Events proved the wisdom of letting us win the right to university rank by actual demonstration. If the growing pains of youth are really due to malnutrition, perhaps it was providential that we were required to fatten up before reaching maturity.

We certainly had the will to grow but without the fostering care of President Low and the munificent support of our Trustees we should have come badly off. The significant fact to note here is that President Low was a layman at the head of an expanding University and that our Trustees were laymen. It was this fortunate juncture of faith and experience that made the Teachers College of today a possibility—faith in the ideals of the undertaking, tempered by practical experience with expert service in public affairs.

One should remember that forty years ago segregated professional schools had barely left the proprietary stage. Theological schools were owned and dominated by sectarian interests; schools of medicine were controlled by groups of practitioners; the Columbia Law School had but recently been taken over from Professor Dwight; normal schools stood by themselves apart and quite generally were restricted to the subject matter and methods of the elementary school.

Such provision as had been made in the universities for the study of education, as in Michigan, Iowa, Columbia, Harvard, California, and Stanford, was the establishment of departments of the usual collegiate type. Nowhere was there a faculty of education comparable to the faculties of law, medicine, and engineering. For a generation the idea of departmental development as the proper organization of a university, an idea imported direct from Germany, had been growing apace. It conformed very neatly with the practice of American colleges of centering the offering in any subject around the person of the professor oldest in service. Newcomers began at the bottom and were subject to the one-man rule of the top.

Quite naturally, too, these ruling elders viewed with suspicion any proposal that tended to spread over a wider field the funds already inadequate for their own needs. Moreover, at a time when mental discipline was held to be the chief end of all education, it could honestly be asserted that subjects of long standing and in practice not found wanting were superior to new and untried ones. Hence every new offering had to force its way into the sacred circle and be held in contempt until death or retirement of its opponents made a vacancy in the hierarchy.

It is also worth noting that the system of one-man control was not confined to the higher institutions. The public schools, particularly those in the Middle West, were in the hands of powerful school superintendents. Looking backward, it does us no credit to belittle the professional contribution of these men. Many of them were exceptionally able organizers and administrative officers who dominated educational thought and practice in an age when order was emerging from chaos in public education—such men as Harris and Soldan of St. Louis, White of Cincinnati, Greenwood of Kansas City, and Maxwell of Brooklyn, later the first superintendent of schools in New York. They were the feudal barons of the pedagogical realm, the educational elite of the golden age of rugged individualism. They were the Rockefellers, the Carnegies, the Morgans of our profession, when giants towered over the common herd.

We were the little fellows, but time was on our side. Dissatisfaction with the aridity and formalism of the schools was finding expression. Henry Adams, writing in his autobiography of his Harvard days, says that if "the student got little from his mates, he got little more from his masters." The bitterest critique of prevailing practice in college preparatory work that I know of was made in President Barnard's Report in 1881, which, as he said a year later, "had (has) lost none of its importance from the fact that its presentation at that time was unattended with the hoped-for success from the favorable consideration of the Trustees."

I can quote only one sentence from this remarkable document: "By immuring an unhappy lad within the four blank walls of a schoolroom, and constraining him to fasten his thoughts upon a series of abstractions to which the power of his intelligence is unequal, we subject his perspective faculties in a long-continued and unnatural inaction, by which, if they are not completely paralyzed, they are certainly dwarfed, and prevented forever from attaining even that degree of development which nature alone, unassisted by educational helps, would have given them."

The famous Committee of Ten had grappled with the problem of the secondary school and later the Committee of Fifteen undertook to instill life into the elementary program. Some teachers were ready to try new methods of dealing with old subjects, and a new type of school superintendent and school principal stood in the offing. This combination of pedagogical unrest, the stirrings of a new social era, our location in the midst of a tenth of the population of the United States, and our association, however tenuous, with a great university, gave us our chance—and we took it.

Professional service, as I conceived it, comprehends not merely the ability to perform certain acts of a highly technical character but also to understand the reason for such action in a particular situation, in order that proper materials and methods be used to attain some worthy end. How and when to act, why a certain procedure is preferable to some other, what knowledge and skill are requisite for the purpose—these are the objectives of professional education. Some skills can be acquired by routine practice, but skills worthy to be called professional are guided by an intelligent appreciation of available materials, of their sources, selection, and adaptation to the business in hand.

It seemed to me, therefore, that we needed to know more about the learner and learning, more about past achievement and present practice at home and abroad, more about possible materials of instruction in schools of all grades, more about school management and administration, and more about the purpose of it all in relation to the teacher, the student, and society at large.

It is now apparent that I was injecting a new tributary into the two streams of influence that had so far determined the career of the College. To the philanthropic influence which had always held first place by virtue of its financial strength, and to the scholastic ideal which would subsume the enterprise as a subject under an academic faculty, I proposed a plan that should incorporate both the scholastic and the philanthropic ideals in a school with its own independent faculty responsible directly to professional needs. The contest between these three ideals for supremacy enlivened the first six years of my administration.

The time intervening between my election as Dean in November and my formal entrance upon the office in January—at least what was left over after conducting classes in psychology, history of education, and general method—was spent in making internal adjustments to the new organization and in scouting for help to implement the scheme.

I was especially anxious to make a bid for advanced students. A course in school supervision and school management was on the program. Occupied as I was—not to say disqualified for obvious reasons—I made bold to approach Superintendent Gilbert of Newark with the argument that inasmuch as he had written a little book on school management he was the man to help us out. Asked what I had in mind, I told him that such a course should be aimed at prospective school principals. He wanted to know how much time would be allotted to the course. I said that to have graduate credit it should run at least two hours throughout the year. His hands went up in astonishment.

"Why," he said, "I can tell all I know in six weeks." My rejoinder was that I wasn't as much concerned with what he could tell as with what the students should learn. "Why not have them investigate what the schools are doing," I asked, "and how school systems are being managed?" "Do you propose," he said, "to have these students visit schools, pry into their methods, and quiz the superintendent about how he conducts his business? If so you are barking up the wrong tree. All that the superintendent wants the public to know can be found in his reports. As for myself, I have never visited another superintendent except as a friendly caller, or perhaps to steal a teacher. Snooping around just can't be done; it isn't ethical." Nevertheless, after prayerful thought and repeated conferences, he gave the course and started us on the road so well paved by Dutton, Snedden, Strayer, and their associates.

During the Christmas holidays I wrote from cover to cover an Announcement of regulations and a list of courses for the following year, and had it printed in time for me to take it, in February, to the meeting of the Department of Superintendence in Chattanooga. I had never attended one of these conferences and had attended only two meetings of the National Education Association. In fact I knew only a few of the leading schoolmen. Nevertheless, I couldn't afford to miss the chance of advertising my wares, even though it were to meet with rebuffs at every turn. One superintendent, whom I cornered on the train, glanced over the catalogue and then curtly remarked, "Young man, you don't seem to know your job. The only way to run a normal school is the way I did it in New Britain. Better look it up."

Nor did I succeed much better with influential heads of departments in Columbia. Even Doctor Butler asked me where I expected to get students for the course on foreign school systems restricted to college graduates with a reading knowledge of French and German. My answer, rather flippant I fear, was that at any rate it looked well in the catalogue.

I can't pretend that I knew better than my elders what was wanted or what was feasible. It may have been the rashness of youth, or possibly the fact that I had only one year to serve, that led me to take desperate chances. Assured, however, by the Trustees of the College that a prospective deficit of $100,000 would be met if necessary to carry out my plans, and with the personal encouragement of Miss Dodge and Mr. Macy, I went ahead.

In January I got the consent of Doctor McMurry to join our staff, but a young instructor in history who was dividing his time between the College and the Horace Mann School was harder to convince that his opportunity lay in the professional field. He doubted that there was such a subject as the history of education. Somehow when he began digging into it he unearthed so much good ore that it required an encyclopedia to describe it. His name was Paul Monroe.

Meantime the Trustees established three fellowships of $500 each which I used as a bait. Some desultory correspondence was had with persons in the West who were interested in Doctor McMurry, but not until midsummer was I assured of three candidates for my pet course on foreign schools. Registration day came. I was not prepared for the time-consuming duty of ruling on exceptional cases referred to the Dean (our administrative staff consisted of a registrar, a bookkeeper, and one stenographer). No one in trouble had asked about my particular course and it looked as if the three who had been bribed with fellowships would constitute the class. Imagine my surprise, therefore, when at the first meeting scheduled for the alcove adjoining the stackroom of the library, I found the place standing full of persons who looked like genuine graduate students—thirty-four of them.

The materials which I had collected abroad were stowed on a shelf convenient to a table seating six, a quite satisfactory arrangement, as I thought, for the expected class. Assuming that a mistake had been made I cited the requirements of the course only to have all present say that they qualified. My only recourse was to ask them to see me individually and after combing over the whole list I still had twenty-three left on my conscience. It being impossible to turn the well-known trick of letting students teach themselves, I had to turn my first seminar into a lecture course.

I cite this personal experience as evidence that we had not misjudged the trend of the times. Doctor McMurry, better known than I was, had a registration of eighty-three in the first semester and two hundred nineteen the second semester. All told in the year 1898–1899 we had eighty-six college graduates, a number more significant than the thousands now on your roll.

While it is true that this influx of graduate students quite overwhelmed us, the fact that they came at all was sufficient answer to the dire forebodings of disaster that had hovered about us for months past. Moreover, tension was relieved by a healthy growth in undergraduate registration despite the lengthening of all curricula from two years to four years beyond the high school. We now had the students. The problem was what to do with them. An account of how we met that problem is the theme of my next lecture, but I want here and now to express my appreciation of the help given by students in reaching a solution.

At first most of the graduate students were teachers or principals in or near New York; others were connected with normal schools or western universities. They brought with them maturity of judgment and a wide diversity of experience. Ambitious they all were, else they would not have been there. What we had to offer was opportunity, and the inducement to join us in opening up new fields was the lure that brought such women as Naomi Norsworthy, Romiett Stevens, and Jean Broadhurst, and such men as

Broome, Cubberley, Elliott, Snedden, Suzzallo, Strayer, Swift, and Payne—to mention only a few of the pioneers. Their co-operation was of inestimable worth not only in their individual achievements but particularly in helping us establish a policy of co-operation between faculty and students which has always seemed to me to be the essence of correct method in professional education. For such a legacy Teachers College should be profoundly grateful.

The establishment of this lectureship by the present Board of Trustees gives me the chance to speak of some former members of that Board whose wise counsel and generous benefactions we still enjoy—Mrs. Bryson, Mrs. Thompson, the Macys (mother and son), the Dodges (father and daughter), and Mr. Milbank, to whom we owe the buildings that bear their names. They and others who helped carry the load of recurring deficits, while the plant was building, equipment was needed, and endowment was hoped for, gave twice in giving early and confirmed their faith by their works.

There is no invidious distinction in singling out two members of the Board with whom I came in closest touch—Grace H. Dodge and V. Everit Macy. Professor Kilpatrick, who is to hold the lectureship next year that alternates with this one, will find in the life of Mr. and Mrs. Macy (I never think of them separately; they worked in team in singular felicity and effectiveness) a practical demonstration of his own ideals of citizenship. My first meeting with Mr. Macy, as I have related, was when we discussed possible affiliation with the University. He was then about twenty-five years of age and had just returned from his honeymoon. Later when I met Mrs. Macy I was welcomed to their home and family life. Many were the visits that I paid to "Chilmark" to get the encouragement that I needed to face the financial problems of a hungry institution. When a new enterprise was proposed or another professor was needed I would present the case to Miss Dodge who would say "We will find the funds"; then I would discuss it with Mr. Macy and get his answer. "Mrs. Macy and I will furnish the cash until college funds can permanently care for it." In this manner, and with Miss Dodge's ability to interest other donors, the Macys either underwrote or actually paid the bills for every advance we made in staff appointment or additions to plant and permanent funds.

Of the many illustrations of the Macy faith in education I will cite only one. Soon after the World War and following a tour of the Mediterranean and the Near East, Mr. Macy came to me with a proposal to provide the means of bringing outstanding students of the Old World, particularly of eastern Europe and the Near East, for a year of study in Teachers College. Despairing of getting mutual understanding and international good will by diplomatic means, he declared the hope of the future lies in education. I am thankful that the year before he died he was able to attend a conference in

Geneva, where some fifty former Macy Fellows demonstrated to his satisfaction that his solution of Old-World problems is more promising than political pacts and diplomatic conferences. Teachers College students in the strategic posts of the school systems of many nations cannot fail to carry over to oncoming generations a better understanding of democratic ideals and a more tolerant international attitude.

Miss Dodge fondly spoke of Teachers College as her oldest child. No mother ever lavished more love upon her offspring or watched more carefully its development. Reared in a family of wealth and social standing, her one mission in life was to aid those less fortunate than herself. From girlhood to the end of a busy life, when she saw something to do she did it. She never waited to formulate a philosophy or to rationalize her action. She embraced no cause and led no crusade. She simply gave herself along with her gift of friendship, her enthusiasm, and her confidence in the Christian virtues of faith, hope, and charity. She was the guiding hand and financial backer of the Kitchen Garden Association and the Industrial Education Association. She nursed the young Teachers College through the perils of infancy and kept her faith despite aberrations of its adolescence. None of us knows the extent of her personal gifts to College funds but I do know that sometimes she went without personal comforts in order that we might be more comfortable. The financial records show hundreds of thousands received from her and her family and at her death she willed us more than a million dollars from her personal fortune. As Treasurer of the College until 1911 she was responsible for meeting the annual deficit which for years together ranged from $60,000 to $100,000. It was faith in our mission and her ability to inspire like confidence in others that brought to us directly or indirectly most of the large gifts for buildings, equipment, salary increases, and endowment. But above all reckoning of dollars, what I prize most is the legacy of her spirit of service. It was already so deeply imbedded in the social life of the College as I found it and so zealously guarded during her life that I trust it will always remain our conscience to check us when tempted to stray into paths of expediency or formal professionalism.

Would you see her monument? Look about you.

Virginia Gildersleeve

1899 BARNARD, '08 PHD

New York City native Virginia Gildersleeve graduated first in her Barnard class. After serving as a lecturer and assistant professor of English, she became Barnard's dean, holding office from 1911 until her retirement in 1947. Gildersleeve used her position to campaign for the admission of women to Columbia's graduate and professional schools and secured privileges such as maternity leave for female faculty members. Her work in international affairs led to her appointment to the United Nations Charter Committee. Her 1954 memoir, Many a Good Crusade, *provides this selection.*

It was on my eighteenth birthday, in October, 1895, that I entered Barnard College, a shy, snobbish, solemn freshman. For six weeks I disliked it intensely. I disliked the shabby, crowded old house. I disliked the basement hall where we hung our overcoats. I disliked particularly the fourth-story front room where the freshman class, twenty-one in number, spent practically all its time, attending the required courses. I even disliked my fellow students. Two moments in my early college career remain vividly and contrastingly in my mind. At the start of the freshman year we had a class meeting to elect officers. I recall sitting alone and aloof in the back row and thinking to myself sardonically, "Well, there's *one* person sure not to be elected to anything, and that's VCG." I was right.

Just one year from that day a different scene occurred. I see myself in the back parlor downstairs surrounded by my classmates. I am sophomore president. I jump upon a sofa (very bad for the furniture!) and exhort them in a brief but zealous speech to prepare to initiate the freshmen. It is already obvious that of all the excellent education I received from Barnard College by far the most valuable part was experience in human relations, the development of an ability to know and understand people of various kinds, to appreciate them and to enjoy helping to organize them.

The class of '99 soon became proud of itself. The twenty-one original members, far less varied in make-up than a college class of today, were conscientious and hard-working. All were more or less on the same social level. All except one came from New York City or the nearby suburbs. The one exception was our poet, Grace Goodale, who came from Potsdam, far up in the North Woods. She has always embodied our class spirit, which she expressed in rattling good verse on the model of Kipling, who was at that time a literary idol of the young. Two members of this original group I grew to know intimately and they remained my lifelong friends,—Edith Striker, gay and laughing and loyal, whose home was in East Orange, and Alté Stilwell, nimble-witted and warmhearted, who lived in a pleasant, dignified Harlem street.

The class had two brilliant additions at the opening of our junior year who both became close friends of mine. The first was Marjorie Jacobi, daughter of two distinguished physicians, herself gifted and witty. The second was Alice Duer. She was several years older than the rest of us, had been "out" in New York society for four years, and had published with her sister Caroline a little volume of poems. She was beautiful and she was brilliant and she was charming. She brought into our classrooms a glamour from the outer world and her friendship gave me the romance of my youth.

Her field of study was mathematics, which I had abandoned, and in it she won all the honors. I can remember her coming back to us from a graduate course, her eyes gleaming with excitement. "We have had a most wonderful time," she explained, "discussing with Professor Keyser whether infinity stretches out in a curve or a straight line." (This was long before Einstein.) Mathematics and poetry remained her real talents. I remember her saying to me once in later years that all her many delightful books of fiction were written with only half her mind. She needed to make money, and it was hard to make any considerable amount out of mathematics or poetry. She came to love the College as much as I did. We remained intimate friends and were associated in its affairs for many years.

At that time there was only one fraternity in the College, Beta Epsilon Chapter of Kappa Kappa Gamma, of which I became a member. It did me lots of good. For one thing it made me act in a play. The only plays given at Barnard in those old days were produced by Kappa in the back parlor on the first floor. The sliding doors served as curtain and the audience sat in the front parlor. The chapter assigned to me, that sophomore year, the part of a young man in a farce by John Kendrick Bangs called *The Bicyclers*. I was horrified. "But I can't act," I protested, "I never have acted. My mother says

I can't." "Never mind your mother," said the chapter, "just go ahead." Thus I learned one of the great lessons I acquired in college,—that you have to do lots of things that you know nothing about and feel quite unable to accomplish. You "just go ahead."

Though the shabby old house at 343 Madison Avenue had become dear to us, it was with a great lift of the heart that we began to become acquainted with our new site on Morningside Heights, to which we moved in the autumn of '97. We rattled around in the great spaces of the new Barnard buildings—Milbank and Brinckerhoff Halls—which later became so cramped and crowded. The Low Memorial Library made a profound impression upon me, as I studied beneath its dome and walked in and out between the great columns of its portico: those mighty and lovely columns which always gave me a thrill as I passed between them.

But best of all was the river—that great river which ever after played a large part in my life. In those early days there was nothing on Morningside Heights except empty fields, a few squatters' cabins, and plenty of goats. No apartment houses cut off our view. We could see far up and down the great stretches of the Hudson. We came to know the sunset flare over the darkened Palisades, and the far lights which sprang up, calling us home at the day's end. Amid these beautiful surroundings, in gay comradeship, I lived two happy years.

Besides my fellow students at Barnard I became acquainted with a remarkable group of young men at Columbia,—the board of editors of a literary magazine, the *Morningside*. We met in a shabby little room on the top floor of one of the old red brick buildings surviving from the days when the Bloomingdale Asylum occupied the site. We had ardent, vigorous discussions regarding literary problems and policies. On that board of editors with me sat Frederick P. Keppel, afterwards Dean of Columbia College and then President of the Carnegie Corporation; Hans Zinsser, distinguished bacteriologist and author; the poet, novelist, and musician, John Erskine; and others who later achieved eminence.

Stimulating human companionship helped me a great deal, but from my courses and my reading I learned most. The freshman class at that time all studied together English, Latin, Greek, mathematics. They had a choice between French and German. I chose French. We were taught by very young men instructors who came down Madison Avenue from Columbia. Most of them became eminent scholars in later years. In English, George Odell, afterwards the distinguished Professor of Dramatic Literature at Columbia University and author of the many-volumed *History of the New York Stage*, began his teaching career with the Class of '99, instructing us in the principles of rhetoric and having us write a theme every week. The principles of

rhetoric gave us an excellent foundation which Dr. Odell enriched and elab-
orated with an amazing amount of quotations from literature. In later years I
became his assistant, and found that I could listen year after year with real
interest to his admirably adorned talks. I recall a great deal of Matthew
Arnold in the examples we had of good structure. He was a kind of guidepost
and beacon for the young writer in those days. My choice of subject for my
first theme was "The Present Political Situation in New York City," typical
sample of my lifelong interest in politics. The second was on Humperdinck's
opera *Hänsel und Gretel*, which had been recently produced for the first time
in New York. A later theme was on our relations with Spain. Apparently I was
already getting started on my concern with public affairs and international
relations.

Far more exciting than English was Greek. The required course dealt
with Homer one term and Plato the other. It was conducted by our brilliant
young Dean, Emily James Smith. A fine scholar with penetrating acumen,
she did a great service for Barnard. The structure and the temper of mind of
the College are largely her creations. As a teacher of freshmen, however, her
rapier-like mind and satiric wit frightened even the solid, conscientious students of the Class of '99. We were inclined to try to avoid being called upon
in class, lest we be made to seem ridiculous.

Once a week there was an hour conducted by a young instructor named
Henry Burchell, in which we read at sight the Phaeacian Episode and other
books of *The Odyssey*. Though it was optional, most of the class attended
regularly. The fascination of the story and the beauty of the poetry carried us
along happily. I can still recite, after more than fifty years, a long quotation
which I learned by heart for my own delectation. Though I never intended
to specialize in Greek, I continued to study it throughout the four years of
my college course. Happily in those days in Greek courses we read rapidly
and widely. In Latin we would spend a whole term analyzing exhaustively,
line by line and word by word, one comedy of Plautus, but in Greek we
plunged adventurously on, so that in my four years I covered a fair amount
of that great literature.

Throughout my life I have remained profoundly grateful that the college
requirements of my time obliged me to take Greek. That lovely language and
literature, so far away in time and space, gave me exhilaration of adventure,
illumination of the mind, and great joy in beauty. As I look back upon this
study it seems to me most like a journey into a different country. It seems
that I lived for a time in a clearer air, under a brighter sky, where minds
played freely, where life was young, where the world was rich with a balanced and exquisite beauty. Perhaps the real Greece was not at all like this
vision of mine. I do not greatly care. Not for much gold would I give up this

memory of a happy journey to a remote and delectable land. I am sorry for the youth of today, cut off by present circumstances from this enlightening and joyous adventure.

After the sophomore year we were allowed considerable freedom of choice in our course. There was no "major" in those days. I wavered between English and history as my principal field of interest. My parents never interfered in any way with my management of my college studies and life. Even my mother, who had had a good deal to do with directing my affairs up to that date, just helped with the social side, gave parties to my classmates and a fireplace to our chapter room. Neither did anyone at College, so far as I can recall, attempt to advise or guide me. I remember asking Dr. Odell once about which of two courses would be better for me, and then failing to take his advice. The college in those days took no interest in "guidance" and cared little about our health, our social life, and our student activities, and nothing at all about our psychological adjustment. The Class of '99 quietly adjusted itself.

Barnard was still small and poor and the array of courses from which we had to choose was of course far smaller than in later years. Some of them were mediocre, but some were excellent. I profited immensely from the third year of required English, a course in argumentation given by Ralph Curtis Ringwalt. In this we had to write long, argumentative briefs—four of them. The instruction was rigorous and the requirements severe. I remember sitting upon the floor surrounded by piles of bits of paper in which I was trying to classify notes on the subject "Should the United States Navy Be Increased?" And I remember pacing up and down the room driving my brain in an agonized effort to analyze the precise issues of the question "Should Vivisection Be Prohibited?" All this was painfully hard work, but it had a good effect on the habits of the student's mind. Thereafter as I read on any subject, I found that the various facts and opinions were inclined to pigeonhole themselves in some sort of order.

Another course that I remember especially was given by Richard Hovey, the poet, in modern English poetry. He seemed to us a rather eccentric person. He used to wear a black Prince Albert coat and a wide-brimmed black felt hat and patent-leather pumps. In this garb he arrived at college on a bicycle. He generally came to class twenty minutes late and left twenty minutes early, but in the interval he read poetry aloud to us magnificently. I remember especially Kipling's *The Song of the Banjo* and the beautiful conclusion to Matthew Arnold's *Sohrab and Rustum*. I began to understand what poetry really is. That is the way to study it,—to hear it read by a poet.

Though the appearance and the conduct of Richard Hovey seemed to us rather strange, with the careless, coldhearted indifference of youth we never speculated about the causes. It was only years afterwards that I learned that this really gifted poet had been pitifully poor at that time, with not a penny to spare towards buying a pair of shoes to replace the patent-leather pumps, and that he had been fighting a fatal disease. His illness made him short of breath, and he could not possibly lecture and read for longer than about twenty minutes at a time. He died within two years after that course. There is a tradition that one day, in spite of his illness, he sat down in the basement of Milbank Hall at Barnard and wrote the first draft of a famous song, one of the gayest and most jovial of drinking songs:

> For it's always fair weather
> When good fellows get together.

Of all this, however, the members of the Class of '99 knew nothing.

On February 15th of my junior year the United States battleship *Maine* was blown up in Havana Harbor. Thus in the peaceful, comfortable security of the Victorian Age we heard the first faint rumblings of approaching wars which were to transform the world. We did not recognize them as portents. The Spanish-American War affected our lives very little. I did not happen to have anyone close to me in the military services, and so, though I was a patriotic American and followed the news in the papers eagerly, I looked upon it all rather objectively.

I remember two great days of triumphant welcome for Admiral Dewey. On one of them I was on a small yacht in the river belonging to one of my early suitors. As the cruiser *Olympia* came up the harbor, we could see the figure of Admiral Dewey on the quarter-deck. There was a terrific uproar of whistles from all the ships and yells from all our throats.

On the other occasion I was sitting up on that vast Egyptian temple which occupied the site of what is now the New York Public Library and which was a reservoir. The parade came swinging up the avenue, and again we gave an uproarious welcome to the triumphant admiral. In our innocence we had little thought for the Philippines, of which we mostly had never heard until he won them for us, and no premonition of the troubled part in world history on which this small war was launching us. Certainly we had no concern whatsoever for our new little possession, the far-away island of Guam, which he had also taken for us and which was, many years later, to occupy much of my attention and interest.

So the Spanish-American War passed over us. My senior year was a satisfying one. Though Barnard was still small and poor, it had the priceless advantage of membership in Columbia University. No other college in the country, I am certain, could have provided me with such excellent and stimulating instruction. Most of my courses were at Columbia, where Barnard and Columbia seniors were taught together. There I had my third course in English composition with Professor Odell and a course by Professor Edward Delavan Perry in Greek lyric and bucolic poets. (How the lovely fragments of Sappho remain, haunting one's memory!) Most notable, however, were three great courses which to some extent dealt with the same ideas and played into one another's hands. One of these, given at Barnard, was in the principles of sociology, conducted by the father of American sociology, Professor Franklin H. Giddings. The second was in the history of philosophy, given at Columbia and conducted by that brilliant young professor, Dr. Nicholas Murray Butler. He was a great executive and became a most distinguished and effective university president. Under him I later served long and happily. As a teacher I thought during the first six weeks or so that he was superb. Then the lectures began to irk me a little. His voice had a slightly rasping quality and his material was so excellently ordered and so lucidly expressed that after a time it seemed to go into one's ears and out at the tip of one's fountain pen without making any great impress on one's mind.

The third notable course was in the history of the French Revolution and the Napoleonic Period, given by Professor James Harvey Robinson. He was by far the greatest teacher I have ever studied under. In later years I remember a brilliant Barnard student saying, "After each lecture by Professor Robinson, I feel as if my brain had been taken out and given an airing." That expressed the effect of his teaching rather well. He largely revolutionized methods of teaching history in American high schools and colleges. That first year that I had him, he was dealing with a subject not very close to him, but even so I found him in his quiet, humorous way electrifying. I wrote my baccalaureate thesis under him on a subject which to some extent combined the contents of my three great courses. Its title was "Ideals of Social Regeneration of the Terrorists, Especially of Robespierre and Saint-Just." (It was not a very good thesis.)

So I came to the end of my senior year, and received the degree of Bachelor of Arts from Columbia University. Looking at a photograph of myself taken at this time, I see a rather self-confident young woman, president of the senior class and leading it in scholarly record, obviously just a bit cocky and pleased with herself. While I was in college people asked me often why in the world I went to college, because at that time it was not a very usual thing for a girl to do. They never believed me when I said I went to please my mother, and I fell into the habit of saying, "Well, I suppose I went to get educated." That always perplexed and annoyed them. Now here I was, educated more or less. What next?

❀ ❀ ❀

Besides administering her own small principality within the big University, the Dean of Barnard College naturally had a responsibility, though this was not provided in the Statutes, for increasing educational opportunities for women in other parts of Columbia. This was not a very hard task, for no other great and ancient American university has been so sympathetic to women, and moreover the trend of the times was towards providing women with more opportunities for acquiring knowledge, enlarging their interests, and training their talents.

As I was not battering at the doors from without, but working from within, it was important to avoid as far as possible creating antagonisms. Most of my male colleagues outside Barnard had to be handled rather gently. Men were opposed to letting women in some courses and professional schools largely because they thought the women would cause trouble, would probably weep and faint at inconvenient moments, expect special consideration and privileges, perhaps lower the standards, and in general be a nuisance. I find that instead of arguing the principles of such matters with men, it is best whenever possible just to get a first-rate woman slipped in as unobtrusively as may be and then let her show that she is not troublesome and that she can do work as sound as the men students and perhaps better.

Over the years, while sitting as the one woman on committees of men at Columbia, I developed a technique of dealing with such situations which proved satisfactory in my University and useful in later years on other councils and commissions. Men dread the prospect of having a woman around. Their worst fear is that she will talk too much and often irrelevantly, that she may get emotional in seeking to have her own way. My natural instinct was to begin very gently. I spent hours and hours just sitting quietly, listening to discussions of the University budget or whatever was before us, speaking rarely and briefly, to comment on the business, to ask intelligent questions, occasionally to make a suggestion. If a woman just sits quietly and says nothing at all, then the men will think she is timid or stupid and uninterested. If she is to gain any influence, she must establish herself as a pleasant, amiable, but intelligent human being, no trouble but rather a help. The men can then turn to her in any puzzling questions involving women, perhaps enjoy her protection in warding off attacks by militant feminists from outside, and in time will lend an attentive ear to her own projects.

This technique of mine, which I drifted into naturally because of my own temperament, was a slow-moving one, not at all spectacular in its results. It required patient months to win the confidence of male colleagues. Meanwhile, the militant feminists outside sometimes accused me of feebleness or indifference or treason against "our cause." In one sense perhaps they were right, for I would always, I think, have placed the welfare of the whole institution above the present advancement of our sex.

My technique would not, perhaps, have been effective for the pioneers in seeking opportunities for women. Probably they had to batter at the doors rather violently and spectacularly before I could get in and sit there peacefully in a friendly atmosphere, "boring from within." Actually, after I got going on any one of these committees or commissions, I was not really "boring from within." I was just one of a group of human beings, all trying together for the best possible solution of the important questions before them.

When I took office, the Dean of Barnard College was officially the Adviser of Women Graduate Students. There were comparatively few of these in those days compared to the vast numbers that later enrolled. There were still a good many graduate courses not open to women. Professor Brander Matthews of the Department of English, I recall, was very obdurate for a long time.. In recompense for having contributed two great scholars to the Faculty of Political Science, Professor James Harvey Robinson in History and Professor John Bates Clark in Economics, Barnard College had secured the admission of women to graduate courses under that Faculty. There remained a number of other departments in which the doors were closed.

To help improve these conditions we organized under the chairmanship of the Barnard Dean a Committee on Women Graduate Students, appointed by the President. We had as members two men who were deeply interested in this cause,—Professor Robinson and Professor John Dewey. There was also an able woman scientist from the Barnard Faculty, Professor Ida H. Ogilvie in Geology. We got as Executive Secretary a newly appointed Adviser to Women Graduate Students, Miss Emma Peters Smith, and we proceeded quietly on our way. We always had the sympathy and support of the President of the University. Some years later, as the result of a study made by this committee and a detailed recommendation, the Trustees of Columbia invested over a million dollars in Johnson Hall, a fine residence for women graduate and professional students.

Meanwhile, we had kept an eye on the great professional schools of the University still closed to women, and meditated ways of getting them opened. The new School of Journalism, just being organized when I became Dean of Barnard, gave us a lift. Its director, Dr. Talcott Williams, announced from the start that it was to be open to women. This was good and showed the drift of the times. Moreover, it enabled us to start at Barnard College what developed into our important Department of Government. The two years of collegiate preparation for the School of Journalism were to be given for women at Barnard College as they were given for men in Columbia College. They included as one of the requirements a course in American government. So we had an excellent reason for introducing what might oth-erwise have been a very controversial course.

How odd that sounds today! But woman suffrage was being discussed actively at the time, with strong differences of opinion, and a course in gov-ernment might to some people indicate that Barnard was aligning itself and influencing its students on one side of this heated controversy. The necessity of meeting the requirements of the School of Journalism gave us an excel-lent excuse. We got an able young man, later widely known, to come over from Columbia to conduct this course in American government, Charles Beard.

Medicine is a profession which naturally appeals deeply to women, as they are instinctively concerned with conserving life. So when the plans for the great new medical center that was to be erected up at 165th Street were first explained to the University Council, I rose and asked whether the School was to be open to women. The representatives of the Medical School replied with warm sympathy that they were highly in favor of having women study medicine. One of them had seen the unit of the Scottish Women's Hospitals at work in the war horrors of Serbia. As soon as our new Medical Center was erected, they said, it would gladly welcome women students. Meanwhile, the crowded old building down at Fifty-ninth Street simply could not accommodate them. Why, there was not even space for them to hang their hats.

Columbia had to raise about thirty-five million dollars to erect those new buildings, and that seemed to involve a very long wait. Meanwhile, I had the perfect candidate for admission,—a charming, sensible, and brilliantly able young Swedish woman, Gulli Lindh, who was to graduate from Barnard in June, 1917. So I took up negotiations with the Dean of the College of Physicians and Surgeons, Dr. Samuel Lambert. I told him about Gulli and I guaranteed that if he would admit her, she would prove a better student than any other in his school. He was sufficiently impressed to be willing to con-sider the suggestion that we might build a small temporary addition to the old buildings down at Fifty-ninth Street to provide some additional labora-tory space and a room where women students could hang their hats. We got estimates and found it would cost $50,000. "Very well," I said, "we will raise $50,000."

The American Women's Medical Association had been deeply interested in all this, and they started in gallantly to help raise the money. I wrote elo-quent letters to the New York newspapers and a few thousand dollars came in, but it was slow going, and June, 1917, was approaching. So I went again to see Sam Lambert, as everyone called him. He was a great character, genial and jolly and forceful and a fine physician. "Look, Dr. Lambert," said I, "here is Gulli Lindh now forced to plan to go to Johns Hopkins. Can't you take her in anyway on faith that the $50,000 will ultimately turn up? If you don't, you'll be sorry in the years to come, when she is a very distinguished medical scientist, that you forced her to study medicine away from her own University."

Shortly after that we got word that the Medical School had admitted Gulli and five other young women to keep her company. And very soon afterward I received a telegram saying that an old gentleman in Texas would give us the $50,000. Some members of the American Women's Medical Association had been trying to persuade him, apparently to no avail. He had been giving large sums of money to the University of Texas, and that institution suddenly did something that offended him deeply. So to peeve them he abruptly contributed $50,000 to us. (I always remember this incident when participating in money-raising campaigns. You just can't guess the motives or the thoughts that will bring you gifts.)

Four years later at Commencement time, as I was crossing South Court in front of Low Library, I met my good friend Dr. William Darrach, who had succeeded Dr. Lambert as Dean of the College of Physicians and Surgeons. He greeted me warmly. "Well," he said, "your girl did it all right. She led her class easily." I learned later that third and fifth places in the class had also been taken by women students.

The Law School proved a much more difficult proposition. Though there are some excellent women lawyers, especially in France, law is not on the whole, I think, a profession which appeals fundamentally to women as does medicine. But there were almost always a few members of the Barnard graduating class who wanted to study law, and it seemed highly desirable that they should have a chance to do that in their own University. As they applied and were refused, we kept thinking up ways of approaching the Law Faculty and persuading them to see the light. In this I had the warm and effective support of the Faculty of Barnard College. The male members of our Faculty were just as eager as were the women to get additional educational opportunities opened to our sex. Once we happened to have in the senior class four daughters of distinguished judges who wished to study law, and we helped them draw up a petition to the Law School asking for admission. It was unsuccessful. Whenever I had a little leisure, which was not often, I tried to think up new approaches to the Law School.

Meanwhile, this question had been discussed among the Columbia University Trustees and the Law Faculty. One night President Butler called a conference at his house to consider the matter. It consisted of the Committee on Education of the Board of Trustees and several of the older and more distinguished members of the Law Faculty. I was the only woman present. The President asked me to explain why members of the Barnard graduating class wanted to study law in their own University, and there followed a good deal of general discussion. The President and the Committee on Education of the Trustees were obviously in favor of the admission of women but they would not force the Law Faculty to take action against its own will. It was Professor Gifford, I think, who spoke for it when he said: "Of course, on general ethical principles women ought to be admitted to the Law School, but we simply cannot do it. It would ruin our school. All our best students, for example the graduates of Amherst and Williams who now come to us, would go instead to Harvard." And there the matter had to rest.

As I thought all this over afterwards, I wondered just what the situation was at Harvard. I knew there had been some discussion of the matter there and that one of the Harvard professors of Law was interested in having women study that subject. I decided to go on to Cambridge and find out. I thought hopefully, "If, when I inquire why they don't admit women, they say it is because if we did our best students would go to Columbia, then I can try to persuade both schools to hold hands and take the dangerous step together. In that case neither would be injured." Accordingly I wrote to my friend Bertha Boody, who was at that time Dean of Radcliffe College, asking her to arrange a meeting for me with the Harvard Law professor who was sympathetic towards women, and presently I went on to Cambridge.

He proved to be indeed kind and interested. I found that his own daughter wanted to study law, and that he was conducting a small class for her and a few of her friends. It seemed that the Harvard Law Faculty, unlike that at Columbia, was on the whole in favor of admitting women, but the Corporation, which roughly corresponded, I gather, to our Board of Trustees, was opposed. He told me that his daughter and one of her friends had called upon every single member of the Corporation to present the case for the admission of women to the Law School, and every one had been absolutely opposed. "And what reason did they give?" said I eagerly. "They all said," he replied, "that it had never been done."

I took the next train back to New York, realizing that whatever difficulties I might have at Columbia, they were as nothing compared to those I should face in the atmosphere of Cambridge, Massachusetts. (This was much changed in later years by Ada Comstock, President of Radcliffe.)

Clearly we had to work it out somehow by ourselves in Columbia University, and it was a group of members of the Faculty of Barnard College who thought up the plan which ultimately proved successful. They drew up a set of resolutions stating that the Faculty of Barnard College found itself in a very embarrassing position in that its students, though thoroughly competent, were not allowed to go on and study law within their own University.

The Faculty of Barnard College found it most awkward to be unable to set forth any valid reason why this should be so. They therefore petitioned their sister Faculty of the School of Law to change this situation.

This document infuriated the Law Faculty. They said it was perfectly absurd; there was no reason whatsoever why the Faculty of Barnard College should feel embarrassed. But somehow, I have never quite understood why, these arguments got under the skin of the Law professors. They went on discussing the question furiously, and they finally came up with this solution. They agreed, because of the petition of the Barnard Faculty, to admit to the Law School graduates of Barnard College who were especially and highly recommended by the Dean of Barnard. I had only one applicant for the Law School that year, by no means as brilliant as Gulli Lindh, but a good and sound student. I recommended her. It was a satisfactory opening wedge.

When I returned to the University the following September, the Dean of the Law School greeted me with some embarrassment. "I hope you won't mind," he said, "but we found it impossible to keep to that agreement that we would admit only graduates of Barnard College. We had applications from two women who had degrees from other parts of the University,—one a Master of Arts and the other a Ph.D. There was nothing against them and we did not see how we could refuse them. So we now have three women students." I assured him that I was not in the least displeased. After that they took in any well-qualified woman. Indeed, during World War II it was really the women students who kept the Law School going, as nearly all the men were off fighting.

There remained the School of Engineering. The Schools of Architecture, Business, and Library Service and of course Teachers College, our school of education, were open to women, but there had been very little discussion about getting women into the School of Engineering. Very few women wanted to go into that field. For a good many years I felt that if a really tip-top candidate appeared, I might be able to insert her in the School, but no one did. Then the Second World War changed the situation drastically. In the year before Pearl Harbor a Barnard Faculty Committee on National Service, under the tireless and enthusiastic leadership of Professor Elizabeth Reynard, began to set up special National Service courses outside the regular curriculum, giving training in skills which might be of use to the country. Among these courses was one in drafting given by two energetic and patriotic members of the Engineering Faculty, Professors Allen and Lee, with the help of the Curtiss-Wright Aircraft Corporation, which was badly in need of draftsmen. Fortunately, the two Barnard seniors who took this course were so extremely good at it, that when they graduated in June, the Curtiss-Wright company promptly engaged them as engineering aides.

The following year, the year of Pearl Harbor, the shortage of engineers became an acute danger to the nation. The clamorous demand for women as engineering aides, especially in airplane factories, grew louder and louder. Happily many of the women who took special courses at Columbia proved able and acceptable, so that the School of Engineering became convinced that a few women, at least, would be competent to go on and become real engineers. Therefore in the year after Pearl Harbor the School was declared officially open to women.

During all these years while more and more doors were being opened to women, I was concerned also with doing everything possible to ensure that women prove themselves worthy of these new privileges in the world of scholarship and the professions. I feared at times that we were not adequately showing our merits. So I joined in various movements to ensure that all the most promising young women scholars should be found and should have every opportunity to go on and develop their ability by advanced study in this country and abroad. As I used to say in speeches,—"If we could produce one or two more Madame Curies, that would accomplish more for the advancement of women than any amount of agitation, argument and legislation."

Lack of money often held back our young scholars. Fellowships and yet more fellowships were urgently needed for them. At that time, before the recent great growth in such aid from many sources, few were available. In a later chapter I say something of the mighty effort made by university women themselves to remedy this situation.

Another obstacle faced us. There was danger at times that women might not be judged by the highest standards, but more leniently because of their sex. "She is a remarkably good chemist—for a woman," you might hear a man say. It seemed to me essential, if the ablest young women scholars were to achieve the best work of which they were capable, that they should be held to the most rigorous standards. This I constantly urged. To advance, a woman must do at least as good work as her male colleagues, generally better.

How about marriage, a home, rearing children? It was obvious that that side of life inevitably affected a woman scholar or other professional worker far more than it did a man, and often held her back from achievement. And more and more generally women scholars and professional workers wanted to marry and have children.

When I was young there were many women in the academic world who cheerfully led celibate lives, somewhat like the nuns of the Middle Ages and today, and dedicated themselves to the education of youth. My colleagues, the heads of other colleges for women in my part of the country,—Miss Pendleton of Wellesley, Miss Woolley of Mount Holyoke, Miss Thomas and later Miss Park of Bryn Mawr, Miss Glass of Sweet Briar, Miss Morriss of

Pembroke, never married, and it was considered perfectly natural and proper that they should lead their active and useful lives in celibacy. Indeed the very idea of their marrying while continuing their professional career was in the early years shocking to many people. I encountered a striking example of this.

Soon after I became Dean a young woman who was an assistant in Physics came to my office to tell me she expected to be married the following summer. "How nice," said I, "I wish you much happiness." "But," said she with a troubled look, "I should like to go on here next year as assistant in Physics, as I've already been appointed." "Well, why not?" I asked in some perplexity. "There's no objection from the College?" she queried. "None at all," I answered, "so far as I can see. As long as you do your work here satisfactorily, your marriage seems to me entirely your personal business."

Thus I spoke in my innocence, from the light of reason, unconscious of the difficulties of the problem. Soon afterwards, when reading some old minutes of the Barnard Trustees, I found that about twelve years earlier, when Dean Emily James Smith announced that she was going to marry George Haven Putnam and would continue as head of the College the Board was rent by controversy. Some of the Trustees felt most strongly that a married woman must devote herself to her home: to carry on a professional career would be shocking and immoral. It was finally decided that Miss Smith might continue, as Mrs. Putnam, to be Dean; but when, a year or so later, she stated that she was expecting a child, everybody, herself included, agreed that she should retire.

Ignorant of all this, I had simply not thought of asking the Trustees about the case of the young assistant in Physics, but had embarked on this policy quite on my own responsibility. We continued to have married women on our staff fairly often; no Trustee objected. From my observations, I began to realize more vividly the difficulty of combining marriage, children, and a professional career; but I realized also that in some cases the combination absolutely had to be made. As a college for women, with a good many women on our staff, I thought Barnard was a suitable place to experiment with trying to adjust this problem. Presently I had a new idea about it.

One day when we were granting a long leave of absence with pay to a male professor who was in the hospital, a woman member of our teaching staff asked me for the usual leave of absence without salary for a semester because she was going to have a child. It suddenly struck me as unfair that you should receive full salary if you went to the hospital because of illness but that if you went in order to provide another citizen for the community, you should lose all your pay. So I propounded this problem to President

Butler, suggesting that under certain circumstances we might grant "maternity leave" with full salary. He looked a bit startled at first. I reminded him that in France they particularly wanted their women teachers to be married and encouraged them to have children. President Butler saw the point. "It's a good idea," said he. "We should have women teachers with fuller lives and richer experience, not so many dried-up old maids."

We made the recommendation to the Executive Committee of the Board of Trustees. I recall that the male members of that committee also looked startled when they first heard the idea, and one of them said: "What about the father of the child? Shouldn't he bear the expense, not Barnard?" Then I noted the two women members, ardent feminists both, Alice Duer Miller and Helen Rogers Reid, preparing themselves for the fray. But there was no fray. The men yielded quickly, and alone among colleges, as far as I know, Barnard has followed this policy of maternity leave with pay ever since.

Of course, such absences are upsetting to a department, but there were not many of them and on the whole the plan seemed to work fairly well. I was glad Barnard had taken this generous attitude towards married women teachers. My observations over the years, however, at college and elsewhere, showed me that the combination of motherhood and a career, especially while the children were young, was extremely difficult. It could be successfully achieved only if the mother was exceptionally strong and healthy, if her husband was sympathetic and helpful, and if there was money enough to secure service in the home and such service to be found. There are some striking examples of successful careers which achieved this happy combination of circumstances, notably that of my successor at Barnard, Millicent Carey McIntosh.

The almost complete disappearance of domestic labor during recent years has, however, made the accomplishment more and more difficult. It is often hard for the most highly trained professional woman to earn enough to pay the exorbitant wages demanded by a competent substitute in the home. And there are very few such substitutes to be found. Indeed, during World War II our country lost the bitterly needed services of some expert women mathematicians and scientists because they could find no reliable person to care for their young children during their hours at the laboratories, and there were no adequate day nurseries at hand.

When the mother is left a widow, or for other reasons compelled to earn money to support her children, she must make some sort of arrangement for the babies; but when the necessity is not so urgent she frequently prefers to drop her professional work for a few years and care for them herself. I used to advise the Barnard seniors on graduation to consider planning in the future, if they married, to discontinue their careers for five or ten years to bear their children and start them on the way to education. This impedes their careers, naturally, but after all you can't eat your cake and have it too. Everything must be paid for.

All this is a large subject which concerned me for many years. I know no easy solution. More part-time jobs for married women, some readjustment of salaries and wages so that a skilled chemist can earn more than a mother's helper, a larger supply of house-workers, more and better day nurseries and nursery schools—all these would help. I watch with interest the development of possibilities for the easier combination of motherhood and career.

Why do I want it made possible for married women to continue their careers in scholarship and the professions? Because it is a deep satisfaction to any human being to develop and use his talents to the utmost of which he is capable; and because the country needs the service of every good brain among its citizens, male or female. There are always far too few of them.

It was right to do what we could at Barnard to aid married women teachers; but of recent years another aspect of the question has troubled me. I have occasionally thought that in schools and colleges there has arisen a particularly cruel and unwholesome discrimination against *unmarried* women for some teaching and administrative posts. This is due in part to the attitude towards the unmarried of certain of the less responsible psychologists and psychiatrists of the day, which tends to voice disrespect for spinsters in the teaching profession as "inhibited" and "frustrated." After all, many of our sex can never marry; women outnumber the men. There are plenty of other lines of work open to them today, where the spinster status is not unwelcome. But why drive them away from a profession which for generations has been natural and congenial to them? In the past hundreds of thousands of pupils have owed and given them deep gratitude and affection. Children have at home married women for mothers, to provide them with maternal instinct and care. Why should they not profit from a different type of nurture in school? The tendency of today to regard celibate teachers as "frustrated"—except the respected and competent nuns in the Catholic teaching orders—threatens deprivation to many children and hardship to women who, like those of past centuries, could give talents and wholehearted devotion to the teaching profession.

Married or unmarried, women's chances of getting professorships in colleges or universities have deteriorated, I fear, during the last thirty years. Most colleges for women, which during their early decades had a large majority of women on their faculties, have during the past quarter-century made great efforts to secure a considerable proportion of men. As it is far from easy for women to obtain a post of professorial rank in a co-educational institution, this has made the situation rather worse than it used to be. I do not know the solution except to try to persuade the men's colleges and the co-educational ones to realize that it is good for young people to be taught by both sexes. Sometimes I think this can be done if we train up a sufficient number of distinguished women scholars and teachers. But can we, if girls are taught almost entirely by men professors and develop a kind of inferiority complex?

A few days ago (December, 1952) I asked a young woman who was a junior with top marks at one of our best universities whether she had any woman professor. "No," she answered, "I haven't. I never thought of a woman professor. I don't believe I should like to study under one."

Nicholas Murray Butler

1882 COLUMBIA COLLEGE, 1884 PhD

A towering figure in Columbia history, Nicholas Murray Butler propelled the University into the highest echelon of scholarship and research. As President from 1902 to 1945, Butler oversaw the creation of five new graduate schools, the consolidation of Columbia-Presbyterian Medical Center, and the establishment of the College's core curriculum. He also sat as president of the Carnegie Endowment for International Peace and shared the 1931 Nobel Peace Prize. His 1939 autobiography, Across the Busy Years, *is excerpted here.*

When the old College was driven by the march of events from its first site on the King's Farm, it had been the intention to place it on the Upper Estate which was then remote indeed from business buildings or even from residences. Renwick, the architect of Saint Patrick's Cathedral, drew a plan for a new Columbia College building, perhaps the largest building which had then been proposed in this country, to stand on the west side of Fifth Avenue and to extend almost from what is now Forty-ninth Street to what is now Fifty-first Street. It was placed back from Fifth Avenue and was shown in grounds charmingly laid out and surrounded by trees. It is of record that Saint Patrick's Cathedral was placed where it is so that it might always face the quiet gardens of Columbia College!

When removal from the King's Farm became urgent and funds were not at hand with which to build the new structure planned for the Upper Estate, the trustees leased that property and purchased the block bounded by Madison Avenue, Fourth Avenue, Forty-ninth Street and Fiftieth Street, then occupied by the Institution for the Deaf and Dumb. This was intended to be but a temporary site while a permanent home for the College was being chosen further north, since there were already signs that the Upper Estate would no long remain remote both from business buildings and from residences. Before anything could be done, however, the Civil War came, the financial situation of the College became more acute and so it was that a site intended to be temporary was occupied for forty years.

Meanwhile the search for a permanent location farther up the Island had never been abandoned. Various individuals took part in it from time to time, but nothing was accomplished. Indeed, just before Henry Villard built the stately brownstone houses on the block north of the College site, it was seriously proposed that Columbia should itself acquire that block and look forward to remaining in that situation permanently. Fortunately, that plan was frustrated, and the search for another and permanent home continued.

During the closing years of the administration of President Barnard, the College was in a great state of ferment and turmoil. New ideas and new projects were being brought forward year by year and almost week by week. While the rentals from the Upper Estate had improved, they were not yet, by any means, adequate or sufficient to give the trustees a free hand in dealing with other problems. During all this period—indeed, from 1754—the College had received but an insignificant number of gifts and bequests, and these uniformly of small amount. The great tide of benefaction which was shortly to begin was not then in evidence or even suspected.

This was the background when John B. Pine, the youngest and most vigorous of the trustees, asked me to join him in the search for a new site. On many successive Sunday afternoons in the autumn of 1890, I went with Mr. Pine all about the upper part of Manhattan Island, searching for a site to be urged upon the trustees as the permanent home of Columbia University. Any proposed site south of 110th Street was rejected, it seeming certain that the march of progress would soon make such a site unsuitable, no matter what attractions it might present at the moment. This applied to property, which was carefully examined, west of the south end of Central Park along what is now Central Park West, and also to several blocks on the east side of Riverside Drive bounded on the south by West Seventy-second Street. The matter soon resolved itself into a choice between three high points on Manhattan Island: Morningside Heights, then generally known as Bloomingdale; a height of land near Audubon Park where the American Academy of Arts and Letters, the American Geographical Society and the Hispanic Society now are; and the high point on what is today Fort Washington Avenue which is now the site of The Cloisters and the very attractive Fort Tryon Park.

Having in mind protection from possible developments in the future, accessibility from east and from west as well as from north and from south, and comparative isolation, we finally settled on Morningside Heights as our choice. The prompt purchase of this property was urged upon President Low and the trustees. It was my fortune to spend several evenings with Mr. William C. Schermerhorn, then Chairman of the Trustees, at his home, 49 West Twenty-third Street, going over maps and discussing future possibilities and developments. Mr. Schermerhorn, who was himself greatly interested in real-estate holdings, followed closely every detail of the suggestions that were made. It was then my urgent proposal, which Mr. Pine shared in theory but thought wholly impracticable, that the trustees should at that time acquire the entire body of land between Morningside Drive on the east and Riverside Drive on the west and between West 110th Street on the south and West 122nd Street on the north, except such part of it as had already been acquired by the Cathedral of St. John the Divine and by St. Luke's Hospital. It seemed to me that since the trustees had had long and successful experience in leasehold property, and since their purchase of any part of this land as a home for the College would greatly and at once increase the value of all the rest of it, they should themselves get this benefit for the College and its future endowment by acquiring and leasing for twenty-one-year periods such parts of the property as they did not or could not immediately use for academic buildings and their surroundings. I remember pointing out that this property was practically an island, since Morningside Park protected it on the east and the Hudson River on the west, while 110th and 122nd streets were both boulevards under the control and maintenance of the Park Department.

At that time this entire tract could have been purchased for a relatively modest sum compared with later values. Had this been done, the future endowment of Columbia would have been made secure through its own foresight and its own act. It must be remembered that there were then no houses or improvements anywhere in the neighborhood, that the Bloomingdale Insane Asylum of the New York Hospital stood in comfortable isolation on a height surrounded by grass and trees, and that the city lots, each twenty-five by one hundred feet, existed only on the map. At that time these lots were thought to be worth from $1600 to $2000. On the day following the announcement of Columbia's purchase of part of this property, their price advanced to $4000 and within two years some of them were being sold at $20,000 to $22,000 each. All this enormous increase in value was given, in effect, to casual holders and to speculators, when a reasonable amount of foresight and courage would have brought it to the coffers of the University.

The first purchase by the University, on which an option was taken in December 1891 and the purchase finally completed in 1892, included that portion of the property between Amsterdam Avenue and Broadway, 116th Street and 120th Street. South Field was acquired in 1903 and East Field in 1910–14 at steadily increasing prices. For each of these purchases the amount paid was several times that for which they might have been acquired in the period from 1892 to 1894.

George W. Vanderbilt had become very much interested in the development of the New York College for the Training of Teachers, now Teachers College, and while this search for a new site for Columbia was going on, I took Mr. Vanderbilt into our confidence and suggested his acquiring for Teachers College the property adjoining whatever land the College might decide to buy. Up to that time Mr. Vanderbilt and I had been looking at the block between Broadway and Central Park West, Sixty-second and Sixty-third Streets, which then seemed very far out in the country. On making his first visit to Morningside, Mr. Vanderbilt's judgment concurred with that of Mr. Pine, that the Morningside Heights site was to be preferred. When the time came, therefore, he was ready to purchase and did purchase for Teachers College the property on the north side of West 120th Street between Amsterdam Avenue and Broadway, to which that institution was moved in 1893 from its original home at 9 University Place.

The acreage which was purchased then and subsequently for the University has long since been outgrown. In particular, the School of Law and the Schools of Engineering have for several years past required greatly increased facilities and accommodation. What was done, however, proved to be of extraordinary significance. It placed the University on one of the highest points of Manhattan Island, protected on either side and away from the chief marts of trade and commerce. It made possible the building of what will some day be regarded, perhaps, as an American twentieth-century Mont St. Geneviève.

The University took possession of that portion of the present site on Morningside Heights which it had then acquired, on October 1, 1894, and at once proceeded to study how it might best be developed. In order to secure legislative action to prevent cutting this site to pieces by opening streets across it, the trustees ceded to the city forty feet of land between Amsterdam Avenue and Broadway in order to give 120th Street a width of one hundred feet. They likewise conveyed to the city a property which was one-half of the present width of 116th Street between Broadway and Amsterdam Avenue. These steps made the unity of the new site secure. The trustees selected three outstanding architects, Richard M. Hunt, Charles C. Haight and Charles F. McKim, to study how the architectural development of the new site might best be planned. Their several projects were carefully studied and then passed upon by the head of the Department of Architecture, Professor

William R. Ware, and by Frederick Law Olmsted of Boston. The Gothic architecture of Mr. Haight was rejected as unsuitable. The reasons were that the cost of the ground made it necessary to erect high buildings and that Gothic windows would not provide adequate light for libraries and laboratories under modern conditions in New York City. It is interesting to recall that one of these architectural projects made the University face to the east, another made it face to the west, while that of McKim, which was finally chosen, made it face to the south. When McKim was asked why he had done this, his answer was most characteristic: "So that Columbia University may always look the City of New York straight in the face!"

The Morningside Heights site was formally dedicated with most impressive ceremonies on May 2, 1896, at which time Abram S. Hewitt, of the Class of 1842, delivered a memorable commemorative oration. Adequate provision by way of buildings was made in time to permit the transfer of the University's educational work from the Forty-ninth Street site on October I, 1897. "No university," wrote President Low, "has a nobler site; no city has a greater opportunity."

John Erskine

1900 COLUMBIA COLLEGE, 1903 PhD

The literary scholar John Erskine taught at Columbia from 1909 to 1937. His notion of a course grounded in the Western classics influenced the humanities component of the College's core curriculum, and more broadly American education in general. Erskine was a gifted teacher whose flamboyant mien set him apart from his colleagues but made him popular among students. He was also an accomplished composer and musician who wrote several books on music and served as president of the then Juilliard School of Music and a board member of the Metropolitan Opera. This selection, in which he recalls his time as an undergraduate, is taken from The Memory of Certain Persons *(1947).*

During the summer of 1897, Columbia moved up to the new buildings on Morningside Heights, and in the complicated migrations a few odds and ends were mislaid or lost—among them a course in chemistry which Harry St. Clair and I had elected. It dropped out of the curriculum, and we spent hours looking for it. Charles Frederick Chandler was to have been the instructor, and his name had attracted us rather more than the subject. We took our problem to Van Am. Chandler's course had lapsed, he admitted, but fortunately there was a substitute, Professor Charles Pellew's lectures for medical students. Pellew was Chandler's son-in-law, and since we were not to have Chandler, it was something to study with so close a relative.

Pellew gave his lectures at the end of the afternoon, from five to six, so that the boys from the College of Physicians and Surgeons could get uptown.

The installation of the new halls was incomplete, especially as concerned electric wiring and bulbs. Pellew's large amphitheatre, after five, faded rapidly from dimness to blind dark. Chandler's son-in-law must have been a chemist or Chandler would not have had him around, but as a lecturer he was nothing at all. Only at intervals could he be heard, and then a certain affectation of speech and manner prevented him from being understood. Some years later, in 1923, he inherited an English title, went back to claim it, became Viscount Exmouth, took his seat in the House of Lords, or wherever viscounts are employed, and no doubt was in his proper place at last. He died in 1945. But meanwhile in 1897, his five o'clock medical students, in grief at his inaudibility, threw spitballs and howled catcalls until six, when they raced for seats in the crowded horsecars southward bound.

Early in November I sought Van Am's permission to desert this kind of chemistry for Professor Ogden N. Rood's physics course, even though it was almost the middle of the term.

"If you change now," said the Dean, "you will flunk."

"I'll flunk if I stay!"

"If it will make you happier," said Van Am, "to do your flunking in Physics, speak to Professor Rood about it."

Rood was a great scientist, and I learned much simply by watching his methods. Research was his passion, but he could teach, as far as was necessary. The physics class came on Mondays, Wednesdays and Fridays, and between sessions the Professor resumed his interrupted experiments. In his laboratory, which was next door to his classroom, he had a couch, where he slept when his experimenting held him too late to go home. On Mondays he came to us fresh and tidy. By Wednesday he looked wilted, by Friday dilapidated. Then he would go home for the week end, and on Monday he would begin the cycle again, refreshed and tidied.

✿ ✿ ✿

The undergraduates at Columbia had a newspaper, *Spectator,* and a magazine, the *Literary Monthly.* When the college moved uptown a third publication was added, *Morningside.* To this last I began to contribute, Melville Cane aimed at *Monthly,* and Sydnor Harrison joined the staff of *Spectator.* By the time we reached senior year each of us was editing his favorite publication, and we all were writing for the two strictly literary magazines. *Monthly,* a conspicuously serious review which permitted itself no more humor than a British quarterly, contained essays, poems (romantically lyrical, tragic, or epic), stories and criticism. *Morningside,* a handsomely printed brochure appearing every three weeks, accepted neither essays nor literary criticism, but showed the broadest kind of hospitality to fiction or verse of any style, provided it had quality. George Hellman edited *Monthly,* in succession to Joseph Proskauer, and Bill Bradley, from Columbia Grammar School, edited *Morningside,* which owed its attractive format to his knowledge of types and page-designing. Though he and Hellman were my academic elders by a year, I learned rather easily to accommodate myself to their exercise of the authority which derives from long-accumulated wisdom.

Of course I am prejudiced, but I think the contributors to *Morningside* were a superior group, some of them to be numbered surely among the great of their time: Hans Zinsser, class of 1899, bacteriologist; Fred Keppel, class of 1898, successor to Van Am as Dean of the College, then Assistant Secretary of War under Newton Baker, then President of the Carnegie Corporation; Joel Elias Spingarn, poet and critic, one of the great authorities on the Renaissance, Assistant Professor of Comparative Literature at Columbia. Every number of *Morningside* had a fresh cover drawn in black and white by some obliging artist who happened to be studying architecture, almost always by Huger Elliott, long a staff-member at the Metropolitan Museum of Art. Without Huger, *Morningside* would have missed some of its habitual excellence. He had talent, and he had the wholehearted joy in our enterprise which marks the true and lovable bohemian, predestined citizen of the Left Bank.

✻   ✻   ✻

Halfway through my sophomore year *Morningside* published some verses of mine, fanciful and light, of no importance except for the impression they made on one man. A few days after the issue came out I found in my mail a flattering note, in a neat but miniature hand, suggesting that I call on the writer in room 509 Fayerweather Hall. That was the building in which I was studying physics with Professor Rood, but the English department occupied an upper floor. I was not sure of the signature, but it seemed to be Thomas R. Price. With an undergraduate's haziness about his elders, I had no idea who Thomas R. Price was, but since he evidently appreciated my peculiar talents, I was glad to encourage him by the sight of me. In this inadequate mood I climbed the stairs and met one of the noblest gentlemen and one of the best friends who ever inspired a sophomore to make the most he could of his life.

I can still see Professor Price, as he opened the door of his office. His manner had a courtliness from another time and place. He was of medium height, rather bald and slightly stooping, with a thick mustache and remarkable black eyes. His sight was not good, but his eyes seemed keen. He received me with expressions of pleasure, and wished me to a seat with something like deference, which overwhelmed me then, and seemed even more incongruous as I learned, through months and years, how great a man he was. But he had a fantastic respect for anyone who could write, especially for anyone who could put verses together.

He was one of the two or three most profound scholars then teaching the English language and literature in America. He had begun as a precocious student at the University of Virginia, with a particularly high record in mathematics. At the age of thirteen he had mastered all of that subject then taught at West Point. After taking his M.A. at the age of nineteen, he went to Germany to study Greek and Oriental languages at Berlin and Kiel, but upon the outbreak of the Civil War he ran the blockade, and received a commission on the staff of his cousin, General J. E. B. Stuart. Immediately after the war he married, and spent his honeymoon in General Lee's house; because of Lee's example, he went into education, to help in the restoration of the South. He taught English and modern languages at Randolph-Macon College, then succeeded Basil Gildersleeve as professor of Greek at the University of Virginia, when Gildersleeve went to Johns Hopkins. At Virginia, Professor Price also taught Hebrew. He had a reading knowledge of some twenty languages, half a dozen of which he could speak fluently.

From my little poem he got the impression that I was destined to be a writer, and he never wavered in that amiable opinion, which no one else then held. He was not himself a writer of the kind he thought I might be; I was later to profit by the instruction of a remarkable poet, and never cease to remember the inspiration with thankfulness. But only Professor Price, before I had accomplished a thing, believed in me, and taught me to believe in myself.

A few weeks after this very first meeting with Professor Price I received from Mrs. Price an invitation to tea. I went, and found myself in a choice representation of the Southern colony of New York City. Professor Price's loyalty to Virginia was extreme. He was never reconciled to the outcome of the Civil War. He and Mrs. Price led their social life either in the University circle or among Virginians who like themselves had come North. I remember the impression made on me that afternoon at tea by the large number of good-looking girls and handsome ladies, and by the prominence of the Southern accent. Mrs. Price was a gracious hostess, and her daughter Elizabeth—Mrs. Frederick Houston—then a young girl, flitted around the room with two or three others of her age. I had not then acquired a gallant philosophy, and to tell the truth, I went to the tea in the hope of seeing the Professor who appreciated my writing. I found him in a corner of the drawing room completely surrounded by the most beautiful girls at the party. As I came up, I saw he was balancing a glass of punch in his fingers without drinking it; he was too busy talking. Obviously his talk was witty, for he had his audience in laughter. When I drew near enough to hear his words, I discovered he was discussing the oddities of Danish grammar. I learned at once two of his main characteristics. He was a born courtier, and preferred not to waste a moment on a man if he could be talking to a woman. And he could turn the driest academic subject into bright material for social purposes.

Whether he was a typical Southerner of the old régime, surviving from pre-Civil War days, I cannot say. I met no one else, whether Northerner or Southerner, quite like him. It was easy to see that he had traveled abroad; he was more likely to speak of Europe than of our own country. If he could, he would avoid all references to American politics. Within the walls of his own home, if he spoke of the President, you knew he was referring to Jefferson Davis. Otherwise he would say with great respect, Mr. McKinley, or Mr. Cleveland.

We had no teacher who was more courteous, but almost my last memory of him illustrates his loyalty to a prejudice. Half a dozen of us in one of his seminars were writing an examination paper. He thought it ignoble to proctor students who were undergoing a test, but the walls of his classroom were lined with cases of books from his overflowing library, and while we were writing he came in to consult a volume. As he turned the pages the janitor came up the stairs with a gentleman who wished to call on Professor Price. The Professor offered the gentleman a chair on the spot, and for a moment they conferred in low tones, the caller explaining his errand, the Professor listening without enthusiasm. All at once something went wrong. The caller arose and backed apologetically toward the door. Professor Price followed him out and across the hall to the staircase. At the top stair the gentleman took a hasty farewell and hurried down, but Professor Price stood there talking after him vigorously, raising his voice to catch up with the fast-disappearing visitor. We in the classroom heard something like this: "No sir! If at any time you ask a favor for yourself in your private capacity, I shall be delighted to oblige you if I can! But as to the present matter—it would be impossible for me to think of anything to say at the funeral of your dead friend which his relatives would care to hear!"

✿ ✿ ✿

With Professor Price, admirer of writers, were associated Professor Brander Matthews and Professor George Edward Woodberry, two younger colleagues whose reputation was well established. They differed sharply in background and temperament, and both differed from Professor Price. Woodberry was the product, somewhat narrowly, of Boston, of Cambridge, of Harvard. Brander was just as narrowly the product of old New York, of that merchandising society—respectability founded on exports and imports—which Henry James and Edith Wharton described. Woodberry, born at Beverly, Massachusetts, from five generations of sea captains, had been brought up in an atmosphere of high thinking but of decidedly plain living. Brander Matthews, heir to a sizable fortune, had been conditioned by social contacts and by wide travel for the life of a cosmopolitan, the kind of world citizen who would feel at home anywhere in the best clubs, the best restaurants, the best theatres. Through my college days Woodberry took his vacations at Beverly, on the ancestral North Shore, or in Italy, which was his spiritual home. Brander liked to rest up in his London clubs or in the Paris theatres.

Brander was a skilled and graceful man of letters. He regarded writing as a craft, an honest way of earning a living. I doubt if his soul ever yearned for self-expression in a more profound sense. His novels were not important, and his plays did not hold the stage, but he was a warm-hearted friend, his acquaintance among celebrated people here and abroad was wide, and he was an excellent raconteur. Also, and perhaps this was his greatest charm, he was of a loyal temperament, and in all his loyalties he remained to the end of his days rather sophomoric. His affection for Columbia, his Alma Mater, expressed itself in typical undergraduate gibes at rival institutions and in exaggerated rooting for the home campus. In this respect, as well as in his love of the theatre, he had points of resemblance with Professor William Lyon Phelps, of Yale. The best portrait of Brander which I have seen is in Lloyd Morris' autobiography, *A Threshold in the Sun.*

Woodberry was a thoughtful scholar, a philosopher, or as Brander would say, an idealistic dreamer—and Brander could say nothing more severe of any man. Woodberry's office in Fayerweather was next door to Price's; Brander's was at the opposite end of the corridor. The two men found each other uncongenial, and the department was threatened with a serious division. Professor Price grieved that his colleagues could not get on together. He was devoted to Woodberry, who admired him greatly. Though he always spoke of Brander with punctilious courtesy, I doubt if he cared much for the New Yorker's self-confident exuberance. Brander was not above telling jokes at the expense of the old and defeated South.

✳ ✳ ✳

In the second semester of sophomore year Will Bradley told me I had been elected to the editorial staff of *Morningside.* From then on I began to learn the routine of getting out a small tri-weekly, and at the board meetings I had good hours with Bradley himself, with Henry Alsberg, my classmate, with Hans Zinsser and Huger Elliott and the Barnard representative, Virginia Gildersleeve, talented and well poised, who contributed fiction to our pages and good sense to our discussions.

One incident made on me a lasting impress. We are often told that the training of character is as important as the training of the mind, but less frequently do we hear just how character can be trained. I had one teacher who knew how to do it. His ostensible but less important job was to acquaint me with the events of American history. He was Harry Alonzo Cushing, afterward

Dean of our Law School. A hard worker himself, he apparently hoped to make slaves of us; the amount of reading he assigned weekly was formidable, and we were to make notes on every page we read and bring our notebooks to class with us, so that Mr. Cushing could examine them immediately if our recitation was unsatisfactory. Unless the volume of our notes convinced him of our industry, we were in trouble. In case a poor recitation was contradicted by a good notebook, I suppose Mr. Cushing attributed to us some defect either of mind or morals. For this disciplinary system of his I had no liking at the time, and I have no respect now. It was based on a number of false premises. The ability to take notes as you read is of no more value than the ability to keep a diary in the midst of exciting experiences. Copious notes, like any other form of long-windedness, can hardly be interpreted as indicative of intelligence or scholarship. In childhood I learned to read with concentration, and the reading which Mr. Cushing assigned was not always interesting. When I became interested I forgot to take notes.

But Mr. Cushing did give me, as I said, a lesson in character, in moral responsibility. Columbia in those days had two literary societies, which frequently met in public debate, and for lack of more experienced debaters my society put me on its team. I found the preparation of my speech more alluring than the lengthy report Mr. Cushing had called for, to be handed in on the very day of the debate. I unfolded my problem as he was writing on the blackboard just before class. He was busy, he had his back to me, he showed no eagerness to turn around.

"Mr. Cushing," I called, "may I hand in my report a week late?"

He glanced, without pleasure, over his shoulder. "Why not hand it in on time?"

I explained why not.

He resumed his blackboard writing. Then with cold deliberation, his back still returned: "You have already decided to debate. If you can also find time for your classwork, do so! If you can't, don't bother me!"

I took my part in the debate, and I handed in the report promptly, and I thank Mr. Cushing for teaching me not to shift, or try to shift, moral responsibility.

* * *

I heard from Melville Cane and other classmates many respectful or even excited references to Professor Woodberry, whose course in Elizabethan literature they were attending. I would have elected that course myself if my attention had not been centered on MacDowell and Professor Price. I resolved to study with Woodberry for the rest of my college years, and to visit his classroom at once, for a taste of his quality. When I went to his office to ask permission, I found myself talking to a quiet person of less than average height, who wore thick glasses but whose glance concentrated on me. He enunciated with leisurely precision, not so much because he wished to be understood as because he loved words for their own sake. He showed no interest in the prospect of an auditor, he may even have been a little on guard, as though I were an intruder, but at last he said I might sit in the back of the room.

There was no need to specify the location of my seat. While he spoke, the good places were already taken. Though the lecture period would not begin for another five minutes, eighty or ninety boys were already assembled. The wiser ones, knowing that Woodberry's voice did not carry well, liked to keep free the hour before his lecture, so that they could arrive early and seize a chair well forward.

I waited patiently with the others until Woodberry came in, about ten minutes past the hour, and the room quickened with a thrill of expectation. At Columbia a teacher who arrived late usually found no class; the students could leave without penalty after five minutes. But for Woodberry they always waited. They knew that when he began at last they would hear at once some quiet-seeming remark which would open their eyes and start them thinking. It was so that morning, as Woodberry lectured on Shakespeare's *Sonnets;* it was so the following year, when I elected his course in nineteenth-century literature; it was so in graduate years, when he lectured on epic poetry.

Others have described the method and the effect of his teaching, and though their accounts seem to me less than adequate, my own attempt may fall just as far short. The truth is that his fantastic success in the classroom was not to be expected and it remains difficult to account for. Of any pedagogical science you might say he was willfully innocent. His voice was so low that it hardly reached to the last row of seats. He might have spoken louder, but he preferred not to make the effort. He was so nearsighted that he could not see what was going on in the classroom, but he probably did not care, so long as a decent silence prevailed. In later years deafness overtook him, but at Columbia his hearing was acute.

He was a fascinating and noble teacher only because what he said to us was fascinating and noble. He always lectured on a high plane, with the obvious assumption that for others as for himself the masterpieces of poetry and the deep things of life would be of consuming interest. His students responded to the generous compliment.

To many scholars imaginative literature is merely one of the graces of life, and the study of books merely a professional occupation, to be pursued during working hours and at other times laid aside. For Woodberry literature was life itself. It could be created by those who were steeped in life, and by no one else; on the other hand, he was concerned with life chiefly under those eternal aspects which are the star dust of poetry. He who would do laudable things in poetry, Milton said, must himself be a true poem; Woodberry believed the doctrine, and his work and his life were of a piece.

We were aware of this unity when he entered his lecture room. Other men, more obviously brilliant, could illuminate literature from the outside, but he made us feel that he was availing himself of an opportunity to speak to his fellow man about what was uppermost in his thought and nearest his heart. His teaching was the overflow of a lifelong preoccupation.

Such subject matter, presented by a teacher so unemphatic, might well have been an excuse for inattention, or even the occasion for classroom disorder. There was indeed a legend at Columbia that Woodberry's first classes, in the early nineties, found something ridiculous in this dreamy, soft-spoken man who conferred with them on equal terms about the spirit of Shelley, or the imagination of Milton, or the moral grandeur of Sophocles, or the divine myths of Plato. Those first students of his, we heard, started a riot, just to see what he would do. In surprise and sorrow he gathered his books and his notes, and retired to his study. He told me of the incident years later. President Low sent for him, and said he understood there had been trouble in the class.

"Indeed there has been!"

"What do you intend to do about it, Mr. Woodberry?"

"Nothing, Mr. President."

Mr. Low was astonished at this detachment.

"No," continued Woodberry, "you invited me to lecture at Columbia on literature, to persons, presumably, who wished to hear. Of course I can lecture to no one against his will."

That held Mr. Low for a moment.

"Perhaps," suggested Mr. Woodberry, "a little discipline might render the students more attentive."

"And who," asked the President, "is to introduce discipline into your classroom?"

"You," said Mr. Woodberry. "I am a teacher. The disciplinary function resides in the college executive."

"Let me ask one more question," said Mr. Low. "When you speak of discipline, what have you in mind?"

"The guillotine."

I asked Mr. Woodberry what happened next, but he had forgotten, or perhaps he never knew. He continued to lecture as before, and his students became aware of what they were listening to. For the word-music of poetry, the phrasing, the verse form, he had extraordinary sensitiveness. Yet the content of the poem was always more to him than the technique and the spirit more than the content. He had a unique gift for making even an unread youth appreciate, at least to a degree, how in some passage of Shakespeare or Keats a very human experience produced in the poet a poetic emotion, and how that emotion dictated the form of the poem. Many of us learned in his classroom, what mature artists sometimes need to re-learn, that technique cannot be acquired or applied from the outside, but must grow out of the experience which the artist hopes to express.

We did not always understand the subtleties of his interpretations, but he imparted the faith that they were not beyond our reach, if we tried. When his students describe him as stimulating, they mean that he sent us away after each class still thinking of the poem or poems he had discussed, and still pondering his criticisms. Though the bell had rung, we could not put his lecture out of mind.

We felt then, what we have thought of more precisely since, his unusual gift for speaking of a poet in the very mood of the poet's own work. This skill of his resembled the art of a musician who can interpret various composers each in his distinctive style. When Woodberry spoke of Shelley, the atmosphere he created was in sympathy with Shelley's genius. When he spoke of Milton, or of Walter Scott, he put us in the mood of those very different writers. Interpretation of this subtle kind is easy to feel, but hard to describe.

No memory of him in his Columbia days would be complete if it did not include his friendship with A. V. Williams Jackson, Professor of Indo-Iranian languages, who collaborated with him in the course on Elizabethan literature. In personality and temperament the two friends supplemented each other. Jackson had a social gift as marked as Woodberry's reticence, and a lightness of touch which offset Woodberry's seriousness. The relation of these two unusual men seemed to us an illustration of those chivalrous loyalties which we had learned to admire in Sidney and Greville, and the other great companions of poetry.

Woodberry was far from being what is called a practical man. His contacts with politics or business or ordinary housekeeping were slim. He was temperamentally destined to the cloister or the study. But it was only in later years that we realized this, and none of us thought the discovery important. We had had teachers in plenty who knew more of the practical world than he, but they taught us far less. He was preoccupied with poetry, in the era of Mark Hanna, but from his lectures on poetry we derived a conception of life in the highest sense realistic. He was the first teacher from whom I got the notion that the public life of the citizen is important as an expression, even as a test, of his private aspirations, and that the business enterprises of a country cannot in the long run be separated from its essential religious or spiritual faith. Having learned from him that poetry is the flower of life but still an integral part of it, we went on to learn that all human activities are related, and—unless one is stupid or a hypocrite—must be harmonious. Perhaps the humanity of this point of view is too magnificent for the jaded or the overcautious or the world-weary, but for boyhood it was a thrilling vision, and in its power many who sat in Woodberry's classes have tried to live.

It was a rare experience to be studying literature with a man who was producing it. In 1899, my junior year, the campus was stirred by *Heart of Man*, and a year later we were quoting to each other lines from *Wild Eden*. I see no reason to change my opinion that *Heart of Man* is one of the great books of our literature. Indeed, it seems more timely now than when it first startled us, more than forty-five years ago. Our country then was dangerously prosperous and self-satisfied; the silly little war with Spain had been won, we were inflated with commercial interpretations of our Manifest Destiny, we were about to shed almost as much blood to subdue the Philippines as more recently to liberate them, and our people were stirred by few moral questions more significant than whether Admiral Dewey should have given to his wife the house which his fellow citizens had presented to him. It was a bleak moment for poets or for youth, but just then, when the need was greatest, Woodberry reminded us that men cannot be, as we have learned to say, isolated; he showed us that poetry, religion, and politics in any noble sense are all rooted—not in the genius of any one race or country—but in the general heart of man. Long before the war agony from which we now emerge, he taught us, and no one has presented the truth with warmer eloquence, that democracy can be limited by no border, no frontier, since all mankind are born into a single world, and in some degree must share a single fate. As though he were speaking to his boys, he reminded his readers that how to live is the main matter, whatever else we may study; our highest intelligence would be to understand our human nature and the ways of our heart; our best fortune would be to share the common lot. And by common lot he made us understand not the constrained inheritance of mediocrity, nor the limited vision of merely local issues, but the whole drama of human experience.

It seemed to many of us a tragedy, the burden of which fell more on us than on him, that when the revival of poetry took place around 1910 the new poets did not value Woodberry's work, and some of them were studiously hostile to it. He had prophesied the revival and had done much to bring it on, but more than one of the younger group took pains to suggest that he was out of date. The verdict described truly enough the external aspects of his art. He spoke with the accent of the older Boston culture, and he had a feeling for the English rather than for the American language. It is true also that he was in the best sense a singer; poetry for him was not conversation but music. But he remained consistently generous toward writers of a different tradition than his, and toward the future in which he might have no part. In one of our last talks, after he had withdrawn from teaching, he asked me what sort of literary background the modern college boy has. I told him my Columbia students came to college with a good fund of reading, but not the reading in which I had been brought up, with slim knowledge, for example, of English literature, or of Greek, or of the Bible. But some of them were widely read in Russian literature, of which I was practically ignorant, and most of them kept up with modern books from all quarters of the globe. Woodberry smiled. "It's not important," he said, "that they should have the same background as you and I. They will belong to another age. Their turn will come to grow old. There will be many other ages."

I must set down here one more memory of the first lecture I heard him give. As he talked he held in his hand a folded sheet of letter paper on which was an outline of what he wished to say, with page references and other reminders. As he came to the end he folded and refolded these notes, and then, as if unconsciously, tore them to fragments and tossed the scraps toward the wastebasket. All his lectures ended with this tearing up of the notes, and I wondered at the destruction of material which a lecturer, I imagined, would be glad to keep. When years later I asked him about it, he said that if he had kept his notes, he certainly would have used them again another year, but his point of view might change. By tearing up his notes, he made sure of having something fresh to say.

⁕ ⁕ ⁕

In my junior year Woodberry's students organized, I believe at his suggestion, a literary circle which we called the King's Crown, after the symbol of royalty on Columbia's eighteenth-century seal. There was also a crown of iron on the old King's College flagpole. King's Crown met twice a month, and he showed further his understanding of his boys in the choice of a meeting place and in the arrangement of programs. Once a month we met in one of the larger classrooms to hear an address by a distinguished writer, a friend of Woodberry's, whom he had persuaded to come. After the talk we adjourned to the College Tavern, for beer and pretzels and an opportunity to exchange ideas with the visitor, if we could think of anything to say. Evenings with William Dean Howells, Edmund Clarence Stedman, Weir Mitchell, John LaFarge, Thomas Wentworth Higginson were a privilege we did not undervalue, nor soon forget.

But I learned even more from the alternate meetings, which were entirely informal, with no guest speaker and no program, but entertainment of quality was sure to offer itself spontaneously. Professor Jackson was always there, and Woodberry himself, and a keg of beer in the middle of the room on the second floor of the Tavern. How much of my education I owe to the Tavern! I grieved when it was torn down to make way for the Union Theological Seminary. Woodberry and Jackson kept the talk on worth-while topics, and drew us into it. We learned then, if we had not known before, how to be both cultured and comfortable. It would be hard to exaggerate the value of an undergraduate "bull session," where boys speak their minds and unconsciously help each other in their gropings. The talks at the King's Crown were, if you please, "bull sessions," with this distinction, that two wise teachers and true gentlemen were present, to set an example of honest thinking, of good taste in thought and speech, of courtesy in discussion.

If any student was called on for a special contribution, the result was memorable. Woodberry was alert to the work of us all, and he usually knew if a boy had something up his sleeve. On one memorable evening Henry (Hank) Alsberg read us a story which, as I happened to know, he had thought of during one of Woodberry's lectures. My seat was next to Hank's, and when Woodberry read a passage from Tennyson's "Lucretius" I heard a muffled exclamation, "God, what a story!" These were the lines:

> Then, then, from utter gloom stood out the breasts,
> The breasts of Helen, and hoveringly a sword
> Now over and now under, now direct,
> Pointed itself to pierce, but sank down shamed
> At all that beauty.

Hank's story was about a beautiful but wicked queen who plotted to kill her husband and give the kingdom to her lover. The loyal prime minister discovered her plan and drew his dagger, but could not strike anyone so beautiful. She remembered the dagger, and as soon as her villainous lover had seized the realm, she put out the minister's eyes and turned him adrift, to beg for a living. Years later, as he crouched in his hovel, he heard a woman's voice praying for shelter. Unable ever to forget that voice, he told her to come in. The country had revolted, her lover was dead, vengeance hunted her. The blind man felt his way along the wall. She did not recognize him till his fingers were at her throat. It was useless for her to scream and struggle; by destroying his sight she had robbed herself of her only defense.

Hank always read his stories bashfully, but this one was superbly written, and its effect was powerful. Woodberry gave it his accolade. "I wonder how you sleep of nights, Mr. Alsberg!"

✧   ✧   ✧

Among the good things of junior year, on another plane, was Professor George Rice Carpenter's course in daily themes. The idea of daily themes was thought up by Harvard teachers, and their pupils went out from Cambridge in all directions, for several decades, preaching the advantages to be derived from writing one page every twenty-four hours. The daily-theme course was not equally successful everywhere, but as Carpenter gave it, at Columbia, it was a remarkable experience.

For the first half-year we handed in a theme every day, each theme being a page in length. The second half-year was devoted, all of it, to writing one essay, of at least five thousand words. The writing of short pieces constantly either left you with not another idea in your head, or it taught you how much there is to say if you keep your eyes open and think about what you see. No doubt the daily themes were good for me, but I learned still more from the long essay in the second half-year. Professor Carpenter asked us to choose a subject, and he gave us a week to think it over. Then he discussed the subjects in public, before the whole class, and in private consultation. He asked us whether our subject was of such significance to us, that we needed five thousand words to do it justice. Then he asked what interest it would have for readers at large. From these preliminaries I learned once for all that nothing worth while can be written on less than a large idea, a great crisis, a genuine problem.

From the subject we passed at once to the treatment—that is to say, to the form. He asked us to bring in a skeleton of the essay, paragraph by paragraph, each paragraph being represented by a single sentence. By the time we had shaped this outline to his satisfaction and our own, nothing remained but to fill out the paragraphs and smooth away the angularities of the frame.

To this day I use no other method in preparing any piece of writing, whether short or long. After training so sound, I do not care to begin a novel or an article before I have worked it out completely in outline. It is easy to write the first sentence when you know what the last sentence will be. I cannot estimate the amount of time I should have wasted, had I not taken that course with George Rice Carpenter.

He taught me other things. He was a gentle soul, with humor and common sense, and he was content to give his life to the teaching of composition because he conceived of the writing process as an exercise in sincere thinking and sincere feeling. Many of my classmates, like me devoted to Woodberry, avoided the daily-theme course because they thought it inculcated a mechanical approach to an art which they conceived of as pure inspiration. I believed they were wrong then, and now I am sure they were, for the simple reason that without the mechanics of writing, which they declined to learn, it is hard to do any writing at all. Many of them have much to say and occasionally squeeze some of it out, but their intervals of silence are too long. A writer is one who writes, as a singer is one who sings—and in either case habitual performance is understood.

Carpenter was no Woodberry, but he loved poetry, and his favorite poet was Dante. He was a good Italian scholar, and he knew the Florentine's compact verses by heart. At the time I wondered at his taste, he coming from New England with much American realism in his blood, but in my graduate years he made one remark which explained himself and opened up to me the essential quality of Dante. I happened to say something about Shakespeare, something full of admiration youthful and undiscriminating, something probably trite and banal, since Shakespeare had been thoroughly admired before I got at him. "Oh yes," said Carpenter. "Very interesting, that Elizabethan poet! He did much for the theatre. But I'm not an antiquarian. I can understand a modern poet like Dante."

❄ ❄ ❄

That fine story of Alsberg's was published in the *Morningside*. The little magazine was at its peak in these years, while the writing fever was running its course in Columbia College, and with almost the same intensity in Barnard. Grace Goodale joined Virginia Gildersleeve to represent Barnard on the editorial board, and they in turn were succeeded by Jeannette Bliss Gillespy, one of the ablest writers in either college, born in Lansingburg, Mother's early home. Miss Gillespy's verse was of a poignant quality much admired and envied by the rest of us. She had a boldness of thought which we could not imitate, and we attributed it to some deep experience withheld from normal mortals. Board meetings of *Morningside* were exciting when she was present; she would say wise things about the manuscripts we considered, she was full of high spirits, when occasion demanded she had a mordant wit, and she might even stoop to a pun. Campus legend declared she had raised the question in a literature class whether "Sphere-born harmonious sisters, Voice and Verse," was not an allusion to the precarious New York pronunciation.

But she was a true poet, and the world lost something when she, mysterious as ever, abandoned the cultivation of her talent, and hid herself in silence.

This miniature foretaste of the writing world suddenly became of secondary interest. At Columbia the seniors each year composed and presented a musical show of variable quality, but always with whatever entertainment value results from seeing female rôles played by boys. In the years preceding our graduation the Varsity Shows had been excellent, and several teams of composers and librettists were grooming for the 1900 production. When the call was sent out for scores and manuscripts, Melville Cane suggested that I write the music to a book by him. Within half an hour Syd Harrison proposed that he write a book to music by me.

In another half-hour we had consolidated forces, and in twenty-four hours—I am sure not later—we were hard at work on *The Governor's Vrouw,* a musical comedy which we said would be in the Gilbert and Sullivan tradition. Syd and Melville were to do the book, Melville the lyrics, I the music. Since the accompaniment would be played by the University orchestra, I had at least one opportunity in a lifetime to score my music and hear what it sounded like.

The book had a good idea, lifted from Washington Irving's *Knickerbocker History.* William Kieft, the Governor who preceded Stuyvesant, was a small man with a quick temper, who had a large wife with a violent tongue, and both of them jointly had a beautiful daughter named Katrinka. My friend George Matthew, from MacDowell's classes, sang Katrinka. He was a gymnast, a specialist on the flying rings, and his biceps were so developed that when he dressed up as a Dutch girl we cautioned him to relax, so his arms would look merely fat. I gave him a tender lullaby, which made quite a hit, especially when he was singing high notes pianissimo. Stage nervousness might at any moment cause him to clench his fists bravely until the astounding biceps ballooned out.

According to Syd and Melville, Governor Kieft won the enmity of the Indians by forbidding the sale or use of tobacco on Manhattan. Mrs. Kieft didn't like the smell. To pacify the Indians, the Governor made wampum legal tender, whereupon the Connecticut Yankees manufactured wampum by the cartload out of discarded oyster shells, and in no time sound money was displaced by bad. The Connecticut Yankees had Amsterdam's gold, the Amsterdam treasury had oyster shells—and Kieft, alas, still had his wife!

The Governor then agreed with the Indians to lift the ban on smoking if they would oblige by abducting Mrs. Kieft. They took her one evening when she stepped abroad for a moment to look at the moon. The Governor called out the trained band, first making sure that they were short of ammunition. To put a proper face on his villainy, he promised to give his beautiful daughter, Katrinka, to any brave gentleman who would rescue her mother. That was the end of Act I.

The handsomest of the Yankees took up the Governor's offer, gathered a few friends, and started out. Before they had gone far they met the Indian band bringing back the unendurable Mrs. Kieft. The young Yankee made a deal with them; they promised to swear he had rescued the lady only after heroic effort. He then took her home, they perjured themselves for the sake of the tobacco trade, the Governor fainted, and the Yankee got Katrinka. Everybody, Indians and all, joined in a loud and amicable chorus, and the friendly audience insisted on many recalls.

The Governor's Vrouw was given for a week at Carnegie Lyceum, beginning Monday evening, February 19, 1900, and for one performance the following Monday in Brooklyn, at the Academy of Music.

My musical and theatre-minded friends were prominent in the cast. George Kelly played the Captain of the trained band, Rutger Planten was the amorous Yankee trader, and William de Mille was the Indian chief.

William C. de Mille had begun his studies in the School of Mines, but toward the end of his course he decided to be a dramatist instead of an engineer, and came over to the College. He was the only non-amateurish actor in the cast; perhaps for that reason he helped himself to the part of the abducting savage, a muscular and gymnastic rôle without dialogue, which as William expanded or inflated it, furnished the exciting moments of the play.

The Governor's Vrouw brought my undergraduate career to a close. At Commencement the award of the Proudfit Fellowship in Letters enabled me to go on to the Graduate School. There would be no break in my life at Columbia but merely, as I assumed, a progress in maturity. I was not likely to think seriously again of music as a profession; I would be a scholar, a teacher—and in time perhaps a writer.

Lloyd Morris

'14 Columbia College

Lloyd Morris was the author of many biographies and plays. His best-known biography was of Nathaniel Hawthorne, The Rebellious Puritan; *his best play,* The Damask Cheek, *co-authored with John Van Druten. This is taken from* Threshold in the Sun, *published in 1943.*

U nlike many another American University, Columbia makes no effort to seduce the eye. It never adopted that composite of confectioner's Gothic and feminine rock gardening which elsewhere advertises the obsequial nature of the higher learning. Its architecture is plain-spoken, prosaic, a trifle tart, and seems to admonish the passer-by that handsome is as handsome does. Set among spinsterish buildings there is a domed and pillared library, very like a pillbox, which hasty sight-seers have been known to mistake for the neighboring sepulcher of General Grant. Far at the back, there is, or was, a "grove"—a strip of greensward with some ancient, noble trees. Outwardly, Columbia's ugliness is sententious; within, brisk and businesslike.

In the midwinter of 1911, having duly matriculated, Morris became a daily commuter to Morningside. Official admission to the university's privileges was an unceremonious transaction; he figured only as a bookkeeping entry. But for him it was touched with romance. He no longer thought of himself as a boy. Each day, traveling up to the Heights by streetcar and

81

subway, he shared the excitement of medieval predecessors who had trudged the slopes of Mont-Sainte-Geneviève. Like them, he felt himself among the privileged and elect. He was a student at a fortunate place, in a prosperous hour.

For, at that moment, there existed at Columbia a constellation of remarkable minds whose effect on the intellectual climate was electric. A student needed only to be receptive to find his own mind the target of ambient energies. But he needed to be hardy to support the intensity of their impact. Mere passive exposure might thus have constituted a kind of education, and perhaps not the worst. However, many of these catalytic forces happened also to be great teachers, for whom mere passivity held a taint of sin. The rewards of such modest collaboration as a student might be equipped to offer were therefore likely to be generous. The campus rang with calls to high adventure. So vivacious seemed the enterprise of learning, that everyone supposed it on the threshold of another Renaissance.

This tonic, buoyant tone pervaded the American academic world. But circumstances made it peculiarly inevitable at Columbia. Among the older American institutions of learning, Columbia is almost uniquely emancipated from its own past. Originally dedicated to the transmission of an official tradition, it seldom recalls this initial purpose except on commemorative occasions. So singular a detachment was bound to breed an exceptional liberty. During Morris's undergraduate years, the university encouraged intellectual disagreement and fostered diversity in its faculty, and thus served a genuinely liberal ideal.

Responsible liberty struck him as the true spirit of the place, and he thought it the most reliable tradition that the institution could hope to transmit. To the teaching staff it had attracted minds of an independent, vigorous cast; a strong tide of renovation was running in scholarship, and the university had already claimed many of its major sources. Another factor likewise helped to invigorate the atmosphere. This was a disposition to level the ancient barriers separating academic precincts from the workaday world. Columbia's metropolitan location furnished one incentive; even then, the strenuous compulsions of New York were relegating ivory towers to antiquarian interest, among sedan chairs and snuffboxes. Perhaps, too, there was stimulus in the daily pressure of a miscellaneous student body, containing representatives of every known nationality, color, creed, and almost every cult—but, as a group, formidably suspicious of authority, dogma, and the example of the past. Certainly a willingness to establish contact with the outside world was conspicuous among the most vigorous minds at the university. On the whole, they appeared to be intensely ambitious; they showed little liking for cloistered insulation, and scant respect for dry-as-dust scholarship; you felt that they were attracted only by creative enterprise.

Faculty participation in a changing world was already notable. The scientific schools had provided an inspiring example in Professor Pupin. The law school offered Dean—now Chief Justice—Stone and Professor Kirchwey, both of whom were shortly to enter public service, and John Bassett Moore, who helped shape American foreign policy. The philosopher, John Dewey, was effecting a revolution in public education, and would presently be invited to devise a school system for China. Charles A. Beard and James Harvey Robinson were quietly scuttling old-fashioned history; this seemed only an innocent academic pastime until, within a very few years, it became apparent that they had radically modified the direction of contemporary thinking.

* * *

Meantime, in the English department, there nested a bevy of fledgling writers, resolutely trying their wings: John Erskine, Carl Van Doren, the playwright Hatcher Hughes, the critic and playwright Clayton Hamilton. Twice each week a burnished coupé, drawn by fat old horses and piloted by a fat old coachman, set down in their midst an aging Cyrenaic, urbane, dryly malicious, often mocking, who was—like the gilded statue of Alma Mater—a distinctive campus landmark.

Brander Matthews held the chair of dramatic literature which an earlier administration had set up for him, possibly feeling that literary extenuation might make the drama itself aseptic. He wore the Legion of Honor in his frock coat, and had a sleek, whiskered feline elegance seldom visible, even then, outside the offices of fashionable physicians, or the wide polished windows of the Union League Club. Worldly, wealthy, widely traveled, and imperturbably a snob, he was a connoisseur of the arts, of food and wine, and perhaps of women. He had been the friend of Stevenson, Howells, Mark Twain, Kipling, and many another literary figure. For almost half a century, he had hobnobbed with such artists, actors, statesmen, and dilettantes as a gentleman might approve, and a scholar not deplore. Thoroughly cosmopolitan, he was soaked in a distillation of London clubs, Paris salons, and the more fashionable greenrooms of two continents—but so long an immersion had only made him hug more tightly to his heart a bundle of invincible prejudices: these were, like a letter of credit, proof of identity, and wherever he might be they attached him firmly to genteel nineteenth century New York.

In his major field of scholarship, the drama, Brander was an American disciple of the French critic, Francisque Sarcey: he held—very soundly—that a play becomes a play only when it is acted on a stage before an audience; and he believed that audience psychology and the physical resources of production at any moment determine the playwright's opportunities. He dismissed as worse than useless any study of the drama apart from the living theater; but, since a professor's chair is based upon the dissemination of tradition, he gave courses in the drama's history, and had founded a dramatic museum of model stage-sets patterned after that of the Paris Opera. In addition to the drama, he claimed American literature as a fief, and occupied it tenaciously. In this field, his critical opinions were less viable; a large portion of the student body, and many of his younger colleagues, accounted them as obsolete as his equipage, his senatorial attire, and his classroom jokes.

No doubt Brander was aware of the mingled affection and impatience that he aroused, and perhaps it constituted the effect he wished to produce. To be considered a reactionary in no way dismayed him; he was fond of remarking that whatever is contemporary is three-fourths temporary; he saw no reason why his personal judgments should be exempt from the ironical mutability of fashion, and appeared quite content to let posterity settle the score as it chose. But his suave invulnerability implied no unfriendliness. As Morris quickly discovered, Brander was readily accessible to any common interest. In the old-fashioned comfort of his West End Avenue home, he was a delightful host, spendthrift of time, worldly wisdom, and pertinent reminiscence. At no time of his life could he have been dissuaded from practicing the "profession of letters" as he called it; but he was conscientiously honest, declaring that he had always commanded independent means; he discouraged others who lacked them from following so wayward a course; writing, he warned Morris, is a poor crutch, though a serviceable cane. Brander, with the inevitable cigarette tilting perilously on his lower lip, perpetually likely to set his whiskers ablaze but never doing so, was the first great talker with whom Morris enjoyed the privilege of conversation. A master of delicate irony, acid wit, and genial humor, he would have considered it merely ill-bred to be solemn as well as serious about human affairs, since this imputes to the human animal a dignity which he does not possess. For his own part, Brander viewed life as a comedy; he maintained an attitude of tolerance toward all that did not trench on his invincible prejudices; but when these were aroused, they shattered his characteristic urbanity like a chrysalis, and he impressed you as being an ill-tempered bigot.

         ❖ ❖ ❖

Philosophers were ubiquitous at the university. They were even to be found in the Department of Philosophy itself which, by consecrated academic tradition, is usually the limbo reserved for professors who expound whatever nobody wishes to know. But chance, or perhaps foresight, had aggregated in the philosophical faculty a group of speculative thinkers as remarkable for diversity of school as for boldness and force. Intellectual disagreement among them ran high, since almost every shade of opinion was vigorously represented. As a student, you enjoyed an unrivaled eclecticism: there, for your peculiar edification, were a pragmatist, an Aristotelian, a transcendentalist, a Thomist scholastic, as well as lively young coveys of two fresh breeds: the new realists, and the radical empiricists. These alternatives were, however, considered inadequate: the university made a vain effort to capture Mr. Santayana, who had retired from Harvard, and then imported Professor Henri Bergson, whose celebrity had penetrated far beyond professional circles.

Having plowed through *Creative Evolution*—nearly unique in philosophical literature as a best seller—Morris devotedly attended the course of lectures which Monsieur Bergson gave throughout a winter. A short, wiry man with a diffident manner, the great Frenchman seemed perpetually astonished by the size and attentiveness of his audiences; one felt that he was, perhaps, slightly embarrassed by the prophet's mantle which fame had thrust on his reluctant shoulders; and one surmised that he would much have preferred to share his insights less formally, with a small and congenial group. He spoke in French, and when your ear had accommodated itself to sustained fluency in a subdued tone, you became aware that you were listening to a poet, whose mind was introspective, subtly discriminating, deeply moralized, but whose imagination soared on joyous wings. Eloquence, vividness, and grace won your interest; what held it, making you return again and again, was the magnanimity of his mind, the limitless prospect which his vision opened before you. Your response was emotional, for Bergson succeeded in making thought an emotional experience, like a journey in some rare upper atmosphere where your sensations became unwontedly acute and your insight abnormally perspicacious, so that values never before perceived were suddenly grasped and understood. In this there was, so to speak, a conjurer's trick: for Bergson was using intelligence, in the efficacy of which he disbelieved, to elicit intuition, the only faculty which he trusted, or regarded as capable of apprehending experience. Intuition lay at the very heart of his system, supporting and amplifying his logical exposition of doctrine; when your intelligence had studied and recapitulated the analysis, it was immediate intuition which yielded the meaning, illuminating his potent concept of a creative, evolutionary life force, and his dramatic theory that duration—the dimension in which our experience occurs, and which constantly grows—is an incessant devouring of the future by the past. Although Morris was unwilling to follow Monsieur Bergson in a renunciation of intelligence, he was grateful for having intuition philosophically justified, and felt that his education had been advanced by the aesthetic pleasure derived from the lectures. Bergson's philosophy, which Morris conceived to be a mystical justification of naturalism and science, appealed to him as a magnificent foundation for great poetry, perhaps a modern epic—but, if there was one thing he really knew, it was that he was no poet. Yet his impression—Monsieur Bergson possibly would have called it intuition—was correct. For even at that very time an unhappy, ill, socially curious Parisian, with a reputation for eccentricity but none for literary genius, was using Bergson's philosophy as the groundwork for a monumental epic novel. But À *la recherche du temps perdu,* and with it the fame of Marcel Proust, were still in the future.

Philosophical authority at Columbia was, by general consent, vested in John Dewey, the most influential and widely reputed American thinker after William James. Professor Dewey was the least cloistered of philosophers. His doctrine was considered characteristically American in its emphasis upon efficacy, expediency, enterprise, and action; his career was no less so in its breadth, variety, and practical achievement. There was a strong native flavor, too, in his briskness, geniality, humor, and unquenchable optimism. It was therefore no surprise to find that his outlook on life was homebred, as fresh and bracing as the American atmosphere itself. Dewey impressed you as believing that the major business of life is living, not reflection, and that philosophy ought to be a useful instrument, a kind of fruitful method, to that end. This conviction, you supposed, explained his impatience with the formal, dialectical "problems" which are regarded as the only appropriate occupation of academic philosophers when not actually instructing the young; an abstruse trivial diversion which restrains them from mischief. Dewey treated them conscientiously, but with distaste; with, as it were, the cold courtesy reserved for an unwelcome relative who will inevitably waste one's time, and quite possibly will borrow one's money. As yet, he had formulated no theory of metaphysics, and in consequence that province of philosophy was in disfavor among his disciples.

In the lecture room, as in his books, Dewey was hard to follow. You felt that he was hounded by the obligation to express himself clearly, precisely, and concretely. But, in spurring him to excessive efforts, it plunged him into interminable verbal qualification and definition, and thus was cheated of fulfillment. Lucidity often deserted him, and style—except for a worried, rugged sincerity—never visited him at all. Nevertheless the impact of his thought, as it reached you, was tonic. His philosophy addressed itself to existence in a democracy, and in a machine age. He situated experience at the dead center of familiar daily enterprise, and invited you to undertake such drastic revision of insight and belief as might be required by this novel transfer, which made action inescapable and efficient action the most meritorious of ideals. If you found the assumption acceptable, Dewey's conclusions followed naturally. Intelligence acquired a pragmatic value; knowledge was made instrumental; thought became an art of discovery. For Dewey, the discipline that is identical with trained power was likewise identical with freedom. "Genuine freedom," he asserted, "is intellectual; it rests in the trained power of thought." Dewey's was a naturalistic world, the world of nature as the modern American envisages it; a world of science, machinery, industry, crowds, democratic controls, and social progress possibly without limit. But by one issue Morris was always puzzled, and Dewey's books seemed to throw little light on it. What, for Dewey, constituted a good life in that world? What might it consist in? So far as Morris could determine, life was an affair of fumbling, presumably efficacious in the end; and experience took on the quality of a universal, perpetual experiment.

The Columbia philosopher to whom he listened with most delight and profit offered no original system of philosophy. Frederick J. E. Woodbridge was a singularly great teacher: powerful, magnetic, humane, in character and temper resembling those classic Greek thinkers whom he so deeply admired. He had lived among them long and lovingly, and had made their culture so thoroughly his own that he preferred, when possible, to lecture in their language. For those students who, like Morris, were ignorant of classical Greek, he lectured on the history of Greek thought in English; but in so doing he left you with an impression that the native language was, in fact, the foreign one.

Woodbridge described philosophy as an attempt at total and reflective thinking, inspired by the immemorial hope of bringing all our actions under a single and unified conception extending, perhaps finally, to embrace a totality of things. Looking at philosophy in this fashion, the history of Greek thought became a dramatic recital, a story of ways of interpreting experience, and ways of dealing with fact, no one of which, in its method of approach, was so obsolete as not to yield some fruitful suggestion, or pertinent analogy, to the modern mind. It was Woodbridge's unique genius as a teacher to involve you, imaginatively, in the drama, to compel your participation in the intellectual enterprise of the philosopher whom he happened to be discussing, so that you lived in, rather than studied, the minds of Empedocles and Anaxagoras, Democritus, Socrates, and Aristotle. This was more than an adventure in ideas; it was, in a very real sense, an experience of civilization.

Though Morris had acquired philosophies, he had, thus far, arrived at no philosophy. A personal philosophy should, and sometimes does, wait on experience, of which he had had next to none; but events and occurrences do not, of themselves, become experience; unless the mind and heart work upon them, they never rise above the incidental level on which they take place; and to do their work, the mind and heart require an instrument, a method or principle congenial to their interests. To arrive at a philosophy, you must begin by borrowing one. You may later discard it. To serve you well, it need only express the compulsions of your mind and heart as you know them.

During Morris's undergraduate years at Columbia, the climate of the mind had been deeply affected by a philosopher whom the university had failed to attract to its service. But so pervasive was the influence exercised by George Santayana that you sometimes suffered the illusion of his presence, as if in an invisible, ghostlike form he had joined Bergson, Dewey, Woodbridge, Felix Adler, Father Clifford, and the others. It was this absent, powerful personality who loaned to Morris—as to so many others of his generation—the needed usable instrument.

The core of Santayana's philosophy appeared in the statement that human reason lives by turning the friction of material forces into the light of ideal goods; that all life is animal in its origin, and all spiritual in its possible fruits. For him, as for the Greeks, existence itself was not a good; it was merely an opportunity. To Morris, the most salient import of *The Life of Reason* was its restoration of the sane conviction that the dignity of humanity consists in being human. The work itself, he read not only as a record and critique of human progress, and epic of intelligence, but an invitation to a theory of life. Like all epics, it offered a reading of the present in terms of the past, and illustrated an ideal of destiny. This ideal, if he understood it correctly, was that of the humane life; life so lived that the maximum of internal harmony shall prevail between the natural world and the mind's aspirations. This ideal assumed a natural world of which intelligence is a function and spirit an expression. In its light, the humane life was necessarily both rational and religious, combining piety with spirituality, and fusing a willing adherence to necessary conditions with a profound devotion to ideal ends. The life of reason consisted in mastering the world scientifically while living in it spiritually. The place of consciousness in the natural world was that of its own ideal products, art, religion, and science; it translated natural relations into ideal symbols by which it interpreted things with reference to its own interests. Such ideals as it was able to evolve were frankly relative; relative to their natural sources, and to the purely human interests which they served. Yet, when rationally conceived and pursued, their beauty, and perhaps their immortality, were not diminished by understanding their origin and use. The humble origin was of itself a high ancestry, and the use was what gave meaning to existence.

The pictures of life made by most modern philosophers offered few reasons for loving it. To Morris, when a college student, Santayana's picture offered many.

                                                           ❁ ❁ ❁

In the midwinter of 1914, three years after a bookkeeper noted his presence at the university, a clerk mailed him its sheepskin. The university, having done what it could for him, considered its obligation discharged. Possibly it had not given him the education that he needed; but it had given him—or tried to give—the one he had asked for. A college, he remembered John Erskine saying, is a collection of diverse minds and natures, strengthening their noblest impulses and their finest knowledge by a communal sharing. A college, people sometimes said, was Mark Hopkins on one end of a log and a boy on the other. On the log which he had occupied for three privileged years, a number of remarkable minds had willingly sat with Morris. He had every reason to be grateful, and none whatever to complain.

Bennett Cerf

'20 COLUMBIA COLLEGE, '20 JOURNALISM

> *Bennett Cerf began his literary career at the* Columbia Daily
> Spectator. *After graduating, he worked briefly for the* New York
> Tribune *before joining a publishing firm. Within a few years he
> went on to become a founding publisher of what became Random
> House, where he also served as an editor for many years. He
> penned a number of books on the side—many for other publishers,
> so as not to create a conflict with his own authors. A well-known
> figure among the literati, Cerf later became a radio host and noted
> lecturer and earned widespread fame as a permanent panelist on
> the television program* What's My Line? *Excerpted here is* At
> Random, *his 1977 memoir.*

On the day before my sixteenth birthday my childhood ended
abruptly. My mother died. She had always been desperately anxious to have another child. She'd had several miscarriages, but she
persisted, and when I was fifteen a little girl was born who lived only about
two weeks. The pregnancy and birth weakened my mother and she never
really recovered.

From the day of my mother's death I became the financial head of the
family. My grandfather, a very shrewd man, had loved my father, but he
didn't trust him with money because he feared Pop would lose it in no
time. Pop was the soft touch of the world, and anybody who asked him for
anything got it. So my grandfather had left money to my mother in trust for
me, and after she died I came into just about $125,000. One of the six chil-
dren who inherited my grandfather's estate was my Uncle Herbert,
Herbert Wise—and when my mother died he came to live with my father
and me, and all three of us adored each other.

At the age of sixteen I decided I was going to learn to be a businessman
and that meant I'd have to go to another kind of school. My handwriting

was very bad and I didn't know anything about bookkeeping, but I was determined to become a tycoon. I hated to leave Townsend Harris for many reasons. By this time I was writing stories for the school magazine and was one of the top students there. Also, I was on the soccer team— even I could see a soccer ball! But I had made up my mind that I was going to make money, so I quit and went to the Packard Commercial School. This enraged Uncle Herbert, but I did it anyway. It was a mighty stupid move in some ways, but luckily it worked out well for me. For one thing, my handwriting improved: they taught the Palmer method in those days. I also learned double-entry bookkeeping and began to know something about the business world. After school I worked for a certified accountant and went around with him to check his clients' books. In this way I got backstage of a big restaurant and learned that all the money's in liquor, not in food. I saw how department stores and various other businesses operated, and I became interested in all of them. Thus I had a lot of experience while I was still in the business school.

During my year at Packard and my job with the accountant, Uncle Herbert continued to talk to me about going to college; and if I hadn't taken his advice, God knows what would have happened to me.

I didn't have enough credits, since I hadn't graduated from high school. I decided in January that I was going to college if I could, so I had until September to get all my entrance requirements. I went to Columbia and took several extension courses, and my uncle coached me in a couple of other subjects.

I quickly decided, after looking at the required courses, that I could never learn Latin or Greek; I had no aptitude at all in that direction. I discovered that at the School of Journalism you didn't need those languages, so then and there I decided that was the place for me. (It was then an undergraduate school. It became a graduate school some years later.) But I still didn't have enough credits. Although I never was good at algebra, I had counted on being able to pass the exam—for the last two points I needed. But I flunked. I simply couldn't do it. So I took an exam in free-hand drawing, which almost anyone could do, and I passed that. That was one point. Then I took advanced French. This was a desperate gamble, because if I didn't get that last extra point, I was dead. But I passed and got into the School of Journalism.

That summer Morty Rodgers had the next locker to me in gym class, and we continued our friendship. Morty's father, Dr. William A. Rodgers, was a very important man in my opinion because one of his patients was my dream girl, Norma Talmadge, the beautiful movie star, and the idea that she was one of his patients dazzled me. I remember pleading with him to let me carry his bag when he went to see her. It was Morty Rodgers who introduced me to the fraternity I joined: Pi Lambda Phi. The head of the fraternity was young Oscar Hammerstein II. A boy named Horace Manges—who became the lawyer not only for Random House but for a half-dozen other big publishers—was also a member. Richard Rodgers soon joined it, and Rodgers and Hammerstein got me more and more interested in the theater.

The School of Journalism in those days was very famous, and while I was there it attracted such young men as my friend Howard Dietz, and George Sokolsky, Morrie Ryskind, Corey Ford and Max Schuster. Richard Simon, the other half of the future Simon and Schuster, was also there, but in the College.

In my freshman year I became pretty well set. First of all, I was already in a fraternity. I didn't have to worry about that, as most freshmen did. Second, I went out for the college newspaper, the *Spectator.* The fellow who had written a column had just graduated, so they had the problem of who was going to take his place. I submitted several samples, and suddenly, and only a freshman, I was the columnist for the Columbia paper! Well, this was an open sesame to everybody and everything. I was elected vice-president of the class.

The *Spectator* column I wrote was called "The Stroller." It was not a gossip column, though there were little pieces about personalities on the campus. I also tried to start controversies about the city government and the dismal subway service, demanding that 116th Street be made an express station—that kind of stuff. "The Stroller" was lively—and it was read! Soon I began sending in little things to *Jester,* the humor magazine, and I became even better known.

Not the least important thing that happened to me was that one of my freshman classes was with a professor named Harrison Steeves, and I will never forget Professor Steeves, because in his course we had to study contemporary authors. In those days the English authors were the popular ones. (This was around 1917. There have been great changes in the publishing business since then, and I like to believe I contributed to them.) There were very few popular Americans. There was one, Henry Sydnor Harrison, two of whose books I remember—a best seller called *Queed* and one called *V. V. 's Eyes.* They're forgotten today, but were then considered outstanding literature. And of course, many Americans were reading books like *Pollyanna.* The professor also introduced me to H. G. Wells and Galsworthy; to Kipling's *Jungle Stories* and *Kim;* and Arnold Bennett's *Old Wives' Tale.* I discovered for myself that there were authors like Anatole France, Theodore Dreiser and James Branch Cabell, and I began to appreciate good writing.

Steeves suddenly popped back into my life many years later. He had written a detective story, *Good Night, Sheriff*, not a very good one, but he brought it down to me, and I was so grateful for what he had done for me that I published it in 1941. It didn't sell very well; it didn't deserve to. But it pleased me to do it. I was making him very happy—this austere English professor who had written a mystery novel.

I soon discovered that if I played my cards right at Columbia, I could get two degrees at the same time—a B.Lit. at Journalism, and a B.A. at the College—without doing too much work. This required manipulating, but I thought that added to the fun. In 1917, right at the beginning of my college career, we got into the war. At that time there was something comparable to the ROTC: it was called the SATC, the Student Army Training Corps. We all became members and wore uniforms. One of my first exploits in the SATC was the day I was commander of the company and I had them in company rank marching across South Field (which is now all covered with buildings). As they were walking toward the grandstand I panicked, and couldn't think of how to stop them. So to their intense delight, they went marching up into the stand, the whole company, while the real officers howled with laughter. I was not cut out for an army career. But anyway, I made a good story of all this in the column.

When the call came for officers' training school, I applied for and was accepted by the infantry training school down in Camp Lee, Virginia, bucking for second lieutenant. Since I was the night editor of *Spectator* when the rule came through that anybody going off to the war would get full credit for any course he had signed up for, without even having to take it, I saw the notice the day before it appeared in the paper. So I rushed over to sign up for all the courses I could and then went to the dean for an okay. He looked at my program and said, "This is an interesting course you've planned out. I figure it would take about sixteen hours of homework a day to really do it right."

I said, "Really, sir?"

He said, "You haven't by any chance seen the rule that you're going to get credit for everything you've signed up for before you go away to camp?"

I said, "I don't know what you're talking about, Dean."

He said, "I didn't think so," and he stamped his approval.

So off I went. I was at Camp Lee until the war ended. I got credit for advanced geometry, something I could never do, and a couple of other science courses where you have to be exact—and I was terrible at those things. In history, economics and literature I was great. I'm very good at adding figures, too, but when it comes to algebra or quadratics or geometry, I'm absolutely hopeless.

Just as I returned to college, Morrie Ryskind, the editor of *Jester*, left Columbia, and in my sophomore year I was made editor in chief of the magazine—that was heady stuff!

Being editor of the *Jester* was a great experience for me, so I was delighted that both my boys worked on a college humor magazine. Chris was the vice-president of the *Harvard Lampoon*, of which Jon later became president. Chris's first book, *The World's Largest Cheese*, was published by Doubleday in 1968; it has all the things he wrote for the *Lampoon* and other pieces done since. He's a great boy. They're both great boys.

To improve the *Jester*, I quickly started both a book-review column and a drama column—the drama column, of course, got us free theater tickets. Then I thought that this could finally be my chance to meet Norma Talmadge, my dream girl. So I wrote a letter asking if I could interview her for the Columbia *Jester*, and a reply came setting up a date. Soon the whole campus knew I was going to meet Norma Talmadge. I was so darn excited about it, but when the day came, I lost my nerve; I was afraid to face her, and I never went. I wrote a glowing interview, anyway—faked the whole thing, ran it in *Jester* and sent copies to Norma Talmadge. I got a warm letter from her in return, saying she had enjoyed meeting me so much and that the interview was masterful and she hoped we'd meet someday again soon. The letter was framed and put up in the *Jester* office.

There was a course at Columbia called Comparative Literature, which was one of those cinches where you got two points for doing practically nothing. The whole football team and the entire staff of *Jester*, including me—all the finaglers—were taking it. The professor who gave the course was Henry Wadsworth Longfellow Dana. He was a great-nephew, or maybe just a nephew, of the poet Longfellow. We had our first class with him, and the next day Dr. Butler kicked him out of Columbia because he was a pacifist. We were just being thrown into a war, and here was Dana making very pacifist statements and joining I-didn't-raise-my-boy-to-be-a-soldier groups. If his name had been Smith or Jones, I don't think Butler or anybody else would have given a darn. He was only an obscure English teacher up at Columbia, but since he was named Henry Wadsworth Longfellow Dana, the papers quoted at length everything he said. It took two lines just to print his name. And Butler was infuriated, so Dana got the heave-ho.

Now all we dedicated students rejoiced: "It will take them a month to get another professor." We went to the next class expecting to see a little white notice on the door saying there would be no class until they got a new teacher. But overnight they did dig one up, and to our disgust, he was standing there, ready for action, when we came in. His name was Raymond

Weaver. He had a very deep, mellifluous voice. He wore one of those long, stiff Arrow collars that met in the front, and he was a very formidable gentleman. We resented his turning up so quickly, and when he started talking, I'm sure we all thought, especially the football team, My God, what are we in for! But this class turned out to be one of the greatest things that ever happened to me, because Raymond Weaver's course in Comparative Literature was extraordinary. Inside of three weeks this man had even the athletes reading Dante and Cervantes and Melville (on whom Weaver was an authority), and discussing them with deep interest. He was a persuasive teacher and a wonderfully nice man.

There were only about thirty people in the class, and I decided I was going to make Weaver one of the most popular teachers at Columbia. I started writing stories about him in my *Spectator* column. There was a baseball player on the Chicago White Sox, Buck Weaver, who was a wonderful player, except that he later became one of the Black Sox in the great baseball scandal. But at the time he was still a great hero, and of course I kept referring to Raymond Weaver as "Buck" Weaver. The dignified Mr. Weaver was not amused. And then I made up stories from whole cloth about him—anything to keep his name in the paper. He used to fuss at me, but I could tell that he was not really displeased. The following spring over a hundred people registered for his course. What at first seemed theatrical about him soon became very attractive to us.

Another thing happened through Weaver. He had rooms in one of the Columbia dormitories, and students would drop in after class once in a while to see him and talk. I met Richard Simon there. Dick was always something of a dreamer. He loved music and played the piano beautifully. He was also one of the most self-centered men who ever lived; he did what he wanted, and what didn't interest him simply didn't exist so far as he was concerned. He read only the assignments he liked, and if we were discussing a book he hadn't read, he'd just get up and play the piano.

My education at Columbia was not only getting a background in literature and history; I also learned at the School of Journalism—mainly through my experience on *Jester* and *Spectator*—how to write a quick story, how to put it down in as few words as possible. Something else that I think is invaluable: I learned not to clutter up my mind with a lot of useless information, because an intelligent man doesn't have to carry all that stuff in his head; he has only to know where to find what he needs when he needs it. I learned where to look for the things I needed and just how to go about getting them. Of course, there was another thing. Those were the years when I was becoming a man, and good teachers like Raymond Weaver and Benjamin Kendrick in the history department were an inspiration to me. I learned a lot just by knowing them.

I made Phi Beta Kappa in my junior year. I earned it because the courses I took were the ones that interested me and I worked on them—English, economics, history.

Irwin Edman

'17 COLUMBIA COLLEGE, '20 PHD

Irwin Edman was a Columbian through and through—a Morningside Heights native who attended the College and Graduate School and taught at the University for his entire adult life. He led well-regarded philosophy classes from 1919 to 1954, helped to develop the syllabus for the first Contemporary Civilization course, and was instrumental in establishing other core courses. He recalls some of his own instructors in this excerpt from Philosopher's Holiday *(1938).*

When one speaks of one's old teachers, it is generally to one's college teachers that one refers. For it is then, if one is lucky, that one comes in contact with men who communicate, and articulate the things and ideas which become the seeds of one's later intellectual and imaginative life. Every college has five or six men who in essence are its educational system. I was very lucky. For during my undergraduate days at Columbia, there was a galaxy of teachers available to the student who in their respective ways and as a group would be hard to duplicate at any college in any period. As a freshman straight from high school, I heard Charles A. Beard lecture on American Government; as a sophomore—and in 1914—I heard Carlton Hayes lecture on European History; as a junior I heard John Erskine talk on Shakespeare, and was in a small class where he taught us, really taught us, writing; and in my senior year I had the unique and irrecoverable experience of traversing the history of philosophy with Frederick J. E. Woodbridge. It was not until my graduate study that I came to know John Dewey.

Charles A. Beard illustrates something very remarkable about the art of teaching. Today everybody, even the literary youngsters, is interested in government. For even literature seems less in the Ivory Tower than it did in 1913. But the study of government, then officially known at Columbia as "Politics," did not, to most of us addicted to poetry and music, seem to be our meat, and there was nothing in the big dark blue tome, Beard's *American Government and Politics,* that seemed arresting. There were endless details about the mechanisms and structure of State and Federal government. It was not the Beard of the *Economic Interpretation of the Constitution.*

But his lectures were another matter. The lanky figure leaning against the wall, drawling wittily with half-closed eyes, made the questions of government seem the most vital that anyone could broach, and touched matters that lay far deeper than the mere forms of constitutional government.

Every good teacher has his own special art; with some, it is a genius for a clarity that sometimes is more lucid than the complexities of the subject justify. Sometimes it is a talent for apophthegm or leading suggestion, a word that evokes a vista or an idea that opens a world. I cannot now quite remember what Professor Beard's special technique was. He was clear, he was suggestive, he was witty. But none of these things could quite account for the hold he had on the smug and the rebels alike, on both the pre-lawyers and the pre-poets. I suspect it was a certain combination of poetry, philosophy, and honesty in the man himself, a sense he communicated that politics mattered far beyond the realm commonly called political, and an insight he conveyed into the life that forms of government furthered or betrayed. One morning he came into class as usual, stood against the wall, and, half-closing his eyes, said:

"Gentlemen, today we are to discuss the budget system in State government. I am sure that must seem to you a dull subject. But if you will tell me, gentlemen, how much *per capita* a nation spends on its Army, on its Navy, on education, on public works, I shall be able to tell you, I think, as much about that nation as if you gave me the works of its poets and philosophers."

We listened with revised and revived attention to an exposition, full of figures and detail, of the State budget system. Charles A. Beard showed us what politics had to do with the life beyond it and which it made possible. And he taught us, too, the difference between the forms of government and the living substance of its operations. Under his easy, drawling manner, we sensed a passionate concern for an understanding of the realities of government, the economic forces and the interested persons involved in it, and the ideal of government: the liberation of the energies of men. Nobody who has ever listened to Beard can disdain the study of politics in favour of the study of "higher things." He has been too well taught, as tragic world events have since shown, how government may nourish or destroy "higher things."

Up to the autumn of 1914 Europe seemed to most American college students a solar system away. In the autumn of 1914, when the war had been going on two months, Europe came for the first time in the imagination of many Americans to be vivid and near. European history ceased to be the anthropology and archaeology of distant peoples who spoke remote languages. It became as alive as yesterday's events: it was what explained today's news. It was, therefore, no wonder that at the beginning of the college year Carlton Hayes's course in "Europe since 1815" had become the most popular course in Columbia College. But it was not only the war that accounted for that. Carlton Hayes had for some time been one of the most popular professors in the college. His lectures were the most famous dramatic spectacle on the campus. Nor was it as a performance alone that they were famous. Everyone had heard that Hayes could actually make clear French political parties; I have never met anybody since who could or can…. The complicated history of Germany in the second half of the nineteenth century took shape as well as drama under his presentation of it. And in the midst of being taught and taught clearly, one had the incidental and additional pleasure of hearing a man to whom the great catastrophe of war had its roots in a past he knew, in the traditions of nations among whom he had lived familiarly, and in the desperate mythologies of nationalism, to which he had given special study and concern. One was treated, besides, to unforgettable vignettes of Disraeli dropping his morning walking stick as the cannons boomed noon at Gibraltar; of the Manchester school of economists, the "spiritual advisers" to the robber barons of early nineteenth-century industrial England; of the black walnut furniture of the Victorian period; of the times and the manners of Louis Napoleon; of the studious German Jew in the British Museum whose studies produced the *Communist Manifesto*. One was shaken out of the smugness of the middle-class world in which most students were brought up and out of the provincial Americanism in which most of us had lived.

It did not matter, it served only as spice, that some of the barbs delivered in a dry voice by this baldish, sharp-featured man in his thirties were directed at us, at our very smugness, at our laziness, or at our fathers: when he was explaining the attitude of the manufacturers of the early Industrial Revolution, he reminded us that we all knew manufacturers; "some of your fathers," he drawled, "are manufacturers." It did matter a little to some of us that he mocked poetry and philosophy (this *in re* Shelley and Godwin) . . . "philosophy is what is taught in Philosophy Hall. . . ." But it did not matter much. For during a whole year, we sat through a whole century of European history, and Bismarck, Garibaldi, Social Legislation in England. Benevolent Tories like Shaftesbury and reformers like Cobden and Bright, "nationalism"—what devastating force Carlton Hayes put and can still put into the word—democracy, the Third Republic, became familiar parts of our imagination. In the midst of cries of "pro-German" and "pro-Ally," "preparedness" and "pacifism," during the three years before America went into the war, we knew somewhat better than many of our older compatriots what had brought the tornado about. Carlton Hayes had brought European history, as Charles Beard had brought American government, from the abstraction of a textbook to an experience lived and a problem to be faced. And it always surprised some of us that, in the midst of the lectures—first-rate theatrical performances, words shot out for emphasis, silences sustained for a moment, gestures and movements deployed like those of a good actor—when we looked down at our notes, they were as ordered and clear as if we had listened to a scholastic metronome. . . . I confess with shame that I achieved only a B.

You were allowed, if you had a fairly good academic record, to take in the senior year a graduate course that was at the time one of the famous academic enterprises of the period. It was James Harvey Robinson's course in the History of the Intellectual Classes in Western Europe. Everyone who had gone to high school knew the two volumes of Robinson and Beard's *Development of Modern Europe*. But the Robinson we came to know as a legend and a rumour by the time we were sophomores was the Robinson who had invented the "new history"—the history of causes and consequences, the history that treated politics as the surface of more fundamental matters, economic and social and cultural, and that regarded the date of the invention of the steam engine as more important than the dates of a king, and the industrial use of steam as more significant than monarchies and dynasties. We had also heard of Robinson, along with Dewey and Beard, as among the intellectual-liberal forces that were making our university famous in some quarters, notorious in others. And, finally, we had heard of the remarkable brilliance of the lectures in History 72.

The latter was a graduate course to which undergraduates, a handful of us, were admitted on sufferance. The majority of the class of over two hundred were graduate students of history, many of them women high school teachers from all over the country, particularly the West and South. Professor Robinson was a short man, with thin, greying hair and a deprecating, half-tired, half-amused, drawling voice. He seemed to be having a half-weary good time examining the origins of human stupidity, and those vestigial remains of our culture that blocked the free and hopeful functioning of human intelligence. It took us a few weeks in the course to get to the beginnings of *intellectual* history. For Robinson, with saturnine delight, liked to show us the mind of the child, the slave, and the animal still functioning in us. Once he brought in a leading editorial from the New York *Times* to illustrate the theme, and another time quoted from a batch of Sunday sermons reported in that journal the next day. The course was not a course in intellectual heroes, but a course in the changing fashions of adult follies taken seriously in various ages. It only gradually became clear what intellectual heroes were presiding over the whole story as he gave it. They were Freud and Marx and Dewey and the anthropologists, and H. G. Wells, the prophet, then, of intelligence reshaping the world. There were only two or three gods of the past left unbesmirched, or whose clay feet were not recognized. They were Lucretius, who saw the diabolism of religion; Francis Bacon, who saw the human possibilities of science; Voltaire, who exhibited the foolishness of superstition. Plato was a man who believed in Truth, Goodness, and Beauty because he saw the actual world as a chaos which, Robinson loved to remind us, he compared to "a man with a running nose. . . . " Aristotle's science was childish (Robinson did not know how soon again it was to be fashionable and how more fundamental than fashion it is); St. Augustine was a most amusingly and scandalously human saint. It was not until the enlightenment of the eighteenth century that anybody, so most of us gathered from the course, was very enlightened.

Many of the graduate students were shocked, especially by the treatment of religion. The undergraduates from Columbia College had heard much of this before and had no faith (as did some of the graduate students) to have taken away. One of the young women complained to Professor Robinson: "You are taking away my faith." He looked at her oddly. "But if I took away a headache," he said simply, "you would not complain."

We undergraduates enjoyed the sallies, the freshness, the irreverence; and enjoyed, too, the fundamental feeling that lay at the basis of it all—that man, if he took his own intelligence into his hands—could make the world less a shambles and an idiocy than it had so often been. It was in the great days of the liberal faith when trust in intelligence was in the ascendant. If Robinson made the world appear a satire to intelligent observation, he made it seem a lyric hope to generosity and understanding. Dixon Ryan Fox, now President of Union College, was the young instructor who took the third quiz hour with the undergraduates. He felt it his special obligation to let us see the other side. And after a week, when he knew Robinson had been "exposing" modern Protestantism, he called in the chaplain as a counterweight. He need not have bothered; we had our own grains of salt. One of the reasons we had grains of salt was that some of us had been studying with a man who will go down, I am quite certain, as one of the great philosophical teachers of our generation. His slender published writings will live, but they will live for a small circle of students. But Frederick J. E. Woodbridge has educated a whole generation of students in philosophy; and a whole circle of them scattered over the country, including Morris Cohen and Sidney Hook and J. H. Randall, Jr., and Herbert Schneider (to mention only a few), are living testimonies to his influence and his power. In my college days, the great thing was to have taken his course in the History of Philosophy. Some of us were taking it at the same time that we took Robinson's History of the Intellectual Classes in Western Europe. It was rather a different story we were told. It was not a story, but a succession of experiences of philosophers whose importance lay "not in their truth but in their power." It was a shock that turned into a liberation for those of us who had come to philosophy looking for *the* Truth with a dogmatic capital letter. There were other shocks, too. Much that was said in the textbooks we never heard in class, or we heard the contrary. Professor Woodbridge, who looked like a bishop and would have made a very eloquent one, talked like a poet whose theme happened to be the human mind. He talked most like a poet on the days when he was most interested; one remembers what days those were: the early Greeks, Plato, Aristotle, Marcus Aurelius, Lucretius, Spinoza with his sovereign detachment, and Locke with his sovereign common sense. He was not an unprejudiced observer and we rather liked the frankness and the brevity with which he dismissed the Germans and Rousseau. But what one was most moved by was the things by which he himself was most moved: the Plato who was the son of Apollo, the poet and the dramatist of ideas; Marcus Aurelius, the disillusioned statesman whistling to keep up his cosmical courage; Lucretius looking out with dramatic sympathy and equable understanding on the eternal nature of things. We were impressed by a mind whose maturity had not dulled its enthusiasms, and an understanding uncorrupted by the technical controversies of the academy, by the routine of the classroom, by the burden of administration of an elder statesman, for Woodbridge was graduate Dean of the University. He taught a whole generation of students of philosophy to keep their eye on the object, to see a thinker in his own terms, to cease to raise foolish and irrelevant questions, and, above all, to raise the central and relevant ones about a man's teaching. On Aristotle's metaphysics, he began by reminding us that Aristotle was asking the simple and the ultimate question: "What does it mean to be?. . ." We found ourselves astonished to be reminded that the Middle Ages were in their own time not the Middle Ages at all. We were made aware of Locke's simple English attempt to be sensible, tolerant, and direct, and learned to understand what Spinoza meant and why he saw it as a liberation to see all things under the form of eternity. For in that wonderful class, as Will Durant (sitting next to me in alphabetical order) remarked, we were listening not to a professor of philosophy but to philosophy itself. It was impossible to feel you were listening to a doctrine; Professor Woodbridge has never founded a school. You were hearing philosophy itself and came to understand it as an attempt to speak in the categories of mind of the categories of things.

I did not—I think not many of us did—understand it all. But we began to understand what understanding meant, in words that had eloquence without rhetoric. We heard great things nobly uttered. We learnt no doctrine but we grasped the significance of intellectual procedure; and to a whole generation of philosophers, though Professor Woodbridge has long since ceased to be their teacher, he remains their teacher still. He made us understand as none else had done, to use one of his own phrases, "the enterprise of learning."

A figure more widely known outside purely academic circles was and is John Dewey. In 1915 his name was already, if not a household, certainly a schoolroom word. His *How We Think* was used in all the normal schools of the country, and even fashionable ladies dipped into his far from easy books. I had read almost all of Dewey I could get hold of by the time I was a senior, but it was not until my first year as a graduate student that I heard, or, I believe, saw him. His familiar figure and speech, seeming at first that of a Vermont farmer, the casual gait, the keen but often absent eyes, seem so familiar now that I can scarcely believe I did not know them before.

I admit the first lecture was quite a shock, a shock of dullness and confusion, if that can be said. It was at any rate a disappointment. I had not found Dewey's prose easy, but I had learned that its difficulty lay for the most part in its intellectual honesty, which led him to qualify an idea in one sentence half a page long. In part also it lay in the fact that this profoundly original philosopher was struggling to find a vocabulary to say what had never been said in philosophy before, to find a diction that would express with exactness the reality of change and novelty, philosophical words having been used for centuries to express the absolute and the fixed. Once one had got used to the long sentences, with their string of qualifying clauses, to the sobriety, to the lack of image and of colour, one sensed the liberating force of this philosophy. Here was not an answer but a quest for light in the living movement of human experience; in the very precariousness of experience there lay open to the perplexed human creature the possibilities that peril itself provocatively suggested. I had found here, as have so many of my generation, a philosophy that, instead of laying down a diagram of an ideal universe that had nothing to do with the one of actual human doings and sufferings, opened a vision of conscious control of life, of a democracy operating through creative intelligence in the liberation of human capacities and natural goods. In *How We Think* I had learned that thinking itself was simply a discipline of the animal habit of trial and error, and of the possible human habit of imagination and foresight. In *Democracy and Education* I had gathered that it was not in the forms of democratic government that true democracy lay, but in the substance of intelligent co-operation, largely dependent on education. Dewey was not easy, but once one had mastered his syntax, a vision of a liberal and liberated commonwealth was one's reward, and a philosophy that was not only a vision but a challenge.

I was naturally prepared, therefore, to expect something of intellectual excitement from the lectures in "Psychological Ethics." Intellectual excitement was the last term to describe what I experienced that September afternoon. The course came, in the first place, directly after lunch. It was well attended; there were even some fashionably dressed society ladies, for Dewey had become a vogue. But this famous philosopher who had written so much on "Interest in Education," as the essence of the educational process, could not, save by a radical distortion of the term, be said at first hearing to sound interesting. He had none of the usual tricks or gifts of the effective lecturer. He sat at his desk, fumbling with a few crumpled yellow sheets and looking abstractedly out of the window. He spoke very slowly in a Vermont drawl. He looked both very kindly and very abstracted. He hardly seemed aware of the presence of a class. He took little pains to underline a phrase, or emphasize a point, or, so at first it seemed to me, to make any. Occasionally he would apparently realize that people in the back of the room might not hear his quiet voice; he would then accent the next word, as likely as not a preposition or a conjunction. He seemed to be saying whatever came into his head next, and at one o'clock on an autumn afternoon to at least one undergraduate what came next did not always have or seem to have a very clear connexion with what had just gone before. The end of the hour finally came and he simply stopped; it seemed to me he might have stopped anywhere. But I soon found that it was my mind that had wandered, not John Dewey's. I began very soon to do what I had seldom done in college courses—to take notes. It was then a remarkable discovery to make on looking over my notes to find that what had seemed so casual, so rambling, so unexciting, was of an extraordinary coherence, texture, and brilliance. I had been listening not to the semi-theatrical repetition of a discourse many times made—a fairly accurate description of many academic lectures—I had been listening to a man actually *thinking* in the presence of a class. As one became accustomed to Dewey's technique, it was this last aspect of his teaching that was most impressive—and educative. To attend a lecture of John Dewey was to participate in the actual business of thought. Those pauses were delays in creative thinking, when the next step was really being considered, and for the glib dramatics of the teacher-actor was substituted the enterprise, careful and candid, of the genuine thinker. Those hours came to seem the most arresting educational experiences, almost, I have ever had. One had to be scrupulously attentive and one learned to be so. Not every day or in every teacher does one overhear the palpable processes of thought. One came to enjoy and appreciate the homely metaphor, "the fork in the road," the child and his first attempts to speak, the New England town meeting, instead of the classical images one had been accustomed to from more obviously eloquent lips. Moreover, if one listened attentively one discovered apophthegm and epigram delivered as casually and sleepily as if they were clichés. I remember one instance. It had been rather a long lecture designed to show that the crucial tests of the morals of a group came in what that group regarded as violations of its conventions. The bell rang. Professor Dewey began to crumple up his notes. "And so," he said, "I think sometimes one can tell more about the morals of our society from the inmates of its jails than from the inmates of its universities." The student next to me who had been semi-dozing stirred in half-alarmed surprise.

I learned later in a seminar to see Dewey's greatest gifts as a teacher, that of initiating inquiry rather than that of disseminating a doctrine. The subject matter of the seminar was innocent enough and removed from the immediacies of current controversy. It was a year's course, meeting every Tuesday afternoon, on "The Logic of John Stuart Mill." The seminar remains in my memory, it must be added, not simply for John Dewey or John Stuart Mill. It consisted, looking back on it and indeed as it appeared then, of a very remarkable group. It included two now well-known professors of philosophy, Brand Blanshard of Swarthmore College and Sterling Lamprecht of Amherst, Paul Blanshard, later to become Commissioner of Accounts under Mayor La Guardia, and Albert C. Barnes, the inventor and manufacturer of Argyrol and collector of French paintings, even then a grey-haired man who used to come up from Philadelphia every week with his secretary expressly to study philosophy with his friend John Dewey.

I don't suppose Professor Dewey said more than five percent of the words actually uttered in that seminar. For the latter consisted largely of papers presented by various members of the group. But one remembered what he said. The subject matter was obviously close to him, for had not Mill been one of the great nineteenth-century leaders of the empirical school of thought; had he not been, in his way, a pragmatist and, like Dewey himself, a liberal? But one notices particularly Dewey's gift for pointing to the exact difficulty or the exact limitations of a man or a paper; his capacity for sympathetically seeing what a student was driving at, even when he did not quite succeed in saying it, and Dewey's candid expression of his own position or his own prejudices.

One instance of Dewey's frankness comes to my mind. There was among the group a young lady who had come from England where she had studied philosophy with Bertrand Russell at Cambridge. She listened patiently for weeks to Dewey's varied insistence that the truth of an idea was tested by its use. One day she burst out toward the close of the seminar in the sharp, clipped speech of the educated Englishwoman: "But, professor, I have been taught to believe that true means true; that false means false, that good means good and bad means bad; I don't understand all this talk about more or less true, more or less good. Could you explain more exactly?"

Professor Dewey looked at her mildly for a moment and said: "Let me tell you a parable. Once upon a time in Philadelphia there was a paranoiac. He thought he was dead. Nobody could convince him he was alive. Finally, one of the doctors thought of an ingenious idea. He pricked the patient's finger. 'Now,' he said, 'are you dead?' 'Sure,' said the paranoiac, 'that proves that dead men bleed. . . .' Now I'll say true or false if you want me to, but I'll mean better or worse."

There are all kinds of talents that go to make up a great teacher. Among those not commonly noted in the textbooks are simplicity and candour. These qualities in Dewey even an undergraduate could recognize and understand.

I cannot say that John Erskine seemed to me a great man in the sense that Woodbridge and Dewey did and do, nor did *The Private Life of Helen of Troy,* for all its bright entertainment, lead me to think I had been obtuse on this point as an undergraduate. But I am convinced he was a very remarkable teacher and it has always seemed to me a pity that he gave up the profession of distinguished teaching for that of the popular novelist. Erskine's quality as a teacher was that of communication by contagion; you felt the quality of the authors he talked about and books seemed to have something to do with life rather than libraries.

Literature was an exercise in imagination, not in archaeology and there must be thousands of students besides myself who learned to read authors in their own terms, to enjoy them for their own sakes, from John Erskine's famous course in Elizabethan Literature. It is true that one enjoyed Professor Erskine for other reasons. He had wit—often malicious—in his own right, and, when he was in the vein, poetry and philosophy, too. He obviously loved poetry and it seemed to him both to matter and a matter of course that we should love it, too. One felt about him something of the prima donna lecturer; it was evidenced by the pointed silence that would occur while some unfortunate late-comer found his way to his seat. It was clear, too, from the way in which, not infrequently, Shakespeare or Marlowe or Castiglione would be the springboards for little bravura lectures by our teacher on the importance of love or of being a cultivated gentleman, the latter one of his favourite themes. But if he was sometimes the prima donna, he always respected the materials he taught, and for many years no one at

Columbia was a more devoted servant to the art and to the love of literature than he. And not the least of his services to that art were, first, the noble and musical way in which he read poetry itself; and, secondly, the pains he took to encourage signs of that art among undergraduates. Other teachers might make literature seem a set of documents to be investigated; no one quite knew why. Erskine made it an art to be lived and loved.

It is occasionally said that a good student needs no teachers and that all that he does need is a library and leisure. Neither the poor nor the good student needs bad teachers or bored ones; he is better off without them. But he is very fortunate indeed if he can look back on his college days and enumerate half a dozen men who, by their passion for ideas, their clarity about them, their love for the communication of them, their exemplification in their own being of intellectual discipline and candour, have given a meaning to facts that, even with leisure and libraries, he would not have been as likely to find by himself.

I feel my college generation at Columbia was very fortunate. Half a dozen good teachers in a college are enough to make it distinguished. We had more than half a dozen very exceptional ones. But then I think current undergraduates at Columbia, if they are discerning, will, looking back, be able to say the same.

Mark Van Doren

'20 PHD

Mark Van Doren was a poet, editor, journalist, scholar, and legendary teacher who inspired Columbia students for more than four decades. He was a founding instructor in Humanities A, which he taught for 17 years, and won the Pultizer Prize for poetry in 1940. This selection is from The Autobiography of Mark Van Doren *(1958).*

B ut I must go back to September, 1920, when I started to teach—with the notion, as I have said, that I would not do it long, although the fact is that I have done it without interruption for almost forty years. I have done other things too, but Hamilton Hall, where Columbia College has its being, is my one professional home that has never changed. I found myself at once in hospitable company. The older professors in the College were not too different, it seemed to me, from the colonels in whose headquarters I had worked as sergeant major and lieutenant. I respected them without being afraid of them. Nor do I remember feeling any panic when I faced my first classes. I must have been nervous, as annually I continue to be; but I was not afraid of freshmen either, for I had learned in the army that they were bound to be at least as apprehensive about the demands I made on them as I was about their opinion of me.

And three of my younger colleagues were old acquaintances: Raymond Weaver, now busy with Herman Melville, his biography of whom (suggested by Carl) would determine that author's vogue for a generation; Emery Neff, who proceeded deliberately, wisely, with his dissertation, *Carlyle and Mill;*

and Roy Dibble, whom recent events had curiously transformed. Rejected by the army for physical reasons, Dibble taught the war through in Hamilton Hall; and since he was required, in addition to teaching his chosen subject, to indoctrinate his students in something called "War Aims," something he had to feed them, as he put it, from a syllabus which left him no discretion in matters either of judgment or of emphasis, his normally vegetative nature had rebelled, so that he now considered himself a literary radical, and fired by the example of Lytton Strachey's *Eminent Victorians* set out to write a series of essays on *Strenuous Americans:* themselves, as essays, strenuous and surprising, and successful enough to call for other work of their kind before he died in 1929 of the weakness that had exempted him from military service. There was Irwin Edman, too, in another department. Carl had known him as an undergraduate in the College, when he amazed his instructors by writing final examinations in rhyme. Now he taught philosophy; and continued to write verses; and for many years was my warm, bright, playful friend.

My elders were benevolent men. George Clinton Dinsmore Odell, who had been a student in Columbia College before it moved uptown, and who did not mind giving us the impression that he had lived much longer than even that, was a massive, genial, smoothly civil and considerate New Yorker whose one passion was the local stage. He was only then beginning to plan the *Annals* of that stage which in many tall volumes would make him famous; but his talk, when it did not have to be about the sections in freshman English which he so leniently administered, was likely to turn back in time to Edwin Booth or Adelina Patti—there had been no soprano worth the name, he said, since Patti. John Erskine, a New Yorker of the next generation, I had known before: as a lecturer in the graduate school, and as a friend of Carl. His energy manifested itself in rougher and directer ways. He was a poet and a musician; as a man he held strong opinions and expressed them without reserve; as a teacher he was powerful; as a colleague he was kind. He was to leave the university after the success of his novel *The Private Life of Helen of Troy,* as Carl had already left it except for the graduate lectures in American literature which for years he came back from *The Nation,* the *Century Magazine,* the Literary Guild, or wherever else he was, to give in Philosophy Hall. Harrison Ross Steeves, no less a New Yorker than Odell or Erskine, impressed me that year, as he would do through all the later time when he administered our College department, by his utter quiet and his impregnable reserve. Speaking always in perfect sentences, and maintaining a decorum which nevertheless could not conceal a dedication to the best that there can be in books, he was not to tell me until I knew him better than I could then that he might just as well have studied law. Precision would have been his strength in any case: precision, and a sense of honor which nobody ever doubted. Professor Trent was no longer one of my immediate superiors. He taught entirely in the graduate school, where I saw him as often as I could, but this was not often, particularly after the long illness set in from which he was to die in 1939. During this illness he wrote me, with difficulty because of his paralysis, letters of touching sweetness and good will.

If I speak of the students last it is not merely because they were the crucial persons with whom I spent my time, as must be true in any college; it is also because no way exists of describing what really goes on in a classroom once the door is closed. What goes on is a kind of secret between him who stands and those who sit. I knew this from the first; it was my secret even more than it was theirs. They had their own responses which I could hear or see them make: they raised their hands, they talked, they shook their heads, they laughed, they looked bored; and special approval or disapproval they expressed—the custom is now obsolete—by stamping or shuffling their feet on the floor. But even then I could believe that if anything of true moment was happening in their minds there was no immediate way for them to show it, any more than I could show, except by talking in the maturest way I could, and following any new idea as far as it would take me, how much our conversations interested me and how much I learned from them.

From the beginning, I think, I assumed experience even in freshmen; and the reward for this assumption was my feeling that I had good students. I had the feeling not only in small classes but in large; for right away I had a taste of what it is like to address rows and rows of faces in rooms like amphitheaters, except that I did not do it myself; I merely assisted Brander Matthews, a fourth New Yorker among my elders who taught an ancient course in American literature which I would recast in time and teach myself. Assisting him then meant taking attendance at his lectures, reading the examinations, and answering students' complaints that they had been given the wrong marks. It also meant walking away with Brander and listening to such stories as he had not told in class. His monologues were witty, and sometimes they sounded as if they had been rehearsed. Their reference was usually to the theater, which Brander knew in his own way as well as Odell. But he was a more professional man, very knowing about authors and playwrights; and if I never thought him profound I knew that he was clever and disposed to help me if I behaved properly, as he seemed never to be positive, however, I would do.

Within two years I had a large class of my own. It was called Six English Authors; it was entirely my invention; and I remember being surprised when upon suggesting it I was permitted to give it and see what happened. It was conceived in reaction against a survey course that skipped too rapidly, I thought, over too many writers. Why not reduce the number to six and read each of them as thoroughly as possible? What happened was that the course succeeded beyond anyone's expectation: certainly beyond mine, for I had not dreamed that as many as 250 students would want to take it. The authors varied from year to year, though Chaucer, Shakespeare, and Fielding were always there; the others might be Milton, Pope, Swift, Byron, Browning, or Hardy (as a poet). I do not know how many of the students listened carefully, but at the moment this did not seem to matter; the readings were copious, and I found that I had a great deal to say, nor did I mind if what I said had been said by others before me. I read aloud, I called attention to good things, I generalized about literature and life to the limit of my capacity. Perhaps the chief novelty consisted in my assumption that nothing was too difficult for the students. I told them not to worry about Chaucer's Middle English but to read him fast for what they could get out of him; they missed a good deal, but I think they got the heart of that master comedian. So with Shakespeare's plays, *Paradise Lost,* and the *Prelude:* I considered each work as a human whole, and ignored many literary problems. I was to teach this course for something like ten years, and was never to grow tired of hearing either myself or the students talk; for I insisted that they continue to talk, in spite of their overwhelming numbers, as if the room were small.

The small room, that is to say, was standard in my mind. And no wonder, for my experience had been chiefly there, with twenty or thirty students considering in seats before me the principles of reading and writing. Professor Odell properly supposed that the two arts went together; so in every section of freshman and sophomore English we read and wrote, which meant among other things my reading aloud what the students wrote, or copying it on the blackboard and discussing its every fault or merit. The small room, indeed, must forever be the model of what teaching is when it is personal and patient and alive. I soon discovered, of course, that my students were persons—in class, that is, where for me it mattered most what they were. I never encouraged intimacy with them outside, and 1 have not done so since; I have no illusion that students and teachers can be friends in the fullest sense, since there is by statute an inequality in their positions; Aristotle is right about that as he is about most things. Yet this has at no time prevented certain ones of them, if they persisted in the effort, from breaking through whatever barrier there was and becoming, if only in after years, some of my finest friends. In college as such I have always taken for granted that what we had to give each other was to be given in the small room we inhabited together for fifty minutes daily; that was where I discovered what I knew, and the same thing would have to be true for them.

Not that the very first class I met was without its young man who engaged me beyond the call of duty. This was Whittaker Chambers, whose eyes were always upon me as if he thought he had found in this strange place a person who would understand him. I cannot claim that I did, for he was continually astounding me. Early in the term he was delinquent with a paper; and when I asked him why, he told me he was busy with politics: he was distributing handbills in favor of Calvin Coolidge, the Republican candidate for Vice President in November. "Why Coolidge?" I asked; and Whittaker asked me in turn whether I had not heard about that great man's action in settling the Boston police strike. I had a different view of this action, for I was a reader of *The Nation* and already a contributor to it of frequent reviews. But the argument did not go on; his politics were not my business, and anyway he was so passionate a Republican that he would not have listened to anybody. Within a year he had ceased to be interested in politics. He was passionate about poetry, philosophy, and all manner of abstract things; and his poems were good. Toward the end of his junior year he published in *Morningside,* the college literary magazine, a little play about Jesus in the tomb, the point of it being that Jesus, called upon to come forth, preferred to sleep forever. During the rumpus that followed I defended in the *Spectator,* the college newspaper, Whittaker's right to publish such a piece; and was rewarded by a word from Brander Matthews that he disapproved of both Whittaker and me. Whittaker himself was expelled from Columbia; and though he was reinstated the next year, he never again felt that he belonged. Shortly after his graduation he wrote me that he had joined the Communist Party. This also had for me an abstract sound, and I could not take it seriously. Dorothy, on the rare occasions when he came to see us after his Columbia days were over, noticed that two or three of his front teeth were broken, and asked him whether he intended to have them fixed. He told her he preferred to leave them as they were: they made him look, he grinned and said, like one of the people. He disappeared from view in time, though cards and letters would come from various places, here or abroad, and not too seldom a poem, able and warmhearted, which I printed in *The Nation.* Then ten years passed during which I never saw or heard from him at all.

An altogether different student must remain anonymous. His writing was so poor that I could not possibly pass it. Not only was it clumsy and incorrect; there seemed to be no mind behind it. He came into my office one day, closed the door, and proceeded to explain. He said he was a physical training instructor in a gymnasium downtown. I looked at him again and realized that he was strong; he was not tall, but by the very way he held out his hands, which were trembling with anxiety and excitement, he expressed muscles I was unable to see. He informed me that with those hands he could bend iron bars; he could even tear a piece two inches square out of the upper left corner of the New York telephone book. I glanced toward the door, wondering what next. But I had misconstrued the man. He had come for no other reason than to tell me what I *could* admire him for. At least he was strong. He was older than the other students; he had thought he could be a student too; but he supposed now there was no use in trying further. Gentle, like most giants, he touched me so deeply that I did my best to spare his feelings. He did not want them spared. He wanted my honest opinion, which I ended by giving him. Before long he left college.

There was no resemblance between him and another student, an able writer, who when he failed to hand in a term paper was furious because I would not overlook the failure. The time was May, and he told me he had been in love all spring. I said: "You don't love her very much." He stared at me with greater fury. "How can you say that?" "You won't sacrifice a mark for her." He could think of no answer to this, and for the time being I am sure he hated me—as still another student must have, for he wrote anonymous letters to all of the New York newspapers saying I had insulted them. He was a journalism student; and it was true that one day, irked by the fact that the composition class of which he was a member seemed incapable of finding subjects other than those suggested to them by the daily press, I had stated Thoreau's opinion of newspapers as if it were my own, and at the moment it more or less was. I even announced that I never read the sheets myself; I preferred books, or even better, my own thoughts. The result of his action was a rush of reporters and photographers to interview me in Hamilton Hall. They left me in peace when I reminded them that his letters had been anonymous, and the incident, which I confess shook me, was closed; except that the *Times* lectured me in an editorial for my addiction to darkness.

It was not long before I found I had the reputation of being partial to Jewish students. I doubt that I was, yet it is true that among the Jewish students in my classes there were many who fascinated me by their brilliance and by the saliency of their several characters. I accent "several"; for it was the variety among these students that impressed me most. Perhaps I had entertained the vulgar notion that as Jews they would be all alike. Of course they were all different, and somehow they did become my friends—so much so that when one of them happened to tell the editor of the *Menorah Journal* about it he invited me to describe them in an article. I did so in 1927, under the title "Jewish Students I Have Known," and those of them I still see tell me I was fairly prophetic as to their futures. The students described—as individuals, for I refused to generalize—were Henry Rosenthal, Clifton Fadiman, Meyer Schapiro, John Gassner, Louis Zukofsky, Herbert Solow, Lionel Trilling, and Charles Prager. I shall not repaint them here; yet to read the article again is to be reminded how early character is formed, and how little it ever changes. In the case of Henry Rosenthal I emphasized the sardonic, satirical genius which his friends still fear in him, though with time he has mellowed. In Clifton Fadiman I noted the gift of mimicry and the fund of knowledge which everybody continues to associate with him. I spoke of Schapiro's "passion to know and make known," particularly in the field of fine art and its history. John Gassner I represented as "drunk with literature"; if I had added, dramatic literature, I would have left nothing out. Louis Zukofsky remains "a subtle poet" with an "inarticulate soul." Herbert Solow, I said, had "brown bored eyes" and was ironic without bitterness. I reported of Lionel Trilling that he was "sensitive" and "fastidious" and that he "spoke diffidently, with a hushed and harmless voice"; I found in him "dignity and grace," and foretold that whatever he eventually did "will be lovely, for it will be the fruit of a pure intelligence slowly ripened in not too fierce a sun." Of Charles Prager, whom I greatly liked, I predicted that he would do nothing so arduous as to become "the man of letters we thought he wanted to be." He never did, nor in fact do I know what he did.

John Erskine, who in France after the war, waiting to come home, had helped organize a program of reading for himself and his friends, decided when he did come home that the same program would be good for the students of Columbia College. It was a revolutionary decision, made at about the same time I came along, and it was not accepted by the faculty without a fight. The revolutionary thing was Erskine's faith, inspired in part by his old Columbia teacher George Edward Woodberry, that the best books are not too good for undergraduates. The opposition said they would never understand them; they would only pretend they did, and the result would be a butchery of the classics, or at the best a travesty upon them. Students should read about them rather than in them; textbooks were still the teacher's most dependable tool. Erskine did not agree. The books he and his colleagues in the French enterprise had read and discussed were the greatest books, from Homer and Plato on, that they could find; he wished he had read them, however imperfectly, when he was young; and he proposed that the education of American youth be no longer neglected. The sooner they made contact with noble minds the better for their own. There is always the first time that any book is read; then in these cases, why not now?

The outcome was a course in the College called General Honors: the ancestor of innumerable courses and even curriculums in Great Books which the colleges of America have created since that day. General Honors was not prescribed, nor could freshmen elect it. Only upperclassmen were invited to the feast. They came, not in great numbers, to sessions conducted weekly for two hours on Wednesday evening; seminar rooms were used so that the students could sit informally around a long table and smoke; and at the end of this table were two teachers, not one, so that benefit might be derived from differences between their views of Aristotle, Euripides, St. Augustine, Dante, Rabelais, Montaigne, Shakespeare, Molière, Voltaire, Goethe, or whoever else was being encountered through one of his masterpieces.

It was at such a table that I learned how powerful Erskine himself was as a teacher, for I sat in with him during my first evenings as a member of the staff. One night the book was Dante's *New Life,* and a student had begun the discussion by saying that so far as he was concerned it was nothing but a story of a man who stood in the gutter and made remarks about some girls who passed. The rest of us, sensible of the outrage, gasped; but Erskine only smiled and said: "Mr.——, will you open the book and read?" "On what page, sir?" "Any page." It was a perfect solution, so quietly arrived at that even the student knew he was refuting himself as he read aloud—I do not remember what, but as I now open the book at random I find this sentence: "And these words said, all this my fantasy vanished suddenly by reason of the great portion of himself that methought Love gave me; and as though trans-formed in my appearance, I rode that day very pensive and accompanied by many sighs." Nor can I forget another time when some student undertook to explain all literature as economically determined. "Can you give me an exam-ple," said Erskine, "of a book or an author so determined?" "Why, yes. Sir Walter Scott. He wrote his last novels to pay his debts." "I would have thought," said Erskine softly—and this was all the more remarkable because he was not soft by nature—"that the sense of honor had something to do with it." There was an answer to that, perhaps. The sense of honor may be a badge of class. But the student did not think of it, and neither have I until this moment.

Before long I was teaching my own section of General Honors with a man younger than I. This was Mortimer Adler, whom I had barely known as a stu-dent in the College but who had reappeared from the department of psy-chology to engage in Erskine's experiment. Mortimer was soon to consider himself a philosopher rather than a psychologist, and as such he has taught me, throughout thirty years of a lasting friendship, more than I am able to add up. But then he seemed to think he was being taught by me, in the inter-vals at any rate of his own inimitable discourse, which was rapid and fiery, and illuminated at every turn by formal logic—itself, as he manipulated it, a shower of sparks. I had not known before, and I have not known since, such high spirits in any man occupied with wholly intellectual concerns. He had other concerns too: trains, girls, movies, food, and indeed all the things that natural people love, for he was entirely natural; but when it came to ideas he blazed with excitement; he would bounce in his chair as he fought to defend a distinction; he would talk so fast that his tongue, as I once told him, fell over itself; he would be deadly serious, and then he would laugh like a happy madman—not that he was ever mad, but he could be happy to the skies over a philosophical discovery. I began to see him away from the university as well as there; he told me of his triumphs and his troubles—mostly his troubles; and I witnessed in him the conversion of a teacher to the cause John Erskine had espoused. Once Mortimer had begun to talk with students about great books there was no need to convince him of their beauty and might.

He professed to believe that I was the only one of us who knew anything about poetry; then when I protested, he talked about poetry in such a way as to fill it with meanings—utmost meanings—I myself had forgotten or never known. To him it was a form of knowledge, and its chief function was to tell stories. He was Aristotelian about the art, as he was in process of becoming about everything. At this point my education under him can be said to have had its beginning. Nor was the end of it in sight three decades later when I wrote "Philosopher at Large" with Mortimer in mind:

> The ancient garden where most men
> Step daintily, in specimen dust,
> He bulldozes; plows deep;
> Moves earth; says someone must,
> If truth is ever to be found
> That so long since went underground.
>
> What truth? Why down? He shakes his head.
> He does not know. But roots and rocks
> Go tumbling, tearing, as his blade,
> Shivering from its own shocks,
> Bites farther, and upturns pure clay
> He does not pause to smooth away.
>
> And horrifies those men, by hedge
> And dust plot, whom the top sufficed.
> They thought the garden theirs. And still
> It is; but the dear air is spiced
> With damp new things dug up. Or old,
> He says; like God, like buried gold.

Margaret Mead

'23 BARNARD, '29 PHD

Coming of Age in Samoa, *an instant best-seller upon its publication in 1928, made Margaret Mead perhaps the most famous anthropologist in the world. Her work addressed problems of child rearing, personality, and culture, and was distinguished by the inclusion of women's and children's perspectives. A student of both Franz Boas and Ruth Benedict, Mead taught at Columbia from 1948 to 1978 and was also affiliated with the American Museum of Natural History for many decades. Her 1972 memoir,* Blackberry Winter, *provides this recollection of her days at Barnard.*

I n the autumn of 1920, I came to Barnard, where I found —and in some measure created—the kind of student life that matched my earlier dreams. In the course of those three undergraduate years friendships were founded that have endured a lifetime of change, and by the end of those years I knew what I could do in life.

At that time Barnard had only one large dormitory, and during preceding years one group of students had been permitted to live in an apartment and do cooperative housekeeping. They were unusual girls, most of whom became well known in later life—Margaret Mayer, Dorothy Swaine Thomas, Betsy Anne Selhayes, Agnes Piel, and Léonie Adams. When I arrived on the scene the group had dispersed and the Coop had been abolished, but the overflow of students still was housed in apartments. Although the space in which we lived was usually very confined, the fact that the cost of rooms varied—the kitchen and the maid's room were the least expensive—meant that a group with unequal financial resources could live together.

In our group Léonie Adams provided a link to the old Coop group and their ethos; out of this we developed our own ideas of unity, based on common tastes and a respect for diversity. Most of the group we formed lived together, in three successive apartments, throughout college. There were always accidents—girls added who turned out not to fit, but we included them, wept with them, and supported them when they dropped out for reasons of their own or were expelled for spending the night in Greenwich Village.

Each year we adopted as a group name some derogatory and abusive phrase that was hurled at us in particular or at the students at large. The first year Miss Abbott, the head of the dormitory apartments, described us as "a mental and moral muss," and we accepted this with a kind of wicked glee. The second year we adopted the phrase "Communist morons," from the angry words of a commencement speaker. "Ash Can Cats," the name that finally stuck, was an epithet bestowed on us by our most popular professor, the vivid, colloquial, contemporary-minded Minor W. Latham, after whom Barnard's theater is named. We all took the course in drama in which she brought together, with a fine human relevance and a contempt for historical sequence, Greek plays, the contemporary Broadway theater, and miracle plays, and we were her partisans against the more conventional members of the English Department, critics ever, who admired creativity only when the creator was dead.

Sophisticated as we were, we were still remarkably innocent about practical matters relating to sex. During that first year, the sixteen-year-old daughter of a friend of my mother's was found in bed with a boarder and was forced by her mother to get married. We knew that she ought not have a baby yet, and we compiled a five-page typed list of home remedies that could be used as a douche. However, our young friend in due course had a baby, and she taught him to sit still on the piano while she practiced. Meanwhile the paint peeled off the plaster wall in the outer living room of our dormitory apartment, and she painted an enormous cartoon on it, in which a huge grinning world invited in a very small miss in cap and gown. The inscription read: "Come in and learn the rest of the alphabet."

But we knew about Freud. Agnes Piel was being analyzed and, although overnight visitors were not allowed and had to be hidden when Miss Abbott pounced, Ag occasionally spent the night with us. The first time she came, I made up her bed for her. Accustomed to being the eldest, that was the kind of thing I always did. Ag looked at me and said, "Well, the man you marry will certainly have an Oedipus fixation on you, which will be all right if it isn't joined to an incest complex."

We learned about homosexuality, too, mainly from the covert stories that drifted down to us through our more sophisticated alumnae friends, through the Coop group, and through Léonie's older sister, who was close to some members of the faculty. Allegations were made against faculty members, and we worried and thought over affectionate episodes in our past relationships with girls and wondered whether they had been incipient examples.

We knew that repression was a bad thing, and one of our friends—not a member of the inner circle—described how she and her fiancé had made up a set of topics to talk about on dates so that they would not be frustrated. When she heard that I had been engaged for two years and did not intend to get married for three years more, she exclaimed, "No wonder your arm hurts!"

Toward the end of my first year at Barnard, I myself, my grandmother, and my sister Elizabeth all developed extreme muscle pains which were then diagnosed as neuritis. One day, while I was going through a routine physical checkup and my grip was being tested, I discovered that all the strength had gone out of my right hand. That spring I wore my arm in a sling, took my examinations orally, and learned—as did my grandmother—to write with my left hand. It was then that my father, short of ready cash, again threatened to keep me home from college.

The pain stayed with me all through college, and I have always been subject to muscle pains of various sorts—in my neck and in my arms and legs. In later years I learned to play with the pain by concentrating on some other part of my body. Still later, Janet Travell's method of treating pain by inserting a needle at the trigger point—so reminiscent of the Chinese method of acupuncture—used to ease the periodic strains. But at the time when the pain first lamed my arm, it appeared to us that I might have suffered some unknown "affectively toned trauma." We liked the phrase, and I wrote a poem called "The Pencil Lines of Pain," which was published in *The Barnacle,* the new freshman paper.

We thought of ourselves as radicals—in terms of our sentiments rather than our adherence to any radical ideology. But there were always staunch conservatives in our midst. Among them were Muriel Mosher, a devoted medievalist, and Viola Corrigan, a Catholic, who found her first year in our group very hard going. Then there were Virginia Huey and K. Wright, two girls from the South, who found very disturbing what they heard in sociology courses about mine workers and Negroes. At the same time Mary Anne McCall, known as Bunny, who was the perfect flapper of the early 1920's, provided us with a running comment on a way of life that was quite alien to the rest of us, either because we were too old-fashioned or because we were too intellectual and idealistic.

The core of our group lived in the dormitory-apartment on West 116th Street, but we provided a center, too, for commuters whom we called, inelegantly, "parasites," because they hung up their hats in our quarters. Of these, two remained lifelong members of the group. One is Eleanor

Phillips, with whom I have carried on running battles, based on our temperamental differences, for fifty years. It was Eleanor Phillips who said that Shelley was not always Shelley to me, while, from her viewpoint, the poet was always, under any circumstances, the poet. The other is Leah Josephson Hanna, who has, I think, a special gift for friendship and who provided all of us with warmth as she listened to us with never-failing, sophisticated sympathy.

Our group was half Jewish and half Gentile. Looking back, it seems to me that the Gentile families were, on the whole, a little more receptive to their daughters' friendships than were the more tightly knit Jewish families. I had enjoyed the few Jewish children I had known earlier, and during college summers I often got very bored with the slower intellectual pace of the Gentile world.

In that first apartment, Léonie Adams lived in the "kitchen," which had a swinging door through which we used to push her when, after endless days of *not* doing a piece of work, the date for completion of a paper became too imminent. The second year she and I shared a room and pinned a sign on the door: "We don't believe in private property, please keep yours out." Each of us chose as a motto lines from a poem in Edna St. Vincent Millay's recently published book, A *Few Figs from Thistles*. The choice Léonie and I made was:

> Safe upon the solid rock the ugly houses stand:
> Come and see my shining palace built upon the sand!

But we liked equally well the three poems that begin "My candle burns at both ends," and "Cut if you will, with Sleep's dull knife," and "Was it for this I kicked the stairs . . ."

When we first began living together I invented a kinship system for the group. Deborah Kaplan, Léonie Adams, and I were the "parents," and Viola Corrigan and Eleanor Pelham Kortheuer—who had an extraordinary gift for sensitive and humorous insights—were the "children." In 1922 we added "grandchildren," only one of whom, Louise Rosenblatt, has remained part of the group, and finally, in 1923, we added a "great-grandchild," Hannah Kahn, whom we called David because of her resemblance to "the shepherd lad." Léonie graduated in 1922. During the third year we lived in a much more imposing apartment at 29 Claremont Avenue.

Throughout the three years our lives were filled with theatrical and literary events. We went to the theater often—to see Robert Edmond Jones' staging of *Macbeth* and to admire Katharine Cornell when she stole the show in A *Bill of Divorcement*. We shared a baby by baby-sitting, in turn, for the daughter of a professor—as much, I think because we wanted to keep in touch with a world with babies in it as for the money each of us earned. Sometimes we read aloud long sections of Milton. Or we worried about whether the new Freudian insights, which seemed to strip life of mystery, could be assimilated and sunk into the unconscious, so that spontaneity in art would again be possible.

Deborah Kaplan became the president of the Hebrew Culture Society and I the president of the Sunday Night Club, which was the only organization on the campus through which young people of both sexes could meet to hear liberal speakers. Before meetings, Deb and I used to buy huge pieces of cardboard that we cut in half to make our posters, and we used to argue vigorously as to whether or not Jews had a "chromosome" for social justice.

All of us took part in a mass meeting for Sacco and Vanzetti during the period of their trial in the spring of 1921. When this netted only $25, Léonie, as editor of *The Barnard Bulletin,* was moved to write an editorial, "Cheer Up, Mr. Coolidge"—her answer to an article the Vice-President had written, "Are the 'Reds' Stalking Our College Women?" for *Delineator.* At different times we also made forays into radical activities, walking on a picket line or stuffing envelopes for the Amalgamated Clothing Workers. We also took a course on the contemporary labor movement with Sylvia Kopald, a brilliant young economist, whose lectures were so elaborately organized that I could outline a point down to 1^{15} in the system with which I was experimenting.

But the most exciting events centered around Léonie's poetry, for while she was still an undergraduate she was already having poems accepted and published. Because we all were interested in literature, we recognized that Léonie was a real poet, whereas none of the rest of us was a real anything as yet; indeed, we were not sure where we were going.

The presence of one highly gifted person whose talent is recognized has an enormous effect on everyone belonging to a group. It makes for a very different affirmation of the values that are being taught in courses and discussed by critics. It also affects one's estimation of one's own talents. I too had been writing verse and I continued to do so for several years, but it became an avocation—an enjoyable way of translating experience for myself and of communicating with friends who were poets. But because Léonie was there, it ceased to be a serious ambition. Without her, I might have gone on much longer, fancying that a slight talent was a real gift. It meant, too, that we had to look at the choices we made in other fields in much stricter terms, evaluating our respective gifts much more critically than we would have been able to do otherwise. And the relationship was not all one-sided; we made a protective and enjoyable shield around Léonie and supported her in whatever she chose to do. This included editing *The Barnard Bulletin;* I followed her, and Louise Rosenblatt followed me. It saddened us when Léonie failed to obtain the Caroline Duror Fellowship, Barnard's only graduate fellowship. I too failed to win it, but finally Louise, as an alternate, received it.

We were a happily captivated audience for Léonie's long narrative anecdotes, many of which are as vivid today in my memory as they were when she told them. I saw myself as a kind of production manager, helping to keep our shifting groups organized around Léonie. I believed that cross-generational continuity among college students, which characterized our own group and which was the one good thing I had perceived in the sorority system at DePauw, was essential to correct the narrow age typing that is so common in American colleges. But I had very little sense that I myself provided a focus for the group, and I remember the surprise I felt, at a college tea during senior year, when I found a group listening to what I said and laughing. I had always been told that I had no sense of humor, and I still don't know how the shift came about so that I could make others laugh, instead of being part of the laughing audience.

Although we were bound together by ties of temperament and congeniality and by a common interest in literature some—but not all—of us also were children of our period and true descendants of the group of girls who had lived in the Coop. We belonged to a generation of young women who felt extraordinarily free—free from the demand to marry unless we chose to do so, free to postpone marriage while we did other things, free from the need to bargain and hedge that had burdened and restricted women of earlier generations. We laughed at the idea that a woman could be an old maid at the age of twenty-five, and we rejoiced at the new medical care that made it possible for a woman to have a child at forty.

We did not bargain with men. Almost every one of us fell in love with a much older man, someone who was an outstanding figure in one of the fields in which we were working, but none of these love affairs led to marriage. Schooled in an older ethic, the men were perplexed by us and vacillated between a willingness to take the love that was offered so generously and uncalculatingly and a feeling that to do so was to play the part of a wicked seducer. Later most of us married men who were closer to our own age and style of living, but it was a curious period in which girls who were too proud to ask for any hostage to fate confused the men they chose to love.

At the same time we firmly established a style of relationships to other women. "Never break a date with a girl for a man" was one of our mottoes in a period when women's loyalty to women usually was—as it usually still is—subordinate to their possible relationships to men. We learned loyalty to women, pleasure in conversation with women, and enjoyment of the way in which we complemented one another in terms of our differences in temperament, which we found as interesting as the complementarity that is produced by the difference of sex. Throughout extraordinarily different career lines we have continued to enjoy one another, and although meeting becomes more difficult as we scatter in retirement, we continue to meet and take delight in one another's minds.

In college, as in earlier years, I had several sets of friends. Although I never tried to keep the Ash Can Cats and other groups in separate compartments, their interests were not the same and often the different groups were mutually incompatible. There was, for instance, a group of girls who liked dancing and who used to go to tea dances, girls for whom I sometimes provided extra dancing partners from among Luther's friends. And there was Marie Eichelberger, who looked younger than many freshmen but who, in fact, came to college very late after curing a severe tuberculosis infection she had contracted in high school. We became close friends and later her home became a focal point in my life. During her college years she remained peripheral to the Ash Can Cats, but afterward many of them became her friends also.

When I went to DePauw, I intended to be a writer, and when I transferred to Barnard I continued to major in English. But the experience was disappointing. Billy Brewster, with whom I took Daily Themes, said I would never be a writer. I took a course on the novel and learned less than I could get out of reading novels by myself. So, although I had been deeply bored by my course in Introductory Psychology, I went on to take the necessary hours for a second major, in psychology.

But I was still uncertain. The experience of knowing Léonie had given me new insight into my talents. Although I could write well, I realized that creative writing would not provide a central focus for my life. I was also interested in politics, especially in bringing about change in the world, and I became a collegiate debater, but I early rejected debating as dishonest. In active politics, debate essentially provides a means of exploiting any weakness in one's opponent and of seizing on any argument, strong or weak, that will bolster one's own position. I had known Scott Nearing as a child and while I was in college I went to hear him debate with the popular radical minister of the Community Church, John Haynes Holmes. Holmes only wanted to win; Scott cared about the issues. I was fairly certain that I could succeed in politics. I could speak well, I had a good memory for people, and I could plan—but I felt that political success was both too short term and too exigent.

Later, by the time the state of the world might have provided a different rationale, I was effectively debarred from political life because I had been divorced twice. Therefore, during World War II, when my friends suggested that I should aim for some political appointment, I could always answer that

I was too vulnerable since I might damage any cause I would be expected to promote or defend.

In a curious way this has both protected me and permitted me a kind of single-minded pursuit of the things I have valued, just as being a woman has protected me from having to accept administrative posts. Otherwise, with my propensity for letting life call the shots, I might easily have been diverted by the argument that it was necessary for me to play a political role. As it was, as long as I did not put myself in the position of being a political target, my private life was not a liability and, in fact, rapidly faded from most people's memories. Today, occasionally, I receive letters attacking me as a spinster without any right to discuss questions of family life. Almost invariably, advocacy of causes on which society is polarized produces the kind of hostility that seizes on any real or apparent vulnerability. Today when I advocate some unpopular point of view, my age is used as target and some fanatic is likely to denounce me as senile.

But I definitely decided, while I was still in college, that I would not make a career out of politics. At the same time my experience with painting and writing had convinced me that I did not have the superlative talent that might not have been necessary in an earlier age but that was crucial for success in the contemporary world. America in the 1920's had no place for the kind of artist who could paint an angel's wing and would leave the painting of the angel's face to someone with a greater gift.

I wanted to make a contribution. It seemed to me then—as it still does—that science is an activity in which there is room for many degrees, as well as many kinds, of giftedness. It is an activity in which any individual, by finding his own level, can make a true contribution. So I chose science—and to me that meant one of the social sciences. My problem then was which of the social sciences?

I entered my senior year committed to psychology, but I also took a course on psychological aspects of culture given by William Fielding Ogburn, one of the first courses in which Freudian psychology was treated with respect. I had also to choose between the two most distinguished courses open to seniors—a philosophy course given by William Pepperell Montague and the course in anthropology given by Franz Boas. I chose anthropology.

I had absorbed many of the premises of anthropology at home as they lay back of what my mother had learned at Bryn Mawr under Caseby and what both my parents had learned from Veblen. I was accustomed to regard all the races of man as equal and to look at all human cultures as comparable. What was new to me was the vista that was opened up by discussions of the development of men from their earliest beginnings. The reconstructions of Stone

Age men with bundles of sticks in their arms had a tremendous power to move me, as they evoked a sense of the millennia it had taken man to take the first groping steps toward civilization and of the many thousands of years the slender flakes from the cores men made into hammerstones had lain unused in paleolithic workshops.

Boas was a surprising and somewhat frightening teacher. He had a bad side and a good side of his face. On one side there was a long dueling scar from his student days in Germany—an unusual pursuit for a Jewish student—on which his eyelid drooped and teared from a recent stroke. But seen from the other side, his face showed him to be as handsome as he had been as a young man. His lectures were polished and clear. Occasionally he would look around and ask a rhetorical question which no one would venture to answer. I got into the habit of writing down an answer and nodding when it turned out to be right. At the end of the semester I and another girl whom I did not know but whose name rhymed with mine were excused from taking the examination for "helpful participation in class discussion."

Ruth Benedict was Boas' teaching assistant. She was tentative and shy and always wore the same dress. She spoke so hesitatingly that many students were put off by her manner, but Marie Bloomfield and I were increasingly fascinated. On Museum trips we would ride down and back on the Broadway streetcar with her. Her comments humanized Boas' formal lectures, as she would remark how like a communist state the Inca Empire had been or satirize the way the Crow Indians invested in visions. She invited Marie and me to the graduate seminar, where we were embarrassed by her shy, inarticulate report on John Dewey's *Human Nature and Conduct*. But we kept on going to the seminar. By the end of the first term I had decided to attend everything Boas taught, as Ruth Benedict said he might retire at the end of the year. I also propagandized the course so thoroughly at Barnard that it doubled in size the second semester and this made it possible for Boas to persuade the Barnard administration to appoint an instructor rather than paying Columbia for each student.

By the spring I was actively considering the possibility of entering anthropology, but I was already launched on my Master's essay in psychology. Then one day, when I was at lunch with Ruth Benedict and was discussing with her whether to go into sociology, as Ogburn wanted me to do, or into psychology, as I had already planned to do, she said, "Professor Boas and I have nothing to offer but an opportunity to do work that matters." That settled it for me. Anthropology had to be done *now*. Other things could wait.

I was slowly getting to know Ruth Benedict when, during the break between semesters, the tragic death of Marie Bloomfield precipitated us into a much closer relationship. Marie, who was the orphaned younger sister of the linguist Leonard Bloomfield, was an awkward girl, intellectually eager but stiff and unresponsive to any kind of physical affection. Although we were not especially congenial, I was moved by her loneliness. And so, when I realized that there was no one to bring her back from the hospital where she had been confined for six weeks with the measles, I felt that I had to take some responsibility for her. I knew how gloomy an empty dormitory could be, especially for someone as isolated as Marie. So I brought her clothes down to the hospital, and when we returned to the dormitory, I installed her in her room.

After that I had to leave her, at least for the time. I had agreed to have lunch with another friend who was taking a physics examination. She emerged from her exam hysterically blind. What was I to do? There was no one to turn to; everyone in the college would be away until Sunday night. This was Friday. I had to make a conscious choice and I chose to take care of the girl who had gone blind and was in need of immediate help. She got her sight back, but on Monday, when Marie did not come down to dinner, we had to break into her room and found that she had taken cyanide. Of course, I could not know what would have happened to the other girl had she been left alone, but I felt that if I had been able to stay with Marie, she might not have been driven by such desperation. All my life, since then, I have been hypersensitive to the possibility of suicide.

Marie's death was spread all over the newspapers. Her face stared up at us from trampled newspapers on the subway floor. Understandably, the college administration was frantic and was determined to convince me—so that I would convince others—that Marie had been insane. I resisted this, feeling very much embattled against the adult world of doctors and deans who cared nothing at all about Marie Bloomfield's plight, but only about keeping the college community quiet.

The one exception was Ruth Benedict. She wrote me a little note and I went to see her. She was the one person who understood that suicide might be a noble and conscious choice. As a child, she herself had wondered why the Roman Cato had been hailed as noble, while in the upstate New York countryside where she grew up, suicides were repudiated. From that time I began to know her not only as a teacher but also as a friend. I continued to call her "Mrs. Benedict" until I got my degree and then, almost imperceptibly, our relationship became one of colleagues and close friends. Nevertheless, I was always aware of the fifteen years' difference in our ages; I always feared that one day I would find a gulf I could not bridge.

By electing anthropology as a career, I was also electing a closer relationship to Ruth, a friendship that lasted until her death in 1948. When I was away, she took on my varied responsibilities for other people; when she was away, I took on hers. We read and reread each other's work, wrote poems in answer to poems, shared our hopes and worries about Boas, about Sapir, about anthropology, and in later years about the world. When she died, I had read everything she had ever written and she had read everything I had ever written. No one else had, and no one else has.

So I came to the end of my years at Barnard. I was engaged to be married in the fall. I was committed to taking my Master's degree in psychology and to finishing the work for this during the summer. I had accepted an assistantship to Ogburn in economics and sociology for the next autumn, when I would also begin my graduate work in anthropology.

At the senior dance Luther and I danced all night and in the damp dawn, which took all the curl out of my small ostrich feather fan, we walked along Riverside Drive, watching the sky brighten over the river.

Sidney Hook

'27 PhD

A City College graduate who taught for many years at New York University, the political theorist Sidney Hook studied at Columbia under John Dewey. A onetime Marxist, Hook would reverse position and became an active anti-communist. He sought to build on Dewey's notion of pragmatism and in later years called himself a secular humanist, telling the journal Free Inquiry *that "Morals are autonomous of religious belief. . . . They are relevant to truths about nature and human nature, truths that rest on scientific evidence." This selection from* Out of Step *(1987) features Hook's remembrance of Dewey and Columbia.*

I have related my memories of John Dewey in many places and on many occasions. Sometimes I suspect that these reveal more things about me than about him. This seems unavoidable because, among other reasons, Dewey was and remains one of the most controversial figures of his age, despite the mildness of his manner, the softness of his speech, and his kindly disposition. When I got to know him well—which was after my student days—we fought in so many causes together that he himself and the ideas he stood for became one of the central "causes" in my life. In some quarters this earned me the sobriquet "Dewey's bulldog," because of my efforts to clarify his views and to defend them against the misunderstandings of critics and sometimes the misstatements of fancied disciples.

In this chapter I shall write of my experiences and observations as a graduate student at Columbia from 1923 through 1927. The time I spent in classes and on the campus was limited until the last year, when I received a university fellowship. Since I was shouldering a heavy economic burden and found it necessary to teach in a Williamsburg public school from 9 A.M. to 3 P.M., I took my courses in the afternoon hours. Consequently, I missed

Dewey's lectures because of scheduling disparities and enrolled in courses with W. P. Montague, F. J. E. Woodbridge, and Irwin Edman.

I had first heard of John Dewey when I was a high school student. Casual references were made to him as an educator. That didn't mean very much to me at the time and for some years to come. As a young Socialist, I was almost automatically an advocate to progressive education or of anything that would break the educational lock step. My own educational experiences, looking back, were devastating confirmations of Dewey's criticisms of conventional education. Elementary school was a period of prolonged boredom, and high school was a succession of nightmares and persecutions.

My familiarity with Dewey's writings began at the College of the City of New York. I had enrolled in an elective course in social philosophy with Professor Harry Overstreet, who was a great admirer of Dewey's and spoke of him with awe and bated breath. The text of the course was Dewey's *Reconstruction in Philosophy*, which we read closely. Before I graduated, and in connection with courses in education, I read some of Dewey's *Democracy and Education* and was much impressed with its philosophy of education, without grasping at that time its general significance. Overstreet was, of course, a colleague of Morris Cohen. In marked contrast to Cohen, however, Overstreet was a devoted follower of Dewey. I have already mentioned the fact that Overstreet was a teacher of great charm and histrionic talent, but I was taken aback by the weakness of his defense of Dewey's views. His enthusiasm outstripped his philosophical sophistication and dialectical skill.

What did impress me about *Reconstruction in Philosophy*, and later other writings of Dewey, was the brilliant application of the principles of historical materialism, as I understood them then as an avowed young Marxist, to philosophical thought, especially Greek thought. Most Marxist writers, including Marx and Engels themselves, made pronouncements about the influence of the mode of economic production on the development of cultural and philosophical systems of thought, but Dewey, without regarding himself as a Marxist or invoking its approach, tried to show in detail how social stratification and class struggles got expressed in the metaphysical dualism of the time and in the dominant conceptions of matter and form, body and soul, theory and practice, truth, reason, and experience. However, even at that time I was not an orthodox Marxist. Although politically sympathetic to all of the social revolutionary programs of Marxism, and in complete agreement with Dewey's commitment to far-reaching social reforms, I had a much more traditional view of philosophy as an autonomous discipline concerned with perennial problems whose solution was the goal of philosophical inquiry and knowledge.

I was prepared to grant that the *acceptance* of philosophical ideas, and sometimes possibly their origin, could be explained by the social interests and struggles of the time rooted in the economic substructure of society. This was also the case for the emergence of certain scientific problems. The motives for some types of scientific theory could be related to extrascientific causes and considerations, but I denied that this had anything to do with the problem of validity or truth in either field. I recall doing a piece of homework for Overstreet, subsequently published in the *Open Court Magazine*, a philosophical dialogue between Pragmaticus, whose position was Dewey's in *Reconstruction in Philosophy*, and Universalus, for whom philosophy was the vision of the world *sub specie aeternitatis* in which time and place had no role. Although fair enough to arouse Overstreet's enthusiasm, the argument clearly showed where I stood.

While taking courses with Overstreet, I was also studying with Morris Cohen. My stimulating bittersweet experiences with him I have described in Chapter 5. Cohen was a highly articulate and harsh critic of pragmatism. For him pragmatism was primarily the philosophy of William James, and the philosophy of William James was primarily the doctrine of the will to believe. To Cohen, the doctrine of the will to believe was simply indulgent, wishful thinking; he damned it as a transparent piece of intellectual dishonesty. Although in his writings Cohen distinguished between the views of James and Dewey, remaining critical of both, in class he lumped them together. He mocked the categories of "life," "experience," and "the dynamic" associated with pragmatists and their writings. He dragged in references to pragmatism at every opportunity, but I do not recall him ever assigning us any specific text to read by James or Dewey. "Pragmatism," he would declare, "is a philosophy for people who cannot think."

A student wandering into a class given by John Dewey at Columbia University and not knowing who was delivering the lecture would have found him singularly unimpressive, but to those of us enrolled in his courses, he was already a national institution with an international reputation—indeed the only professional philosopher whose occasional pronouncements on public and political affairs made news. In that period he was indisputably the intellectual leader of the liberal community in the United States, and even his academic colleagues at Columbia and elsewhere who did not share his philosophical persuasion acknowledged his eminence as a kind of intellectual tribune of progressive causes.

As a teacher Dewey seemed to me to violate his own pedagogical principles. He made no attempt to motivate or arouse the interest of his auditors, to relate problems to their own experiences, to use graphic, concrete illustrations in order to give point to abstract and abstruse positions. He rarely provoked a lively participation and response from students, in the absence of which it is difficult to determine whether genuine learning or even comprehension has taken place. Dewey presupposed that he was talking to colleagues and paid his students the supreme intellectual compliment of treating them as his professional equals. Indeed, if the background and preparation of his students were anywhere near what he assumed, he would have been completely justified in his indifference to pedagogical methods. For on the graduate level students are or should be considered junior colleagues, but when they are not, especially when they have not been required to master the introductory courses, a teacher has an obligation to communicate effectively. Dewey never talked down to his classes, but it would have helped had he made it easier to listen.

Dewey spoke in a husky monotone, and although there was a sheet of notes on the desk at which he was usually seated, he never seemed to consult it. He folded it into many creases as he slowly spoke. Occasionally he would read from a book to which he was making a critical reference. His discourse was far from fluent. There were pauses and sometimes long lapses as he gazed out of the window or above the heads of his audience. It was as if he were considering and reconsidering every point until it was tuned to the right degree of qualification. I believe it was Ernest Nagel who first observed that Dewey in the classroom was the ideal type of a man thinking. His listeners sometimes feared that, because of his long pauses, Dewey had lost the thread of his thought, but if they wrote down and then reread what Dewey had actually said, they would find it amazingly coherent. At the time, however, because of the absence of fluency or variation of tone in his speech—except for an occasional and apparently arbitrary emphasis upon a particle word like *and* or *of*, which woke many of his auditors with a start—the closely argued character of his analysis was not always apparent.

Every experienced teacher knows that, because of the vicissitudes of life he or she sometimes must face a class without being properly prepared. This is not always educationally disastrous. Some individuals have a gift for improvisation, and a skillful teacher can always stimulate fruitful discussion. Dewey never came to a class unprepared, and there were plenty of family crises in his life. Rarely did he miss a class. There was an exemplary conscientiousness about every educational task he undertook, all the more impressive because it was so constant. His posthumous papers reveal draft upon draft of lectures and essays.

Despite the distracting extrinsic features of Dewey's teaching, the high seriousness of his concentration, unrelieved by any irrelevant humor, affected us in the same way it did his colleagues. Dewey seemed to exemplify not only man thinking, but nature itself thinking. After Bertrand

Russell's first meeting with Dewey in 1914, when their paths crossed at Harvard, Russell wrote of him: "To my surprise I liked him very much. He has a slow moving mind, very empirical and candid, with something of the impassivity and impartiality of natural force." (Josiah Royce he dubs "a garrulous old bore.") In a subsequent letter, he refers to Dewey's criticisms of a paper read before the New York Philosophical Club at Columbia, "The Relation of Sense-data to Physics," as very profound, and all others as worthless. This turned out to be the high point of Russell's appreciation of Dewey. From that time on, save for an extended article on Dewey's *Essays in Experimental Logic* in 1918, Russell's strictures on Dewey were an expression of misunderstanding and malice.

During the first year of my study with Dewey—the course may have been Types of Logical Theory—I constituted myself, so to speak, as the official opposition. I did the apparently unprecedented thing of interrupting him from time to time with questions that reflected the metaphysical and logical standpoints, as I understood them, of Russell and Cohen. This annoyed some of my fellow students, whom I awoke out of their somnolent drowse. Others informed me after class, with some acerbity, that they had paid good money to hear John Dewey speak, not to hear me ask him questions. But Dewey showed not the slightest annoyance or impatience. Before the year was out, there were others too who had questions. All I remember about these questions is that, whenever they caught him up on a terminological inconsistency or on a purely dialectical difficulty, he would smile and with a twinkle in his eye resolve it with an easy dexterity. Years later I asked him whether he had resented my persistent questioning, which must sometimes have interrupted his trend of thought. "No," he replied, "it was obvious to me that you were eager to find out and struggling to come to grips with a position unfamiliar to you." He had easily divined the quarter from which my questions had come.

Nothing Dewey said in class convinced me of the validity of his general position. It was only at the end of the year, when I sat down to write a definitive refutation of pragmatism, that I discovered to my astonishment, as I developed my argument, that I was coming out in the wrong place. Instead of refuting Dewey's views, I was *confirming* them! They involved judgments of perception, the nature of theories, and the ultimately existential character of the laws of logic. My point of departure was Peirce's fallibilism and his theory of leading principles, to which I had been introduced in CCNY days by Morris Cohen. I was intellectually distressed by this outcome, and the first thing I did was to repair to Cohen to find out what was wrong with the way the argument was coming out. He shrugged off my complaint that he had not done justice to Dewey's views about the nature of being "practical"—Dewey made the practical synonymous with the "experimental" and not with the "useful"—and that in some respects he had not sharply enough differentiated Dewey's theories of meaning and truth from those of James. After he read the draft of my article, to my astonishment, Cohen said: "What you have written is true enough. If that's pragmatism, I'm a pragmatist. But it isn't Dewey." I then went to see Dewey, whose office I had been reluctant to visit until then because of my critical role in his class, and said in effect: "I started out to criticize your positions, but I seem to have come to the conclusion that they can very well be squared with Peirce's arguments, his rejection of Cartesian dualism, and his doctrine of leading principles. I think something is wrong, for instead of refuting your views, here I am confirming them." I can still remember his grin as he took the paper and suggested that I return later. When I did, he handed the paper back to me with the smiling observation: "I don't see anything wrong with it."

Subsequently I was to come to the conclusion that Dewey rarely found anything wrong with the position of anyone who was moving philosophically in his direction. At the time it was clear to me that, although kindly and amused, Dewey was really pleased with my development. I suspect that this was not so much because it strengthened his convictions of the validity of his own views as because someone who had been close to Cohen and sympathetic to Russell's Platonic realism, and who had advertised himself as a resolute opponent to Dewey, had found some of Dewey's most formidable critics wanting. To outsiders it looked as if Dewey had won over one of Cohen's disciples. It certainly looked that way to Cohen himself, who never really forgave me despite my published encomiums about him as a great teacher and philosopher. It had a bearing on our subsequent relations. We rarely met without heatedly disagreeing with each other about Dewey, whenever his name came up.

During those years at Columbia, we graduate students never socialized with our professors. What we got to know about them was largely hearsay or inferred from public prints, reviews, association meetings, sometimes news stories. Dewey, and especially F. J. E. Woodbridge, dominated the department at Columbia. Too much so. The degree of their agreement and difference on key issues was the subject of much speculation and debate among us, something that could have easily been ascertained had they and the other members of the department talked back to each other in joint meetings with us. Only William Pepperell Montague would occasionally in his classes venture on indirect criticisms of the views of his colleagues, but he was the odd man out and, I believe, remained in a state of genuine puzzlement about the strange doctrines his eminent colleagues propounded. Montague was devoted to Dewey as a human being, supported all his liberal views, but was baffled by his technical philosophical doctrine. Morris Cohen, who had an unerring critical eye for the weaknesses of his fellow philosophers, trenchantly observed about Montague: "What he sees he sees clearly; what he doesn't see, he doesn't see at all."

The primary difficulty with the teaching of philosophy at Columbia when I was a student was that it was insufficiently systematic. Woodbridge was a thinker of deep insight, thoroughly steeped in the history of philosophy, who was convinced that epistemology was a mistake. He was always asking "simple" questions that had, he insisted, "simple answers," but it required considerable philosophical sophistication to understand the meaning of the questions and preternatural powers of intuition to grasp the "right" answers—which we did by guessing. Dewey at the time was challenging the confusion between cosmic and ethical issues central to the Greek classical tradition in philosophy and the mistaken theories of experience on which the whole of the modern philosophy of empiricism rested. Long before Wittgenstein, he denied that there was any philosophical knowledge and dissolved questions like the existence of the external world, the traditional mind-body problem, etc., by showing that on their own assumptions they were insoluble or question begging. This approach, as well as that of Woodbridge, would have been stimulating and challenging to students already well trained in the analysis of the traditional problems, but to the miscellany of theological students, social workers, teachers, seekers of wisdom, beauty or social salvation that in those days constituted a considerable part of the classes in philosophy, Dewey and Woodbridge were obscure. Their junior colleagues, some of whom were just as mystified by them, could not dissipate the obscurity.

But to return to the teaching scene. I doubt that the teaching staff got much philosophical stimulation or challenge from those taught, except in a few small seminars. There was not enough intellectual feedback. Woodbridge enjoyed asking questions that stumped his class but didn't fancy getting questions in return. Montague was always wary of the philosophical quarter from which a dissenting query came. The younger men were suspicious, when questions were asked of them, that someone was trying to catch them out. Everyone except Dewey and Montague seemed to me to be trying to understand why the philosophers of the past said the odd things they did, not whether what was said was true or even formally valid. In later days the pendulum may have swung to the other extreme, and the historical dimensions of philosophical problems were not sufficiently appreciated when linguistic analysis became the rage. No one who was genuinely interested in philosophy was discouraged. If he caught fire, it was from an outside source, usually from something read. A few of us kept abreast of the professional periodicals, which in perspective seemed more exciting than those today, possibly because the issues discussed seemed larger and not so specialized.

Dewey was the soul of kindliness to questioners whenever they were bold enough to interrupt him, which they did with greater frequency as the course wore on. He never put any student down. If a question was obscure or made no apparent sense, he would find an intimation of relevant significance in it that encouraged some students to take themselves more seriously as thinkers than was warranted. As a rule I have discovered that students seem to resent classmates who ask questions more than their teachers do.

In my own case, I recall an act of extraordinary kindness on Dewey's part, which was all the more surprising to me since at the time I had little contact with him. During that period, to qualify as a doctoral student, one had to pass a preliminary oral examination of two hours on four philosophers, two ancient and medieval and two modern. I selected Plato, Plotinus, Schopenhauer, and Charles Peirce. We were required to hand in questions or extended topics on each of them, which would indicate the area and range of our interests, although the faculty could question us about anything if it chose. Usually I am in good form with interlocutors, but for the first hour and a half I was conscious that I was not doing well. I tangled with Montague on Plato, who was nettled by my rejection of the subsistence doctrine of universals to which he subscribed. I answered inadequately a question from Woodbridge on the relation between Plotinus and Christian theology because I had concentrated on some of the more difficult points in the *Enneads*. (The course on Plotinus was the first one I took at Columbia with Irwin Edman whom, I fear, I terrified because I had read the same secondary sources he consulted. Neither of us knew Greek.)

By the time Dewey began the questioning on Peirce, I was rather rattled. Dewey began in words that I still recall, at least in part. "I wish I could take the time to read all the questions Mr. Hook has submitted on Peirce's doctrines. They reveal a thoroughgoing grasp and mastery not only of Peirce's doctrines but of their revolutionary impact on traditional philosophy," and he went on in this vein for a minute or two before he put his own questions. It restored my nerve, and I finished with fine rhetorical flourishes about Pierce's seminal ideas that I owed to Cohen. I am confident that Dewey would have done the same thing for any other student in the same position.

I began publishing while a graduate student, and reactions from Harvard and elsewhere were favorable. By the time I faced the department at the final examination in defense of my dissertation, *The Metaphysics of Pragmatism*, which I had stitched together out of the articles I had published, everything went smoothly.

Although at the time the world seemed in turmoil, looking back from where we are today, and despite the hurried quality of our student days, Columbia during those golden years seemed an island of peace and calm and yet of intense intellectual excitement. We were filled with hope and a tremendous expectation that great things were in the offing, that the ideas we were debating would play a role. Memories of the First World War and the inglorious postwar years in America, when the worst cultural excesses in American history had occurred, were receding. We sensed the presence of intellectual giants on the campus—not only Dewey, but of Robinson and Beard (who had been in recent residence), of Mitchell, Boas, and others.

The only extra-academic issue that mildly stirred the campus was the Sacco-Vanzetti case. Together with a few other students and the help of a young woman from the Sacco-Vanzetti Defense Committee, I organized a demonstration for Sacco-Vanzetti on the steps of the Low Library. It was a mild and tepid affair that attracted few passersby, drawn more out of curiosity than sympathy. One of the junior members of the Department of Philosophy, although in sympathy with our view, was outraged by our action. Such things, he told me, "were in bad taste." I replied, "To hell with taste when men's lives are at stake."

At that time I was convinced that Sacco and Vanzetti were innocent, but ten years or so later Carlo Tresca, the Italian-American Anarchist leader, who ought to know, told me that Sacco was guilty. It was indisputable, however, that neither he nor Vanzetti ever got a fair trial. Like many radicals, then as now, I was prepared to believe the worst about American justice. I recall that Dewey was deeply affected by their fate. As events were moving toward the end, he once told me in a tone of wonder and despair, "She was right after all. She kept telling me that they would never let them go, regardless of the appeals." I didn't know to whom "they" referred. "She" was Celia Polisuk, who had come to see him to enlist his aid in the defense of Sacco-Vanzetti and who had helped with our meeting.

I don't know how the notion got about at Columbia that I was a dangerous radical. I never concealed my strong interest in Marx, whom hardly anyone read or cared about and whose views were considered irrelevant to any particular philosophical issues. Dewey had never read Marx systematically and was inclined to judge him by the doctrinaire vulgarisms of his orthodox proponents. Again and again, however, I was struck, in studying Dewey, to find worked out in detail certain views that Marx had expressed in cryptic and undeveloped form.

What excited me more than anything else was Dewey's revolutionary approach to philosophy that undercut all the assumptions of the classical tradition in philosophy. This view had held that man was primarily a knower and that knowledge reflected the antecedent structure and truths of the world. The mind was a spectator of what was given and discovered the truth when its ideas corresponded with the facts. The great difficulty in this approach was to account for the warranted everyday belief that thinking makes a difference to the outcomes of experience, that thought could be practical, that ideas count for something, and that ignorance and error have a price. If ideas were images, impressions, or mere effects of an external world on an organism, how could they ever change the world or modify the conditions into which we are born? The whole of education and other aspects of human experience presuppose that human reflection plays an active role in redetermining within limits not only ourselves but our society and to some extent even our natural environment. Yet the traditional conceptions of mind from Plato to Descartes make a mystery of it. For Dewey man is an integral part of nature, whose thinking is a form of behavior, of doing guided by words and symbols that direct and redirect differential responses. Thought is an outgrowth of the world, not a mirror image of it, as most previous empiricists believed. It cannot be explained by any unbridgeable dualisms or supernaturalisms. By guiding our action in problematic situations, thought changes the world but not the laws by which the changes are made. When we are truly thinking about a problem involving existence, we are involved with ways of operating upon things or experimenting with them in the light of their anticipated fruits and consequences. Literally it makes no sense, according to Dewey, for ideas "to correspond" with existences except possibly in the sense in which a key corresponds with a lock when the emphasis is on the activity of the key. Ideas are plans of action rather than maps of antecedent reality. Even maps are not isomorphic, or simulacra, of the regions mapped. They are instruments whose adequacy or validity is to be judged by the adequacy of their use in enabling us to achieve our purposes and goals. Something like this was intimated in the writings of Marx, and without some view of this kind, his call upon philosophers to change the world, not merely understand it, was rhetoric. For Dewey, knowing or understanding was a mode of activity in which something in the world is changed.

All great visions in philosophy are based on simple ideas, but Dewey's philosophic vision was revolutionary in its outlook and conclusion: It denied that there was any such thing as philosophical knowledge, denied that we ever have immediate or certain truths of fact, even of sense perception, denied that we ever learn from experience, ours or others', unless we bring ideas to that experience. On the other hand, he opened up a view of the world in which human beings did not regard themselves as slaves of fate, history, or necessity, or lose themselves in the fantasies of magical idealism, but became aware of genuine possibilities and novelties and their own responsibilities, however limited. Although he repudiated philosophy in the grand manner, he restored the conception of philosophy as a quest for wisdom. Every distinctive philosophical doctrine of Dewey's could be derived from this approach. He wrestled to the end of his days with a multitude of technical details and difficulties that in the eyes of his critics confront this bold reconstruction of the philosophical enterprise.

My dissertation, *The Metaphysics of Pragmatism,* was an attempt to give a realistic cast to Dewey's views contrasting them with the subjective and voluntaristic expressions of pragmatism in the writings of James and F. C. S. Schiller, the Oxford pragmatist. That Dewey offered to write a preface to the book in which I seriously discussed some of this ideas, I interpreted then, and for many years to come, as an expression of his kindness. It enabled me to find a publisher—and a respectable philosophical one at that—and to deposit a hundred published copies in the Columbia libraries, at that time a prerequisite for the degree, without cost. It came as a great surprise to me (and as a shock) to learn a few years ago of the existence of a letter from Dewey to his old friend, James H. Tufts, written during my last year at Columbia. He told Tufts that he was ready to resign his post and withdraw from the field of philosophy because he had found a successor. And he named me as that successor!

The surprise results from the fact that I had not yet taken to the field to combat critical attacks on Dewey. I wasn't aware that I had added anything significant to his thought or deepened it. He credited me with more insight than *I* ever claimed or was aware of. I always thought I was merely expounding him. To many of Dewey's readers this was a service, for they professed to find my exposition clearer than Dewey's own, even if they couldn't agree with it. Much has been made of Dewey's crotchety style. This seems to me to be a manifest injustice to his writings on social, ethical, and educational problems, which are written in vigorous—if not limpid—prose. His technical philosophical writings were sometimes obscure, because Dewey was handicapped by our linguistic traditions, whose idioms reflect the categories of Aristotle and the dualism of Descartes. Dewey's stress on the ongoing development and evolution of forms runs counter to the linguistic habit of speaking of substances, natures, essences, just as Dewey's conception of experience, which includes the envisioning situation suggested by the noun *an experience*, is almost invariably misinterpreted by Dewey's critics as something inner, private, incommunicable, and unshared. "Whose experience?" they always ask, "yours or mine?"

If professional philosophers had difficulty understanding Dewey, it is not surprising that laymen are often confused. John Dewey's brother, an economist of some standing, once took me aside and said: "It's strange. I've been trying to read John's work for years, but I can't make heads or tails of it. Can you explain it?" None of Dewey's children, with the exception of Evelyn (his eldest daughter) who collaborated with him on *The Schools of Tomorrow*, had any realization of the scope and revolutionary character of his ideas. The same was true of Dewey's second wife, Roberta. All of the children seemed to me a little mystified by the great fuss made over their father outside the field of education.

Dewey's letter to Tufts was a shock to me, because it made me feel that I had failed him—not so much in not living up to this fantastic, unrealistic expectation that I could ever come closer than a sympathetic expositor of his vision, but because I had not done more to amplify and defend his technical doctrines, resolve their difficulties, and carry out his ambitious program of philosophical reconstruction and deconstruction. After many years of eclipse, philosophers are beginning to rediscover him, but the Dewey they rediscover in many aspects seems strange to me. Dewey believed that much of traditional metaphysics and epistemology were elaborate and ingenious attempts to solve problems that were not genuine or that resulted from dubious assumptions about man, nature, and society, but he believed that buried in the dialectical thicket were either genuine questions that only scientific inquiry could illumine or confrontations of different normative standards or values that each generation had to resolve for itself.

I am confident that, had I not returned from Europe convinced that Germany would soon erupt into a new threat to the world, I would not have thrown myself so wholeheartedly into the political movement of the thirties, and would instead have done more work in academic philosophy to justify Dewey's faith in me. I cannot now guess what in my writings and thought led him to praise me so extravagantly. In the last twenty-odd years of his life, I read all his manuscripts and acted as a kind of sounding board, since I could anticipate the difficulties and objections of the philosophical opposition. I believe that, out of loyalty—and unconsciously—I wasn't critical enough of him. He probably had me in mind when he remarked, "People pay too great a price for intellectual loyalty; it gets in the way of justified criticism." Once when Dewey had made some kind remarks about what I had written—something not unusual—I observed: "I don't know why you should make a fuss about it. All I was doing was restating what you have said." I have always treasured his reply: "Well, Sidney, when I read what you write about me, I understand myself better."

It is not relevant to his philosophy, but I must say something about Dewey as a human being. He was world famous when I first got to know him, but he didn't seem to know it. He was the soul of kindness and decency in all things to everyone, the only great man whose stature did not diminish as one came closer to him. In fact it was difficult to remain in his presence for long without feeling uncomfortable. He seemed too good to be true, and I still recall my relief when I found a moral fault in him—his tolerance of Albert Barnes, of whom we shall hear more later on. He never seemed to begrudge his time to anyone, often perfect strangers, despite his busy life. He was too kind, kind to a fault. If anyone asked him to read a manuscript, he would begin by saying, "No, I'm too busy," but once the author got his foot into the door of Dewey's office and kept on pleading, it was a cinch that he or she would leave his manuscript. There is no doubt that he encouraged too many people in their thinking and their writing. He would justify himself by saying that one could never know what would come of the effort.

There was an air of abstraction about Dewey that made his sensitivity to others surprising. It was as if he had an intuitive sense of a person's authentic, unspoken need. Anyone who thought he was a softie, however, would be brought up short. He had the canniness of a Vermont farmer and a dry wit that was always signaled by a chuckle and a grin that would light up his face.

When I was still a student at Columbia, he invited me to his home for Sunday dinner. His daughters, son, and daughter-in-law were there, and it seemed to me a rather formal affair. It was my first visit, and I was naturally nervous. When I rang the bell, he himself came to the door. The first thing he did when I had shed my hat and overcoat was to point out the bathroom. I had no experience with dinners as elaborate as this seemed to me and don't remember whether I talked too much or too little. I wasn't sure what all the knives and forks were for, and my lack of ease must have been quite apparent. At the end of the meal, when the nuts were passed around, I took only one lest I be considered greedy. "Sidney," remarked Dewey, "you remind me of the man who kept a bee."

Before many years had passed, I felt so much at home with Dewey— though this is running ahead with my story—working closely with him on his manuscripts and his public activities in behalf of good causes, that I even ventured suggestions to relieve him of what seemed to me needless, time-consuming burdens. He was, as I have mentioned, besieged by requests to write introductions for all kinds of books, and I got him to stop after he agreed to do one for a book called *The Lazy Colon*. I questioned the trouble he took to answer every letter he received. To him it was a matter of simple courtesy, but I noted with satisfaction that he did take to replying by post card more and more. He encouraged me to comment upon the invitations he should accept, the books he should read and review, and the criticisms to which he should reply. Sometimes he ignored my advice, but mostly he agreed. The only thing I kept my mouth shut about was his relationship with Roberta Lowitz Grant, which separated him from his children and their families and led to an abrupt and unhappy break with them, when he married her, after almost a decade of association (much of it devoted to nursing care), at the age of eighty-eight.

The story of Roberta when she was a Lowitz, then Mrs. Grant, and then Mrs. Dewey, her life with Dewey and her difficulties with his children, are more appropriately part of Dewey's biography. Unfortunately, until now, none has been written on a plane and in a manner worthy of its subject.

The character of John Dewey became more manifest to a wider public in its quiet heroism and unfailing goodness during the thirties and forties, both in defending the heritage of American democracy and in resisting the advance of totalitarian thought and practice. At a time when age and achievement had earned him the right to retire from active political life, he devoted all his energies and most of his husbanded hours of leisure in the fight for freedom, from which many younger colleagues turned away.

Whittaker Chambers

Whittaker Chambers was a journalist and translator who served a term as foreign news editor of Time *magazine. A member of the Communist Party from the mid-1920s, Chambers broke with the party in the late 1930s and eventually became a strident anti-communist. He gained a measure of fame—or notoriety—by serving as a witness against Alger Hiss, the subject of a series of controversial prosecutions in the late 1940s. Toward the end of his life he was a senior editor for the nascent* National Review. *The following, which describes his leaving college in 1925 before graduating, is excerpted from Chambers's best-selling autobiography,* Witness *(1952).*

In the fall of 1920, I entered Williams College. A room was assigned to me and my furniture had been shipped. But one or two days on that beautiful and expensive campus told me that Williams was not the place for me, that my parents could never stand the cost of that little Harvard. I saw that I had a quick and difficult decision to make. I took a night train for New York. The next morning, before going home, I entered Columbia University. There I could live at home and all expenses would be less. Since I lacked certain requirements for entrance, I took a general intelligence test and passed without difficulty. I also used the occasion to rid myself at last of the name, Vivian. In its place, I took my mother's family name: Whittaker.

I remained at Columbia until my junior year. When I entered I was a conservative in my view of life and politics, and I was undergoing a religious experience. By the time I left, entirely by my own choice, I was no longer a conservative and I had no religion. I had published in a campus literary magazine an atheist playlet, of which the Hiss defense was to make large use twenty-six years later. The same year, I went to Europe and saw Germany in the manic throes of defeat. I returned to Columbia, this time paying my own way. In 1925, I voluntarily withdrew for the express purpose of joining the Communist Party. For I had come to believe that the world we live in was dying, that only surgery could now save the wreckage of mankind, and that the Communist Party was history's surgeon.

At Columbia, like all freshmen, I was at once assigned a faculty adviser. In my case, he was Mark Van Doren, then a young instructor in the English department. Like all really first-rate teachers, Mark Van Doren's personal influence on his students was great—in my case, powerful and long-lasting. We quickly passed to a first-name basis and developed a friendship of respect and common interests, which, no doubt, was stronger on my side than on his. Mark was not then a nationally known literary critic and poet. He was working on his first book of poems, *Spring Thunder,* of which he sent me a copy as soon as it was published. All problems of writing, but especially of poetry, touched him profoundly, and he brought to them incisive judgment, humor and exceptional common sense.

I soon began to bombard him with the poems I was writing, very bad poems, most of which he rejected out of hand, but with such understanding that he never left any wound, only a disappointment that I could not measure up to his standard, and a determination to do so.

Mark Van Doren (and certain of my fellow students) first developed in me the belief that writing poetry is not, as my mother and many other people supposed, a somewhat disreputable pursuit, but a way of life—one of the highest to which a man can be called. I thought that I was called. Mark Van Doren agreed with me, or led me to suppose so.

When I returned from Europe in 1923, I began to arrange my life so that I could devote most of my time to writing verse. I took a part-time job at the New York Public Library, where I worked at the desk in the newspaper room at night. The rest of my time was my own. I was living at home. I set about a definite poetic project. Its purpose was twofold. I wished to preserve through the medium of poetry the beautiful Long Island of my boyhood before it was destroyed forever by the advancing City. I wished to dramatize the continual defeat of the human spirit in our time, by itself and by the environment in which it finds itself. With my deep attachment to the earth I grew up on, the spread of the tentacular towns across it, felling the little woods, piping the shallow brooks through culverts, burying the little farms under rows of identical suburban houses, struck me an almost physical blow. Those sprawling developments, without character or form, destroying the beauty that had been for an ugliness that had no purpose but function and profit, seemed to epitomize all that I dreaded in the life around me. By defacing the one part of itself that had been intimately mine, it cut my roots and left me more than an alien, a man without soil, and, therefore, without nation. I called the book: *Defeat in the Village*. It was to be an autobiography of mood, but not of factual reality. Each of the poems in it bore some relationship of tone or feeling to the next poem, and all were intended to build up to a climax of despair. Few of the poems were autobiographical in any other sense. Few were based on real occurrences, though some were touched off by them. Many of them were inspired by places, and in the years when I was composing them, I took to wandering a great deal at night, especially around the little Long Island harbor of East Rockaway, where the tides of my childhood still exerted a strong pull, and the mists and the darkness blotted out the ugliness of the present and helped me to recall the Long Island of the past.

In time, I had written a fair-sized book. I submitted it to a national poetry contest where *Defeat in the Village* was just "nosed out" of first place (I was duly informed) by *Chinese White*, a book of poems by the wife of the *Daily Worker* cartoonist, William Gropper.

I concluded, after several years of trying, that I never could write poetry good enough to be worth writing. My natural development had, in fact, settled the matter for me. For as soon as I began to shake off the influence of authentic poets, I found myself writing prose. I used to think, sometimes, that those versifying years were a complete and stunning waste. But I came to see that I was mistaken. Those were the years of apprenticeship, during which, by trial and error, I was beginning to learn the difficult, humbling, exacting art of writing.

They were more. They were the years in which my mind first awakened to one of the languages of the soul. It filled me with a strange elation. I realized at last that I had been listening to it all my life without knowing what it was, and that its unheard logic blended in a consistent tone all that was most personal in my experience. I was like an adult who first learns to speak. Awkwardly, I fumbled, in my early manhood, to give expression to the strongest impression of my earliest childhood—the enfolding beauty of the external world. It was the flooding and ebbing tides, the sense of the ocean, beating on its beaches as on the edge of the world, or of its mists, folding the houses and streets of my childhood under silence, that I groped to express in verse. I remained a babbler, in part because I grasped the outward effects of that language, but not its inward principle. I continued to hear it in the highest moments of my life long before I recognized what voice spoke it to me.

* * *

One day, early in 1925, I sat down on a concrete bench on the Columbia campus, facing a little Greek shrine and the statue of my old political hero, Alexander Hamilton. The sun was shining, but it was chilly, and I sat huddled in my overcoat. I was there to answer once for all two questions: Can a man go on living in a world that is dying? If he can, what should he do in the crisis of the 20th century?

There ran through my mind the only lines I remember from the history textbook of my second go at college—two lines of Savinus', written in the fifth century when the Goths had been in Rome and the Vandals were in Carthage: "The Roman Empire is filled with misery, but it is luxurious. It is dying, but it laughs."

The dying world of 1925 was without faith, hope, character, understanding of its malady or will to overcome it. It was dying but it laughed. And this laughter was not the defiance of a vigor that refuses to know when it is whipped. It was the loss, by the mind of a whole civilization, of the power to distinguish between reality and unreality, because, ultimately, though I did not know it, it had lost the power to distinguish between good and evil. This, failure I, too, shared with the world of which I was a part.

The dying world had no answer at all to the crisis of the 20th century, and, when it was mentioned, and every moral voice in the Western world was shrilling crisis, it cocked an ear of complacent deafness and smiled a smile of blank senility—throughout history, the smile of those for whom the executioner waits.

Only in Communism had I found any practical answer at all to the crisis, and the will to make that answer work. It was not an attractive answer, just as the Communist Party was not an attractive party. Neither was the problem which had called it forth, and which it proposed to solve, attractive. But it had one ultimate appeal. In place of desperation, it set the word: hope. If it was the outrage, it was also the hope of the world. In the 20th century, it seemed impossible to have hope on any other terms.

When I rose from the bench, I had decided to leave college for good, and change the whole direction of my life. I had decided to join the Communist Party. The choice was not so much for a program that promised to end war, economic chaos and the moral enervation of the West. I had already said to myself what Lenin had already said better: "We do not presume to maintain that Marx or the Marxists can show us the way to socialism in perfectly concrete terms. That would be absurd. We know the direction of this road: we know which class forces lead to it. But in actual practice, only the experience of millions of men and women can show it when they begin the actual work."

The ultimate choice I made was not for a theory or a party. It was—and I submit that this is true for almost every man and woman who has made it— a choice against death and for life. I asked only the privilege of serving humbly and selflessly that force which from death could evoke life, that might save, as I then supposed, what was savable in a society that had lost the will to save itself. I was willing to accept Communism in whatever terms it presented itself, to follow the logic of its course wherever it might lead me, and to suffer the penalties without which nothing in life can be achieved. For it offered me what nothing else in the dying world had power to offer at the same intensity—faith and a vision, something for which to live and something for which to die. It demanded of me those things which have always stirred what is best in men—courage, poverty, self-sacrifice, discipline, intelligence, my life, and, at need, my death.

I went to my campus friends who had so long and patiently worked to convert me to Communism and said that at last I was ready. I asked them where the Communist Party could be found. To my great surprise, they did not know. For I was then unfamiliar with that type of fellow traveler who also serves Communism, but chiefly by sitting and talking.

I remembered that there had once passed across the Columbia campus a high-strung, red-headed boy from an upstate college. He had slept overnight on the bare floor of a friend's room in one of the residence halls. He talked incessantly in a voice like a teletype machine; and what he talked about was the Soviet Union and Communism. His name was Sender Garlin. I thought that Sender Garlin would probably know where to find the Communist Party. Presently I located him.

Garlin said that, in fact, there was no Communist Party. For reasons of expediency, the Communist Party which had just come up from underground, now called itself the Workers Party. He was not sure that he knew how to contact it or that he knew anyone in it. But if it turned out that he did, he would mention my name, and a man might presently come to see me.

I decided that Garlin knew exactly where to find the Communist Party and was telling me that he would put me in touch with it.

William O. Douglas

'25 LAW

William O. Douglas was appointed as an associate justice of the U.S. Supreme Court in 1939 and went on to serve the longest term in history—36 years, six months. He taught at Columbia for a year before moving on to Yale, where his work on bankruptcy and reorganization made his reputation and led to a position with the Securities and Exchange Commission. As a justice, Douglas championed free speech, privacy rights, and environmental protection. A devoted naturalist, he wrote several books on the outdoors in addition to his legal scholarship. Go East, Young Man, *a 1974 memoir of his early life, is excerpted here.*

In September, 1922, having decided to go to Columbia Law School, it was time to go East. After two years of teaching I had saved seventy-five dollars and, of necessity, my transportation across the country was to be by freight train. I had arranged to go to Wenatchee, Washington, to take over two thousand sheep owned by a Yakima firm and see them safely on the Great Northern Railroad to the Chicago stockyards.

The night before I left, Mother, my sister, my brother, and I gathered for a final evening together. I remember sitting on the stool by the organ that Mother often played for us, my heart heavy. This seemed like a permanent parting of the ways, as I would be gone three years. There were tears in my eyes as I took an old battered suitcase with a suit and change of clothes in it and left by the back way to the railroad yards, where I would catch a freight to Wenatchee.

* * *

When I finally pulled into the freight yards in New York City, I had only six cents of my seventy-five dollars left in my pocket. I was grimy and weary, and I'd had very little to eat for several days. I had had no bath since

Chicago, no change of clothes, and doubtless looked like a bum. My clothes were tattered, my hat was nondescript, my battered brown suitcase was held together by a piece of rope. I was utterly lost. As I walked along a broad avenue lined with tall apartment buildings, I tried to stop a man, asking, "How do I get to Columbia?" His eyes swept by me and he kept going. Over and over again I tried to stop people to ask directions, and each time I was rebuffed. No one would even speak to me. It would have been different in Yakima or Walla Walla. The stranger who asked a native for directions might even end up as a luncheon guest. Not so in New York City. The stranger—especially the one with no badge of affluence—knew only the rough back of the hand. I quickly saw the cold side of New York City and I never got over it.

Somewhere in my suitcase was a slip of paper on which I'd written the address of the New York headquarters of Beta Theta Pi. After untying the rope that held my bag together, and rummaging around, I found the address and, eventually, made my way to the staid and rather elegant Beta Club.

I went up to the clerk, told him I was a fraternity member, and asked, "Do you have a room for the night?"

The fellow took one look at the dust-covered specimen before him and answered with an abrupt "No." Furthermore, he didn't believe I was a member of the fraternity.

As we stood arguing, a Whitman friend, William M. Wilson, came down the stairs. He was passing through New York on his way to Johns Hopkins University in Baltimore to study medicine.

I greeted Bill with great joy, and in high indignation turned to the clerk and said, "Ask *him* who I am."

Bill Wilson said, "This is my friend Bill Douglas, from the Whitman College chapter of Beta. Put him up."

In addition to that intercession, Bill loaned me seventy-five dollars as seed money to get me started in New York.

The next day I registered at the Columbia Law School and was assigned a room in Furnald Hall. Then I scurried around to try to find work. In this hungry time, I often had only one meal a day. I sold newspapers and waited on tables, but I still could not get far enough ahead to pay my tuition and my room rent at Furnald Hall.

Miss Breed, head of the university's employment agency, tried to help me. She was perhaps in her thirties, an exceedingly attractive brunette, well educated and adroit with people. She carefully interviewed each student who sought work. I gave her Jim Donald's letters, but she had few doors to open for me. Finally the bursar of Columbia called me into his office and said,

"You have not paid your tuition or your dormitory rent. I have consulted the regulations of the university and learned that I will violate none of them if I drop you from the Law School."

I was stunned, and saddened. Now it seemed that my legal career would have to wait. But before accepting that, I thought I would get advice from the dean, who was then Harlan F. Stone. I went to Dean Stone's office and was ushered to him at once. I would never have given credence to anyone who would have prophesied that he, an eminent law teacher, and I, fresh from the freight yards, would, in seventeen years, be sitting together on the Supreme Court. Of course, there was no such prophet.

Years later, on the Court, I told Stone of my arrival at Columbia by freight. He asked the name of the railroad. I said it was the Great Northern most of the way to Chicago. "Then you should always ride the Great Northern, paying first-class fares." After a pause he added, "Come to think of it, why not send them a check for your Law School transportation?"

Stone, then as later, was a portly man with a broad face and twinkling eyes. A mop of hair usually hung down his forehead. All in all, he had somewhat the appearance of a farmer. His voice was soft and he was patient with people. He never begrudged an hour with a student, mulling over personal problems. He talked to me as a father, and I listened as a son. His advice was to drop out, get a job, save my money, and come back in a few years. He had nothing to offer in terms of a scholarship or a loan.

So I went from the dean's office across to New Jersey and got a job as a teacher of Latin and English in a high school. I packed my bag, said good-by to a few friends, and left Furnald Hall. But on my way to the subway and New Jersey, I made one last stop at the Appointments Office. "Not a thing," said Miss Breed. "Now wait a minute—what's this?"

Picking up a memo, she read a message from her assistant. A man with offices in Columbus Circle ran a correspondence school. He was doing well with various courses, including one on hemstitching. Now he wanted a course in law. Could a third-year law student be sent down to help him?"

"I'll go," I said.

"But you're not a third-year man," Miss Breed said.

"Let me try," I implored.

She gave in, handed me a note of introduction, and agreed to keep an eye on my bag while I visited Columbus Circle. I reached it by subway in less than a half-hour. The proprietor did the talking, and in five minutes I realized that I knew more law than he did. He handed me a textbook on business law, saying he thought he would start with that.

"Let's be modern," I said. "Let's make it a case law course. We'll divide the book into fifty parts and prepare fifty lessons."

The idea had suddenly come to me to assign five pages of text, say, for Lesson No. 1, sending each student a true legal problem taken from a prominent New York decision. The student would read the text, study the question, and write his answer, returning it for grading. We would give the citation to the law report so that he could, if he wished, go to a library and read it. In thirty minutes we agreed on this format. He would sell each course for twenty-five dollars—five for the book, twenty for the questions and answers. Did I want a part of the profits?

"No," I said, and quickly adding up my cash requirements for the year, I announced I would do it for a flat six-hundred-dollar fee, but I needed a two-hundred-dollar advance. Within the hour I walked out of the office at Columbus Circle with a check for two hundred dollars and a contract that would pay me four hundred dollars more on delivery of the manuscript within six weeks.

I repaired at once to Columbia, paid two hundred dollars to the bursar, picked up my bag, moved back into the dormitory, and canceled my New Jersey employment.

Preparation of the correspondence course was such a formidable undertaking that I did not go to law classes for six weeks. I spent practically every working hour of every day in an alcove in the library of old Kent Hall putting my case material together: finding the best illustrative cases and making digests of them. At the end of six weeks I had finished the job and resumed classes, working feverishly to catch up.

When I turned in the manuscript and received the balance of the fee, I realized what a foolish bargain I had made. The proprietor had already sold a thousand courses on which I could easily have had a quarter or more interest. For a while I graded the papers for him at a normal hourly rate. Then I got others to do it, for soon I was in big-money tutoring. I saw my correspondence-course friend frequently. He was making money fast and never realized that the chap who had prepared his course in law had had less than six weeks of legal education.

I was in New York City for six years altogether; I attained considerable professional achievements there—as a student, as a practitioner, and as a teacher. So logically, perhaps, I should have only happy associations with New York. But those six years developed in me a deep dislike for the city. That feeling goes back, no doubt, to my early reception when I first walked Park Avenue. Later, I was often feted in New York apartments and came to know the warm-hearted people who live there. But though warm-hearted, they are still far, far removed from the miserable people of the ghettos that surround them. New York City is highly stratified, as are most metropolitan areas, and it is run largely for the middle and upper classes. During those first few miserable, starving months in New York, I saw the ugliness of the city.

Moreover, I felt alien to the city because I came from the wide-open spaces, where only the haunting call of the coyote or wind in the pines broke the stillness of night. Now whenever I awoke, I heard nothing but the roar of traffic. This constant noise always grated on my ears. In one of my early years in New York, I had a room looking onto an air shaft. The only green thing in it was a miserable geranium plant struggling to survive. The sun touched the shaft only briefly each day and never reached the room. For me this was as depressing as I imagine a prison would be. Even when I acquired a sunny room, the depression never left me. The din of the city was still present. The only bird I ever saw was a pigeon. I longed for the call of the meadowlark, the noisy drilling of the pileated woodpecker, the drumming of the ruffed grouse. I would sleep well, I thought, if I could only hear the music of a wilderness creek flowing over ledges. But all I ever heard above the distant rumble of the city was the dripping of a faucet.

I needed grass and earth under my feet. But unless I traveled far—either west or north—all I found was concrete. I saw block after block of apartment houses—some standing in splendor, most in squalor—with no tree, no touch of grass to adorn them, no playground except a paved one, no nature trails.

The earth and all its wonders were too much a part of me to shake off. I needed them as a daily diet. When I thought of the babies being born and raised in these unlivable concrete prisons, I became even more depressed.

I was able to live very cheaply in New York, though it was supposed to be an expensive city. I found real warmth in places like the Horn & Hardart restaurants. Until recently, they had food on display in machines with glass doors that could be opened with a coin. For ten cents I could get a dish of pork and beans; for five cents, a glass of milk, or bread and butter, or a piece of apple pie. That was a good twenty-five-cent supper, which carried me through many a day during the first few rough months of my first year in Law School. The food was good and it was nourishing, as good and as nourishing as the twenty-five-dollar meals that I later ate in Sardi's or the Oak Room at the Plaza or other high-class restaurants where the head waiters would bow and scrape.

I liked the people who ate at Horn & Hardart. Most of them were open-faced and friendly. I always seemed to be on the same wave length with them.

There was a Child's Restaurant at Broadway and 110th, where one day by chance I met the famous John Bassett Moore, leading international-law expert who taught at the Law School. I met him only because the sole empty chair in the crowded restaurant was at his table and he asked me to join him. That was the beginning of a warm friendship. He was short and rotund and bald, and at the time, sported a gray goatee. His eyes always seemed to dance to the excitement of his ideas as he talked.

There were, of course, other kind people in New York City. One of the friendliest was a chap, also in Law School, who had the room next to me in Furnald Hall. He was so friendly that he barged into my room full of talk all night long. It was not long before he was marched off to a mental institution as a psychotic.

A tall amiable chap counted the prices of the items on our trays at the university cafeteria and always gave me a wink as I said "Touch me lightly, Joe."

The decrepit man who sold roasted chestnuts and pine nuts on Broadway at 116th Street reminded me of my old Wobbly friends. He was a compassionate person with wide interests in politics and literature, a man who never made the grade due to some idiosyncrasy that I never comprehended.

There was much sadness among the people I knew. I had known Jews in the West; and some of them were my dear friends. But the Jews in New York City were more numerous and inclined to be clannish. They faced the problem of discrimination organized in a way that I had never seen before. The power structure was against them.

There were six Blacks in my class, Paul Robeson being the most memorable. Paul worked his way through Law School by boxing professionally. The Blacks, of course, knew severe discrimination, but their organized opposition to it had not yet jelled.

One of my classmates in Law School was Carrol Shanks, later to become president of the Prudential Life Insurance Company. Alfred McCormack, who later nosed me out as Justice Stone's law clerk, was a warm friend. So was Tom Dewey, who had a fine baritone voice and worked his way through school by singing at the Cathedral of St. John the Divine.

Another close friend was Simon Rifkind. My friendship with Si has been long and enduring. Si, too, worked his way through school, and after graduation, became a partner of Senator Robert Wagner of New York. He later served as district judge in New York from June 6, 1941, to May 24, 1950, making a very outstanding record on the Bench, as he did before and afterward at the Bar. It was Si who nearly fifty years later represented me in impeachment proceedings launched in 1970 by Nixon, Agnew, and Gerald Ford.

Hiram C. Gill had been a turbulent mayor of Seattle from 1910 to 1918, and when I was in Law School, his widow moved to New York City. Her son, Stanley Gill, was in chemical engineering at Columbia. Howard Meneely, later president of Wheaton College, was working for his Ph.D. in history; Delbert Obertauffer, later head of the Department of Physical Education at Ohio State, was getting his M.A.; George C. Watson of Petersburg, Virginia, was at the Columbia Business School. The five of us used to gather at "Miss Gill's" almost every Friday night for a home-cooked meal and poker. The poker I later played with FDR in Washington, D.C., I learned at Columbia.

Later, I made the acquaintance of other classmates, among them Hal Seligson, Law Comstock, Arthur Schwartz, and Alvin Sylvester. In time I came to be on intimate terms, although still a student, with Dean Harlan F. Stone, Professor Underhill Moore, and Professor Huger Jervey. These three were the ones to whom I turned for advice when my financial problems seemed insoluble.

                      ❀ ❀ ❀

Once my tutoring jobs began, they seemed never to stop. I prepared students for college-entrance examinations for Princeton, Yale and Columbia. To obtain my services, or the likes of them, students needed to be both stupid and rich. My boast was that I never failed to get even a dumb student into Princeton. None of my students *ever* failed, except one in law. And as my success mounted, my fees rose. I started at five dollars an hour and got as high as twenty-five. The latter was paid by a lady who ran a boys' school in the South. She was out of date when it came to elocution. She and her husband had a suite at the Waldorf-Astoria, and it was there that I had her recite again and again before her husband and me "The Cremation of Sam McGee." She demanded a certificate of proficiency. So I had one made of sheepskin that looked like a genuine diploma but was only a personal citation.

                      ❀ ❀ ❀

Through my tutoring service, I struck it rich at Columbia. I not only paid all my expenses, I also banked a couple of thousand dollars, enough so that in 1924 I was, for the first time in my life, fairly well set up financially. That summer I returned West and married Mildred Riddle, graduate of the University of Oregon, resident of LaGrande, Oregon, and Latin teacher in the Yakima High School, where I had met her. She was related on her mother's side to Thomas Stone, one of the signers of the Declaration of Independence.

While we were living in New York, Mildred taught in suburban schools around the metropolitan area, though never in the city itself. We lived in New York during the school year, but would spend part of each summer on the small farm of Mildred's parents in Oregon.

She was a lifelong scholar of Latin and rated high in the teaching profession for her achievements in that area. She had teacher's certificates in Oregon, Washington, New Jersey, and New York and she taught Latin for a while in a private school in Connecticut before the children were born. She was a quiet, retiring lady of beauty who liked to sit in green meadows beside purling waters; but she never really enjoyed the hard exhausting journeys into the high wilderness.

If someone had told me then that I would be divorced, not once, but three times, I would have been horrified. Divorce was, in my Presbyterian heritage, a sin, and I looked down on those who had gone that way. It is, it seems to me, the worst ordeal a man can suffer and it has for me a strong sense of shame—shame because of great failure. There is nothing in life brighter than a lifelong marriage. Yet often the mysterious amalgam is lacking, and when that happens, no one is at fault. Over the years I saw couples who were complete misfits but whose religion or stubbornness or weakness held them together—at least formally. Sometimes the husband, sometimes the wife, became alcoholic. Sometimes one or both were on the "make," seeking sub rosa partners. Sometimes the mounting energies were expended in outside endeavors and projects which left the home empty, and made it necessary for the children to shift for themselves. It took years for me to resolve that those conditions were much worse than divorce, that divorce, especially for the young wife, can well be the beginning of a new, full life.

At the end of my first year in Law School, I made the Columbia *Law Review,* then, as now, a student publication. We had rooms in the basement of Kent Hall and there edited eight issues a year. We wrote unsigned student "Notes" and "Comments" and polished up or revised articles submitted by outsiders. When I joined the *Review,* Samuel Nirenstein was editor in chief, and during my third year, Alfred McCormack held the post. Never, up to then, did I have a brighter, happier moment in my life than the day I received notice that I was an editor of the *Review.* That achievement turned not on pull, family, influence, or politics, but on grades alone. But the burden it added to an already busy life was considerable, with the result that my second happiest day was when we put the last issue of the *Review* "to bed" and turned over our jobs to the oncoming group of eager-beaver second-year men.

I got my law pretty much on the run during those three years at Columbia. In addition to the *Law Review,* which demanded time, during my last two years I tutored, and also worked for one of the professors, Underhill Moore.

Underhill Moore's mind had a cutting edge, sharper than any other. He was in the field of commercial law, and a year at his feet was a prodigious experience—in the exactitude with which he dealt with minutiae; in the broad dimensions of the practical world where he framed his questions; in his concern with the roots of the law and their modern incidence. Moore was Teutonic in appearance. He was almost bald, which helped emphasize his massive appearance in head and shoulders. He was Teutonic in method also, very demanding and very precise. He had a thundering voice and he emphasized his points by pounding the table with his fist.

Trade associations were at the time under fire from the Department of Justice for antitrust violations and some cases involving their practices were before the U.S. Supreme Court. It looked as though the cement associations would be next. So the industry hired Underhill Moore to write them a treatise. He took me as his assistant, and we not only did library research and economic analysis, but toured the East as well. We went by car, visiting all the cement plants and interviewing executives. We had an expense account and this was the very first time in my life that I knew what "eating high on the hog" meant.

On one leg of this junket, Moore and I were somewhere in Maine riding a caboose, the only way to reach a remote cement plant. It was a warm spring day and Moore sat by an open window. The benches in the caboose, as usual, ran along each side of the car. Moore sat with one leg under him and *The New York Times* held by his two hands in front of him. He was absorbed in reading when the brakeman, sitting opposite, let go a wad of tobacco juice that passed between Moore's face and the newspaper and went smack out the window. Moore ruffled his paper and muttered something inaudible and returned to his reading. In a few moments the brakeman let go another wad of tobacco juice, and it also passed between Moore's face and the paper, neatly clearing the open window. Moore, flushed with anger, turned to the brakeman and shouted, "What goes on here?" The brakeman rose to his feet, cleared his throat, and said, "I'm sorry, sir, if I upset you. But I think you must admit it was some spitting." I could no longer contain myself and broke into loud laughter, to which first the brakeman and then Moore succumbed.

The men on the Columbia Law faculty were mostly hard-hitting teachers with sharp minds. They were not lecturers but teachers who used the Socratic method, a brand-new technique in my experience.

Stone himself was an excellent teacher in this method; no one was better at it than he. He never made an affirmative statement as to what the law was. Not once did he put into black type, so to speak, any fundamental principle of the subject matter. All he did was question, question, question. Finally, one caught on—at least those who did well in the course—to the stages in the law's development by the intonation of Stone's voice. The way he would say "So you think, Mr. Douglas, that such and such is the governing principle" was the only guidepost through his course, except the voluminous materials, including cases, which he assigned for reading.

Herman Oliphant, with his pointed nose and piercing eye, had an incisive mind. He had the skill of a brain surgeon in dissecting a legal problem. It was Oliphant who, on my very first day in Law School, embarrassed me before the class of 365 students. He came into the room, placed his notes on the lectern, polished his glasses, and then paced the room—up one aisle, around in back, down the center aisle where he stopped at my row. I was on the aisle and, therefore, an easy victim. He asked my name, had me stand, and then asked, "Mr. Douglas, what is an estoppel?" My mind was a blank. All I could say was, "I know it's not anything you find in the woods. Whether it is a legal principle or a disease, I haven't the least idea." I sat down, crushed and humiliated, certain that I was doomed as a lawyer, though by term's end I had earned myself an A in Oliphant's course.

Young B. Smith—bright, affable, and conservative—taught Torts. Later, when I was elected to the Columbia faculty, he was to be my nemesis, as I shall describe.

Harold Medina, who later served on the Court of Appeals for the Second Circuit, taught New York Practice. Medina was bright, able, and a ham actor. One shining principle was his admonition: "When you practice law, get a piece of wood that you can force into the letter slot on your door, so you won't be served with a subpoena when out to lunch."

Medina had a cram course preparing one for the New York Bars—which we all took at the end of our third year for fifty dollars apiece, and which made Medina a small fortune.

Ralph W. Gifford's courses were Criminal Law, Wills, and Evidence. He, too, was an actor who could turn the class into stitches over a juicy sex case.

Richard Powell was a terrier who taught Property and was expert at resolving such mysteries as limitations on cross-remainders.

Huger Jervey taught Personal Property, Trusts, and Mortgages. Jervey was so bored with his duties that he hired me to correct all the examination papers in his classes—at fifty cents a paper. I read at least six hundred for him every May.

Professor George Folger Canfield taught Corporations. He was old and feeble and his classes were very disrespectful of him. Eventually, the time came for him to retire. A few of us passed the hat and bought him a lovely pipe set at Dunhill's. Then, at the end of the last class, we had a little party and I presented the gift to the old professor. I made a little parting speech of appreciation and Canfield was so touched he cried. The next day the dean thundered at me, "What did you do to Canfield?" When I told him, the dean shouted, "I've been trying to get rid of Canfield for years. Now he says he's going to stay on. Why in hell do you go around giving no-good people presents?"

Thomas Reed Powell, who was to become a spokesman for the Establishment when he reached Harvard in 1925, was then an iconoclast. He was the offbeat intellectual who could cut the Supreme Court into ribbons in any field of constitutional law. I had taken his course in my third year in Law School and turned in a paper feeling completely confident I would get an A. It might, I thought, turn out to be the best paper I had ever written.

To my surprise, I received a C. I was both stunned and humiliated. Years later, when I was named to the Court, Powell wrote a congratulatory note in poetry, the first stanza of which was a reminder of that grade:

> In days of yore
> In old Kent Hall
> He took some law from me.
> And rumor has it
> That his grade was just a
> Modest C.

I replied in a long, rambling poem, the last stanza of which read:

> Yes, when I am not one of five
> But only one of four
> Then truth and light will go for naught
> As once it did before
> When at the feet of T.R.P. I only got a
> Modest C.

Meanwhile, I had formed the Powell C. Club. Combing school records, I collected the names of men who had received a C from Reed Powell and who later became prominent in the law. One, I recall, was Wesley A. Sturgis, who was a Yale Law professor of note and later dean of that school. These men and I formed the club, elected officers, and had stationery printed. For a few years we had an annual powwow, the guest of honor being Reed Powell. Our purpose was to remind him of his fallibility in handing out grades in constitutional law.

I did not learn until years later, when his daughter Mary Lee wrote me an amusing letter, that Powell, when a student at the University of Vermont in 1898, got a C in history!

While several of my classmates, like Si Rifkin, were extraordinarily able, on the whole, the intellectual competition at Columbia was not as keen as I had expected.

This is not to say I did not have to compete. In fact, to my everlasting chagrin, I graduated second in my class, having lost out on first place to Al McCormack. The two of us, throughout Law School, constantly tried to edge past each other, but we remained good friends. In fact, I was later to be best man at his wedding.

Al was a poor boy, with brains and ambition, who was determined to make good. He married a girl whose family was said to have fifty million dollars, and I had the feeling that her father looked askance at his daughter's penniless groom.

To add to the father's discomfort, on the day of the rehearsal for the wedding, those of us in the wedding party took an alcoholic bracer to prepare ourselves for the coming ordeal. We were, I'm afraid, late in arriving, and by the time we approached the church, Al's future father-in-law was in a fury, standing at the top of the stairs waiting for us. As Al went to greet him, the bride's father grabbed him by the collar and the seat of the pants and threw him down the steps.

We were outraged. We threatened to kidnap the bride and run away to Cuba, and later proposed that the matter needed third-party negotiations. In general, we thoroughly riled the dear man.

Al eventually became wealthy and his political views tended to become more conservative. Al, however, always defended me against those who disliked my views and one of his sons has grown up to be a liberal whose politics are very different from those he saw around him as a child.

Still, I was terribly hurt that when we graduated, Al was selected as Justice Stone's law clerk. Stone had left the deanship of the Law School for a partnership in Sullivan and Cromwell in the summer of 1923. When the Teapot Dome scandal broke in Washington, D.C., and Henry M. Dougherty, the Attorney General, resigned under fire, President Coolidge, who had gone to Amherst with Stone, called Stone to take over that office. So Stone went to Washington and became Attorney General of the United States in 1924. The action at the Department of Justice for which Stone is best remembered was his appointment of J. Edgar Hoover to head the FBI.

Shortly thereafter Mr. Justice McKenna died and Coolidge named Stone to the Court, where he took his seat March 2, 1925.

Stone decided to take, each year, a Columbia Law man as his clerk, and I thought surely I would be chosen. But Al McCormack nosed me out. The news reached the Law School in April, and I was so unhappy that for two weeks the sun never came out for me. The world was black and I was unspeakably depressed that for all those years and all that work, I had so little to show. The one opportunity I had wanted had passed me by—a year in the nation's capital before I went West to practice law.

Grant S. Bond, a lawyer in Walla Walla, had a partnership waiting for me. But he graciously said he would hold it for me when I decided to stay in New York City for another year to sample law practice there. So I started to walk the city streets, looking for a job. I made the rounds of the Wall Street firms, covering many of them. I was interviewed by Emory Buckner, an eminent trial lawyer, spending an hour with him after he returned from lunch. I decided against Buckner because I could smell liquor on his breath, and I did not think liquor and the serious business of law mixed. I saw John Foster Dulles and decided against him because he was so pontifical. He made it appear that the greatest favor he could do a young lawyer was to hire him. He seemed to me like a high churchman out to exploit someone. In fact, I was so struck by Dulles' pomposity that when he helped me on with my coat, as I was leaving his office, I turned and gave him a quarter tip. I finally signed up with Cravath, deGersdorff, Swaine, and Wood at 15 William Street, because everyone there seemed earnest and frank, and not at all pretentious. I took and passed the New York Bar examinations.

When I graduated, the faculty at Columbia asked me to teach three courses—Bankruptcy, Damages, and Partnership. I agreed, and worked it out so that I could meet these classes in the early morning and get to Cravath's by nine-thirty or ten o'clock. That meant teaching law and practicing law on the run. Of the three courses, I had taken only Partnership, so there was a lot of digging to do, for which I had very little time. As a result, I barely kept one hour ahead of my Columbia students.

I was terribly nervous as I entered each classroom to give a course. Law as taught at Columbia University was not the gentle discourse of English classes at Whitman. The students were the lions and the teacher was the tamer. Utter precision was demanded and sarcasm plus occasional humor was the technique. I got no calmer as the year progressed. So I stopped Oliphant in the hall one morning and asked him what to do about nervousness just before combat with the students. "I wish I knew," he replied. "I have been teaching twenty years and the palms of my hands are always moist when I meet my class." After a pause, he added, "The truth is that if you're not nervous, you're no damn good as a teacher." I found out that he was right.

My brother Art came to Columbia after I graduated. He inherited my tutorial business, which put him through school as it had paid for me. By the time Art arrived, the tutoring service was "big business."

Art took my course in Damages, and was surprised when he got an A.

Morris Lapidus

'27 ARCHITECTURE

The Russian-born architect Morris Lapidus designed hundreds of buildings over his long career; he is best known for stylish New York and Florida hotels built in the 1950s and '60s. His designs featured innovative use of light and color and were a great influence on modern architecture, perhaps most notably in Las Vegas. Following is a selection from Too Much Is Never Enough, *his 1994 autobiography.*

O n my first day at Columbia University's School of Architecture I took the uptown I.R.T. and got off at the 116th Street station. Autumn leaves were drifting across the campus and up a broad flight of monumental steps, at the top of which sat a statue of Alma Mater gazing serenely at the new crop of students hurrying to their first classes. Charles Follen McKim's stately library acted as an imposing backdrop for the students climbing the steps to reach their various schools—engineering, law, or architecture. I hurried past the library and St. Paul's Chapel to Avery Hall where the School of Architecture was housed. My first class, An Introduction to the History of Architecture, was on the fourth floor. There were thirteen of us in the class. I slipped quietly into my seat. I wanted to look around and see who my classmates would be for the next four years, but I thought it best to keep my eyes on the empty lecture podium. The classroom door opened, and a short elderly gentleman entered the room. He walked quickly to the desk and stood there looking over the class. He was a perfect example of what I thought an architecture professor should look like. Professor A. D. F. Hamlin must have been in his seventies. He had unruly white hair, which looked as if he had been running his fingers, rather than a comb, through it. His mustache and carefully trimmed goatee framed a pair of pursed quizzical lips—half smile, half frown. His cheeks were ruddy, a pair of piercing blue eyes looked through steel-framed spectacles, which sat perkily on his small button nose. His tie was, in fact, a knotted black scarf flowing over a well-worn tweed jacket.

He stood there examining each of us. His eyes went from one to another. His expression seemed to say, "So this is what architecture has come to." Finally he spoke:

> Gentlemen, I see before me thirteen young men who have decided that they want to become architects. I presume that, since I am the senior professor, it is my prerogative and duty to welcome you to Avery Hall and to start you on the road to becoming members of an ancient and honorable profession. Now gentlemen, there must be some specific reason why each of you has decided to follow in the footpaths of such men as Vitruvius and Christopher Wren. Vitruvius, that ancient Roman architect, summed up the profession by saying that buildings should be designed to embody three principles: firmness, commodity, and delight. I might as well start my lecture by explaining these three esoteric words.

By firmness, he meant the building would have to be strong enough to stand there without collapsing. By commodity, he meant that the building would function properly. And by delight, he meant that a building should be designed to be something pleasant to look at, something to be enjoyed, a thing of joy.

Professor Hamlin welcomed us to the profession, in a manner of speaking. He emphasized that architecture had been, and continued to be, a gentlemen's profession, and that no one would ever become rich practicing architecture. He recommended that any of us who might be entering the profession as a means of achieving wealth should choose another profession; for those of us who might remain, he asserted that the study and practice of architecture would be highly rewarding in every way but financially. He then left the room for ten minutes to give us time to think about what he had just said.

I really had no visions of ever becoming wealthy. I had assured my father, when I decided to study architecture, that I could "make a living" at it. I stayed. I do not know what the other twelve thought, but they all remained.

The other men were graduates of Ivy League colleges—Princeton, Harvard, and Yale. I had had only two years of liberal arts, most of which was devoted to studying drama at Washington Square. All of my classmates were what Professor Hamlin called "gentlemen" who were entering a gentleman's profession. I was the outsider, a prisoner of my own deep-rooted sense of inferiority.

There was only one classmate with whom I seemed to have any rapport. He was an Austrian named André who had decided to come to the United States to study architecture. He was as Germanic as a young man could be, not only in his speech and his manners, but also in the way he thought. Since we were two outsiders, we found time to discuss many differences between Americans and Europeans. One of the earliest courses required in the study of architecture was the copying of the classical orders: the Doric, the Ionic, the Corinthian, and the Composite. The first step was the preparation of a precise pencil drawing with all the crispness of a steel engraving. At this type of work, André was perfection itself. My pencil lines could never achieve the precision and the uniformity of André's, but when it came to rendering these orders, it was another matter.

Rendering is the term used to indicate the coloring or toning of a drawing which gives it a third dimension by the use of shades and shadows. A five-month course was devoted to that one subject, the study of shades and shadows using Chinese ink. Chinese ink is made by taking a stick of hard Chinese ink, which looks like a stick of sealing wax, and grinding it with water in a slate mortar. The result is a gray or black liquid, depending on how much ink was ground into the water. This liquid could be applied to appear almost black or, by thinning it down with water, it could be applied to create an almost imperceptible gray transparent tone. The column, the capital, the cornice, the frieze, and the entablature were rendered, or painted, with the Chinese ink to give them a third dimension to show the delicate modeling and to create crisp shadows.

I loved every phase of my studies in architecture except the courses in engineering. To begin with, I was never much good at mathematics; in fact, I hated the entire subject. I knew that I would never receive my degree in architecture unless I passed them so I gritted my teeth and studied those ridiculous formulas, saying to myself, "Just get through it and get a passing mark. After all, I will never have to figure the strength of a column or a beam or a footing. Who needs it? I am going to design theater settings."

Our curriculum was largely based on our professors' own early studies in Paris or Rome. Our courses included perspective, watercolor, drawing in charcoal of classic plaster casts, and life drawing. The most important texts we used were written by A. D. F. Hamlin: *The History of Architecture* and *The History of Ornament* in two volumes.

And, of course, a major part of our work was design. We took elementary design the first year, then intermediate, and finally senior design. Three design presentations were required of us each semester. We were to present the plans for a building, as well as a picture of the building, in any medium—Chinese ink, watercolor, or tinted pencil. As we worked on our projects, a critic (usually a practicing architect) was designated to oversee and make suggestions as the problem advanced from rough sketches and studies to the final presentation. Some of the finest architects came to the drafting room two or three afternoons a week. They went from table to table and spent about a half hour talking with the students and often sketched their ideas on what the student should do. The final presentation was judged and marked by a group of practicing architects together with some of our critics. If the design did not meet with their approval, the design was X'd—meaning no credit points. If the design was accepted, it was given a "passed," which meant three credit points. If the design was above average it was given a "first mention," which earned the student four points. If the design was exceptional, it received a "first mention placed," which earned the student five points.

Our first project was the design of a garden dome used as a small shelter. All the students used classical ornament and designs. Some were in the Greek style, some in the Roman style with classical columns and entablatures around the bottom of the dome. I searched for something different—the beginning of my rebel phase. I noticed that the subway stations all had peculiarly shaped domes for a roof. I decided to adapt the odd domelike structure as my design concept. My critic was not sure he liked it, but he let me have my way.

In the end, my presentation was given a "first mention placed" for my originality and the colorful presentation. I wondered if any of the jury even noticed the subway domes that I had copied. I was beginning to earn a reputation as a innovative designer.

I remember another elementary project in which we were asked to design a "Cemetery Gateway." Most of the students who were studying Greek and Roman architecture designed a Greek or Roman section of a wall with a classical arch, complete with flanking columns, crowning the walls with a classical cornice. My design was not a classical expression of a cemetery gateway. I started with a large circular fountain around which arriving cars circled to the cemetery entrance. In the center of the fountain I placed a figure which to me symbolized Grief. It was a tall figure dressed in a monk's robe and hood. The shoulders were bent, the hands covered a bowed face. This tall figure was rendered in almost black Chinese ink. At the cemetery gateway, I used two flanking walls of marble with no adornment. In the central space between the two walls which curved with the driveway, I used a tall, wrought-iron grill which I copied from a cathedral screen. At least a hundred marble blocks formed the walls. I rendered each block separately with

Chinese ink in varying tones. Using a principle I had learned in my water-color class, I left a white paper hair line at the left and the top of each stone. It was a tedious chore, each block taking a long time to render.

One day, while absorbed with my task, I felt as if somebody was behind me. I put down my brush and turned around. About forty students were watching me. One of them, noticing my embarrassment, spoke up and told me that Dean Williams Boring had been watching my work and had gone through the drafting room telling the entire school about a first-year student so devoted to his tedious work he never looked up. He suggested they come to my table and watch what a dedicated student was doing. I was truly embarrassed, but I was given a "first mention placed" in the final judgment.

During the years that I studied architecture at Columbia, a great revolution was beginning to take place in the profession. I was actually living through the death throes of an era. As far as architecture was concerned, the nineteenth century did not end until the 1920s were over.

The period is known as the eclectic era—an era in which architects copied what had been done before. Architects throughout the world were copying everything in sight. The École des Beaux-Arts in Paris was doing its damnedest to keep the seventeenth- and eighteenth-century styles alive. Victorian Gothic was simply a copy of the true thirteenth-century Gothic with a great deal of meaningless ornamentation added. The great American architect Henry Hobson Richardson was finding his inspiration in the Romanesque style of the twelfth century. Banks were designed to look like Greek or Roman temples of the time of Pericles or Caesar and colleges to look like fourteenth-century cathedral towns. Smart suburban mansions masqueraded as thatch-roofed, half-timber English country homes of the time of Shakespeare, or as French chateaux, or Italian Renaissance villas. Addison Mizner was convincing his millionaire friends that a castle from Castile was what they should live in—down in Palm Beach. Millionaires in Newport had their mansions designed like tremendously magnified shingled cottages, which one associated with the stories of Hansel and Gretel. Here and there, small, still voices were heard, like the Greene brothers in California, who were trying to create a contemporary regional style. Frank Lloyd Wright was designing houses in the Midwest that are now recognized as great monuments of architecture but were then most unacceptable to the American public. At the time Americans were much happier with a reproduction of a Cape Cod saltbox or an ante-bellum mansion from the deep South.

As architecture students, we studied all the great styles of the past. One of the design problems we were given to work out was a ten-room house in the suburbs. Our design critic for this project was a Mr. Hirons, a graduate of the École des Beaux-Arts. As our mentor, what was the suggestion he made to his class? "Look at the magazines and copy a house! There is nothing new, gentlemen, so copy a good one." Some of us timidly asked about the houses being designed by the German architects or by Frank Lloyd Wright. "That crackpot!" Hirons said. "Don't be misled. The poor chap is doing weird things. Steer clear of him."

We studied the classic styles so assiduously that we could recognize a thousand famous buildings at a glance. If we had been taken to any city in Europe blindfolded, we could have told you where we were by simply looking at a cathedral or a palace or a mansion. I recall questioning our senior design critic, Harvey Wiley Corbett, about the modern skyscrapers. These after all, were a product of the twentieth century. Why, I wanted to know, were they being clothed in Renaissance or Gothic styles? Our curiosity had been aroused by the International Competition for the Chicago Tribune Building. The first prize and the commission had been won by Raymond Hood. The winning design still stands next to the Chicago River, a stretched-out, attenuated version of a Gothic cathedral. The second prize was the one that fascinated us. It was designed in the new *modern* style. The architect was Eliel Saarinen. If a building like a skyscraper is modern architecture, why use a classic style? Why not develop a modern idiom? Corbett's answer to us was: "If you dress a Chinese in Western clothes, he is still an Oriental. So what difference does it make if we dress a building like the Woolworth Building in Gothic clothes? It is still a modern skyscraper." But the seeds of discontent had been sown.

We saw pictures of the Paris World's Fair of 1925—L'Exposition Internationale des Arts Décoratifs et Industriels Modernes—and were excited by this new architecture, which eventually gave birth to the term *art deco*. We looked at designs of Mies van der Rohe's German Pavilion for the Barcelona World's Fair. Erich Mendelsohn was creating buildings with free-flowing lines in Germany; Le Corbusier, the Swiss, was making sketches of wild-looking buildings that we thought no one would ever build. The Dutch architect Willem Dudok was creating a new school of design. The group of German architects who had founded the Bauhaus were advocating stripping buildings of all adornment to produce what they called an honest structure. All of this was forbidden territory for us. But eventually Professor Boring decided to give seniors one lecture on the modern movement. During this speech, the dean appeared actually embarrassed to talk about the new architecture, as if it were a lewd subject.

I wanted to experiment with these new modern styles. I wanted to get into the twentieth century. I wanted excitement and resolved that if ever I got a chance to design a building, I would kick over the traces and take off in this new medium. All of that, however, would have to wait, and who knew if I would ever be an architect and be trusted to design a building? I was still determined to be a set designer.

In my third year, a new critic was assigned to our class. His name was Wallace Harrison, and he had recently returned from Rome, where he had been studying at the American Academy. He came to my drawing table and told me that he had decided to make me his assistant critic. I was pleased and astonished by this offer, but I told Mr. Harrison that I had my own projects to work on. He said, "You can design and render your project in two weeks— so do that and become my assistant critic." He had been studying my work and was sure that I could handle my own projects and still make the rounds with him as his assistant critic.

During my four years in Avery, I was especially proficient in presentation drawings. These drawings were perspective views of our designs. Using water color or pencil, I made a picture of how my proposed building would look. I often wondered whether my designs were as good as they should be, but my renderings were about the best that anyone in my class could produce. I sometimes think that the jury of architects was more influenced by my skill in presentation than my skill in designing, because I had more grades of "first mention placed" than any of the others in my class. I was able to finish my major work in design in the School of Architecture in three years, thus finding myself with only two courses in engineering to take during my fourth year. I decided to go to work during that fourth year in the office of an architect and finish the two engineering courses at night.

Zora Neale Hurston

Zora Neale Hurston received a scholarship to Barnard courtesy of founding Trustee Annie Nathan Meyer. The anthropologist Franz Boas later arranged for her admission to the Graduate School and served as a mentor; while she did not complete a dissertation, she later published a series of folklore collections that drew on her fieldwork there. One of the leading authors of the Harlem Renaissance, Hurston saw her popularity fade as the years passed; her work was rediscovered in the mid-1970s thanks in large part to novelist Alice Walker. Excerpted here is Hurston's correspondence with Meyer, from Zora Neale Hurston: A Life in Letters *(2002), collected and edited by Carla Kaplan.*

TO ANNIE NATHAN MEYER
260 W. 139th St—
New York City
Sept. 28, 1925

Dear Mrs. Meyer,

Not thru registration yet, but hope to be O.K. by the tune this reaches you. Miss Libby's letter will explain a lot. I have the duplicates now and turned them in to the Registrar's office today. So I think things will move off smoothly. But I never took any records away from the office. I never dreamed of even asking to see them. She probably confused my case with some other. It has made me several days late, anyway. I hated to contradict her—it looked too much like accusing her of either lying or carelessness or both—so I have said very little. I merely telegraphed for duplicate.

I have a letter from Dr. Durkee with his note to sign. I want to live at

International House very much. And if any money is left after tuition is paid would you be in favor of it? I wish the contacts to be had by living there. I don't know whether I can make it or not. room rent $5–$9 per week a cheaper scale than Harlem's. I think I have some after school work also.

Your criticisms were just the things I needed on the stories. I am doing them over but cant do much until the worry of registration is over.

I received the MSS. O.K.

Thanking you again for your magnificent work for me, I am—

Yours most humbly & gratefully,
Zora—

TO ANNIE NATHAN MEYER
260 W. 139th St.
New York City
Oct. 12, 1925.

Dear Mrs. Meyer,

No, I am certain that the next semester will not be so expensive. You see, if I am to get a degree, there are certain subjects that I must have and so Miss Meyer put them on my program as absolute necessities. I expected to be a full fledged Senior but I have lost some points in the transfer (one always does) and there is a half year's work more for me. I have thought things over pretty thoroughly and concluded that this term is about all that I can do unless some more of the people to whom I have appealed send in something substantial. You see I am in class until 5 oclock three days in the week—so the job is out of the question if I am to prepare my lessons. There is no point in going to class unprepared. All I can do is make the most of this semester and then take a job. I am gaining a more secure footing in New York all of the time and I am sure of places. There are two rather good ones open to me now. The time I spend at Barnard will enhance my reputation considerably and boost my earning power. So it will do some good at that. I would love to graduate of course, but I can keep taking two or three subjects at the time in Extension and offer them towards a degree when I have enough. I can do that in about a year and neither strain myself mentally nor financially. I am going to try to sell something after this week. My routine is beginning to work smoothly now.

I shall be so very happy to have you to lunch with me! Will you return soon? Miss Fannie Hurst has just written to say that she will have me at her home for tea and visit—lunch with me at Barnard. Isnt she kind to me?

I had to spend so much money for necessities—books, gym outfit, shoes, stockings, maps, tennis raquet, I still must get a bathing suit, gloves and if I am here in the Spring, I will need a golf outfit. It is cheaper to "elect" that than riding. I <u>could</u> elect canoeing tho instead, I suppose.

You have been very kind, you are being warm and staunch. I hope that I can deserve you and never let you regret.

Yours humbly and gratefully,
Zora—

TO ANNIE NATHAN MEYER
260 W. 139th St—
N.Y.C.
Oct. 17, 1925

My dear Mrs. Meyer,

Your very kind letter of three days ago came to me.

Yes, I would be glad if you would write to Miss Hurst. I am sure she would help but I felt a little 'delicate' about asking her.

I am still trying to match a job to my schedule. The one I had, I lost because they wanted me by three oclock at least and on three days of the week I could not get there until 5:30. Today I have 11 cents—all that is left of my savings, so you see there is some justification for my doubts as to whether I can remain there. I must somehow pay my room-rent and I must have food.

You see, Mrs. Meyer, I have been my own sole support since I was 13 years old. You will appreciate the tremendous struggle necessary for me to merely live to say nothing of educating myself in a community indifferent to anything except creature comfort. Being "different" has its drawbacks in such an atmosphere. You can see then, that nothing would be done to soften my circumstances. For them that would be encouraging me in my freak-ishness. I've taken some tremendous loses and survived terrific shocks. I am not telling you this in search of sympathy. No melodrama. If I am losing my capacity for shock absorbing, if privation is beginning to terrify me, you will appreciate the situation and see that it isnt cowardice but that being pounded so often on the anvil of life I am growing less resilient. physical suffering unnerves me now.

I will be glad to come whenever you say that I may.

Everything is going on very well at school. French is hardest for me, but I am getting that much better every day.

Hoping to see you soon, I am

Most humbly and obediently yours,
Zora.

TO ANNIE NATHAN MEYER
27 West 67th St
New York City
November 10, 1925.

My dear Mrs Meyer,

I have been with Miss Hurst one week today. I am very happy with the arrangement and I think that she is satisfied, too. I answer letters for her, the telephone, go errands and anything she wants done.

I am enclosing the letter from Mrs. Malone from whom I had hoped so much. Mr. Schomburg has not even answered so it does not look so bright. I love it at Barnard, but if it requires a great deal of your time and effort, please dont let me be too selfish. You have done more for me than anyone else on earth. It is a splendid demonstration of pure disinterested service. You, and thru you yours have done for me what none of mine would never consider. If the money is not easily forthcoming, Miss Hurst will keep me and let me learn to be a good secretary, she says.

How is the novel coming on? Miss Hurst has a new one coming out in Jan. I am reading the proof now.

My French is improving. I shall write my next letter to you in that language. Oh, Barnard is the thing. I am getting a great deal out of it. It was a little difficult at first, but by now I [am] getting my sea-legs and expect my grades to climb steadily.

Will you come to see me here, please? If so, when? I should love nothing better.

I have made a number of friendships now. Two that I particularly enjoy. One is Miss Florence Friedman of Jersey City, and the other Miss Claire Barkman of Morristown N.J. Oh yes, a Miss Sorrell of this city who is coming to see me on Friday. I have been out to Morristown to see Claire, and Florence has been here to see me. Claire is coming here on Sat. And next Wed. she is having me to tea in Brooks Hall.

The Negro Art Theatre of Harlem is fairly launched now and the first program will include my "Color Struck" I am hoping that you will find time to come. It will be near the end of the year, the presentation. Do come and like a good Zora rooter Yell "Author, author".!!

All, everything I owe to you. I strive so much harder now for those things that I want. You see, being at Barnard and measuring arms with others known to be strong increases my self love and stiffens my spine. They dont laugh in French when I recite, and one of those laughers ha[s] asked to quiz with me. I knew getting mad would not help any, I had to get my lessons so well that their laughter would seem silly.

Have you given up the idea of coming to lunch with me at Barnard? I hope not.

This telephone number is Trafalger: 4157.

Hoping to see you soon, I am

> Your most humble and obedient servant,
> [unsigned]

TO ANNIE NATHAN MEYER
108 West 131st Street
December 13, 1925.

My dear Mrs. Meyer,

I shall be very happy to get the dinners for Mrs. Levy. On the days suggested, I am practically free half a day. I only wish it were three days instead of two. I shall call her and make the engagement for Tuesday afternoon. Again I am indebted to you.

Oh, Mrs. Meyer, the girls at Barnard are perfectly wonderful to me. They literally drag me to the teas on Wednesdays and then behave as if I am the guest of honor—so eager are they to assure me that I am desired there. At the Senior tea on Friday to Freshmen and transfers, the President of Student Govt. asked me why I did not live in Brooks Hall, and wouldnt I come in for the Next semester. They have urged me to come to the Junior prom at the Ritz-Carlton in Feb. and several girls have offered to exchange dances with me if I will bring a man as light as myself. Their frankness on that score is amusing, but not offensive in that dancing is such an intimate thing that it is not unreasonable for a girl to say who she wishes to do it with.

I do not yet know how many credits I shall be given by Barnard, but I shall be pretty well off Miss Meyer assures me, which I take it, means that I shall be a Senior. They have held back on giving me a count until they could see what kind of a student I would make. I shall know at the end of this semester. Oh, how I hope for the best! She told me that all of my instructors had given me a good report for the midterm, so that'[s] that.

Have you begun your new novel yet? I hope so. Also I wish you a speedy recovery. Miss Hurst is going to take two articles and a story to the Editors for me this week. She says she will always do that for me. She suggested certain changes which I have made with reservations. I do not wish to become Hurstized. There would be no point in my being an imitation Fannie Hurst, however faithful the copy while the world has the real article at hand. I am very eager to make my bow to the market, and she says she will do all she can for me with her Editors. Victory, O Lord!

In one of the articles, I am mentioning you.

I have spared you the French letter, but do not begin to gloat over your escape, I am merely waiting for a little more technique.

Thanking you again for your your marvellous care of me, I am

Your humble and obedient servant,

Zora

TO ANNIE NATHAN MEYER
108 West 131st Street
New York City
Dec. 17. [1925]

My dear Mrs. Meyer,

I have done my First afternoon's work wity [sic] Mrs. Levy. She is very, very nice I think. Now I must look around and find another place for the rest of the week.

No doubt you are right about the Prom. But even if things were different, I could not go. Paying 12.50 plus a new frock and shoes and a wrap and all the other things necessary is not my idea of a good time. I am not that 'Ritzy' yet. If I can simply continue to exist until June, I shall award myself the Croix de Guerre with palms. I was pleased, however that the girls tried to make me feel good about it. Of course I dont want to make any false steps and I am most fortunate in having you to halt me before I sprout donkey ears.

I shall send you a copy of the article as soon as Miss Hurst hands it back. If she doesnt care for it at all, I'll not send it. It will not be an article then, but just so much paper and time wasted.

Hoping that you will soon be able to start on your new novel, I am

Cordially yours,

Zora

TO ANNIE NATHAN MEYER
[winter 1925/26]
108 W. 131st St—
Saturday

Dear Mrs. Meyer,

I have written [Mrs.—x-ed out] Mr. Shay. I have been scouting around for material. For the greater part, I am trying to pick them up off of Lenox Ave. because one is likely to find a great deal of talent that will be easily handled—that is, free from great ideas of their own great worth, and from complexes and inhibitions.

Thanks for the money. Thru Miss Weeks the College is granting me $76 to finish out the year. I could not have gone on otherwise. They were eager for me to stay! Isnt that splendid? Miss Weeks is a jewel, is she not? And the Dean was splendid. They would rather let me have it than have me either drop out, or endanger my record by too much work. One really needs ones time at Barnard.

Oh, I hope Mr. Shay can see me. I want to be the principal's wife so badly.

Most Cordially yours,

Zora

[on back of letter] Went down to Hotel McAlpin to Glee Club luncheon and everything went off well. The other members insisted on my being there.

TO CONSTANCE SHEEN
Barnard College
116th Street and Broadway
New York City
Jan. 5th [1926]

My dear Constance,

I have just returned from my vacation—we got out on the 18th and returned to class on the 4th—and found your card waiting for me. I assure you, it was mighty welcome.

Do you remember how we used to talk of Fannie Hurst? Well I am secretary to her now. Of course she could get a better one, but she just likes me and so I sit up and peck her letters out on the machine. All this, of course after school hours.

I suppose you want to know how this little piece of darkish meat feels at Barnard. I am received quite well. In fact I am received so well that if someone would come along and try to turn me white I'd be quite peevish at them.

Here is a [letter—x-ed out] match container of Miss Hurst's. I took out the remaining matches for fear of fire in the mails. It was used on the evening of Dec. 19th by Fannie Hurst, Stefanson(the explorer) Chas. Morris, and myself. Irvin S. Cobb was there but he used another pack. with Jesse L. Lasky and Margaret Anglin. You can get one of your brothers to put in another pack of matches. I just thought you might like a souvenir of F.H. since you admire her so much. Her new novel APPASSIONATA will be out Jan. 23rd.

I am glad that you remembered me. Write me a line sometimes when you have some moments to kill.

Sincerely and cordially,
Zora Neale Hurston.

TO MELVILLE HERSKOVITS
43 West 66th Street
New York City
July 20th [1926—library dated]

My dear Dr. Herskovits,

I am getting on but not so fast as at first. so many of the wives and children are going away that I am unable to finish the families at once. I am getting the fathers though. Dr. Boas told me to search a little harder for families of more than one child and to be very discriminating as to economic rating, since you and King had gotten the others. So I am trying to be very selective.

A number of people remember you and send regards. George Schuyler is back in town and eager to talk to you. I am sending copies of the papers carrying your article under separate cover.

Family number: Z57
Ind.   ”   Z149

Hoping that you are having a great vacation, I am

Sincerely yours,
Zora Neale Hurston

TO FRANZ BOAS
1663 Evergreen Ave
Jacksonville, Fla
March 29, 1927

My dear Dr. Boas,

Arrived in town today to meet Dr. Woodson who is here for Negro History
Week, and found your letter.

I am not borrowing any money. I suppose that came out of looking into
the matter of buying a used car for $300. They asked me for whom I worked
as a matter of routine, and I told them. I am getting the car because it is terribly hard to get about down here. The places I ought to go are unusually far
from transportation, and it is discouraging to walk. So I thought that I would
get it, since I felt that I could keep up the monthly payments—26.80—even
when the work was over. I had no idea that it would cause you any worry at
all. In fact, I thought I was doing business with the Martin-Nash Motor
Company, I have had no dealings, nor communication with this Investment
Securities Corporation at all. But someone is telling me that that is the way
cars are sold if not bought for cash.

Enclosed [on side: "under separate cover"] find all of the material that I
have transcribed into ink. It is fortunate that it is being collected now, for a
great many people say, "I used to know some of that old stuff, but I done forgot it all." You see, the negro is not living his lore to the extent of the Indian.
He is not on a reservation, being kept pure. His negroness is being rubbed
off by close contact with white culture.

I have a "hand," a powerful piece of conjure for the museum, and I have
bargained for two more pieces, from a still more powerful "doctor." By the
way, I found in Fernandina, a man [Brooks Thompson] seventy years old,
who is a most marvelous wood-carver. Born a slave, unable to read or write.
The interior of his house is all carved, <u>every</u> <u>inch!</u> His doors and casements
are of such wondrous beauty, that in my opinion they compare favorably with
the best that has come out of Africa. He is doing a 2 ft. square piece for you
to see.

I am sorry that I have kept you waiting, I have a great deal of material in
pencil, and I am transcribing it in odd moments. The reason that it is not
typed, is that it is hard for me to lug a machine along country roads in addition to my bag. That was one of the first things, in addition to the fatigue,
that made me think of getting the used car. I knew that there was not

enough—that I could not get a car furnished me, so I decided to do as Dr. Reichard had done—and buy an old one cheaply. I can sell it again when I am thru.

Respectfully yours,

Zora Neale Hurston

Next towns, 1Armstrong, 2 Palatka. (general delivery) 3Sanford.

John Berryman

'36 COLUMBIA COLLEGE

A student of Mark Van Doren, the poet John Berryman lectured at various colleges before accepting in 1955 a position at the University of Minnesota, where he would finish his career. Two years earlier had seen the publication of Homage to Mistress Bradstreet, *the product of five years' work that sealed Berryman's reputation as an important literary figure. Over the years, his volumes of poetry won numerous awards, including the 1965 Pulitzer Prize. This poem, "In & Out," is taken from 1989's* Collected Poems 1937–1971.

IN & OUT

Niceties of symbolism & identification.
The verve I flooded toward in *Don Giovanni*
A shroud, a spade.
Sense of a selfless seeker in this world.

I gave up crew and track after Freshman Spring.
I had my numerals & no more time.
No politics.
I was watching Corbière doomed, John Davidson doomed, their
frantic aplomb.

Shapes of the white ape & his irresistible companions.
My birthday the same as Burroughs',
I had a letter on 'Tarzana' stationery.
He lost his knack later on.

Corridors deep, near water. The surgeon looks over the parapet
& looks straight down in the water. '*Mordserum* sie habe sagen.
Wo ist Doktor Dumartin? Doktor Dumartin
muss Doktor Dumartin *finden!*'

When was I most afraid? Of eerie Wither,
his nonchalance abandoned. Of fragile Elspeth's opinion.
Of a stabbed lady in a drawer at Bellevue
one Saturday afternoon, we peered at Starr Faithful's

stomach in a jar, Exhibit H, avocado-green
Down to the Princeton game with no brakes to speak of
stopping by coasting into cars ahead
I'd never seen such traffic

Princeton had two complete Sophomore backfields
& took us 19–0. But the Brown game,
the last quarter ticking out, 7–0,
a freezing rain on their 2-yard line

& couldn't bull it over
neither Cliff Montgomery nor Al Barabas
my friend with shoulders & bright
who scored the only touchdown at the Rose Bowl.
I still hear from him, wanting me to contribute.

Money? for Columbia?? They use my name
now & then. That's plenty.
I make a high salary & royalties & fees
and brother I need it all.

I sent $100 it's true to Montana
to fund a poetry prize in the name of a girl
I liked in hospital, named Rita Lux,
a suicide, witty & masochistic

who was trying to get her priest to leave the Church
& marry her, she beat a punching bag
with bare fists until her knuckles bled
cursing with every blow 'John Berryman! . . . John Berryman! . . .'

I learnt in one week more about prose from Pascal
than ever from any Englishman I learnt
though from John Aubrey something, Pascal's polar.
I was tickled by Whitman's also.

And the live magazines were gone,
The Dial, Symposium. Where could one pray to publish?
The Criterion's stories & poems were so weak.
Solely *The Southern Review,* not *Partisan* yet.

After my dismal exile at my school
I made at Columbia a point of being popular,
by mid-November already I knew by name
most of the nearly 500 men in my class,

including commuters, touchingly pleased
to have a soul recognize them.
I liked them, a man of the world, I felt like them,
barring my inordinate desire.

Morose and slovenly, Zander thought like a tank
the only man in college who understood Hegel
agile enough too for the *Tractatus*
I used to stop by his room, which he never left.

Vistas ahead of what must be endured,
cold girls, fear, thoughtless books . .

'Dear Mr C, A reviewer in *The Times*
considering 200 poems of yours
produced over a period of fifteen years
adjudged them "crushingly dull"; my view too,

though you won't suppose of course I read them all.
Sir, you are trivial.
Pray do not write to me again. Pitch defileth.
Yours faithfully, Henry.'

James Wechsler

'35 COLUMBIA COLLEGE

James Wechsler edited the Spectator *while at Columbia and went on to write for* The Progressive, The Nation, *and* PM, *liberal publications all. He joined the* New York Post *in 1946 and within a few years was promoted to editor, subsequently using the newspaper as a tool to challenge figures such as J. Edgar Hoover and Senator Joseph McCarthy. In 1961, Wechsler moved to the editorial pages, for which he served as editor (until 1980) and also wrote a signed column (until 1983). This selection comes from* Revolt on the Campus *(1935).*

I f Kentucky had captured the imagination of thousands of American students, the expulsion of Reed Harris from Columbia University set free even more sweeping currents. It may have been less of a spectacle than the invasion into the land of Bourbon rule; yet the Harris case, localized, with a single Campus for background, indicated trouble close enough to home to atone for its conventional setting. Terror in the Kentucky coal regions was, to some extent at least, a remote consideration even to those aroused by the reports. However much they may have been astonished or chagrined by the fate of the student investigators, however intensely they might have become aware, for the first time, of such conditions, there were many who did not sense any genuine relation to the Campus.

But Harris was an American undergraduate, a member (in not very good standing) of the Phi Gamma Delta fraternity, the editor of a student newspaper at a major University. These were familiar items to any student, whatever his institution. Moreover, Harris was hardly unknown; a series of incidents prior to his expulsion had established his repute beyond the Columbia Campus. And finally, coming directly in the wake of the celebrated Kentucky furor, this episode found the Campus world already partially sensitized to the conflict of which it was a stormy symptom.

When the affair had at last subsided, Dr. John P. Neal, a Columbia alumnus of Knoxville, Tennessee, wrote that "this was the most significant event which has occurred in the colleges in a decade. . . . The students of Columbia have fired a shot which will be heard around the college world."

When Harris assumed the editorship of *The Spectator* in April, 1931, his unobtrusive arrival seemed no excuse for jubilation. The paper had always behaved in the best tradition of American college journalism: unhesitant pandering to the Administration, only intermittent and usually uninformed comment on affairs outside the realm of the University, devout catering to the institutions made sacred by Trustees, Alumni and their subordinates. The most illuminating example of this heritage has been furnished by Nicholas McD. McKnight, now associate dean of Columbia College but in 1920 a crusading editor of *The Spectator*. His ardor was directed most frequently against those who insisted upon witnessing football games from their dormitory rooms overlooking the field, rather than taking their places in the cheering section.

On October 28, 1920, he turned his virile pen upon these iconoclasts and wrote: "We also take the attitude that those dormites . . . are showing very poor college spirit. A man who comes to college should put something into it for what it gives him. And it certainly is not too much to ask him if he cannot play himself to at least lend his full support to the men who represent Columbia on the field of play.

"No matter how hard a man may exhort from Livingston or Hartley (dormitories), the team cannot hear him and he cannot help them. Where his cheer will help, is in the cheering section of South stand. And that is where he belongs if he is to call himself a Columbia man."

Whatever may have been the troubled state of the world two years after the war, no matter how infinite were the changes being wrought in certain patterns of civilization, the problem of indolent football rooters remained uppermost in the minds of the editorial department of *The Spectator*. But Mr. McKnight was not alone; he set the standard for a decade and his own prodigious efforts were equalled and often excelled by ensuing editors. The college press throughout the country was, on the whole, absorbed by topics of similar weight.

The background is important if we are to contemplate the outcries which greeted Harris' declarations. Mr. McKnight may have been apoplectic at the desecration of pages he once edited; there were hundreds of others accustomed to his treatises who must have been startled into confusion by these first rays of light.

In November, 1931, Harris questioned the eternal verities of high-pressure football, intimating that certain more valiant gridmen were receiving more than honor as their reward; whereupon Ralph Hewitt, quarterback par excellence, loudly offered to sock Mr. Harris in the eye. But when Harris asked for publication of the books of the Athletic Association to prove his charges, there was concerted silence in the camp of the enemy. (Now, four years later, despite efforts by every ensuing editor to achieve the same end, the books are still firmly shut.) From football Harris proceeded to evaluate critically the sacrosanct senior society, Nacoms, of which he was a member. Nacoms is a secret "honorary" body, addicted to all the mumbo-jumbo of such institutions and dedicated to the ideals of the better people. This attack was no small irritation to those Alumni whose very life was dependent on mumbo-jumbo. Anti-semitism, rife in almost every quarter of the University, was not, presumably a topic for public discussion; Harris discussed it fully and comprehensively. Although several high administrators were known to be in opposition to the Kentucky trip, Harris gave his editorial support and substantial news space. The awarding of jobs by the Appointments office, still an operation shrouded in considerable mystery, was probed for the first time. Nicholas Murray Butler, the highest monarch of all, was not immune to criticism. Nor did Harris confine himself to an estimate of institutions at Columbia. The world which his predecessors had so conveniently ignored was introduced as a subject of editorial analysis; the existence of R.O.T.C. units at other colleges was mercilessly attacked; repression in education became a field of inquiry. Finally, Harris approached more forbidden territory—the administration of the college dining halls, which had been mildly scrutinized the previous year. He merely reprinted the charge that the halls, ostensibly run for the service of students, were actually being manipulated for profit, and that student waiters were receiving far less than benevolent treatment. Citing these allegations, Harris demanded an investigation; and with this demand went his editorship of the paper. It becomes obvious, however, that his expulsion did not arise from that isolated incident but climaxed a series of Administrative grievances.

For Harris had broken the shell. Many of his writings—and those of Donald Ross, the editorial associate—might today be regarded as groping and undefined in terms of objectives; in 1931 he was speaking out amidst a dead silence. No wonder that one irate alumnus snapped: "Harris is too grown-up." His words summarized the view of the whole network of Columbia administrators. Accustomed to deal with the subservient and the credulous, who took what was offered without examining the contents, they were appalled by a critic who resisted them. Harris was marked for departure.

*   *   *

Dean Herbert E. Hawkes did not know, to his everlasting sorrow, that the Friday he expelled Reed Harris was the day of the election of Harris' successor. Had he been aware of this, he would hardly have taken such drastic action; he would have placed his faith in the board which was to come into office the following Monday. But this sad lack of information about the affairs of his college was to plague him for the rest of his life. In the words of a prominent faculty man, he committed a bull.

On the last three days of March, 1932, *The Spectator* republished articles criticizing the preparation and serving of food in the John Jay dining hall, condemning the treatment of the student waiters and summarizing the results of previous investigations of the dining-room. On March 31 Harris was summoned to the Dean's office and substantiation of the charges was demanded—within the next twenty-four hours. Harris then wrote a letter of explanation to the Dean preceded by an expression of surprise at the Dean's dictatorial attitude. He said:

"Before submitting the explanation regarding a statement made in *The Spectator*, I want to protest against the manner in which I was 'demanded' to produce an explanation. You have repeatedly said to me that my mode of presentation in my editorial column has been unmannerly. Surely the dictatorial tone you adopted yesterday was not an example for me to follow in changing the tone of that column. In spite of the fact that we have had, almost constantly, major differences of opinion, I believe that I have acted in a gentlemanly fashion while in your office during my term as editor of *The Spectator*. That you should have adopted a tone suited only to a sergeant in the Marine Corps surprises me."

The letter then outlined the basis of the accusations against the dining hall. Its contents should be observed because subsequently this document was used by the University as a last, desperate excuse for the ouster of Harris.

The following day, Harris, suddenly called to the Dean's office, was informed that he had been expelled. Startled by the abruptness of the pronouncement, he asked for a reason. Whereupon the Dean read him a statement prepared for the press, the substance of which was:

"Material published in *The Spectator* during the last few days is a climax to a long series of discourtesies, innuendos and misrepresentations which have appeared in this paper during the current academic year and calls for disciplinary action."

Having explicitly informed Harris of his dismissal, Dean Hawkes then took him before the Committee on Instruction for a "hearing," although that committee had no authority to veto or modify the expulsion order. This was later explained by Harris, who quoted Dean Hawkes as saying that he had conferred with President Butler and the latter had cautioned him to give Harris "the pretense of a hearing." It was obvious, at any rate, despite Dean Hawkes' later repudiation of this statement, that there was to be no genuine hearing for the dissenting editor. And when the news appeared in the afternoon papers, Alumni, Trustee and administration rejoiced that the rebel was at last gone.

But his departure did not bring peace and quiet to the University. By the next morning the case had become a nationwide issue; any hope that Harris' ouster would still the waters he had troubled must have fled swiftly from Columbia's administrative halls.

So instantaneous and pronounced was the protest against the University's action that it became evident that her original defense would not suffice. The Dean had already admitted that more than a single editorial was involved in the expulsion, that Harris' whole editorial policy was the source of his discharge. Confronted with the dissatisfaction this explanation had caused, he reversed himself in mid-field—very likely after consultation with more authoritative groups. He informed a delegation of conservative students that Harris' "personal misconduct" prompted the ouster. To another delegation he gave the publication in *The Spectator* of the following paragraph as his reason:

> "Waiters asserted that the personnel in charge of the dining room evidently were working only for profit, serving poor food, attracting organizations not strictly student in character and otherwise changing the character of the organization from one of student service to one of personal profit."

This was a tragic blunder which the Dean will not soon forget—and which was carelessly repeated by President Butler in an interview with another group. They had apparently been very negligent in preparing their alibis, for precisely that paragraph had been published in *The Spectator* a year before under a different editor and without any reprisals against him. The republication occurred in the course of an historical survey on previous inquiries into the dining-halls.

Neither Dean Hawkes nor Dr. Butler was ever able to explain why, if a previous editor could make this statement without punishment, Harris would have to be expelled for it. If all the other testimony could be forgotten, this phase alone would have demonstrated beyond dispute the real motivation behind the dismissal.

That was Dr. Butler's only direct statement on the case— his reference to "slanders" against the dining hall management. After that had proved a boomerang, he retired behind the scenes, resuming the attitude he had adopted on April 3 when interviewed by *The Herald-Tribune:*

"Would you make a statement on the expulsion of Harris," Dr. Butler was asked.

"Of whom?" he queried.

"Harris, Reed Harris, editor of *The Spectator*."

"Oh," said Dr. Butler, "I don't know anything about that. That hasn't come to me at all."

He was, by Dean Hawkes' earlier statement, not telling the truth. He had been consulted. Moreover, the event had been broadcast over the radio and spread over the newspapers; only a recluse could fail to have heard of it three days later.

Student indignation crystallized on the Monday after the expulsion, when a mass meeting was held on the Library Steps with more than 4,000 students present. Columbia had never witnessed—since the war years when R.O.T.C. men had held their review in exactly the same place—so impressive an outpouring of serious and determined students. And there, a University strike of major proportions was voted, to take place on Wednesday.

Since that time students in other colleges, faced with similar situations, have adopted the procedure of those thousands who massed on the Steps in the warm April afternoon. In 1931 that was a bold and almost unprecedented move.

Simultaneously the first hint of opposition developed. Its origin, tactics and appeal is worthy of note because, in subsequent years, almost every college has been visited by a similar bloc. At Columbia in 1931 the group styled itself "The Spartans"; later we are to see them as "Vigilantes" and even as "Silver Shirts." It was perhaps too early to comprehend their full meaning; yet some intimation of their later nature could be discerned.

Part of this opposition did not follow the action of "The Spartans" on the day of the strike when a meeting "to uphold the Dean" was held in front of his office under the auspices of that group. The "loyalists" preferred to attend the strike meeting, to hurl eggs, provoke fist-fights and attempt to disperse the assemblage. When one of their number was urged to express his sentiments verbally to the crowd, he rose and shouted: "I think it's a lot of boloney," then fled before the disgust of the audience. Another rose up to defend him, crying, "We all know what Harris said was true. But he didn't have to say it in public."

With these two eloquent contributions, the invaders, recruited primarily from the football team and Fraternity Row, then returned to their egg-throwing. At the meeting of "The Spartans," equally eloquent orators swore their fealty to the Dean and then devoted most of their time to a valiant assault on "communism." One of them later admitted the essence of his feeling on the matter: "The only way to run a corporation or a university or a government is to have discipline or authority vested in one person." He also confessed that, like most of his fellow-supporters of the Administration, he was an athlete, residing at the Manor House and otherwise enjoying a remunerative college career.

"The Spartans" and their sympathizers were plainly outnumbered. If a few hundred followed their leadership, close to seventy-five per cent of the 1800 students in the college, augmented by hundreds from other schools of the University, went on strike. The Dean's loyal lackeys could not carry the day despite the red menace, eggs and a substantial number of powerful football players.

On the steps of the Library several thousand students were demanding the reinstatement of Harris and a probe of the dining-halls.

The appearance and methods of the opposition was nevertheless ominous. It is equally significant that those who sought to break up the strike and provoke a riot were never censured by the Administration. They were its handmaidens and, if their tactics were crude, their intentions were noble. No sentimental Dean could have penalized such boyish devotion. They came from what we shall discover to be the accustomed seats of reaction—from Fraternity houses, from the athletic field and from that group which, in return for its willing and unquestioning loyalty, receives the numerous favors an Administration can afford to dispense.

Two days after the strike Dean Hawkes departed for a "long planned" trip to England. He told reporters at the boat that there was no possibility of Harris' reinstatement.

But the pressure did not cease. As one periodical wrote at the time, "This issue agitated the student body of the country for almost two weeks. From Maine to Texas, literally, letters and telegrams of protest came pouring into Columbia."

On April 20th prolonged negotiations between the Civil Liberties Union, representing Harris, and the University came to an end. Harris was reinstated. As he had originally intended, he immediately submitted his resignation to the University. In addition, he had previously sent a note of apology to the Dean for any personal injury the Dean may have experienced.

But, as the Civil Liberties Union commented in reviewing the case: "Columbia University's reinstatement of Reed Harris is a plain confession of error despite its face-saving conditions."

Student editors had been disciplined before; in the five preceding years, however, no case of expulsion had been reported.

The severity of the reprisal unquestionably served to project it into public notice. There were, however, more basic aspects to the protest. For Harris had become the standard-bearer of incipient student revolt, of a campus awakening from its stupor. His editorial policies had declared what others everywhere, in increasing numbers, were beginning to think. The restlessness caused by the perceptible inroads of economic uncertainty, the news of the Kentucky delegation—these had launched the downfall of "isolationism." Now there arose an unceasing uproar over Harris' expulsion. The event, moreover, served to dramatize the need for organized student force to combat similar moves, an emphasis continually set forth by the National Student League members who capably and energetically led the strike. They warned that this was the beginning of a crisis in students' rights—in the course of which students would be compelled to realize that their rights existed only so long as they defended them.

In the aftermath of the controversy its full significance was profoundly appreciated. One commentator remarked: "Teachers and others familiar with American student life agreed that the Columbia strike was the most militant student demonstration of recent years. It was noted far and wide that at last American college students were becoming excited over something more important than football and crew."

Its effects were visible in the amount of space which college journals in every community devoted to it. Thousands in eating-clubs and fraternity houses hundreds of miles from New York discoursed upon the issues involved. The sessions of undergraduate liberal clubs were occupied by similar discussion.

Perhaps more important than the mere fact of undergraduate thought—however extraordinary—was a conviction of power which the triumph of the strike engendered. When the resort to this weapon was first proposed, students ridiculed it, contending that it would be a lame, "undignified" gesture and nothing more. Now the move was vindicated. Faculty members had urged undergraduates to "bide your time" and "allow us to talk it over quietly with the administration." Their reticence was something which the strike participants will never forget. Only one man, Donald Henderson, gave unhesitant and vigorous public support to the walkout. When John Dewey was approached for aid, he said that he "knew nothing about it"—a rebuff which some of his disciples bitterly remembered. This was an hour, it was felt, when the faculty should have recognized an identity between its own welfare and that of the students in the face of so outright an invasion of an allegedly cherished principle. Instead there was almost hushed silence; some deplored "hasty action"; others cited their "loyalty to the Dean." Throughout the whole university only sixteen men, mostly young instructors, consented to sign a petition for Harris' reinstatement.

The reluctance of the teaching staff only enhanced the victory of the students. With the entire administrative machinery mobilized to affirm the expulsion, the University was eventually forced to surrender. Certainly the threat of legal action accelerated its retreat. On the other hand, without the pressure of nationwide opinion and the attendant glare of publicity, it is highly doubtful that Columbia's capitulation would have been so sweeping and swift. At the outset there were those who sought to "keep the affair among ourselves"; they resented the intrusion of "outsiders"—students and teachers from other schools who readily avowed their support. But the hostility slowly evaporated; in its stead was the acknowledgment that precisely such joint agitation had been effective and that, moreover, the disagreement could not be isolated from the academic scene as a whole. The outcome of the Columbia conflict, it was admitted, would condition activities of administrators everywhere.

These were broad truths; the extent to which they were accepted, of course, varied with individual cases. What was uniform and of prime consequence was the crystallization of opinion. The Columbia strike of April, 1932, was an inspiration and a model for the rest of the country and one which was to have its counterparts in the months to come. It established the place of the student movement and the paths of procedure for it to follow, arousing students in other areas to the imminence of parallels on their own campuses and outlining the strategy of counter-attack.

When Dean Hawkes blundered on that Friday in April, he served a far more distinguished purpose than was then supposed. The revolt was penetrating the "intellectuals" and the "collegians" alike.

Erwin Chargaff

The pioneering biochemist Erwin Chargaff is credited with a groundbreaking finding in the study of heredity—namely that it is not protein but DNA that carries genetic information. A wide-ranging researcher, Chargaff worked and taught at Columbia's College of Physicians and Surgeons from 1935 to 1974. His memoir Heraclitean Fire *(1978) is excerpted here.*

A few years after I had joined Hans Clarke's Department of Biochemistry at Columbia University, a visitor told me that, on getting off the elevator on the fifth floor of the College of Physicians and Surgeons, the quaint eighteenth-century designation of the medical school, he thought he was in a madhouse. People ran past him, some screaming, others carrying weird vessels or apparatus; a door opened, and an elderly professor ejected, brachially and in a loud Germanic falsetto, a graduate student who, with faked dismay and in a great hurry, rushed to hide among his equals. Most doors were open, and a rich mixture of Brooklynese, Bostonese, but mostly Hamburg-American, filled the air.

Traffic density was high in the shabby corridors and laboratories, but some individuals stood out from the general disorderly and aimless fervor of Insanity Square. There was, for instance, one who seemed to rehearse a bizarre ballet: surrounded by a copious array of various motionless apparatus and empty vessels, he poured nothingness from one into the other. An empty beaker was raised and slowly and carefully emptied into an empty separatory funnel, the noncontents of which, after being shaken, divided into two layers

189

of nonentity, separating nothing from nothing. Both nothings were then collected cautiously, each in its own vessel. A visitor, seeing all this, would, of course, have been baffled, but those who had observed the beautiful spectacle before knew that this was a "dryrun" for an experiment to be performed on one of the subsequent nights. There were, in fact, more acts to this dumb show: many other operations—crystallization, distillation, sublimation—partook of the ghostly pantomime. That most of this activity did not lead to anything handed on to posterity was perhaps a pity. But does this count in the face of a human life? Does not the great *corpus mysticum* of the world contain all that was once felt or thought, suffered or overcome, created or forgotten, whether written or unwritten, made or destroyed? Are we not in this sense parts of a greater organism, kept alive through the ever more vividly circulating blood of an enormous past?

A large part of the population seemed to be marginal: they came and they went. A few did nothing, a few worked hard; others—owls of Minerva—flew only at night. The place was very crowded, the laboratories were in part quite irregular in shape, and some of the inmates were stacked away in the oddest corners. My wayward memory throws up many iridescent bubbles: a short man with a blue-black beard speaking, for unknown reasons, with a Maltese-British accent; a charming Chinese lady, not unconnected with one of the greatest historical undertakings of our time—Joseph Needham's awe-inspiring *Science and Civilisation in China;* a benign walrus presiding somewhere and intermittently over a sort of kymograph. The latter—tolerated in the department but not really belonging, and later separated from it—now reveals himself as the discoverer of a very important group of physiologically active substances, the prostaglandins. This was the good-hearted Raphael Kurzrok, an excellent and friendly obstetrician, dear to our family annals for having delivered our son Thomas in 1938. At that time I was taken to task for not handing out cigars: I was stingy, poor, and averse to any form of folklore.

A department at an American university is, or was when I began my life, something entirely different from a German "Institut." It reflected some of the most admirable qualities of the American character, which at that time had not yet been entirely submerged or denatured by the overpowering moral and physical noises that the drumfire of the mass media, including all that is called government or administration, set loose on a good-natured and helpless people. I know, in fact, no other nation that is as little represented by its representatives—public or private, business or art or science—as is the American people. In any event, the openness and informality, the absence of pomposity, the helpfulness and true collegiality, the resigned recognition that we were all in the same leaky boat, the good-humored lack of ambition: all this and much more must have impressed every newcomer from Europe.

The last-mentioned attribute explains, in part, the relatively low quality of the science departments. This was actually not due to the low caliber of the individuals who constituted the departments, but to the feeling on their part that nothing they could do counted on the scientific stage, which was occupied by the loud-mouthed and conceited European heavyweights. They took it for granted that all beauty contests would be won by the decibelles from Germany and England. In other words, university departments in the United States, pleasant as they were in their well-ordered family lives, lacked all power of percussion.

I believe it is no exaggeration to say that, as concerns biochemistry, this was changed radically through Clarke's coming to Columbia University. It is time for me to say a few words about him.

Hans T. Clarke (1887–1972) was born in England of American parents and educated there and in Germany. He received his training in organic chemistry in London and worked subsequently in Emil Fischer's celebrated laboratory at the University of Berlin. At the outbreak of the First World War, he came to the United States and spent fourteen years as an organic chemist with the Eastman Kodak Company in Rochester, New York. During that time he was instrumental in developing the imposing line of organic chemicals sold by this firm, a huge repository of often difficultly accessible substances without which the great advance in organic chemistry in this country would have been impossible. In 1928, when the medical school moved uptown to Washington Heights, to form part of the Columbia-Presbyterian Medical Center, Clarke came to the Department of Biochemistry as chairman. He remained there for twenty-eight years.

When I first saw Clarke in 1935, I met a rather tall, aristocratic-looking man with a human face and friendly eyes. His British upbringing, or perhaps his innate temperament, had endowed him with the special kind of shy aloofness that has baffled continentals in their dealings with the English upper class since times immemorial. In his case, it did not go all the way to stammering, the true attribute of the empire-builders who, while the rest of the world looked at them with bewilderment, managed to stutter away entire continents. For this reason, Clarke was not a good lecturer. But he was a very good organic chemist of the old observance; one of those who liked to putter around in the laboratory with test tubes and small beakers and watch glasses and who was happy when crystals appeared. He belonged to a vanishing species, when science was young and adventurous, when real experiments could still be performed, when the sense of smell still served to identify classes of compounds.

In contrast to the eager beavers among whom I have spent most of my life—all surface and polished professionalism—there was a very private side to Hans Clarke: he loved music and was an ardent clarinetist. I often heard him play chamber music with his first wife, who belonged to the Max Planck family.

He published very little and knew more than he showed. He belonged to the conscientious generation: every day of his long life he came in early each morning, and there he sat in his shabby office, door open to the corridor; you could see him and speak with him by sticking your head in. His dignity required no ceremony. When I think of my slick contemporaries in thick plush—receptionists and intercom and all the abstract art that foundation money can buy, cars with chauffeurs, private dining rooms—I can gauge the long, devilish way that we have traveled in forty short years.

Clarke would not have impressed one as very bright, nor was he a profound scientific thinker. He was, perhaps, the most unselfish scientist I have encountered, and I have often wondered whether in science a certain lack of passionate involvement is not the only way to true disinterestedness. But he had an uncanny sense of quality. After a short interview with an aspiring graduate student, in which he mostly asked the young man how he would make sulfuric acid or something of similar import, he arrived at a judgment which, at least nine times out of ten, was correct. He may have rejected a few who did not deserve to be, but he was almost never wrong in those he took. In my later years I have often envied him this gift, which I lack completely. The graduate students whom Clarke assembled in the department were, therefore, of high quality on the whole, and their subsequent careers have borne this out. He showed the same feeling for quality in selecting the members of the department with whom he surrounded himself, but of this more later.

Like many well-to-do people, Clarke was frugal and had little appreciation of the importance of money for those who had none. The salaries which he negotiated for his faculty members—one of the foremost functions of a department head in an American university—were largely below the average and mostly insufficient; he had no understanding of the material difficulties that beset some of his younger colleagues, and he did little to keep those who were pushed or pulled away.

He built the foremost department of biochemistry in the United States. The group that he had assembled and that he led benevolently through non-leading—faculty members, guests, and students—represented the first serious group in this science, which lifted biochemistry way above its previous status as an ancillary discipline in the education of physicians. Clarke's ideal was F. G. Hopkins, who had done something similar at the University of Cambridge. I had met Hopkins first in Cambridge in 1934 when he showed me his laboratories with absent-minded and paternal friendliness. I saw him again during the war, when he called on Clarke at Columbia, and I know how happy Clarke was about that visit. Hopkins was a wise and decent man, and so was Clarke. They both had what I would call the wisdom of the heart.

When, in 1956, the time had come for Hans Clarke to retire from his university chair, he asked to be let remain at Columbia in a small laboratory. The request was refused.

◦ ◦ ◦

In the beginning of October, 1935, I entered Columbia, as almost everybody did, through one of its many back doors. In the first part of this brief memoir I recounted my return to the United States at the end of 1934. This was made possible by the hospitality of The Mount Sinai Hospital of New York and especially through Harry Sobotka, who was in charge of biochemistry there. I spent a few months in his laboratory, doing almost nothing except listening to his pleasant conversation and to his many jokes. He had been a student of the two great Richards of Munich, Willstätter and Kuhn, and later a collaborator of another great and unpleasant biochemist, P. A. Levene of The Rockefeller Institute. Like many scientists who came to this country prematurely, i.e., of their own choice and before being propelled by the Great Migration, Sobotka never really fitted into what he had, and his quick intellect went to waste on petty matters.

It was through Sobotka that I made the acquaintance, at about that time, of the only genuine genius of my life, Bertolt Brecht. He had come to New York to supervise the unsatisfactory performance of his play _The Mother,_ which he had adapted from Maxim Gorki's novel. I spent one unforgettable afternoon with Brecht, mostly fighting about our very divergent views of the blackest monster of these horrible times, Adolf Hitler. In retrospect, I must concede that I was wrong in that discussion: I had not realized that, in gauging the historical importance of a potentate, his weight must be increased by that of all the corpses he has created. This insight, acquired later, has helped me to do justice to the historical significance of some of our own congenitally insignificant statesmen.

The first few months of 1935 were spent on a search for a job. I already had thirty papers to my credit, but did not know anybody who could be of much use. After unprofitable visits to Boston, Philadelphia, Baltimore, and Chicago, it occurred to me to visit Hans Clarke and to present myself as a former collaborator of Rudolph Anderson at Yale, with whom Clarke was on good terms. I underwent the same baffling interview, at the likes of which I later assisted innumerable times, but nothing seemed to be on the horizon. My knowledge of sulfuric-acid manufacture must, however, have satisfied Clarke, for a few weeks later he telephoned me asking that I come to see him again. He suggested that two surgeons at Columbia were looking for a biochemist and that I might be suitable for this position. This proved to be the case: Drs. Frederic W. Bancroft and Margaret Stanley-Brown of the Department of Surgery had received a small grant from the Carnegie Corporation to help them in research on blood coagulation. I was given the job, at $300 a month.

This was, then, the back door through which I entered Columbia; and since nobody ever called me away, I stayed there throughout the rest of my professional life. I had been promised the title of assistant professor of biochemistry, which, in view of my having been on the way to a *Privatdozentur* in Berlin and of my advanced age, thirty years, was the least to be expected. But when I moved in with my spatula and my notebook, Clarke hemmed and hawed and disclosed to me that they had decided to start me at a lower rank, that of research associate. Always meek before the inevitable and caring, in fact, very little about such things, I acquiesced. It was an unpropitious beginning of a far-from-brilliant academic career: assistant professor at thirty-three, associate professor at forty-one, professor at forty-seven. I suppose that, at some time during this dazzling ascent, I received tenure; nobody told me and I did not ask. As so many other things, that grail of the American academic escaped me entirely.

I found myself in what would be called a happy place: a chief one could respect, colleagues one could admire. The title of this chapter requires, therefore, some justification. To begin with, such words as "happy" or "happiness" —done to death by the advertising jargon of our times—are not easily understood by someone brought up in a Latin, Germanic or, for that matter, Slavic language. I remember my surprise when, on learning English, I first read about "the pursuit of happiness." *Glückseligkeit, félicité?* Other languages do not possess a single word expressing the complete absence of malaise. In any event, looking around the happy department, I noticed that its members were far from a state of bliss. This was partly due to the human condition, partly to Clarke's disregard of the future of the people under him, which I mentioned before, but mostly to the fact, which took a long time dawning on me, that we were working in the middle of an American medical school. The education of health-care delivery boys is actually the function of a trade school, and that is what the medical schools were in the course of becoming. Sincere or excellent as some faculty members may have been—I remember with affection Palmer of Medicine and Whipple of Surgery—the ridiculous technicolor aureoles glued to the physicians' heads by their busy medical chamber of commerce or by a gullible and deadly afraid public have corrupted them all.

It is regrettable that most biological research has become concentrated in the medical schools; a development furthered by an insane funding policy on the part of government. Although I recognized this early, I remained. What else could I have done? I am, perhaps, the most impatient stoic there ever was, but I am a stoic. Since then, things have become much worse: the medical schools have been taken over by a particularly virulent type of scientific entrepreneur, those who are best described as wheeler-healers or, if you prefer, as healer-dealers. The inchoate mob which is called the public suffers them gladly; but when the water gates of what goes by the name of "biomedical research"—MD's getting the money, PhD's doing the work—once are opened, there will be quite a flood.

o   o   o

Turning now to what I found in Clarke's department when I joined it, in 1935, I enter, happily and fearfully, the realm of the living. I am certain that my colleagues or, as one says in the United States, my friends, who still eat their shabby pensions, will be glad if I do not describe or characterize them. The old precept *de mortuis nil nisi bonum*, which undoubtedly was coined by a Neolithic undertaker, ought not to be converted to something like *de vivis nil nisi malum*. On the other hand, Cassandra should not be invited to address the Kiwanis. Even the most heartfelt panegyric sounds false when uttered in public. So let us assume that I am saying the best of everybody.

The supreme council of the department, as it were, was composed of three older, helpful, and friendly men: Clarke, Edgar G. Miller, and G. L. Foster. They were not old at all—forty-eight, forty-two, and forty-four, respectively—but to me they appeared old. They undertook most of the teaching load, which consisted mainly of rather poor lectures for the medical students. As the graduate students received practically no formal instruction, this left much time for us younger ones. Several already had reached distinction or were soon to do so, although the university showed little recognition of this fact: an old Columbia habit.

When one grows old, one is surrounded by an ocean of unremembered names and of young familiar faces. When you remember the names, they are forgotten; when you see the faces, they have grown old and sad. The only way to cross this Malebolge—and without a Vergil as your guide—is to tell yourself that what was is; that once young, always young; once beautiful, always beautiful; once bright, always bright; that what lived cannot die.

I lay, therefore, my hand in that of Mnemosyne, the goddess of remembrance, and let her guide me. There were several who had already established themselves as scientists of high rank: Michael Heidelberger, the founder of immunochemistry, a new branch of biochemistry—it was only the day before yesterday that I sat in the bus next to him, nearly ninety years old, on his way to work, and admired again the handsome face of a humanist scholar who should have been painted by Quentin Matsys or Holbein. Perhaps because Heidelberger also played the clarinet very well, Clarke had a low opinion of immunochemistry. For that reason, Heidelberger was, in my time, never really in the department. His laboratory was two floors higher up, in the department of medicine; and there I visited him often to speak about sugars or the world, more about the first. He gave rise to an entire school of excellent researchers in the field of immunology.

There was Oskar Wintersteiner, a fellow Austrian, who played the piano beautifully. He had already done very good work on progesterone and was to do more in many fields of the steroid hormones and other complex natural substances. At that time he collaborated with J. J. Pfiffner, who later went into the pharmaceutical industry. Wintersteiner was, like many Austrians, a quiet, sensitive, retiring, and slightly melancholy man. I was very fond of him, and so was Clarke; but instead of urging the promotion of one of the best organic chemists we had seen, he let him go. Wintersteiner went to Squibb, where he had a distinguished career.

The prize exhibit, when I came, was, however, Rudolf Schoenheimer. Not long before, he had come to Columbia from Germany, where he had been the chemical assistant in Aschoff's famous department of pathology at the University of Freiburg. From there he had brought with him a brilliant idea which he had the good luck and the energy to transform into reality in Clarke's department. The professor of physics in Freiburg, G. von Hevesy—later, I was to know him well—had been the first, before the 1914 war, to introduce isotopes as markers in biological reactions. Those available until the early thirties were, however, of no great interest in biology. The elements of the greatest importance for biological studies are hydrogen, oxygen, carbon, nitrogen, phosphorus, and sulfur. When Schoenheimer came to New York, the heavy hydrogen isotope, deuterium, had become available, thanks to the work of Harold Urey at Columbia, and Schoenheimer began an ambitious program on the use of this isotopic marker in the study of intermediary metabolism. He was helped in the work by one of Urey's former students, David Rittenberg, who had joined Clarke's department a short time before I did. Their work—the first consistent use of stable isotopes in the investigation of biological reactions—is of lasting historical importance. Science has, however, moved so fast in my lifetime that the actual has become the historical almost before the print has dried, and even the youngest scientists are condemned to survive themselves. Many must go around pitifully, clowns of their own achievement, beating a drum that long ago had gone out of tune. This is why I have often compared the sciences of my time to soap sculpture.

Schoenheimer had an interesting, histrionic face. He was a marvelous lecturer, an ambitious, assertive, but at the same time a very nervous and easily wounded man. In 1941, at what would appear the height of his success, he took his own life; he was only forty-three years old. Universities being notoriously gossipy places, there were many rumors, none of any interest. Not given to boring into souls, neither my own nor those of others, I can only deplore the circumstances that drove this gifted man to so deep a despair. In my cool and witty way, I had never realized the misery in which he lived.

There were others when I came, and each explored, or began to explore, a field of great significance. Erwin Brand, an irascible, kind-hearted, protein chemist, a former pupil of the great Max Bergmann; Warren Sperry, who worked on lipids; Karl Meyer, who was just about to make his first important discovery in the chemistry of connective tissue. These people, together with three or four more, made up the department as I saw it before me. There were few areas of biochemistry, as it was then understood, to which the group of men chosen by Clarke was not making distinguished contributions.

In addition, there were the graduate students, not many, but of excellent caliber. I mention just a few of the early crop and more or less haphazardly: Joe Fruton and David Shemin, Ernest Borek and deWitt Stetten, Konrad Bloch and Bill Stein, Elvin Kabat and Seymour Cohen, who was my first graduate student at Columbia.

When I came, the migration from Europe had barely got under way. Great numbers of scholars and scientists arrived during the next few years, and Clarke took several into the department. It would be a great mistake to believe that they were received with open arms in those days. It was not too difficult for the young ones, with little offended pride to swallow; but the more distinguished, the more famous a man was, the greater was the reluctance to welcome him. These poor luminaries had a hard time. Their manners were imperial, their accents ridiculous; their cant was entirely different from the one practiced in the country to which they had come.

✧ ✧ ✧

When I entered the biochemistry department of Columbia University, the population density of American science was extremely low. Clarke's group was one of the larger ones. In the spring of 1935 I attended my first "Federation meeting" in Detroit. The abstracts of the papers read there occupied a thin booklet of one-hundred pages that fitted into my breast pocket. The corresponding yearly publication of the "Federation of American Societies of Experimental Biology" now is the size of the New York telephone directory. The friendly, but lugubrious and slightly depressed, tone of the gathering showed to what extent American science then vegetated at the outskirts of society. This has changed radically, to the benefit of neither science nor society.

Few people have the strength, or the temerity, to decide early what they want to do in their life and then to attempt to follow it through. I am certainly not one of those. The gusts that pushed me in one direction or another are an important, perhaps the most important, part of my life. I never had a choice, or I never could afford to wait for an alternative to appear. Clarke's offer was the first I got, and so I accepted it without hesitation. Man's fate, I believed early, comes from his own heart; and this heart, as I learned later, is not programmed for him by his DNA. The conditions under which I was taken on demonstrated to me, however, the precarious position of a practitioner of pure scientific research—but is there such a thing?—in a medical school. There were, for instance, two kindly surgeons who had received a grant to study thrombosis and embolism, two important clinical complications of undoubted interest to surgery. Since biochemistry then was highly quoted on the medical stock market, a biochemist was hired to help them consume the meager gift. As I was that biochemist, I took the direction of studying the mechanism of blood coagulation: a biological system that has remained fascinating to this very day, and one from which the natural philosopher can learn as much as the natural scientist. With three joint publications the obolus was paid. From then on I was a free agent, and have remained one until very recently, when a much worse and more degrading form of servitude, namely to the public hand doling out the research money, made itself felt. But of this more will be said later.

In any event, between 1936 and 1948 I published a large number of papers on various aspects of the coagulation of blood, first unaided and later with the help of several gifted younger colleagues. The manner in which the animal organism manages and regulates the fluidity of its circulating blood presents a most interesting and instructive biological dilemma. I have tried to state it in the opening sentences of the lecture on the biochemistry of blood clotting that I gave to the Columbia medical students between 1942 and 1957. "Blood coagulation is an eminently protective mechanism, but there is a curious antinomy: blood must stay liquid in circulation; it must clot when shed. Otherwise, there are indications of pathological conditions." In all of my lectures, on many different topics, I have tried to stress the dialectical character of the life processes. One-half of a generation of physicians must have heard me; but I wonder how much of an impression I made.

Our work in this field gained quite a bit of recognition at that time; but it now seems to be forgotten. This is one of the many wilted flowers forming the bunch that lent its name to the title of this chapter. To be a pioneer in science has lost much of its attraction: significant scientific facts and, even more, fruitful scientific concepts pale into oblivion long before their potential value has been utilized. New facts, new concepts keep crowding in and are in turn, within a year or two, displaced by even newer ones. We worked on the activation of clotting by tissue lipids; we isolated and purified the tissue factor that triggers the physiological coagulation process, the so-called thromboplastic protein; we were among the first to introduce the anticoagulant heparin into clinical application, studied its mode of action, and discovered that circulating heparin can be inhibited by the injection of protamine. I shall mention here only one review article on blood coagulation that I wrote in 1944.

It is quite possible that the clotting of blood represents only one example of coagulation processes of a much more general biological importance. In what manner the living organism controls these coagulation processes is completely unknown. One may assume that the various factors that constitute the clotting phenomenon, although continually formed and destroyed and continually acting on each other, are held in a delicate equilibrium. This is, in fact, what constitutes both the difficulty and the fascination of the problem: the difficulty, because it is a borderline problem, involving some of the most refractory and least explored substances and reactions; the fascination, because in the coagulation of blood there is brought into the open, as it were, one of the innumerable systems through which the organism maintains, by predetermined oscillations, the condition of life.

What I have taught about all this may be outdated and surpassed, but not what I have learned from it. This is, in fact, the great predicament of the scientist: that what he leaves behind is his experiment, not his experience.

The lipids—those intriguing and complicated fatlike cell constituents whose real biological function still is obscure—play an important role in blood clotting. In addition, other representatives of this class formed the object of my initial research work, as I mentioned in the first section of this account. It was natural for me to continue work in that direction, as well. There were quite a few panels to this polyptych. One had to do with the chemistry of various lipids, work that went on to the middle Sixties. Another line dealt with a group of important high-molecular cell components designated as lipoproteins. This is the form—a complex combination with certain proteins—in which some of the lipids occur in the body. I wrote one of the first reviews on the subject. Clarke's esteem for me, never at fever heat, was increased considerably by that article; he told me that he found it written most amusingly— which shows that even lipids can be funny to the prepared mind.

Another series of investigations, which at that time had the charm of great novelty, concerned itself with the metabolism of the phospholipids. The radioactive phosphorus isotope ^{32}P was beginning to be available, although with difficulty. It was simultaneously used for such metabolic studies by a few other people, especially by Camillo Artom, a charming, lovable man, dried and concentrated by the sun of Sicily, but swept by the turbulent hurricanes of our century all the way to Winston-Salem, North Carolina. When I took up this work, one had to prepare one's own radioactive phosphorus, and I was helped in this home-industry alchemy by a young Columbia physicist, John Dunning, who was later to go on to a distinguished career. Although we were excited at that time, the results, as I look back on them, were uninspiring: it was to be expected that the different phosphorylated lipids of the body were not all formed at the same rate. Were I to expose the details of our findings to the uninitiated, they would perhaps say what a Shah of Persia is reputed to have answered when refusing an invitation from Emperor Franz Joseph to attend a horse race: "That one horse runs faster than another, I have always known. And I don't care to know which." It is, however, the very business of science to "know which." At any rate, I thought so when I was young, although much later I began to change my mind.

There was, however, a curious by-product of the work: I published the first synthesis of a radioactive organic compound. The few times I tried to preen myself on this feat, I encountered angry disbelief and ridicule. But there it is: "Synthesis of a radioactive organic compound: alpha-glycerophosphoric acid."

A few more dusty specimens out of my mournful herbarium, and I shall have done. Blood clotting, lipids, lipoproteins, and radioactive tracers were not the only things on which I worked. I should like to mention three more areas of research. We did considerable work on the inositols, a group of sugarlike substances, of which one is nearly ubiquitous in living nature and is often listed among the vitamins. We worked on the biological fate of the hydroxy amino acids. We also studied the mechanisms of the inhibition of mitosis.

In everything I did I was impressed by the marvel of the cell, in which I saw nothing but order and beauty. I did not believe that we could ever unravel the plan of construction in which cohesion and crowding were only two of the many elements that we were forced to destroy in order to investigate them. Although I am now told that this plan has become clear to us, I cannot help feeling that it is not what I was dreaming of in those long-gone days. My laboratory was one of the first to prepare mitochondria and look at their chemistry, and also to use the high-speed centrifuge to isolate the organelles of the cytoplasm, such as the microsomes. It is not surprising that a little later, when I got a group of laboratories of my own, I called them the Cell Chemistry Laboratory.

This far from complete list of my activities covers the first twelve years of my stay at Columbia. The more than sixty regular papers published during that period dealt with a very wide field of biochemistry, as it was then understood; and a few of them may even have contributed a little to the advance

of the science, which, at that time, was still slow, i.e., it had human proportions. The work was done with very little outside support: a small grant from
the Markle Foundation and, during the war years, a little money from the
Office of Scientific Research and Development. There was no publicity; I
have never given a press interview. In fact, the "gentlemen of the press"
have, on the whole, stayed away from me: a rare instance of the rabbit hyp-
notizing the snakes.

All was done with human hands: four graduate students, one or two postdocs, one technician. Almost the only use of electricity was for rather prim-
itive centrifuges. Substances still were isolated, and even crystallized, in a
visible form. The marvelous power of chemistry to demythologize and sub-
stantialize mysterious phenomena of nature was invoked. No claims were
made that went beyond the evidence of reality. No questions were asked that
only God can answer, nor were answers given on His behalf. No attempt was
made to improve on nature.

Nevertheless, when I look back on what I did during those miraculous
years, there come to mind the words ascribed to St. Thomas Aquinas: *Omnia
quae scripsi paleae mihi videntur.* All he had written seemed to him as chaff.
When I was young, I was required—and it was easy—to go back to the origins of our science. The bibliographies of chemical and biological papers
often included references to work done forty or fifty years earlier. One felt
oneself part of a gently growing tradition, growing at a rate that the human
mind could encompass, vanishing at a rate that it could apprehend. Now,
however, in our miserable scientific mass society, nearly all discoveries are
born dead; papers are tokens in a power game, evanescent reflections on the
screen of a spectator sport, news items that do not outlive the day on which
they appeared. Our sciences have become forcing houses for a market that
in reality does not exist, creating, with the concomitant complete break in
tradition, a truly Babylonian confusion of mind and language. Nowadays, scientific tradition hardly reaches back for more than three or four years. The
proscenium looks the same as before, but the scenery keeps on changing as
in a fever dream; no sooner is one backdrop in place than it is replaced by an
entirely different one.

The only thing that experience can now teach is that it has become
worthless. One could ask whether a fund of knowledge, such as a scientific
discipline, can exist without a living tradition. In any event, in many areas of
science which I am able to survey, this tradition has disappeared. It is, hence,
no exaggeration and no coquettish humility if I conclude that the work we
did thirty or forty years ago—with all the engagement that honest effort
could provide—is dead and gone.

Thomas Merton

'38 COLUMBIA COLLEGE, '39 MA

Influenced by his study of medieval philosophy, the essayist and poet Thomas Merton converted to Catholicism shortly after finishing his undergraduate work. He later became a Trappist monk and wrote extensively on a variety of subjects until his death in 1968. In 1948 Merton penned The Seven Storey Mountain, *a surprise best-seller that recounted, among other things, the tale of his conversion—and also provides this selection.*

I t was bright, icy-cold afternoon when, having passed Nantucket Light, we first saw the long, low, yellow shoreline of Long Island shining palely in the December sun. But when we entered New York harbor the lights were already coming on, glittering like jewels in the hard, clear buildings. The great, debonair city that was both young and old, and wise and innocent, shouted in the winter night as we passed the Battery and started up the North River. And I was glad, very glad to be an immigrant once again.

I came down on to the dock with a great feeling of confidence and possessiveness. "New York, you are mine! I love you!" It is the glad embrace she gives her lovers, the big, wild city: but I guess ultimately it is for their ruin. It certainly did not prove to be any good for me.

With my mind in the ferment in which it was, I thought for a moment of registering for courses at the New School for Social Research, in the shiny, black building on Twelfth Street, but I was easily persuaded that I had better finish out a regular university course and get a degree. And therefore I entered upon all the complicated preambles to admission to Columbia.

I came out of the subway at 116th Street. All around the campus were piles of dirty snow, and I smelled the wet, faintly exhilarating air of Morningside Heights in the winter time. The big, ugly buildings faced the world with a kind of unpretentious purposefulness, and people hurried in and out the glass doors with none of the fancy garments of the Cambridge undergraduate—no multicolored ties and blazers and scarfs, no tweeds and riding breeches, no affectations of any kind, but only the plain, drab overcoats of city masses. You got the impression that all these people were at once more earnest and more humble, poorer, smarter perhaps, certainly more diligent than those I had known at Cambridge.

Columbia was, for the most part, stripped of fancy academic ritual. The caps and gowns were reserved for occasions which, as a matter of fact, nobody really had to attend. I only got mixed up in one of them purely by accident, several months after I had acquired my degree, rolled up in a cardboard container, through one of the windows of the post-office-like registration bureau in University Hall.

Compared with Cambridge, this big sooty factory was full of light and fresh air. There was a kind of genuine intellectual vitality in the air—at least relatively speaking. Perhaps the reason was that most of the students had to work hard to pay for every classroom hour. Therefore they appreciated what they got, even when there was not much in it to appreciate. Then there was the big, bright, shiny, new library, with a complicated system of tickets and lights, at the main loan desk: and there I soon came out with a great armful of things, books which excited me more than I now can understand. I think it was not the books themselves but my own sense of energy and resolve that made me think everything was more interesting than it was.

What for instance, did I find to enthrall me in a book about esthetics by a man called Yrjö Hirn? I cannot remember. And even in spite of my almost congenital dislike for Platonism, I was happy with the *Enneads* of Plotinus, in Marsilio Ficino's Latin translation. The truth is that there is a considerable difference between Plato and Plotinus, but I am not enough of a philosopher to know what it is. Thank God I shall never again have to try and find out, either. But anyway, I dragged this huge volume into the subway and out on the Long Island railroad to the house in Douglaston, where I had a room with a big glass-enclosed bookcase full of Communist pamphlets and books on psychoanalysis, in which the little Vulgate I had once bought in Rome lay neglected and out of place . . .

For some reason I became intensely interested in Daniel Defoe, and read his whole life and dipped into most of the strange journalistic jobs of writing which he did besides *Robinson Crusoe*. I made a hero for myself out of Jonathan Swift, because of his writing. Towards May of that year I remember going in to the Columbia Bookstore and selling them a copy of T. S. Eliot's essays and a lot of other things which I was getting rid of in a conscious reaction against artiness—as if all that were too bourgeois for my serious and practical new-self.

Then, because of the wide general curriculum of an American university, which, instead of trying to teach you any one thing completely, strives to give its students a superficial knowledge of everything, I found myself mildly interested in things like geology and economics, and interiorly cursing a big, vague course in current events called "Contemporary Civilization," which was imposed on all the sophomores whether they liked it or not.

Soon I was full of all the economic and pseudo-scientific jargon appropriate to a good Columbia man, and was acclimated to the new atmosphere which I found so congenial. That was true. Columbia, compared with Cambridge, was a friendly place. When you had to go and see a professor or an advisor or a dean about something, he would tell you, more or less simply, what you needed to know. The only trouble was that you usually had to wait around for about half an hour before you got a chance to see anybody. But once you did, there were no weird evasions and none of the pompous beating about the bush, mixed up with subtle academic allusions and a few dull witticisms which was what you were liable to get out of almost anybody at Cambridge, where everybody cultivated some special manner of his own, and had his own individual and peculiar style. I suppose it is something that you have to expect around a university, this artificiality. For a man to be absolutely sincere with generation after generation of students requires either supernatural simplicity or, in the natural order, a kind of heroic humility.

There was—and still is—one man at Columbia, or rather one among several, who was most remarkable for this kind of heroism. I mean Mark Van Doren.

The first semester I was at Columbia, just after my twentieth birthday, in the winter of 1935, Mark was giving part of the "English sequence" in one of those rooms in Hamilton Hall with windows looking out between the big columns on to the wired-in track on South Field. There were twelve or fifteen people with more or less unbrushed hair, most of them with glasses, lounging around. One of them was my friend Robert Gibney.

It was a class in English literature, and it had no special bias of any kind. It was simply about what it was supposed to be about: the English literature of the eighteenth century. And in it literature was treated, not as history, not as sociology, not as economics, not as a series of case-histories in psychoanalysis but, *mirabile dictu,* simply as literature.

I thought to myself, who is this excellent man Van Doren who being employed to teach literature, teaches just that: talks about writing and about books and poems and plays: does not get off on a tangent about the biographies of the poets or novelists: does not read into their poems a lot of subjective messages which were never there? Who is this man who does not have to fake and cover up a big gulf of ignorance by teaching a lot of opinions and conjectures and useless facts that belong to some other subject? Who is this who really loves what he has to teach, and does not secretly detest all literature, and abhor poetry, while pretending to be a professor of it?

That Columbia should have in it men like this who, instead of subtly destroying all literature by burying and concealing it under a mass of irrelevancies, really purified and educated the perceptions of their students by teaching them how to read a book and how to tell a good book from a bad, genuine writing from falsity and pastiche: all this gave me a deep respect for my new university.

Mark would come into the room and, without any fuss, would start talking about whatever was to be talked about. Most of the time he asked questions. His questions were very good, and if you tried to answer them intelligently, you found yourself saying excellent things that you did not know you knew, and that you had not, in fact, known before. He had "educed" them from you by his question. His classes were literally "education"—they brought things out of you, they made your mind produce its own explicit ideas. Do not think that Mark was simply priming his students with thoughts of his own, and then making the thought stick to their minds by getting them to give it back to him as their own. Far from it. What he did have was the gift of communicating to them something of his own vital interest in things, something of his manner of approach: but the results were sometimes quite unexpected—and by that I mean good in a way that he had not anticipated, casting lights that he had not himself foreseen.

Now a man who can go for year after year—although Mark was young then and is young now—without having any time to waste in flattering and cajoling his students with any kind of a fancy act, or with jokes, or with storms of temperament, or periodic tirades—whole classes spent in threats and imprecations, to disguise the fact that the professor himself has come in unprepared—one who can do without all these non-essentials both honors his vocation and makes it fruitful. Not only that, but his vocation, in return, perfects and ennobles him. And that is the way it should be, even in the natural order: how much more so in the order of grace!

Mark, I know, is no stranger to the order of grace: but considering his work as teacher merely as a mission on the natural level—I can see that Providence was using him as an instrument more directly than he realized. As far as I can see, the influence of Mark's sober and sincere intellect, and his manner of dealing with his subject with perfect honesty and objectivity and without

evasions, was remotely preparing my mind to receive the good seed of scholastic philosophy. And there is nothing strange in this, for Mark himself was familiar at least with some of the modern scholastics, like Maritain and Gilson, and
he was a friend of the American neo-Thomists, Mortimer Adler and Richard
McKeon, who had started out at Columbia but had had to move to Chicago,
because Columbia was not ripe enough to know what to make of them.

The truth is that Mark's temper was profoundly scholastic in the sense
that his clear mind looked directly for the quiddities of things, and sought
being and substance under the covering of accident and appearances. And
for him poetry was, indeed, a virtue of the practical intellect, and not simply
a vague spilling of the emotions, wasting the soul and perfecting none of our
essential powers.

It was because of this virtual scholasticism of Mark's that he would never
permit himself to fall into the naive errors of those who try to read some
favorite private doctrine into every poet they like of every nation or every age.
And Mark abhorred the smug assurance with which second-rate left-wing
critics find adumbrations of dialectical materialism in everyone who ever
wrote from Homer and Shakespeare to whomever they happen to like in
recent times. If the poet is to their fancy, then he is clearly seen to be preaching the class struggle. If they do not like him, then they are able to show that
he was really a forefather of fascism. And all their literary heroes are revolutionary leaders, and all their favorite villains are capitalists and Nazis.

It was a very good thing for me that I ran into someone like Mark Van
Doren at that particular time, because in my new reverence for
Communism, I was in danger of docilely accepting any kind of stupidity, provided I thought it was something that paved the way to the Elysian fields of
classless society.

*   *   *

There was a sort of a legend in New York, fostered by the Hearst papers,
that Columbia was a hotbed of Communists. All the professors and students
were supposed to be Reds, except perhaps the president of the university,
Nicholas Murray Butler, living in solitary misery in his big brick house on
Morningside Drive. I have no doubt that the poor old man's misery was real,
and that his isolation from most of the university was very real. But the statement that everybody in the university was a Communist was far from true.

I know that, as far as the faculty was concerned, Columbia University was
built up in concentric rings, about a solid core of well-meaning, unenlightened
stuffiness, the veterans, the beloved of the trustees and the alumni, and
Butler's intellectual guard of honor. Then there was an inner circle of sociologists and economists and lawyers, whose world was a mystery to me, and who
exercised a powerful influence in Washington under the New Deal. About all

of them and their satellites I never knew anything, except that they were certainly not Communists. Then there was the little galaxy of pragmatists in the school of philosophy, and all the thousands of their pale spiritual offspring in the jungles of Teachers College and New College. They were not Communists either. They cast a mighty influence over the whole American Middle West, and were to a great extent conditioned by the very people whom they were trying to condition, so that Teachers College always stood for colorlessness and mediocrity and plain, hapless behaviorism. These three groups were then the real Columbia. I suppose they all prided themselves on their liberalism, but that is precisely what they were: "liberals," not Communists, and they brought down upon their heads all the scorn the Communists could pour upon them for their position of habitual compromise.

I do not understand much about politics. Besides, it would be outside the scope of my present vocation if I tried to make any political analysis of anything. But I can say that there were, at that time, quite a few Communists or Communist sympathizers among the undergraduates, and especially in Columbia College where most of the smartest students were Reds.

The Communists had control of the college paper and were strong on some of the other publications and on the Student Board. But this campus Communism was more a matter of noise than anything else, at least as far as the rank and file were concerned.

The Spectator was always starting some kind of a fight and calling for mass-meetings and strikes and demonstrations. Then the fraternity boys, who elected to play "Fascist" in this children's game, would get up in the classroom buildings and turn the firehoses on the people who were standing around the Communist speaker. Then the whole thing would come out in the New York *Journal* that evening and all the alumni would choke on their mock turtle soup down at the Columbia Club.

By the time I arrived at Columbia, the Communists had taken to holding their meetings at the sundial on 116th Street, in the middle of the wide-open space between the old domed library and South Field. This was well out of the range of the firehoses in the Journalism building and Hamilton Hall. The first meeting I went to, there, was very tame. It was against Italian Fascism. There were one or two speeches—by students practising the art. Those who stood around were mostly members of the National Students' League, who were there out of a sense of duty or partisanship. A few curious passers-by stopped a while on their way to the subway. There was not much excitement. A girl with a mop of black hair stood by, wearing a placard pronouncing some kind of a judgement on Fascism. Someone sold me a pamphlet.

Presently I picked out the quiet, earnest, stocky little man in the grey overcoat, a hatless, black-haired Communist from downtown, who was running the affair. He was not a student. He was the real article. This was his assignment: forming and training the material that offered itself to him at Columbia. He had an assistant, a younger man, and the two of them were kept pretty busy. I went up to him and started to talk. When he actually listened to me, and paid attention to my ideas, and seemed to approve of my interest, I was very flattered. He got my name and address and told me to come to the meetings of the N.S.L.

Soon I was walking up and down in front of the Casa Italiana wearing two placards, front and back, accusing Italy of injustice in the invasion of Ethiopia that had either just begun or was just about to begin. Since the accusation was manifestly true, I felt a certain satisfaction in thus silently proclaiming it as a picket. There were two or three of us. For an hour and a half or two hours we walked up and down the pavement of Amsterdam Avenue, in the grey afternoon, bearing our dire accusations, while the warm sense of justification in our hearts burned high, even in spite of the external boredom.

For during that whole time no one even came near the Casa Italiana, and I even began to wonder if there were anyone at all inside it. The only person who approached us was a young Italian who looked as if he might be a Freshman football player, and tried to get into an argument. But he was too dumb. He went away mumbling that the Hearst papers were very excellent because of the great prizes which they offered, in open competition, to their many readers.

I forget how the picketing ended: whether we waited for someone else to come and take over, or whether we just decided we had done enough and took off our signs and went away. But any way I had the feeling that I had done something that was good, if only as a gesture: for it certainly did not seem to have accomplished anything. But at least I had made a kind of public confession of faith. I had said that I was against war—against all war. That I believed wars to be unjust. That I thought they could only ruin and destroy the world. . . . Someone will ask where I managed to get all that out of the placard I was carrying. But as far as I remember, that was the party line that year—at least it was the line that was handed out to the public.

I can still hear the tired, determined chanting of students at campus demonstrations: "Books, not Battleships!" "No More WAR!" There was no distinction made. It was war as such that we hated and said we wanted no more of. We wanted books, not battleships, we said. We were all burned up with the thirst for knowledge, for intellectual and spiritual improvement. And here the wicked capitalists were forcing the government to enrich them by buying armaments and building battleships and planes and tanks, when the money ought to be spent on volumes of lovely cultural books for us students. Here we were on the threshold of life, we cried: our hands were reaching out for education and culture. Was the government going to put a gun in them, and send us off on another imperialistic war? And the line of reasoning behind all this definitely held, in 1935, that all war was imperialistic war. War, according to the party line in 1935, was an exclusively capitalist amusement. It was purely and simply a device to enrich the armament manufacturers and the international bankers, coining fortunes for them with the blood of the workers and students.

One of the big political events of that spring was a "Peace Strike." I was never quite able to understand by virtue of what principle a student could manage to consider himself on strike by cutting a class. Theoretically, I suppose, it amounted to a kind of defiance of authority: but it was a defiance that did not cost anybody anything except perhaps the student himself. And besides, I was quite used to cutting classes whenever I felt like it, and it seemed to me rather bombastic to dress it up with the name of "strike." However, on another of those grey days, we went on "strike," and this time there were several hundred people in the gymnasium, and even one or two members of the faculty got up on the platform and said something.

They were not all Communists, but all the speeches had more or less the same burden: that it was absurd to even think of such a thing as a just war in our time. Nobody wanted war: there was no justification for any war of any kind on the part of anybody, and consequently, if a war did start, it would certainly be the result of a capitalist plot, and should be firmly resisted by everybody with any kind of a conscience.

That was just the kind of a position that attracted me, that appealed to my mind at that time. It seemed to cut across all complexities by its sweeping and uncompromising simplicity. All war was simply unjust, and that was that. The thing to do was to fold your arms and refuse to fight. If everybody did that, there would be no more wars.

That cannot seriously have been the Communist position; but at least I thought it was. And anyway, the theme of this particular meeting was the "Oxford Pledge." The words of that pledge were written out in huge letters on a great big placard that hung limply in the air over the speakers' platform, and all the speakers waved their arms at it and praised it, and repeated it, and urged it upon us, and in the end we all took it, and acclaimed it, and solemnly pledged ourselves to it.

Perhaps everybody has, by now, forgotten what the Oxford Pledge was. It was a resolution that had been passed by the Oxford Union, which said that they, these particular Oxford undergraduates, simply would refuse to fight for King and Country in any war whatever. The fact that a majority of those who happened to be at a meeting of a university debating society, one evening, voted that way certainly did not commit the whole university, or even any one of the voters, to what the resolution said, and it was only other student groups, all over the world, that had transformed it into a "pledge." And this "pledge" was then taken by hundreds of thousands of students in all kinds of schools and colleges and universities with some of the solemnity that might make it look as if they intended to bind themselves by it—the way we were doing at Columbia that day. All this was usually inspired by the Reds, who were very fond of the Oxford Pledge that year. . . .

However, the next year the Spanish Civil war broke out. The first thing I heard about that war was that one of the chief speakers at the 1935 Peace Strike, and one who had been so enthusiastic about this glorious pledge that we would never fight in any war, was now fighting for the Red Army against Franco, and all the N.S.L. and the Young Communists were going around picketing everybody who seemed to think that the war in Spain was not holy and sacrosanct and a crusade for the workers against Fascism.

The thing that perplexes me is: what did all the people in the gymnasium at Columbia, including myself, think we were doing when we took that pledge? What did a pledge mean to us? What was, in our minds, the basis of such an obligation? How could we be obliged? Communists don't believe in any such thing as a natural law, or the law of conscience, although they seem to. They are always crying out against the injustice of capitalism and yet, as a matter of fact, they very often say in the same breath that the very concept of justice is simply a myth devised by the ruling classes to beguile and deceive the proletariat.

As far as I can remember, it seems that what most of us thought we were doing, when we took that pledge, was simply making a public statement, and doing so in sufficient numbers, as we hoped, to influence politicians. There was no intention of binding ourselves under any obligation. The notion never even occurred to us. Most of us probably secretly thought we were gods anyway, and therefore the only law we had to obey was our own ineffable little wills. It was sufficient to say that we did not intend to go to war for anybody: and that was enough. And if, afterwards, we changed our minds—well, were we not our own gods?

It's a nice, complex universe, the Communist universe: it gravitates towards stability and harmony and peace and order on the poles of an opportunism that is completely irresponsible and erratic. Its only law is, it will do whatever seems to be profitable to itself at the moment. However, that seems to have become the rule of all modern political parties. I have nothing to say about it. I do not profess to be either amazed or broken-hearted that such a thing should be possible. Let the dead bury their dead: they have certainly got enough to bury. It is the fruit of their philosophy that they should: and that is all that they need to be reminded of. But you cannot make them believe it.

I had formed a kind of an ideal picture of Communism in my mind, and now I found that the reality was a disappointment. I suppose my daydreams were theirs also. But neither dream is true.

I had thought that Communists were calm, strong, definite people, with very clear ideas as to what was wrong with everything. Men who knew the solution, and were ready to pay any price to apply the remedy. And their remedy was simple and just and clean, and it would definitely solve all the problems of society, and make men happy, and bring the world peace.

It turned out that some of them indeed were calm, and strong, and had a kind of peace of mind that came from definite convictions and from a real devotion to their cause, out of motives of a kind of vague natural charity and sense of justice. But the trouble with their convictions was that they were mostly strange, stubborn prejudices, hammered into their minds by the incantation of statistics, and without any solid intellectual foundation. And having decided that God is an invention of the ruling classes, and having excluded Him, and all moral order with Him, they were trying to establish some kind of a moral system by abolishing all morality in its very source. Indeed, the very word morality was something repugnant to them. They wanted to make everything right, and they denied all the criteria given us for distinguishing between right and wrong.

And so it is an indication of the intellectual instability of Communism, and the weakness of its philosophical foundations, that most Communists are, in actual fact, noisy and shallow and violent people, torn to pieces by petty jealousies and factional hatreds and envies and strife. They shout and show off and generally give the impression that they cordially detest one another even when they are supposed to belong to the same sect. And as for the intersectional hatred prevailing between all the different branches of radicalism, it is far bitterer and more virulent than the more or less sweeping and abstract hatred of the big general enemy, capitalism. All this is something of a clue to such things as the wholesale executions of Communists who have moved their chairs to too prominent a position in the ante-chamber of Utopia which the Soviet Union is supposed to be.

❉   ❉   ❉

My active part in the world revolution was not very momentous. It lasted, in all, about three months. I picketed the Casa Italiana, I went to the Peace Strike, and I think I made some kind of a speech in the big classroom on the second floor of the Business School, where the N.S.L. had their meetings. Maybe it was a speech on Communism in England—a topic about which I knew absolutely nothing; in that case, I was loyally living up to the tradition of Red oratory. I sold some pamphlets and magazines. I don't know what was in them, but I could gather their contents from the big black cartoons of capitalists drinking the blood of workers.

Finally, the Reds had a party. And, of all places, in a Park Avenue apartment. This irony was the only amusing thing about it. And after all it was not so ironical. It was the home of some Barnard girl who belonged to the Young Communist League and her parents had gone away for the week-end. I could get a fair picture of them from the way the furniture looked, and from the volumes of Nietszche and Schopenhauer and Oscar Wilde and Ibsen that filled the bookcases. And there was a big grand piano on which someone played Beethoven while the Reds sat around on the floor. Later we had a sort of Boy Scout campfire group in the living room, singing heavy Communist songs, including that delicate anti-religious classic, "There'll be pie in the sky when you die."

One little fellow with buck teeth and horn-rimmed glasses pointed to two windows in a corner of one of the rooms. They commanded a whole sweep of Park Avenue in one direction and the cross-town street in another. "What a place for a machine-gun nest," he observed. The statement came from a middle-class adolescent. It was made in a Park Avenue apartment. He had evidently never even seen a machine-gun, except in the movies. If there had been a revolution going on at the time, he would have probably been among the first to get his head knocked off by the revolutionists. And in any case he, like all the rest of us, had just finished making the famous Oxford Pledge that he would not fight in any war whatever . . .

One reason why I found the party so dull was that nobody was very enthusiastic about getting something to drink except me. Finally one of the girls encouraged me, in a businesslike sort of a way, to go out and buy bottles of rye at a liquor store around the corner on Third Avenue, and when I had drunk some of the contents she invited me into a room and signed me up as a member of the Young Communist League. I took the party name of Frank Swift. When I looked up from the paper the girl had vanished like a not too inspiring dream, and I went home on the Long Island Railroad with the secret of a name which I have been too ashamed to reveal to anyone until this moment when I am beyond humiliation.

I only went to one meeting of the Young Communist League, in the apartment of one of the students. It was a long discussion as to why Comrade So-and-so did not come to any of the meetings. The answer was that his father was too bourgeois to allow it. So after that, I walked out into the empty street, and let the meeting end however it would.

It was good to be in the fresh air. My footsteps rang out on the dark stones. At the end of the street, the pale amber light of a bar-room beckoned lovingly to me from under the steel girders of the elevated. The place was empty. I got a glass of beer and lit a cigarette and tasted the first sweet moment of silence and relief.

And that was the end of my days as a great revolutionary. I decided that it would be wiser if I just remained a "fellow-traveler." The truth is that my inspiration to do something for the good of mankind had been pretty feeble and abstract from the start. I was still interested in doing good for only one person in the world—myself.

May came, and all the trees on Long Island were green, and when the train from the city got past Bayside and started across the meadows to Douglaston, you could see the pale, soft haze of summer beginning to hang over the bay, and count the boats that had been set afloat again after the winter, and were riding jauntily at their moorings off the end of the little dock. And now in the lengthening evenings the dining room was still light with the rays of the sun when Pop came home for dinner, slamming the front door and whooping at the dog and smacking the surface of the hall table with the evening paper to let everybody know that he had arrived.

Soon John Paul was home from his school in Pennsylvania, and my exams were over, and we had nothing to do but go swimming and hang around the house playing hot records. And in the evening we would wander off to some appalling movie where we nearly died of boredom. We did not have a car, and my uncle would not let us touch the family Buick. It would not have done me any good anyway, because I never learned to drive. So most of the time, we would get a ride to Great Neck and then walk back the two or three miles along the wide road when the show was over.

Why did we ever go to all those movies? That is another mystery. But I think John Paul and I and our various friends must have seen all the movies that were produced, without exception, from 1934 to 1937. And most of them were simply awful. What is more, they got worse from week to week and from month to month, and day after day we hated them more. My ears are ringing with the false, gay music that used to announce the Fox movietone and the Paramount newsreels with the turning camera that slowly veered its aim right at your face. My mind still echoes with the tones of Pete Smith and Fitzpatrick of the Travel-talks saying, "And now farewell to beautiful New South Wales."

And yet I confess a secret loyalty to the memory of my great heroes: Chaplin, W. C. Fields, Harpo Marx, and many others whose name I have forgotten. But their pictures were rare, and for the rest, we found ourselves perversely admiring the villains and detesting the heroes. The truth is that the villains were almost always the better actors. We were delighted with everything they did. We were almost always in danger of being thrown out of the theater for our uproarious laughter at scenes that were supposed to be most affecting, tender and appealing to the finer elements in the human soul—the tears of Jackie Cooper, the brave smile of Alice Faye behind the bars of a jail.

The movies soon turned into a kind of hell for me and my brother and indeed for all my closest friends. We could not keep away from them. We were hypnotized by those yellow flickering lights and the big posters of Don Ameche. Yet as soon as we got inside, the suffering of having to sit and look at such colossal stupidities became so acute that we sometimes actually felt physically sick. In the end, it got so that I could hardly sit through a show. It was like lighting cigarettes and taking a few puffs and throwing them away, appalled by the vile taste in one's mouth.

In 1935 and 1936, without my realizing it, life was slowly, once more, becoming almost intolerable.

In the fall of 1935, John Paul went to Cornell, and I went back to Columbia, full of all kinds of collegiate enthusiasms, so that in a moment of madness I even gave my name for the Varsity lightweight crew. After a couple of days on the Harlem River and then on the Hudson, when we tried to row to Yonkers and back in what seemed to me to be a small hurricane, I decided that I did not wish to die so young, and after that carefully avoided the Boat-House all the rest of the time I was in college.

However, October is a fine and dangerous season in America. It is dry and cool and the land is wild with red and gold and crimson, and all the lassitudes of August have seeped out of your blood, and you are full of ambition. It is a wonderful time to begin anything at all. You go to college, and every course in the catalogue looks wonderful. The names of the subjects all seem to lay open the way to a new world. Your arms are full of new, clean notebooks, waiting to be filled. You pass through the doors of the library, and the smell of thousands of well-kept books makes your head swim with a clean and subtle pleasure. You have a new hat, a new sweater perhaps, or a whole new suit. Even the nickels and the quarters in your pocket feel new, and the buildings shine in the glorious sun.

In this season of resolutions and ambitions, in 1935, I signed up for courses in Spanish and German and Geology and Constitutional Law and French Renaissance Literature and I forget what else besides. And I started to work for *The Spectator* and the yearbook and *The Review* and I continued to work for *Jester* as I had already done the spring before. And I found myself pledging one of the fraternities.

It was a big, gloomy house behind the new library. On the ground floor there was a pool-room as dark as a morgue, a dining room, and some stairs led up to a big dark wainscoted living room where they held dances and beer-parties. Above that were two floors of bedrooms where telephones were constantly ringing and all day long somebody or other was singing in the showerbath. And there was somewhere in the building a secret room which I must not reveal to you, reader, at any price, even at the cost of life itself. And there I was eventually initiated. The initiation with its various tortures lasted about a week, and I cheerfully accepted penances which, if they were imposed in a monastery, for a supernatural motive, and for some real reason, instead of for no reason at all, would cause such an uproar that all religious houses would be closed and the Catholic Church would probably have a hard time staying in the country.

When that was over I had a gold and enamel pin on my shirt. My name was engraved on the back of it, and I was quite proud of it for about a year, and then it went to the laundry on a shirt and never came back.

I suppose there were two reasons why I thought I ought to join a fraternity. One was the false one, that I thought it would help me to "make connections" as the saying goes, and get a marvelous job on leaving college. The other, truer one was that I imagined that I would thus find a multitude of occasions for parties and diversions, and that I would meet many very interesting young ladies at the dances that would be held at that mausoleum. Both these hopes turned out to be illusory. As a matter of fact, I think the only real explanation was that I was feeling the effects of October.

Anyway, when John Paul went to Cornell the whole family, except me, drove up to Ithaca in the Buick and came back with words and concepts that filled the house with a kind of collegiate tension for a couple of weeks to come. Everybody was talking about football and courses and fraternities.

As a matter of fact, John Paul's first year at Cornell turned out to be sad in the same way as my first year at Cambridge—a thing that was not long in becoming apparent, when the bills he could not pay began to show up at home. But it was even more obvious to me when I saw him again.

He was naturally a happy and optimistic sort of person and he did not easily get depressed. And he had a clear, quick intelligence and a character as sensitive as it was well-balanced. Now his intelligence seemed a little fogged with some kind of obscure, interior confusion, and his happiness was perverted by a sad, lost restlessness. Although he maintained all his interests and increased them, the increase was in extent, not in depth, and the result was a kind of scattering of powers, a dissipation of the mind and will in a variety of futile aims.

He stood for some time, with great uncertainty, on the threshold of a fraternity house at Cornell, and even let them put a pledge pin on him, and then after a couple of weeks he took it off again and ran away. And with three friends he rented a house on one of those steep, shady Ithaca streets, and after that the year was a long and sordid riot, from which he derived no satisfaction. They called the place Grand Hotel, and had stationery printed with that title, on which desultory and fragmentary letters would come to Douglaston, and fill everyone with unquiet. When he came back from Cornell, John Paul looked tired and disgusted.

I suppose it is true, at least theoretically, the brothers watch over one another and help one another along in the fraternity house. In my fraternity house at Columbia, I know that the wiser members used to get together and shake their heads a little when somebody was carrying his debauchery too far. And when there was any real trouble, the concern of the brothers was sincere and dramatic, but it was useless. And there is always trouble in a fraternity house. The trouble, which came in the year after I was initiated, was the disappearance of one of the brothers, whom we shall call Fred.

Fred was a tall, stoop-shouldered, melancholy individual, with dark hair growing low on his brows. He never had much to say, and he liked to go apart and drink in mournful solitude. The only vivid thing I remember about him was that he stood over me, during one of the peculiar ceremonies of the initiation, when all the pledges had to stuff themselves with bread and milk for a special reason. And while I tried with despairing efforts to get the huge mouthfuls swallowed down, this Fred was standing over me with woeful cries of: "EAT, EAT, EAT!" It must have been sometime after Christmas that he disappeared.

I came into the house one night, and they were sitting around in the leather chairs talking earnestly. "Where's Fred?" was the burden of the discussion. He had not been seen anywhere for a couple of days. Would his family be upset if someone called up his home to see if he was there? Evidently, but it had to be done: he had not gone home either. One of the brothers had long since visited all his usual haunts. People tried to reconstruct the situation in which he had last been seen. With what dispositions had he last walked out of the front door. The usual ones, of course: silence, melancholy, the probable intention of getting drunk. A week passed and Fred was not found. The earnest concern of the brothers was fruitless. The subject of Fred was more or less dropped and, after a month, most of us had forgotten it. After two months, the whole thing was finally settled.

"They found Fred," somebody told me.

"Yes? Where?"

"In Brooklyn."

"Is he all right?"

"No, he's dead. They found him in the Gowanus Canal."

"What did he do, jump in?"

"Nobody knows what he did. He'd been there a long time."

"How long?"

"I don't know, a couple of months. They figured out who it was from the fillings in his teeth."

It was a picture that was not altogether vague to me. Our famous course in Contemporary Civilization had involved me, one winter afternoon, in a visit to the Bellevue Morgue, where I had seen rows and rows of iceboxes containing the blue, swollen corpses of drowned men along with all the other human refuse of the big, evil city: The dead that had been picked up in the streets, ruined by raw alcohol. The dead that had been found starved and frozen lying where they had tried to sleep in a pile of old newspapers. The pauper dead from Randalls Island. The dope-fiend dead. The murdered dead. The run-over. The suicides. The dead Negroes and Chinese. The dead of venereal disease. The dead from unknown causes. The killed by gangsters. They would all be shipped for burial up the East River in a barge to one of those islands where they also burned garbage.

Contemporary Civilization! One of the last things we saw on the way out of the morgue was the hand of a man pickled in a jar, brown and vile. They were not sure whether he was a criminal or not, and they wanted to have some part of him, after they had sent the rest of him up to the ghats. In the autopsy room a man on the table with his trunk wide open pointed his sharp, dead nose at the ceiling. The doctors held his liver and kidneys in their hands and sprayed them over with a trickle of water from a little rubber hose. I have never forgotten the awful, clammy silence of the city morgue at Bellevue, where they collect the bodies of those who died of contemporary civilization, like Fred.

Nevertheless, during that year I was so busy and so immersed in activities and occupations that I had no time to think for very long on these things. The energy of that golden October and the stimulation of the cold, bright winter days when the wind swept down as sharp as knives from the shining Palisades kept driving me through the year in what seemed to be fine condition. I had never done so many different things at the same time or with such apparent success. I had discovered in myself something of a capacity for work and for activity and for enjoyment that I had never dreamed of. And everything began to come easy, as the saying goes.

It was not that I was really studying hard or working hard: but all of a sudden I had fallen into a kind of a mysterious knack of keeping a hundred different interests going in the air at the same time. It was a kind of a stupendous juggling act, a tour-de-force, and what surprised me most was that I managed to keep it up without collapsing. In the first place, I was carrying about eighteen points in my courses—the average amount. I had found out the simplest way of fulfilling the minimum requirements for each one.

Then there was the "Fourth Floor." The fourth floor of John Jay Hall was the place where all the offices of the student publications and the Glee Club and the Student Board and all the rest were to be found. It was the noisiest and most agitated part of the campus. It was not gay, exactly. And I hardly ever saw, anywhere, antipathies and contentions and jealousies at once so petty, so open and so sharp. The whole floor was constantly seething with the exchange of insults from office to office. Constantly, all day long, from morning to night, people were writing articles and drawing cartoons calling each other Fascists. Or else they were calling one another up on the phone and assuring one another in the coarsest terms of their undying hatred. It was all intellectual and verbal, as vicious as it could be, but it never became concrete, never descended into physical rage. For this reason, I think that it was all more or less of a game which everybody played for purposes that were remotely esthetic.

The campus was supposed to be, in that year, in a state of "intellectual ferment." Everybody felt and even said that there were an unusual number of brilliant and original minds in the college. I think that it was to some extent true. Ad Reinhardt was certainly the best artist that had ever drawn for *Jester*, perhaps for any other college magazine. His issues of *Jester* were real magazines. I think that in cover designs and layouts he could have given lessons to some of the art-editors downtown. Everything he put out was original, and it was also funny, because for the first time in years *Jester* had some real writers contributing to it, and was not just an anthology of the same stale and obscene jokes that have been circulating through the sluggish system of American college magazines for two generations. By now Reinhardt had graduated, and so had the editor of the 1935 *Spectator*, Jim Wechsler.

My first approach to the Fourth Floor had been rather circumspect, after the manner of Cambridge. I went to my adviser, Prof. McKee, and asked him how to go about it, and he gave me a letter of introduction to Leonard Robinson who was editor of *The Columbia Review*, the literary magazine. I don't know what Robinson would have made of a letter of introduction. Anyway, I never got to meeting him after all. When I went to the *Review* office I gave the note to Bob Giroux, an associate editor, and he looked at it and scratched his head some bit and told me to write something if I got an idea.

By 1936 Leonard Robinson had vanished. I always heard a lot about Robinson, and it all adds up to nothing very clear, so that I have always had the impression that he somehow lives in the trees. I pray that he may go to heaven.

As for *Review*, Robert Paul Smith and Robert Giroux were both editing it together, and it was good. I don't know whether you would use the term "ferment" in their case, but Smith and Giroux were both good writers. Also,

Giroux was a Catholic and a person strangely placid for the Fourth Floor. He had no part in its feuds and, as a matter of fact, you did not see him around there very much. John Berryman was more or less the star on *Review* that year. He was the most earnest-looking man on the campus.

There was not an office on that floor where I did not have something to do, except the Glee Club and Student Board and the big place where all the football coaches had their desks. I was writing stories for *Spectator*, and columns that were supposed to be funny; I was writing things for the year-book and trying to sell copies of it—a thankless task. The yearbook was the one thing nobody wanted: it was expensive and dull. Of this I eventually became editor, without any evident benefit to myself or to the book or to Columbia or to the world.

I was never particularly drawn to the Varsity show: but they had a piano in their room, and the room was almost always empty, so I used to go in there and play furious jazz, after the manner I had taught myself—a manner which offended every ear but my own. It was a way of letting off steam—a form of athletics if you like. I have ruined more than one piano by this method.

The place where I was busiest was the *Jester* office. Nobody really worked there, they just congregated about noontime and beat violently with the palms of their hands on the big empty filing cabinets, making a thunderous sound that echoed up and down the corridor, and was sometimes answered from the *Review* office across the hall. There I usually came and drew forth from the bulging leather bag of books that I carried, copy and drawings which I put into the editor's hand. The editor that year was Herb Jacobson, and he printed all my worst cartoons very large in the most prominent parts of the magazine.

I thought I had something to be proud of when I became art-editor of *Jester* at the end of that year. Robert Lax was to be editor and Ralph Toledano managing editor, and we got along well together. The next year *Jester* was well put together because of Toledano and well written because of Lax and sometimes popular with the masses because of me. When it was really funny, it was not popular at all. The only really funny issues were mostly the work of Lax and Bob Gibney, the fruit of ideas that came to them at four o'clock in the morning in their room on the top floor of Furnald Hall.

The chief advantage of *Jester* was that it paid most of our bills for tuition. We were happy about it all, and wandered around the campus with little golden crowns dangling on our watch chains. Indeed, that was the only rea-son why I had a watch chain. I did not have a watch.

I have barely begun the list of all the things that occupied me in those days. For example, I gave my name to Miss Wegener at the appointments office. Miss Wegener was—and I hope she still is— a kind of a genius. She sat all day long behind her desk in that small, neat office in the Alumni house. No matter how many people she had talked to, she always looked unruffled and at peace. Every time you went to see her one or two phone calls would come in, and she would make a note on a little pad of paper. In summer she never seemed to be worried by the hot weather. And she always smiled at you with a smile that was at the same time efficient and kind, pleasant and yet a little impersonal. She was another one who had a vocation and was living up to it!

One of the best jobs she ever got for me was that of guide and interpreter on the observation roof of the R.C.A. building, Rockefeller Center. It was an easy job. So easy in fact that it was boring. You simply had to stand there and talk to the people who came pouring out of the elevator with all their questions. And for this you got twenty-seven and a half dollars a week, which was very good pay in 1936. I also worked in another office in Radio City, for some people who handled publicity for all the manufacturers of Paper Cups and Containers. For them I did cartoons that said you would surely get trench mouth if you ever drank out of an ordinary glass. For each cartoon I was paid six dollars. It made me feel like an executive, to go walking in and out of the doors of the R.C.A. building with my pockets full of money. Miss Wegener would also send me off on the subway with little slips of paper with the addresses of apartments where I would interview rich Jewish ladies about tutoring their children in Latin, which meant that I got two or two and a half dollars an hour for sitting with them and doing their homework.

I also handed in my name for the Cross Country team. The fact that the coach was not sorry to get me is sufficient indication of one reason why we were the worst college Cross Country team in the East that year. And so, in my afternoons, I would run around and around South Field on the cinder path. And when winter came, I would go round and round the board track until I had blisters all over the soles of my feet and was so lame I could hardly walk. Occasionally I would go up to Van Cortlandt Park and run along the sandy and rocky paths through the woods. When we raced any other college, I was never absolutely the last one home—there were always two or three other Columbia men behind me. I was one of those who never came in until the crowd had lost interest and had begun to disperse. Perhaps I would have been more of a success as a long-distance runner if I had gone into training, and given up smoking and drinking, and kept regular hours.

But no. Three or four nights a week my fraternity brothers and I would go flying down in the black and roaring subway to 52nd Street, where we would crawl around the tiny, noisy and expensive nightclubs that had flowered on the sites of the old speakeasies in the cellars of those dirty brownstone houses. There we would sit, for hours, packed in those dark rooms, shoulder to shoulder with a lot of surly strangers and their girls, while the whole place rocked and surged with storms of jazz. There was no room to dance. We just huddled there between the blue walls, shoulder to shoulder and elbow to elbow, crouching and deafened and taciturn. If you moved your arm to get your drink you nearly knocked the next man off his stool. And the waiters fought their way back and forth through the sea of unfriendly heads, taking away the money of all the people.

It was not that we got drunk. No, it was this strange business of sitting in a room full of people and drinking without much speech, and letting yourself be deafened by the jazz that throbbed through the whole sea of bodies binding them all together in a kind of fluid medium. It was a strange, animal travesty of mysticism, sitting in those booming rooms, with the noise pouring through you, and the rhythm jumping and throbbing in the marrow of your bones. You couldn't call any of that, *per se*, a mortal sin. We just sat there, that was all. If we got hangovers the next day, it was more because of the smoking and nervous exhaustion than anything else.

How often, after a night of this, I missed all the trains home to Long Island and went and slept on a couch somewhere, at the Fraternity House, or in the apartment of somebody I knew around town. What was worst of all was going home on the subway, on the chance that one might catch a bus at Flushing! There is nothing so dismal as the Flushing bus station, in the grey, silent hour just before the coming of dawn. There were always at least one or two of those same characters whose prototypes I had seen dead in the morgue. And perhaps there would be a pair of drunken soldiers trying to get back to Fort Totten. Among all these I stood, weary and ready to fall, lighting the fortieth or fiftieth cigarette of the day—the one that took the last shreds of lining off my throat.

The thing that depressed me most of all was the shame and despair that invaded my whole nature when the sun came up, and all the laborers were going to work: men healthy and awake and quiet, with their eyes clear, and some rational purpose before them. This humiliation and sense of my own misery and of the fruitlessness of what I had done was the nearest I could get to contrition. It was the reaction of nature. It proved nothing except that I was still, at least, morally alive: or rather that I had still some faint capacity for moral life in me. The term "morally alive" might obscure the fact that I was spiritually dead. I had been that long since!

Louis Simpson

'49 GENERAL STUDIES, '59 PHD

> *For a time, the poet Louis Simpson addressed contemporary themes using traditional poetic structures, but it may have been his experimentation with new forms that brought him the 1964 Pulitzer Prize for his collection* At the End of the Open Road. *Simpson also wrote a novel, critical studies, and memoirs and taught for many years, primarily at the University of California Berkeley and the State University of New York at Stony Brook. Excerpted here is* North of Jamaica *(1972).*

The first time I saw snow I ate a handful.

Ted Hoffman remembers the incident, and much more besides. Ted was my best friend at Columbia. He too felt out of place. He came from Brooklyn, a long way from the Ivy League.

Recently I wrote Ted asking him to help me rediscover what I felt about Columbia at that time, before the war, and he answered in a long letter that was full of incident and character analysis.

He wrote:

You sought a true education because your childhood prison had postulated it as desirable salvation, but you also succumbed to the injunctions of your parents and elders, without knowing why. "Parents are necessary evils," I do recall discovering and explaining to you once then, and receiving from you great gratitude for my wisdom. Which is to say you feared your mother. You couldn't bear her appearances, her orders . . . she would show up from those Helena Rubinstein trips commanding you to appear at a good restaurant. I must say for all the time I knew you,

222

you had abominable taste in food and liquor, willing to take anything set before you. . . . She would also buy you clothes, usually based on some ridiculous Broadway concept. Why you didn't buy your own clothes I don't know, I guess because you were happy in pants and sweater; I recall watching you dress and pick out any shirt *and any tie*, which even in the depths of Brooklyn was a sign of grossness, which much distressed me when I was counting on your instinctive tastes to define life. I guess you didn't dig money. You didn't seem to know how much you had (*in toto* or at your immediate command) and I'd explain the price of things to you (but values. . . ?). Anyhow it was winter, and you were shivering in the top coat she bought you for fall. I have a mental image of you sweeping a handful of snow off the fender of a car during the first snowfall, licking it and tossing it up in the air, whether out of natural joy or prescribed gesture I can't guess now, and probably didn't consider then. Anyhow, back you came from one of those visits, miserably encased in a big boxy, nubbly tweed overcoat and a big grey, snap-brim fedora hat (neither Bogart nor Capone, but assuredly the worst of each). I said you looked like a gangster—Louie—and you almost cried, truly in anguish, feeling doomed to walk the campus in that monstrosity because your mother had put it on your head. "Look at it!" you pleaded. "Whatever can I do about it?" "You can take it off right now and throw it in that garbage can," I said. And you did, with great relief, and a Cheshire cat grin. I let you keep the coat, which after all was expensive and warm and you were acclimatized to the Caribbean, and we expected you foreigners to be a little garish.

❋ ❋ ❋

The snow drifted down on my windowsill, forming a sculpture of white grains, millimetre by millimetre. By the end of the day the ledges would be filled with white, sparkling snow, and the street covered with a carpet, inches deep.

Children would be out, sledding down snowbanks with loud cries. I knew them by their boots, earmuffs and mittens. They were figures out of the Montgomery Ward catalogue I had looked at years ago on a veranda. They were part of the American landscape. Some day I too would have merged with the landscape, if I could stand the cold.

❋ ❋ ❋

The instructor's hands were thin and the green veins stood out. The index and third finger were stained with nicotine.

He had been talking for some time, explaining Ricardo's theory of value, and I was not following what he was saying. I was listening to the sound of his voice rather than what he actually said, noticing his hands which moved about as he talked. Now and then he would jump up from the chair and write on the blackboard. Sometimes he sat on the edge of the table. He lit another cigarette. Then, in the middle of a sentence, he began to cough. His chest heaved and he snatched a handkerchief out of his pocket and coughed into it. He sounded as though he had consumption.

This man had written books that had been translated into several languages. He was teaching a course called Contemporary Civilization. But it seemed from the nicotine stains on his fingers and the way he coughed that what he liked best was smoking.

When he had finished coughing it seemed that he sensed what we were thinking, for he strode to and fro, glaring first at one then at another, and speaking more vehemently. Then he settled on the edge of the table again and crossed his legs and clasped his right knee in his hands. Hands which for forty years had crawled over sheets of paper, writing so many books. The man himself had been only the attachment to a hand that wrote and wrote. A hand that got up in the morning to write.

After these classes I could hardly remember what had been said. The instructor had uttered a great number of words on a subject he knew well, but it is necessary to experience something for oneself in order to know it. The instructor dealt in abstractions. He provided the student with quantities of words which signified a number of things. If the student remained for a long time in the university he would be encapsulated in words, like the instructor, and there would come a day when he would not have to deal with anything but the shell of words surrounding him. He would touch the smooth walls on every side and think this was reality.

*   *   *

Besides Contemporary Civilization, I was required to take a course called the Humanities. This consisted of reading and discussing great books from Herodotus to Dostoievsky. Our instructor was Lionel Trilling. He had hazel eyes and a charming smile. He conducted the discussions gracefully and always seemed to have something more to say than he actually revealed. The object of our reading seemed to be to find ideas we could argue about. Ideas were what we were after, not feelings or a sense of the way the work was written. We were certainly not reading for pleasure. I kept finding things that pleased me, however, and Trilling corrected me every time. My pleasure in the work itself was not to the point. He brought the discussion back to the idea we were pursuing. It seemed that we were about to find it when the bell rang and our instructor vanished. On Monday next it would be another book and another great idea.

I was also taking a course in English literature, with Raymond Weaver. Weaver would make a dramatic entrance, then sit at his desk without saying a word for a minute or so. Then, glaring at a student and in a deep, resonant voice, he would launch a question. The questions were intended to mystify. Once when he did this—"What is Aristotle's *Poetics* about?"—I answered immediately, "How to write a play." As this spoiled the suspense he was aiming at, he pretended not to have heard.

Weaver wore dove colours; he was an aesthete, and would have been at home in the nineties. As is common with such people, he was suspicious of those who, like himself, were aesthetes; he favoured the unimaginative, athletic types. He had a trick that underlined this prejudice. He would recite "Casey at the Bat."

> Ten thousand eyes were on him as he rubbed his hands
>   with dirt,
> Five thousand tongues applauded when he wiped them on
>   his shirt;
> Then while the writhing pitcher ground the ball into
>   his hip,
> Defiance gleamed in Casey's eye, a sneer curled Casey's
>   lip.

Then he would recite Dowson's poem about Cynara.

> I cried for madder music and for stronger wine,
> But when the feast is finished and the lamps expire,
> Then falls thy shadow, Cynara! the night is thine;
> And I am desolate and sick of an old passion,
>   Yea hungry for the lips of my desire:
> I have been faithful to thee, Cynara! in my fashion.

Then he would ask which was poetry. Inevitably some poor fish would bite, saying that "Cynara" was poetry and "Casey" wasn't. Whereupon, in his booming voice Weaver would explain the pretentiousness of "Cynara," its insincerity, its essential vulgarity.

※ ※ ※

I would meet Ted for lunch at the New Asia. My freshman year at Columbia had a distinct flavour of soy sauce. The history of the Peloponnesian War came with an egg roll and fried rice, and the cogitations of Ricardo were mixed with Chinese vegetables. Now that I think about it these surroundings were suitable, for the liberal arts at Columbia were served simultaneously in little portions, like dishes in a Chinese restaurant— a mouthful of St. Augustine, a spoonful of Spinoza, a small helping of Huxley. The object, I suppose, was to make you hungry later.

Ted and I discussed current events. I said, with my mouth full of noodles, "Poor little Finland! I don't give a damn about Finland, what's important is the Russian army. Let's face it, they are the ones who are going to have to fight the Nazis. At least we know now that their artillery is good."

I was one of the leading authorities on Marxism among College freshmen. Also, as I had been in a revolution in the Caribbean and had seen the workers shot down in cold blood—this was the impression my friends had gathered, and I did not try to correct it—I was the leading authority on street fighting and military strategy and tactics. I was ruthless in my attitude toward the Finns. Individuals and small nations didn't matter. Only the future mattered.

Sometimes we were joined for lunch by Bob Shafner. He had an easy, superior manner. Bob was very much the New Yorker. He had gone to Horace Mann high school and was now getting A's in Columbia College. There were dozens of Bobs at Columbia; they seemed to have learned all the answers long ago. They ran campus activities and were going into journalism, law, or medicine. Already in his freshman year Bob was taking professional courses.

A few years after graduating he would be established in his profession. He would have married a good-looking girl. They would have an apartment on Park Avenue and rent a house in the Hamptons every summer. Bob would take up sail-boating. Their living-room would be decorated with paintings by Larry Rivers, and Norman Mailer would come to one of their parties. If Mailer couldn't make it, Gore Vidal.

But I am anticipating. We are still in the New Asia restaurant. Ted, in the plaid sports jacket, is exchanging Joycean puns with Bob Shafner, who is more suitably dressed for the Ivy League, in grey flannel. The author of *Ulysses* is one of their heroes—Groucho Marx is another.

The third man, myself—we have already seen how he dresses—is trying to get a word in edgewise. When he does, it will be some enthusiastic outburst; it will probably be off the point, and it will probably be about Marcel Proust, whom he has been reading again. They will listen to him tolerantly, then Ted will say something to modify the outburst and make it more acceptable, or Bob Shafner will dispose of it with a witty remark. But tolerantly, for Shafner is a well-rounded man, and this is his day for seeing his literary friends. Back at the fraternity when they twit him with it, he says, "It takes all kinds."

"This talk of war . . ." Bob said, "you don't know what real trouble is. I have to go see Sammy Kaye's agent this afternoon and persuade him to let Sammy play for us."

Ted and I looked at him in silence. The man of affairs.

"The prom is only a few months away," he explained.

Not only did Bob have to get a band for the prom, but also he had to see Dean Hawkes that afternoon and plead the case of a fraternity brother who had got into trouble and was on the verge of being expelled from the college.

"What kind of trouble?"

He put his finger to his lips. A man of important secrets.

"And tonight I'm taking Betty to see *Pal Joey.* I had a helluva time getting tickets. They charge an arm and a leg. But I had to . . . she's been after me. Women are expensive, let me tell you."

A man of the world.

When Bob left to see the Dean, Ted and I were subdued. I had a class in French that afternoon, but after listening to Bob's real-life activities, I wondered if it was worth studying French. Those long drifting sentences of *La Recherche du Temps Perdu.* . . . What was it someone had said about Proust and his interminable explorations of the psyche? Proust was like a man in a bathtub, wallowing in his own dirty bath water.

I had once met Bob with his Betty—or was it another girl? He dated several. This was a pretty brunette, with a sparkling, humorous face. She shook hands with me, interested to be introduced to "my friend the poet," but I couldn't think of anything to say. She looked at me and waited, but I couldn't think of anything.

Bob said, "Well now, keep at it," and they walked off. I saw him handing her into a taxi.

I consoled myself with thinking that she would be unfaithful to him. All women were unfaithful, and love was a disease. I knew that from my reading in Proust.

❀ ❀ ❀

I was tutoring two children. When they had done their homework I would take them to Riverside Drive with their dog.

It was so that I met Bonnie. She watched me throwing a ball, and the dog and Hans and his sister Amelie scampering after it. One or the other of them would return panting with the ball, and I'd throw it again.

Once the dog brought the ball back to Bonnie, and so she joined in the ball-throwing. Her legs were too fat, but she had a lovely face, bright eyes, black hair. It was a pity about her legs, but this one defect made it possible for me to talk to her. If she had been perfect I would have been speechless.

Every afternoon she happened to be there, on the walk near the Soldiers' and Sailors' Monument. Little Hans grew sulky because I would be rapt in conversation with Bonnie and no longer willing to discuss the American Civil War and the Far West and other matters that his parents, having escaped from Germany, wanted him to be familiar with, in order to be Americanized. While I talked to Bonnie, Sister Amelie looked downright jealous behind her thick glasses.

Bonnie was in high school and was impressed with everything I said about college life. At this time I had discovered a teacher I liked—Mark Van Doren. I was in the seminar he gave in the poems of Thomas Hardy and W. B. Yeats. I aired my ideas about poetry on the Drive, with Bonnie for an audience.

It occurred to me that I could see her when I was not with the children. I asked her to come up to Columbia and look around, and she said yes as though there were nothing unusual about the request. I was to pick her up at her apartment.

The person who opened the door wasn't the girl of the Soldiers' and Sailors' Monument, with red mittens and earmuffs. This one was dressed like an Easter rabbit, in pink, with ribbons and bows. When I took her on the trolley up to Columbia, and when I walked her around the campus, everyone stared. I passed two or three people I knew—I nodded stiffly and they looked surprised. I caught them looking back at us.

Bonnie was gay. She wanted to know who the bronze lady was, holding up one of her hands with the palm open.

"Alma Mater," I said.

"She looks as if she's saying, Don't blame me."

I took her down to the Lion's Den. This was where the College men brought their girls. Bob Shafner came over to our table. "Mind if we join you?" he said. He was with a girl with red hair. I said not at all, and soon we were all talking. Bob kept deferring to me for my opinion on this and that—I had never seen him so deferential. Bonnie rolled her eyes and made little mouths of approval or disapproval. Now and then she would be convulsed with laughter and have to wipe a tear from the corner of an eye.

The redhead wasn't so talkative. She kept looking at her watch. Then she got up suddenly and left. Bob got up too and hurried after her. They spoke together briefly, then he returned to the table, shrugging his shoulders.

When we left the Lion's Den, Bob walked us over to Broadway. He waved a cheery goodbye.

"Take care of him, Bonnie," he said. "Mind now! He's a wonderful guy."

* * *

I wasn't in love with Bonnie. I just had a feeling of excitement when I went to the Drive, and a sinking feeling if she were late, and a feeling of relief when she appeared. But she was too flamboyant for my taste, and the two or three times I took her out—to Columbia, to the movies—I was actually embarrassed to be seen with her. And her bell-like laugh . . . I wished she wouldn't laugh like that, so that people turned around.

She thought I was a scream. Once when we were looking at a parade, and a platoon came marching by in the costume of the old British redcoats, with high bearskin hats, I said, "I thought we won that war." Bonnie went off in a peal of laughter and the redcoats nudged each other in the ribs.

Once when I picked her up to take her to the movies she had put on a new dress and looked so beautiful that I said, "What's this? Hallowe'en?" And Bonnie went off in a scream.

⚬ ⚬ ⚬

I hadn't ever kissed her. I did hold her hand, however, crossing streets, and I wrote a few poems in which love was mentioned in a rather cynical manner. Sometimes it was the cynicism of Hardy in his *Satires of Circumstance*—a woman burying her husband and going off with a lover. At times the cynicism was French, in the manner of Laforgue—the gentleman visitor thinks that the lady has become a little stale.

It was always assumed that, for one reason or another love was an illusion. Either the lover was betrayed or the loved one died.

Life imitates art. Or is it simply that art mirrors the tendencies which determine life? One day I was coming back to the dormitory in the dusk, from the library where I had been reading. It was drizzling. It had been one of those days that seemed to express the monotony of a scholar's life—in which any page you turned was like the rain outside, dismal and repetitious.

I heard a peal of laughter. Then two figures went past me in the rain—a man and a girl. She was sheltering under his raincoat. It was Bonnie, and the man was Bob Shafner. They didn't see me—they were too engrossed in each other.

I went up to my room and paced to and fro. I was unable to sit down for more than a few seconds. I lay down on the bed and immediately stood up again. I tried reading, but it was no use. I was filled with bitterness and rage. Then . . . calm resolve—I would never speak to her again.

When next she appeared on Riverside Drive, coming toward me with a light in her eyes—I said, "I don't want to see you again." I turned away, with little Hans and Amelie and the dog, and left her standing there.

⚬ ⚬ ⚬

I got back into Columbia by a rear door, by way of the School of General Studies. I could take courses there in the evenings and get a degree. It was so that I met younger students and writers who had not been in the war and whose attitudes were new to me. There were others I met at parties in the Village and in cold-water flats on the East Side. One night I gave a party of my own—I was living on West End Avenue—to which came a number of my new friends, bringing friends of their own. There was a thin, sallow young man with staring eyes and a puzzling smile, Allen Ginsberg. He'd been at Columbia while I was away. There was a burly fellow with an all-American face, Jack Kerouac. Another named Neil Cassady. The party got rough and they threw glasses out of the window to shatter on the pavement ten floors below. Ginsberg appeared from my bedroom carrying the sheet of a poem I had been trying to write, tripping rhymes about a little German girl. He read it aloud to my embarrassment. It seemed that Ginsberg, too, was trying to write poetry, and Kerouac had written a novel comparing the city and the country.

The next day I found that a copy of Henry Miller's *Tropic of Cancer* that I'd picked up in Paris was missing. I've sometimes thought that, in this small way, I contributed to the growth of the Beats.

There was a man named John Hollander who seemed to know everything about poetry, especially metrics, and music. He would sit at the piano playing T. S. Eliot—that is, singing the words of "The Waste Land" to an arrangement of his own. And Ted Hoffman was living on Barrow Street in the Village; he was specializing in theatre, mentioning names I'd never heard of—Bertolt Brecht and Eric Bentley.

There were a few girls who came to the parties, wild young things who had been educated at progressive schools. They were always talking about *avant-garde* painting and music and books. They dressed in hand-me-downs and came and went at odd hours.

I was invited to take part in a poetry-reading at Columbia. The other readers were Allen Ginsberg and John Hollander. The famous English poet Stephen Spender would make the introduction. Spender's name meant a great deal to me. He was one of the so-called Oxford poets—W. H. Auden, Stephen Spender, C. Day Lewis and Louis MacNeice. Many poets of the thirties and forties wrote in imitation of these men's style—a mixture of prep-school flippancy and private jokes—and borrowed their Marxist and Freudian attitudes, their symbolism of images taken from machinery. Spender's poems were quite sentimental, but they were bedecked with pylons, factory chimneys and locomotives. My own early poems had been alliterated like Auden's and brought up to date with Spenderesque references to machinery.

> Life is a winter liner, here history passes
> Like tourists on top-decks, seeing the shore through
>   sun-glasses . . .

Introducing us, Spender said a few words about the poetry of the day. The main difference between English and American poetry was that Englishmen had experienced the war and Americans hadn't. I listened to this description with some astonishment. Spender's other remarks were made with the same off-hand air of authority, and for the first time I began to wonder if famous English authors knew as much as they seemed to.

Ginsberg read some poems about North Africa; he'd been there on a boat as a member of the crew. Later we walked down the Drive together talking about poetry. It was a hard life. He showed me holes in the elbows of his jacket.

✿   ✿   ✿

Ginsberg hasn't much changed, from that day to this. I doubt that people ever do change fundamentally. They may go off in directions that seem contrary, but in a while you see that these were only digressions; the main direction is unaltered. Twenty years later, people are pretty much what you might have expected them to be; it is the ways by which they have arrived that are astonishing. In order to be true to themselves, poets have to go far afield and discover new ways of speaking. Apollinaire says:

> Sacrifice taste and keep your sanity
> If you love your home you must make a journey
> You much cherish courage and seek adventure . . .
> Don't hope for rest risk everything you own
> Learn what is new for everything must be known . . .

The world does not see the necessity of this. But poets know that their most extravagant actions are dictated by a need to be perfectly simple.

Jack Kerouac

Recruited as a football player, Jack Kerouac attended Columbia College in the early 1940s and became a mainstay of the so-called Beat Generation along with schoolmates Allen Ginsberg and Lucien Carr. His signature work is of course On the Road, *the semiautobiographical novel that became an instant literary sensation upon its publication in 1957. Excerpted here is Kerouac's recollection of Columbia in* Vanity of Duluoz *(1968).*

B ut now some old buddies, the Ladeau brothers, proposed to drive me to New York for my school year because they were going to see the World's Fair at Flushing Meadows and might as well take me along for the ride and I could help with the gas instead of taking a bus. And who comes along, riding in the rumbleseat in back of the old 1935 coupe, hair blowing in the wind, singing, "Whoooeee, here we come New York!" if it wasn't my old Pop himself, Emil? Me and 350 pounds of Pop and baggage in a rumbleseat, all the way with the car veering here, veering there. I guess from the unsuitable disposition of weight in the back, all the way to Manhattan, 116th Street, Columbia campus, where me and Pa got out with my gear and went into my dormitory, Hartley Hall.

What dreams you get when you think you're going to go to college! Here we stood in this sort of drear room overlooking Amsterdam Avenue, a wooden desk, bed, chairs, bare walls, and one huge cockroach suddenly rushing off. Furthermore in walks a little kid with glasses wearing a blue skullcap and announces he will be my roommate for the year and that he is a pledge with the Wi Delta Woowoo fraternity and that's the skullcap. "When they rush you

you'll have to wear one too." But I was already devising means of changing my room on account of that cockroach and others I saw later, bigger.

Pa and I then went out on the town, to the World's Fair too, restaurants, the usual, and when he left he said, as usual: "Now study, play good ball, pay attention to what the coach and the profs tell you and see if you cant make your old man proud and maybe be an all-America." Fat chance, with the war a year away and England already under blitz.

It seems I had chosen football and come to the brim of the top of it just at that time when it would no longer matter to anybody or his uncle.

There were always tears in my Pa's eyes when he said goodbye to me, always tears in his eyes those latter years, he was, as my mother often said, *"Un vrai Duluoz, ils font ainque braillez pi's lamentez* [A real Duluoz, all they do is cry and lament]." And rage too, b'God, as you'll see later when my Pa finally got to meet Coach Lu Libble of Columbia.

Because from the start I saw that the same old boloney was going to be pulled on me as in Lowell High School. In the freshman backfield there was a good blocking boy called Humphrey Wheeler, but slow, and a slow plodding fullback called Runstedt, and that's about it. Absolutely nobody of any real ability and nothing like the gang at HM. In fact one of the boys was small, slow, weak, nothing at all in particular, and yet they started him instead of me and later on I talk to him and discover he's the son of the police chief of Scranton. Never in my life have I ever seen such a bum team. The freshman coach was Rolfe Firney who had made his mark at Columbia as a very good back who'd made a sensational run against Navy that won the game in 1934 or so. He was a good man, I liked Rolfe, but he seemed to keep warning me about something all the time and whenever the big coach, famous Lu Libble went by, all sartorial in one of his 100 suits, he never even gave me the once-over.

The fact of the matter is, Lu Libble was very famous because in his very first year as coach at Columbia, using a system of his own devised at his alma mater, Georgetown, he won the bloody Rose Bowl against Stanford. It was such a sensational smash in the eye all over football America nobody ever got over it, but that was 1934, and here it was 1940 and he hadnt done anything noteworthy since with his team and went clear into the 1950's doing nothing further either. I think it was that bunch of players he had in 1934 who carried him over: Cliff Montgomery, Al Barabas, *et al.,* and the surprise of that crazy KT-79 play of his that took everybody a year to understand. It was simply . . . well I had to run it, anyway, and you'll understand it when we run it.

So here I am out with the Columbia freshman team and I see I'm not going to be a starter. Will admit one thing, I wasnt being encouraged, as I'd been by Coach Ump Mayhew at HM, and psychologically this made me feel lackadaisical and my punting, for instance, fell off. I couldnt get off a good kick anymore and they didn't believe in the quick kick. I guess they didnt believe in touchdowns either. We practiced at Baker Field in the one field in back. At dusk you could see the lights of New York across the Harlem River, it was right smack in the middle of New York City, even tugboats went by in the Harlem River, a great bridge crossed it full of cars, I couldnt understand what had gone wrong.

One great move I made was to switch my dormitory room from Hartley Hall to Livingston Hall where there were no cockroaches and where b'God I had a room all to myself, on the second floor, overlooking the beautiful trees and walkways of the campus and overlooking, to my greatest delight, besides the Van Am Quadrangle, the library itself, the new one, with its stone frieze running around entire with the names engraved in stone forever: "Goethe . . . Voltaire . . . Shakespeare . . . Molière . . . Dante." That was more like it. Lighting my fragrant pipe at 8 P.M., I'd open the pages of my homework, turn on station WQXR for the continual classical music, and sit there, in the golden glow of my lamp, in a sweater, sigh and say "Well now I'm a collegian at last."

* * *

Only trouble is, the first week of school my job began as a dishwasher in the diningroom cafeteria sinks: this was to pay for my meals. Secondly, classes. Thirdly, homework: *i.e.,* read Homer's *Iliad* in three days and then the *Odyssey* in three more. Finally, go to football practice at four in the afternoon and return to my room at eight, eating voracious suppers right after at the training table in John Jay Hall upstairs. (Plenty of milk, plenty of meat, dry toast, that was good.)

But who on earth in his right mind can think that anybody can do all these things in one week? And get some sleep? And rest war-torn muscles? "Well," said they, "this is the Ivy League son, this is no college or group of colleges where you get a Cadillac and some money just because you play football, and remember you're on a Columbia University Club scholarship and you've got to get good marks. They cant feed you free, it's against the Ivy League rules against preference for athletes." In fact, tho, the entire Columbia football gang, both varsity and freshmen, had B averages. It was true. We had to work like Trojans to get our education and the old white-haired trainer used to intone, "All for glory, me boys, all for glory."

It was the work in the cafeteria that bothered me: because on Sundays it was closed and nobody who worked got to eat anything. I s'pose in this case we were s'posed to eat at the homes of friends in New York City or New Jersey or get food money from home. Some scholarship.

I did get invited to dinner, formally with a big formal card, by the dean of Columbia College, old Dean Hawkes, in the house on Morningside Drive or thereabouts right near the house of Nicholas Murray Butler, the president of Columbia. Here, all dressed up in Ma's best McQuade-Lowell-selected sports coat, with white shirt and tie and pressed slacks (the cleaner was on Amsterdam across the street), I sat and ate my soup by gently lifting the saucer away from me, spooning away from me, smiled politely, hair perfectly combed, showed suave interest in jokes and awe in the dean's serious moments. The entree was meat but I cut it delicately. I had the best table manners in those days because my sister Ti Nin had trained me back in Lowell for these past several years; she was a fan of Emily Post's. When, after dinner, the dean got up and showed me (and the three other special lads) his prized Dinosaur Egg I registered actual amazement; whoever thought I'd get to see a billion-year-old egg in the house of an old distinguished dean? I say house, it was a sumptuous apartment. He thereupon wrote a note to my mother saying: "Your son, John L. Duluoz, may I say with pride, Mrs. Duluoz, has absolutely the best and most charming table manners it has ever been my pleasure to enjoy at my dinner table." (Something like that.) She never forgot that. She told Pa. He said "Good boy," tho when Pa and I used to eat late-night snacks in Lowell it was eggs this way, butter that way, hell be damned, up on the ceiling, EAT.

But I loved Dean Hawkes, everybody did, he was an old, short bespectacled old fud with glee in his eyes. Him and his egg . . .

       ❉ ❉ ❉

The opening game of the season the freshman team traveled to New Brunswick N.J. for a game against Rutgers' freshmen. This was Saturday Oct. 12, 1940, and as our varsity defeated Dartmouth 20-6, we went down there and I sat on the bench and we lost 18-7. The little daily paper of the college said: FRESHMEN DROP GRID OPENER TO RUTGERS YEARLINGS BY 18-7 COUNT. It doesn't mention that I only got in the game in the second half, just like at Lowell High, and the article concludes with: "The Morningsiders showed a fairly good running attack at times with Jack Duluoz showing up well. . . . Outstanding in the backfield for the Columbia Frosh were Marsden [police chief's son], Runstedt and Duluoz, who was probably the best back on the field."

So that in the following game, against St. Benedict's Prep, okay, now they started me.

But you remember what I boasted about how, to beat St. John's, you gotta have old St. John on the team. Well I have a medal, as you know, over my backyard door. It's the medal of St. Benedict. An Irish girl once told me: "Whenever you move into a new house two things you must do according to your blood as an ancient Gael: you buy a new broom, and you pins a St. Benedict medal over the kitchen door." That's not the reason why I've got that medal now but here's what happened:

After the Rutgers game, and Coach Libble'd heard about my running, and now his backfield coach Cliff Battles was interested, everybody came down to Baker Field to see the new nut run. Cliff Battles was one of the greatest football players who ever lived, in a class with Red Grange and the others, one of the greatest runners anyway. I remember as a kid, when I was nine, Pa saying suddenly one Sunday "Come on Angie, Ti Nin, Ti Jean, let's all get in the car and drive down to Boston and watch the Boston Redskins play pro football, the great Cliff Battles is running today." Because of traffic we never made it, or we were waylaid by ice cream and apples in Chelmsford, Dunstable or someplace and wound up in New Hampshire visiting Grandmère Jean. And in those days I kept elaborate clippings of all sports and pasted them carefully, among my own sports writings, in my notebooks, and I knew very well about Cliff Battles. Now here all of a sudden the night before the game with St. Benedict and we freshmen are practicing, here comes Cliff Battles and up to me and says "So you're the great Dulouse that ran so good at Rutgers. Let's see how fast you can go."

"What do you mean?"

"I'll race you to the showers; practice is over." He stood there, 6 foot 3, smiling, in his coach pants and cleated shoes and sweat jacket.

"Okay," says I and I take off like a little bird. By God I've got him by 5 yards as we head for the sidelines at the end of the field, but here he comes with his long antelope legs behind me and just passes me under the goalposts and goes ahead 5 yards and stops at the shower doors, arms akimbo, saying:

"Well cant you run?"

"Ah heck your legs are longer than mine."

"You'll do allright kid," he says, pats me, and goes off laughing. "See you tomorrow," he throws back.

This made me happier than anything that had happened so far at Columbia, because also I certainly wasn't happy that I hadnt yet read the *Iliad* or the *Odyssey,* John Stuart Mill, Aeschylus, Plato, Horace and everything else they were throwing at us with the dishes.

* * *

Comes the St. Benedict game, and what a big bunch of lugs you never saw, they reminded me of that awful Blair team a year ago, and the Malden team in high school, big, mean-looking, with grease under their eyes to shield the glare of the sun, wearing mean-looking brown-red uniforms against our sort of silly-looking (if you ask me) light-blue uniforms with dark-blue numerals. ("Sans Souci" is the name of the Columbia alma mater song, means "without care," humph.) (And the football rallying song is "Roar Lion Roar," sounds more like it.) Here we go, lined up on the field, on the sidelines I see that Coach Lu Libble is finally there to give me the personal once-over. He's heard about the Rutgers game naturally and he's got to think of next year's backfield. He'd heard, I s'pose, that I was a kind of nutty French kid from Massachusetts with no particular football savvy like his great Italian favorites from Manhattan that were now starring on the varsity (Lu Libble's real name is Guido Pistola, he's from Massachusetts).

St. Benedict was to kick off. They lined up, I went deep into safety near the goal line as ordered, and said to myself "Screw, I'm going to show these bums how a French boy from Lowell runs, Cliff Battles and the whole bunch, and who's that old bum standing next to him? Hey Runstedt, who's that guy in the coat next to Cliff Battles there near the water can?"

"They tell me that's the coach of Army, Earl Blaik, he's just whiling away an afternoon."

Whistle blows and St. Benedict kicks off. The ball comes wobbling over and over in the air into my arms. I got it secure and head straight down the field in the direction an arrow takes, no dodging, no looking, no head down either but just straight ahead at everybody. They're all converging there in midfield in smashing blocks and pushings so they can get through one way or the other. A few of the red Benedicts get through and are coming straight at me from three angles but the angles are narrow because I've made sure of that by coming in straight as an arrow down the very middle of the field. So that by the time I reach midfield where I'm going to be clobbered and smothered by eleven giants I give them no look at all, still, but head right into them: they gather up arms to smother me: it's psychological. They never dream I'm really roosting up in my head the plan to suddenly (as I do) dart, or jack off, bang to the right, leaving them all there bumbling for air. I run as fast as I can, which I could do very well with a heavy football uniform, as I say, because of thick legs, and had trackman speed, and before you know it I'm going down the sidelines all alone with the whole twenty-one other guys of the ball game all befuddling around in midfield and turning to follow me. I hear whoops from the sidelines. I go and I go. I'm down to the 30, the 20, the 10, I hear huffing and puffing behind me, I look behind me and there's that selfsame old longlegged end catchin up on me, like Cliff Battles done, like the guy last year, like the guy in the Nashua game, and by the time I'm over the 5 he lays a big hand on the scruff of my neck and lays me down on the ground. A 90-yard runback.

I see Lu Libble and Cliff Battles, and Rolfe Firney our coach too, rubbing their hands with zeal and dancing little Hitler dances on the sidelines. But St. John ain't got a chance against St. Benedict, it appears, because anyway naturally by now I'm out of breath and that dopey quarterback wants me to make my own touchdown. I just can't make it. I want to controvert his order, but you're not supposed to. I puff into the line and get buried on the 5. Then he, Runstedt, tries it, and the big St. Ben's line buries him, and then we miss the last down too and are down on the 3 and have to fall back for the St. Benedict punt.

By now I've got my wind again and I'm ready for another go. But the punt that's sent to me is so high, spirally, perfect, I see it's going to take an hour for it to fall down in my arms and I should really raise my arm for a fair catch and touch it down to the ground and start our team from there. But no, vain Jack, even tho I hear the huffing and puffing of the two down-field men practically on my toes I catch the ball free catch and practically say "Alley oop" as I feel their four big hands squeeze like vises around my ankles, two on each, and puffing with pride I do the complete vicious twist of my whole body so that I can undo their grip and move on. But their St. Benedict grips have me rooted to where I am as if I was a tree, or an iron pole stuck to the ground, I do the complete turnaround twist and hear a loud crack and it's my leg breaking. They let me fall back deposited gently on the turf and look at me and say to each other "The only way to get *him*, don't *miss*" (more or less).

I'm helped off the field limping.

I go into the showers and undress and the trainer massages my right calf and says "O a little sprain wont hurt you, next week it's Princeton and we'll give them the old one-two again Jacky boy."

◦   ◦   ◦

But, wifey, it was a broken leg, a cracked tibia, like if you cracked a bone about the size of a pencil and the pencil was still stuck together except for that hairline crack, meaning if you wanted you could just break the pencil in half with a twist of two fingers. But nobody knew this. That entire week they told me I was a softy and to get going and run around and stop limping. They had liniments, this and that, I tried to run, I ran and practiced and ran but the limp got worse. Finally they sent me off to Columbia Medical Center, took X rays, and found out I had broken my tibia in right leg and that I had been spending a week running on a broken leg.

I'm not bitter about that, wifey, so much as that it was Coach Lu Libble who kept insisting I was putting it on and told the freshman coaches not to listen to my "lamentings" and make me "run it off." You just can't run off a broken leg. I saw right then that Lu for some reason I'll never understand had some kind of bug against me. He was always hinting I was a no-good and with those big legs he ought to put me in the line and make "a watch charm guard" out of me.

Yet (I guess I know now why) it was only that summer, I forgot to mention, Francis Fahey had me come out to Boston College field to give me a tryout for once and for all. He said "You really must come to B.C., we've got a system here, the Notre Dame system, where we take a back like you and with a good line play spring him loose down the field. Over at Columbia with Lu Libble they'll have you come around from the wing, you'll have to run a good twenty yards before you get back to the line of scrimmage with that silly KT-79 reverse type play of his and you'll only at best manage to evade maybe the end but the secondary'll be up on yours in no time. With us, it's *boom,* right through tackle, guard, or right or left end sweep." Then Fahey'd had me put on a uniform, got his backfield coach MacLuhan and said: "Find out about him." Alone in the field with Mac, facing him, Mac held the ball and said:

"Now, Jack, I'm going to throw this ball at you in the way a center does; when you get it you're off like a halfback on any kinda run you wanta try. If I touch you you're out, so to speak, and you know darn well I'm going to touch you because I used to be one of the fastest backs in the east."

"Phooey you are," I thought, and said "Okay, throw it." He centered it to me, direct, facing me, and I took off out of his sight, he had to turn his head to watch me pass around his left, and that's no Harvard lie.

"Well," he conceded, "you're not faster than I am but by God where'd you get that sudden takeoff? Track?"

"Yep." So in the showers of B.C. afterward, I'm wiping up, I hear Fahey and Mac discussing me in the coaches' showers and I hear Mac say to Fahey:

"Fran, that's the best halfback I ever saw. You've got to get him to B.C."

But I went to Columbia because I wanted to dig New York and become a big journalist in the big city beat. But what right had Lu Libble to say I was a no-good runner. And, wifey, listen to this, what about the night the winter before, at HM, when Francis Fahey had me meet him on Times Square and took me to William Saroyan's play *My Heart's in the Highlands,* and in the intermission when we went down to the toilet I'm sure I saw Rolfe Firney the Columbia man watching from behind the crowd of men? On top of which they then sent Joe Callahan to New York to take me out on the town too, to further persuade me about Boston College, and eventually Notre Dame, but here I was at Columbia, Pa had lost his job, and the coach thought I was so no-good he didnt even believe I'd broken my leg in earnest.

Years later I published a poem about this on the sports page of *Newsday,* the Long Island newspaper: fits pretty good: because it also involves the later fight my father had with Lu about his not playing me enough and some arrangement that went sour whereby Lu was s'posed to help him get a lino-typist job in New York and nothing came of it:

TO LU LIBBLE

Lu, my father thought you put him down
 and said he didnt like you
He thought he was too shabby for your
 office; his coat had got so

And his hair he'd comb and come
    into an employment office with me

And have me speak alone with the man
    for the two of us, then sigh

And repented we home, to Lowell; where
    sweet mother put out the pie
        anywye.

In my first game I ran like mad
    at Rutgers, Cliff wasnt there;

He didnt believe what he read
    in the *Spectator* "Who's that Jack"

So I come in on the St. Benedicts
    game not willing to be caught by them bums

I took off the kickoff right straight at
    the gang, and lalooza'd around

To the pastafazoola five yard line,
    you were there, you remember

We didnt make first down; and I
    took the punt and broke my leg

And never said anything, and ate hot
    fudge sundaes & steaks in the
        Lion's Den.

Because that's one good thing that came of it, with my broken leg in a cast, and with two crutches under my good armpits, I hobbled every night to the Lion's Den, the Columbia fireplace-and-mahogany type restaurant, sat right in front of the fire in the place of honor, watched the boys and girls dance, ordered every blessed night the same rare filet mignon, ate it at leisure with my crutches athwart the table, then two hot fudge sundaes for dessert, that whole blessed sweet autumn.

And I never did say anything, so as to say, I never sued or made a fuss, I enjoyed the leisure, the steaks, the ice cream, the honor, and for the first time in my life at Columbia began to study at my own behest the complete awed wide-eyed world of Thomas Wolfe (not to mention the curricular work too).

For years afterward, however, Columbia still kept sending me the bill for the food I ate at training table.

I never paid it.

Why should I? My leg still hurts on damp days. Phooey.

Ivy League indeed.

If you dont say what you want, what's the sense of writing?

* * *

But o that beautiful autumn, sitting at my desk with that fragrant pipe now taped like my leg was taped, listening to the beautiful Sibelius Finnish Symphony which even to this day reminds me of fragrant old tobacco smoke and even tho I know it's all about snow, and my dim lamp, and before me laid out the immortal words of Tom Wolfe talking about the "weathers" of America, the pale-green flaky look of old buildings behind warehouses, the track running west, the sound of Indians in the rail, the coonskin cap in his hills of old Nawth Caliney, the river winking, the Mississippi, the Shenandoah, the Rio Grande . . . no need for me to try to imitate what he said, he just woke me up to America as a Poem instead of America as a place to struggle around and sweat in. Mainly this dark-eyed American poet made me want to prowl, and roam, and see the real America that was there and that "had never been uttered." They say nowadays that only adolescents appreciate Thomas Wolfe but that's easy to say after you've read him anyway because he's the kind of writer whose prose poems you can just about only read once, and deeply and slowly, discovering, and having discovered, move away. His dramatic sections you can read over and over again. Where is the seminar on Tom Wolfe today? What is this minimization of Thomas Wolfe in his own time? Because Mr. Schwartz could wait.

But there I am sitting at my desk, book open, and I says to myself: "Now it's almost seven thirty, we'll hobble down to ye olde Lion's Den, have filet mignon, hot fudge sundaes, coffee, and then hobble on down to the one hundred sixteenth subway stop [remembering Prof Kerwick and his mathematics series numbers] and ride on down to Times Square and go see a French movie, go see Jean Gabin press his lips together sayin *"Ça me navre,"* or Louis Jouvet's baggy behind going up the stairs, or that bitter lemon smile of Michele Morgan in the seaside bedroom, or Harry Bauer kneel as Handel praying for his work, or Raimu screaming at the mayor's afternoon picnic, and then after that, an American doublefeature, maybe Joel McRae in *Union Pacific,* or see tearful clinging sweet Barbara Stanwyck grab him, or maybe go see Sherlock Holmes puffing on his pipe with long Cornish profile as Dr. Watson puffs at a medical tome by the fireplace and Missus Cavendish or whatever her name was comes upstairs with cold roast beef and ale so that Sherlock can solve the latest manifestation of the malefaction of himself Dr. Moriarty. . . .

Lights of the campus, lovers arm in arm, hurrying eager students in the flying leaves of late October, the library going with glow, all the books and pleasure and the big city of the world right at my broken feet. . . .

And think of this in 1967: I even actually used to get on my crutches and go to Harlem to see what was going on, 125th Street and thereabouts, sometimes to watch spareribs turning in the spareribs shack window, or watch Negroes talk on corners; to me they were exotic people I'd never known before. I forgot to mention earlier, on my first week at HM in 1939, hands clasped behind my back I'd actually walked all over Harlem one whole warm afternoon and evening examining all this new world. Why didnt anybody hit up on me, say to sell me drugs, or hit me, or rob me: what did they see? They see a tweeded college boy studying the street. People have respect for those things. I must have been an awfully weird-looking character anyway.

So I'd go into the Lions Den, sit in my regular chair in front of the fire, the waiters (students) would bring me the supper, I'd eat, watch the dancers (one beauty in particular, Vicki Evans, interested me, Welsh girl), and then I'd go down to Times Square for my movies. Nobody ever bothered me. I always had, of course, nothing, but something like sixty cents on me anyway and must have looked like it with that innocent face.

Now also I had time to start writing big "Wolfean" stories and journals in my room, to look at them today it's a drag but at that time, I thought I was doing allright. I had a Negro student friend who came in and boned me on chemistry, my weakness. In French I had an A. In physics a B or C-plus or so. I hobbled around the campus proud like some heroic skimaster. In my tweed coat, with crutches, I became so popular (also because of the football reputation now) that some guy from the Van Am Society actually started a campaign to have me elected vice-president of next year's sophomore class. One thing sure I had no football to play till the sophomore year, 1941. To while away the time that winter I wrote sports a little for the college newspaper, covered the track coach interviews, wrote a few term papers for boys of Horace Mann who kept coming down to visit me. Hung around with Mike Hennessey as I say on that corner in front of the candy store on 115th and Broadway with William F. Buckley Jr. sometimes. Hobbled down to the Hudson River and sat on Riverside Drive benches smoking a cigar and thinking about mist on rivers, occasionally took the subway to Brooklyn to see Grandma Ti Ma and Yvonne and Uncle Nick, went home for Christmas with the crutches gone and the leg practically healed.

Sentimentally getting drunk on port wine in front of my mother's Christmas tree with G.J. and having to carry him home in the Gershom Avenue snow. Looking for Maggie Cassidy at the Commodore Ballroom, finding her, asking for a dance, falling in love again. Long talks with Pa in the eager kitchen.

Life is funny.

A cameo for size: one night in the Phi Gamma Delta fraternity house, where I was a "pledge" but refused to wear the little blue skullcap, in fact told them to shove it and insisted instead on giving me the beer barrel, which was almost empty, and raised it above my head at dawn and drained it of its dregs . . . all alone one night, in the completely empty frat house on 114th Street, except maybe for one or two guys sleeping upstairs, completely unlighted house, I'm sitting in an easy chair in the frat lounge playing Glenn Miller records fullblast. Almost crying. Glenn Miller and Frank Sinatra with Tommy Dorsey "The One I Love Belongs to Somebody Else" and "Everything Happens to Me," or Charlie Barnet's "Cherokee." "This Love of Mine." Helping paralytic or spastic Dr. Philippe Claire across the campus, we've just been working on his crossword puzzles which he writes for the New York *Journal-American,* he loves me because I'm French. Old Joe Hatter coming into my dormitory room one drenching night, with battered hat all dissolved in rain, bleary-eyed, saying, "Jesus Christ is pissing on the earth tonight." At the West End Bar Johnny the Bartender looking over everybody's heads with his big hands on the counter. In the lending library I'm studying Jan Valtin's *Out of the Night,* still a good book today to read. I wander around the Low Library wondering about libraries, or something. Told you life was funny. Girls with galoshes in the snow. Barnard girls growing bursty like ripe cherries in April, who the hell can study French books? A tall queer approaching me on a Riverside Park bench saying "How you hung?" and me saying "By the neck, I hope." Turk Tadzic, varsity end of next year, crying drunk in my room telling me how he once squatted on Main Street in a Pennsy town and shat in front of everybody, ashamed. Guys pissing outside the West End Bar right on the sidewalk. The "lounge lizards," guys who sit in the dormitory lounge doing nothing, with their legs up on other chairs. Big notes pinned to a board saying where you can buy a shirt, trade a radio, get a ride to Arkansas, or go drop dead more or less. My legs better, I'm now a waiter in John Jay dining hall, that is, I'm the coffee waiter, with coffee tray balanced in left hand I go about, inquisitively, gentlemen and ladies give me the nod, I go to their left and pour delicate coffee in their cups; a guy says to me: "You know that old geezer you just poured coffee for? Thomas Mann." My legs better, I saunter over Brooklyn Bridge remembering that raging blizzard in 1936 when I was fourteen years old and Ma'd brought me to Brooklyn to visit Grandma Ti Ma: I had my Lowell overshoes with me: I'd said "I'm going out and walk over the Brooklyn Bridge and back," "Okay," I go over the bridge in a howling wind with biting sleet snow in my red face, naturally not a soul in sight, except here comes this one man about 6 foot 6, with large body and small head, striding Brooklyn-ward and not looking at me, long strides and meditation. Know who that old geezer was?

Thomas Wolfe.

Go to Book Five.

Herman Wouk

'34 COLUMBIA COLLEGE

Herman Wouk drew on his Navy experience in the World War II Pacific theater in writing The Caine Mutiny—*excerpted here—for which he received the 1952 Pulitzer Prize in fiction. Wouk also authored the widely popular* The Winds of War *and* War and Remembrance, *both praised for their richness of detail, along with other novels and plays.*

He was of medium height, somewhat chubby, and good looking, with curly red hair and an innocent, gay face, more remarkable for a humorous air about the eyes and large mouth than for any strength of chin or nobility of nose. He had graduated from Princeton in 1941 with high marks in all subjects except mathematics and sciences. His academic specialty had been comparative literature. But his real career at Princeton had consisted of playing the piano and inventing bright little songs for parties and shows.

He kissed his mother good-by on the sidewalk near the corner of Broadway and 116th Street in New York City, on a cold sunny morning in December 1942. The family Cadillac was parked beside them, its motor running, but maintaining a well-bred silence. Around them stood the dingy gray-and-red buildings of Columbia University.

"Don't you think," said Mrs. Keith, smiling bravely, "that we might stop in that drugstore first and have a sandwich?"

She had driven her son to the midshipmen school from their home in Manhasset, despite Willie's protests. Willie had wanted to take the train. It would have seemed more like departing for the wars; he did not like being escorted to the gates of the Navy by his mother. But Mrs. Keith had prevailed as usual. She was a large, wise, firm woman, as tall as her son, and well endowed with brow and jaw. This morning she was wearing a fur-trimmed brown cloth coat instead of mink, to match the austerity of the event. Beneath her mannish brown hat her hair showed the dominant red strain that had reappeared in her only child. Otherwise there was little resemblance between mother and son.

"The Navy'll feed me, Mom. Don't worry."

He kissed her for the second time and glanced nervously about, hoping that no military men were observing the overtender scene. Mrs. Keith pressed his shoulder lovingly.

"1 know you'll do wonderfully, Willie. Just as you always have."

"Aye aye, Mother." Willie strode along the brick walk past the School of Journalism, and down a few steps to the entrance of Furnald Hall, formerly a dormitory for law students. A grizzled, pudgy Navy chief with four red service stripes on his blue coat stood in the doorway. Mimeographed papers in his hand flapped in the breeze. Willie wondered whether to salute, and swiftly decided that the gesture did not go well with a brown raglan coat and green pork-pie hat. He had completely forgotten his mother.

"You V-7?" The chief's voice was like a shovelful of pebbles dropped on tin.

"Aye aye." Willie grinned self-consciously. The chief returned the grin and appraised him briefly with, it seemed, an affectionate eye. He handed Willie four sheets clipped together.

"You're starting a new life. Good luck."

"Thank you, sir." For three weeks Willie was to make the mistake of calling chiefs "sir."

The chief opened the door invitingly. Willis Seward Keith stepped out of the sunshine across the threshold. It was done as easily and noiselessly as Alice's stepping through the looking glass; and like Alice, Willie Keith passed into a new and exceedingly strange world.

At the instant that Mrs. Keith saw Willie swallowed up, she remembered that she had neglected an important transaction. She ran to the entrance of Furnald Hall. The chief stopped her as she laid a hand on the doorknob.

"Sorry, madam. No admittance."

"That was my son who just went in."

"Sorry, madam."

"I only want to see him for a moment. I must speak to him. He forgot something."

"They're taking physicals in there, madam. There are men walking around with nothing on."

Mrs. Keith was not used to being argued with. Her tone sharpened. "Don't be absurd. There he is, just inside the door. I can rap and call him out."

She could see her son plainly, his back toward her, grouped with several other young men around an officer who was talking to them. The chief glanced dourly through the door. "He seems to be busy."

Mrs. Keith gave him a look appropriate to fresh doormen. She rapped on the glass of the outer door with her diamond ring and cried, "Willie! Willie!" But her son did not hear her call from the other world.

"Madam," said the chief, with a note in his rasping voice that was not unkind, "he's in the Navy now."

Mrs. Keith suddenly blushed. "I'm sorry."

"Okay, okay. You'll see him again soon—maybe Saturday."

The mother opened her purse and began to fish in it. "You see, I promised—the fact is, he forgot to take his spending money. He hasn't a cent. Would you be kind enough to give these to him?"

"Madam, he won't need money." The chief made an uneasy pretense of leafing through the papers he held. "He'll be getting paid pretty soon."

"But meantime—suppose he wants some? I promised him. Please take the money—Pardon me, but I'd be happy to give you something for your trouble."

The chief's gray eyebrows rose. "That won't be necessary." He wagged his head like a dog shaking off flies, and accepted the bills. Up went the eyebrows again. "Madam—this here is a hundred dollars!"

He stared at her. Mrs. Keith was struck with an unfamiliar sensation—shame at being better off than most people. "Well," she said defensively, "it isn't every day he goes to fight a war."

"I'll take care of it, madam."

"Thank you," said Mrs. Keith, and then, vaguely, "I'm sorry."

"Okay."

The mother closed with a polite smile, and walked off to her Cadillac. The chief looked after her, then glanced at the two fifties fluttering in his hand. "One thing," he muttered, "we're sure as hell getting a new kind of Navy." He thrust the bills into a pocket.

Meanwhile, Willie Keith, spearhead of the new Navy, advanced to war; which, for the moment, took the form of a glittering array of inoculation needles. Willie was not angry at Hitler nor even at the Japanese, though he disapproved of them. The enemy in this operation lay not before him, but behind. Furnald Hall was sanctuary from the United States Army.

He was jabbed swiftly for several tropical ailments. The bugs thus liberated whirled down his bloodstream. His arm began to ache. He was ordered to strip naked, and his clothes were carried off in a heap by a burly sailor.

"Hey, when do I get those back?"

"Who knows? Looks like a long war," the sailor growled, and mashed the green hat under his arm. Willie followed with anxious eyes as his old identity was hauled away to camphor balls.

With forty other upright pink animals he was herded into a large examination room. His lungs, liver, heart, eyes, ears, all the apparatus he had been using since birth, were investigated by hard-eyed pharmacist's mates, who prodded and poked him like suspicious women about to buy a turkey in a market.

"Stand up straight, sir." The last pharmacist's mate of the line-up was eying him critically. Willie stiffened. It unnerved him to see, out of the corner of his eye, that the examiner looked very dissatisfied.

"Bend over and touch your toes."

Willie tried, but years of overeating barred the way. His fingers hung eight inches from his toes. He tried the ancient mode of cheating—

"*Without* bending the knees, please."

Willie straightened, took a deep breath, and tried to snap himself double. Something gave in his spine with an ugly crack. There were four inches to go.

"You wait." The pharmacist walked away, and returned with a lieutenant characterized by a black mustache, puffy eyes, and a stethoscope.

"Look at that, sir."

"That" was Willie, erect as he could get.

"Can he touch?"

"Hell, no, sir. Hardly gets past his knees."

"Well, that's quite a breadbasket he's got."

Willie hauled in his stomach, too late.

"I don't care about the breadbasket," said the pharmacist's mate. "This joker has a hollow back."

The naked candidates behind Willie on line were fidgeting and murmuring.

"There is a lordosis, no doubt of it."

"Well, do we survey him out?"

"I don't know if it's that serious."

"Well, I ain't gonna pass him on my responsibility. You can, sir."

The doctor picked up Willie's record. "How about the pulse?"

"I didn't bother. What's the point if he's a lordosis?"

The doctor took Willie's wrist. His eyes emerged in surprise from the red puffs. "Ye gods, boy—are you sick?"

Willie could feel his blood galloping past the doctor's fingers. Various tropical bacteria, and above all, the shadow of the United States Army were pushing up his pulse rate.

"No, just worried."

"I don't blame you. How on earth did you get past the receiving station? Did you know the doctor?"

"Sir, I may be chubby, but I play six hours of tennis at a stretch. I climb mountains."

"There's no mountains at sea," said the pharmacist's mate. "You're Army meat, my friend."

"Shut up, Warner," said the doctor, noticing in the record that Willie was a Princeton man. "Leave pulse and back vacant. Send him down to Captain Grimm at the Navy Yard for a recheck."

"Aye aye, sir." The doctor left. Sullenly, the pharmacist's mate took a red pencil, scrawled on a memo pad, "Lordosis—Pulse," and clipped the crimson indictment to Willie's record. "Okay. Report to the exec's office right after inspection tomorrow, Mister Keith. Best of luck."

"Same to you," said Willie. They exchanged a look of pure hate, remarkable on such short acquaintance, and Willie moved off.

The Navy now dressed him in blue jumper and trousers, black shoes, black socks, and a perky sailor hat, marked with the special blue stripe of a midshipman. Then it filled his arms with books, of all shapes, colors, sizes, and degrees of wear. As Willie left the book-issuing room, seeing his way with some difficulty over the pile of prose in his arms, a sailor at the door laid on top a stack of mimeographed sheets which brought the heap level with his eyebrows. Willie craned his neck around the corner of his burden, and sidled crabwise to the elevator—the "HOIST," said a freshly lettered sign over the push buttons.

When the elevator reached the top floor, only Willie and a skinny horse-faced sailor remained. Willie walked down the hall, scanning the names posted outside each room, and found a door labeled:

ROOM 1013
KEEFER
KEITH
KEGGS

He went in, and dropped the books on the bare springs of a cot. He heard the twang of springs again directly behind him.

"My name's Keggs," said the horse face, poking an arm toward him. Willie shook the hand, which enveloped his in a big moist grip.

"I'm Keith."

"Well," said Keggs mournfully, "looks like we're roommates."

"This is it," said Willie.

"I hope," said Keggs, "that this Keefer doesn't turn out to be too much of a drip." He looked at Willie earnestly, then his face maneuvered its length into a slow smile. He picked up *Naval Ordnance* from the pile on his cot. "Well, no time like the present." He sat on the only chair, put his legs up on the only desk, and opened the book with an unhappy sigh.

"How do you know what to study?" Willie was surprised at such industry.

"Brother, it makes no difference. It's all going to be too much for me. Might as well start anywhere."

A heap of books entered the door, walking on stout legs. "Make way, gentlemen, heah Ah come," spoke a muffled voice. The books fell and bounced all over the remaining cot, unveiling a tall, fat sailor with a cherry flushed face, small crinkling eyes and a very large loose mouth. "Well, fellas, looks like we're in for a lot of Shinola, don' it?" he said, in a high, musical Southern cadence. "Ah'm Keefer."

"I'm Keith."

"Keggs."

The fat Southerner shoved a number of his books off the cot to the floor, and stretched himself out on the springs. "Ah had me a farewell party last night," he groaned, inserting a happy giggle into the groan, "to end all farewell parties. Why do we do it to ourselves, fellas? 'Scuse me." He rolled his face to the wall.

"You're not going to *sleep!*" Keggs said. "Suppose they catch you?"

"My boy," said Keefer drowsily, "Ah am an old military man. Four years at Gaylord Academy. Don' worry about ol' Keefer. Punch me if Ah snore." Willie wanted to ask the old military man how serious lordosis might be in a war career. But as he searched for a delicate way to open the subject, Keefer's breath grew regular and heavy. Within a minute he was sleeping like a hog in the sun.

"He'll get bilged, sure," mourned Keggs, turning the pages of *Naval Ordnance*. "So will I. This book is absolute gibberish to me. What on earth is a cam? What do they mean by an interrupted screw?"

"Search me. What do you mean, 'bilged'?"

"Don't you know how they work it? We get three weeks as apprentice seamen. Then the top two thirds of the class become midshipmen. The rest get bilged. Straight to the Army."

The fugitives exchanged an understanding look. Willie's hand crept around to his back, to ascertain how hollow his hollow back really was. He began a series of frenzied efforts to touch his toes. At every bend he came nearer. He broke out in a sweat. Once he thought the tips of his fingers brushed his shoelaces, and he gurgled in triumph. With a swoop and a groan he brought his fingers squarely on his toes. Coming erect again, his spine vibrating, the room spinning, he found that Keefer, rolled over and awake, was staring at him with frightened little eyes. Keggs had backed into a corner. Willie attempted a lighthearted laugh, but he staggered at the same moment and had to clutch the desk to keep from falling over, so the effect of nonchalance was marred. "Nothing like a little setting-up exercise," he said, with drunken savoir-faire.

"Hell, no," said Keefer. "Especially three o'clock in the afternoon. Ah never miss it myself."

Three rolled-up mattresses came catapulting through the open door, one after another. "Mattresses!" yelled a retreating voice in the hall. Blankets, pillows, and sheets flew in, propelled by another disembodied voice shouting, "Blankets, pillows, and sheets!"

"Couldn't imagine what they were less'n he told us," growled Keefer, untangling himself from a sheet which had draped itself on him. He made up a bed in a few moments, flat and neat as if it had been steamrollered. Willie summoned up boys' camp experience; his cot soon looked presentable. Keggs wrestled with the bedclothes for ten minutes while the others stowed their books and clothes, then he asked Keefer hopefully: "How's that, now?"

"Fella," said Keefer, shaking his head, "you an innocent man." He approached the cot and made a few passes of the hand over it. The bed straightened itself into military rigidity, as in an animated cartoon.

"You're a whiz," said Keggs.

"I heard what you said about me bilging," said Keefer kindly. "Don' worry. I be there on the great gittin'-up morning."

The rest of the day went by in bugles, assemblies, dismissals, reassemblies, announcements, marches, lectures, and aptitude tests. Every time the administration remembered a detail that had been omitted in the mimeographed sheets the bugle blared, and five hundred sailors swarmed out of Furnald Hall. A fair-haired, tall, baby-faced ensign named Acres would bark the new instruction, standing on the steps, jutting his chin and squinting fiercely. Then he would dismiss them, and the building would suck them in. The trouble with this systole and diastole for the men on the top floor ("tenth deck") was that there wasn't room for them all in the elevator. They had to scramble down nine flights of stairs ("ladders"), and later wait wearily for a ride up, or else climb. Willie was stumbling with fatigue when at last they were marched off to dinner. But food revived him wonderfully.

Back in their room, with leisure to talk, the three exchanged identities. The gloomy Edwin Keggs was a high school algebra teacher from Akron, Ohio. Roland Keefer was the son of a West Virginian politician. He had had a job in the state personnel bureau, but, as he cheerfully phrased it, he didn't know personnel from Shinola, and had simply been learning the ropes around the capitol when the war came. Willie's announcement that he was a night-club pianist sobered the other two, and the conversation lagged. Then he added that he was a Princeton graduate, and a chill silence blanketed the room.

When the bugle sounded retreat and Willie climbed into bed, it occurred to him that he had not had a single thought of May Wynn or of his parents all day. It seemed weeks since he had kissed his mother that same morning on 116th Street. He was not far, physically, from Manhasset, no further than he had been in his Broadway haunts. But he felt arctically remote. He glanced around at the tiny room, the bare yellow-painted walls bordered in black wood, the shelves heavy with menacing books, the two strangers in underwear climbing into their cots, sharing an intimacy with him that Willie had never known even in his own family. He experienced a most curiously mixed feeling of adventurous coziness, as though he were tented down for the night in the wilds, and sharp regret for his lost freedom.

Jacques Barzun

'27 COLUMBIA COLLEGE, '32 PHD

Jacques Barzun served on the Columbia faculty for more than six decades, including a tenure as dean of faculties and provost from 1958 to 1967. Over the course of his career, he wrote or edited dozens of critical and historical works for both academic and general readerships; his most recent book, From Dawn to Decadence, *was a surprise best-seller in 2000. The following is from his* Teacher in America *(1945).*

> Oh that mine enemy had
> founded a college!
> —*Job*, revised

I have done with specifications for subject matters. If in so doing, I have had to generalize critically about certain practices, in order to set in relief what I felt were more desirable ways, it should not be inferred that all the evils I spoke of were concentrated in any one place or kind of institution. And now that I am going on to discuss institutional arrangements, let me begin by saying that in normal times it is possible to obtain in this country a thoroughly satisfactory college training. As with the evil, so with the good. There is not one choice spot where wisdom holds an exclusive salon. There are several varieties of the good and they may be had in every kind of natural setting or architecture. The small country college, the state university, the small-town big place, the big-town big place, the progressive, the old-fashioned, and the middling, all provide, under favorable conditions, a type of instruction which easily matches that given

252

abroad, and which certainly surpasses the instruction given in the same places fifty years ago.

What is to be deplored is that the facts about any institution, facts which no one tries to conceal, should nevertheless remain hidden from parents interested in educating their sons and daughters. This is one great difference between higher learning here and abroad. Educated Europeans know their schools. They hear of it at once when Bovril College, Oxbridge, loses its best tutors. The heads not only of universities but of preparatory schools are, by virtue of their office, national figures. They are accordingly subjected to a public scrutiny that is valuable to them, to their schools, and to the country.

Over here, it is not uncommon to find a reputation outlast the grounds for it—good or bad—by twenty to thirty years. I am thinking of two sizable neighboring institutions, one of which is generally considered a "serious" place and the other rather a country club. It so happens that the academic eminence of the first has somewhat declined, though not dangerously, and that—what is more important—the second has emerged in every respect superior to the first. "How do you know that?" One knows it chiefly by comparing the teaching staffs in each branch, and by observing on the spot the practical arrangements in use as well as the products of the system.

Similarly, given the absence of serious interest on the part of the public, it is possible for an institution to publicize changes of plan or "new" features without any chance of verification by those most interested. Almost anything passes for "new" and there is no checkup on the extent to which plans become facts. One can imagine, for instance, a university quite sincerely, making much of its devotion to the principle of teaching, and yet continuing the bargain-counter method of holding huge classes without adequate supervision of individual work. Practical reasons may forbid it, but that is not the point: the point is that the student or his parent is led to think he is going to be taught personally, whereas he finds that he is lectured at, graded, and "put through" impersonally.

Let me take an actual case of the reverse ignorance, though it affects what may at first seem a trivial point. Everybody has heard of a place called Columbia. The name is in the papers, the institution is in New York, and every novelist who wishes to "locate" a metropolitan character makes him either an instructor or a student "at Columbia."

These fictional persons add to the general impression of size, so that new acquaintances who find that I teach "at Columbia" ask me without a smile whether I ever get to know my students; seeing that I lecture to thousands at a time. When I reply that most of my teaching is done in classes of twenty-five and that I am in fact attached to one of the smallest of men's colleges in the East, they can only stare and suspect me of irony. I explain to them that there is a part of Columbia University called Columbia College, founded nearly two centuries ago and consisting of one thousand seven hundred and fifty male undergraduates, taught by a faculty of about one hundred and thirty. For the space of five minutes they believe me. At the end of that time, their mind snaps back and they burst out with one invariable question, which is: "How is it that with thirty thousand students to choose from, your football team is always so poor?" At this point, I either explain again, or I do not.

Does it matter, after all, whether the public knows that the enrollment figures in Columbia's undergraduate college are less than those of Harvard, Princeton, or Yale? It does in one sense, namely that if it is impossible to get over this first hurdle and take it as cleared for good, it is certainly impossible to explain a scheme of instruction which, with all its shortcomings, *is* a going concern and has steadily and noticeably influenced practice elsewhere.

It might save breath if I had small cards printed with the following statistics: —

Enrollment Fall of 1940

Harvard	3,561 men
Yale	2,375 men
Chicago	3,512 men and women
Princeton	2,405 men
Wisconsin (College of Letters and Science)	6,142 men and women
COLUMBIA COLLEGE.	1,672 men

I have already spoken of John Erskine's reading course in great books, after which others have been patterned, and the latest offspring of which is the radio program, "Invitation to Learning." There may be good enough reasons why Erskine has not yet received due credit for his innovation of 1919, but it is obvious that no one can begin to grasp what that idea was if one's imagination pictures him at that time discussing Dante informally with thirty thousand students of all ages and sexes.

Perhaps I am unduly sensitive on the point; if so, it is not because I have an abstract dislike of large numbers. If I had, I should never have done any radio broadcasting. My reason is rather that I believe in hand-to-hand, mind-to-mind encounters as an indispensable part of teaching, and the undying *idée fixe* of the public concerning that nonexistent thing "Columbia" puts me in the mood of the British undergraduate who, being a member of an unfashionable College at Oxford, got into the habit of supplying the right response: "I'm from Wadham—Oh!" I could paraphrase it: "Men only—one, seven, five, o!"

Oddly enough—and this is why I dwell on its true character—Columbia College is highly representative of modern instruction throughout the country.

Whether it be the Honors programs, the many introductions to the history of civilization and to the humanities, the abandonment of loose electives, or the interdepartmental devices for staffing small classes and reading groups, they all owe something to the ideas of the late Dean H. E. Hawkes and his associates in Columbia College. Yet it seems to be only at that college that these separate improvements have been fitted together into an established whole, and the sense of the innovation accepted in its fullness. This has come about partly because the college is small enough to permit flexible arrangements, partly because the resistance of older traditions of teaching has been amicably overcome during a period of twenty years.

Still using Columbia College as an epitome of changes now well entrenched in many places, I should say that "modernism" in the American college began towards the end of the First World War. At Columbia the need to explain war aims generated a course known as An Introduction to Contemporary Civilization in the West, compulsory for all freshmen. A year later, in 1919, came Erskine's reading course, for selected juniors and seniors. Ten years after that, the Contemporary Civilization course was extended to cover two years, and very soon after it was supplemented by two new courses, also obligatory and also covering two years—one in the Humanities and one in the Sciences.

The sense of the plan can be seen at once by starting, not from the college, but from the world. What are the broad divisions of thought and action in that world? There are three and only three: we live in a world saturated with science, in a world beset by political and economic problems, in a world that mirrors its life in literature, philosophy, religion, and the fine arts. In all reason, a college can but follow this threefold pattern. To this extent, the problem of "What shall we teach?" is nonexistent. This is what we must teach. To quote the present Dean of Columbia College on the teaching of science, social science and the humanities, "Any one of them without the other two gives a lopsided, incomplete, dangerously ignorant product. A false specialization that chooses to neglect even one of these fields is like a three-legged stool with only two legs."

If this is true, it would seem logical to ask that all freshmen and sophomores in the liberal arts should be required to take courses introducing them to these three matters of ancient and modern learning. In the Columbia Introduction to Contemporary Civilization they are shown the historical development of the modern world since 1200. By studying the institutions, ideas, and ways of making a living prevalent during that period, they are prepared to go on with courses in economics, government philosophy, and history. The second year of this Introduction concentrates on America and ends with an analysis of the world about us, its politics and its economic structure.

In a parallel Humanities course, the students must read books, hear music, and see pictures. The books, ranging from Homer to Goethe, are read in their entirety, include fiction, history, poetry, and philosophy, and take up the whole of the freshman year. The sophomore year serves to introduce music and the plastic arts, with a choice for the student to take more hours of the one than the other. But both he must have. I indicated above the kind of instruction that is possible and profitable in the arts.

Finally, the freshman must make acquaintance with the physical and logical sciences. He can do so in two ways. If his bent is scientific to begin with, he can choose the mathematics and other sciences that suit his purpose. But if he is to remain a layman, he must take the two-year introduction to scientific concepts and techniques. The first year includes geology, astronomy, physics, and chemistry; the second, biology, botany, mathematics, and logic. Needless to say, the course does not "cover" these vast subjects: it describes their contents and viewpoints and relates them. In the present state of quasi-universal ignorance of science, it is a great thing to have liberal-arts students learn accurately what biology is concerned with, how the biologist leans on the chemist and the geologist, and what a cell or a syllogism is for.

The first two years, then, take the student and show him a mirror of the world. He not only fills his head with fair pictures of reality, but he can begin to think with tolerable good sense about what he himself wishes to do, both in his next two college years and later on. Any part of this program, suitably altered to fit local needs, is undoubtedly good in itself, as adaptations of the Columbia College scheme have repeatedly proved. It is moreover generally acknowledged that teaching individuals is better than lecturing masses; and the recognition of intellect through Honors work has proceeded apace. But there is a virtue peculiar to the full introduction, obtainable only from the deliberate and protracted hand shaking with all the muses in turn, for in teaching the whole is more than the sum of its parts.

To be sure, this initial dose of instruction sounds formidable. It taxes the powers of both students and instructors but it produces genuine students capable of really advanced work. But before sketching the character of this advanced work, I want to point out the drawbacks and difficulties of the introductory stage; drawbacks and difficulties that must be cheerfully faced and fought, if the whole arrangement is to be kept from turning into hokum.

The chief need and the hardest to fill is a good staff, willing to work like dogs with small discussion groups. They must be well-informed, active, interested in students, conscientious in their preparation, and committed to the idea of interdepartmental work. The next biggest difficulty is to make the three main required courses fit into the time available. For of necessity, freshmen and sophomores have other demands made upon them as well.

They must write English prose, continue a foreign language, and they should, if possible, engage in extracurricular activities and acquire some physical skill.

As things stand, modern languages and English prose undoubtedly suffer. Both are dealt with by asking "proficiency" rather than by following courses. The student writes English or learns German until he can pass the set examination. Usually he has to take one or two courses in the language to pass it. But it is bad to put foreign languages on the footing of a nuisance to be got rid of; and it is equally bad to make the writing of English an isolated performance which is also to cease after "passing." It will take work and thought—and they have begun to be applied—to iron out these major blemishes. It is perhaps only fair to add that other plans in force elsewhere reveal the same weakness in languages and composition. Again, the techniques for teaching music and the plastic arts to every kind of mind are still in their infancy. Trial has been followed by error and this by trial again. Some improvement is noticeable, substantial enough to suggest that the right road has at last been struck. But success here also depends on gifted teachers.

Finally, the third conflict of desires comes from the situation of the scientific and engineering students. Their specialized preparation, as now outlined by the professional schools, demands a large allotment of time to science courses. These must come in a set sequence and naturally require much laboratory and outside work. Hardship cases are frequent and have to be dealt with as they come. But the situation is fundamentally unstable and something must topple over: either the basic, required *collegiate* preparation will be seriously breached, or the basic required *vocational* preparation will have to yield. This is true generally over the country, and the curriculum I describe only reflects it more vividly because it has gone farther than most in prescribing the work of the first two years. It is surely not fair to subject young men to the drawing-and-quartering of incompatible demands. It verges on the immoral to compel a choice between education and professional competence, and if the American college cannot reconcile them it will deserve all the hard words that normally accompany superannuated institutions to the grave.

Two things strike me as possible: either the engineering and pure science vocations will choose to follow the lead of medicine and law and reduce their demands on undergraduate time; or, keeping the requirements the same, they will recast their courses. I tread on mined ground in saying this but I should not be surprised if an overhauling of lecture contents and laboratory manuals could not be made to yield precious time. No doubt some of the acceleration done during the war emergency went much too far: I heard of a Qualitative Chemistry course being given by lecture alone; but an occasional upsetting of the apple cart may show administrators that the regular way is not necessarily immutable. One can understand, even honor, men so devoted to science that they put it before all other things, but it is poor political arithmetic to go on to say, like most scientists, that science should share the student's time half and half—one half for science, one half for all the rest. I say poor *political* arithmetic, because under this assumption the future American Citizen, the voter, the democrat, the parent of later generations, will be quite simply a half man.

*　*　*

To the point where I have taken him, the undergraduate has not yet heard a lecture—unless he has replaced the Introduction to the Sciences by specialized courses. Nor has he taken part in a seminar or colloquium. In his junior and senior years, he will probably experience both. He will be put in charge of a senior adviser, who will act in concert with his previous counselor, to whom he was assigned as a freshman on the basis of professional plans. The senior adviser's task is to fit the resources of the College—and of the University, for the upperclass man may with permission take graduate work—to the individual interests and purposes of the man in his charge.

This will probably mean the choice of a dominant interest in one branch of study, accompanied by two lesser interests. A student once compared this to Aristotle's golden mean and when I asked him what he meant, he said, "One virtue flanked by two vices." In the main subject, the student will take one or two courses plus a seminar—such as the junior or the senior seminar in economics. There he will do research and reading and receive training designed either to top off his preparation or to lead to graduate work. The lesser subjects usually bear some relation to the main one. An economist may take statistics and political theory; an historian will be advised to choose philosophy and English literature. The permutations are endless, and indeed, the student is not to be thought of as "an historian" or "an economist." He is still the raw material for an educated man. But the tradition of "going on to an M.A." is so strong in the American college population that it is advisable to make of the senior year the working half of a universal joint.

Interestingly enough, at Columbia College the unspecialized "Colloquium on Great Books"—the Erskine course—seems to draw steadily from all ranks of special interest. Future doctors seem to favor it especially, thinking perhaps that bedside books go with the bedside manner. Mathematicians come and dispute over Berkeley; poets endure Adam Smith so as to rhapsodize over Milton and Hardy; and engineers express the hope that they will imbibe style and the sense of beauty from viewing so many masterpieces in different tongues and genres.

In connection with this reading course, a long and careful attempt has been made to teach writing on the principles I indicated earlier. Each colloquium student writes one short paper each month on a topic of his own choosing and dealing with any aspect of the readings or discussions. The paper is submitted in duplicate; it is fully annotated by the two instructors in charge, and returned for later reference or immediate rewriting. After three papers, most students begin to think, talk, and write in less boyish fashion, and after six of them, half the class can write with a sureness of touch affording pleasure to both author and reader.

It remains to say a word about lecture courses. They are of two kinds: courses given by members of the College Faculty exclusively for college students, and courses open to graduate and undergraduate students alike. The virtue of the latter kind is that it offers college men the opportunity of studying with well-known authorities in the field of their choice, even when these men are attached primarily to the Graduate School. Conversely, certain College teachers offer courses for Graduate students. Thus another artificial gap in the ladder of learning is bridged over, and the truth recognized that the unceasing aim of teaching should be to let the instruction fit the class.

In all lecturer courses, however, the undergraduate contingent is responsible for more written work than the graduates, and for one additional hour, spent with the lecturer for the purpose of thrashing out left-over difficulties. How well this third hour is handled, how closely the written work is checked, how suitably the three or four lecturers that each student hears supplement or contradict one another—these are matters left to chance, and perhaps not to be regulated without loss of desirable freedom.

The Columbia College curriculum is anything but perfect. As in all working machinery breakdowns occur, parts wear out and have to be replaced. "Efficient" teaching is an absurd aim, though doubtless "effective" teaching is not. In any case, perfectionism in education is a false idol which too often induces paralysis or meddlesome bustling about. The particular form which weaknesses in language and composition study take in the Columbia College scheme, I have stated. Other failures, personal ones, are only too evident at the end of each term, and with them comes the sense that it takes two to fail, just as it takes two to teach. Diversity of aims, temperaments, and opportunities, which makes for various kinds of success, also allows mishaps that in gloomy moods seem preventable. But risks of this sort are not to be conjured away by system. The strength of this specimen institution seems to me to reside in two things: one, it teaches in close coordination the three live subject matters in modern life—science, social science, and the humanities; and two, it does not undertake to "process" men for the sake of any single virtue.

Columbia College does prescribe a much greater part of the four-year course than do other institutions. But the required work is concentrated in two years and its contents are designed to help the student choose wisely in his upper years. The unrestricted right to shop among electives may look like freedom, but it may actually be confining, as a student from the Middle West confessed when I asked what his preparation in history had been. "I was going to be a minister, so I took Pre-Theological Rural Sociology." Custom tailoring is excellent for the human form, but in collegiate teaching it can soon become patchwork. Besides, its appearance of perfect adaptation is deceptive. There is no such thing as a separate sociology for rural ministers. The title betrays the touch of the salesman, doubtless well meant, but more congenial to the catalogue maker than to the teacher.

Otto Luening

Musician, composer, and conductor Otto Luening authored the opera Evangeline *in the early 1930s before helping to found the American Composers Alliance, which promoted composers' rights. An early advocate of electronic music as an art form, Luening became chairman of the music department at Barnard in 1944 and taught at Barnard and Columbia until 1970. Excerpted here is his autobiography,* The Odyssey of an American Composer *(1980).*

In late January, Douglas Moore invited me for an interview in his Columbia office. Accustomed to the Jennings mansion at Bennington, I wasn't impressed by his tiny room or the other, cramped offices, each shared by two instructors, or the unattractive classrooms and the shabby second-hand furniture.

Moore told me Columbia was planning an Arts Center or School of the Arts.

"How long have you been planning?" I asked.

Moore cleared his throat twice. "Since Edward MacDowell came to Columbia in 1896."

He went on about the department's hopes and plans for the future. I asked about my future chances. After a carefully timed pause he made a salary offer of $5,000. I explained I needed $500 more.

Professor Moore's face fell. "You wouldn't want the whole deal to fall through for a measly five hundred dollars, would you?" he asked.

"Well, perhaps," I said.

What an administrator, I thought, but that $500 would put me into a higher salary bracket and affect my future eligibility for promotions, pensions, and other fringe benefits. I was by no means so tired of Bennington that I simply could not stand working there, so I stood firm. Professor Moore's lips tightened and he excused himself to phone Dean Gildersleeve.

After an interval, he returned, saying that Dean Gildersleeve would like to have a luncheon conference with us in two days. He described her as a real bluestocking, a Barnard graduate, a very good administrator, a great lady, and a fine scholar.

*   *   *

I arrived at the Barnard Deanery at twenty-five minutes past twelve noon. Moore was waiting. At twelve twenty-nine and a half, the door opened silently and in glided an impressive lady who greeted Moore with just the right degree of cordiality and administrative reserve. At exactly twelve-thirty the clock chimed eight times, and I was introduced. We went through the small talk and then the sherry-and-crackers ritual with style and academic abandon.

A quick glance around revealed that the Deanery was furnished in 1910 eclectic style, probably with gifts from trustees. There was a reproduction of *Whistler's Mother* and some 1890s bric-a-brac on a table. Dean Gildersleeve, at first rather shy, soon relaxed and spoke of the weather. I felt at home and reasonably safe in my formal blue suit, white shirt, blue tie with diagonal white stripes, and well-shined shoes.

"How long have you been at Bennington?"

"Ten years."

"You have accomplished much. Do you think you could do as well here?"

"That depends on student and faculty cooperation."

"We haven't done much in the arts." She looked sad, then brightened. "Of course, we have the Greek games."

Moore broke in to say, "I'll tell Mr. Luening about the games later."

The dean went on. "Our English department is very fine; they believe all students are illiterate until they graduate." She then asked how music related to other subjects.

I explained. "Songs, operas, and oratorios use words—Goethe, Schiller, Heine, Pushkin, and the Elizabethans wrote the words for thousands of these. Professor Moore has set Stephen Vincent Benét, I have composed Blake and Whitman songs . . ."

"I didn't know musicians were that literary!"

"Some prefer the physics of sound—you know—acoustics. A fundamental tone has a certain number of vibrations and upper partials." The Riverside Church tower clock obliged by striking sixteen bells before one. "If you listen carefully, Dean Gildersleeve, when the clock strikes one you will hear the big boom and several higher sounds all at once."

The clock boomed one. She listened attentively. "Gracious—I hear them—and to think that until now I've missed all the overtones!"

"Only consciously, Dean Gildersleeve—subconsciously you heard them."

"I hope so—Shall we have lunch?"

The luncheon talk reminded me of Sunday dinner at Aunt Gretchen's in Milwaukee. No ideas intruded on our gustatory enjoyment. After a cheerful discussion about the annual rainfall in New Hampshire and Vermont, Moore and I took our leave. Dean Gildersleeve gave me a knowing look and a special hand pressure somewhat like the secret grip of my Boy Scout troop in Madison.

"She likes you," said Moore.

"And I like her—she's great."

Moore mumbled, "Very scholarly. . . . Would you like to be guest conductor for the premiere of Bernard Wagenaar's opera, *Pieces of Eight*, in May? Have Bennington give you a three-month leave."

I agreed to try for it.

"Let's visit Dr. Milton Smith, the director of Brander Matthews Theatre," Moore said. "We cooperate with him and the Columbia Theatre Associates."

Brander Matthews was a tiny, attractive theater, seating about two hundred. At a rolltop desk piled high with manuscripts, clippings, cigarette butts, costumes, and letters sat Dr. Milton Smith. "My arthritis is killing me," he groaned and cracked his neck.

"Sorry Milton," Moore said. "Meet Otto Luening, guest conductor of our coming *Pieces of Eight* opera premiere."

"Another one of those lousy operettas. *Paul Bunyan* was a flop, but Benjamin Britten and W. H. Auden had talent. *A Tree on the Plains* by Ernst Bacon and Paul Horgan was a near miss, and now Wagenaar! The only good 'operetter' was the *Burglar's Opera* by Munday and Eager. All about the Macy's store." Chuckling, he recited the synopsis, which sounded mighty corny to me. As he steered us onto the stage, Dr. Smith impressed me as a mixture of country editor, country storekeeper, and country doctor.

The stage was large and the shop was roomy, but the sunken orchestra pit was two feet too narrow for comfort. The conductor would have to conduct the orchestra with one hand and the singers with the other; possible, of course, but difficult.

"Why don't you use a piano and keep those impertinent orchestra musicians out of the theater?" Smith growled. "They are always too loud."

"We must be going," said Moore nervously.

I shook hands with Smith, who sneered, "It's not too late to quit."

On our way across campus I asked Moore if Dr. Smith was always in such a good mood.

"He pretends to hate music but he runs a tight ship, is a good carpenter, and has his crew build houses, outdoor scenes, and interiors by the dozen. His wife, Helen Claire, is a fine professional actress, and sometimes she and Broadway actors like Alfred Drake do leads here, for the fun of it."

That afternoon, I met Lewis Jones, the Bennington president, at a cocktail party and told him I was thinking of going to Barnard. "That skunk; that cheapskate!" he roared.

"Who?"

"The Barnard trustee I dined with three weeks ago. I bragged about you and our music department. Now he steals you."

"All for the best, I hope."

"So do I. Well, good luck."

"Wait a minute; I haven't accepted formally."

"You will. Columbia, Juilliard, New York—too much glamour."

In ten days, I showed Wagenaar's score to the conductor, Professor Dittler, and to my assistant. In two hours Dittler returned the music and stated that his orchestra could not play it if they practiced a hundred years. My assistant announced the workshop had almost no men, but he phoned around to arrange auditions. I mentioned the orchestra problem to Moore.

"You'll have to get on the phone and find your own group."

"Does the job pay anything?"

"It's a great opportunity for the singers——show window, press reviews—they are glad to volunteer. The orchestra is made up of students—we allow ten dollars for meals and taxis."

Pieces of Eight, a Riverside Drive–Long Island version of Gilbert and Sullivan, was not an opera but a comic operetta. Bernard Wagenaar was an experienced European composer living in the United States. His music was moderately difficult, his vocal writing singable, and his melodies and harmonies agreeable. The libretto, by Edward Eager, an experienced Broadway wordsmith, was about eighteenth-century pirates, New England spinsters, and Captain Kidd. It was dominated by low comic rhyming and by references to the visceral organs. At times the jokes became scatological. It was too late for me to suggest changes so I recruited my forces by telephone, and began rehearsing.

The singers, all then unknown, included Patricia Neway, who later made a career at City Center and internationally in Menotti's *Consul* and his other works. From then on, I picked a few winners for each of my productions. Wagenaar played rehearsals to keep his opus from falling apart, and I did all the coaching.

During our long stage rehearsals, Milton Smith and Eager would whinny their approval after each witty line. I didn't, because I had nothing to whinny about: I had only four two-hour orchestra rehearsals. I memorized the score and nursed the players along, scene by scene, at a slow tempo. Attendance was irregular because of examinations. One singer was in service at the Brooklyn Navy Yard and was often called up for duty. There were no male understudies because of the war. I had to put it together like a jigsaw puzzle.

The dress rehearsal went well—and when it was over, Smith hollered, "Now that I have seen it, I know it will be a flop—the timing is off."

On opening night the theater was packed with singers, conductors, stage directors, students, and the press. As I entered the pit, Dr. Smith whispered, "You've got a turkey on your hands. Good luck."

The performance was rewarded by enthusiastic applause. Some reviewers reported a flop or at best a near-miss because of the libretto, but fortunately they praised my musical direction and my "conviction, understanding, verve, and animation," and the beautiful playing of the orchestra. Moore said I was a "howling success" and Wagenaar said I had done one swell job. I was lucky. My professional reputation was saved by the skin of my teeth and Barnard formalized my appointment.

Now I was an associate professor at Barnard College, Columbia University in the city of New York. We returned to Bennington to pack and found a card from Edgar Varèse: "Glad to have you with us. Cordially, Varèse."

After winding up business in Bennington, we visited Carl Ruggles at the Arlington Inn on our drive to New York. On the third day, he bellowed, "Are you staying in Vermont or going to New York? If you are going, tell Varèse I'm composing a piece that will blow the goddamn audience right out of their seats . . . and pants, too."

He roared, we howled, Mrs. Ruggles said, "Now, Carl," and we went on our way at last.

* * *

I found an apartment at 119th Street and Claremont Avenue. F. Scott Fitzgerald had once lived in the neighborhood and Ferruccio Busoni had had an apartment at 116th and Riverside in 1914. Riverside Park and the Hudson River were magnificent; Douglas Moore lived around the corner and my Barnard office was a short walk away.

Ethel's studio on 67th Street had a telephone, and she was hoping daily to hear favorable news about her audition at the Metropolitan Opera. The new apartment had no phone because of the war. It was roomy and quiet so I could work.

Two days later, I visited Barnard. Professor Cady, who shared my office, showed me around. We entered a large, beautifully furnished room, with a

Steinway concert grand at one end, a collection of baroque and Renaissance instruments in locked cases around the walls, and attractive oil paintings and Gobelins on the walls. There was a striking portrait of Dean Gildersleeve.

"A perfect room for chamber music," I said. "What happens here?"

"This is the College Parlor. The music club meets here, the faculty has teas, and there are large faculty meetings."

"No concerts?"

"Mr. Swan of Buildings and Grounds wants to preserve the valuable equipment."

"By not using it?"

"Why don't you visit him in his downstairs office?"

Mr. Swan's secretary said that he could give me an appointment in ten days. I called him on the public phone in the lobby.

"Come right in," said Mr. Swan, and to the astonishment of his secretary I walked into his office.

"I'm the new music chairman, and I would like to know how many pianos Barnard owns."

Mr. Swan fished out a chart marked PIANO MAP. "Twenty-four," he said.

"Where are they? I have seen only two."

He pointed to the map of Barnard buildings, which bore twenty-four crosses.

"Are they being used?" I asked.

"Don't know," he said, lighting his pipe. "They are all gifts and we just store them."

"Can I look?"

"Sure," he said, and he handed me the map.

The next hour was spent finding the pianos. They were in coal bins, in dormitories, in storerooms, in the gymnasium, under the elevator shaft, and behind the boiler room. Six seemed usable, eighteen were covered with dust and had broken keyboards and split sounding boards. Mice had enjoyed chewing up the felt hammers of three. I suggested repairing some of the pianos and discarding the others.

I walked through the campus to have lunch with Moore. The Faculty Club, our luncheon rendezvous, was post–World War I modern. It looked as though the furnishings and the library itself were mostly gifts, a very mixed selection of not-too-attractive armchairs, sofas, and old books.

The dining room was soon crowded with energetic faculty members. The food was academic—not very tasty, but nourishing. The fragments of conversation that floated around the hall were on a high plane: "But the tse-tse fly . . ." "More eliptic, differential operators on manifolds . . ." "MIT is ahead in principles of statistical inference . . ." "But ancient Near Eastern tests will be very practical in the future . . ."

Moore looked disinterested as I told him about my Barnard visit. "Yes, yes, but it is only the branch store; here is something more interesting. President Butler appointed me to the Alice M. Ditson Fund committee a few years ago, and I am nominating you. Now let's visit the Columbia music department."

I had seen McMillin Theatre previously. In the elevator of the Journalism Building, Moore introduced me to Dean Ackerman, then whispered on our way out, "Dean Ackerman is with the School of Journalism. He is a famous World War I correspondent. He lets us have rooms on the sixth floor."

We went into the office area. He showed me my studio, room 604, with a grand piano and shelves for scores and books. Classrooms were drab and made Bennington seem luxurious by comparison.

Moore sent the secretary in the main office to round up the faculty. Everyone was very friendly. After introductions were over, the professors pulled out their watches, mumbled about other appointments and disappeared either into their offices or into the elevator.

"Here's your schedule," Moore said. "I put you down for an evening class in General Studies, Music I. It will pay three hundred dollars extra for the semester." Moore looked at his watch and rushed for the elevator.

I went upstairs to examine the music library. It was a small but very good collection of books and scores, without much contemporary music and with a rather small record library, not as good as the one at Bennington. I went home to think.

At the beginning, the Columbia music department seemed strange. Professor Lang was building a musicology empire. Professors Willard Rhodes and William Mitchell were my friends. The practicing musicians on the faculty seemed restricted by their surroundings. The music scholars discussed unknown music authoritatively and they were impressive with their course outlines, schedules, textbooks, and esoteric tidbits. I once lost control and said that musicology was "words without song." My remark was not appreciated but was widely quoted.

Moore arranged a party to introduce Ethel and me to the music faculty. Ethel performed her favorite arias, and I accompanied. Our colleagues were enchanted. Then Moore, a rather mischievous executive officer, suggested that I do musical impersonations like those he had seen at Yaddo. I demurred, but he insisted. I did takeoffs of a French tenor singing Fauré, a German baritone singing a Strauss song, the famous German musicologist Dr. Hasenschweiss lecturing about and performing a fugue for the Apfelorgel (an unknown baroque instrument), some contemporary songs and poems, and Hindemith explaining how music flowed in currents and undercurrents.

My indiscretions were received with guffaws, cackles, and cheers. Apparently everyone at the Columbia music department had been waiting a long time for just such an evening. My slightly barbed lampoons seemed to be what was needed to loosen things up and at the same time establish my position at Columbia. The piano and vocal improvisations were accepted as my musical credentials, my improvised lectures as my scholarly credentials. Professor Lang was overheard saying, "That man could be dangerous."

✿   ✿   ✿

At our initial Ditson Committee meeting, Moore and I proposed that we schedule the first Annual Festival of Contemporary American Music at Columbia University for May 1945, devoted to the performance of signifi-cant chamber and orchestral compositions by contemporary American com-posers, and an opera premiere. We would begin by commissioning American composers for orchestral and chamber music works, and a librettist and com-poser to do an opera. The programs would be selected by a committee con-sisting of the advisory committee of the Alice M. Ditson Fund, Pulitzer Prize winners in New York, and the Department of Music of Columbia University.

The first Columbia Festival began with an orchestral concert by the NBC Symphony Orchestra conducted by Dr. Howard Hanson, who won the 1945 Ditson Award for an American conductor. The University of the Air of the National Broadcasting Company, station WEAF, broadcast the orchestra concert nationally. Two chamber music concerts were broadcast over station WNYC.

The orchestral program included *Rounds for Strings* by David Diamond, in which he used canonic and fugal devices with an expressive lyric adagio between two fast movements. The piece is today a part of the permanent reper-tory. Hanson's Symphony no. 4, a Pulitzer Prize winner, with movement titles Kyrie, Requiescat, Dies Irae, and Lux Aeterna, was received respectfully. Sigmund Rascher played Henry Brant's *Concerto for Saxophone and Orchestra,* a piece I liked because of the masterly way Brant handled the orchestral balances, and because of Rascher's brilliant performance. Walter Piston's Symphony no. 2, a Ditson Fund commission, had flowing themes developed canonically, a slow movement with a quiet lyric development of a motive from the beginning, and a vigorous rhythmic, marchlike finale. Piston's symphony, academic writing in the very best sense of the word, was widely praised.

Recruiting orchestra and cast for the festival opera and arranging for reg-ular attendance was difficult during World War II. I was feeling the pressure, when, one day, Dean Gildersleeve asked me to come to her office.

"Professor Luening, I have five hundred dollars in my discretionary fund that I want to place at your disposal. Use it as you please. I think you are overworked. Hire a secretary, take a vacation, or get some help with the operas you are conducting."

I was speechless. "Can you afford it?"

"Contingency."

She held out her hand. I took it between mine. She looked straight at me. She reminded me of my sister, Helene.

I used $250 to pay debts and engaged Jack Beeson to be my opera assistant—the beginning of our long professional association and friendship. When I told the Columbia faculty about my windfall, they went into shock.

The festival opera was Normand Lockwood's *The Scarecrow*. The libretto by Dolly Lockwood was an adaptation from Percy MacKaye's play of the same name based on Hawthorne's story "Feathertop," about witchcraft in a small town in Massachusetts Bay Colony in the seventeenth century—a fable dealing with humanization through the love of a magically vitalized scarecrow for a lovely but spell-cursed girl. It reminded me of certain E. T. A. Hoffmann tales.

I was happy when Lockwood told me that I was carrying the torch and keeping the flame burning for American opera, that I responded to what composers were driving at, and that I understood their music. A distinguished audience came to the opening, including many conductors, stage directors, and singers. The audience reception was cordial.

The general reaction was that Lockwood's first operatic venture showed technical mastery, dramatic feeling, and sensitivity for the text that underlined the drama—and that he wrote beautiful melodies. The staging, which projected the fantastic, eerie quality of the work, was a credit to Milton Smith. *The New Yorker* spoke of the work as having "clarity, movement, and sense." My conducting was described as being "highly commendable," "expert," "effective," and "competent." The now defunct *New York Sun* wrote that it was "prophetic and encouraging to promote the performance of a work based on an American scene, historic event, and folklore." This success made my Columbia teaching job much easier. I was told confidentially that public recognition when positive had a real place in the academic environment. I kept this in mind during my entire academic career.

I was appointed music director of Brander Matthews Theatre in 1944. A year later Assistant Professor Willard Rhodes was appointed music director of the Opera Workshop. Former assistant conductor with the American Opera Company and with the Cincinnati Zoo Opera, he was an excellent musician.

The overall direction of opera productions was in the hands of Milton Smith and myself, as director of Opera Projects for Columbia University.

The main productions were under the auspices of the Columbia Theatre Associates and the music department, with grants from the Ditson Fund.

Smith ran Brander Matthews like a provincial German repertory theater, with a training school for theater and the opera workshop. The theater school taught everything that was needed to put on a show: building scenery, acting, making costumes, stage designing, running the box office, painting posters, and tending to publicity. The opera department did not provide voice lessons, but concentrated on stage action, body movement, and the production of scenes and entire operas—some with piano accompaniment and some completely mounted with costumes, scenery, and orchestra.

My job as music director was somewhat like being General-musikdirektor in a small Swiss or German city. I saw it as a great opportunity to develop an apprentice system for the musical theater. Dr. Smith consulted with me quite regularly about all musical matters that took place in the theater. I cooperated with Willard Rhodes and the Opera Workshop and gave the workshop singers first consideration for the larger productions in Brander Matthews Theatre. I tried to lend support to good projects when the workshop ran into problems with money or personnel.

At the 1945 Ditson Fund meeting, I proposed that we commission an opera from Gian Carlo Menotti. I knew that he had a good sense of the theater and had had some success with his operas. The committee agreed, so Douglas Moore arranged a conference with him.

Menotti arrived at Moore's apartment at precisely five o'clock. I liked him immediately. Moore offered drinks but Menotti, looking very businesslike, declined. He was handsome and wore his clothes with casual elegance. I thought he resembled an Italian marchese and was a bit like a Latin movie star, or perhaps like a very rich member of the jet set who was interested in the arts. His face had the mobile expression of an intellectual, sophisticated young Italian. His eyes were expressive. When Douglas and I tried to be humorous, he sometimes looked very sad and troubled, but when we were serious, he often laughed. He apparently enjoyed taking the other side of the subject.

When we offered him a commission, Menotti said that he was fed up with composing operas and wanted simply to compose instrumental music. His reason was that stage directors never carried out his intentions.

We assured him that *we* would.

"Could I produce and direct my own opera?" he asked.

"Yes, certainly, that would be marvelous."

"Could I also conduct it?"

"I'm the music director, but if you want to conduct, go ahead and I will help in every way. I don't recommend, it, though. It's too dangerous"—and I explained the Brander Matthews pit problem to him.

After our discussion, he relaxed with a vermouth and said he was interested and would get in touch with us. A week later he accepted the commission, and decided on Oliver Smith as stage designer, himself as stage director, and myself as conductor.

Meanwhile, Paisiello's *Barber of Seville*, translated by Phyllis Mead, was scheduled for February 13, 1946. This opera, first performed in 1782, had remained a popular favorite in Europe until 1816. It had last been performed in the United States in French in New Orleans in 1810. The work, based on Beaumarchais' *Barbier de Seville*, was charming; the music was somewhat Mozartian, but without Mozart's sophisticated counterpoint and orchestration. As far as we knew, our production was the first twentieth-century public revival of this piece. Milton Smith's crew built a two-story house as a set. He trained the cast to climb ladders, run over roofs, jump out of windows, and leap from turrets, all with fascinating lighting effects. In fact, the lively acting style did not help the musical ensemble one bit. We provided musical color by having a harpsichord and a mandolin join the string orchestra.

The music delighted the audience and critics. The *Herald Tribune* found the performance sufficiently lively to "demonstrate that a cultural institution like Columbia University can take a very real part in the active, producing art world [and] be a stimulus to that world by raising the intellectually low level on which that world habitually operates." WNYC broadcast the dress rehearsal.

In January 1946, Menotti had finished his opera, *The Medium.* Moore, Milton Smith, and I met him in Moore's apartment. Menotti outlined the story of his phony fortune-teller who is finally tripped up by her own deceptions, and proceeded to play and sing it for us. We were immediately taken by the validity of his dramatic conception and by the original theatrical and musical qualities of his score.

Milton Smith was relieved that Menotti was staging the work. He predicted a near-flop: "It's great, but the second act is exactly like the first, and you can't do that in the theater. You've got a half-turkey on your hands, Otto." Moore and I didn't agree.

Menotti, Beeson, and I put out a dragnet around town and we heard about one hundred and twenty singers in February. Menotti was friendly, tactful, and meticulously fair in the auditions. He spent weeks looking for the perfect face, the perfect type, the perfect voice for the lead. One afternoon, a woman with an imposing figure and an expressive face came for an audition. Her voice was as thrilling as her appearance. Clara Mae Turner was also a fine musician and looked just right for the role of the Medium. Menotti was ecstatic. She soon knew her part musically, so we began stage rehearsals.

From the first rehearsal on, Menotti proved to be an extremely adroit, skillful, and original stage director. He was kind and fair to the artists and always gave the understudies enough rehearsal time. He was almost psychic in his reactions. He often wandered around the theater with his back turned to the stage and would suddenly about-face with "You were too far stage left" or "This scene must be more realistic." It was as though he was trying to get the mental image he had of his opera into focus. This image was what he projected to the people on the stage. He was unlike Vladimir Rossing, who had to push the singers around to get his productions into shape. Menotti was more like a bard composer, or playwright who wanted the performance to fit an inner image.

On sizing up the Brander Matthews pit, Menotti had wisely held his orchestra down to twelve players plus piano four hands. I picked an excellent group of Columbia and a few Juilliard players. Besides the dress rehearsal, I had six two-hour orchestra rehearsals. Menotti was behind schedule with his orchestral score and was entangled with other performances that had developed for him. In the initial rehearsal, the orchestra was still reading the first act while he passed out parts for the second. I kept right on and suddenly found myself conducting a section for which Menotti had not yet notated the score. Fortunately I knew it by memory from the piano score. There I was, conducting the orchestration that had not yet been notated!

Menotti wanted to achieve a powerful musical-theatrical unity. *The Medium*'s story—of a fortune teller who makes money as a spiritualistic phony and who, one evening, thinks she feels a cold hand at her throat and is made to wonder whether her fraudulent séances are not perhaps real— was masterful in its conception. As a librettist, Menotti created situations and incidents that led to credible climaxes. Individual sections of the opera were carefully conceived; they were musically complete in themselves and colorful in orchestration. The melodic invention was clean and transparent.

As stage director, Menotti brought out every event on the stage with dramatic clarity and precision. I think I matched him musically. He insisted from the first rehearsal that the total theatrical effect be the main drive of the piece. When it was a matter of theatrical effect versus musical precision, he would tell me to forget the musical precision. But we rehearsed so carefully that in the performances, it was a pleasure to control the whole operation from the pit.

By now, Brander Matthews had made a reputation as a tryout theater. Many prominent conductors, stage directors, singers, and actors came to openings and even to dress rehearsals. For the premiere Serge Koussevitsky, Dimitri Mitropoulos, Alfred Wallenstein, and Artur Rodzinski sat in the second row.

The performance was remarkably smooth; not one slip. The singers, who were beautifully costumed, acted with animation. The performance was described as *"grand guignol"* in style. The work was an immediate hit. There were favorable reviews in the national press, and plans were made to perform the work on Broadway. Clara Mae Turner was engaged by the Metropolitan Opera and began a distinguished career. Later, *The Medium* moved to the New York City Center where, with Thomas Schippers conducting, it had a successful run. The entire cast was used in a movie that brought international fame to the work. It became part of the permanent repertory and was recorded, and Menotti's publisher reports that it now has had around four hundred performances annually. Menotti considers it his most personal work, important in the development of his style; he feels this work and *The Consul* are his best. Some composers thought the work gave the right direction to American chamber opera.

❁ ❁ ❁

From 1941 to 1958, forty-one operas and plays, either premieres or classical revivals, were produced in Brander Matthews Theatre. Besides the ones mentioned earlier, the opera premieres included *Paul Bunyan,* by W. H. Auden and Benjamin Britten, conducted by Hugh Ross, a work that is now being revived; *A Tree on the Plains,* by Paul Morgan and Ernst Bacon, conducted by Nicholas Goldschmidt; and *Acres of Sky* by Zoë Schiller and Arthur Kreutz. I conducted the last one.

Willard Rhodes conducted *Sir John in Love* by Vaughan Williams, *Giants in the Earth* by Arnold Sundgaard and Douglas Moore, and *Hello Out There* by William Saroyan and Jack Beeson. Emerson Buckley conducted *The Boor* by John Olan and Dominick Argento and *Gallantry* by Moore.

Plays with music included *Iphigenia in Tauris* and *Euripides*, translated by Witter Bynner, with choral settings by Claude Latham; *Poor Eddie,* a dance drama with songs, book by Dooley, music by Albert Rivett, choreographed by Doris Humphrey, and starring Charles Weidman; and *The Dream,* a multimedia show by Reich and Sergievsky.

There was a special performance of Stravinsky's *Histoire du soldat,* produced by the International Society for Contemporary Music and Columbia Theatre Associates, and conducted by Mitropoulos.

In 1959 the theater was razed and the Columbia Law School was built on the site. Columbia has been unsure about what to do with the arts program ever since Mozart's librettist, Lorenzo Da Ponte, arrived in New York in 1805 and won $500 in a lottery, which he spent buying Italian books for the Columbia library. A worm-eaten volume of Boccaccio with a broken binding was the only Italian book there, and Da Ponte was rewarded for his gift by being made honorary professor, an appointment that did not include stipend or students. Da Ponte solved his academic problems by opening up a vegetable and fruit market, a speakeasy in Elizabeth, New Jersey, and a bookshop, and by giving private lessons. Ever since Edward MacDowell tried to establish a School of the Arts at Columbia early in the century, there have been many discussions and proposals. In 1965, Jacques Barzun and Davidson Taylor finally got such a school underway. After twenty-two years of discussions, a Columbia University Music Press was also established. Schuyler Chapin is now dean, and Chou Wen-chung, a former composition student of mine, associate dean, of the School of the Arts.

¤ ¤ ¤

One of my jobs at Columbia was to teach and develop a master of arts seminar for musical composition, under the Faculty of Philosophy. After some conversations with possible degree candidates, I saw that their backgrounds were so diverse and sometimes so deficient in certain areas that I admitted them only after a personal interview. Academic records were a poor description of a candidate's abilities and deficiencies. I developed a system of individual musical diagnoses and prescription. I gave personalized aptitude tests, from which I drew musical and psychological portraits—a slightly offbeat system, but it seemed to work.

I quickly realized that there were not enough courses in the university to supply each one of the candidates with what is needed to survive and be reasonably contented in the academic world or in the professional world of music. Remembering my own experiences, I tried from the outset to develop in all my students the habit of self-study. In the seminar, when I detected weaknesses I would suggest whatever studies were necessary for the candidate to overcome them. I also suggested that the great musical resources of New York City should be used by the student and that he or she should, in some way, become an active participant in the musical life of New York.

The seminar met for several hours weekly, and when necessary I held private conferences. It was a kind of apprentice system, for I was more interested in establishing myself as an older professional and more experienced colleague than as a maestro or a professor who knew all the answers. Candidates brought works in progress almost every week. I read everything through at the piano. I felt my job was first to understand what the composer was trying to express. If, after my best efforts, a passage or a section was unclear to me, we would try to determine why. Sometimes the student was at fault, and the piece needed reworking; sometimes it was my fault, and I needed to study and play the piece again.

I would often suggest procedures that would strengthen each student's musical background. These included analyzing obscure works from the sixteenth or seventeenth centuries, reading through nineteenth-century

German song literature, studying Berlioz scores, examining Rimsky-Korsakov's *Foundations of Orchestration,* examining compositions of Weber, scanning a score of Harry Partch or Joseph Matthias Hauer, and reading Busoni's *Sketch of a New Esthetic of Music.* I also made such mundane suggestions as the need for composers to practice piano, to join a chorus, or to attend rehearsals of the student orchestra. I avoided analyzing most contemporary music and never played my own, for I wanted my students to select their own influences and make up their own minds. After all, they would be stuck with themselves, and not with me, for the rest of their lives.

There were required classes for all composers in the fields of theory and music history. They needed this background if they planned to teach, and for a number of years the musicologists—and particularly William J. Mitchell, the theory professor—were quite cooperative in developing the program. We often suggested specific contemporary and older works for study outside the class. I was just as interested in my students' works as I was in my own, and in their successes and failures as well.

All in all, it was a strong enough approach in music training that many of my students were active in New York music life while still in school. The graduates branched out into many music fields and a number of them later became or remained my friends and co-workers, and in some instances took over jobs that I had started. I believe I avoided the usual teacher–student fixation without losing sight of what I thought was necessary to teach and to learn. I think I learned at least as much from my students as they did from me, perhaps more.

Some careers of graduates have been interesting and parallel to mine. Robert Kurka graduated in 1948. His well-formed thesis composition, *Concerto for Violin and Chamber Orchestra,* was not premiered until 1978. His opera *Good Soldier Schweik* has been in the world repertory for some time. He died at the age of thirty-five. Peter Davis reviews for the *New York Times.* Marvin Levy's opera *Mourning Becomes Electra* was performed by the Metropolitan Opera in New York. William Hellerman is president of the Composers' Forum. William Kraft became assistant conductor of the Los Angeles Philharmonic and is a prominent West Coast composer. After my retirement Roy Travis, Ezra Laderman, and Karl Korte each invited me to conduct their classes during their sabbatical leaves. John Corigliano, whose works attracted much attention when they were performed by the New York Philharmonic, was a very lively undergraduate. So was Eric Salzman, who has written extensively about contemporary music. I often worked together with former students; my compositions were both rejected and accepted by them, and some students even wrote letters of recommendation for me.

John Hollander

'50 COLUMBIA COLLEGE, '52 MA

John Hollander is a distinguished poet, editor, teacher, and critic. The author of A Crackling of Thorns *and many other collections and the editor of the anthology* American Poetry: The Nineteenth Century, *Hollander taught for many years at Yale, where today he is a professor emeritus. This poem, "West End Blues," is from 1993's* Selected Poetry.

WEST END BLUES

The neon glow escapes from
Inside; on a cracked red leather
Booth poets are bursting
Into laughter, half in
Death with easeful love. They
Feign mournful ballads
Made to their mistresses' highbrows

"Lalage, I have lain with thee these many nights"
For example (but I hadn't,
Really, only once, and
When we got to the room
I'd borrowed from a logician
We left all the lights off,
And so in the cloudy morning

She gasped at the sudden, grey sight
Of the newspaper picture of Henry
Wallace tacked up on the wall)

You bastards, my girl's in there,
Queening it up in the half-light

O salacious tavern!
Festus taught me the chords of "Milenberg Joys" there
Far from mid-western places where red sunsets fall
Across railroad tracks, beyond the abandoning
Whistles of trains.

They've taken out the bar that lay along the wall
And put one in the middle
Like a bar in Indiana
(Not the old Regulator where there were hardboiled eggs)

"Approchez-vous, Néron, et prenez votre place"
Said Gellius, and there I was, skulking like Barrault
After his big dance in *Les Enfants du Paradis*
When Lemaître takes him out for coffee: "Yes, Ma," I said
While the frightfully rare breed of terrier waddled
From lap to lap, ignoring his dish of sorrowful beer.
And later on in the evening, swimming through the smoke,
Visions of others came upon us as we sat there,
Wondering who we were: Drusus, who followed a dark
Form down along the steps to the water of the river,
Always seemed to have just left for his terrible moment;
Gaius in Galveston, setting out for Dakar,
Was never away. As a bouncy avatar
Of "Bye, Bye Blackbird" flew out of its flaming cage
Of juke-box colored lights yet once more, finally
I would arise in my black raincoat and lurch my way
Out to the street with a shudder. The cold and steamy air
Carrying protein smells from somewhere across the river
Hovered about me, bearing me out of Tonight into
A late hour like any other: as when at five in the morning,
Clatter of milk cans below his window on the street
Measured with hushed, unstressed sounds of her long hair,
Her pillowslip, beside his window on the bed,

Suddenly the exhausted undergraduate sees his prize
Poem taking its shape in a horribly classical meter
—So would the dark of common night well up around me
As the revolving door emptied me onto the street.

Salax taberna! And all you, in there, past the third
Corner away from Athena's corny little owl
Hiding for shame in the academic skirt-folds of Columbia,
Alma Mater, who gazes longingly downtown—
All you, all you in there, lined up along the bar
Or queening it up in the half-light,
Listen to me! No, don't!

Across Broadway and down a bit, the painfully bright
Fluorescence and fierce tile of Bickford's always shone
Omnisciently, and someone sad and crazy said
"God lives in Bickford's"

But that was after we had all become spectres, too,
And eyes, younger eyes, would glisten all unrecognizing
As heads turned,
Interrupting the stories innocently and inaccurately
Being told about us, to watch the revolving door make a tired,
Complete turn, as the shape huddled inside it hardly
Bothered to decide not to go in at all,
Having been steered there only by the heart's mistakes
In the treasonable night; by a kind of broken habit.

Charles Townes

Charles Townes taught at Columbia from 1948 to 1961, research-
ing early microwave physics. In 1954 he developed the first
"maser," coining with his students the acronym for microwave
amplification by stimulated emission of radiation. Townes later
co-wrote a theoretical paper on optical and infrared masers, bet-
ter known as lasers. His work on what became known as the
maser-laser principle won him the 1964 Nobel Prize in physics,
and is described in his memoir, How the Laser Happened *(1999).*

On January 1, 1948, I joined the Columbia University physics department as an associate professor with a $6,000 salary, only a bit lower
than what I was being paid by Bell Labs. By then our second
daughter, Ellen, had been born, but Frances and I thought we could get
along in New York City on such a salary.

The department was busy putting itself back together after the disruption
of the war. Some faculty members came back, and a few moved on. I filled
a vacancy left by Norman Ramsey's departure to Harvard. Overall, I found a
group with scientific interests perfectly in tune with my own.

It was not as large a physics department as some, such as Berkeley's, but
it was first rate. I was pleased to be a member. Rabi was top man, both
chairman of the department and head of the Columbia Radiation
Laboratory, created during the war as a center for the generation of
microwaves. I arrived shortly after the Radiation Laboratory had turned back
to basic physics, including Rabi's research on molecular and atomic beams.
Polykarp Kusch worked on magnetic moments of atoms and nuclei, using
techniques similar to those of Rabi. Willis Lamb explored the energy levels

of the hydrogen atom (work I had thought about trying myself, but Lamb had gotten to it first). A student there, Bill Nierenberg, had just finished an excellent thesis in spectroscopy of atomic nuclei, which was close to some of my own work.

That period in the Columbia physics department was to be even more remarkable than I could have realized at the time. When I arrived, I knew only that the department seemed interesting; it was both stimulating and comfortable for me. Yet only in retrospect do I fully appreciate the enormous productivity of the scientists then at Columbia.

During the 12 years I was a full-time member of the department, in addition to Rabi, Kusch, and Lamb, other professors there included T. D. Lee, Steve Weinberg, Leon Lederman, Jack Steinberger, Jim Rainwater, and Hideki Yukawa; all were to receive Nobel Prizes. Rabi was the only one so recognized when I arrived. Students during that period included Leon Cooper, Mel Schwartz, Val Fitch, Martin Perl, and Arno Penzias, my doctoral student who, in 1965, was codiscoverer (with Robert Wilson) of the cosmic background radiation (CBR), the relic photons from the big bang. All these were also to receive Nobel Prizes. Hans Bethe and Murray Gell-Mann were visiting professors there before receiving their Nobel Prizes. Then there were the young postdocs Aage Bohr, Carlo Rubbia, and my postdoc and close associate, Arthur Schawlow, now Nobel laureates.

Had I been a theorist, at my age—32—I should perhaps have been expected to have already done much of my best work. According to popular belief, theorists excel in their 20s. Experimentalists, however, have staying power. It takes time to get clever with instruments, and experience counts. The wartime detour had given me rich and crucial experience with electronics, with electromagnetic generators such as klystrons and magnetrons used in radar, and with practical engineering.

My research interests took no sudden new turn; the only change was the location of my lab and the opportunity to interact with students and a new group of interested senior physicists. The basic physics I did at Bell Labs, associated as it was with applied industrial and military work, gave me a good idea of what I wanted to do at Columbia. I was deeply fascinated with a number of lines of work which could be done with microwave spectroscopy. Those included highly precise examination of molecular structure, exploration of fundamental properties of nuclei, and improvements in the measurement of time. In addition, microwaves and radio spectroscopy provided new theoretical insights into the interactions of electromagnetic waves and matter.

Getting the equipment and team together was not a big problem. Today, a newly hired faculty member is often expected to bring along his or her own sources of support for a research program—and to find new ones as time goes by; usually this means a great deal of time putting together grant applications to government agencies. There are some advantages to today's competitive grants system. Nevertheless, writing proposals for supporting funds does drain time and energy from the lab.

The Columbia Radiation Laboratory had, by contrast, a secure source of support: a block grant from the joint services—the Army, Navy, and Air Force—administered by the Army Signal Corps. The grant's roots were based in the military's wartime interest in radar. Columbia's radar-related magnetron projects had led to wide-ranging physical research in the radio wave and microwave fields. Rabi told me about the workaday fashion in which the grants had been initiated and renewed. An Army representative came around one day shortly after the end of the war, took stock of all the magnetron work under way, and asked, "Would you be willing to keep this laboratory going, and do some physics with it? We can give you some money, something like a half million dollars a year." Rabi was very impressed by the generous offer, so much so that he told them half a million dollars was too much. They obligingly cut it down some!

The same kind of thing went on all around the country shortly after the war. The Office of Naval Research, under Alan Waterman from Yale, was the largest source of government money for basic science, and it was enormously important to research in U.S. universities. Waterman's philosophy, held also by such wartime research organizers as Vannevar Bush of MIT, was that a strong scientific establishment is important to the nation's future, important enough to the military specifically to justify such support. The result was a remarkably fruitful period of generous, open, and effective support of university research.

Military grants initially included considerable freedom over how to spend them. The system gradually became smaller and more rigid. This was partly because, somewhat later, the government set up the National Science Foundation (NSF), largely owing to Bush's inspiration; Waterman was the natural person to become its first director. Thereafter, the military could and did somewhat reduce its sponsorship of basic science. Still later, rules arose that required strict goals and accountability of military grants. Many universities began to find military-sponsored work to be more restrictive, and during the Vietnam war more politically burdensome, than it was worth. Yet in the first ten years or so after World War II, very few people had any reservations about doing civilian-type tasks with Pentagon money, and such support was a great boon to the nation's science.

In the same vein, in the late 1940s and in the 1950s, still fresh in people's minds were the important roles of the wartime Manhattan Project and radar programs. This gave physicists considerable social prestige, a great contrast to the years before the war, when most people never thought about physicists or physics at all. Suddenly, physics had an aura and physicists were popular at dinner parties. (The onus of nuclear dangers was to weigh on physicists heavily some time later, particularly in the 1960s and onward, after public interest took still another turn.)

We moved into an apartment at 120th Street and Morningside Heights with our two daughters, Linda and Ellen. Two more daughters, Carla and Holly, were born while I was at Columbia. Except for the worry Frances and I had over the extra care and attention it took to raise small children in the city, Columbia provided exactly the rich, challenging, and questioning environment I had sought. With weekly colloquia and other talks by faculty, visiting professors, and eager students, it was perfect. And before our fourth daughter Holly was born, we had managed to move into a house with a nice yard in the Spuyten Duyvil area of the Bronx.

My office on the tenth floor of Pupin, the physics building, looked out over the Columbia campus and, in the distance, the Empire State Building. When I got there my laboratory space—a large dusty room—was one floor up from my office. It was empty except for a big, man-sized metal box. The box provided a purely coincidental but very physical connection to my years at Bell Labs. It held a test apparatus that Columbia physicists had used to measure water vapor absorption of 1.25-centimeter radar waves. The tests were inspired by the doubts, associated with work on radar systems and already mentioned, that such waves could go far in moist air.

My immediate goals were to continue to extend microwave spectroscopy, including moves to shorter and shorter wavelengths. This would let me examine the behavior of many more molecules, plus the shapes, masses, and spins of nuclei. During my early work at Bell Labs, I had encountered some skepticism from other physicists that I was on a productive path. While ammonia had produced good results, several of my colleagues believed that its prominent microwave spectrum was such an oddity that it might be the only one we could usefully study. They simply doubted that there would be techniques sensitive enough to use in studying other molecules. Rabi also kept impressing on me his deep doubts about my theoretical interpretation of the effects of nuclear quadrupole moments, or shapes, on molecular spectra.

But microwave spectroscopy was already catching on before I arrived at Columbia. The chemistry departments at Berkeley and Harvard, plus the physics groups at MIT and at Duke and Oxford universities, were getting important results. Early work also was done at the industrial laboratories of General Electric, Westinghouse, and the Radio Corporation of America (RCA) in addition to my own work at Bell Labs. Within a few years we had found useful spectra in many gases. These included organic molecules, some diatomic molecules, quite a few salts that became gases at high temperatures, and a free radical, OH (water with a hydrogen atom torn off). An idea proposed by Bright Wilson, a chemist at Harvard, produced large improvements in sensitivity. With readily available klystrons and magnetrons—leftovers from the war—we found spectra that revealed new and interesting ways to determine the masses, the spins, and the shapes (quadrupole moments) of a variety of nuclei, as well as ways to get very detailed information about the structure, dipole moments, and interaction between molecules and electric fields.

By this time, a special abstract sort of friendship was arising from my research. Any devoted scientist develops a deep intimacy with the problems, concepts, or devices in his field. As for me, starting somewhat at Caltech, more and more at Bell Labs, and most richly at Columbia, my career brought growing familiarity and fascination with molecules. How molecules absorb and emit energy, their motions, and the behavior of their electrons and nuclei—all those things, while never actually seen by anyone, became real for me and easily visualized. When I try to figure out how a molecule behaves under particular circumstances, it seems almost like a friend whose habits I know. Ammonia, without a doubt, has been my favorite. Its simple arrangement of a single nitrogen and three hydrogen atoms has been pivotal in many important moments of my career. I have met this very familiar molecule in the insides of masers, as the mainspring of atomic clocks, in clouds among stars at great distances from Earth, and in the atmospheres surrounding some stars.

My molecular friend stood out in those highly productive first years at Columbia. This was partly because ammonia interacts strongly with microwaves. In addition, its unusual inversion (turning itself inside out like an umbrella in a high wind) and rotation, when combined with the effects of nitrogen and hydrogen nuclei, generated effects that demanded new theoretical explanations and careful measurement. Working with ammonia and other molecules in those early years at Columbia made it among the most satisfying periods of my career.

Not that I found myself in a perfect utopia. The military was still paying the freight, so there were gentle suggestions that I should do something in tune with the Pentagon's interest in magnetrons. Pushing spectroscopy to ever-shorter wavelengths or work with more difficult molecules did not quite fit the bill. Several times, Rabi or other members of the department asked me whether I really might like to work a bit on magnetrons. My reply was always no. The pressure never became intense, but it was there. For me, the magnetron was not particularly interesting in itself. A magnetron was merely a tool.

❖ ❖ ❖

The military was not the only group outside the academic world interested in what we were doing. Private industry also paid attention. One unusual example came in the person of H. W. ("Hap") Schulz. A chemist at Union Carbide and Carbon Corporation, Schulz had been blinded as a result of a lab accident while a student at Columbia. He focused mostly on theory, including abstractly pondering the theoretical aspects of reactions.

One day in 1948, Schulz appeared in my lab with a proposition. I had never heard of him before, but I learned soon enough that he was a brilliant and inventive person. This visit was a lucky day for me. He had an idea for generating very specific molecular reactions with infrared radiation, radiation that has wavelengths shorter than 1 millimeter and occupies a portion of the electromagnetic spectrum between optical (visible) light and microwaves. Schulz noted that, if properly tuned, infrared could excite some molecules in particular ways, while directly causing no other changes in them. This selective alteration of molecular energies could provide a new way to control chemical reactions. In a mixture of reacting molecules, he hoped, infrared radiation could selectively speed up some chosen reactions. In principle, it was a very appealing idea. However, infrared wavelengths at suitable intensities were unavailable. Schulz had $10,000 from Union Carbide to offer to a knowledgeable scientist willing and able to try to produce such radiation. He asked me to give it a try. In effect, he had the $10,000 check right there in his hand. That was then a considerable amount of money—as much as scientists like me made in a year. It would be a great help in research. But I told Schulz that while my own interests certainly included development of waves still shorter than 1 millimeter, I saw no immediate way to do that. I told him it would be a bit false of me to take the money and to say I was going to do something for him with it. I did not want to interrupt my own work to make such an effort unless I felt I had a good idea to work on. At that, he left.

Within a couple of days, Schulz was back. He said he had been to other labs and decided he would simply like to give me the money anyway, because he thought what I was doing was impressive and was at least somewhat related to his initial aims for the money.

He had one question. What would I do with such a donation? To me, the answer was obvious. I would use $5,000 to finance a fellowship for a young postdoc to work with me, and the other $5,000 for research equipment. But of course I would continue to work on whatever I found interesting. Amazingly, this was fine with Schulz. I got the money, and it was renewed annually as long as I was at Columbia.

My first postdoc on the Carbide and Carbon fellowship was a young South African, Jan Loubser. He had trained at Oxford with my friend Brebis

Bleaney, who was well known for microwave work. Jan worked on using the harmonics of magnetrons for molecular spectroscopy. The next year, the fellowship went to a highly recommended young optical spectroscopist from the University of Toronto. His name was Arthur Schawlow. He came to work with me to learn this new form of spectroscopy done with microwaves. Art was to become a major collaborator with me on many developments. Together we wrote a definitive text on microwave spectroscopy. He married my younger sister, and thus became a family member as well. And he was to play a key role in eventually making a revolutionary reality of Schulz's hopes for sources of intense infrared radiation—the laser.

Other visitors to the lab included, a few times every year, investigators from the military services. They routinely dropped in simply to take a look at what we were doing. One of these fellows was a Navy man, Commander Paul Johnson. He knew I wanted to study short wavelength microwaves and asked if I would consider forming an advisory committee to evaluate and stimulate work in the field of millimeter waves. This is the part of the spectrum just shorter in wavelength than the microwaves studied at the time, which were typically in the centimeter region or longer.

At that time, the Navy had no clear goal for millimeter waves. Johnson's committee proposal merely demonstrated that a few people in the Navy, familiar with the general directions of scientific research, wanted to be sure that no fruitful avenues for practical technologies were missed. The Navy and the military in general also knew for certain they did not want the United States to be surprised by enemy weapons that were based on techniques whose applications Americans had failed to recognize. It was an attitude toward science that contrasted sharply with feelings before the war, when most military organizations had been skeptical about needing some professor for advice on the way to go about the practical business of fighting wars. Yet during World War II, with its new radars, atomic bombs, ballistic missiles, jet aircraft, and electronic control and communication systems, the military developed a respect for science that it has never lost.

I had myself been stubbornly pursuing shorter and shorter wavelengths. Because they interacted more strongly with atoms and molecules, I was confident they would lead us to even more rewarding spectroscopy. Johnson's suggestion of a committee to consider ways that millimeter waves might be generated and used matched my professional interests quite well. He was not asking me to take up new projects in the lab, but only to put together a committee to look at potentials in a field in which I was interested already. I agreed, and the Navy gave Columbia money to finance the effort.

In early 1950, I sorted through names and asked senior people like John Slater and Al Hill at MIT and Leonard Schiff at Stanford University for advice on individuals at their institutions who might best contribute. The committee included only seven members, but they represented a wide spectrum of researchers. Besides myself there was John Pierce from Bell Labs, Marvin Chodorow from Stanford, Lou Smullin at MIT, and Andrew Haeff of the Naval Research Laboratory, all well-known microwave engineers. John Strong of Johns Hopkins University, a very important expert on infrared radiation, was on the team, as was John Daunt of Ohio State University, who worked on detection of infrared with low temperature devices.

We spent a good part of our time contacting industrial, government, and university laboratories to talk with people in the general field. At the committee's urging, Pierce wrote an article for the journal *Physics Today*, reviewing the importance of millimeter waves. We hoped to flush out, from physicists or engineers who read the article, concepts that we might miss on our own.

We racked our brains to think up ways to justify military support for research and development of millimeter waves. We didn't think of many. One drawback of millimeter waves, just like that of the 1.25-centimeter radar that took up so much of my time during the war, is that they don't go very far in the atmosphere. We tried to turn this shortcoming inside out, suggesting that it might actually be an advantage for short range communication. The dissipation of the signal would make things tough on eavesdroppers! We also noted that a wavelength of a few millimeters would allow antennas to be very small, a possible plus for packaging communication gear into aircraft or other vehicles. Space travel did not exist then, but we did note that in the low-density atmosphere of high altitudes, millimeter waves would not be absorbed and could therefore be very useful for communication, an advantage for very high-flying airplanes.

Primarily, we pondered how to produce the millimeter waves. One notion I had was that electron-spin resonances in very high magnetic fields would generate signals in the millimeter regime. That is, electrons would process, or oscillate, as they interacted with the magnetic field at millimeter-wave frequencies. But I didn't see a very productive way to harness this process and we didn't pursue it very far. I had already in the laboratory worked on magnetron harmonics and on Cerenkov radiation to get millimeter waves. The latter involved electrons skimming the surface of magnetized materials.

The main problem, which Pierce pointed out in his article, was that generating millimeter waves by conventional means required a very small resonant cavity, only a wavelength or a small multiple of a wavelength in size. Making precise, delicate parts about a millimeter across is not easy, and to generate significant power one would have to pump considerable power through it, which wasn't easy. It would have to be strong and able to cope with a lot of heat. We did not in fact dig up any very great ideas for beating such problems. It was out of a sense of frustration over our lack of any substantial progress that the conceptual breakthrough finally came.

The Navy millimeter committee met several times in Washington, D.C. For one of our meetings, we chose April 26, 1951, to get together, because we could take advantage of an American Physical Society meeting at the same time. Art Schawlow was also there to present a paper. To save money, he and I shared a room at the Franklin Park Hotel. I felt that the committee was nearing the end of its useful life, and I was frustrated by our relatively meager list of new ideas or recommendations.

With small children at home, I was used to getting up early. Shortly after dawn on the day of the meeting, I awoke. So as not to disturb my late-sleeping bachelor companion—and future brother-in-law—I quietly dressed and crept out of the room to enjoy the early morning. In the back of my mind, I mused over the committee meeting and how we could be effective in our mission. In the fresh morning air of nearly deserted Franklin Park, I took a bench among beautiful red and white azaleas, in full bloom and laden with dew. It was a strikingly tranquil and lovely place, free of distractions. The problem turned over and over in my head. "Why is it that we just haven't been able to get anywhere? What is basically stopping us from being able to do this?" I asked myself. My mind first went back over the practical problems of tiny electron tubes or other resonators and of getting enough power through them to get decent signals out. As they had often done before, my thoughts drifted to a realm that was comfortable and natural for me, to physical mechanisms involving solids or molecules, especially the molecules to which I had devoted so much of my career and which I knew best.

The committee members and I knew from the start that some molecular transitions involve absorption and emissions at millimeter energies. I mused that, instead of trying to make small resonators, we really should somehow use molecular resonances, already provided by nature. I went through the usual arguments about why this would not work—that any collection of molecules would absorb more energy from a source of moderately high intensity than it would emit. One never shines a light or sends a signal through a gas, or anything else, and expects a stronger signal coming out! By heating a gas enough, one can make it radiate at many wavelengths, but to get the microwave portion of the spectrum radiating enough energy to be useful, the molecules would have to be so enormously hot that they would disintegrate into individual atoms. The requirement for an enormously high temperature results from a basic physical principle known as the second law of thermodynamics, which had always blocked me in previous forays down such avenues of thought.

I was well enough acquainted with the theory that radiation, even in a cool gas, can stimulate an excited atom or molecule to emit photons at exactly the same frequency as the stimulus, thus boosting the signal. This process is just the inverse of the absorption of radiation by an atom or molecule in a lower energy state; and for every atomic or molecular downward transition that contributes a photon to a passing wave, there are even more at lower energy levels to absorb the same energy photons in upward transitions. So, if a substance is in thermal equilibrium, this process is a net loser. That is what the second law of thermodynamics directly implies. The material soaks up more photons than it surrenders.

I cannot reassemble exactly the sequence of thought that pushed me past that conundrum, but the key revelation came in a rush: Now, wait a minute! The second law of thermodynamics assumes thermal equilibrium; but that doesn't really have to apply! There is a way to twist nature a bit.

Left to itself, as the second law describes, a collection of molecules does always have more members in lower energy states than in higher energy states, but there is no inviolable requirement that all systems be in thermal equilibrium. If one were, somehow, to have a collection entirely of excited molecules, then, in principle, there would be no limit to the amount of energy obtainable. The greater the density of excited atoms or molecules, and the longer the distance through them that the radiation wave goes, the more photons it would pick up and the stronger it would get. A few years earlier, I had even toyed with the idea of demonstrating this physical phenomenon but decided it was rather difficult to do and, because there was no reason to doubt its existence, I felt that nothing new would be proven by such a test.

On that morning in Franklin Park, the goal of boosting energy gave me an incentive to think more deeply about stimulated emission than I had before. How could one get such a nonequilibrium set up? Answers were actually well known; they had been in front of me and the physics community for decades. Rabi, right at Columbia, had been working with molecular and atomic beams (streams of gases) that he manipulated by deflecting atoms in excited states from those of lower energies. The result could be a beam enriched in excited atoms. At Harvard, Ed Purcell and Norman Ramsey had proposed a conceptual name to describe systems with such inverted populations; they had coined the term "negative temperature," to contrast with the positive temperatures, because these "negative" temperatures inverted the relative excess of lower-level over upper-level states in equilibrated systems.

It is perhaps a hackneyed device among dramatists to have a scientist scribble his thinking on the back of an envelope, but that is what I did. I took an envelope from my pocket to try to figure out how many molecules it would take to make an oscillator able to produce and amplify millimeter or submillimeter waves. All the required numbers about my friend, the ammonia molecule, were in my head. Ammonia appeared to be the most favorable medium. I quickly showed that we still needed a resonator, but now we would not have to pump electromagnetic energy into it. We could merely send a stream, or beam, of excited molecules through it, which would do the work! Any resonator has losses, so we would need a certain threshold number of molecules in the flow to keep the wave from dying out. Beyond that threshold, a wave would not only sustain itself bouncing back and forth, but it would gain energy with each pass. The power would be limited only by the rate at which molecules carried energy into the cavity.

A month earlier, I had coincidentally heard the German physicist Wolfgang Paul gave a colloquium at Columbia. He described a new way to focus molecular beams, by using four electrically charged rods to form a quadrupole field—a field with four-fold symmetry. This system focused and intensified the beam better than Rabi's system with two flat plates, which had only a two-fold symmetry. Sitting on that bench, I calculated just how lossy the cavity resonator could be and still have oscillations produced by a beam of ammonia focused by Paul's method. That is, at what rate could the cavity lose energy because of imperfect conductivity and still allow an energy build up? The results indicated that it was just marginally possible the idea would work with ammonia. Using Paul's technique, one should be able to put enough excited ammonia molecules through a cavity to produce an oscillator that would operate at shorter wavelengths than could be achieved by any other known means. My calculations were for the production of electromagnetic waves in the far-infrared region, with wavelengths about $\frac{1}{2}$ millimeter long that corresponded to the first rotational resonance of ammonia. But there was, in fact, no sharp limit that I saw to how short the wavelengths could be.

The signal, I also knew, would be coherent. The wave resonating in the cavity, reflecting back and forth, picking up strength from the molecules through which it passed, would maintain itself almost perfectly in phase and at a very nearly constant frequency, or wavelength.

I stuffed the envelope back in my pocket. In the hotel room, Art was up by the time I returned. I told him what I had just been thinking. He said, "That's interesting." He seemed only moderately impressed. To tell the truth, I also was not sure how far it would go. It would work in principle, but could we get one going, and if so how well?

*   *   *

When I got back to Columbia from Washington, I felt the idea for stimulated radiation was good enough that, first, I had to double-check the basics.

I wanted to be completely certain that there were no mistakes in fundamental physics. I went and found my notes from a course in quantum mechanics that I had taken in 1939 at Caltech, from W. V. Houston. Yes, the equations there showed clearly that stimulated emission of radiation would permit amplification, and it indeed would produce a signal that was in phase, or coherent. The principles were all there in a course taught before the war to graduate students.

The characteristics of the resonant cavity also demanded more detailed thought. Waves needed to bounce back and forth in the cavity without losing energy too quickly to the cavity walls, a property described by what is called the quality factor, or Q, of the cavity. Calculation showed that, yes, a copper cavity could probably provide the needed Q (or low enough loss per bounce), even without lowering its temperature to achieve better conductivity characteristics. Most important, the calculation seemed to make it clear that I would not need to attempt the rather far-out possibility of using superconducting materials in the cavity; they would require very low temperatures and cause additional complications. Room temperature copper should do the job.

I satisfied myself that my idea employed only standard, known physics. In the years since, I have continued to learn the degree to which physics history was littered with hints that one could, in fact, use molecular and atomic transitions to make an amplifier. A few scientists suggested it explicitly; some had even undertaken experiments, though none seems to have thought of using a resonator and, in most cases, coherence of the amplification had been ignored. Here is a brief summary of these unappreciated clues.

Einstein in 1917 was first to explain how radiation could induce, or stimulate, still more radiation when it hits an atom or a molecule. The requirement is that the energy of the incoming photon, or quantum of radiation, approximately equals the energy that can be lost by an atom (or a molecule) that is making a transition from a higher to a lower energy state. Thus, Einstein described a process that would feed energy to the triggering radiation. He never considered coherence, but I feel sure that if asked, Einstein would have quickly concluded there must *be* coherence and that, if one had enough atoms in an appropriate upper state, one would get net amplification. Einstein, of course, was thinking of systems in thermal equilibrium. I don't have any evidence that he thought about non-equilibrium conditions. If prompted to think in such terms, he surely couldn't have missed the implications for amplification and coherence.

At Caltech, among my more interesting teachers was Richard Tolman, a physicist and chemist who worked in both general relativity and statistical mechanics. In 1924, he carefully discussed stimulated emission and absorption of radiation in a *Physical Review* article, calling the stimulated emission "negative absorption" (which is the same as amplification). For example, he wrote:

> The possibility arises, however, that molecules in the upper quantum state may return to the lower quantum state in such a way as to reinforce the primary beam by "negative absorption.". . . it will be pointed out that for absorption experiments as usually performed the amount of "negative absorption" can be neglected. (vol. 24, p. 697)

In one of his books of the period, he also commented that the stimulated emission must be coherent with the stimulating radiation, while at the same time he recognized that there was not yet any good mathematical proof of it. Thus the general ideas behind stimulated amplification were already fairly well understood in the mid-1920s by some physicists dealing with the quantum mechanics and the thermodynamics of radiation.

In 1932, Fritz Georg Houtermans, a German physicist, was told by an experimenter who studied gaseous discharges in his laboratory about the unusual intensity of a particular spectral line. Houtermans told me, long after the fact, that he remembered distinctly thinking that it might be a light (or photon) avalanche. This is a vivid way of envisioning stimulated emission in a gas that is out of thermal equilibrium. Houtermans said he didn't think about coherence and dropped the idea after another, more prosaic (and correct) explanation was found for the unusually bright emission line. More important, he evidently did not consider the phenomenon interesting enough to publish anything about it at the time, but he did publish his recollections of the event and the physics behind it after seeing the paper that Art Schawlow and I later wrote on "Optical Masers" and published in the *Physical Review* in 1958.

In 1939, a Russian, V. A. Fabrikant, published a rather obscure thesis describing the absorption and emission of light radiation in a gas in which he explicitly looked for what was called "negative absorption," or amplification. He did not discuss coherence or resonant cavities, but did suggest trying to obtain the necessary distribution of states by "collisions of the second kind," a mechanism now commonly used in gas lasers. However, he was not able to achieve any amplification, and his work was quickly forgotten. After our own maser idea was revealed, Fabrikant claimed a patentable version, dated June 18, 1951. That patent claim was published only in 1959, but I learned that Soviet law allowed patents to be rewritten and backdated. Fabrikant was definitely working on relevant concepts as early as 1939, but unfortunately he did not get very far and no one picked up his work as being particularly interesting.

A somewhat different type of energy-level inversion also got some study before that day in Franklin Park. A number of scientists had inverted nuclear-spin populations, using radio-wave excitation—though nowhere near enough to provide a net amplification, and had studied the results. This was the work that led the group at Harvard—Purcell, Ramsey, and Pound—to talk about "negative temperatures."

It was about 1948 when I had my own first idea to amplify radiation with a molecular beam, primarily as a demonstration of the physical principles. I did not couple it then with the idea of including a resonant cavity or of making an oscillator. A year or so later, John Wilson Trischka, a young postdoc at Columbia, got the same idea for demonstrating stimulated emission with a molecular beam containing inverted energy levels. He talked with me and worked at it on paper for some time before he decided that it would be very difficult and really would not prove much.

In 1950, Willis Lamb and Robert C. Retherford published a review of their study of the fine structure of the hydrogen spectrum. In describing the behavior of the atom they noted, in one sentence, that if the atom's higher energy levels were more populated than that at lower levels, "there will be net induced emission (negative absorption!)." They had not known that Tolman had already pointed out such a process, using the same terminology, as early as 1924. Willis was clearly aware of the process and understood phenomena such as coherence more completely than Tolman could in his day.

The Russian astrophysicist Vitaly Ginzburg has written of his professor, S. M. Levi:

> As far back as the 1930s Levi understood clearly the sense and the possible role of induced emission. Levi told me straightforwardly, "Create an overpopulation at higher atomic levels and you will obtain an amplifier; the whole trouble is that it is difficult to create a substantial overpopulation of levels." But why lasers were not created as far back as the 1920s, I do not understand. Much becomes obvious in hindsight.

Ideas about stimulated emission were thus floating around, but they were not being pursued. And although the basic physics was understood, no one had any idea that it could be useful. It seems clear that the study of microwave spectra of molecules was a key catalyst for putting together the various ideas needed for practical amplification or oscillation—probably because the needed concepts and skills emerged from a combination of practical experience with microwave engineering and devices and familiarity with quantum mechanical effects. At two other places in addition to our lab at Columbia, there were people working with such spectroscopy who had serious ideas about useful amplification by stimulated emission. One was Joe Weber, at the University of Maryland. He gave a talk to electrical engineers in 1952 about the possibility of amplifying by stimulated emission. He didn't have a cavity or a useful amount of amplification, but he certainly understood and suggested the basic idea.

In addition to Weber's short publication, and quite unknown to me until the spring of 1955, Alexander Prokhorov and Nicolai Basov at the Lebedev Institute in Moscow published a paper in 1954 describing how a molecular beam of alkali halide molecules might be passed through a cavity to produce a microwave oscillator. It was published somewhat after our publication on the ammonia maser, but it had been submitted before our paper came out. Their concept was remarkably like my own, except that they suggested using alkali halide molecules and a beam method that, as they showed, required a very high cavity quality, or Q, that was not very practical at the time. Because Weber and the Russians published after our system had been described in the Columbia Radiation Laboratory's quarterly progress reports, and since Weber visited me from time to time, one can wonder to what extent their ideas may have, perhaps subconsciously, been affected by our work. However, I see no reason to believe their work was not independent. The Russians proceeded toward building such a system and were later jointly awarded the 1964 Nobel Prize, with me, for contributions they made to the field.

By the 1950s, then, the idea of getting amplification by stimulated emission was already recognized here and there, but for one reason or another, nobody really saw the idea's potency or pushed it, except for me and the Russians, whose work was then unknown to me. A critical new idea that I added in Franklin Park was to use a resonant cavity so that the signal would go repeatedly through the gas, bouncing back and forth, picking up energy each time. This process would provide effectively infinite amplification, or oscillations limited in power only by the amount of molecular excitation that could be provided and the ability of the material to withstand so much energy passing back and forth through it. The whole plan only required properly putting together a number of ideas that were already known and floating around. Also critical was the recognition that this plan could be important.

✧ ✧ ✧

Essentially all of my research at Columbia was done with graduate students. To tackle the amplifier project I needed a good person, someone who was not only bright but who would have a few years to work at it. Jim Gordon had recently come from MIT, where he worked on atomic and molecular beams; and clearly he was a hardworking and quick student. "Here is an idea I think would be very interesting if we can make it work," I recall saying. "I can't be sure we can get it going on the time-scale needed for a thesis. Nevertheless, if you feel like working on it, I think it could pay off." Even if we could not get amplification out of it, I assured him, there were opportunities to do some very high-resolution spectroscopy with the apparatus, which would make for a fine doctoral thesis. The Carbide and Carbon Fellowship, which Hap Schulz had provided, allowed me to take on as the third Fellow another bright young postdoc, Herb Zeiger. He had done his thesis with Rabi in the field of molecular beams, and brought some of that expertise to the new project.

The general outline of the device seemed fairly clear. We needed a resonant cavity and an intense beam of excited molecules streaming through it. A key question was, what wavelength should we try first?

Because I was trying to get to shorter wavelengths, my first idea was to use ammonia with a rotational transition in the infrared region of the spectrum, for which the wavelengths—a few tenths of a millimeter—are much shorter than any that could be produced by other generators then available. There were many molecular transitions to choose from and such a generator, I felt, could be a real boon to further spectroscopy. It didn't take long, however, before we decided this was a hard nut to crack the first time out. We adopted the easier task of making a system work in the normal microwave region, for which we already had equipment and experience. We could then work our way down to shorter wavelengths and higher frequencies.

We set our aim on the strongest of ammonia's 1.25-centimeter transitions—one of the same group of ammonia resonances that Cleeton and Williams had measured back in the 1930s. This was the same wavelength region we had worked with for the radar that the wartime military establishment had wanted and which had been thwarted by water-vapor absorption. By the early 1950s, we knew quite a bit about the ammonia spectra, about techniques useful at this wavelength, and we had experience making good resonant cavities. Also, ammonia was my old friend. Today, it is almost laughable to think how easy it is to build a molecular or atomic amplifier, but the first one did not look so easy. Since this project was for a student thesis, it was also not done in a great hurry; it took more than two years to build up the equipment and work through the needed modifications and refinements.

The basic experiment involved a rectangular metal box, evacuated but with a tube leading in to introduce the ammonia gas. The gas diffused in through multiple small tubes to form a beam of molecules. Inside the box we mounted the molecular focuser, made of four parallel tubes about one inch in diameter and arrayed in a square. Downstream from this was the cavity, with a hole in each end to let the molecules go through. After the molecules flowed beyond the cavity, they were removed by either a vacuum pump or a surface at liquid nitrogen temperature, which condensed them as fast as they hit it.

George Dousmanis, a student who had made his way to Columbia from the Greek Peloponnesus, also did some preliminary work with Jim Gordon. We all wrote the first formal plan for the device in the lab's quarterly report of December, 1951. This was not a public report in the usual sense; it was not, strictly speaking, a publication. Yet copies of it circulated around and we sent them to anybody who asked for them. Later, this quasi-publication would become an issue in battles over patents, but that was far from our minds at the time.

We were still working under a Joint Services contract, managed by the U.S. Army Signal Corps, and we had spent about $30,000 on the project during the first two years. I worked from time to time with Gordon and Zeiger, overseeing the project, as I did the other dozen or so graduate student theses I was supervising. We hardly rode a wave of encouragement. When we showed the experiment to lab visitors, they would say "Oh, yes, interesting idea," and leave.

One day after we had been at it for about two years, Rabi and Kusch, the former and current chairmen of the department—both of them Nobel laureates for work with atomic and molecular beams, and both with a lot of weight behind their opinions—came into my office and sat down. They were worried. Their research depended on support from the same source as did mine. "Look," they said, "you should stop the work you are doing. It isn't going to work. You know it's not going to work. We know it's not going to work. You're wasting money. Just stop!"

The problem was that I was still an outsider to the field of molecular beams, as they saw it. It was their field and they did not think I fully appreciated the pertinent physics. Rabi was particularly assertive. On major scientific issues and debates, he was a wise and public-spirited man, but he could be combative over smaller arguments or day-to-day tasks. As far as he was concerned, he and Kusch were the beam experts, I was the molecular spectroscopist. Yet I had gone over the numbers very carefully with Gordon and Zeiger. I knew that the chances for quick success were somewhat marginal, but that the physics undergirding the concept was sound and the numbers promising. Rabi and Kusch, I felt, were going more on instinct. I simply told them that I thought it had a reasonable chance and that I would continue. I was then indeed thankful that I had come to Columbia with tenure.

After two years of work on the idea, Herb Zeiger's fellowship ran out and he took a job in solid-state physics at the Lincoln Laboratory. He told me later that in the meantime Professor Kusch had berated him for wasting two years on this hair-brained project, when he could have been publishing some solid papers in more conventional research areas. This apparently didn't divert Herb's thinking permanently, however, because at Lincoln Laboratory he was to later do pioneering work toward a semiconductor laser.

At Columbia, we kept working hard on our ammonia-beam device. Even though we had talked about the possibility of this new kind of oscillator and had had many visitors to the lab, and even though a few universities had put our internal laboratory reports on their open shelves, nobody else pursued the idea. It was not the only project in the lab, of course. I had a dozen Ph.D. students, quite a few for a physicist, to keep me busy with a variety of projects in microwave spectroscopy. But the oscillator got steady attention, because I felt it could provide a terrific tool for spectroscopic work.

The experiment was in my main laboratory room, so I saw Gordon and Zeiger frequently. We regularly talked over the design and plans. We worked particularly hard on improving the input of molecules and on making a cavity whose energy losses were less than the gains that would be picked up from the molecular beam. We started getting indications of stimulated emission almost as soon as we looked for it, and this provided some interesting spectroscopy of exceptionally high resolution. A good thesis for Jim Gordon was assured. The problem was that our cavities were a bit too lossy (too low in Q) to allow a resonant wave to build up as it bounced back and forth. We solved this problem little by little.

The idea all along was that, as we sent the molecular beam from one end of the cavity to the other, amplification would occur in microwaves reflecting back and forth across the cavity, more or less at right angles to the direction of flow in the molecular beam. Originally, we felt the whole cavity should be as enclosed as possible, but this was inconsistent with the job of getting molecules in and out. If holes in the cavity to let molecules through were too large, the resonating radiation might leak out the ends faster than it could build up. Adequately sealing the cavity to microwaves while getting molecules through it was a tricky problem. We kept trying different metal rings fitted into the necessary holes in the ends of the cavity. They could perhaps keep microwaves from escaping too fast while letting molecules pass. The solution, when it came, was simple. One day, Jim Gordon opened the ends almost completely; that was what put it over the top. Without a ring in each end, we could get plenty of molecules through the cavity. Our worry over too much radiation leaking from the ends was unnecessary. Apparently, without the rings, the pattern of radiation in the cavity became simpler and more efficiently confined. The cavity was quite long, and radiation largely bounced back and forth between the sidewalls, so not much leaked out the perfectly circular, large holes in the ends. Probably, the slitted rings, which had previously been fitted on the cavity, had neither been perfectly circular nor well enough connected to the cavity, thereby distorting the fundamental resonance pattern of radiation in the cavity and actually enhancing the loss of energy.

During a seminar with most of the rest of my students in early April of 1954, Jim Gordon burst in. He had skipped the seminar in order to complete a test with the open ends. It was working! We stopped the seminar and went to the lab to see the evidence for oscillation and to celebrate.

At lunch with my students some time later, as work on the new oscillator continued, I commented that we needed a name for the new device. We tried Latin and Greek names, but they seemed too long, so we settled on an acronym, based on the description: *m*icrowave *a*mplification by *s*timulated *e*mission of *r*adiation. The first "maser" had been born. This was about 3 months after Poly Kusch had insisted it would not work. When it did work, he was gracious about it, commenting that he should have realized I probably knew more about what I was doing than he did.

This history—including the subsequent impact of the maser and its optical version, the laser—leads to an important point that must be in the forefront of any long-term scientific or technical planning. Some science historians, looking back on those days, have concluded that we were being in some way orchestrated, managed, manipulated, or maneuvered by the military, as though the Navy already expected explicit uses for millimeter waves and even anticipated something like the maser and laser. Politicians and planners, managing the budget, also generally believe plans must be focused by funding agencies on specifically useful directions. From our vantage point, the Navy didn't have any specific expectations at all about something like the maser or laser. Whatever new came out of the field was up to us. The military seemed quite uninterested in my maser work until some time after it was proven. What was critical was that I was free to work on what I thought was interesting and important. When one looks back in time, cause and effect sometimes get turned around. Industry and the military were important sources of generous support, but—in an experience shared by many academic scientists—throughout my career I have had to convince others, including sponsors, to let me keep following my own instincts and interests. Very often, this pays off.

Norman Podhoretz

'50 COLUMBIA COLLEGE

A longtime editor of the political and cultural journal Commentary, *Norman Podhoretz is best known as one of the founders of the modern neoconservative movement. He broke with the 1960s New Left over Vietnam and joined the Republican party in the 1970s, all the while advocating in the pages of the magazine for a more forceful and activist foreign policy. Excerpted here is Podhoretz's first memoir,* Making It *(1968).*

Oddly enough for a boy of literary bent, I had read almost nothing before Columbia but popular novels and a few of the standard poets. I had never heard of most of the books we were given to read in Humanities and Contemporary Civilization—the two great freshman courses for which the college is deservedly famous—let alone of the modern authors whose names were being dropped so casually all around me. Though I had been writing poems and stories ever since I could remember, I did not know what men were doing when they committed words to paper. I did not know that there was more to a poem than verbal prettiness and passion, or that there was more to a novel than a story. I did not know what an idea was or how the mind could play with it. I did not know what history was, thinking of it as a series of isolated past events which had been arbitrarily selected for inclusion in the dreary canon of required knowledge. I did not know that I was the product of a tradition, that past ages had been inhabited by men like myself, and that the things they had done bore a direct relation to me and to the world in which I lived. All this began opening up for me at Columbia and it set my brain on fire.

Columbia College, unlike the university of which it forms the undergraduate liberal-arts division (for men), is a small school. Total enrollment in my day was about two thousand and classes were rarely larger than twenty—which, of course, permitted them to be run as seminars rather than lecture courses. The other unusual characteristic of the college which is relevant here is that many of the university's most distinguished faculty members taught these small classes. This meant that most of us, even as freshmen, came into intimate contact with such important senior professors as Moses Hadas, Irwin Edman, and Mark Van Doren.

I yearned with all my soul to be equal to them and what they stood for, and I feared with all my soul that I wasn't. Accustomed to effortless preeminence in school, I suddenly found myself as a Columbia freshman staggering under an incredibly heavy load of assignments and surrounded by classmates who knew more about everything than I did or clearly ever would. I was sure I would fail. They would take my scholarship away. I would be disgraced. Amazingly, it did not work out that way. After a shaky start and many night-long porings over strange and difficult books, I gradually learned to pace myself; and after a few initially timid ventures in classroom discussion had elicited a certain familiar glow in the eyes of several professors, I began jumping in with both feet whenever I could get the chance. This did not endear me to my classmates, but that was a small price to pay for catching the attention of my teachers, which I certainly succeeded in doing.

Utterly open, limitlessly impressionable, possessed of something like total recall and a great gift for intellectual mimicry, I also succeeded, and without conscious intent, in writing papers for each of my professors in a different style—one which invariably resembled his own. And finally, it turned out that I had a remarkable talent for examinations of the essay type. Where others were semiparalyzed by the impossibility of showing how good they were in a mere three hours, I was never so fluent, never so coherent, never so completely in command of my powers of imitation as when I opened a blue book and started racing the clock. Given all this, and given also the intensity with which I worked, it is no wonder—though it was a great and glorious wonder to me then—that A +'s (an unusual grade at Columbia outside courses in the sciences) should have begun appearing on my record almost as regularly as A's.

Nor, given all this, is it any wonder that I aroused so much hostility among certain Columbia types: the prep-school boys, those B students who rarely said anything in class but who underwent such evident agonies over the unseemly displays of pushiness they had to endure from the likes of me; the homosexuals with their supercilious disdain of my lower-class style of dress and my brash and impudent manner; and the prissily bred middle-class Jews who thought me insufferably crude. All of them were lumped indiscriminately together in my mind as "snobs," and though their hostility got to me often enough to cause me considerable pain, I had friends of my own to lean on who, while they too regarded me as something of a barbarian and perhaps also something of an opportunist, at least regarded me as a likeable one: a Julien Sorel or a Rastignac, let us say (Columbia literati having been very fond of such analogies), rather than a Sammy Glick or a Flem Snopes.

I can see now, of course, that I must have caused the "snobs" as much pain as they caused me. If I envied them their social composure and their apparent self-assurance, they must have envied me my freedom from the scruples which governed them and the consequent torrent of unhindered energy on which I was able to call. These scruples had nothing to do with morality; they had to do only with the code of manners governing ambitiousness which seemed to bind everyone at Columbia but me. It was a code which forbade one to work too hard or to make any effort to impress a professor or to display the slightest concern over grades. Since most of the "snobs" in question were serious students, however, the code hemmed them in, and since most of them were also ridden with ambition—quite as much, I think, as I—it forced them into secret transgressions, made them feel guilty, hypocritical, and ashamed. Yet I, a flagrantly open violator, instead of being punished, was being rewarded; I would probably even wind up, a "snob" once bitterly remarked to one of my friends, with Columbia's choicest prize, a Kellett Fellowship: "Can you imagine *him* at Oxford or Cambridge? Sammy Glick in the *Agora!*" (Columbia literati were not only fond of analogies, they also tended to a romantic Anglophilia, entertaining, as I was later to discover, an altogether exaggerated idea of the polish of English society.)

There was, to be sure, nothing unusual in the prevailing attitude toward ambitiousness at Columbia: it was a fair reflection of a widespread American sentiment. And yet it does seem odd that in America, where the word ambition has traditionally been used as an honorific, ambitiousness itself should be so generally considered an unattractive quality and the signs of it looked upon as a personal deformation. According to William H. Whyte in *The Organization Man,* overt ambitiousness has even come to be frowned upon among businessmen, the very class of people who have been held responsible for exalting it to the status of a major virtue. Whyte, of course, ascribes this change to the growth of organization; in a large corporation, he says, the young executives compete with one another in being cooperative. But it is entirely possible that the new attitude toward ambition represents not a revolutionary development at all, but rather a return to normal after an aberrant historical episode brought about by the rapid and uncontrolled industrialization of the country following the Civil War. There is enough reason, God knows, for thinking that it is in the nature of man to be ambitious, but this quality has, after all, more generally been associated with the darker than with the lovelier side of human nature. Thus it is altogether typical that in the contest for popular support between Brutus and Mark Antony after the assassination of Julius Caesar, Antony (at least in Shakespeare's version) should have been able to win by refuting Brutus' charge, advanced in justification of the murder, that Caesar had been an ambitious man.

So far as the characteristic upper-class disdain for ambitiousness is concerned—the species of disdain I encountered in youthfully exaggerated form at Columbia—no doubt it was originally adopted as a weapon to be used by those whose wealth was inherited or whose position was secure against those who were occupied with accumulating the one or acquiring the other. To become aware of the origins of this disdain is to be let in on the comedy of certain situations whose humor might otherwise not be apparent: for example, the frequently voiced complaint of old-stock Massachusetts Yankees, privileged descendants of some of the most rapacious merchants history has ever known, over the terrible "ruthlessness" of the Kennedy family.

This same "ruthlessness" also bothered many liberals whose discomfort over it probably derived from more strictly ideological considerations. But whatever the source of their discomfort, they dealt with it while John F. Kennedy was still alive by persuading themselves that the President was exempt from the family stigma, the whole of that unworthy legacy having been inherited by his brother Robert. This, in spite of the fact that John F. Kennedy, like any man who goes far, and especially in the vocation of politics, must not only have been ambitious but also not inconveniently troubled by delicate scruples in the pursuit of his ambition. Once in the White House, of course, Kennedy did carry himself like a *gentleman* (the kind of person, as Yeats once said, who is thought not to be too much occupied with getting on), and taking him for such (his famous "style"), most liberals finally came to adore him. Ambition, ruthlessness, unscrupulousness—all these unpatrician-like qualities were simply projected onto Bobby, who, we can be sure, is richly endowed with them, but, as we can be equally sure, no more than his brother was and possibly even less. If Bobby had not existed, the liberals would either have had to invent him or forgo the luxury of worshiping Jack.

Such attitudes toward ambition were not, when I was an undergraduate, without their effect on me; nor was I anywhere near as free of the Columbia code as the "snobs" believed me to be. But my hunger for success as a student, which was great enough in itself but might yet have yielded to discipline, became absolutely uncontrollable when I began to realize that I would never make the grade as a poet. I had a small talent for verse, yet try as I did for more than two years, there was finally no concealing the fact from myself that as compared with Allen Ginsberg, John Hollander, and a dozen other Columbia poets of the time, I rated at the most generous estimate a grudging honorable mention. (Even Mark Van Doren, who admired *everyone's* poetry, clearly thought little of mine: the only B I ever got in English at Columbia was in a creative writing course I took with him.) This was not an easy discovery to take for a boy who since the onset of puberty had been in the habit of telling girls that he would kill himself at twenty-five—Keats again—if he had decided for certain by then that he was not a great poet. Yet there was a truth concealed in those adolescent histrionics: the truth was that I could not bear the idea of not being great. Poetry had once seemed the only way to greatness, but now Columbia taught me that it was neither the only nor the right way for me.

Then what do you want to be now when you grow up, little boy? *A literary critic.* An unlikely answer today, perhaps, for anyone so ambitious as I was at nineteen, but in the late 1940's, the opening years of what Randall Jarrell was later to call "The Age of Criticism," nothing could have been more natural for an undergraduate who was doing well in English than to look forward to a career as a critic, while supporting himself, of course, by teaching. The physical sciences apart, literary criticism in those days was probably the most vital intellectual activity in America, and the most vital branch of literature itself; or if it was not in actual fact more significantly alive than philosophy or theology or history or the social sciences or poetry or fiction or the theater, it was certainly felt to be so by a great many young men of the time who aspired to the academic life. In my circle at Columbia, for example, we awaited the arrival of the quarterlies in which criticism flourished— magazines like *Partisan Review* and *Kenyon Review*—with the avidity of addicts, and we read the essays of such "New Critics" as Cleanth Brooks, R. P. Blackmur, and Allen Tate with an excitement that equaled, if indeed it did not surpass, the passion we brought to the poems and novels they were writing about. If we could all quote at length from the poetry of T. S. Eliot, we could also quote at length—and with, in truth, a greater feeling of assurance—from his critical essays.

And so with the critics on the Columbia faculty itself—the late Andrew Chiappe, the late Richard Chase, F. W. Dupee, and especially Lionel Trilling—who became our mentors, our models, our gods. In the classroom as on paper, the critics were not only our guides to the secret riches of literature, they were our guides to philosophy, theology, and politics as well. As explicators of difficult texts, they taught us a method of reading and gave us a veritably gnostic sense of power; as theoreticians of literature, they introduced us to the thrilling metaphysical categories which, banished from the philosophy department by the triumph of logical positivism, found a new home in criticism. As implicit polemicists for a neo-conservative (the New Critics) or neo-Marxist (the *Partisan Review* critics) point of view, they extended the boundaries of literature in general and their own work in particular to take in this world, as it were, along with the next.

In such an atmosphere, the vocation of critic-teacher seemed a genuine alternative to the vocation of poet, and with the record I already had behind me in English as I entered my senior year, there was every reason to believe that it was the right career for me. But it was only the ultimate certification I received that year from Trilling and Dupee that settled the matter for good. Trilling in particular was known as a tough grader and he was said to be automatically suspicious of students who came to his classes with great reputations behind them. The A+ he gave me in his course on the English Romantics, coupled with another A+ from Dupee in a course on contemporary literature, removed any lingering doubt as to what my future would be. All that remained for the moment was to decide where I would go to graduate school, and that question was settled—the "snobs" had been right—by a Kellett Fellowship and then a Fulbright Scholarship to boot.

The first lap of that journey I was making from Brooklyn to Manhattan had most definitely been completed; the second lap would be a generously financed three-year stay at the ancient university of Cambridge.

Charles Peters

'49 COLUMBIA COLLEGE, '51 MA

Charles Peters is the founding editor of The Washington Monthly. *A former West Virginia state legislator and Peace Corps administrator, he is a longtime foe of bureaucracy and Washington special interests and a self-proclaimed "neoliberal." Joining the several books on public affairs that he has edited is* Tilting at Windmills, *his 1988 autobiography, which is excerpted here.*

I was discharged from the army in January 1946 and immediately went to New York City to enter Columbia College. While in the hospital, I had read *Teacher in America* by Jacques Barzun, one of the luminaries of the Columbia faculty. Barzun's description of the college was seductive. It was not gigantic, like the university of which it was a part but had only 1,750 students and small classes, averaging twenty students or so. More surprising, those small classes were taught, even at the freshman level, by the brightest stars of the faculty—people like Barzun and Lionel Trilling and Mark Van Doren—rather than by the graduate students my friends who went to other prominent universities often got stuck with.

As Barzun's book implied, teaching was important at Columbia. In the fall of 1946, for example, Trilling taught eleven hours a week. Today's average in the Ivy League is more like five hours. And, as Barzun explained, this teaching served an overall educational objective, which was to make sure that every student was introduced to the basics of Western civilization. All students were required to take courses that introduced them to the major works of literature, art, and music as well as to the thought of the great philosophers, economists, and historians. Having leafed through the bulletins of other colleges, which listed a bewildering array of electives with no discernible purpose, I welcomed this deprivation of free choice.

As an intellectual experience, Columbia more than met my expectations. Most of the classes *were* small; most of the teachers *were* outstanding. But I had come to Columbia not just to be educated but to live the life of a New Yorker. I had access to that life because it was cheap. Even a student of modest means could enjoy the city. Tuition was $225 per term. A glass of beer cost a dime, so you could have a full evening of intense discussion and fairly intense drinking for a dollar or so. The subway was only a nickel as 1946 began. One snowy night in late January, I took the IRT from the Columbia stop at 116th and Broadway to Greenwich Village, getting off at Sheridan Square and buying a copy of the *Daily Worker*. I felt deliciously radical with my upturned coat collar and my scarf blowing in the wind. Later, in April and May, the same nickel would buy a ride on an open-topped double-decker bus that would take you down to Washington Square or up to the Cloisters—a perfect answer to those warm spring afternoons when you weren't going to get any studying done anyway. There were lots of inexpensive French and Italian restaurants, like Le Champlain, La Fleur de Lis, and Barbetta's, where dinner with a glass of wine could be had for less than three dollars.

✻ ✻ ✻

One of the most impressive things about Columbia in the late forties was the brainpower of its students. They were, for the most part, not from the social elite—Jason Epstein was the only person I knew who had gone to prep school. They were drawn largely from two groups. One was World War II veterans. Several of them were my friends: Bob Williams, who had endured the frightening disintegration of the 106th Division during the Battle of the Bulge; John Uhl and Don Kirchoffer, who had served in the navy; and Ned Gatchell, who had been a bomber pilot and had flown those hair-raising daylight missions over Germany. I was nineteen when I entered Columbia, but most of the other veterans were two to six years older and therefore more mature and much less likely to waste time than the average college student. They were tough competition.

Only a little less tough, however, was the next largest group of students, the bright high school graduates from New York City, like my friend Steve Marcus. Because there were so many applicants from the city, they were subjected to more demanding admission standards than the rest of us. Columbia had a Jewish quota then, which meant that if you were from New York and Jewish, you had to be even brighter to get in. To those of us who were their less diligent classroom competition, these New Yorkers seemed demonic in their devotion to academic excellence—they'd get off the subway at 8:00 A.M., go directly to the library in South Hall, and stay there, except for meals and classes, until it closed, studying every minute. Norman Podhoretz, who later became editor of *Commentary* and a leading neoconservative, was a member of this group.

I knew Podhoretz as someone who attended a class with me, not as a friend or even an acquaintance. The course we took together was in twentieth-century fiction, taught by Harrison Steeves. Since the lures of life in New York often left me less than prepared for the morning's discussion, I sat in the back of the room. Podhoretz sat in the front and was always prepared. He was constantly waving his hand, constantly talking, constantly trying to impress the professor.

The problem was that Podhoretz was a Jew from Brooklyn and Steeves was a snobbish old Wasp with little patience for the upwardly mobile. However brilliant Podhoretz might be, Steeves would not give him the recognition he so avidly sought. Steeves bestowed his regard, instead, on one Donald Maher, a reserved young man with the right accent.

The juxtapositon of Podhoretz and Steeves was hilarious to those of us on the back benches. But our laughter did not reflect personal animosity (as Podhoretz suggests in his book, *Making It)*. Indeed, most of us were grateful to him for deferring the dread moment when Steeves might ask, "Well, Mr. Peters, you haven't said much lately. Why don't you tell us what you think Proust is trying to say?"

Several of my other classmates later made their marks on the world. One who did, and who probably influenced me more than anyone, I met on an October afternoon in 1946. I was with about twenty other students in Trilling's Humanities 3 class, discussing William Blake's *Songs of Innocence.* I noticed that some of the most thoughtful observations were being made by a dark, slight young man who was sitting in that day.

When the class broke up, I wanted to ask him about some of the things he had said, and I spoke with him as we walked out of Hamilton Hall, around to 116th Street, and on to the Amsterdam Avenue bus stop. Apparently we were headed in the same direction, for, still talking, we boarded the same bus. The conversation continued until I reached my stop. "I get off here," I said. "So do I," he said. We walked from the bus stop to my apartment building at 200 West 92nd Street. "Well this is where I live," I said. "So do I," he said. It was time to introduce ourselves. His name was Allen Ginsberg. He lived on the second floor; I lived on the fourth.

Allen and I became friends. He opened up a new world for me, introducing me to people like Jack Kerouac and Neal Cassady, people who were much more open and much less careerist than the typical Columbia student of that time. Sometimes I thought they were crazy, but more often I found myself liking their unconventionality.

One of the most appealing aspects of their unconventionality was that they didn't push it. Once, at a party, Kerouac took me into a bedroom to show me pictures of Arab boys in various postures of sexual abandon. It was obvious that Jack thought they might stimulate certain thoughts in my mind. But when I asked him instead about an attractive girl in the front room, he cheerfully put away the pictures and told me, "She works for United Press and is from Mt. Airy, North Carolina. I'll introduce you."

I liked Allen best. When you talked to him you knew he really heard what you were saying. The barriers of pride and self-image that inhibit real communication between people were so slight in Allen that he could strip them away instantly when you were trying to get through to him. In his gentleness and his indifference to material things, he was almost otherworldly. One day we went to the Frick Museum, where, directly opposite the El Greco that occupies the most prominent position in the main room is a St. Francis by Bellini, and we stopped to look at it. As we stood there I thought, of course there aren't saints any more, but Allen comes closer than most of us. I may have idealized Allen and Jack and Neal—Jack and Neal, in particular, had tormented undercurrents in their lives that I was unaware of—but my idealized version provided what was, for me, an important alternative to the Podhoretzes and the veterans, who were all preparing to don gray flannel suits.

* * *

We often had guests for dinner at 92nd Street— friends from Columbia or the theater or people like Doctorow, who went to Kenyon College with Dick and Billy. Occasionally, someone would just appear. One of these was Herbert Huncke, whom we knew through Ginsberg. Allen had met him in the Automat on 42nd Street between 7th and 8th Avenues, which was a headquarters for junkies and petty criminals. Herbert was both. He was slight, dark, and fine-featured. He moved, Kerouac once observed, like a movie Arab. You could easily picture him sneaking into a house or picking a pocket. When he appeared at 92nd Street, good fellowship was not his only motive. He was usually trying to sell us something, and that something, one suspected, often was not in the hands of its rightful owner. If he was especially impecunious, Herbert would ask for the empty bottles in the apartment, which he could sell for a few cents apiece. Tiny always gave him the bottles and occasionally bought his merchandise, although the buying was done with a mournful sigh and an upward roll of the eyes as she contemplated the current penalty for receiving stolen goods.

Allen's taste for minor criminals once nearly got me in trouble. In April 1948 I moved to an apartment of my own. One night around 2:00 A.M.,

Ginsberg, Kerouac, and Huncke arrived for a visit. That wasn't unusual, except that this time they brought along an exotic young woman—I'll call her Susie instead of using her real name, since her life has subsequently taken a respectable turn.

Susie and I hit it off. The next night, she called and asked if she could come by and take a bath. I said fine. When she emerged from the bathroom, she said she had had an inspiration. My apartment would be a perfect place for her to use for scoring with johns. Susie, it seemed, was a prostitute. She had a notebook full of clients. All she needed was a place to do business—a "pad," as she put it. Although I was anxious to make a favorable impression on Allen's friends, I said no.

Allen was not as successful at avoiding trouble. A few weeks after Susie visited my apartment, I was on the subway, reading the *Daily Mirror* over the shoulder of the person standing next to me. When he turned to the back page, I saw a large photograph of four people staring out of the rear of a paddy wagon—Allen, Susie, Herbert, and their friend Little Jack Melody.

They had been driving around Queens with Little Jack at the wheel when they were stopped by a policeman who wanted to tell them they were going the wrong way on a one-way street. Little Jack, mindful of the possible misunderstanding that might arise from the fact that the car was stolen, did not wait to hear the officer out. Instead, he jammed the accelerator to the floor and sped off into the night. As he attempted to negotiate a sharp corner, the car turned over, and its occupants quickly scattered. Allen returned to his apartment on York Avenue. He opened the door, thinking he was safe at last, only to be greeted by several city officials in blue uniforms. It seems that Allen had left his diary in the car and that it contained his address. (I can't explain why he took his diary on a joy ride through Queens or, for that matter, why they chose Queens in the first place.) Allen had made another mistake: he had permitted Little Jack and Herbert to use his apartment for storage, and, you guessed it, among the stored goods there were few that were the legal property of either Herbert or Little Jack. To beat the rap, Allen had to commit himself to the care of psychiatrists at Payne Whitney.

There are dramatic differences between Charleston and New York, and by the end of my first year at Columbia, those differences were beginning to have an effect on me. Charleston is the small town where practically everyone knows you or your family. The good side of this is that it encourages you to behave thoughtfully toward others. If you're a clerk in a store and you're rude to Mrs. Jones, it is likely that she knows several people who know you and that she will tell them about it. Also, when people have known you well for your entire life, they aren't likely to mistake you for either the purest saint or the most evil sinner. Their knowledge of you is protection against unjust accusation as well as unwarranted praise.

But all this is limiting, too, which is why many people want to escape small towns. They want to be more than they have been. Someone in New York might hire them to do great things, while the small-town employer would know their limits all too well. In other words, the song's promise—"If you can make it there, you'll make it anywhere"—is misleading. Some people make it in New York because they *couldn't* make it back home. They never would have gotten the chance.

New York also offers anonymity. Your private life can be your own business and no one else's in a way that's impossible in a small town. But anonymity also means that, even after living in New York for years, you can walk all the way down Fifth Avenue and not be recognized by a single human being. This may explain why so many people who go to New York thinking that they want anonymity end up trying to be celebrities or envying those who are. Some even seek identity through contact with celebrities. The most extreme example is the horde of autograph-seekers that follows in the wake of anyone famous. Telling their friends about having seen a celebrity, and proving it by showing his autograph, endows them with importance and gives them something to talk about.

I was not immune to celebrityism. Having met a few of the famous during my years in New York—including Grace Kelly, John Huston, Ingrid Bergman, and William Faulkner—I became skilled at casually weaving these brief encounters into conversations with my friends and acquaintances. I could get a sense of importance even by knowing someone who knew a celebrity—"She's a close friend of Tennessee Williams, you know." A similar sense of self-importance can come—and this is especially so in the case of intellectuals—from knowing something others don't, from being among the first to divine what's in and what's out in literature and in the arts.

By 1947, I was getting pretty heavily involved in this sort of thing. In other words, I had become a snob. One reason was the transfer of my career interest from politics to the theater, which had happened the previous summer. In politics, snobbery is likely to lose you votes. In the arts, it can be viewed as evidence of your higher powers of discrimination.

But a more important cause in my case was insecurity. From the secure world of Charleston High School, where I was "most likely to succeed" in my class, I had entered a world where what I considered my exceptional promise was not instantly recognized. There were a lot of very bright students who were better prepared for Columbia than I was.

During my first term I puzzled over the phrase "perne in a gyre" in "Sailing to Byzantium." Should I confess, I wondered, that I hadn't a clue as to what it meant? Of course not—I would only confirm that I was a hick from West Virginia. So I slipped off to the library to consult *A Vision*, the book in which Yeats explains his philosophy. But instead of enlightenment, I encountered even greater obscurity in those bewildering diagrams of intersecting cones, and my anxiety became worse.

I finished the first term with two As and four Bs. Although a perfectly respectable record in retrospect, it opened a crack of doubt in my academic self-assurance. At Charleston High School I had gotten As without unseemly sweat. Now it was clear that I would not get many unless I became a grind. I enjoyed the pleasures of New York far too much to take that possibility seriously.

Instead, I gradually became a snob, trying to impress others not with my performance but with my awareness of what was intellectually chic. I could talk knowingly about the latest literary controversy or casually drop the names of the authors who were "in." In the library I would feign total immersion in Baudelaire, especially if a Barnard girl was sitting nearby. The only movie theater I would deign to enter was the Thalia on West 95th Street. It featured ancient classics as well as the work of the French and Italian directors who were fashionable in the forties and who seemed to have a special fondness for overexposed film and scratchy sound tracks.

This was a period during which you could not, as I secretly did, admire a Victorian house or the beaux arts splendor of Grand Central Station. Picasso was in, and so was Henry James. I liked neither, but I pretended that I did. The first minutes of an encounter with someone you wanted to impress were spent flashing your taste badges. And your worst fear was that you might flash the wrong one, that you might be praising last year's poet instead of this year's. So you made sure to keep abreast of those publications that could keep you informed of what was in and what was out—the *New Yorker* and the *Partisan Review* were the essential ones.

My grades began to plummet. I was afraid to commit myself to the effort that might produce an A and then have to face the fact that I couldn't make it even when I was really trying.

In January 1948 I got a call from the dean's office about my sinking grades. This resulted in a referral to a psychiatrist. I knew I had lost my way and needed help. I was turning into someone I didn't like at all, and I was ready to open myself to someone who wanted to come to my rescue. I was lucky enough to find a really kind and caring doctor.

At the same time that I was seeing the psychiatrist, another benign influence appeared in my life. That spring, Van Doren offered a remarkable course that began with Kafka's *The Trial* and *The Castle,* continued through

The Divine Comedy, and ended with *Don Quixote.* It was a progression from lost bewilderment to what became my true faith—that I had to pursue my own vision even if the rest of the world thought I was only tilting at windmills.

Max Frankel

'52 COLUMBIA COLLEGE, '53 MA

Max Frankel began writing for The New York Times *while a student at Columbia. He would go on to spend his entire professional career with the newspaper—rising to Washington bureau chief, editorial-page editor, and, ultimately, executive editor. Frankel, who won the 1973 Pulitzer Prize for international reporting, remembered Columbia (and the* Spectator) *in his 1999 autobiography,* The Times of My Life and My Life with The Times, *now available in a paperback edition.*

I think I knew that Carl Van Doren, the world federalist among historians, had a brother, a poet named Mark, who taught at Columbia University. And I knew that Columbia passed out awards each year to competing high school newspapers. But otherwise, I knew Columbia only as the fourth station down from home on the Broadway subway. I'd never heard of Joseph Wood Krutch, Lionel Trilling, Jacques Barzun, Irwin Edman, Dumas Malone, David Truman, Moses Hadas, Charles Frankel, C. Wright Mills, and all the other celebrated scholars who became my mentors when oh so ignorantly I decided to enroll in Columbia College and chanced upon what was probably the country's finest undergraduate curriculum. Like General of the Army Dwight D. Eisenhower, who arrived at the same time to be the university's president, I picked Columbia for essentially unworthy reasons. And like Ike, I exploited the place shamelessly.

Bright New York youngsters from poor families were supposed to go to CCNY, the City College of New York, which Jews called "our Harvard," and with reason. City College fielded a gifted faculty and offered a first-class education at taxpayer expense. It opened access to the finest graduate schools—more so than other colleges when you consider that Ivy League bastions still used informal quotas to hold down their number of New York Jews. But CCNY served only city kids, and the still striving refugee inside me mistook that for provincialism. I yearned to cross yet another frontier and invested extraordinary energy in the journey. Unlike CCNY, the private colleges demanded that I take the College Board entrance exam, an alarming prospect.

My desultory reading habits were finally taking their toll: I could not recognize half the words on the sample vocabulary test the College Board sent me. I could not begin to match word pairings like "hammer:nail" with "despot:peon." Self-help manuals, like *Thirty Days to a More Powerful Vocabulary*, did not relieve the crisis. And the College Board boasted that cramming was useless; it was testing a "lifetime of learning."

My vocabulary may have been shallow, but my skepticism ran deep. I resolved to cram and somehow prove them wrong. I discovered that the library at Columbia's Teachers College housed a file of all College Board exams ever devised. In just half a dozen visits, I copied out every unfamiliar word and word pairing, filling two shoe boxes with index cards that bore the strange words on one side, their definitions on the other. For months, I traveled everywhere with some of those cards until I had memorized, although in no true sense acquired, this new vocabulary. When I came upon the boxes a decade later, I was startled to find how many of those once intimidating words appeared routinely in *The New York Times*, and in my own writings. But at the time, the cards were cork to a drowning swimmer. When I finally took the board test, I recognized three fourths of the words, enough to qualify for all three of the private colleges to which I had applied.

At the top of the list was the University of Chicago, whose curriculum struck me as suitably bohemian and whose campus was attractively far from home. Chicago taught the Great Books without even requiring that you attend class. It was led by Robert M. Hutchins, the university's president before he was thirty, who banished football and not only favored world government but composed and published its constitution. Then, too, Chicago would let me hover near Sandy, a high school flame who had incomprehensibly committed herself to a rival suitor. Mom's prayers against Chicago were answered only when it denied me financial aid. I would have to stay inside the borders of New York after all and take advantage of the state's scholarship, worth a significant $350 a year. That was almost enough to cover tuition at NYU and more than half the cost of Columbia.

Pop argued fervently for Columbia. It was famous even in Europe, he insisted, so its degree would always be worth more. His endorsement would have surely soured me on Columbia if I hadn't heard the siren songs of

David Wise, my predecessor as editor of *Overtone* at Music & Art. Dave had followed his father to Columbia and told rhapsodic tales about writing for *The Columbia Daily Spectator*—the *Monday-to-Friday Spectator!* As a daily, he emphasized, *Spec* was hungry for new recruits; NYU and City offered only weeklies, he scoffed. Besides, at Columbia you met "downtown journalists" who came to cover campus events and to teach at the Graduate School of Journalism. Dave had already sold two features to International News Service!

That's how I chose Columbia; I followed the ink. I reported for duty at the *Spectator* a full week before the start of classes, an order of priority that remained immutable for four fateful years.

In just one week, Columbia bleached out all my frustrated ambitions for elective office. Though shy, chubby, and unimposing, I'd been emboldened by Mom's faith to believe that I could be a popular as well as articulate leader. But the absurdity of it dawned at the first meeting of the freshman class, when we were invited to nominate ourselves for the posts of class president and secretary-treasurer. The winners would cast votes on the Student Board, arrange assorted "smokers" with professors and dances with Barnard girls, and, of course, get a leg up on admission to good medical and law schools. A dozen classmates ran eagerly toward the stage, and I, too, felt the undertow of high school campaigns yanking at me. In an epiphanous moment, still vivid a half century later, I stopped in midmotion for a rush of calculation: stick with journalism and you'll be writing about these clowns; give up frivolous self-promotion and deal instead with "real" issues. With a memorable thud, I sat back down, never to feel the candidate urge again.

My immersion in campus journalism seemed to have the university's highest sanction. In Ike's first speech to our class, he promised a new gym and a better football field and stressed the importance of "nonacademic" pursuits. "The day that goes by that you don't have fun, that you don't enjoy life," Eisenhower said, with a syntax prophetic of his political career, "is to my mind not only unnecessary but un-Christian." Indeed, we non-Christians were drawn in great numbers to the fourth floor of John Jay and the adjacent offices of the *Spectator,* the chess club, the debate team, the *Review,* the *Jester,* and the Varsity Players. Religious or not, we devoutly believed in extracurricular fun and turned those rooms into bustling fraternity houses, and more: a place where individual growth also produced communal value.

Sniffing out the trustees' secret plot to raise tuition and spreading the news turned out to be more gratifying even than deciphering a Shakespeare sonnet. Embarrassing the dean about the girls-in-the-room rule—*Could the order to keep doors open by at least "the thickness of a book?" be satisfied with a slim volume of poetry?*—was far more amusing than defining the comic nature of Don Quixote. I could not resist the lures of journalism: the license to pry into all corners of campus life, the chance to champion remedies for discovered wrongs, the easy access to persons of every rank, and the reliable armor to shield an otherwise debilitating shyness.

Columbia, with a wisdom since abandoned, did not then require undergraduates to "major" in any one subject, so we prejournalism dilettantes majored aggressively in *Spec.* We hung around its shabby offices, eager to take any reporting assignment or to run photographs to the engravers, to dummy page layouts or to change typewriter ribbons. Although I slept at home and was due in my first freshman class at 8:00 A.M., I cheerfully volunteered for frequent duty at Cocce Press down in Greenwich Village, where we cobbled stories into their pages until dawn, then hastily skimmed a Saint Augustine essay on the subway ride home. I soon suspected that I lacked the necessary devotion for a career in scholarship.

Even so, the seductions of Columbia's core curriculum were not easily resisted. Two freshman courses in particular imposed massive nightly readings and opened our minds to an intoxicating flood of ideas. Each met four times a week in intimate settings of about fifteen students. Humanities Lit burdened us with a big book a week, from Aristophanes to Zola. And with so few targets in the room, there was no ducking the provocations of senior professors: *How would you compare Yahweh's character in Genesis with that of the gods of Sophocles, Mister Frankel?*

Still more demanding was "CC"—Introduction to Contemporary Civilization in the West. It dragged us through a parade of Western ideas with excerpts from the writings of scores of philosophers like Aquinas, Machiavelli, Hobbes, Kant, Mill, and Adam Smith. Despite the density of these texts, they magically transformed our adolescent sense of history. The ancient Greeks ceased to be just authors of myths and fairy tales and became impressive tutors in the meanings of tyranny and democracy. Europe's past ceased to be a tiresome succession of monarchs and emerged instead as a cascade of speculations about the nature of man and the ideologies that might tame him. These readings let us connect the debates of sages like Plato and Marx, Aquinas and Kant. We were encouraged to join in this chain of conversation across the ages and taught the fundamental laws of disputation. My clarifying moment came in an encounter with Prof. Charles Frankel (no relation), in an instruction that has focused all my reading ever since. Explaining why he, a liberal, and C. Wright Mills, a Marxist, were willing to wrestle so publicly and passionately in our weekly philosophy seminar, he said: *"You never know what anyone is for until you know what he is arguing against."*

That whole categories of humanity, especially women, were left out of our readings and discussions did not then strike us as remarkable. In our sense of the natural order of things, the girls across Broadway at Barnard College, with obvious exceptions, were preparing for mate- and motherhood; they were the engines of biology, not of philosophy. Little did we realize that those very women would become a driving force in our generation's history.

* * *

Though *Spec* remained my major, Ideas were at least my college minor. And together these interests shaped both my political stance and my personality. I became a secular liberal, plainly more devoted to political analysis than to action.

I made the satisfying discovery of Moses, who commanded the worship of law instead of the golden calf, and of Jesus, who proclaimed the equality of mankind in God's love. And I came to understand that since people are not in fact equal in talent and strength, their equal rights to life, liberty, and opportunity had to be defined and secured by law. It took four years to get from that first sentence to the second, but it was an exhilarating journey.

The ultimate riddle of these formative years was how the worshipers of Moses and Jesus could have abandoned their prophetic teachings and succumbed to a pathetic, murderous tribalism. I finally found the answer in my year-long study of a single book, *The Open Society and Its Enemies*, Karl R. Popper's investigation during World War II of the roots of totalitarianism. My guide, once again, was Prof. Charles Frankel, who held out Popper as our century's most relevant prophet of liberalism. He was even more than that for me because he finally resolved my youthful struggle to link the tyrannies that had shaped our family's fortune.

The doctrines that produced both Hitler and Stalin, Popper observed, could be traced through Hegel and Marx all the way back to Plato, to a family of ideas that proclaimed Utopian truths and certitudes whose imposition by force required the construction of "closed" societies. The Utopian tyrannies insisted that history had "Meaning" and that it imposed an inexorable logic on events. The Nazis proposed to reach a Platonic Golden Age by purifying a racial tribe, Popper taught, while the Communists idealized a single tribe or class of proletarians. But their doctrines were equally wicked:

> The more we try to return to the heroic age of tribalism, the more surely do we arrive at the Inquisition, at the Secret Police and at a romanticized gangsterism. Beginning with the suppression of reason and truth, we must end with the most brutal and violent destruction of all that is human. *There is no return to a harmonious state of nature. If we turn back, then we must go the whole way—we must return to the beasts.*

I found that to be the only plausible explanation of the Holocaust. Popper persuaded me that the claim that history has a single Meaning leads inevitably to the rule of brutes and the closed society. The only defense was to recognize that "History" had no purpose or meaning, no Utopian past or future, and that social justice had to be found in the present, through a process of "piecemeal social engineering"—constant experiment, debate, and corrections of course. Only in an "open society" could reason prevail and violence be curbed, because experiment required universal skepticism and the freedom to dissent.

Thus did Professors Popper and Frankel ratify my commitment to Journalism. For once you conclude that freedom requires society to live by reason—by experiment, analysis, correction, and piecemeal engineering—then language and discourse become more than instruments of self-expression. As Popper put it:

> Rationalism is therefore bound up with the idea that the other fellow has a right to be heard, and to defend his arguments. . . . Also the idea of impartiality leads to that of responsibility; we have not only to listen to arguments, but we have a duty to respond, to answer, where our actions affect others. Ultimately, in this way, rationalism is linked up with the recognition of the necessity of social institutions to protect freedom of criticism, freedom of thought and thus the freedom of men. And it establishes something like a moral obligation towards the support of these institutions.

So working for *Spec* became not only fun but a duty. Journalism became not just gratifying but a moral imperative.

✣ ✣ ✣

As I began my sophomore year, Dave Wise was blazing a new trail to journalistic glory. The chum who had lured me to Columbia and the *Spectator* had succeeded Richard Dougherty as campus stringer for the *Herald Tribune*. Besides attending class and reporting for *Spec,* Dave now traveled downtown most days to write for the *Trib* about tiresome education conferences at Teachers College, about new habits being pulled out of rats in Columbia's psychiatry labs, and about Eisenhower homilies to alumni concerning God and country. And Dave brought back to campus the irreverent celebrations of such news from veteran *Trib* reporters, stoking our ambition to labor among them.

Dave plotted his life the way he eventually plotted his spy novels and pathbreaking exposés of the CIA—elaborately and furtively. In his most conspiratorial manner, he summoned me to lunch one day to report that crusty Nancy Edwards, a graduate student then covering campus news for *The New York Times,* had received a humiliating but nonetheless tempting offer from that paper: to write up wedding notices in its Society Department. Nan, who had developed a bark worthy of Hildy Johnson in *The Front Page*, pined like all of us to cover cops and politicians, but staff was staff, and so she was likely to settle for brides and births. If she did, Dave said, she would let Dave choose between staying at the *Trib* and succeeding her at *The Times*. Whatever his choice, they had agreed to try to pass the remaining job to me.

Dave had already cast me as the more Timesian by temperament, a judgment that I stuffily took to be a compliment. More practically, we both believed that young men rose faster on the livelier—and stingier—*Tribune*. We both aspired to cover politics, progressing from general assignments to stalking the mayor, the governor, and finally the president in the White House. We reckoned that, with luck, reaching those heights would take maybe six years at the *Trib* but ten, or even fifteen, at *The Times*. So Dave decided to stay at the *Trib* and encouraged Nan to nominate me for *The Times*.

Bob Garst, *The Times*'s city editor, was politely incredulous. A courtly Virginian, he blushed and patiently explained his demurral. The campus correspondency had occasionally gone to a college senior, he recalled, but a mature graduate student, like Nan, was best. If she knew no one better than a sophomore, he could surely interest one of his students at Columbia's Graduate School of Journalism; several even had professional experience with smaller papers.

Garst spoke with such courteous deliberation that Nan had time to invent a final argument. Well, yes, she said, there are undoubtedly good reporters at the J-School, but they're busy all day chasing assignments around town. Frankel, by contrast, spent all day and many nights at the *Spectator*, and in this Eisenhower era, with so much news at Columbia, *The Times* would be getting not one pair of legs but fifty!

A rarity among editors, Garst enjoyed contradiction. Even in society news, he welcomed imagination and spunk. He smiled appreciatively at Nan. *Well, all right, send him down. We'll take a look.*

Buttoned into my most Timesian jacket, I followed Nan into the marble lobby on West Forty-third Street and into the vast third-floor newsroom that stretched a full city block from Garst's chair at the City Desk. I expected him to explore my knowledge of Columbia, but Garst chose to test my maturity. How would I ever find the time to work for both *Spec* and *The Times* while going to school? I said Dave Wise had proved it was possible; in any case, I would never let an amateur interest interfere with a professional obligation. Since I hoped one day to join the staff of *The Times*, I would not dare to cheat on my responsibilities.

That was that. It was my first regular job, and my last.

The pay was twenty dollars a week, nearly twice the cost of tuition. Unlike most newspaper stringers—so called because they were part-timers paid by

the measurement of a string, or ruler, at the rate of a dollar or two per inch—
I would be earning only about fifty cents an inch, or a penny a word. But the
steady income meant that I could be trusted not to press for the printing of
worthless news and not to pad every item just to enlarge my income.
Overnight, I had become a news professional, empowered to discard the
chaff churned out by the university's public relations office. Overnight, I had
become a sophomore of renown, familiar to campus authorities as the lad
who could spread their boasts and promotions around the world. And
overnight I had become a wage earner, freed from parental cash subsidies. I
could afford dinner at Toffenetti's in Times Square while awaiting *The
Times*'s first edition with my cherished prose—and the early *Trib*, to make
sure that I hadn't been scooped by Dave. I could even afford an occasional
steak at Bleeck's, at the *Trib*'s back door, where the biggest bylines in New
York gathered to trade stories too bawdy to print, all delightful, some even
true. It was a heady transformation. And occasionally, my beat produced
some very delicious news.

* * *

Ike's Beer and Hot Dogs speech was that kind of news. It was also a memorable demonstration of how journalism, like science, progresses by hypothesis, by shrewd conjecture that anticipates events and evidence.

Around the *Spectator*, our most persistent hypothesis was that Dwight D.
Eisenhower had been brought to Columbia by a cabal of influential trustees
to be "demilitarized" for an eventual run at the White House. Democrats
and Republicans alike had clamored to run him in 1948, but he'd put them
off, refusing even to hint at his political philosophy and surprising everyone
by taking the Columbia presidency instead. He had no prior connection to
the university and obviously lacked any interest in scholarship or scholars.
And his speeches were insipid models of the platitudinous: "As a fellow
freshman at Columbia, let me just say this: I have learned on the field of battle what I think you can learn more easily in these pleasant surroundings.
Our need is for moral rectitude and a spiritual rededication to the principles
upon which this great nation was built."

Whenever Dave and I heard Ike pronounce on the country's "need," we
would immediately mutter "moral rectitude and spiritual rededication" and
strain to suppress our snide front-row laughter. Maybe Ike enjoyed begging
for donations from alumni or courting publicity for Columbia. But we suspected that the ringleaders on the board of trustees, including Arthur Hays
Sulzberger, the publisher of *The Times*, hoped to use Columbia as a platform
to launch Ike's career as a Republican. They needed him to rescue the party
from Midwest isolationists and from the irresponsibility bred by the party's
twenty years in opposition.

The evidence for our hypothesis was skimpy but intriguing. As only a few of us had noticed, a *Spectator* photograph of the trustees' black-tie welcome for Eisenhower in 1948 had shown a single alien figure standing at the edge of the group; it was Henry Cabot Lodge, a Republican who lacked any connection to Columbia but who became an early advocate of "drafting" Ike for the White House and then served as his campaign spokesman. Meanwhile, at Eisenhower's elbow in his Columbia office, sat retired Col. Kevin McCann, for many years the general's most trusted confidant, speechwriter, and political counselor. Stephen Ambrose, Ike's admiring biographer, doesn't think much of our theory, noting that most of Columbia's trustees supported Thomas Dewey in 1948 and expected him to win and serve eight years. But Columbia's first offer to Ike was made in 1946, and the deal was sealed in mid-1947, when Sen. Robert Taft, the Ohio isolationist, looked to be in firm command of the GOP.

And a most remarkable offer it was, clearly foreshadowing Eisenhower's casual approach to the White House. Ambrose reports that Ike was promised no "involvement" in academics, no "responsibility" for fund-raising, no "excessive" entertaining, and no "burdensome" administration. Even so, Ike confided to a friend five months into the job that he'd made a mistake, never realizing what a "big operation" Columbia was.

Eisenhower was relieved of his misery by a wily President Truman, who did his best to keep Ike in uniform, maybe because he needed him but maybe also to restrain him politically. Truman summoned the general to Washington for half the 1948–49 academic year and early in 1951 sent him back to Europe as supreme commander of the Allied armies. From the start, these absences made a mockery of Eisenhower's academic pretensions, and we *Spectator* reporters could not get even an off-the-record commitment from him that he planned eventually to return to the university. Like most Columbia teachers and students, we were openly contemptuous of Ike's campus caper.

Ever the cool professionals, Dave and I were less interested in mocking Ike than in teasing out evidence of the political plans that we were sure existed. That is why the rumors of a few overlooked sentences in one of Ike's off-campus speeches, to the Saint Andrews Society at the Waldorf-Astoria, struck us, and us alone, as pregnant with significance. Buried in a text that an amused Colonel McCann eagerly provided, we found unmistakable evidence that Ike was ready to be labeled a Republican, a fervent opponent of the New Deal and Fair Deal social policies. He had defined a liberal as "a man in Washington who wants to play Almighty with your money," and he'd chided liberals, meaning Democrats, for encouraging folks to want "champagne and caviar when they should have beer and hot dogs."

How colorfully our hypothesis had found supporting evidence! Ike's campaign had begun, we concluded. But no one downtown had noticed. So we gave our little scoop to *Spec,* never expecting it to gain a second life when the seniors in charge of the student paper wrote an editorial assaulting the general as no one had assaulted him since the Battle of the Bulge:

> General Eisenhower, who doubles as president of this University, delivered himself of several remarkable statements last Wednesday evening. . . . If the speech was a trial balloon, we think public reaction will soon flatten it. . . . Being content with beer and hot dogs has never been part of the American tradition we know. The one we know assures any citizen that he may some day eat champagne and caviar, and in the White House at that. We don't know, of course, but we are willing to bet that beer and hot dogs weren't on the menu at the Waldorf-Astoria last Wednesday night either.

The Times and the *Trib,* having missed the story on the first bounce, were delighted to let their campus stringers resurrect it now. Though I was new to the job, my article about *Spec*'s editorial—"Student Daily Chides Eisenhower as Belittling 'Personal Security'"—ran prominently, and the news reverberated through press and radio. So great was the excitement that *The Times* a week later took three more of my paragraphs on the subject, reporting that eight frankfurters and rolls had mysteriously appeared in the cupped right hand of the campus statue of Alexander Hamilton. And a week after that, *The Times* admitted yet another short dispatch, this one about the campus Christmas party at which Ike tried to disarm his now loud critics. He said he couldn't give a sermon because the chaplain was present; he couldn't address "scholarly things" because scholars were present; and, to much applause, "certainly I'm not going to talk about politics. . . . I never have."

Neither Ike's eight years in the White House nor my forty-five at *The Times* would wipe away the memory of the Beer and Hot Dogs excitement. That was my first successful deduction of a truth about power and my first thrill of shouting news through the megaphone that is *The New York Times.* For the first time, I applied Prof. Charles Frankel's philosophical counsel—*"You cannot know what a man is for until you know what he's against"*—to journalism. And for the first time I understood that a reporter is no mere stenographer, that facts and quotes are not necessarily truthful until they have context.

❉ ❉ ❉

In my college years, our most analytical and meaningful journalism was practiced uptown, at *Spec.* And what a media-mad crew we were. Dave Wise became the editor in chief of *Spec* and, as we had figured, was hired after graduation by the *Trib*; he reached the White House via City Hall and Albany as planned, in six years. When I succeeded him at *Spec*, my deputies included two future presidents of network news, Richard C. Wald and Lawrence K. Grossman; a third, Roone Arledge, labored down the hall editing our yearbook.

We used both the news and editorial columns of *Spec* to decipher the double-talk by which our college deans for too long tolerated the exclusion of blacks and Jews from fraternities. We decoded and denounced a university decree celebrating academic freedom but slyly barring Communists from appearing on campus. We questioned the fairness of deferring brainy students from the Korean draft. Uptown, we practiced being Reston, examining the complexities of community life. Downtown, we were dull apprentices, learning to polish mostly pallid, parochial news of little consequence:

EISENHOWER OPENS TERM AT COLUMBIA.
Again Calls for U.S. Faith in Democratic Aims

COLUMBIA SETS UP ISRAELI STUDY UNIT

10 "BORING CLASSICS" VOTED BY READERS.
Bunyan Wins First Place

Occasionally, of course, I would bag some news of major consequence, but in the stream of trivia, it attracted little notice:

George F. Kennan, counselor of the State Department, charged here last night that the "witch-huntings" of Communists in this country had dimmed considerably our understanding of the Russian people—a people, he said, that is "saturated" with liberal and moral concepts that "must some day" assert themselves and lead to the collapse of the present Soviet regime.

✻   ✻   ✻

Even in my last year at college, however, there was nothing distinctive about my writing except its volume. I was writing a lot, in three different venues, each demanding a different voice.

Over the summer, *The Times* had hired me as a full-time reporter, to serve mostly as a lobster-shift replacement in police "shacks." That meant sitting from 8:00 P.M. to 3:30 A.M. among friendly competitors who shared a rented apartment across the street from police headquarters in Manhattan and other boroughs and also across from the East and West Side command precincts. We would count fire bells, alert for four- or five-alarmers and lesser conflagrations in tony neighborhoods. And we'd listen to the chatter on police radios for crimes worth pursuing. The permanent shack dwellers enjoyed tutoring new kids from *The Times;* they would drive me, their own pistols at the ready, to the seedier parts of town to watch a tenement fire, an auto chase, or a crime-in-progress collar. We talked cop talk with cops and racist talk to racists; all our papers felt then that a "black-on-black" crime had little or no "news value." Only once or twice a week did I get a reportable incident; *The Times* favored jewel thefts—or anything worse—at fancy addresses or crimes that provided a certain anecdotal cuteness: MAN IN VICTIM'S SUIT SEIZED AS MURDERER or 2 JITTERY ROBBERS GET $10,000 IN LOOT—VICTIM CALMS THEM DOWN.

Back in school that fall, I had to muffle this vernacular voice to produce learned essays with titles like "On Equality" or "Mill's Epistemology." My classes were mostly once-a-week seminars in classical readings. I learned best in small discussion groups and welcomed the freedom to write the required papers at my convenience, in predawn somnolence. Now that I was editor of the *Spectator,* Mom and Pop were able to rationalize my moving out, even to a campus just forty-five blocks from home. I shared an apartment with *Spec's* managing editors, Larry Grossman and Charlie Jacobs, whose courses overlapped with mine and permitted collaborations that our economics text called "efficiencies of scale."

I rarely had trouble tracking a material argument by John Locke or a mystical passage in Franz Kafka, but the simple syntax of news writing downtown interfered with my production of suitably intricate, footnoted essays uptown. Perversely, my instructors seemed to find my colloquial approach to scholarly themes refreshing and gave me grades that were rarely warranted by the intellectual weight of my ideas.

If these extremes of uptown and downtown expression ever merged, it was in the editorials that our gang wrote for *Spec.* We disdained the pomposity of some of our predecessors, but the war in Korea also cured us of excessive frivolity. The now worldwide struggle against communism was claiming the lives of our generation and some of our freedoms, and we could hear the future's challenge: Where were *you* when it mattered?

Why, indeed, were we sitting out the war in college? We wrestled with that one until we figured how to eat our cake and have it too: We urged students to take the IQ tests for deferment from the draft so long as they were available, like tax loopholes. But we opposed the policy that sent mostly poor and undereducated men to fight our battles.

✻ ✻ ✻

Opportunists we were. But pop historians notwithstanding, we were not a "silent generation." We wrote mostly about campus affairs, but we yielded nothing in fervor. When the college refused to shut down fraternities whose national leaders insisted on racial and religious discrimination, we named the offending chapters and implored freshmen to boycott them. When the university tried censoring campus speakers by disqualifying "radical" organizations, we exposed the hypocrisy and urged alumni contributors to resist a threat to academic freedom. We chided Ike for refusing to forswear politics and not promising to return to Columbia when his European duties ended. We invented a comparison shopper, Charlie Marketwise, who found student loans at Chase National for 3.83 percent without collateral while the university was soaking students at 4.00 percent. We published the names, including our own, of seniors chosen for membership in "secret" service societies, praising their work but shattering their hurtful aura of mystery. And we preached liberty in the cheeky but civil spirit of Columbia's liberal values:

We were pleased to see the other day that the charming ladies of Sapulpa, Oklahoma, have decided to revive the felicitous custom of burning books. The ladies were quite surprised that their disposal of "books about sex and socialism" (there is some sort of connection, you know) raised such a fuss in outlying districts. . . . The appropriate fuel in ancient Rome was Christians, but this is no longer the style. One no longer burns individuals—one burns ideas. This is much more sanitary, humane, and final. Individuals have been known to die of their own accord, but the tenacity with which ideas cling to life in books is startling.

When the time came to surrender our *Spectator* pulpit, we ended with a closing thought that finally connected the three worlds of my Columbia experience:

It is to our great surprise that we find in the last 130 issues of *The Spectator* a theme . . . that to print the news and record ideas is a positive good . . . that there is nothing to be gained by secrecy, collusion and suppression of thought and deed, but that much is lost by such practices. In a year characterized by increased popular acceptance of the path of least resistance—the path of repression, conformity and shortsightedness—we have tried to convince our community that it must retain its liberal vitality.

Carolyn Heilbrun

'59 PhD

Carolyn Heilbrun taught literature at Columbia beginning in 1960 and became a professor emerita in 1993. Early in her career she wrote a number of literate mystery novels under the pen name Amanda Cross, but kept her identity hidden until she had received tenure. She later made her mark in feminist scholarship and is known for books such as Reinventing Womanhood *and* Writing a Woman's Life, *a modern classic of feminist literary theory. She remembers various instructors in a 2002 memoir,* When Men Were the Only Models We Had, *excerpted here.*

The critic of the opposite sex will be
genuinely puzzled and surprised by an attempt to
alter the current scale of values, and will see in it not merely
a difference of view, but a view that is weak, or trivial,
or sentimental, because it differs from their own.
—VIRGINIA WOOLF, *Women and Fiction*

Once upon a time there were three men who exemplified, without knowing it, my ideal life. All of them became famous as writers, influential thinkers, and public figures. Their names are Clifton Fadiman, Lionel Trilling, and Jacques Barzun. They met in college, they remained aware of one another—as friends or, if less than friends, companions and fellow crusaders on behalf of similar ideals. What I recount here is only part of their story, a small part of their significance, their accomplishments. They, however, were a large part of my story, and the place they occupied in my life is what I have set out to convey here. Although one of them never knew of my existence, the second ignored it, and the third treated me with formal kindness, without them I would have had no concrete model in my youth of what I wanted to become.

Indeed, until I was past forty they remained my guides. It is hardly too much to say they were my motivation, my inspiration, my fantasy. Theirs was the universe in which I wished to have my being. When I first encountered them, however, the fact that no woman could have her being in the world where they prevailed evaded my consciousness; the impossibility of that particular dream did not present itself to me as an inexorable fact. Like women before me, I hoped against all evidence that I, an exception, might join that blessed circle. Had it not been for the women's movement of the twentieth century's last three decades, I would have had to choose, as women in academia and elsewhere had long chosen, between my inevitable exclusion from this brilliant, beckoning world or my half-life as an "exceptional" woman— never a full member of these men's fellowship but clinging to the edges of it.

Fadiman, Trilling, and Barzun were, when it came to women, men of their time, at least in their published sentiments. All three of them witnessed the early years of the women's movement, although Trilling died soon after the explosive beginnings of modern feminism. Yet neither Barzun, who has lived into the twenty-first century, nor Fadiman, who missed that turning point by only half a year, took serious notice of women's new place in their universe. The question for me now, in the light of the failure of even these two to change profoundly, is why did I revere only men then, and why those three? Why do I remember my veneration of them as the single most compelling passion of my youth?

Lovers are supposed to serve as milestones, as markers on the road to maturity or old age; if not lovers, then jobs, children, marriage, adventures of one kind or another. But for me Fadiman, Trilling, Barzun are the markers; they were the significant events. Oddly, even when I finally understood that I could never be a colleague in their eyes, my admiration for them, my devotion to them, if qualified, did not abate. Even today, I remember my preoccupation with their world, or what I glimpsed of it, exactly as if these three men had been a palpable part of my life rather than actors in my dream—a dream not of romance but of vocation.

"How do you feel writing about guys?" a friend asked me when I told her about this book. It was a fair question. At the start of my professional life I had written about guys—Edward, Richard, and David Garnett, as well as Christopher Isherwood. True, a woman, Constance Garnett, had been included in my Garnett family history, but through no venture of mine: she simply belonged there, with her group of guys. But thereafter I wrote only of women, their writings, their lives, their status in the world, earlier and now.

Yet, before that time, of course I wrote about guys, and thought about guys, and read as a guy: what else was possible? If I wanted a prototype, an example of the sort of career and accomplishment I sought, where was there to look except at men? True, at Columbia where I studied and taught, as at most other universities, there were a few women professors, but they tended toward type. As we callow students saw it then, they were unmarried, hence unloved—that they might have loved women did not so much as occur to us—and while that fact alone did not disturb me, who had few illusions even then about marriage as the only suitable destiny for women, the sense of their incompleteness was palpable. If we assumed that their apparent unfulfillment arose from their single state, we had no other terms in which to describe what we observed. Now, I can perceive that the wound those women displayed did indeed have to do with deprivation of their womanhood, but not sexually or maternally. The deprivation arose from their having, of necessity, determined not to act or write as women. They had become what I would later call honorary men; they presented themselves and their ideas in male attire. One did not choose them as models; the aura of deficiency was too tangible.

So guys it had to be. They filled my imagination; they occupied all the room in my mind devoted to hope, ambition, emulation. And, what is more, they continued to hold sway over me even after feminism had rescued me both from the hope of becoming one of the boys and from the realization of that role's high cost. When it had become possible to be a woman among women, to have women friends and colleagues, to speak, teach, read, and write as women, their magic still prevailed.

Having placed these men and their accomplishments as the exemplars of my aspirations, I was asked if I ever desired them sexually, ever had fantasies about them in that role. Strangely enough, I never did, either at first encountering them, or in the years since. Those casting a disbelieving eye at this response have asked why not? There are a number of possible reasons. I never at any time in my life was attracted to older men; every man for whom I felt desire was close to my own age; these men were over twenty years my senior. Also, if the longing for a nurturing father explains a woman's passion for older men, having had a supportive father all my early life perhaps enabled me to escape this route toward infatuation. Another possible reason: I was married, and not, as they say, on the hunt. Not long after beginning my graduate studies, I had a child and, soon after, two more. A life as busy as mine hardly left time for sex, let alone sexual fantasies. (I have since learned that this configuration of time and sex under those circumstances is far from universally true; nonetheless, it was true for me.) The main reason, however, is simplest of all: I needed them as exemplars, not as lovers. Freud had written that men experience ambition and the erotic as separate desires; women experience only erotic desire. For me, in this case (*pace* Freud), it was with those men only the ambitious desire that operated.

But surely I felt affection for them, however expressed or experienced? Not even that. They were beyond affection from such as me: admiration was what they deserved and what they got. What made their gift to me greater, I now believe, than any with which they endowed their male followers was the fact that I knew I could not become like them. When the women's movement finally freed me from the choice between playing at being male or remaining outside the boundaries of male accomplishment, I combined what I had learned from them with the pleasure of thinking and writing as a woman. The male acolytes merely imitated their models and, I suspect, inevitably fell short. For my three guys were not readily imitated, and in the nick of time I was enabled to understand this and not to try to become them, in however pale or awkward a replication.

I had wanted to be a doctor for most of my childhood; specifically, I wanted to be like Banting and discover the equivalent of insulin. At college, an aptitude test revealed my capacities for the law. But women were not welcome in either of these spheres in the 1940's, and it was literature—reading—that occupied and restored me, though it took me a while to admit this, despite the fact that I had been enthralled by books as long as I could remember. (I'm always amazed today to discover that perfectly bright children, even those with highly educated parents, have not yet learned to read fluently even by the age of eight. Probably the regime in schools has changed, or perhaps television, computers, video games render reading inessential.) For me, as for so many then, there was reading and there was life, and they neither competed with nor noticeably affected one another. Fadiman, in *Reading I've Liked,* would insist that "commuters' wives—there are tens of thousands of them—were not really in any active sense doing any reading at all. They were taking their daily novel in a numbed or somnambulistic state. They were using books not for purposes of entertainment, but as an anodyne, a time-killer, a life-killer."

I shall consider this condemnation later, in the light of Fadiman's prevailing and consistent scorn for women in his literary world, but for now let me say that, whether or not this kind of reading is true of "commuters' wives," it was not true of me. Nor do I think it is true of many child readers: we read, I think, to peek outside the boundaries of our world, eventually to step outside those boundaries, but not by means of fantasy or mainly for escape. Rather, I think, with the intentions of explorers, psychologists, and archaeologists, children seek not anodynes but more examples of a moral language than a child's life can give them. I fear that the moral ideas—in the largest sense of moral—that children today receive from videos, television, and computer games are hardly concerned with truth, trust, courtesy, or personal courage in any subtle sense. But, being old, I try to refuse the temptation to damn the occupations of youth—a temptation neither Trilling nor Fadiman resisted; Barzun has contented himself with damning most of the twentieth century and trying to rescue the English language and the ideals of art from decimation.

And so, like many young people who "live in books," I got a job in publishing, about which the less said the better, although publishing in those days had not yet become the property of corporations mainly producing almost anything but books. Then one day in 1949 my husband and I were in Chicago; having already visited the site where he had attended midshipman's school in World War II, we went to look at the University of Chicago. We sat on the grass in the "midway" between the Gothic buildings, and I became convinced that I must go back to school and study literature. We lived in New York, which meant, at least to me in those days, Columbia. I had no intention of continuing for a Ph.D. I would get an M.A. I was merely putting my toe in.

In that first year at Columbia, I attended many lectures, though not the ones I signed up for; no notice was taken of any student apart from his or her appearance in a seminar. My seminar was in Modern Studies, the term then encompassing the years from 1890 to 1950—a rough demarcation. The professor was William York Tyndall, a man frightened of women and devoted to Joyce with a passion equaled only by those dedicated to Freud. Tyndall barely tolerated women students or women writers: recently, I was amused to come across this recollection in a book by Herbert Marder, who was also a graduate student of his:

> [I] decided to work on Virginia Woolf, "women and fiction"—it was then an uncluttered field, without the sludge that encrusted Yeats and Eliot. My adviser at Columbia [Tyndall] said: "Not much mileage in feminism these days. Virginia Woolf was not a political animal. She was a lady, you know—disliked working-men, Negroes, and Jews."
> "There are subversive, radical ideas all over her books," I said.
> He puffed decisively on his unlit pipe. "E. M. Forster says she was a snob and proud of it—true Brit. Could generate some heat. I think you should go ahead." So it was settled.

Tyndall, however, was not as adamant on the question of women as was Trilling. Later, I would learn that he and Trilling had been classmates at Columbia, and that Tyndall deeply resented Trilling's greater fame. In Tyndall's seminar I joined in the general fascination with Joyce, and in fact did admire some of his stories, and the first half, together with the Ithaca chapter, of *Ulysses*. I played at analyzing Joyce as others play at bridge or chess. Occasionally I wondered why we worked so hard to find out what Joyce had put into his book on purpose to puzzle us, but I hardly mentioned this doubt, even to myself.

The only part of the studies for my master's degree that enthralled me and that would, as a direct result, commit me to doctoral studies was Lionel Trilling's lectures. He spoke as a prophet—no less dramatic a word will suffice. He made acceptable what we believed, but had thought improper to believe. When, for example, he described how Hyacinth in Henry James's *Princess Casamassima* learned the profound pleasure to be taken in large rooms with high ceilings—a pleasure that those who were both poor and revolutionary had told him contained no virtue—we too suddenly admitted the attraction of space and elegance, if not luxury. Hyacinth kills himself because of his inability to resolve the terrible dilemma that had also tortured me and, I suspect, many others: that art was worth experiencing, that the greatest art did not come from the purest minds, that the rich exploited the poor but at the same time made art possible. If all this was too much for Hyacinth, it was also profoundly distressing to me.

I had grown up liberal in my inclinations despite my politically conservative parents. Hyacinth, lonely like me, like me split in his deepest loyalties, revealed to me, through Trilling's analysis, that the essence of literature was in the tensions of the thinking life. Trilling himself embodied tension, though I could not, in those early days, have so identified the energy that flowed from him. It was only twenty-five years after his death that I would learn of what pulled him, first this way, then that, and of the impossibility of reconciling those conflicts. I remember him saying—or perhaps I read it as I began to read everything he had published—how Freud knew that we paid for everything life gave us with more than equal coin. Long before I came to distrust some of Trilling's obiter dicta, I had learned to distrust Freud, because of his views of women and because of the Freudian psychoanalysts I had come to know. Yet, even distrusting Freud, I agreed with him that tragedy is what most marks us if we are thinkers—a central concept of Trilling's worldview.

Never once in anything he said did Trilling admit women to the fellowship of learning. Men were what it was all about, men struggling for some assurance—these were the actors in Trilling's drama. Trilling readily published comments like this:

> Truth, we feel, must *somewhere* be embodied in man. Ever since the nineteenth century, we have been fixing on one kind of person or another, one group of people or another, to satisfy our yearning—the

peasant and the child have served our purpose; so has woman; so has the worker; for the English, there has been a special value in Italians and Arabs. (*Gathering of Fugitives*, Trilling's emphasis)

Even if Trilling was using "man" to mean humankind, it is still noticeable that on his list of individual subcategories of human beings (exotics, naifs, all of them), we find "woman"—exotic, naive, other—always an object, never the subject.

Usually when Trilling said "we" he meant men like himself, or younger men learning from him. Some years later, Trilling would take a lot of flak for his use of "we," his assumption that anyone reading him was part of his "we." I never was part of "we," and even in my earliest times of infatuation I knew it to be an impossibility. Later, wistfully, I wondered, though not with much hope, if I could somehow persuade Trilling to include women in his intellectual community. I think I always sensed that this was as probable as persuading Orthodox Jews or Muslims to admit women on an equal basis to their religious life.

It astonishes me now to recognize that almost from the beginning I wanted to confront him, to force him to recognize that I, a woman, was, at the least, not prevented from embodying truth, even if I could not embody it for him. It is clear to me now, and was clear then, that when he spoke of woman or others as embodying truth, it was to deny the possibility of their doing so; his only question was where should "man" look for confirmation. I never confronted him, but it was because of the power he had seized over me, and because of the quality of mind and the persuasiveness he demonstrated in his lectures, that I decided to go on for the doctorate. Perhaps, I must have thought—indeed, I remember thinking—one day he will confirm my right to be a part of the struggle he embodied, of the yearning he expressed.

I would, however, soon have to face the truth that there was no chance of women entering into his union of thinkers. Long before the question of admitting women to Columbia College came to be seriously considered, Trilling declared—and his announcements were always widely quoted—no women at Columbia: he liked the idea of a men's college. It was reported that he even opposed a woman's presence at college faculty meetings.

In the early 1950s, the most important event in my years as a graduate student occurred: I was persuaded by a fellow graduate student—a future professor of literature, although he never went on to get his doctorate (which, particularly if one was a published poet, was not absolutely required in those halcyon days)—to apply for admission to the by then famous Trilling-Barzun seminar. Admittance was strictly limited: the seminar was intended to be small, cohesive, and hardworking. I was accepted into the seminar, as was my friend. There was at least one other woman in the group. I tried once, when she and

I met many years later, to ask her how many women members there had been, but she flatly dismissed the question by saying she didn't share my interest in such matters; she remains to this day an unflinching deplorer of feminism.

The seminar was carefully structured by its two instructors. I recall this with amusement when I read of seminars these days where the reading list, the schedule, and the conduct of the class are all under the direction of the students; Trilling did not live to know this, and by the time this fashion took hold Barzun was long gone from the university. We read a book each week, and each week one of us wrote a paper discussing that book from any angle we chose.

My book was *Jane Eyre*. It is strange to remember that in 1953 not much notice was taken of *Jane Eyre*. No books by women were studied in the honors courses; yet Trilling and Barzun included Brontë in their seminar, the only woman on the list. I wrote a paper on the contemporary critical reception of the book, a subject often repeated once feminist criticism entered the academy, but I had then launched myself on a maiden voyage, having simply chosen a topic that seemed to provide an opportunity for both research and interpretation. The practice in the seminar, a method firmly established, no excuses accepted, was for the writer of that week's essay to leave a copy of the paper in the library for the other students to read and to give a copy to each of the instructors. We were true library workers in those days. There were few paperback books, no copy machines: one took notes on reserved books and typed papers with carbons. Did we leave a carbon copy in the library, give one of the exalted men a carbon? Did we type out two clean copies, one for each of them? I can recall only that Barzun liked my paper and Trilling didn't, but that hardly registered; they discussed it as though my opinions and ideas mattered. Even more astonishing, they each annotated each paper, making comments in the margin, as no other paper I wrote in graduate school was ever marked, perhaps ever read. The respect they showed for us was invigorating, and full of the promise of what an academic life might afford. Once, I remember, Trilling responded to something I had said or written, and I must have looked troubled. "Did I traduce you?" I remember him asking.

From that seminar I came away with another vision of what I might find in the life of the mind: friendship, intimacy as it existed between Trilling and Barzun, for they were, famously, friends. By "intimacy," I meant a mutual trust, consultations, laughter, conversation, perhaps private or personal, but not necessarily so, above all the knowledge that they were part of the same group; they were "we." Recently I have learned more of that friendship—I did not earlier even know that they had both attended Columbia College— and discovered that it was indeed, as I had imagined it, a close professional companionship such as I would one day know with female colleagues and the occasional male. Did I dream then that I might one day be their friend? I doubt it, except perhaps as an idle fantasy.

Perhaps I hoped to be a disciple. Trilling had disciples, young men whom he honored, supported, took pleasure in; no woman ever played that role in his life. Barzun did not, I think, have disciples in that sense, neither men nor women, but he continued to welcome women into his graduate seminars in history. Barzun, unlike Trilling, did not strike one as a lovable man. This was odd, since Trilling was also obviously distant and disdainful; one sensed, however, that once one was accepted into his affections he could be lovable. Barzun was always kind, but distant, cool—qualities I eventually came to attribute to his Frenchness; but of that, more anon.

Oddly enough from my point of view, a number of Trilling's "disciples" went on to teach, as I did, at Columbia, to gain tenure, as I did, and to be my colleagues. They all idealized him and referred to him often, long after, so I thought, what he had stood for had ceased to be appropriate. None of his disciples could touch him; indeed, I soon determined that their having idolized him had limited them in their achievements and in their dispositions. Even those who did not teach seemed to betray something essential in Trilling: Norman Podhoretz, for example, became a neoconservative whose opinions seemed altogether foreign to Trilling's as I read him.

I remember reading in Trilling's essay on George Orwell in *The Opposing Self* his account of a discussion about Orwell with a student, and the student's remarking that Orwell was "virtuous." This seemed to Trilling exact and profound, as indeed it was. Yet I often thought, in later years, that these younger men, Trilling's disciples, like Trilling himself, could not recognize virtue in a woman or in any but a certain kind of man. I well remember Trilling sadly remarking about Victorian men—he may have been quoting Chesterton—that, since there had for so long been no wars, men were not risking their lives in battle while women were risking theirs in childbirth; this was a failure of their manhood. Long before feminism I disliked having a woman's life defined exclusively by childbirth. But that was what women were for: I read Chesterton who averred that when women ceased to have children there would be no reason for their existence. Trilling might not have put it quite that definitively, but he was prepared to deny women "the peculiar reality of the moral life." "They seldom exist as men exist—as genuine moral destinies," he famously wrote in his 1957 introduction to *Emma*. Nor was that all. "It is the presumption of our society that women's moral life is not as men's," he declared—and certainly "we" women could hardly deny the point at that time. While I longed to convince him of women's "genuine moral destinies," that wish quickly became less a hope than a dream. Trilling's views on women were unchangeable, and in fact never changed.

What he and Barzun, however, could and did teach me in those student years was that to be highly intelligent, persuasive, and knowledgeable as a thinker and writer, it was essential to write readable, clear, elegant prose and to avoid jargon. "Jargon" was their favorite pejorative term; its misuse arose from the inclusion in prose for a general audience of the specific, technical terms of a particular discipline. When it came to writing, even all those years before incomprehensible "theory" took over, Barzun and Trilling taught us how to write without shame or condescension for an audience as intelligent as we, though not perhaps as professionally trained.

They wrote as I wanted to write, but they were not my first or only models in that important skill. My first exemplar in writing was Clifton Fadiman, whose precise but unpedantic prose I had encountered while still in high school. Fadiman had been at Columbia College with Barzun and Trilling—he was born in 1904, Trilling in 1905, Barzun in 1907—and when I was fifteen, he showed me how one might write intelligently while avoiding the traps of excessive erudition and garbled syntax. Fadiman wrote as though he wanted to entertain the reader, and perhaps, by chance, persuade him (there were no "or hers" for Fadiman or Trilling) of the delights of intellect.

Looking back now I can see that these three men identified for me what I aspired to. What other model had I? Rereading their works today has enabled me to identify the distinct aspects of these men's lives and ideas that I early intuited but could not then have accurately delineated. In writing of them here, I am not attempting biographies, and shall use only published, public materials. I wish only to capture, if I can, that ideal of the life of the mind they represented, and the way that model was eventually translatable to a female possibility. All were, as I wished to be and in a sense became, reformers, seeking to change those aspects of society they saw as limiting and diluting. Two of the three men—Fadiman and Trilling—were, like me, Jewish and suffered from that condition in pre-World War II academia. Barzun, born in France, was also, to some slight extent at least, an outsider. I knew none of this when I first encountered them.

Because they all attended Columbia College, because two of them remained at Columbia throughout their professional lives, they provide me, who also devoted my professional life to that institution, an opportunity to construe their accomplishments in the particular conditions and profound limitations Columbia offered. For Columbia produced these three men, two of whom became part of Columbia's establishment, as in turn it produced me, who became a feminist.

It is worth reemphasizing that none of these men was feminist; Barzun alone seemed capable of respecting female accomplishment and eschewing stereotyped views of women. Trilling frankly admitted no interest in teaching women or in considering their destinies beyond the domestic sphere. Fadiman's many anthologies and introductions hardly indicated any devotion to questions of female destiny; indeed, women writers, as we shall see, were his favorite target when he was scattering literary scorn. Yet these three men, all unconsciously, made my professional life possible by representing both what I wished to join and what I needed to struggle against. Since there was no woman inviting me to the destiny I sought, these three stood in such a woman's place. One male model might have become the unwilling mentor of a confused young woman. Because there were three of them, I avoided that trap—the betrayal of the mentor—and scattered my hopes among the triad.

They knew each other well; me they scarcely knew at all.

Now, midway through my seventies, I find myself thinking back, remembering the time when only men seemed able to represent the life a woman not attracted by conventional female destinies might aspire to. I find it possible to keep distinct my views of these men at the time when they held the greatest sway over my mind—the 1950s and '60s—but at the same time I have discovered the urge to ponder their lives beyond those years, when their influence on my thought did not abate even as my judgment of their ideas became more critical, more confrontational. I want to follow them into the time when the modern feminist movement made feasible a career few in the earlier decades could have imagined possible. What were they writing and propounding in those years?

During the heady beginnings of the feminist movement, when being a woman seemed to encourage rather than limit my professional accomplishment, had that revolution which altered my life in any way affected the thought and the writings of my three models? And if it did affect them, how, and to what extent? Trilling was dead at seventy, but Fadiman worked well into his nineties, and Barzun, now in his nineties, has never ceased to publish and to think. What were they thinking in the late years—what had Trilling been thinking before his death? Did they think about women at all, and was I able to follow their interpretations of modern life half as fervently as I had done at the time of my earliest professional aspirations?

Dan Wakefield

'55 COLUMBIA COLLEGE

> *After graduating from Columbia, Dan Wakefield wrote for* The
> Nation *and then* The Atlantic Monthly *through the early 1980s.*
> *He is the author of the nonfiction* Island in the City *(1959), an*
> *account of life in Spanish Harlem; the novel* Going All the Way
> *(1970) and its 1997 screenplay adaptation, and numerous other*
> *books and articles. Wakefield is currently a lecturer and writer-in-*
> *residence at Florida International University. This selection*
> *recalling his well-known professors comes from 1992's* New York
> in the Fifties.

W hen New Yorkers said "train" it meant the subway. As in Duke
Ellington's "Take the A Train," you took the train to go down-
town to Greenwich Village or uptown to Columbia, on
Morningside Heights. I took the IRT line to the local stop at 116th and
Broadway and got off there to go to college. Crash and toot of congested traf-
fic, underground earthquaking rush of the subway, faces black, yellow, and
swarthy, voices speaking in foreign tongues, made the place seem as alien as
Rangoon, yet I felt at home, sensing it was where I should be.

Columbia bore no resemblance to the idyllic, pastoral campuses of the
movies, or the ones I knew in the Midwest, where ivy-clad buildings were set
on rolling hills with ancient elms, and chapel bells tolled the slow passage of
time. The quad of dormitories and classroom buildings that made up
Columbia College was set in the gritty heart of the city, and the catalogue
boasted, "New York is our laboratory." I loved it. What could be more
removed from the rah-rah frat-house collegiate life I had fled?

Because I was a transfer student, I had to make up required courses I had
missed, but my faculty advisor allowed me, as a reward, to take the elective

Introduction to Poetry course of Mark Van Doren my first semester. The morning that began a new term—and for me a whole new life—I went for breakfast at the drugstore my roommates recommended on Amsterdam Avenue (the eastern boundary of the campus, opposite Broadway), squeezing into a packed counter of students crying orders to the friendly pharmacist, Mr. Zipper, who reminded me of a plump Groucho Marx. I picked out something soft and sweet called a French cruller, a doughnut fancier than any I'd dunked in Hoosierdom, and washed it down with sugar-and-cream-laden coffee, hoping to dispel the butterflies I felt before going to meet for the first time the teacher whose words drew me halfway across the country.

Van Doren had become a prototype of the American author-scholar-sage as college professor. Winner of the Pulitzer Prize for his *Collected Poems* in 1940, he had influenced such gifted students as John Berryman and Louis Simpson (as well as young renegade poets still to be heard from, like Allen Ginsberg and Lawrence Ferlinghetti), the critics Maxwell Geismar and Lionel Trilling, the editors Robert Giroux and Clifton Fadiman, and the novelist Herbert Gold. He appeared in Whittaker Chambers's political autobiography, *Witness,* and in Thomas Merton's spiritual autobiography, *The Seven Storey Mountain.* After getting an A in Van Doren's course on Shakespeare, a football player named Jack Kerouac quit the Columbia team to spend more time studying literature. Before his retirement at the end of the decade, Van Doren would be described by *Newsweek* as "a living legend."

When I saw Van Doren in class that morning for the first time, his hair was gray and I had no idea of his age (fifty-eight), which was anyway irrelevant for he didn't seem old but ageless, like the visage of one of the presidents on Mount Rushmore. His face had that craggy granite look of being hewn or chiseled by hard-won experience and knowledge, but it wasn't grim or set in a stare of stony, locked-away wisdom. His eyes gave off a love of his work (which included the students seated before him) and the world, and he had a playful and wry sense of humor. To Allen Tate he was "the scholarly looking poet who always looks as if . . . he were going to say grace, but says instead damn."

The Noble Voice was the title Van Doren gave one of his books, and it was also an apt description of his own way of speaking—mellow, thoughtful, dignified without being formal. His voice was familiar to radio fans across the country, who heard him discuss great works of literature on "Invitation to Learning." Van Doren retained a flat midwestern accent (he was the fourth of five sons of an Illinois country doctor) that made me feel at home. He wasn't afraid to sound his r's, and he spoke at a measured, leisurely pace, letting the words come out without being clipped at the end or hurried along like the New York traffic. He anglicized foreign words when he pronounced them, speaking of *Don*

Quixote as "Quicks-ott," with the *x* sounding, rather than in the Spanish manner of "Key-ho-tay." He said with a wry smile that if we followed that style, we would have to call the capital of France "Paree," and he preferred plain "Paris."

Hearing that plain midwestern accent, as well as the plain thinking behind it, bolstered my confidence, proving that people from the hinterlands could make it in East Coast literary circles. It gave me courage to speak to some of my new classmates, jostling down the steps of Hamilton Hall after a lecture.

"Hey, Van Doren's great, huh?" I said.

One of them shrugged, and in a nasal New Yorkese said, "I dunno, he's a little too midwestuhn."

"Yeah, that's it!" I blurted out.

It was not just the familiar accent that made it easier to knock at the door of Van Doren's office and introduce myself later that semester. It was also the kindness in the older man's eyes, in his whole demeanor.

"May I come in?"

"Please."

Professor Van Doren greeted me as a fellow midwesterner and fellow lover of words and stories. I told him about the impact of reading his essay "Education by Books" and mentioned that a friend of mine from high school, John Sigler, had been one of his student hosts when he gave a reading at Dartmouth. Van Doren said he wished he'd known: "I would have told him you were a student of mine."

I left his office in Hamilton Hall not only feeling welcomed and acknowledged but somehow made safe in that alien place, intimidating city and sophisticated college. I had the reassuring sense that because such a man was here, no deep-down harm could come to me, no malevolence invade the grace of his plain goodness.

A student whose poetry Van Doren had encouraged (this was four years before I met him myself) came running into the office of the Columbia English department saying, "I just saw the light!" Most of the professors there thought the student's claim of a visionary experience meant he had finally cracked. The only one who wanted to hear about it was Mark Van Doren. More than forty-five years later, that former student, Allen Ginsberg, tells me, "At Columbia I found nourishment from Van Doren—spiritual nourishment. He had a spiritual gift."

Van Doren's kindness to students did not equal sentimentality, or excuse sloth. One morning in his poetry class he called on a student who confessed he had failed to read the assigned poem. Van Doren's face transformed, tightening, turning a deep and outraged red, and the voice, still measured and controlled, but stern as that of a ship's captain charging mutiny, ordered the student to leave the room. In the breath-held silence that followed, the hapless, hangdog fellow fumbled together his books and fled.

I downed a cold chocolate milk at Chock Full O' Nuts on Broadway to calm my anxiety after class, for I hadn't read the assignment myself, and I wondered what I'd have done if he'd called on me. From then on I was always prepared, but I wondered more deeply if the anger of this good man was an aberration or a part of his personality, a necessary component of being a great professor. I knew I'd learn the answer; Van Doren would teach me.

A hush of respect and excitement came over Van Doren's Narrative Art class when he said he was going to take time out from the great books we were studying to discuss a story written by one of our own classmates, Ivan Gold. Heads turned to Ivan, who slumped down in his seat just in front of me as Van Doren explained to the class that Mr. Gold's story, "A Change of Air," which had won the fiction prize of the student literary magazine, *The Columbia Review,* was worthy of our attention.

The story was about a promiscuous young woman from the Lower East Side who voluntarily engaged in sex with members of a teenage gang. She was so traumatized she was sent to a mental hospital, saw a psychiatrist, and eventually returned to her neighborhood a transformed person who politely refused to have sex with any of the old gang. "That must have been one hell of a psychiatrist," one of the boys remarked with wonder.

Van Doren wanted to know what the force or power of change was behind this story. He educed or drew out of us (for that was his method of education) the realization that this new force in the world was psychiatry, which now was our accepted system for effecting change, just as in the writers of the past we had studied, like Homer, Dante, and the authors of the Bible, God was the source of transformation in people's lives.

Through our own classmate's story of a teenage sexual trauma, Van Doren taught us something not only about writing and literature but also about one of the major shifts in modern man's understanding of himself and his world, a shift just being recognized and acknowledged in my own generation.

"I didn't know what the story was about until Van Doren told me in class that day," Ivan Gold says. "I thought it was about these guys pissing away their time, but he showed me it was about the girl, and what changed her."

Ivan later learned that Van Doren had sent the story to an editor he knew at *New World Writing,* a prestigious literary periodical of the day, where it was published at the end of that year, 1953.

"Jesus was the most ruthless of men," Van Doren said in a tone as hard as a struck bell, and I came to tingling attention. The modern image of Jesus,

Van Doren said, was of a man almost unrelated to the one described in the New Testament as a strong and stern leader, ruthless in following his conception of truth and iron in his will. "He was not," Van Doren said, "an easy man to follow. He was certainly not like our ministers now who try to be one of the crowd and take a drink at a cocktail party to prove it, or tell an off-color joke. That seems to be their approach today." The professor paused for a moment, and then he said, "Maybe that's why we hate them so much."

I remembered Van Doren's anger at the student who hadn't done his homework, and I realized it was no aberration but that Van Doren, too, was ruthless in his teaching, and respected those who demanded the most of the people they led. I quoted some of his comments on Jesus in an article I wrote a few years later in *The Nation*, "Slick Paper Christianity," and sent Van Doren a copy. I enclosed it with a letter in which I acknowledged the gift of his teaching, and recalled the New York student's saying he was "too midwestuhn." He wrote back thanking me for telling him of the student's judgment: "I was afraid I had changed."

I waited until my junior year to take a course with Lionel Trilling, fearing I wasn't yet up to the intellectual level of this professor, who was described by his peers as "the most intelligent man of his generation" and "the intellectuals' conscience." *The Liberal Imagination*, Trilling's book of essays published in 1950 which dealt not only with literature but also with Freud, Kinsey, and American society, had became a touchstone of the decade. I was equally impressed with his novel, *The Middle of the Journey*, especially when I learned the main character was based on his former student Whittaker Chambers, the controversial ex-Communist.

Trilling himself was as elegant as his prose. He looked the part of the aristocratic critic as he stood before us at the front of the class in his three-piece suit, his hair already a distinguished gray at forty-eight. He had the darkest circles under his eyes I had ever seen, so dark they reminded me of the shiners produced by a well-placed punch in a street fight. I assumed these circles were results of the deep study he engaged in, the heavy-duty intellectual battles.

Professor Trilling took a significant drag on the cigarette he inevitably held, sometimes gesturing with it like a wand, sometimes holding it poised just beyond his lips, like people did in the old movies of New York high life, where all the men seemed to wear only tuxedos or dressing gowns and subsisted entirely on caviar and champagne. Twin streams of smoke flowed from his nostrils, like an underlining of his words.

"We shall not read any criticism of the work of the poets we are going to study this semester," he announced. "We shall only read the work itself— *all* the poems written by Wordsworth, Keats, and Yeats."

There were intakes of breath as we absorbed the shock of hearing that our most distinguished literary critic wasn't going to assign us any criticism. When Trilling said we were going to read all the poems of Wordsworth, Keats, and Yeats, he didn't mean just once. "Until you have read a poem at least a dozen times," he explained, "you haven't even begun to get acquainted with it, much less to know what it means."

Ideas became as real as stories in the poetry of Yeats, as I learned to read it in Trilling's class, and by the end of the term I had other lines of verse running through my mind than the ones that I brought to college from childhood. "Little Orphan Annie came to our house to stay / To wash the cups and saucers and brush the crumbs away" had been replaced with Crazy Jane's "Wrap that foul body up / In as foul a rag / I carry the sun in a golden cup / The moon in a silver bag." The comforting time "When the frost is on the punkin / And the fodder's in the shock" was supplanted by the soul-shaking vision of a world in which—as I recited to myself in the roar of the hurtling IRT express and in the early morning hours in the dorm after studying Marx and Freud, Kierkegaard and Nietzsche, in our course in Contemporary Civilization—"Turning and turning in the widening gyre / The falcon cannot hear the falconer."

If Van Doren's course introduced me to poetry, Trilling instilled it in me, making it part of my consciousness, accessible for the rest of my life. Though the two teachers were different in style and manner—Harold Kushner describes Van Doren as "the populist" and Trilling "the aristocrat"—their approach to teaching was much the same. It made sense when I learned years later that Trilling had been Van Doren's student. It wouldn't have occurred to me in college, for both men looked to my youthful eyes like contemporaries; I assumed the great men of our faculty all sprang from the womb as full professors.

The only undergraduates who were barred from studying with Trilling, Van Doren, and the other stars of that golden age of Columbia's English department were the Barnard students. Women were not yet first-class citizens in academia, and college classes were segregated according to sex—though on isolated occasions a Columbia boy brought a girl to sit in on a popular professor's class like a date.

Marion Magid, who was a student at Barnard in the fifties, says, "We weren't allowed to take the famous Columbia courses—in retrospect it's the only thing I feel resentful about. You never questioned that Trilling was for the boys and you were a girl, so you had to make do. Barnard was its own little world on the other side of Broadway. One was aware that high-class thinking was going on across the street."

Lynne Sharon Schwartz—who would write a brilliant novel, *Disturbances in the Field,* which followed the lives of three Barnard students through middle age—says that as a student she didn't take any courses with Van Doren or Trilling because "I felt that was for the men. I felt very cut off from all that, what was going on across the street." She believes that Barnard's hiring of two young working writers as faculty members—Robert Pack, a poet, and the novelist George P. Elliot—helped nurture a creative "outburst" in fiction among Barnard students of the late fifties, whose literary ranks included Lynne herself, novelists Rosellen Brown, Joyce Johnson, and the late Norma Klein, poet Judy Sherwin, and dance critic Tobi Tobias.

Though Trilling's donnish manner made some people think him aloof, he was always accessible and supportive of his students, especially the aspiring writers. On a spring day in 1953, Trilling walked in the park along the Hudson River below the campus, holding the hand of his four-year-old son, James, and talking with his student Ivan Gold. Ivan was going to graduate in June, and wondered, if his goal in life was to write fiction, whether he should go to grad school for an M.A. in literature, which would also get him a draft deferment from service during the ongoing Korean War (or "conflict," as it was called), or whether he should go ahead into the Army. Trilling admitted that he, too, wanted most of all to be a fiction writer, and said he regarded the literary criticism he did as secondary to the novel and short stories he had written. He didn't see academic life as the best route to Ivan's goal. "If you want to write, Mr. Gold," he said, "stay away from graduate school."

Ivan took the advice and was drafted after graduation. "Trilling was right, of course, the way those guys [our Columbia professors] always were," he says, looking back nearly forty years later. "After I got back from the Army and living in Japan, I did go to graduate school on the GI Bill for a while, but I couldn't hack it."

Ned O'Gorman, who met Van Doren and Trilling while he was a graduate student at Columbia in the fifties, says, "I sent Mark Van Doren every poem I ever wrote, and he sent me a postcard or letter the next day with his comments. Lionel met my adopted son, Ricky, at the Aspen Institute, and I have a picture of him cutting a watermelon with him. Trilling didn't know how to cut a watermelon, and he's cutting it the wrong way. It's a picture I treasure. Those men were surrogate fathers for many of us."

When Sam Astrachan was a junior at Columbia and his father died, Trilling got him a scholarship that lasted until graduation. When Sam showed Trilling part of his first novel, the professor got his student into Yaddo, the writers' colony, to finish it, and then sent the book to another former student, Robert Giroux, who published Astrachan's *An End to Dying* at Farrar, Straus.

In a letter Sam Astrachan wrote me last year from his home in Gordes, in the south of France, he said of Trilling, "When he died, I felt I had lost a father."

Van Doren and Trilling were more to us than lions.

The young lion of Columbia's faculty in the fifties was a brash, dynamic sociologist up from Texas, C. Wright Mills, who had made a name for himself beyond the academy with a provocative new book on the American middle class called *White Collar,* and was working on a similar but even more controversial critique of the upper classes called *The Power Elite.* If Mark Van Doren and Lionel Trilling epitomized in their personal style and the thrust of their work the best of traditional values, C. Wright Mills was a harbinger of the anti-establishment future.

Impossible to picture in the confinement of a three-piece suit—he even rebelled against wearing a tie—Mills roared down to Columbia on the BMW motorcycle he drove from his house in Rockland County, outfitted in work boots, helmet, flannel shirt, and heavy-duty corduroys. His broad chest was crisscrossed with canvas straps of duffel bags bearing books, a canteen, and packages of the prepared food he took on camping trips, which he heated up in his office to save time. He looked like a guerrilla warrior ready to do battle, and in a way he was.

I first became interested in Mills when my classmate Mike Naver pointed out to me an ad for *White Collar* that was part of an enticement for joining the Book Find Club, and I signed up to get Mills's work as a bonus. *White Collar* moved and excited me, as it had so many readers who, I'd heard, wrote letters to the author, responding to the issues he raised and also seeking his advice on problems, for the book seemed to address the deep discontent people felt about their jobs and their circumscribed futures. With its sharp critique of the growing impersonality of white-collar work, it touched my own typical fifties fear, shared by many of my fellow students, that we'd lockstep into some automated, sterile future. But the very articulation of the fear raised hope that we might transcend it.

I was eager to see the author of this powerful work in action in the classroom, but I had to get his permission to take his seminar, which was limited to "qualified" students. I waited for my quarry in the cold, cheerless lobby of Hamilton Hall, ambushed Mills on the way to the elevator, and squeezed in beside him. Riding in an elevator with Mills felt like riding in a Volkswagen with an elephant, not so much because of his size—he was a little over six feet tall and weighed two hundred pounds—but because of a sense of restlessness and ready-to-burst energy about him.

Mills fired the requisite questions at me in a rather aggressive, discouraging tone, and I'm sure my answers made obvious my lack of academic qualifications for the course, which I compensated for with enthusiasm. I trotted out my credentials as a journalist and threw in my admiration for *White*

Collar. When the elevator ejected the crowd at his floor, Mills glanced back at me and said simply, "O.K."

Mills at thirty-eight was an exhilarating teacher. He stalked the room or pounded his fist on the table to emphasize a point, surprising us with ideas that seemed utopian, except he was so convinced of their practicality you couldn't dismiss them as mere theory. He shocked us out of our torpor by challenging each of us to build our own house, as he had done himself. He even insisted that, if he applied himself, any man could build his own *car*—a feat not even Mills performed, though he made an intensive study of German engines and loved to tinker with them.

Mills urged us, as part of a new generation coming of age, to abandon the cities, which he felt were already hopelessly dehumanizing, and set up small, self-governing units around the country. His vision of communities where people could develop crafts and skills and work with their hands was in some way acted out in the communes of the sixties, though the drug culture would have been completely foreign to Mills. The yearning for such an independent and self-sufficient way of life that Mills expressed in the fifties was part of the message that so excited his audience.

Inspired by his challenge to think for ourselves, I tried an experiment in his course. Instead of cranking out the usual dry précis of one of the heavyweight books we read each week, I let my imagination go to town, comparing Ortega y Gasset's *Revolt of the Masses* with a Hemingway story.

When Mills handed back the papers, he scanned the classroom and asked with sly curiosity, "Which one is Wakefield?"

I took a deep breath and held up my hand.

"See me after class," he said.

In his office, I waited in suspense while Mills sat behind the desk, stoked up his pipe, and looked me over. Finally he asked what had made me write a paper comparing Ortega and Hemingway. I confessed I was bored by simply recounting the contents of the book in précis form.

"My God, I'm bored too, reading the damn things," he said, and we both laughed.

He told me to "do some more," continue to experiment. I started going to his office after class to talk about the latest paper, and these discussions broadened into friendly inquiries about my plans and goals, and even—to my flattered surprise—a sharing of his own work and concerns. I think he felt a bond with me because of our similar backgrounds as middle-class boys from the hinterlands who made it to the intellectual center, New York. I told him how my admiration for *White Collar* had inspired me to take his course, and he said what the book meant to him personally.

"I met a woman at a cocktail party who really understands me," he said. "She told me, 'I know you, Mills. I've read *White Collar* and I know what it's all about.' I asked her to tell me, and she said, 'That's the story of a Texas boy who came to New York.'" Mills paused, frowning, and then broke into a giant grin and said, "My God, she was right." As he later wrote, *White Collar* was "a task primarily motivated by the desire to articulate my own experience in New York City since 1945."

☉   ☉   ☉

Mills became a friend whose help and guidance would see me through the early years in New York. Columbia had not only provided me with an education but a new family as well, in the city I'd adopted as home.

☉   ☉   ☉

If the real lions of Columbia were its star professors, I sensed very soon that some of my fellow students were future lions. They had come to the university to excel, to learn at the feet of great men in order to aim for greatness themselves, or at least to ascend to the highest ranks in their field. The college was a training ground for ambitious and talented cubs, especially those who would find careers in the media, whose national headquarters were based in New York—which, after all, was our laboratory. In 1952, the year I arrived at Columbia, the editor of the student newspaper was Max Frankel, who eventually became executive editor of the *New York Times;* the editor of the literary magazine was Robert Gottlieb, the future editor of *The New Yorker;* and the editor of the college yearbook was Roone Arledge, who years later became president of ABC News.

Some undergraduates already had a leonine aura about them, an air not of arrogance but of mission, as if they were ready to stride from the classroom to the IRT downtown local and take their places in New York, which was the world. I was awed most of all by Frankel, who was not just editor of the *Spectator* but also served as campus correspondent for the *New York Times.* I was further impressed because he was the first student I knew who always seemed to be wearing a suit. It was usually dark, worn with a white shirt and dark tie, and I took it as a symbol of the dignity of his office, a kind of uniform for those who bore the honor of representing the stately *Times.*

As a cub reporter when he was a senior, I didn't get to know Frankel well, but found him to be a serious, soft-spoken man whose intensity about his job did not prevent him from being gracious to a newcomer from the wilds of the Midwest. I immediately assumed—and reported this back to my high school journalism teacher—this man would someday be editor of the *Times.*

☉   ☉   ☉

Going out for *Spec* was my own entrée into the life of Columbia, and soon I was covering stories I'd never seen in Indiana, from crew races at Cornell to

Broadway and TV actresses, who would appear in the Lions' Den, the dorm restaurant, to be crowned queen of some prom or other. " 'That ain't Dagmar,' said a confused Columbia man" was the lead of my first story, quoting a student who stumbled into the wrong coronation while looking for the famously buxom blonde who was one of the first celebrities created by television.

I elbowed my way through the homecoming crowd on assignment from *Spec* to get photos of Ike, on leave from the presidency of Columbia to run for the U.S. presidency. He was making a campaign stop at this pregame picnic lunch by the football field, and I snapped my Rolleiflex as he gnawed fried chicken with the faculty and tried to smile.

Homespun Ike never seemed comfortable at intellectual Columbia. "Dammit, what good are exceptional physicists . . . exceptional anything, unless they are exceptional Americans?" he fumed, questioning a university scholar. In the rah-rah fifties rhetoric he helped create, Eisenhower urged Columbia to become "a more effective and productive member of the American national team." He surely felt even more out of tune with Columbia's student body that fall, when the *Spectator* published a front-page editorial supporting Adlai Stevenson for president and described the Eisenhower campaign as "the Great Disenchantment."

* * *

Who was the glamorous girl with Sam Astrachan, our fledgling novelist who paced Broadway late at night with his hands clasped behind his back? Sam was standing outside the College Inn restaurant on Broadway one early February evening in 1955 with this tall, attractive girl who had shiny black hair, bright red lipstick, and a long black coat with a fur collar. Sam, in his customary black suit and white shirt with no tie, was smiling more broadly than usual, and invited me to come to the West End Bar & Grill and have a drink with him and "Zelda."

She was really Jane Richmond, and she could have passed for a twenties flapper that night. She loved the legend surrounding Zelda and Scott Fitzgerald, our generation's idols of literary glamour and doom. Jane had published a story in *Focus*, the Barnard literary magazine (the undergraduate women's counterpart to *The Columbia Review*, as the *Barnard Bulletin* was their *Spectator*). Gender segregation of publications, as well as classrooms, was taken for granted; the problem was, Jane told us, there was no equivalent of Columbia's humor magazine. She and her friends wanted to start their own, a Barnard version of *Jester*. "We want to call it *Shvester*," she said. "It's Yiddish for 'sister.'"

We agreed it was a great idea, but it never came to be.

"I was a literary girl, a writing major," Jane says, looking back. She won the Elizabeth Janeway Writing Prize when she graduated, started writing for the satirical television show of the sixties, "That Was the Week That Was," wrote scripts for "Kate and Allie," and continued her lifelong love of writing short stories, which have appeared in *The New Yorker* and other magazines.

Though Barnard girls were segregated from Columbia's undergraduate classes and publications, they were welcomed at the West End, whose notorious allure was unintentionally enhanced by Diana Trilling, Lionel's wife and herself a literary critic. Mrs. Trilling immortalized the place in a *Partisan Review* piece as "that dim waystation of undergraduate debauchery on Morningside Heights." She compared it unfavorably to the "well-lighted" Stewart Cafeteria, a popular literary hangout in *her* day.

With a horseshoe-shaped bar, a steam table offering stews and other student bargains, plus wooden booths and a jukebox, the West End was the all-purpose off-campus hangout for Columbia and Barnard. It provided a respite from academia as a place to go for drinks, dates, and fun, and also served as a haven where students could moan about their troubles over a beer. When the threat of being drafted to fight in Korea struck Columbia men at the start of the decade, they knew where to go for comfort. The editors of *Spec* reported: "Rumors that the college ranks would be depleted by the end of the year [1951] caused many to lose faith and many more to find solace in the West End."

The West End owed its literary rep to Ginsberg, Kerouac, and other beats who frequented the place in the forties, and some of them reappeared in our own time. Jane Richmond saw Kerouac there just after *On the Road* came out and she was a senior at Barnard. "He loved women with dark hair," she says. "He'd look at me and say, 'You Greek girl? Why you all look like that?'" She had also met Ginsberg, "one of the sweetest people I've ever known. He told someone I always looked like I was wearing a big picture hat."

Ginsberg got the right image for Jane—a sense of largesse, bigness of spirit, a celebratory air. Her smile, her ability to make you laugh, her very presence, lit up the time and place.

I didn't meet Ginsberg at the West End back then, but I knew about him. He was a personage on the Columbia scene, a mixture of mystery and legend even before the publication of *Howl* had made him famous. A rumor buzzed among literature students that he'd been the inspiration for the brilliant, troubled student in Lionel Trilling's short story "Of This Time, of That Place," though Trilling later denied the character was based on any real people.

No one denied that Ginsberg had been suspended from the college and spent time at the Columbia Presbyterian Psychiatric Institute: "The people here see more visions in one day than I do in a year," he wrote his student friend Jack Keroauc. Both Trilling and Mark Van Doren testified for

Ginsberg when he was brought to trial for possession of stolen goods. He had gotten mixed up with friends who pulled a robbery and stored the loot at his apartment; Van Doren told him he had to choose between criminals and society ("Some of us here have been thinking that it might be a good thing for you to hear the clank of iron"). Ginsberg was later cleared of the charge.

Besides such notorious escapades, Ginsberg was known for his talent as a poet, and was even recognized as such by Norman Podhoretz, a fellow student who became his literary arch-rival. "What I remember about him was his virtuosity with metrical forms," Podhoretz recalls. "I remember him writing something in heroic couplets, and he wrote in other traditional forms, so when he busted loose it was not as if he couldn't write conventional verse. He was more like an abstract painter who was good at figurative stuff."

Ginsberg was starting to read Whitman then, and felt at odds with the prevailing academic attitude toward poetry. "When I was at Columbia," he says, "Shelley was considered a jerk, Whitman 'an awkward prole,' and William Carlos Williams wasn't in the running." Ginsberg felt alienated from the faculty in other ways as well: "I told Trilling I smoked grass and he was horrified. He thought it was a nineteenth-century disease."

My friends and I at Columbia in the fifties would have been as shocked. "I was surprised by the beats coming out of Columbia," Max Frankel says. "That was a side of the college I never knew, and it was just a few years before me. We were such innocents. There wasn't any dope around, and a beer party was a big thing."

Because we were serious students who hit the books not out of a sense of duty but from a driving curiosity to find answers, to understand, didn't mean we spent all our time holed up in the library. "New York is our laboratory" was a jocular toast, as we winked knowingly and clinked glasses of draft beer at the San Remo in the Village, swilling it to give us the courage to pick up the wistful girls at another table whose long hair and sandals we hoped were signs of bohemian belief in free love (it more likely indicated a sophisticated disdain for college boys).

New York was not just our laboratory but our theater, our art museum, our opera house. It was one thing to take a music appreciation course—students at any college did that—but quite another to have the music of great professionals performed live. Mike Naver got us standing-room tickets for *Don Giovanni* at the Metropolitan Opera (the old one, on 39th and Broadway), and we looked over the massive, gilt-embellished tiers of boxes under jeweled chandeliers. This was the real thing.

Courtney Brown

'40 PhD

> *Courtney Brown worked for Bankers Trust, Chase National Bank, and Standard Oil before becoming Dean of Columbia Business School, a position he held from 1954 to 1969. An authority on business ethics and economic statistics, Brown also served on a number of private boards and both state and federal commissions. This excerpt is from his memoir,* The Dean Meant Business *(1983).*

I t was with some trepidation that I arrived on the Columbia campus on February 1, 1954, for my first day as dean. It had been more than thirteen years since my previous Morningside Heights days. In the intervening years, a world war and much else had occurred to change the perspective that I had had when I left. I wondered how that absence would affect my efforts.

The faculty of business as a department at Columbia was founded in 1916. From its earliest days under Lester Egbert as department chairman, the masters and doctors degrees had been awarded, but the major interest had been on the undergraduate baccalaureate degree, and the main emphasis on accounting. That, however, had ended in 1947; no more undergraduate degree candidates were being matriculated. The new program was characterized as graduate level, but as I looked at the total operation of the School, I was not happy with what I saw.

When I was an instructor at Columbia between 1937 and 1941, I had known the Business School and many of its faculty. Several of them were distinguished in their fields of special interest and had national reputations:

Montgomery and Kester in accounting, Bressenden in labor, Shoup in taxation, Bonbright in corporation finance, Mills in statistics, Willis in banking, Graham and Dodd in finance. By the mid-1950s, however, some of these stars had departed. The lack of growth in enrollments and the absence of development in the academic program had resulted in a sorry state of faculty morale. "All we need to be among the best in the nation is a few million dollars," was a comment often heard. Yet, shortly after my arrival, an alarmed assistant dean of admissions, without notifying me, had admitted all of his earlier rejects to fill an entering class.

A week after my arrival a senior faculty member asked me, "Are you frustrated yet?" When I expressed surprise, he continued, "Well, you will be." After which he added, "I have been trying for months unsuccessfully to get the fly specks removed from my windowsill." The mood of the faculty, it seemed to me, bordered on the masochistic. For example, after a little used room was furnished as an attractive faculty lounge, they approved the action by only a very narrow margin. I discovered that some of the faculty did not even know all their colleagues. Several members told me that that was impossible until one of them failed to identify a casual passer-by to a Faculty Club lunch table. "He's a member of our faculty," I said impatiently.

My doubts about the advisability of having accepted the job of dean of so demoralized a faculty were replaced after a little delay by a resolve to attack the major deficiencies of the School. There is more than one way, I discovered, to develop the academic program of an institution of higher learning. One is to identify scholars of outstanding competence in specialized fields of learning, then give them the uninhibited opportunity to construct a program of research and instruction in their field of interest, with adequate resources and associates. That is the dream of most academics, and it seems to have been the way used to recruit the initial Business School faculty. Most were outstanding. The result, at one time, was quality work in each field of study. Somehow the student interest did not last. An unfortunate lack of balance and comprehensiveness in the students' total program had developed. As the academic stars departed, they left a curriculum that failed to achieve increasing enrollments or to identify the School as uniquely attractive.

The full-time faculty in 1954 consisted of twenty-eight men and no women; part-time lecturers brought the total to a full-time equivalency of forty-four. There were fourteen academic divisions in the School, each a specialized field of business, such as banking, insurance, real estate, or transportation. And there were divisions for subjects that cut across all the fields of business, such as finance, marketing, and accounting. Each academic division was more or less autonomous, staffed by a professor, an associate chosen by that professor, and the additional part-time and junior faculty required to staff the instructional program. The offerings of each division typically consisted of an introductory course, several intermediate courses (that fitted the particular interests of the instructors), and a terminal seminar.

Course development had become an individual matter over the years. As might be expected, overlaps appeared in the instructional material of many courses. Four or five attempts had been made in previous years to eliminate these redundancies, but the results had been minimal. Moreover, when the School had decided to abandon its undergraduate program, some of the content of the courses had been upgraded, but sad to say many had not been. In a number of cases, undergraduate courses had become graduate level simply by changing the catalogue numbers. In a curious way, the existence of these glaring defiencies was widely recognized—and tolerated.

I soon began to hear about a Committee on Instruction, of which my newly acquired executive secretary was the administrative assistant, but I was discouraged from making a detailed inquiry about its "work." What I did find out, nonetheless, was that it had little to do with the curriculum. Each part of the curriculum, it turned out, was controlled by a faculty division. Descriptions of its courses were usually submitted for printing in the catalogue without further approval or amendment. In fact, each member of the faculty, subject to the approval of the senior professor in the division—would determine what he wished to teach and when. There were really fourteen little czars for the fourteen divisions, or "departments." The minimum teaching program was set by the curriculum requirements of each division. The end result was an overall School curriculum without balance of content and a class schedule designed for the convenience of the faculty—certainly not for the students.

Since the chairman of the department of economics had served concurrently as dean of the Business School in past years, doctoral candidates in economics who looked promising were often assigned to teach in the Business School. If they showed ability, they would return to the economics faculty or move to another institution's economics or business department. It was not unlike the farm-out system in major-league baseball. Several business faculty members who later became conspicuously distinguished followed this path. But however useful it was as a training ground for the economics department, it did nothing to build the prestige of the Business School—and little for its students.

There had been limited opportunity to refresh the faculty through expansion for there had been little growth in the number of classroom hours for more than a decade. Faculty turnover had been almost nonexistent. On occasion I heard the hollow boast that no member of the faculty had been lost except for retirement for a decade or more. When a rare vacancy occurred, the senior man in the division would pick the replacement—usually someone a notch below his own intellectual capacities—discuss the matter with his acquiescent peers, and recommend the name to his passive dean.

The Business School building was shared by the School of General Studies. I was told by a senior member of the faculty that its vigorous and aggressive dean, Louis M. Hacker (who had his office in our building), had boasted that he would take over the Business School in two years. The physical and administrative arrangements of my office were symptomatic. The desk had been badly battered over the years. The office sofa suffered from protruding springs and hair stuffing. More telling was the arrangement of the inter-office buzzer system. Since an earlier dean, Roswell McRea, as chairman of the University's department of economics, was absent from his office for long spells, the School was, in effect, held together by his assertive executive secretary. When I arrived, there was an inter-office buzzer between her desk and mine—but she had the button and I had the buzz!

To add to our difficulties, I discovered that the School had no money. To be specific, there was only about $200 of unexpended and uncommitted funds remaining in the year's budget. The School's development officer, who resigned after my arrival, had had no success. After deducting for his budgeted expenses, he left a $30,000 deficit. The alumni were poorly organized, and both the membership and resources of their association were declining. It was little wonder that this was so, for they had been deliberately neglected.

The business faculty was underpaid even by the generally low standards of those days—and they were much underpaid in comparison with their peers in other faculties of Columbia University. There was little research money available, and not much was being published by members of the faculty, useful or otherwise.

Many of the students were attending part-time and had no degree aspirations. Others were working for the ten-course M.S. degree, still fewer for the twenty-course MBA degree. Degree candidates usually limited their interests to a specialized field. Scholarships and fellowships were few in number. Where the normal program for a full-time graduate student was five courses, Columbia business students of 1953–54 averaged about half that course load. The whole orientation of the business program for students seemed to be half-hearted, unfocused, and not up to the level of a serious effort.

Acrimonious faculty sentiments were directed toward other faculties of the University, particularly toward the School of General Studies. The state of relations between the two schools was illustrated by an event that took place early in my days as dean. When I innocently had a cold water fountain installed in the entrance lobby, I was scolded by my faculty for having it placed on the

General Studies side of the lobby, even though that was where the water pipes happened to be located. But, the core of the difficulties with that school stemmed from the fact that it was offering courses that competed with courses offered by the Business School. Personal relationships among the several divisions within the School were also often less than amicable. Longstanding feuds existed between the accounting and finance faculties, and between the marketers and the statisticians. Very few of the rest of the faculty failed to envy the student popularity of the general management division.

In addition to these problems, there was only a qualified acceptance by the other Columbia faculties of the existence of a graduate business school. This was attributed to Nicholas Murray Butler's early reluctance to include business subjects in the Columbia University curriculum. Once the School had been established, the view became widespread that its main function was to be a financial contributor to what were perceived to be the more important faculties of the University, in short, to be a "milk cow."

This second-rate citizen image and posture of the Columbia Business School contrasted sharply with the attitudes toward business schools at several leading universities. At Harvard, the Business School was treated as a major ornament. There and at Pennsylvania's Wharton School and the University of Chicago, the level of business education as well as the level of acceptance of the graduate business school was much higher than at Columbia. But on many university campuses, including Columbia's, business education as an academic discipline was at an incipient—and unpredictable—state of development and acceptance. Vocational trade school courses were still evident in most curricula. Indeed, the Columbia Business School had a large classroom assigned to shorthand and typing instruction in 1954. This hardly conformed with my idea of a graduate business school as the training ground for senior officers of major worldwide corporations.

This—not wholly unjustified—attitude of the other faculties and the central administration at Columbia seemed to have permeated the psyches of the business faculty. They had become disgruntled through sheer lack of change and development. Yet, I discovered as I talked to members of the faculty that the dean was expected, as one professor put it, "to keep the place nourished and count the paper clips." President Grayson Kirk in his persuasive invitation had encouraged me to take my time and get to know the school. And for a very short period I fell in with this approach. To those to whom I talked, I expressed the tentative view that I anticipated few changes for six months or so, while I learned my new tasks. As it turned out, the serious condition of the School—and an impatient disposition—decreed otherwise.

Had I been more knowledgeable of academe and more aware of the School's actual condition, I might well have lacked the courage to accept the responsibilities of the deanship. I knew from my prewar teaching days that change—even widely desired change—would not be easy or comfortably accommodated at Columbia. As a new dean, I was often to hear the cliché explaining why some problem on campus could not be solved: "But it has always been done that way." When I delved further I usually found that the underlying reason was that, first, vested personal interests and, then, the lack of money prohibited significant change or experimentation. But still deeper than these human and economic reasons, there was an emotional commitment to the established ways of the School as an institution, a characteristic of organizations everywhere.

The administrative staff was as much shadow as substance. Two assistant deans, one for admissions and one for fund raising, a full-time assistant for "housekeeping," and a director of our newly established program for executives were supplemented by part-time assignments of members of the faculty to different tasks. Fortunately, I was able, with some delay, to enlist several administrators with talent.

o   o   o

Apart from creating an orderly administrative staff, I realized at an early stage, rebuilding would require four major efforts: (1) strengthening the faculty, (2) upgrading the quality of the students admitted, (3) revising the curriculum, and (4) providing a more suitable building to house the School's activities. Each was necessary to support the other efforts. *Failure to achieve any one purpose would impair success in the other three.* All four were accomplished in the course of time.

Of these, building additional strength in the faculty was the most urgent. A cluster of retirements was just ahead. One of my first efforts was to try to correct two major faculty deficiencies: inadequate salaries and the deplorable lack of research funds. My experience with the contributions program of Jersey Standard had suggested that we should try to get corporate support of $1,000 to $5,000 a year from a diversified and expanding list of leading business firms. An Affiliated Business Fellows program of corporate members was established to supply both needs. With the premise of a continuously expanding list of contributors, I was permitted by the University administration to use 20 percent of the annual contributions for salary increments instead of the then customary 5 percent that was earned on endowment investments, which meant that only 80 percent of the annual receipts that were assigned to salary support was held in reserve.

As the newly raised funds began to come in, salary increases were awarded in January so they would be identified apart from the salary adjustments provided by the University budget, which were awarded in June. In the course of several years, we got the business faculty salaries up to those of the rest of the University for similar grades. At that point we stopped these off-University budget increments to faculty salaries. It was quite clear that the central administration would not permit us to go beyond campus levels; compensating downward adjustments in the School's annual budget allotment from the University would assure against that. We were, however, ultimately permitted to transfer the accumulated 80 percent salary reserve to an endowment for a named professorial chair.

From that point on, all receipts from the Affiliated Business Fellows program were applied to enlarging the scope of faculty research. At the start of the program, a faculty committee had been elected to review research proposals from their colleagues. When a proposal was approved, possibly after modifications, the dean's office would then allot modest financial support to the applicant's free-time research work.

By 1957, it seemed clear to me that the conventional academic calendar with a summer interregnum was outdated for the faculty and inefficient for the best use of classroom space and administrative staff. After review with the faculty, we restructured the academic calendar to the so-called trimester system of three full terms, each of four months per year. The academic program of the School thus ran through the full year. The rule for the faculty was that they were to teach four four-month terms in twenty-four months, which is the equivalent of the traditional two semesters in twelve months. The total faculty time in the classroom was thus unchanged. The gain was in flexibility. A member of the faculty could choose to teach three consecutive terms, take two off back-to-back, and return to teaching for one; thereby earning eight consecutive months of class-free time every two years. We did not permit four terms of teaching consecutively. Faculty research projects began to blossom, and the level of intellectual endeavor in the school rose noticeably.

The salary rises, the revised academic calendar, and the research funds made it possible to attract additional full-time faculty of quality. It was necessary, and always will be, to continue some part-time instructors. But, by 1957–58, the full-time faculty had grown from twenty-eight to forty-one, and full-time equivalent members from forty-four to sixty-one. The important thing was that faculty morale had been boosted. The essence of education is what happens in the classroom and in informed association between faculty and student. Nothing was of more concern to us than finding just the right additions to the faculty as the School expanded, including senior and mature scholars.

All of the early additions, of course, were made with the orderly procedures of faculty recruitment. Search committees were appointed with instructions to find the "best men in the nation" that met our specifications. We would have liked to have employed some women, but it did not then seem realistic. The guidelines included recognized academic credentials, but they also contained what we called character and the ability to relate comfortably with others. We were conscious of being a school for young people preparing for a career in business. This concern for qualities additional to those of a strictly scholarly nature at times got us in mild difficulties with colleagues in other parts of the University for whom the academic record was paramount. Experience in the business community was a positive factor if the academic background was solid, but there were not many then available with experience in both worlds.

* * *

Our interest in a strong faculty was accompanied by a desire for committed students of quality, who could be expected to earn degrees. Financial assistance was essential if we were to have full-time enrollment. I went to the School's alumni organization, which had not been previously cultivated. My thought was that it might come to life if given a challenging job. The response was gratifying. The first annual alumni fund drive raised only about $10,000, but it made consistent growth in successive years. By 1982, it was running at over $500,000 annually. Much of the subsequent success of the alumni program was due to Harris Wofford's early efforts.

To help students finance their business education, a novel grant-loan program was devised to cover the full cost of tuition; the funds offered were 40 percent grant, 60 percent loan. The grant, supported by the newly established annual alumni fund, was made available only if the student took the personal loan at subsidized rates from Bankers Trust. The loan was repayable on a monthly schedule after graduation. The credit experience proved to be excellent with only 2 to 3 percent defaults.

We wanted to be able to say that whoever could pass the admissions gate could attend full-time without financial constraint. The results were first-rate: the quality of applications improved and the total number of degree candidates increased by 50 percent during the initial five-year period. By 1958–59, more than half of our students were registered for the four-term, twenty-course MBA degree. The total number of classroom hours grew by 27 percent and the number of degrees awarded had jumped by 77 percent, from 240 to 425.

As important as it was to press ahead with these several changes, we felt that much of the educational experience occurred outside the classroom. Efforts were made to encourage students to arrange social events, contribute to student publications, and organize informal lecture sessions. Student associations concerned with marketing, finance, personnel and industrial relations, international business, and foreign country affiliations were started and soon humming. The wives of the faculty and teaching staff (WOFTS) served tea and cookies four times a week. A sign read, "Here's Tea for You and Cookies *Two!*" Students are always hungry and ours were known to fill their pockets at tea time.

∘ ∘ ∘

In turn, the School's academic program required a major commitment of time and effort. In February 1954, there were 635 degree candidates registered in the School but only 240 degrees were awarded in the 1953–54 academic year. Nearly three quarters of the degree candidates had been matriculated for the two-term, or ten-course, MS degree. There were also 475 "non-classified" part-time students who took one or two specialized courses. This required the School to offer 130 to 135 separate courses, quite a few of which were no longer of interest to students, but which were nonetheless continued.

Once a course had been designed and "accepted" by the faculty, it had come to be something of an insult to the professor to take it out of the catalogue. So there it stayed, no matter how long it atrophied. Languishing courses were one of the wasteful drains of our academic resources. More professorial time—and therefore money—could be saved, I felt, by rationalizing the curricula than in any other way. The large number of specialized courses offered were a weakness, not a strength. They were absorbing our scarce resources like a sponge. Very early I made up my mind that only a complete curriculum reform would do.

The curriculum was no longer suitable for the revised program of the School. Yet the course material that had been developed over a quarter of a century could not be lightly abandoned. While at Jersey Standard I had formed some ideas of how a graduate business program should be organized, but those thoughts had not evolved in collaboration with my new-found faculty—or with any other faculty for that matter. My thinking was somewhat fragmented and nebulous, but I did have a general sense of the direction I thought we should go. That direction was toward a study of the corporation and its role in society, a theme that had been a major part of my thinking during the Jersey Standard days. I knew that business had a large influence on the cultural, as well as the material, life of the contemporary world. On the other hand, I knew that I did not fully understand the corporation and its place in the world—but then I doubted if anyone really did.

It was pretty clear that the economists did not understand the institutional impact of the corporation. They were still living in the world of the single enterpriser and of Alfred Marshall's traditional supply and demand curves as modified by E. H. Chamberlain and Joan Robinson. Behavior in the marketplace was still interpreted in terms of the single buyer-seller transaction instead of the continuous flow of business in stabilized relationships with other businesses and customers. Accountants saw the corporation through its financial records, but missed much of the rest. Lawyers dealt with management-stockholder relations, the corporation's contracts, interpretation of regulations, and lawsuits, but hardly grasped the impact on society, if indeed many of them cared. Engineers were concerned with material processes and physical structures, but rarely thought about social structures. Sociologists were just discovering the corporation as a laboratory to test their theories. And the general public was largely uninformed or misinformed.

It seemed to me that there was a wide open field and a great challenge to achieve a better understanding of the corporation and its limitations as well as its opportunities to serve society. I was especially eager to stimulate investigation of the relationship of the institutions of business to the value structure of the society that gives business its right to exist and thrive. This was the approach that, I hoped, should guide the formation of a new graduate curriculum at Columbia Business School. We were to succeed only in part.

Faculty control of the curriculum is one of the sacred cows of the academic world. There are, of course, very good reasons for this. They come out of the long evolution of the university, institutions that started in Europe in the thirteenth and fourteenth centuries as collegiums. Clusters of scholars gathered in population centers to offer their own courses and admit their own students, from whom they would collect their fees. The faculty-student relationship was very personal. What was taught was the result of each professor's study, inquiry, and reflection.

To some extent similar attitudes guided the initial shaping of the academic program in the Columbia Business School. This made a collective revision of the curriculum no easier. Nothing is more highly prized on the campus than intellectual independence and integrity along with the opportunity to follow one's broadly informed interests and carefully derived convictions with unrestricted objectivity. A professor builds his intellectual capital in much the same way that a businessman builds his skills and productive capital.

The Columbia business faculty had been accumulating an inventory of intellectual capital for nearly four decades when the new dean arrived. Only naiveté could explain my initial intention to get right to the job of revising the curriculum. I had not at that time heard the comment attributed to Woodrow Wilson when he was at Princeton: "Reforming a college curriculum is like moving a graveyard." Had it not been for the frequent expressions of discontent from individual members of the faculty, it would have been pure bravado. What I did notice was that the expressed dissatisfaction of one faculty member about the curriculum always referred to the contents of another professor's courses, not his own. Another complaint was the lack of balance and integration in the whole instructional program.

Business education in the United States had gotten its start at the Wharton School of the University of Pennsylvania in 1898. The pattern for organizing the curriculum initiated there was still followed in the mid-1950s by most business schools, including Columbia. Indeed, many of the members of the Columbia business faculty had been recruited from Wharton during the presidency of Nicholas Murray Butler. The functional studies of accounting, statistics, personnel practices, and administration were supplemented by the study of a specialized field of business on which the student spent the largest block of time.

Harvard was the first to modify this basic pattern with its heavy use of the case method of instruction, a method appropriated from the nation's law schools. The Columbia Business School had looked at the case method and rejected its use as the dominant means of instruction, wisely in my judgment. It was, of course, deemed to have merit. In fact, it had been adopted for some of our advanced courses after the degree candidate had acquired enough knowledge to support meaningful participation in a case discussion. But the case method as the principal way of presenting instructional materials, it was felt, was too wasteful of the limited time available. The price paid in neglected subject matter was seen as too great, as well as financially costly. Rather, our faculty was dedicated to a combination of the interrupted lecture, plus the case method, and student presentations in seminars. The adoption of each method was determined by the nature of the subject matter, and to a certain extent by the propensities of the instructor.

Four or five attempts at curriculum revision had been made before my time. Professors would compare their courses for overlaps. Many were found, but curiously they were always in the other fellow's courses. Little was done to investigate significant areas of business that did not happen to coincide with a faculty member's major interest. Needless to say, the efforts of the past had not been successful. Faculty discontent with the curriculum was matched by that of the students.

It was clear that another round of attempts would be futile if the same approaches were tried. Something new had to be done. It had to be subtle, avoiding by all means the implication that the ideas of the dean were being imposed. It must avoid simply copying the efforts of others; that had also been tried before without success. Whatever was done had to derive from fresh thinking. What was required, it seemed to me, was an analytical consideration of the needs and opportunities in the current business world, arrived at from extended discussions by the faculty, individually and collectively. With only a modest bit of nudging from the dean, we decided to adopt a novel *procedure* that, so far as we were aware, had not been tried before in curriculum building.

To begin, we rejected a comparison of our course offerings with those of other business schools, regardless of their quality. We were not even interested in analyzing what we ourselves had been doing. But as a business school desiring to operate at advanced levels of instruction, we were keenly interested in what *business* was doing, what *business* was thinking, and which problems of *business* were important.

Only after a comprehensive examination of the entire business spectrum would we be ready to assign its most important parts to specific courses of study that could be further developed. The initial faculty effort was not to adopt, modify, or eliminate in-place course materials, but to accept a *new procedure*. It would start with the totality of business, then move to phases of that totality, and finally to the design and selection of specific course materials, which would be constructed as needed by members of the faculty itself. Only then would we be ready to appraise the new curriculum for balance and comprehensiveness.

It was an ambitious undertaking, and everyone felt a bit threatened. But it was a group exercise that created its own momentum, esprit de corps, and requirements as it evolved. The faculty was constituted as a committee of the whole to review the successive progress reports. With a grant from the Ford Foundation, we were able to engage several visiting scholars from other faculties to teach some of our classes. This released certain of our own scholars to do the research and writing demanded by our new project.

Three major sectors of business life were soon identified: (1) the *environment* in which business operates, (2) the organizational *arrangements* for the internal management of business, and (3) the communicating and analytical *tools* used by business. A third of the faculty was assigned to each of these sectors with a senior man as chairman. Each group made frequent and comprehensive reports that were reviewed and discussed by the entire faculty. Out of these review sessions we gradually identified the content of the three areas that were important to the business community.

Concerning the first major sector, we concluded that the environment in which business operates is conditioned by three main forces: the state of the economy, the legal concepts and social attitudes inherited from the past, and the interplay throughout the world of specific kinds of resources: physical, technological, and human. That meant that there were three basic courses that all degree candidates should take. The first was economics, including both macroeconomics (the study of economic aggregates on the national level) and microeconomics (the analysis of specific variables), which were well-established subjects with us. The other two areas of interest in the business environment would require fresh approaches and, therefore, new courses.

The second area was an unusual study of the attitudes, ideas, and cultural practices, largely inherited from England and Western Europe, that had resulted in the evolution of the modern corporation. We called it the "Conceptual Foundations of Business." It was our way of presenting the societal and ethical issues that today increasingly confront business decision making. The material has proved to be reasonably successful. I wanted very much to have Charles Malik of Lebanon and Sterling McMurrin of the University of Utah, two leading philosophical thinkers, join the faculty to help us with these materials, but, as noted earlier, the faculty found the proposal a bit too imaginative.

We gave the task of studying the third area, the several interrelated world resources, to our geographers. The results were disappointing for their training had covered physical resources and their location, rather than a comprehensive analysis of all resources including demography and technology. Ultimately, our geography division was made a department in the nonprofessional graduate faculties of the University.

We also found it necessary to build a new course in our second major sector, namely the internal organizational arrangements of business. Behavioral science was a subject much discussed in the mid-1950s by academics. We thought that in a new course we could relate this body of emerging knowledge to behavior and decision making in business. This we did, but the results were only partly successful.

Another course in this second sector, the administrative structures of business firms, had long been a part of the curriculum and fitted nicely with the study of behavioral patterns. The legal framework within which the corporation is managed, including taxation and the strengths and weaknesses of regulation, provided supplementary material for a modified course to round out this second major segment of business interests. It was agreed by the faculty that our graduate students should also be exposed to all three courses in this second sector.

The tools of business, our third sector, was already in the curriculum and presented less of a challenge to innovate. An attempt was made to blend the subjects of accounting and statistics as is frequently done in business. But we were not successful in this; the two teaching staffs had lived too long in their separate compartments. The mathematics of operations research had a fascination, however. Several members of the faculty structured a course that made extensive use of the newly emerging computer to test business assumptions and decisions with simulation models and fast computation. Comprehensive exposure to all the tools of business, the faculty concluded, was essential to graduate business study.

The study of these three major segments of business life produced a total of nine courses. Several of these would require new syllabi, a very large task if adequately done. But the faculty was not through. It was concluded that, as a capstone in the last or fourth term of study, the student should be exposed to the processes of group decision making, based on the knowledge acquired in earlier terms. This was accomplished through a course on business policy that used the case method of instruction. In short, it was an attempt to duplicate the reality of decision making in the corporation.

Together these formed a core of ten required courses, half of the twenty stipulated for the MBA degree. Another five courses, it was decided, could be taken in a student-selected field of concentration—we did not call it a specialization—such as finance, marketing, international business, transportation, etc. International business was a newly introduced field that students could select for concentration, based on the rapidly emerging multinational corporation. The remaining five courses of the total of twenty the student could select at random from offerings of the faculty of business or of other graduate faculties.

The adoption of this program of study did several things. It achieved the integration and balance long sought by the faculty. It approached the study of business as a comprehensive activity with an emphasis on the reciprocal influences between business and society at large. It shifted the primary goal of graduate business education at Columbia from preparation for the first job to preparation for a business career. And as a significant by-product, it made redundant many of the specialized—sometimes antiquated—course materials that had accumulated to serve different purposes. The total number of courses offered was reduced from 130 to 80. We had constructed an integrated program of study that had a far lower expenditure of time and money per classroom hour.

No longer was the curriculum suitable for the occasional student looking for a particular topic or two that he could squeeze in at night. There is a place for such a program, but we did not think that place should be at inconveniently located Columbia. Nor was the ten-course MS degree compatible with our newly adopted curriculum. Accordingly, we no longer accepted the part-time student except in unique circumstances, we stopped the matriculation of candidates for the MS degree, and scheduled no further evening classes. The whole complexion of the School changed.

Had the dean disclosed his personal ideas of curriculum revision to the faculty, it would have been resented and properly so. We might have gone nowhere. But getting agreement on a *procedure* led to success. It resulted in a curriculum revision that had the intellectual integrity to attract widespread faculty and student attention throughout the nation, and we were told, abroad as well.

The experience of organizing and living through this curriculum revision was one of the most exhilarating of my life. My first five years as dean were exciting; but it cannot be said that they were serene. To use an expression often heard on the campus, "a bit of blood was left on the floor." There was a continuous chorus of dissent by a small but sincere group that protested vigorously change of any kind. I particularly felt bad about a conflict with an old friend and colleague, Haggott Beckhart, that ended in his retirement several years before he had planned. Despite the determined efforts of that small group, it bordered on the inspirational to observe a majority of mature scholars deliberately deciding to scrap, or fundamentally to modify, more than a quarter century of established course construction and venture into new and untested territory. In the end almost everyone—but not all—felt a sense of satisfaction. Numerous faculties in other colleges and university business schools have since been influenced by this Columbia business curriculum.

Moreover, the new curriculum gave greater flexibility to the University's total study program. With the provision that the five elective courses could be taken in other graduate faculties of the University, joint degree programs were worked out with Law, International Affairs, Journalism, Urban Land Use, Public Health, Teachers College, and others.

These joint programs brought to the surface the recognition that what the School of Business was teaching was basically management, an occupation by no means limited to business. Some even suggested that the School change its name to the Graduate School of Management. But the time was not yet ripe for that.

Dwight D. Eisenhower

Dwight D. Eisenhower, leader of the Allied forces in World War II and 34th President of the United States, served as Columbia's president from 1948 until early 1953. The following account is from his 1967 book At Ease: Stories I Tell to Friends.

When a committee from the Board of Trustees of Columbia University asked me to consider becoming President of that great institution, I said (as I did later when other people had ideas about another Presidency) that they were talking to the wrong Eisenhower. My brother Milton was uniquely fitted for leadership because of his scholarly depth and his lifelong work in principal areas of American life—governmental, economic, and academic.

Without any disparagement to Milton, the committee, of which Thomas Watson, Sr. was chairman, countered that I had a broad, varied experience in dealing with human beings and human problems, a fundamental concern of the University; that I knew at first hand many areas of the earth and their peoples; that my interest in the training of young Americans and my wish to spend the rest of my life in such work offset my lack of formal preparation. They said that their invitation had the complete approval of Columbia's former President, Nicholas Murray Butler, and they were anxious to put my name before the Board for confirmation. I declined to accept because I felt the post should go to a man who was not only a good executive but was known as a scholar. The committee was not discouraged. For months its members applied pressures which would have been worthy of most super salesmen. I agreed, after a time, that if and when I left the military service, I would at least confer with the Board of Trustees before I made any move.

My preference, as I've said, inclined me toward a small school in a rural setting. In such a place, where friendly ties with students and faculty could be easily developed, I felt I might hope to share with them the lessons in hindsight from a reasonably full life. Possibly I visualized myself as a campus character whose lack of scholarly achievements would be offset by an ability to talk freely and fully about the world. Such a role I would have loved and it would have been easy. Columbia, on the other hand, was a formidable challenge.

Located in the world's greatest city, Columbia University was an international mecca for students and scholars. All sorts and conditions of men and women walked the campus. Its twenty-six or so acres crowded with buildings, a self-contained and even self-centered community, were a microcosm of the intellectual world, as Abilene had been of small-town America.

Famed philosophers, scientists, historians were familiar figures on the sidewalks. "Names" in every field of human knowledge and research studded the University directory. The students, who in the undergraduate and graduate schools numbered around thirty thousand, were variety itself, in race, dress, speech. In all this diversity, a single concern—the search for knowledge and its dissemination—gave the Columbia community homogeneity. As everywhere, Columbia had its share of freeloaders, of students who were happy just to get by, of faculty and staff members who cherished the shelter of a rut to the windy and dangerous slopes leading up to peaks. But these were a small minority. Most were concerned with intellectual excellence.

My difficulty in reaching a decision was a natural fear that I could hardly hope to discharge the responsibilities in an enterprise so different from all my own experience and already so richly endowed with leadership in its deans and senior faculty. After all, I was approaching sixty years of age and although I still thought myself capable of adjustment to new scenes and new circumstances, Columbia would require a transformation in my way of life. The severity of the change might have been one element that tipped the scale against searching out a small college where life would have been, on the surface, at least, easier.

Above all, I saw in Columbia, because of its standing among American educational institutions and its influence on the educational process, opportunities as large and rewarding as the environment might be strange and difficult. If the faculty could stand me, I decided, I could stand the job.

* * *

Possibly I had worried too much about their reaction. Despite a surface excitement or curiosity or trepidation about the newcomer and what he might do to hallowed traditions, an old and great university takes a new president in stride with an aplomb and serenity that marks no other institution. As students come and go, so do presidents; but the university continues. Columbia, however, should have been an exception. For more than half a century, Nicholas Murray Butler had been its chief, as scholar and builder, as spokesman and showpiece.

The identification of the University with one man from the nineties of the nineteenth to the mid-years of the twentieth century could have spawned worries and fears when he departed the scene and a new face appeared in his place. After my selection as President was announced, there must have been rumblings and grumblings about the danger that a professional soldier might corrupt academic standards. But I soon learned that deep within the University structure, my arrival had caused little stir at all.

On Friday evening, for example, Low Library, where the University administrative offices were concentrated, closed its doors until Monday morning. Saturday, for me, was just another day in the week when I expected to put in at least a few hours at the desk. My peculiar attitude about schedules made no difference in the University's practice. For a while I did not realize this; on Saturday mornings I walked from our residence to the Library with a faculty or staff member who knew his way about campus, who knew the doorways, and who had the proper keys. One Saturday, without companion or guide, I attempted to penetrate the vastness of Low only to be confronted by a campus policeman who refused me entrance.

"I'd like to get into the President's office," I said.

"There won't be anybody there," he said.

When I added that my name was Eisenhower, his countenance and firm stand against my entrance changed not an iota. Nor did it when I assured him that I was President of the University. Whatever the outcome might have been of this confrontation between stalwart sentry and the new man, I have not the slightest idea. At that point, another policeman, who had apparently seen my picture in the paper, came along and vouched for me. The ivory towers of learning on Morningside Heights were guarded by other than venerable philosophers.

This was not the end of it. On another weekend during an austerity period when we had cut back on heating and lighting in all buildings not in use, I visited old East Hall late one evening. It housed the studios of the Fine Arts Department. I had heard about the work of one of the painters there and wanted to see it. During the visit, a watchman, opening the first floor door of the building that should have been unoccupied as well as unheated and unlighted, shouted up the stairs. He wanted me to identify myself.

My name, shouted back as loudly as I could, probably seemed a Germanic garble. He wanted to know my business. When I called down the staircase that I was President of the University, a look of vigorous disbelief crossed his face and he was prepared to order my instant departure had not the artist, a well-known fellow, with his brilliant red beard, come out of his studio to urge my continued presence.

Later I learned that the watchman had reported to his senior that he had discovered in East Hall an elderly man who claimed to be the President of Columbia but did not look like it. The guard was undoubtedly accustomed to Nicholas Murray Butler, who looked the role to perfection. Butler, with his many-sided career, personified Columbia in the public eye. A scholar, as I have said, but no scholarly recluse, the world was a platform on which he played many roles. He had been all his adult life active in the Republican Party and in 1912 was its candidate for the Vice-Presidency. His money-raising talents were enviable and some thought him a bit of a Machiavelli who seldom disclosed his hand as he moved and maneuvered to augment the prestige—and wealth—of Columbia. My own nomination might have been of his own doing, although the committee of trustees never hinted this to me. Whatever the case, he certainly supported the trustees' selection—and a good thing for me, too.

When Mamie and I first saw our future residence on Morningside Heights, I was a little disturbed by the mansion-like appearance of the place. Sixty Morningside Drive, in all its weight of marble and dark oak, was a grand and formal structure architecturally. It could be brightened, even warmed up, and Mamie immediately took on that task with Elizabeth Draper, the decorator. Even at that point, I saw that there was no room in which I could hope to flee grandeur. If there had been an attic I could have remodeled, I might have designed such a room. But there was no attic and the basement was beyond redemption. On the roof, which had once housed a water-tank as insurance against collapse of public supply, was a sort of "penthouse." From it, you could see all Harlem and on clear nights the lights of Long Island.

In this room, even as in the barn loft of my boyhood or my attic "command post" when I was a student at Leavenworth, I could find high above the street escape from the insistent demands of official life. Into the re-done water room, Mamie and I moved furniture utterly ineligible for a place in the gracious rooms below but dear from long association and worn by the years. A piano dominated one corner.

Access to the retreat was by a tiny elevator, unpredictable in operation, in which four passengers were a crowd. Up there, we were as cut off from the great city about us as we would have been on a remote island, and it was the one place where I could be myself.

An artist, Thomas E. Stephens, of New York, began a portrait of Mamie. I was an interested spectator. Having completed a sitting for the day, he asked Mamie to go with him through the house so that they could agree for a proper place for the portrait, when finished. Sitting alone after the two of them left, it occurred to me that I might as well make use of the paints remaining on his palette to try poking away on my own. The problem was to find anything on which to begin. It happened then that my old companion, Sergeant Moaney, came into the room and I had an idea. "Sergeant," I said, "in my room there is a little box about twelve inches on each side. Will you please knock out the sides, take any kind of white cloth you can find, and stretch it on the board by tacking the edges?" Within a matter of minutes, Moaney was back with a clean dust cloth and the bottom of the box. Together, we fastened the cloth to the board.

The only subject I could think of was right before me—Mamie's unfinished portrait. So I started out and kept going until the two explorers came back about forty-five minutes later. I displayed my version of Mamie, weird and wonderful to behold, and we all laughed heartily. Tom Stephens, for some reason, urged me to keep on trying. I did not even bother to argue; painting was beyond me. So when he said that he wanted my "painting" as a keepsake, I was glad to give it to him, this product of my first grand venture into "art."

A few days later a package arrived. Opening it, I found a present from Mr. Stephens: everything I could possibly need—except ability—to start painting. I looked upon the present as a wonderful gesture and a sheer waste of money. I had never had any instruction in painting; the only thing of possible help was a working knowledge of linear perspective, a subject we had studied at West Point.

I left the open package in my room. Each day I seemed to develop a little more curiosity about painting a picture. The result was that I took the plunge, to find that in spite of my complete lack of talent, the attempt to paint was absorbing. My most urgent need at the start was a generous-sized tarpaulin to cover the floor around the easel. The one thing I could do well from the beginning was to cover hands, clothes, brush handles, chair, and floor with more paint than ever reached the canvas. With the protection provided by the tarp, and with my painting clothes always stored in a dark recess of a closet, I succeeded in avoiding total domestic resistance to my new hobby.

The penthouse retreat at Columbia was an ideal studio. A professional might have objected to its lack of north exposure and a skylight. But privacy and quiet were more important to me than lighting. After eighteen years, I am still messy; my hands are better suited to an ax handle than a tiny brush. I attempt only simple compositions. My frustration is complete when I try for anything delicate. Even yet I refuse to refer to my productions as paintings. They are daubs, born of my love of color and in my pleasure in experimenting, nothing else. I destroy two out of each three I start. One of the real satisfactions is finding out how closely I come to depicting what I have in mind—and many times I want to see what I am going to do and never know what it will be.

In spite of this, I have frequently wished for more daylight hours to paint. Its only defect is that it provides no exercise. I've often thought what a wonderful thing it would be to install a compact painting outfit on a golf cart.

In the White House, in bad weather, painting was one way to survive away from the desk. In a little room off the elevator on the second floor, hardly more than a closet, the easel, paints, and canvases were easy to use. Often, going to lunch, I'd stop off for ten minutes to paint. In Gettysburg, I've tried many landscapes and still lifes but with magnificent audacity, I have tried more portraits than anything else. I've also burned more portraits than anything else.

The first member of the University family to greet Mamie and me at 60 Morningside when we arrived there in May 1948 was David Syrett. He was outfitted in cowboy togs with a toy pistol in a holster at his side. David, the son of a faculty member, was nine years old. Meeting us at the front door of our new home, he made a good picture for the waiting photographers. Better still, the informality—and the age of the University's unofficial greeter—set the right tone. I think David was more interested in getting an autograph than anything else. Our picture made page one in eight New York newspapers the following day, I am told.

Fifteen years later, when I was in New York for the 1963 Alexander Hamilton dinner, David appeared again, we were photographed together, and the six newspapers that had survived from the original eight ran a "then and now" layout. At least one of them pointed out that young Syrett had developed much more than I since our first meeting; he was preparing for graduate work in history at the University of London.

The years between the two meetings had been for both of us, I think, exciting, unexpected, and rewarding. Despite Columbia's worldwide reputation as a prestigious center of learning, with its unspoken suggestion that the University would be far removed from the intimate, personal pursuits of daily life, David Syrett, on that May day almost twenty years ago, crystallized for me the idea that humanity would be present among the humanities and sciences. A small boy had set himself one mission and wanted proof of its accomplishment. In his eager curiosity, forthright warmness, and initiative, he got it. My autograph was an urban counterpart to the jack-rabbit a country boy might have exhibited after a chase in field or forest.

I arrived at Columbia determined to enjoy a firsthand association with the students and faculty. I insisted on a change in the location of the President's office. Nicholas Murray Butler had worked on the second floor of Low Library, reaching it by a private elevator from the office of the University's secretary. This protected him against intrusion by the crowds that often thronged the rotunda, usually sightseers; it also made him inaccessible to visitors who had not gone through the red tape of appointment-making. The office was moved to the first floor. There, I hoped, both students and faculty might have direct and easy access to their President and I would not feel immured in a remote citadel.

Duties and responsibilities, whose scope I had not fully realized before I arrived, soon sealed me off from all but formal or brief association with the students. This fact became a source of vast annoyance to me. Students, the chief reason for a university's being, and for me the paramount appeal and attraction in campus life, were in danger of becoming numerical figures on forms and passing, unknown faces on campus. Supervising the management of a vast endowment that included one of the largest real estate empires in New York; administrating an economic enterprise that employed more maintenance people, to mention just one category, than most colleges had students; satisfying the demand for speeches, alumni appearances, ceremonial functions; correcting an appalling deficit that threatened academic standards, salary scales, and Columbia's traditional objective of excellence—all these, as ravenous of energy as they were of time, fast became a moat against communication with the young men and women.

In the Army, whenever I became fed up with meetings, protocol, and paper work, I could rehabilitate myself by a visit with the troops. Among them, talking to each other as individuals, and listening to each other's stories, I was refreshed and could return to headquarters reassured that, hidden behind administrative entanglements, the military was an enterprise manned by human beings. As a university president, perhaps less sure of myself, I did not at first permit myself as much freedom as I enjoyed in Army command. The invisible and intangible rules of academic propriety and procedure were partial shackles on my personal inclinations.

With the advantages of hindsight, I know now that I should have tossed the rules into the trash can, abandoning my office and its minutia more frequently.

In one period, I set myself the goal of visiting every classroom, office, and laboratory. Under the guidance of deans and faculty, I spent a morning or an afternoon each week dropping in on lectures, poking into corners, and occasionally getting a chance to chat briefly with students or teachers. Climbing stairs was good exercise, I suppose; at least I was usually a little tired once back in the office, and I did come to know more than I had before. But a guided tour is seldom fun and often profitless; you are apt to see only what the guide deems proper.

There were countless ways, on the other hand, in which I might have enjoyed myself and possibly done some good—if only by a voluntary return to coaching, and looking in over Lou Little's shoulder while he worked out with the squad, or advising married students on the GI bill how to decorate their apartments. I never succeeded in liberating myself from the traditional decorum and occasional pomp of the university president's role although eventually I think I would have burst my way into thoroughly enjoying life there. But I remained chief officer of everything from ritual to rentals.

During the years as an Army officer, I had met outstanding men; my command in World War II had brought me into association with great men. Columbia was a concentration of outstanding characters and superior intellects. Here and there was a bore, to be sure. But most of the men and women who make up that complex of culture and learning and buildings called Columbia were brilliant in their talk, profound in their thoughts, and enthusiastic about the University and its work. They immensely broadened my horizons. Among them, I felt myself a student who learned more from them than I could ever hope to give in return.

* * *

At Columbia, I not only made friends but was fortunate to be able to take several there with me. Certain men were invaluable to me during my time at the Pentagon. One of these was Kevin McCann, whose interest in education was deep and who was sharply sensitive to the rapidly changing conditions of the postwar years. Another was my administrative aide, Major Robert Schulz, who had joined me in the Pentagon shortly after the war. The others were Master Sergeant John Moaney and his wife Delores, who are regular members of our household, and Sergeant Leonard Dry, my principal driver.

Two trusted confidants in University affairs were Albert Jacobs, the provost, and Kevin, who, as Assistant to the President, was tireless in his efforts to help me, a man whose background was completely governmental and military, understand the needs and sensitivities of a faculty and others in our educational institution. Learning how to take a place in academic life was not simple but learning to like the people of Columbia was; I conceived an instant liking for many faculty members and administrators. I had only known one, Lou Little, before my arrival.

In the number of friendships made, the Columbia period was one of the richer periods of my life. But an attempt to name each individual who became a friend would be a list marred by omissions. Nevertheless I should mention some of those I saw most often.

Harry Carman, who never walked when he could run, and a scholarly authority in American history, possessed a zest for Columbia College and for living a full life that he communicated to everyone associated with him, including myself. Bob Harron, Columbia's Director of Public Relations, began his professional career as a sports writer—one of his books was Knute Rockne's biography—but he had moved to Morningside Heights because the education of young people became his paramount interest. George Cooper, before World War War I a Columbia great in water polo (when that sport was still organized mayhem), spent much of his time and resources in organizing the University's alumni clubs and in introducing me to them around the country.

In the management and raising of money respectively my chief counselors were Joseph Campbell and Paul Davis, two men who were masters of their fields. The former, who knew to the last dollar and the bottom brick the recesses of Columbia finances and real estate, I later appointed to the Atomic Energy Commission and then Comptroller General of the United States. Paul Davis was the most vigorous and informed exponent of voluntary giving for education I have ever encountered.

All the trustees became my close friends. Among them, however, I saw most frequently, Douglas M. Black, whom I first met in connection with *Crusade in Europe;* Marcy Dodge, the senior among them in years of service and the youngest in his enthusiasm about Columbia; George Warren, whose common sense and wisdom were dependable sources of support; Frank Fackenthal, Acting President between the death of Dr. Butler and my arrival, who was my chief link with the Columbia administrative tradition.

To keep me up-to-date in matters as diverse as medicine, literature, science, and alumni affairs I looked for the latest information to Willard Rappleye, Dean of the College of Physicians and Surgeons; John Henry Hobart Lyon, who well into his seventies memorized a new poem every morning and rated all other colleges and universities on their resemblance to Columbia. George Pegram, a scientist's scientist, occupied an office immediately above mine and was always ready to drop in to chat about anything from common fractions to nuclear fission and fusion; Frank Hogan, the oft-elected New York District Attorney, was as good at solving alumni problems as in prosecuting criminals.

Two men, dedicated to teaching as a vocation and a profession, gave up their professional chairs, at my request, for the worries and frustrations and burdens of administrative duty. They were Lawrence Chamberlain, who became Dean of Columbia College, and Grayson Kirk, who became Provost, succeeding me as President of the University in 1952. For their willingness to subordinate their preference to my and Columbia's need, I am indebted to them.

Charles Swift, manager of the Men's Faculty Club, was my host whenever I ate or attended a University function there. Although he was devoted to Columbia, I later learned his enduring ambition was to manage the Thayer Hotel at West Point. Had he lived and had a vacancy occurred there, I would have done everything in my power to help him fill it.

My personal secretary at Columbia, and an extremely good one, was Marilyn MacKinnon. Only her decision to become a full-time housewife separated us. Another in the office, Alice Boyce, did accompany me to France and later to the White House where she occupied extremely sensitive positions through both terms. Secretaries like these two multiply a man's official effectiveness.

o o o

When Lou Little was football coach at Georgetown University, back in the twenties, I was coaching an Army team that lost to Georgetown by one point. While I was still Chief of Staff, and on the eve of my departure to take up duties at Columbia, I was given the mission of saving Lou for the University. He had been offered the head coaching job at Yale. Columbia alumni panicked. They decided that only I could persuade Lou to stay on. A group of them, headed by Bill Donovan, of the OSS in World War II, and Frank Hogan, the New York District Attorney, escorted Lou to Fort Myer for a talk. I had no professional or financial arguments to offer. I was reduced to a personal appeal. It was not at all eloquent:

"Lou, you cannot do this to me," I said. "You're one of the reasons I am going to Columbia."

The coach seemed a little flustered. But he recovered quickly and, asking for time to consider his future, we talked football, reminisced, and had a general discussion of the state of the game. For once all the years that I had spent coaching seemed to make sense.

I continued to be uneasy about Lou's decision. And then I learned that immediately on his arrival at his hotel in Washington, he called his wife, Loretta, and said:

"Stop packing. We're not going!"

To the alumni, that success in saving Columbia from depredation by Yale might have been my largest contribution to Columbia's stature. At least I am told that whenever the alumni got together during my time there, my triumph was cited as convincing proof that I had leadership potential. Those of the Columbia family who were less concerned with football may have assessed it with a colder eye. Nevertheless, there was, I think, a substantial academic by-product, one that not everyone could see at the time.

Columbia was pitifully short of ready money. The salary scale, formerly one of the highest in the country, had been static for years. Other universities, with ready cash, were raiding the talent pool of Columbia's faculty and staff. Had Lou Little, a fixture at Columbia, been lured to a rival campus, faculty and staff recruiting by other schools might have hurt the University. Against such raids, the University had, at the time, little protection except appeals to loyalty. More than once, I found such appeals exceeded the bait of dollars.

Some time later, for example, the Nobel Prize winner Isidor Rabi was offered a position at the Institute for Advanced Study in Princeton. There, he would not only enjoy a much larger salary, he would be free from metropolitan pressures and campus schedules, with an opportunity for creative thinking and reflection in an environment of scholarly quiet. He would enjoy daily association with his close friend, Albert Einstein. Such a partnership of brains, I knew, could be highly productive in its contribution to science. As President of Columbia, I had to protect the University against the disastrous effect of faculty morale and academic standards should Dr. Rabi leave.

We were in no position to match Princeton's offer financially. Could I have, it would have been futile, for Dr. Rabi praised intellectual challenge above money. I could only present to him the probabilities of what might happen to Columbia should he leave, in the hope that his concern for the institution and its future would save him for us. I stressed that, to the academic world, he symbolized pure science on Morningside Heights. His departure, I continued, would deprive the University of its chief drawing card—to use layman's language—to bring in brilliant graduate students for whom his presence on our campus meant excellence in science. If their numbers diminished and they were replaced by average or mediocre students, faculty members would soon lose the zest and excitement they knew and they would begin looking for other places. The chain reaction, I pointed out, could do serious damage to the institution.

My arguments were simple. I could not speak as one scientist to another; our conversation was man to man. I was only sorry that I could not find the splendid phrases such an appeal and such a figure deserved.

Then Dr. Rabi delighted me and assured Columbia against sudden deterioration in science by agreeing to stay on.

Although our alumni body was one of the largest in the country and many of its members successful and affluent, alumni support was relatively meager. One reason was the widespread conviction that Columbia was immensely rich. Another was the notion, among those who equated physical growth with quality, that Columbia was stagnant. No new building had been erected since the depression. Some Columbia College graduates pointed out that the gifts they had already made for a field house at Baker Field had been banked by the University. They suspected that Columbia's officers were more concerned with the interest the money earned than in using it for the purpose intended.

This complaint had to be dealt with. I investigated and having learned that the money had in fact been hoarded, I went to the trustees and urged approval of a new field house. The amount of money involved was around $650,000, petty cash by present spending standards in many colleges.

No one could argue that the new building added to the academic stature of the University. Realistically examined, it only made life more convenient for the athletic squads. But as it went up, it brought down the alumni grievances. And it was at least a hint that the University might be ready for new expansion. I pushed its construction as hard as I could.

More important than bricks and mortar to me was the moral and intellectual strength of Columbia, a power for good throughout the country and the Western World. To extend this strength, to channel it better to serve the nation, new growth—I thought—should be rooted in the chief asset of any university, its faculty.

The Columbia faculty, I believed, was capable of taking the lead in studying and analyzing the national viewpoint on the vast social, political, and economic problems thrust upon us after World War II. With such a venture, they would amplify the University's role so that its influence would not be restricted to campus classrooms or scholarly conferences. Among the nationwide problems that concerned us at the time were:

The mental and physical health of our young people. Weakness of mind and body among far too many of them had been startlingly revealed during the war years when hundreds of thousands were rejected from the country's service because they were below minimal educational and physical standards.

The role of pressure groups in every area of our social and economic life. I would later make this the subject of my last address as President of the United States but even then the aggressive demands of various groups and special interests, callous or selfish, or even well intentioned, contradicted the American tradition that no part of our country should prosper except as the whole of America prospered. Unless there were changes, I felt that eventually only the promises of the extreme right and the extreme left would be heard in public places.

Third—there was a sort of torpor about individual responsibility and a disbelief that an enlightened and dedicated individual could, on his own, accomplish much for the good of all. This seemed to suggest a disregard for the meaning of American citizenship, and its obligations as well as its rights, or an ignorance of the opportunities for self-expression and self-development in our country.

For examining these and other problems, I saw on the Columbia faculty an immense pool of talent, scholarly and humane in its comprehension of human needs and aspirations, above the bias of sect and party. At first I thought of it as a sort of intellectual Supreme Court which could search through the entanglements of the problems before us and by dispassionate study, and with imaginative and profound thought, propose solutions that would win acceptance. I found that when I began to speak out on this point, many—even within the faculty itself—thought my notions were too idealistic. They may well have been right.

In any case, with Dean Philip Young of the Graduate School of Business, I began to elaborate the idea of a truly national assembly where we could mobilize in addition to the University's educational and intellectual resources other experts from every walk of life. Gathered together free from telephone calls and urgent summons to make instant decisions, they might examine the larger problems, find a common ground of agreement about answers, and arrive at working conclusions.

There was little or no co-ordination or joint effort among the schools within the University at that time. The real co-ordination was with the student himself, who picked out courses, and drew on the various disciplines. But the various faculties did little together. Young and I got them working on problems and drafting papers, and then brought in businessmen, encouraging an atmosphere of the free exchange of ideas. My own education at Leavenworth and at the War College had been in the "case method" and I understood its usefulness.

Working toward this idea became an absorbing pursuit for me through most of 1949. I talked about it, wrote about it, thought about it almost incessantly. Till late in the year, I got no farther than a name—the American Assembly. Then, Averell Harriman became interested. He offered the family home, Arden House, with superb surrounding acreage, high on a ridge near the Hudson as a site for the Assembly. I visited the place and found it a mansion of delightful drawing rooms and endless corridors. I was enthusiastic and the property was soon transferred to Columbia.

Now known as the Harriman campus of Columbia University, the old mansion has witnessed scores of meetings concerned with almost every aspect of human society. Throughout the years, its influence, although difficult to measure, has been far reaching beyond my dreams of almost two decades ago. Much of the time I think its beginnings were my principal success as University President. The American Assembly, however, was not the only venture that meant much to me during my short academic career.

Another project undertaken at Columbia, called the Conservation of Human Resources, had its beginnings, too, in my wartime realization that we had seriously neglected the full education and preparation of our young people to be vigorous and productive members of society. This neglect was tragically tabulated, among young men, in those armed forces rejection records of the years 1940–1945. I suspected that a fair study of these records, while they were still easily available, could produce guideposts for our future conduct as a nation. Dr. Eli Ginzberg, whose profound scholarship did not in the slightest blunt an almost boyish enthusiasm about any proposal for the betterment of human living, took over this project with a passion. This support I was able to produce in furthering his research and advancing his proposals is still one of my proudest memories of life at Columbia.

The Institute for the Study of War and Peace, the new Engineering Center headed by Dean John Dunning, the Citizenship Education Project were innovations we worked out during my Columbia years. One innovation was less a matter of intellect than of the senses. It reflected the distaste for concrete and macadam of a big-city University President who had started out as a country boy.

Our campus of twenty-six acres or so was, by New York standards, an immense real estate holding. The original planners probably thought they had ample room for buildings and open lawn. They had not foreseen an enrollment of thirty thousand. By the time I arrived, despite a few trees and small patches of lawn, we were a "campus" of buildings and paving.

The factory yard appearance distressed me most of all. Leaving my office by the front entrance of Low Library on a hot day, I looked down the long flight of stone steps, across 116th Street crowded with parked cars and creeping traffic, over the dry gravel and clay of tennis courts to Butler Library, grassless, treeless. This was the physical center and heart of the University. It should be a green oasis. In my eye, I could see the hot and noisy street converted into lawn, with automobiles forever barred.

An improvement would take a little time and only a small expenditure of money. When I first presented the idea to city officials, all of them, including Mayor William O'Dwyer, were sympathetic. I quickly learned that stopping the flow of traffic through a single block of the main artery on Manhattan Island presents the city authorities with problems they think appalling and unsolvable. For one thing, New Yorkers through generations have been accustomed to free movement on 116th Street. To restrict their use of it would provoke an outraged reaction expressed in meetings and at the polls. I countered that most of the traffic was University-centered and our people would adjust their driving patterns for the sake of an attractive park.

The second objection was that fire equipment could not be barred from the street. Although I suspected that such equipment did not use 116th Street once a year, I suggested that the barrier to other traffic would be the flimsiest sort of fencing which, in an emergency, would be no obstacle to any public vehicle. At times it seemed that settling one problem spawned the birth of two or three more. The project that I thought could be accomplished within a very few months dragged on eternally. I was living in the White House, surrounded by lawn, before the dream became reality and 116th Street a pleasant mall.

All the ideas I had for changes, all the projects for advancing Columbia, were so different from the tasks of my earlier years, so novel and fresh in their appeal, that I found the work fun—or would have, if only I could have concentrated without the distraction of other demands.

Instead, I found myself caught up in a whirl of additional duties. My life at the University, exhausting enough for a neophyte in education, was complicated by a presidential summons in the fall of 1948. I was asked to go to Washington regularly to serve as senior adviser to the Secretary of Defense. When these new duties were first presented to me, the usual assurances were made that they could be done in my spare time. Politicians thought the academic life was marked by an abundance of that! I was assured that even if my new task called for long hours occasionally, the work would still be compatible with my University role and even profitable to Columbia.

In the first flush of my arrival on campus, knowing that the trustees would expect me to be an active spokesman for the University, I had accepted numerous invitations to speak during the winter months. On the campus itself, I had become involved in enough developments to consume all my waking hours when I was not in front of the microphone. Now, the "part-time" duty in Washington turned out to be no less than a major role in the reconstruction of the military establishment.

Sometimes I was an umpire between disputing services; sometimes a hatchetman on what Fox Conner use to call Fool Schemes. It was true that both my jobs, at the University and in Defense, were somewhat compatible; each was concerned with the expanding future and security of the nation. Most of the time they were a tolerable load, and frequently inspiring and rewarding.

But commuting by plane and train between Washington and New York ate up a good many hours. Making half a dozen speeches a week was something of a burden although, to be sure, if prepared texts were not required, the speeches were harder on the audience than on the speaker. And the ride between New York and Washington, although a soon-familiar monotonous and dreary process through familiar train yards and past endless billboards, did offer occasional leisure for relaxation, reading, or a nap.

* * *

Columbia was threatened by a strike. While the law provided that eleemosynary institutions were not required to permit their employees to organize, the University, during World War II, had agreed to the unionization of maintenance workers. Now the workers wanted a wage increase. If denied it, they threatened a walkout.

I checked our lawyers to learn what measures were possible. First I found that, although the union was recognized by the University, we could, if the maintenance force quit, enlist the services of students on a part-time basis. But before taking such a step, I had to find out whether the workers' demands were justified.

There was some justice in them and if a compromise could be reached, both sides might be satisfied. The Columbia maintenance workers were part of the New York Transport Workers' Union, headed by Michael Quill. Mike Quill, a tough, blustering fellow that some people described as a "professional Irishman," came to see me. I told him that the University would do its best to meet a reasonable request because I realized that costs had gone up and the workers were entitled to an increase in pay. But I pointed out that Columbia was not making money, we were basing all our budgets on frugality, and were not yet making ends meet. Unless he was prepared to be reasonable, we would have to part right then and there.

Mike Quill grinned and said, "Look, General, I'm not going to have any trouble with you. I've got more sense than to be taking on an opponent who is as popular as you seem to be in this city."

We quickly settled the strike and had no further difficulty.

A new turn of events might well have brought the University crashing down. Louis Hacker, Dean of the School of General Studies, was quite successful in securing distinguished outside lecturers for subjects in which his classes were interested. Then he made a mistake of coming to me one day to ask that I be one of them.

I told Lou Hacker emphatically that this was ridiculous. All I could talk about was military history, military training and operation, the mobilization of a nation for war, or the problems of demobilization. He said that the students, particularly in history and economics, would be interested. With considerable diffidence, I finally agreed to try a talk before an evening group.

I specified that because I always despised long, dreary lectures, I would talk for not more than twenty minutes and would be prepared to answer questions, if any were forthcoming. I said also that I would have to leave no later than 9:30, if we began at 8:00 P.M. I was certain that a longer stay would produce a sleeping student body.

When the time came to deliver the lecture, the room was filled with several hundred students. They listened attentively as I went through a sketch of some of the major aspects of war, from its historical beginnings to the tactics and weapons we employed in World War II. Then I went a little further to speculate about the prospects of future wars now that the atomic bomb existed. I talked about the methods used by government in time of war to keep the fighting forces and the productive capacity of the nation in balance, so that neither should be exhausted. When I finished, I was astonished to find dozens of students on their feet, ready to ask questions. As each was answered, a half dozen more were ready. This went on for an hour, and finally, the professor stood up to say that he had promised to get General Eisenhower out of the lecture room by 9:30, it was already 9:45, and time to adjourn. I got out as gracefully and quickly as possible—and perspiring from every pore. I had really been "through the wringer" and wanted only a quiet corner where I could regain my equilibrium. The questions had been searching. But there were no mean or loaded questions, none designed to trip up the old soldier; these people wanted to learn.

Next morning Dean Hacker called to say that I'd done well. In fact he asked that I sign up on an annual basis for two or three of these lectures. I was complimented but I silently determined that in coming years I'd be unavailable.

It was just as well. At another point, Gabriel Silver, a friend of Columbia University, said that he would endow an annual lecture on the general subject of peace and war, but he made the stipulation that the endowment money would be forthcoming only if I would give the first lecture. Well, I could not allow an opportunity for a contribution of that sort to go by the board, so with the valuable help of Kevin McCann, I set about preparing the lecture. My previous attempt at professorship had been completely extemporaneous. Giving the new lecture was a more studied effort and, being written out, it did not put quite so much strain on me. But it put a tremendous strain on the listeners. It went on for about an hour, which was probably fifty minutes too long, and there were no demands for an encore. Fortunately, the good benefactor provided the promised endowment.

So far as I can recall, these were my only ventures into the realm of the classroom lecturer. All my other talks and addresses were ceremonial or official as the University's chief spokesman. At one point I attended a dinner where there were three previous speakers. Each had gone on at considerable length and as the evening threatened to become morning, I decided to set aside my own text. When the time came to speak, I stood up, said that every speech, written or otherwise, had to have punctuation, "Tonight, I am the punctuation—the period," and sat down. It was one of my most popular addresses.

Patrick J. Buchanan

'62 JOURNALISM

Pat Buchanan wrote for the editorial pages of the St. Louis Globe-Democrat *before becoming a spokesman for Richard Nixon's 1968 presidential campaign. He went on to serve Nixon as a White House speechwriter and later worked for President Ronald Reagan as well. After making his name as a television pundit—he helped start CNN's* Crossfire—*Buchanan sought the Republican nomination for president in 1992. A high-profile conservative who consistently advocates economic protectionism and traditional family values, Buchanan ran again in 1996 but has since returned to his role as a commentator and critic. This selection comes from his memoir,* Right from the Beginning *(1988).*

The Graduate School at Columbia was in 1961—and remains today—the finest journalism school in America. When I arrived, I was probably the least prepared student in the class of '62.

I had never worked on a newspaper, high school or college; I had never had anything published, not even a letter to the editor; I could not type. Though my straight A's in early senior year, and my "experience" as an auditor had helped to win me the $1,500 Clapp-Poliak fellowship for "economic writing," I had never taken a course in economics. Soma Golden, who had won the $1,000 Clapp-Poliak fellowship (and who now is national editor of the *New York Times*) had been graduated *summa cum laude* in economics from Radcliffe. Twenty-five years later, as I reviewed my personnel file at Columbia, the commentaries of my teachers suggested that they saw me as a rude amateur, dropped in among young professionals. Students like Joe Salzman of U.S.C. and Arnie Abrams of Columbia were award-winning editors of their college papers; others, like Tony Sargent and Don Oliver, both of whom had had years of on-air experience, were already well into their careers.

Everything at Columbia was new to me: how to report, how to write a lead, how to put together a story, how to write a headline, how to edit copy, how to piece together a magazine article. Only crusty George Barrett, the assistant city editor at the *New York Times,* seemed to think this student had promise. And George was a contrarian. The curt and dismissive comment on my midterm report, by copy editor Betsy Wade, was not untypical: "I met this student 12/7 and 12/14 and had to take him by the hand for every single thing that needed doing. He seems not to have any motive power of his own."

The most memorable teacher at Columbia in those years was Professor John Hohenberg, who taught advanced news writing to the class of '62. Hohenberg was an institution at the "J" School; his fine book, *The Professional Journalist,* was scriptural text.

An intense, emotional man, for whom journalism was a calling, not an occupation, and an honored calling at that, Professor Hohenberg began his hours-long morning course with a brief lecture on what this particular writing exercise was all about. Then, we were handed "fact sheets" from which to produce a news story at our desks. "Editors," many of them active newspapermen and women, would start down each aisle, lean over our typewriters, and criticize and correct what we had written.

Years later—after I had penned Vice President Agnew's famous attack on the networks at Des Moines, November 13, 1969, and his follow-up assault on the *Washington Post* and *New York Times* ("The day when . . . the gentlemen of the *New York Times* enjoyed a form of diplomatic immunity from comment and criticism of what they said is over. Yes, gentlemen, that day is past.")—John Oakes, editorial editor of the *Times,* was chatting with me at a party. When I volunteered that *New York Times*'s reporters and editors had taught me at Columbia most of what I knew about news writing, he mused, "That must have been quite painful for you."

The very opposite is true. Whatever their politics, the men and women who worked for the *Times* were thought, by all of us at Columbia, to be the New York Yankees of American journalism. "If the *Times* went on strike in the morning," one of my professors told me, "every afternoon paper in the city would have to shut down," so dependent were they on the Gray Lady of 43rd Street.

We may have rankled beneath their airs of superiority, but, liberal or not, the *Times* was considered the finest newspaper in the world, setting a standard of excellence against which other newspapers should measure themselves. Students taken on as night copy boys were envied; upon graduation, they might be hired as apprentice reporters, and soon have their by-lines in the greatest newspaper in the world. To have the most respected journalists in America take a personal interest in my miserable copy was what I had come to Columbia for.

The Journalism School was everything I had hoped it would be; and I have always taken a measure of pride that, after nine months at the toughest graduate school in America, I was competitive with young journalists who had started years ahead of me. That liberalism was in vogue, with respectable dissent coming from the fashionable left, made the experience all the more cherished. "Pat, how did you ever survive up there at Columbia?" conservative friends would ask me, years later.

I did not just survive; I had the time of my life.

About the ideological predilections of the best and brightest in the profession I had chosen, I was never in doubt. (Some of my professors, like Penn Kimball, refused to cross a picket line set up by students outside the campus bookstore, even though they were simply passing through the store to get to class. They walked all the way around the building to come in another entrance, lest they be *perceived* as crossing a picket line!) The chasm that opened wide and deep between the Establishment press and the American people during Vietnam and Watergate came as no shock to me; I was present at the creation.

The first time I got one of those long fact sheets, I read it over carefully and began ruminating silently about my lead. Two minutes had not elapsed, however, before I heard one typewriter start up, then another; then, what sounded like a battery of machine guns was firing in the newsroom. All the cocky young journalists were breezing through this easy calisthenic. As I could barely type, I panicked, tearing page after page out of the big Underwood, until Professor Larry Pinkham came down the aisle and told me to calm down and take some of the aspirin I kept on my desk and ate like jelly beans because of the arthritis.

One of the earliest fact sheets described an elderly philanthropist and art collector, a friend of the publisher, who had taken as his third wife an eighteen-year-old coed. We were asked to write up this delicate item in a style suitable to the Sunday *Times.* My lead ran something like this: "Dr. Harold Ross, noted philanthropist and contributor to New York's Metropolitan Museum, added a new piece to his celebrated collection this afternoon. The objet d'art is Miss Becky Woodham, an eighteen-year-old graduate of the Student Art School; Becky and Dr. Ross were wed, etc. etc."

The *Times* editor working my aisle that day, bug-eyed, ripped the copy out of my typewriter, and ran it up to Hohenberg, who read it to the class, which howled with delight. A gracious man, John Hohenberg declined to divulge the name of the author.

From the day classes opened, I felt I was in over my head; I was nervous and tense in class and had serious doubts as to whether I could catch up with the other students, before the faculty caught up with me. Each afternoon, I would go home and work on my assignments (and typing) until all hours of the night.

My personal best, however, came on election day in November, the night the ethnic dream ticket of Lefkowitz, Fino, and Gilhooley went down to defeat before Mayor Robert Wagner, who had campaigned brilliantly for reelection against the bosses who had put him in office, and whose tool he was said to have become.

The election for Bronx borough president was being held the same evening, and I was assigned to cover the almost certain winner, a protégé of Democratic machine boss Charley Buckley. Sitting in the Democratic headquarters from six until after nine, talking with the pols, I sensed this crowd did not have the feel of a winner. Operating on a hunch, I found out from a telephone operator the address of Joe Periconi's headquarters and took a cab over to assess the mood in the Republican reformer's camp. When I arrived, the returns were bringing in the upset of the night. Flushed with a victory they had not anticipated, Periconi and his people were ebullient, talkative, and quotable. Before the metropolitan press arrived, I had Periconi's quotes phoned in to our "city desk."

Exhausted but quite pleased with myself, I left the Bronx around midnight and headed for the West End bar across from Columbia, arriving back at my room near three in the morning. The next day when I walked into the 9 A.M. class five minutes late, Hohenberg, who was speaking, did not appear angry. He looked over and nodded with a smile, as I walked back to my desk. Don Oliver, who had the desk in front of me and who was now a constant companion, whispered loudly, "Your ears should have been burning."

Hohenberg had related to the class, apparently in gratifying detail, the exploit of the intrepid and savvy young reporter who had had the initiative to drop his given assignment and go get "the story" of the night. Great reporters get their start that way, Hohenberg had explained to the class. The "objet d'art" incident was forgotten; I knew I was going to make it.

During that election campaign, the professors and teachers did little to disguise their political bias. They didn't like the ethnic bosses, the Charley Buckleys and Carmine DeSapios; and they loved the reformers. When Congressman John V. Lindsay, then forty, held a news conference in front of the class, arguing indifferently the case for the mayoral candidacy of Louie Lefkowitz, one professor asked Handsome John, "Why didn't you run yourself?"

The professors and teachers, gathered in the front of our large "newsroom," purred with pleasure. Smiling at the suggestion, Lindsay was coy in his response, but, even though he was chairman of the failing Lefkowitz campaign, he seemed not at all displeased with the question. When Lindsay departed, they spoke of him as a future mayor and even a future President of the United States, a Republican JFK. And, although Lindsay was on the far left of the Republican party, I had to concede they had a point. Compared with some of the Republicans whose golf bags I had carried around the fairways of Burning Tree, the handsome, debonair liberal from Manhattan's "silk-stocking district" did indeed strike me as a man with a future.

The aspect of Columbia I found most puzzling and off-putting was the seriousness, bordering on stuffiness and sanctimony, that pervaded much of the faculty and student body. We were young; we were gifted; we had our whole lives in front of us; but one would have thought many of us had just been condemned to a life of mortification and prayer with the Carthusians. Some students and teachers seemed to carry the weight of the world; a look of barely suppressed pain was forever in their faces. Some were downright grim.

Growing up with my family, with my friends, laughter was a part of life. Even the worst of the troubles into which we had gotten ourselves invariably yielded up a rich harvest of humor and anecdote. Among the reasons I had gone into journalism was because I wanted an enjoyable life; and newspapering was known to be an occupation where *le bon temps* was never far away. To many of my classmates and professors, however, journalism was their religion; and they had adopted the aspect of mournful missionaries, sent out to certain martyrdom, to save a sinful world.

All too often, an overdeveloped social conscience is accompanied, *pari passu,* by an atrophied sense of humor.

Oliver, who was from Montana and studied even harder than I, and I were forever on the lookout for ways to lighten things up. When, in our history of journalism course, each of us was assigned to write about some journalistic institution and the contribution it made to our profession, I chose the *New York Graphic,* the most outrageous daily ever published in the United States.

The delinquent child of millionaire health nut Bernarr Macfadden, the *Graphic* in the Roaring Twenties faked composite photographs ("composographs"); its reporters had the manners and ethics of barnyard animals; and it libeled everybody. In the world of "gutter journalism" the *Graphic* was in a class all by itself. Once, when the tabloid's lead story was about a lunatic who had escaped from an insane asylum and gone on a rape spree, a senior editor had to sprint to the composing room to take down the screaming banner headline his copy desk had sent over: NUT BOLTS AND SCREWS! Macfadden and his editor had once been hauled into court—by the New York Society for the Suppression of Vice.

Even though the daily *Graphic* had perished thirty years before, however, the teacher did not think my paper funny, or me funny, or the subject funny. The *New York Graphic* had been an unpardonable affront to American journalism, a throwback to a dark age, and I had exhibited a juvenile tolerance of the outrage. (Presumably, he wanted yet another essay on the importance of James Gordon Bennett and the *New York Herald.*)

Told to write an editorial imitating the style of a major daily, Oliver and I collaborated on "Ransom for Red Beard," an editorial crafted in the brawling 1962 style of the *New York Daily News*—carving up JFK for his plans to ransom the Cuban patriots he had left stranded at the Bay of Pigs. Some of the students thought it a clever enough imitation of what the *News* would produce to win the editorial writing award; but some of the professors let us know that the *Daily News* editorial style was something we had come to Columbia not to emulate, but to change. We didn't even come close. (Less than a decade and a half after Oliver and I penned "Ransom for Red Beard," the executives of the *Daily News* sounded me out on becoming their editorial editor.)

✺ ✺ ✺

The two subjects in which I was given a C- that first semester at Columbia were "copy editing, typography, and newspaper makeup"—about which I knew nothing—and "basic issues in the news." The grade is understandable. My views on such questions as the U.N., a revered institution at Columbia, must have been considered neolithic (I was not that far removed from the John Birch bumper-sticker position of "Get the U.S. out of the U.N. and the U.N. out of the U.S."); and my thoughts about "urban problems" were nonexistent. (Growing up in D.C., with no home rule, my friends and I were probably the principal "urban problem" in Northwest.)

Hohenberg gave me a C+ in "advanced news writing," which was more than fair. While no longer writing about comely "objets d'art" being added to the collections of philanthropists, I often missed the "lead" completely in the stories I wrote. Handed, for example, FCC Chairman Newton Minow's famous philippic against network television as a "fact sheet," I left his now-anthologized phrase, "vast wasteland," out of my first two paragraphs. My "news judgment" was not what it ought to be. In economics and libel law, academic subjects and more familiar turf, I got A's; and was given an A- in mechanics of expression and magazine writing. A couple of teachers (with professors, instructors, deans, and so on, there must have been a score of them who graded us) felt I had some native ability to communicate. All the other grades were B.

It was in that magazine writing course that I first came to feel I could actually "write." Far into the morning hours at the "I" House, one night, I wrote a long piece about the 1920s I can remember to this day, all about the "confident young men who had roared into the nineteen twenties in their Stutz Bearcats and raccoon coats, and departed via the upper floors of Wall Street skyscrapers."

For ten minutes, the teacher read long passages to the class, and he read it well; to me, it rolled beautifully. The class listened in silence. When he was done, Glenn Mitchell, the young black from Shaw College with the lilting Caribbean accent, said, "We have a writer in the class!" Some of the other students, including Anna Kisselgorf, now dance editor at the *New York Times,* and the late Judy Klemesrud, a friend from Iowa (who would also spend most of her career at the *Times),* agreed that it was beautifully written.

"What exactly is the point?" the magazine editor blurted impatiently. "This may be nice writing," but what he had assigned us to do was go to the library, plagiarize the best "anecdotes" from other magazine articles, and string them together in our own. That was the way professional writers produced and sold magazine stories. And that's what this course was supposed to train us to do. Even though he seemed frustrated by my failure to follow the course he had recommended, I was not at all displeased; fellow students, whose judgment I respected and whose approval I relished, were saying Buchanan was a "writer." The old self-confidence was coming back.

Looking back on that year, that tightly organized program at Columbia was immensely productive. Instead of hanging around Columbia for two academic years working toward a master's degree, the course work was intensified and completed in nine months. There were only eighty students in the school—sixty-five Americans and fifteen foreign students from countries like Japan, Indonesia, Pakistan, Aden, Germany, Holland, Canada, and Nicaragua. (India, with three students, had the largest foreign contingent.) There were three blacks and eighteen women; and Jewish students were probably the largest ethnic contingent. While there were no black teachers, women taught in virtually every area.

Almost every day, we went to school from nine in the morning until five in the afternoon, shifting from one course to another; and we studied and wrote far into the night. It was baptism by immersion; we were introduced to every form of journalism: radio and television broadcasting, news reporting and writing, copy editing, movie and book reviews, editorial writing, photography, newspaper management and production. We were taught the theory and history of communications in America, and were solidly grounded in libel law. As my scholarship was for economic writing, that was where I had to specialize, not foreign affairs, which is where I had wanted to be. While the economic writing seminar was meeting under the guidance of

Dean Richard T. Baker, and we discussed and wrote about the theories of David Riccardo and Karl Marx and Thorsten Veblen, Penn Kimball's class on national issues was shooting the bull with Theodore H. (Teddy) White, who had just completed *The Making of the President, 1960,* and who regaled students with stories of the Nixon–Kennedy campaign. But because I arrived with so much less skill and knowledge than the other students, I took away much more from Columbia. The assignments they found boring and redundant, I found fresh, interesting, and challenging.

❖ ❖ ❖

When Father McNamee had recommended me to Columbia, he had been asked to "handicap the applicant." The truthful old Jesuit priest put down a single word: "Irascibility."

Under "additional comments," he explained: "This applicant has only one drawback—the temper of the Irish! Yet it is this very intensity of spirit that gives him his drive and ambition. He wants to be a journalist because of his recognition and ready acceptance of the challenge of the work. He could move into a comfortable position in his father's firm. I think he will be a success at journalism."

Irascibility, the old priest had said; and he was dangerously close to the truth.

At the Christmas party, before our departure home for the holidays, Oliver, a "streetcorner conservative" like me who would have meshed nicely with the Homers, told me he had had about enough of Kim Willenson, a superior student who would seek out occasions to demonstrate that superiority. As a member of the "entertainment committee" for the party, Oliver had suggested the class sing some old cowboy songs he recalled from Montana days, such as "I Ride an Old Paint." Willenson had mocked the idea in front of the other students, and thus, Oliver said, had mocked him. As we went to buy more beer for the class midway through the party, Oliver informed me he was going to take Willenson out.

While I had nothing against Willenson, I had nothing going for him either. However, Oliver was my best friend at school and I now recalled darkly that, when Willenson had been "slot man" on our copy desk, he had flipped back a headline he had assigned me to write, with a contemptuous remark about its stupidity. This was something I would have accepted from a *Times*man, but not from a contemporary. *"Nemo me lacessit impune!"* (no one wounds me with impunity!), is, after all, the motto of the Scot.

So, I associated myself with Oliver's grievance. With you all the way, I told him. Then, I forgot about it. Later that night, as we partied in the World Room and the library, I tried out the Christman Game on a female student, in whom I had taken no prior interest. Lo and behold, who should amble up and begin exhibiting an interest of his own, but Kim Willenson. When I commented caustically on his behavior, he sent a short burst of obscene invective in my direction. Which was all I needed.

Willenson never cleared the holster. After I sucker-punched him, Willenson was on the library floor at the feet of Dean Baker, who was staring quizzically at me, wondering what in God's name he had let into his Graduate School. The whole class stormed in.

While I was relaxed about the episode, Willenson was enraged and had to be restrained. So, Oliver and I decided to call it a night. As we departed, however, I paused, turned back toward Willenson, who was still being held by a couple of students and glaring angrily at me, and said in a sweet voice, "Good night, Kim." It worked. Willenson wrestled himself free of his retainers and charged. I was waiting for him; and, now, he was on the deck a second time, with half the faculty staring incredulously and Oliver standing over him, yelling that if he tried to attack me again, he, Oliver, would "beat the shit" out of him. Which, at that point, would have been redundant.

Oliver and I laughed all the way down Broadway to Fred Appel's apartment (and after-party party) on 110th Street.

On Monday, Willenson showed up in class with a large black patch covering his eye, which, I was told, had been severely damaged. I started getting nervous; and by late afternoon, a dozen students, including several of the girls, escalated the affair by wearing black eye patches in a show of solidarity—with me.

Came word from the fifth floor that Dean Barrett wanted to see me in his office, immediately; and I could feel the old volleyball return to the abdomen. There was no doubt who had thrown the first punch; indeed, I was unsure Willenson had thrown any. The thought occurred that Dean Barrett was inviting me up to inform me he did not want me back for the second semester. Willenson, after all, was at or near the top of the class, and, as a journalist, I was, at best, expendable. I did not know how I would handle a second expulsion.

But, when I got there, the dean, who had already consulted with class president Chris Trump, was anguished only about the "destruction of class unity." Class unity was something important and vital for our future, Dean Barrett said; and he had worked tirelessly to build it. Whatever the cause, the Buchanan–Willenson fight had exposed and deepened divisions that he felt already existed within the class. Now, these eye patches, mocking Willenson, showed the class was choosing up sides. All this was deeply disheartening.

"Pat, what can we do about it?" he said.

My relief was total: "Whatever I can do to restore class unity," I said, "Dean Barrett, you've got it."

"Excellent, Pat," he said. With that, I raced downstairs, walked over to Willenson, shook hands, and implored my buddies to drop the eye patches. Which they did.

For a dozen years, after we left school, I never saw Kim Willenson. Then, in 1974, I was coming down the steps of a hotel in Yalta, during President Nixon's final summit, and there was Kim Willenson in the lobby. He had spent much of the preceding decade in Southeast Asia, and was now a respected, veteran correspondent for UPI. We had a couple of beers together in the hotel bar.

         * * *

Elected to the student affairs committee the second semester, I went to the dean's office and asked that, among the fifty or so speakers and panelists to be brought to the Journalism School at year's end, conservative journalists also be included.

"Excellent idea, Pat," Dean Barrett said, "why don't you go work me up a list?" I thought and thought—and went to him with only two names: William F. Buckley, Jr., and George Sokolsky, whom I had heard debate Senators Ken Keating and Harrison Williams on campus. (Afterwards, I had gone up and introduced myself to Sokolsky, who had been my father's journalistic hero after Pegler. Though Sokolsky had a thundering voice, he seemed old and frail and his grip was feeble when I shook hands with him. Still, to me, he was a historic figure who had actually been inside Russia only a few years after the revolution; and had personally known Stalin, Trotsky, Bukharin, Zinoviev, Kamenev, and all the old Bolsheviks who had launched the Ten Days That Shook the World.)

The dean nodded at my two names, said both were acceptable, and then said, "Fine, Pat, now which of the two would you like us to invite?" He was not joking and he was not being hostile; that was the attitude at the school. We conservatives were Hare Krishnas. Of course, we had a right to our strange beliefs, and we must not be discriminated against. But we were not taken seriously, as representing other than some aberrant strain of thought that had resurfaced somehow in the Eisenhower years and that was difficult to accord any great respect.

Students who wrote tough articles about the John Birch Society were praised; they were "out there—on the cutting edge of social change," as one professor repeatedly put it.

Once, when I covered a Ban-the-Bomb demonstration, I decided to follow the participants into a bar. (They thought I was sympathetic.) There, the demonstrators confided, while I listened and took notes, how indispensable it was, to euchre good publicity, to bring along a baby in a baby carriage as a prop—even if they had to borrow someone else's baby. The press would always photograph a woman pushing a baby carriage, they said; this tactic always got them into the paper. "Was this papoose a ringer?" I asked. No, they said; but we've used one before. So, I wrote up both what they had demonstrated about, and how they manipulated the press. I was led to understand I was letting my opinion get in the way of the real story.

But while I had different beliefs and heroes, the professors and teachers graded me as fairly as I had a right to expect. Penn Kimball, an unapologetic liberal (who later discovered some of his liberal colleagues had blacklisted him for a government job, by falsely suggesting he was a security risk, and who wrote a book about it called *The File*), gave me an A in his course. Virtually all my other grades the second semester were B and B+; I was improving by the week, and George Barrett even thought they should consider me for one of three traveling fellowships given the top students in the class. And the dean at Columbia, Edward Barrett (no relation to George), who had served as Assistant Secretary of Defense in the Eisenhower Administration, was always gracious.

When I went to Columbia, I had determined to sever all ties of economic dependency, and make it on my own. So, I wrote the school that I could expect no financial help from my parents. The $1,500 Clapp-Poliak scholarship I had won covered the $1,400 tuition; the money I had earned as an auditor, plus a $1,000 student loan, covered room and board at International House. But, as the spring of 1962 approached, I was tapped out. So, I went home one weekend and retrieved my sole asset, my DKW, and brought it to New Jersey for my cousin, Bucky Boy, to unload. (A pretty little German car, the color of a lemon, the DKW—the initials were Bavarian for "remarkable little wonder"—had been sold to me for $1,700 by the manager of Capitol Cadillac, Howard Jobe, when I had gone there to buy a Renault. That DKW was no end of trouble. It sounded like a washing machine that had thrown its bearings; and the tires were the size of Soap Box Derby wheels. Once, the air-cooled engine had overheated on the way home from Somers Point, New Jersey. With Peter Sommer and Hatchet in the car, the DKW exploded on the Baltimore–Washington Parkway, splitting the engine block. For two years, the little lemon had eaten up my savings, but it had become my trademark. You could spot it a mile away maneuvering beautifully in traffic. In one humorous incident, Cricket and I had taken it back, for the umpteenth time, to Capitol Cadillac for repairs, and while I was walking toward the showroom, I saw the salesmen looking out at me with apprehension in their faces. Absentmindedly, I had brought along my squash racket, which I was swinging energetically back and forth. The salesmen thought I was coming to settle accounts with Howard Jobe, for having sold me the little lemon.)

After running ads for several weeks, dropping the price every few days, Bucky Boy finally dumped my DKW for $300 on "Smiling Sam" Rosenberg, "the Fairview Cowboy," a used-car dealer and the only man I ever knew who had his picture on his checks. When I showed the check to the dean, with "Smiling Sam's" photograph on it, in a cowboy hat with a cigar, he said, "I'd cash that right away."

Still, I was short. So, I went back to the dean, and told him my situation.

"We have a special scholarship fund for students who have shown great improvement," he said; "I think you qualify." He made out a check for $100 to me to finish the year. It was an act of generosity and graciousness, for which I am permanently grateful.

In yet another sense, Columbia in the early '60s was more a challenge to me than to the other students. Where conservative clichés were ridiculed, by faculty and students alike, liberal clichés were accepted as recitals of the catechism in which all educated men and women supposedly believed. The total disparagement with which Columbia viewed my heavily Catholic education is something I inadvertently discovered, going through my records twenty-five years later. On my Georgetown transcript, sent to the admissions committee, a line had been drawn through all my theology and philosophy grades from college, crossing out some forty hours of course work. As though these grades were for basket-weaving, they were not even factored into Columbia's assessment of my true grades from Georgetown. A knowledge of Catholic theology and Christian philosophy was apparently irrelevant to the making of a modern journalist.

That liberals were unprepared for the radical onslaught of the '60s, and for our conservative counterreformation in the '70s, came as no surprise. They had it too easy. They rarely had to defend their beliefs in the colleges and universities they attended. Liberal opinions were received as revealed truth, while I was ideologically embattled night and day in the newsroom, at the West End Bar, at classmate Fred Appel's TGIF parties, at the International House—with everybody and about everything.

When Khrushchev detonated his fifty-eight-megaton superbomb over Novaya Zemla, the greatest man-made explosion in history, and laughed about how his scientists had miscalculated the force of the explosion, some of the professors almost "freaked out," in the parlance of the time. I can recall Larry Pinkham expostulating about what would happen to Manhattan if that bomb were dropped on us.

But, to me, Khrushchev was a blusterer; this superbomb was set off for propaganda effect; and, from Pinkham's reaction, it was working. From my reading of history, the Soviet Union had never attacked a prepared and powerful nation; they had cut a devil's bargain with the Third Reich; they had preyed upon weak and defenseless countries like prostrate Poland, Finland, the tiny Baltic Republics, Romania, and Iran; and they had only attacked Imperial Japan after the United States had broken Japan completely. We had nothing to fear from the Soviet arsenal—so long as we kept our own nuclear gun pointed at their head and were prepared to retaliate if they dared to attack. Materialist to the core, they wanted to die even less than we did.

Another day Larry Pinkham told us how shaken he had been, when, working in daily journalism, he saw a fourteen-year-old Puerto Rican kid, who had been charged with murder, described by all the tabloids as "the Umbrella Man"; and he spoke in anguish of how such terrible journalism precluded a fair trial. But where were his priorities? Tabloid labeling seemed to me less of a problem than rising crime, when Columbia girls were being warned to stay out of Morningside Heights for fear of being raped by some of the little Umbrella Men below, whose adverse publicity so exercised the sensitive social conscience of Professor Larry Pinkham.

❖ ❖ ❖

Looking back, while I was indeed an oddity at that elite school— right-wing student in a citadel of liberalism, a Goldwaterite studying to become a journalist, an educational product of nuns and Jesuits who accepted as true what Columbia regarded as mystical nonsense—it was they who were falling out of touch with America.

Repeatedly, students would come up to me and say, "Now, tell me, Pat, why did you hit Willenson?" When I told them the abusive language he had thrown into my face, it was clear that they felt this could not be the *real* reason. "It was political, wasn't it?" they would press.

But, my brothers and the friends I grew up with would have understood in a second. They would have reacted the same way; a thirty-second fistfight was no big deal. Indeed, their question to my classmates who accepted that kind of abusive language would have been, "Why the hell didn't you hit him?" To us, someone who threw that kind of language in your direction was insulting you and looking for a fight; and, if you took that without responding something was wrong with you, not him. The only reason America sits still for the kind of abuse vomited upon us routinely at the U.N. is because, too often, we have had the wrong kind of Americans sitting there.

Philosophically and politically, the young-journalist and student-editor types at Columbia may have been compatible with the professors, but they and the professors were living in another country, as far as Middle America was concerned. The politicians they admired—Stevenson Democrats and Lindsay-Rockefeller Republicans—were on the way out. Both would become irrelevant, as the years went by; as would many of the causes in which they devoutly believed, like the U.N.

Half a century ago, the newsmen who wrote for major papers, as often as not, were high-school graduates or dropouts, tough men from working-class families who had never cut their roots, and who respected the values they had learned in neighborhood and home and church. In Washington, today, the journalists all come from somewhere else; but most consider themselves at home here. Part of our permanent governing elite now, they are never going back whence they came. But their views on social, political, and foreign policy issues are further and further removed from the convictions of the heartland. The gulf between the American people and their national press is not closing; it is widening; and the distance is breeding a distrust "out there" deeper than anything dreamed of in 1962.

Mary Gordon

'71 BARNARD COLLEGE

The writer Mary Gordon won the 1997 O. Henry Award for her short story "City Life." She has been compared to figures as diverse as Jane Austen and Jean-Paul Sartre; among her novels are Final Payments *(1978) and* The Other Side *(1989). In 2000, she wrote a collection of autobiographical essays,* Seeing Through Places, *excerpted here.*

From the place where I stand at the top of this hill there is a view, a glimpse, rather, of river. In some seasons, like this one, late summer, it is far more glimpse than view. There is a thick curtain of trees and then, cut out, a hand-size triangle of pewter or of tin.

This hill is not really a hill but a narrow street beginning at the gates of a university campus. Columbia: designed by the murdered Stanford White, shot by a madman for a woman's love. Even the blueprints of the place are soaked in narrative.

The first time I stood at the top of this hill was in the spring of 1966. My two friends and I had just been admitted to Barnard and we were coming to look in on some classes on a day off from our Catholic school in Queens. It must have been a Holy Day of Obligation, otherwise there would have been no reason for Barnard to be in session while we were free. Perhaps it was Holy Thursday or the Feast of the Ascension. Perhaps we lied to our parents and said we would go to Mass first.

Was it a punishment for that lie that led us to get off the subway at the wrong One Hundred Sixteenth Street—One Hundred Sixteenth and Lenox

Avenue? The man in the token booth took one look at our clothes and faces and guessed our mistake without our having to say anything. "This isn't Broadway, girls," he said, as if we were hick starlets with straw valises. He told us to take the subway back down to Forty-second Street, then the shuttle, then the West Side train uptown. We didn't listen. We walked across One Hundred Sixteenth Street, through Harlem, through Morningside Park, fearless, pretending we felt at home, knowing that our parents would be appalled.

I remember seeing the green roofs of Columbia and feeling a sense of rightness that stayed with me as I crossed the street to Barnard's Millbank Hall, where I climbed the marble staircase to the admissions office. From there I was sent to Barnard Hall, where the English classes were. I got off the elevator and looked in the mirror on the fourth floor of Barnard Hall. I said to myself, Yes, I'm here.

Thirty-two years later (almost the entire life span of Jesus Christ) I stand in front of the same mirror, a teacher now, waiting for the same elevator. And again I say to myself, Yes (but perhaps with more emphasis on the monosyllable), yes, I'm here.

But what do I mean by here? And how did I get here? Or more properly, how did I get back?

                        * * *

When I first came here, in 1967, the world that I thought I was traveling to, a world of formality, embellishment, grandeur, and fineness, was in the process of disappearing. Or at least of being so radically questioned in precisely those aspects I had dreamed of that I had no time to revel in my dearly bought reward.

No sooner had I arrived at Barnard, in the clothes I'd saved my summer wages to buy, clothes whose labels I had coveted—Villager, Papagallo, Pendelton—that I realized they were all wrong, and a person wearing those clothes was not the person I wanted to be at all. I had hardly got to know my new friends—non-Catholics from places like Missouri and North Dakota—when I was, along with my two old friends from high school, riding on a bus to Washington to the Pentagon march, for which I bought a new pair of bell-bottomed jeans.

Only now do I understand the speed at which we then were forced to travel. In six months, we went from processions where we crowned a statue of the Virgin with a wreath of flowers to linking hands with strangers, learning what to do in case of tear gas or cops run amok. The same girls who in the spring had been singing, "O Mary we crown thee with blossoms today/Queen of the Angels, Queens of the May," were chanting, the following autumn, "Hey, hey LBJ, how many kids did you kill today?"

And in my second semester of freshman year at Columbia, the riots occurred. A year earlier I had been presiding over student council meetings where we had to decide on an appropriate punishment for girls who'd been caught getting into a car with a boy while still in uniform; now I was sitting in on teach-ins on the lawn in front of Butler Library where we contemplated "burning the whole fucking place down."

I had to hide my horror at the idea of destroying those marble staircases, the reading room with its long, monastic tables and its crystal chandeliers and its beautiful books that smelled of learning. But I had to believe that property was less important than the flesh of children, which was being burned by the napalm that was manufactured by Dow Chemical, from which the university accepted money. I had to understand that the ornate green roofs remained intact, the lights in the chandeliers were kept lit, because of money earned from the burning flesh of children. And I knew that if I had to cast my lot with some group, it had to be the group pledged to stop the burning of children's flesh. I knew this, not from my new friends, or from what I was learning in my classes or in teach-ins, but from the words of the Gospel: "Where your treasure lies, there also doth your heart lie."

I prayed that the beautiful buildings would not be burned down, that the beautiful books would not be destroyed. I prayed furtively, guiltily; I wouldn't have dreamt of going into a church. The archdiocese was presided over by Cardinal Spellman, a great supporter of Vietnam. If I went into a church, everyone would know I was having sex, and would order me to stop, and I knew I wouldn't because I liked it much too much. I understood that there were priests who opposed the war, but they were saying folk masses, and I couldn't stand singing about transubstantiation to the tune of Peter, Paul and Mary songs, and I suspected they loved themselves too much for consecrating whole wheat bread instead of Hosts, and that, despite the antiwar protest and the whole wheat bread, they would still be telling me to stop having sex. I needed formality, but formality was in the hands of men who were shouting about communism and free love, just as the country was in the hands of men who were lying about burning the flesh of children.

It was hard for me to recognize the world. Not only was I not a virgin, I was in love with a homosexual; my friends were dealing drugs and having abortions. Some days we lay around all day in an apartment on One Hundred Nineteenth Street, where not only the walls but the windows were painted black. We listened to Joplin and Hendrix and the Stones; *Marjorie Morningstar* and Bloomingdale's and the Museum of Natural History were never mentioned. We were sometimes surprised when we went outside to find that the sun was still shining.

But I did not stop going to my classes, except during the riots. Except for those weeks, I went on entering the buildings of Barnard, which comforted me with their solidity—their bookish smell, the width of the staircase, the cool stone of the banisters. I was taught by women who told me I was gifted, well-born women with hair hanging down their backs or in coiled blond knots at their napes, who introduced me to Chaucer and Spenser and Auden, elegant men in houndstooth jackets who smoked pipes and told of people whose names I confused: Arthur Henry Hallam, Arthur Hugh Clough.

I discovered that the Romantic poets were not romantic and that I did not like them, except for Keats; that I preferred the Renaissance. So after reading Sidney and Donne and Herbert and Marvell and the Revenge Tragedians, I took a course on Tasso and Ariosto, taught by an Italian, and on Ronsard, taught by a Russian Jew brought up in France. I would hear a snatch of Hindemith or Monteverdi and spend the day in the library listening to music, earphones on my head like a radio announcer. I discovered the paintings of Van Eyck and took the bus across town on Friday afternoons to the Metropolitan to see them, forgetting that, only a short time before, I had prayed to the Madonnas that the other people in the museum only looked at and that because of that I had more in common with the kneeling donors than I did with the people I stood beside.

I could sense the material of my mind thinning, spreading, growing transparent; sometimes I was feverish with the excitement of what I was learning and my eyes felt dry and hot and overlarge, the skin around them felt abraded. After hours studying in the library, I would walk outside and the color of the sky at six o'clock on an October evening—slate blue, shot through with black— seemed as inviting and dangerous as if I were a child playing too late, too hard, and at any minute I might be called in. But I was not called in. I was told to stay out later, to travel farther: the world of ideas was mine. I belonged there; I could inhabit any region of it. My body, both overexcited and repressed from all that reading, would insist on movement. I would run down the hill toward Riverside Drive and let the wind bite into me, hear the buzz of the cars and watch the lights come on across the river.

My friends and I took the subway downtown to see movies starring Holly Woodlawn and we speculated that she might be a real genius and that maybe drag queens were on the existential cutting edge, and we wondered if we had to listen to the thinkers who told us that if we really loved our bodies we would eat our own menstrual blood. I knew myself a poet, but I didn't want to be a fake, like some others I suspected, so I set myself tasks so that I could honor my calling. I wrote villanelles and curtal sonnets and ghazals and translated from the Italian and revised all night. A teacher suggested that I might really be a fiction writer and I said, "No, of course I'm not, I'm a poet":

I am (can't you see) in love with form and its restrictions, so different from the unrestricted life which, as a poet, I intended to live.

And, most every night, unless I lied and said I was at a girlfriend's studying (I was probably in someone's bed, someone I may or may not have known well), even after days which I spent occupying buildings, I took the train back to my mother's house. My grandmother's house. Every night when I came home, my mother made us supper in the increasingly ramshackle kitchen, then went to bed where she drank herself into a stuporous sleep. In the room that my high school boyfriend and I painted yellow, where the skeleton of the dead bird might, for all I knew, still have been, I talked on the phone to my friends coming down from bad acid trips or coming home from parties at Warhol's Factory.

But I turned in my papers; and I wrote more poetry than anyone, and Barnard rewarded me. I won all the literary prizes. One summer I was given a grant so that for the first time since I was fifteen I didn't have to work in an office for a whole summer. Instead, I studied Italian, like one of the girls who could go home to Central Park West. That summer I told my mother I was getting a room in the newly built dorm, on One Hundred Twentieth Street and Amsterdam, that I would pay for it. The week before I was to move in, she fell and fractured her leg in three places. Heartlessly, I refused to give up my plans for the dorm, and I arranged for one of her cousins to care for her. The cousin made it clear that she thought I was a selfish monster. I paid no attention. I came home every weekend to a house where the dust made me asthmatic and I ate sweet foods to the point of nausea, and past it, to the point of retching in the toilet of the gray bathroom that I had never liked.

Paul Auster

'69 Columbia College, '70 MA

> *Today Paul Auster is best known as a novelist, but he worked for a number of years as a poet and translator before the 1985 publication of* City of Glass. *In 1994, he collaborated with the director Wayne Wang on two films,* Smoke *and* Blue in the Face, *set in Brooklyn and rooted in an Auster short story. His most recent novel is 2003's* Oracle Night; *his 1989 novel* Moon Palace *provides the following selection.*

Throughout the winter and early spring, I had stored my food on the windowledge outside the apartment. A number of things had frozen solid during the coldest months (sticks of butter, containers of cottage cheese), but nothing that was not edible after it had thawed. The main problem had been guarding against soot and pigeon shit, but I soon learned to wrap my provisions in a plastic shopping bag before leaving them outside. After one of these bags was blown off the ledge in a storm, I began anchoring them with a string to the radiator in the room. I grew quite adept at managing this system, and because the gas was mercifully included in the rent (which meant that I did not have to worry about losing my stove), the food situation seemed well under control. But that was during the cold weather. The season had changed now, and with the sun lingering in the sky for thirteen or fourteen hours a day, the ledge did more harm than good. The milk curdled; the juice turned rank; the butter melted into glistening pools of yellow slime. I suffered through a number of these disasters, and then I began to overhaul my diet, realizing that I had to shun all goods that perished in the heat. On June twelfth, I sat down and charted out my new regimen.

Powdered milk, instant coffee, small packages of bread—those would be my staples—and every day I would eat the same thing: eggs, the cheapest, most nutritious food known to man. Now and then I would splurge on an apple or an orange, and if the craving ever got too strong, I would treat myself to a hamburger or a can of stew. The food would not spoil, and (theoretically at any rate) I would not starve. Two eggs a day, soft-boiled to perfection in two and a half minutes, two slices of bread, three cups of coffee, and as much water as I could drink. If not inspiring, the plan at least had a certain geometrical elegance. Given the paucity of options to choose from, I tried to take heart from this.

I did not starve, but there was rarely a moment when I did not feel hungry. I often dreamt about food, and my nights that summer were filled with visions of feasts and gluttony: platters of steak and lamb, succulent pigs floating in on trays, castlelike cakes and desserts, gigantic bowls of fruit. During the day, my stomach cried out to me constantly, gurgling with a rush of unappeased juices, hounding me with its emptiness, and it was only through sheer struggle that I was able to ignore it. By no means plump to begin with, I continued to lose weight as the summer wore on. Every now and then, I would drop a penny into a drugstore Exacto scale to see what was happening to me. From 154 in June, I fell to 139 in July, and then to 123 in August. For someone who measured slightly over six feet, this began to be dangerously little. Skin and bone can go just so far, after all, and then you reach a point when serious damage is done.

I was trying to separate myself from my body, taking the long road around my dilemma by pretending it did not exist. Others had traveled this road before me, and all of them had discovered what I finally discovered for myself: the mind cannot win over matter, for once the mind is asked to do too much it quickly shows itself to be matter as well. In order to rise above my circumstances, I had to convince myself that I was no longer real, and the result was that all reality began to waver for me. Things that were not there would suddenly appear before my eyes, then vanish. A glass of cold lemonade, for example. A newspaper with my name in the headline. My old suit lying on the bed, perfectly intact. Once I even saw a former version of myself blundering around the room, searching drunkenly in the corners for something he couldn't find. These hallucinations lasted only an instant, but they would continue to resonate inside me for hours on end. Then there were the periods when I simply lost track of myself. A thought would occur to me, and by the time I followed it to its conclusion, I would look up and discover that it was night. There was no way to account for the hours I had lost. On other occasions, I found myself chewing imaginary food, smoking imaginary cigarettes, blowing imaginary smoke rings into the air around me. Those were the worst moments of all, perhaps, for I realized then that I could no longer trust myself. My mind had begun to drift, and once that happened, I was powerless to stop it.

Most of these symptoms did not appear until mid-July. Prior to that, I dutifully read through the last of Uncle Victor's books, then sold them off to Chandler up the street. The closer I got to the end, however, the more trouble the books gave me. I could feel my eyes making contact with the words on the page, but no meanings rose up to me anymore, no sounds echoed in my head. The black marks seemed wholly bewildering, an arbitrary collection of lines and curves that divulged nothing but their own muteness. Eventually, I did not even pretend to understand what I was reading. I would pull a book from the box, open it to the first page, and then move my finger along the first line. When I came to the end, I would start in on the second line, and then the third line, and so on down to the bottom of the page. That was how I finished the job: like a blind man reading braille. If I couldn't see the words, at least I wanted to touch them. Things had become so bad for me by then, this actually seemed to make sense. I touched all the words in those books, and because of that I earned the right to sell them.

As chance would have it, I took the last ones up to Chandler on the same day the astronauts landed on the moon. I received a little more than nine dollars from the sale, and as I walked back down Broadway afterward, I decided to stop in at Quinn's Bar and Grill, a small local hangout that stood on the southeast corner of 108th Street. The weather was extremely hot that day, and there didn't seem to be any harm in splurging on a couple of ten-cent beers. I sat on a stool at the bar next to three or four of the regulars, enjoying the dim lights and the coolness of the air conditioning. The big color television set was on, glowing eerily over the bottles of rye and bourbon, and that was how I happened to witness the event. I saw the two padded figures take their first steps in that airless world, bouncing like toys over the landscape, driving a golf cart through the dust, planting a flag in the eye of what had once been the goddess of love and lunacy. Radiant Diana, I thought, image of all that is dark within us. Then the president spoke. In a solemn, deadpan voice, he declared this to be the greatest event since the creation of man. The old-timers at the bar laughed when they heard this, and I believe I managed to crack a smile or two myself. But for all the absurdity of that remark, there was one thing no one could challenge: since the day he was expelled from Paradise, Adam had never been this far from home.

For a short time after that, I lived in a state of nearly perfect calm. My apartment was bare now, but rather than discourage me as I had thought it would, this emptiness seemed to give me comfort. I am quite at a loss to explain it, but all of a sudden my nerves became steadier, and for the next three or four days I almost began to recognize myself again. It is curious to use such a word in this context, but for that brief period following the sale of Uncle Victor's last books, I would even go so far as to call myself *happy.* Like an epileptic on the brink of a seizure, I had entered that strange half-world in which everything starts to shine, to give off a new and astonishing clarity. I didn't do much during those days. I paced around my room, I stretched out on my mattress, I wrote down my thoughts in a notebook. It didn't matter. Even the act of doing nothing seemed important to me, and I had no qualms about letting the hours pass in idleness. Every now and then, I would plant myself between the two windows and watch the Moon Palace sign. Even that was enjoyable, and it always seemed to generate a series of interesting thoughts. Those thoughts are somewhat obscure to me now—clusters of wild associations, a rambling circuit of reveries—but at the time I felt they were terribly significant. Perhaps the word *moon* had changed for me after I saw men wandering around its surface. Perhaps I was struck by the coincidence of having met a man named Neil Armstrong in Boise, Idaho, and then watching a man by the same name fly off into outer space. Perhaps I was simply delirious with hunger, and the lights of the sign had transfixed me. I can't be sure of any of it, but the fact was that the words *Moon Palace* began to haunt my mind with all the mystery and fascination of an oracle. Everything was mixed up in it at once: Uncle Victor and China, rocket ships and music, Marco Polo and the American West. I would look out at the sign and start to think about electricity. That would lead me to the blackout during my freshman year, which in turn would lead me to the baseball games played at Wrigley Field, which would then lead me back to Uncle Victor and the memorial candles burning on my windowsill. One thought kept giving way to another, spiraling into ever larger masses of connectedness. The idea of voyaging into the unknown, for example, and the parallels between Columbus and the astronauts. The discovery of America as a failure to reach China; Chinese food and my empty stomach; thought, as in food for thought, and the head as a palace of dreams. I would think: the Apollo Project; Apollo, the god of music; Uncle Victor and the Moon Men traveling out West. I would think: the West; the war against the Indians; the war in Vietnam, once called Indochina. I would think: weapons, bombs, explosions; nuclear clouds in the deserts of Utah and Nevada; and then I would ask myself—why does the American West look so much like the landscape of the moon? It went on and on like that, and the more I opened myself to these secret correspondences, the closer I felt to understanding some fundamental truth about the world. I was going mad, perhaps, but I nevertheless felt a tremendous power surging through me, a gnostic joy that penetrated deep into the heart of things. Then, very suddenly, as suddenly as I had gained this power, I lost it. I had been living inside my thoughts for three or four days, and one morning I woke up and found that I was somewhere else: back in the world of fragments, back in the world of hunger and bare white walls. I struggled to recapture the equilibrium of the previous days, but I couldn't do it. The world was pressing down on me again, and I could barely catch my breath.

I entered a new period of desolation. Stubbornness had kept me going until then, but little by little I felt my resolve weaken, and by August first I was ready to cave in. I did my best to contact a number of friends, fully prepared to ask for a loan, but nothing much came of it. A few exhausting walks in the heat, a pocketful of squandered dimes. It was summer, and everyone seemed to have left the city. Even Zimmer, the one person I knew I could count on, had strangely vanished from sight. I walked up to his apartment on Amsterdam Avenue and 120th Street several times, but no one answered the bell. I slipped messages into the mailbox and under the door, but still there was no response. Much later, I learned that Zimmer had moved to another apartment. When I asked him why he hadn't given me his new address, he said that I had told him I was spending the summer in Chicago. I had forgotten this lie, of course, but by then I had made up so many lies, I could no longer keep track of them.

Not knowing that Zimmer was gone, I kept going to the old apartment and leaving messages under the door. One Sunday morning in early August, the inevitable finally happened. I rang the bell, fully expecting no one to be there, even turning to leave as I pushed the button, when I heard movement from within the apartment: the scraping of a chair, the thump of footsteps, a cough. A flood of relief washed through me, but all came to nothing an instant later when the door opened. The person who should have been Zimmer was not. It was someone else entirely: a young man with a dark, curly beard and hair that hung down to his shoulders, I gathered that he had just woken up, since he didn't have anything on but a pair of undershorts. "What can I do for you?" he asked, studying me with a friendly if somewhat puzzled expression, and at that moment I heard laughter from the kitchen (a mixture of male and female voices) and realized that I had walked in on some kind of party.

"I think I'm in the wrong place," I said. "I was looking for David Zimmer."

"Oh," said the stranger, not missing a beat, "you must be Fogg. I was wondering when you'd turn up again."

It was a brutal day outside—scalding, dog-day heat—and the walk had nearly done me in. As I stood in front of the door now, with sweat dripping into my eyes and my muscles feeling all spongy and stupid, I wondered if I had heard the stranger correctly. My impulse was to turn around and run away, but I suddenly felt so weak that I was afraid of passing out. I put my hand on the doorframe to steady myself and said, "I'm sorry, but would you say that again? I don't think I caught it the first time."

"I said you must be Fogg," the stranger repeated. "It's really quite simple. If you're looking for Zimmer, then you must be Fogg. Fogg was the one who left all the messages under the door."

"That's very astute," I said, letting out a small fluttering sigh. "I don't suppose you know where Zimmer is now."

"Sorry. I don't have the slightest idea."

Again, I began mustering my courage to leave, but just as I was about to turn away, I saw that the stranger was staring at me. It was an odd and penetrating look, aimed directly at my face. "Is something wrong?" I asked him.

"I was just wondering if you're a friend of Kitty's."

"Kitty?" I said. "I don't know anyone named Kitty. I've never met anyone named Kitty in my life."

"You're wearing the same shirt she is. It made me think you must be connected to her somehow."

I looked down at my chest and saw that I had a Mets T-shirt on. I had bought it at a rummage sale earlier in the year for ten cents. "I don't even like the Mets," I said. "The Cubs are the team I root for."

"It's a weird coincidence," the stranger continued, paying no attention to what I had said. "Kitty is going to love it. She loves things like that."

Before I had a chance to protest, I found myself being led by the arm into the kitchen. There I came upon a group of five or six people sitting around the table eating Sunday breakfast. The table was crowded with food: bacon and eggs, a full pot of coffee, bagels and cream cheese, a platter of smoked fish. I had not seen anything like this in months, and I scarcely knew how to react. It was as though I had suddenly been put down in the middle of a fairy tale. I was the hungry child who had been lost in the woods, and now I had found the enchanted house, the cottage built of food.

"Look everyone," announced my grinning, bare-chested host. "It's Kitty's twin brother."

At that point I was introduced around the table. Everyone smiled at me and said hello, and I did my best to smile back. It turned out that most of them were students at Juilliard—musicians, dancers, singers. The host's name was Jim or John, and he had just moved into Zimmer's old apartment the day before. The others had been out partying that night, someone said, and instead of going home afterward, they had decided to burst in on Jim or John with an impromptu housewarming breakfast. That explained his lack of clothing (he had been asleep when they rang the bell) and the abundance of food I saw before me. I nodded politely when they told me all this, but I only pretended to be listening. The fact was that I couldn't have cared less, and by the time the story was over, I had forgotten everyone's name. For want of anything better to do, I studied my twin sister, a small Chinese girl of nineteen or twenty with silver bracelets on both wrists and a beaded Navaho band around her head. She returned my look with a smile—an exceptionally warm smile, I felt, filled with humor and complicity—and then I turned my attention back to the table, powerless to keep my eyes off it for very long. I realized that I was on the verge of embarrassing myself. The smells from the food had begun to torture me, and as I stood there waiting for them to invite me to sit down, it was all I could do not to grab something off the table and shove it in my mouth.

Kitty was the one who finally broke the ice. "Now that my brother is here," she said, obviously entering into the spirit of the moment, "the least we can do is ask him to join us for breakfast." I wanted to kiss her for having read my mind like that. An awkward moment followed, however, when no extra chair could be found, but again Kitty came to the rescue, gesturing for me to sit between her and the person to her right. I promptly wedged myself into the spot, planting one buttock on each chair. A plate was set before me along with the necessary accoutrements: knife and fork, glass and cup, napkin and spoon. After that, I entered a miasma of feeding and forgetting. It was an infantile response, but once the food entered my mouth, I wasn't able to control myself. I chomped down one dish after another, devouring whatever they put in front of me, and eventually it was as though I had lost my mind. Since the generosity of the others seemed infinite, I kept on eating until everything on the table had disappeared. That is how I remember it, in any case. I gorged myself for fifteen or twenty minutes, and when I was done, the only thing left was a pile of whitefish bones. Nothing more than that. I search my memory for something else, but I can never find it. Not one morsel. Not even a crust of bread.

It was only then that I noticed how intently the others were staring at me. Had it been as bad as that? I wondered. Had I slobbered and made a spectacle of myself? I turned to Kitty and gave her a feeble smile. She did not seem disgusted so much as stunned. That reassured me somewhat, but I wanted to make amends for any offense I might have caused the others. That was the least I could do, I thought: sing for my grub, make them forget I had just licked their plates clean. As I waited for an opportunity to enter the conversation, I became increasingly aware of how good it felt to be sitting next to my long-lost twin. From the drift of the talk around me, I gathered that she was a dancer, and there was no question that she did a lot more for her Mets T-shirt than I did for mine. It was hard not to be impressed, and as she went on chatting and laughing with the others, I kept on sneaking little glances at her. She wore no makeup and no bra, but there was a constant tinkling of bracelets and earrings as she moved. Her breasts were nicely formed, and she displayed them with an admirable nonchalance, neither flaunting them nor pretending they were not there. 1 found her beautiful, but more than that I liked the way she held herself, the way she did not seem to be paralyzed by her beauty as so many beautiful girls did. Perhaps it was the freedom of her gestures, the blunt, down-to-earth quality I heard in her voice. This was not a pampered, middle-class kid like the others, but someone who knew her way around, who had managed to learn things for herself. The fact that she seemed to welcome the nearness of my body, that she did not squirm away from my shoulder or leg, that she even allowed her bare arm to linger against mine—these were things that drove me to the point of foolishness.

I found an opening into the conversation a few moments later. Someone started talking about the moon landing, and then someone else declared that it had never really happened. The whole thing was a hoax, he said, a television extravaganza staged by the government to get our minds off the war. "People will believe anything they're told to believe," that person added, "even some rinky-dink bullshit filmed in a Hollywood studio." That was all I needed to make my entrance. Jumping in with the most outrageous remark I could think of, I calmly asserted that not only had last month's moon landing been genuine, it was by no means the first time it had happened. Men had been going to the moon for hundreds of years, I said, perhaps even thousands. Everyone tittered when I said that, but then I launched into my best comico-pedantic style, and for the next ten minutes I showered them with a history of moon lore, replete with references to Lucian, Godwin, and others. I wanted to impress them with how much I knew, but I also wanted to make them laugh. Intoxicated by the meal I had just finished, determined to prove to Kitty that I was not like anyone she had ever met, I worked myself into top form, and my sharp, staccato delivery soon had them all in stitches. Then I began to describe Cyrano's voyage to the moon, and someone interrupted me. Cyrano de Bergerac wasn't real, the person said, he was a character in a play, a make-believe man. I couldn't let this error go uncorrected, and so I made a short digression to tell them the story of Cyrano's life. I sketched out his early days as a soldier, discussed his career as a philosopher and poet, and then dwelled at some length on the various hardships he encountered over the years: financial troubles, an agonizing bout with syphilis, his battles with the authorities over his radical views. I told them how he had finally found a protector in the Duc d'Arpajon, and then, just three years later, how he had been killed on a Paris street when a building stone fell from a rooftop and landed on his head. I paused dramatically to allow the grotesqueness and humor of this tragedy to sink in. "He was only thirty-six at the time," I said, "and to this day no one knows if it was an accident or not. Had one of his enemies murdered him, or was it simply a matter of chance, of blind fate pouring destruction down from the sky? Alas, poor Cyrano. This was no figment, my friends. He was a creature of flesh and blood, a real man who lived in the real world, and in 1649 he wrote a book about his trip to the moon. Since it's a firsthand account, I don't see why anyone should doubt what he says. According to Cyrano, the moon is a world like this one. When seen from that world, our earth looks just like the moon does from here. The Garden of Eden is located on the moon, and when Adam and Eve ate from the Tree of Knowledge, God banished them to the earth. Cyrano first attempts to travel to the moon by strapping bottles of lighter-than-air dew to his body, but after reaching the Middle Distance, he floats back to earth, landing among a tribe of naked Indians in New France. There he builds a machine that eventually takes him to his destination, which no doubt goes to show that America has always been the ideal place for moon launchings. The people he encounters on the moon are eighteen feet tall and walk on all fours. They speak two different languages, but neither language has any words in it. The first, used by the common people, is an intricate code of pantomime gestures that calls for constant movement from all parts of the body. The second language is spoken by the upper classes, and it consists of pure sound, a complex but unarticulated humming that closely resembles music. The moon people do not eat by swallowing food but by smelling it. Their money is poetry—actual poems, written out on pieces of paper whose value is determined by the worth of the poem itself. The worst crime is virginity, and young people are expected to show disrespect for their parents. The longer one's nose, the more noble one's character is considered to be. Men with short noses are castrated, for the moon people would rather die out as a race than be forced to live with such ugliness. There are talking books and traveling cities. When a great philosopher dies, his friends drink his blood and eat his flesh. Bronze penises hang from the waists of men—in the same way that seventeenth-century Frenchmen used to carry swords. As a moon man explains to the befuddled Cyrano: Is it not better to honor the tools of life than the tools of death? Cyrano spends a good part of the book in a cage. Because he is so small, the moon people think he must be a parrot without feathers. In the end, a giant black man throws him back to earth with the Anti-Christ."

I rattled on like that for several more minutes, but all the talk had worn me down, and I could feel my inspiration beginning to flag. Midway through my last speech (on Jules Verne and the Baltimore Gun Club), it abandoned me entirely. My head shrank, then grew enormously large; I saw peculiar lights and comets darting behind my eyes; my stomach began to rumble, to bulge with dagger-thrusts of pain, and suddenly I felt I was going to be sick. Without a word of warning, I broke off from my lecture, stood up from the table, and announced that I had to leave. "Thank you for your kindness," I said, "but urgent business calls me away. You are dear, good people, and I promise to remember you all in my will." It was a deranged performance, a madman's jig. I staggered out of the kitchen, knocking over a coffee cup in the process, and groped my way to the door. By the time I got there, Kitty was standing next to me. To this day, I still don't understand how she managed to get there before I did.

"You're a very strange brother," she said. "You look like a man, but then you turn yourself into a wolf. After that, the wolf becomes a talking machine. It's all mouths for you, isn't it? First the food, then the words—into the mouth and out of it. But you're forgetting the best thing mouths are made for. I'm your sister, after all, and I'm not going to let you leave without kissing me good-bye."

I started to apologize, but then, before I had a chance to say anything, Kitty stood on her toes, put her hand on the back of my neck, and kissed me—very tenderly, I felt, almost with compassion. I didn't know what to make of it. Was I supposed to treat it as a genuine kiss, or was it just one more part of the game? Before I could decide, I accidentally leaned my back against the door, and the door opened. It felt like a message to me, a secret cue that things had come to an end, and so, without another word, I continued backing out the door, turned as my feet crossed the sill, and left.

After that, there were no more free meals. When the second eviction notice arrived on August thirteenth, I was down to my last thirty-seven dollars. As it turned out, that was the same day the astronauts came to New York for their ticker-tape parade. The sanitation department later reported that three hundred tons of trash were thrown to the streets during the festivities. It was an all-time record, they said, the largest parade in the history of the world. I kept my distance from such things. Not knowing where to turn anymore, I left my apartment as seldom as possible, trying to conserve whatever strength I still had. A quick jaunt down to the corner for supplies and then back again, nothing more than that. My ass became raw from wiping myself with the brown paper bags I carried home from the market, but it was the heat I suffered from most. The air in the apartment was intolerable, a sweat-box stillness that bore down on me night and day, and no matter how wide I opened the windows, I could not coax a breeze to enter the room. My pores gushed constantly. Even sitting in one place put me in a sweat, and when I moved in any way at all, it provoked a flood. I drank as much water as possible. I took cold baths, doused my head under the tap, pressed wet towels against my face and neck and wrists. This offered scant comfort, but at least I was able to keep myself clean. The soap in the bathroom had shrunk to a small white sliver by then, and I had to keep it in reserve for shaving. Because my stock of razor blades was also running low, I limited myself to two shaves a week, carefully scheduling them to fall on the days when I went out to do my shopping. Although it probably didn't matter, it consoled me to think that I was managing to keep up appearances.

The essential thing was to plot my next move. But that was precisely what gave me the most trouble, the thing I could no longer do. I had lost the ability to think ahead, and no matter how hard I tried to imagine the future, I could not see it, I could not see anything at all. The only future that had ever belonged to me was the present I was living in now, and the struggle to remain in that present had gradually overwhelmed the rest. I had no ideas anymore. The moments unfurled one after the other, and at each moment the future stood before me as a blank, a white page of uncertainty. If life was a story, as Uncle Victor had often told me, and each man was the author of his own story, then I was making it up as I went along. I was working without a plot, writing each sentence as it came to me and refusing to think about the next. All well and good, perhaps, but the question was no longer whether I could write the story off the top of my head. I had already done that. The question was what I was supposed to do when the pen ran out of ink.

The clarinet was still there, sitting in its case by my bed. I am ashamed to admit it now, but I nearly buckled under and sold it. Worse than that, I even went so far as to take it to a music store one day to find out how much it was worth. When I saw that it wouldn't bring in enough to cover a month's rent, I abandoned the idea. But that was the only thing that spared me the indignity of going through with it. As time went on, I realized how close I had come to committing an unpardonable sin. The clarinet was my last link to Uncle Victor, and because it was the last, because there were no other traces of him, it carried the entire force of his soul within it. Whenever I looked at it, I was able to feel that force within myself. It was something to cling to, a piece of wreckage to keep me afloat.

Several days after my visit to the music store, a minor disaster nearly drowned me. The two eggs I was about to place in a pot of water and boil up for my daily meal slipped through my fingers and broke on the floor. Those were the last two eggs of my current supply, and I could not help feeling that this was the cruelest, most terrible thing that had ever happened to me. The eggs landed with an ugly splat. I remember standing there in horror as they oozed out over the floor. The sunny, translucent innards sank into the cracks, and suddenly there was muck everywhere, a bobbing slush of slime and shell. One yolk had miraculously survived the fall, but when I bent down to scoop it up, it slid out from under the spoon and broke apart. I felt as though a star were exploding, as though a great sun had just died. The yellow spread over the white and then began to swirl, turning into a vast nebula, a debris of interstellar gases. It was all too much for me—the last, imponderable straw. When this happened, I actually sat down and cried.

Struggling to get a grip on my emotions, I went out and splurged on a meal at the Moon Palace. It didn't help. Self-pity had given way to extravagance, and I loathed myself for surrendering to the impulse. To carry my disgust even further, I started off with egg drop soup, unable to resist the perversity of the pun. I followed it with fried dumplings, a plate of spicy shrimp, and a bottle of Chinese beer. The good this nourishment might have done me, however, was negated by the poison of my thoughts. I nearly gagged on the rice. This was no dinner, I told myself, it was a last meal, the food they serve up to a condemned man before they drag him off to the gallows. Forcing myself to chew it, to get it down my throat, I remembered a phrase from Raleigh's last letter to his wife, written on the eve of his execution: *My brains are broken.* Nothing could have been more apt than those words. I thought of Raleigh's chopped-off head, preserved by his wife in a glass box. I thought of Cyrano's head, crushed by the stone that fell on it. Then I imagined my head cracking open, splattering like the eggs that had fallen to the floor of my room. I felt my brains dribbling out of me. I saw myself in pieces.

I left an exorbitant tip for the waiter, then walked back to my building. When I entered the lobby, I made a routine stop by my mailbox and discovered there was something in it. Other than eviction notices, it was the first mail that had come for me that month. For a brief moment I fancied that some unknown benefactor had sent me a check, but then I examined the letter and saw that it was merely a notice of another kind. I was to report for my army physical on September sixteenth. Considering my condition at that moment, I took the news rather calmly. But by then it hardly seemed to matter where the stone fell. New York or Indochina, I said to myself, in the end they came to the same thing. If Columbus could confuse America with Cathay, who was I to quibble over geography? I entered my apartment and slipped the letter into Uncle Victor's clarinet case. Within a matter of minutes, I had managed to forget all about it.

I heard someone knocking at the door, but I decided it was not worth the effort to see who it was. I was thinking, and I did not want to be disturbed. Several hours later, I heard someone knock again. This second knocking was rather different from the first, and I did not think it could have been made by the same person. It was a coarse and brutal pounding, an angry fist that rattled the door on its hinges, whereas the other had been discreet, almost tentative: the work of a single knuckle, tapping its faint, intimate message on the wood. I turned these differences over in my mind for several hours, pondering the wealth of human information that was buried in such simple sounds. If the two knocks had been made by the same person, I thought, then the contrast would seem to indicate a terrible frustration, and I was hard-pressed to think of anyone who was that desperate to see me. This meant that my original interpretation was correct. There had been two people. One had come in friendship, the other had not. One was probably a woman, the other was not. I continued thinking about this until nightfall. As soon as I was aware of the darkness, I lit a candle, then went on thinking about it until I fell asleep. In all that time, however, it did not occur to me to ask who those people might have been. Even more to the point, I did not make any effort to understand why I did not want to know.

The pounding started again the next morning. By the time I was sufficiently awake to know I was not dreaming it, I heard a jangle of keys out in the hall—a loud, percussive thunder that exploded in my head. I opened my eyes, and at that moment a key entered the lock. The latch turned, the door swung open, and into the room stepped Simon Fernandez, the building superintendent. Sporting his customary two-day beard, he was dressed in the same khaki pants and white T-shirt that he had been wearing since the beginning of summer—a dingy outfit by now, smudged with grayish soot and the drippings of several dozen lunches. He looked directly into my eyes and pretended not to see me. Ever since Christmas, when I had failed to give him his annual tip (another expense struck from the books), Fernandez had turned hostile. No more hellos, no more talk about the weather, no more stories about his cousin from Ponce who almost made it as a shortstop with the Cleveland Indians. Fernandez had taken his revenge by acting as though I did not exist, and we had not exchanged a word in months. On this morning of mornings, however, there was an unexpected reversal of strategy. He sauntered around the room for several moments, tapping the walls as though inspecting them for damage, and then, passing by the bed for the second or third time, he stopped, turned, and did an exaggerated double-take as he noticed me at last. "Jesus Christ," he said. "Are you still here?"

"Still here," I said. "In a manner of speaking."

"You gotta be out today," Fernandez said. "Apartment's rented for the first of the month, you know, and Willie's coming with the painters tomorrow morning. You don't want no cops dragging you out of here, do you?"

"Don't worry. I'll be out in plenty of time."

Fernandez looked around the room with a proprietary air, then shook his head in disgust. "You've got some place here, my friend. If you don't mind me saying so, it reminds me of a coffin. One of those pine boxes they bury bums in."

"My decorator has been on vacation," I said. "We were planning to do the walls in robin's egg blue, but then we weren't sure if it would match the tile in the kitchen. We agreed to give it a little more thought before taking the plunge."

"Smart college boy like you. You got some kinda problem or what?"

"No problem. A few financial setbacks, that's all. The market has been down lately."

"You need money, you gotta work for it. The way I see it, you just sit around on your ass all day. Like some chimp in the zoo, you know what I mean? You can't pay the rent if you don't have no job."

"But I do have a job. I get up in the morning just like everyone else, and then I see if I can live through another day. That's full-time work. No coffee breaks, no weekends, no benefits or vacations. I'm not complaining, mind you, but the salary is pretty low."

"You sound like a fuck-up to me. A smart college boy fuck-up."

"You shouldn't overestimate college. It's not all it's cracked up to be."

"If I was you, I'd go see a doctor," said Fernandez, suddenly showing some sympathy. "I mean, just look at you. It's pretty sad, man. There ain't nothing there no more. Just a lot of bones."

"I've been on a diet. It's hard to look your best on two soft-boiled eggs a day."

"I don't know," said Fernandez, drifting off into his own thoughts. "Sometimes it's like everybody's gone crazy. If you wanna know what I think, it's those things they're shooting into space. All that weird shit, those satellites and rockets. You send people to the moon, something's gotta give. You know what I mean? It makes people do strange things. You can't fuck with the sky and expect nothing to happen."

He unfurled the copy of the *Daily News* he was carrying in his left hand and showed me the front page. This was the proof, the final piece of evidence. At first I couldn't make it out, but then I saw that it was an aerial photograph of a crowd. There were tens of thousands of people in the picture, a gigantic agglomeration of bodies, more bodies than I had ever seen in one place before. Woodstock. It had so little to do with what was happening to me just then, I didn't know what to think. Those people were my age, but for all the connection I felt with them, they might have been standing on another planet.

Fernandez left. I stayed where I was for several minutes, then climbed out of bed and put on my clothes. It did not take me long to get ready. I filled a knapsack with a few odds and ends, tucked the clarinet case under my arm, and walked out the door. It was late August, 1969. As I remember it, the sun was shining brightly that morning, and a small breeze was blowing off the river. I turned south, paused for a moment, and then took a step. Then I took another step, and in that way I began to move down the street. I did not look back once.

David Lehman

'70 COLUMBIA COLLEGE, '78 PhD

David Lehman is a poet and nonfiction writer who has served as general editor of the annual Best American Poetry *anthology series since its initial publication in 1988. His poems are distinguished, in some cases, by their humor; the most recent collection is* The Evening Sun *(2002). Lehman is also the author of* The Last Avant-Garde: The Making of the New York School of Poets *(1999), among other works, and is a core faculty member in writing programs at Bennington College and New School University. The following poems, "April 2" and "June 8," are taken from his collection* The Daily Mirror: A Journal in Poetry *(2000).*

APRIL 2

What I like about reading in the dark is
you can't see what you're reading
and must imagine verses equal to your longing
and then Keats shows up with "La Belle Dame
Sans Merci" and Yeats wonders whether
"you" will ever be loved for yourself alone
and not your yellow hair
when I was a Columbia freshman
we had to compare those two poems
I wish I were asked to do that today
for I have finally figured it out
but at the time all I could think to say
was both women, the one whose eyes

were shut with kisses four
and the one with the yellow hair,
were the same woman, and I knew her

JUNE 8

It's three days before my birthday
I think I'll rent *Doctor Zhivago*
tonight (Hilton Obenzinger said
he liked the music) and read the novel
today and write a poem tomorrow about
the Russian Revolution as performed
by the students of Columbia College
in 1967 Aaron Fogel had a beard
David Shapiro a mustache Les Gottesman
went to Poland for the summer
and Hilton Obenzinger bought a pound
of ground chuck and walked to Hamilton Hall
where a class on Plato was in progress
he threw the meat into the room
yelled "meat!" and ran away

James Simon Kunen

'70 COLUMBIA COLLEGE

James Simon Kunen has written four books and contributed to magazines as diverse as Esquire, Mademoiselle, *and* Sports Illustrated. *A self-described radical leftist who participated in the 1968 student protests, Kunen wrote about the experience in* The Strawberry Statement *(1968), excerpted here.*

Columbia used to be called King's College. They changed the name in 1784 because they wanted to be patriotic and *Columbia* means *America*. This week we've been finding out what America means.

Every morning now when I wake up I have to run through the whole thing in my mind. I have to do that because I wake up in a familiar place that isn't what it was. I wake up and I see blue coats and brass buttons all over the campus. ("Brass buttons, blue coat, can't catch a nanny goat" goes the Harlem nursery rhyme.) I start to go off the campus but then remember to turn and walk two blocks uptown to get to the only open gate. There I squeeze through the three-foot "out" opening in the police barricade, and I feel for my wallet to be sure I've got the two I.D.'s necessary to get back into my college. I stare at the cops. They stare back and see a red armband and long hair and they perhaps tap their night sticks on the barricade. They're looking at a radical leftist.

I wasn't always a radical leftist. Although not altogether straight, I'm not a hair person either, and ten days ago I was writing letters to Kokomo, Indiana, for Senator McCarthy; my principal association with the left was that I rowed port on crew. But then I got involved in this movement and one

416

thing led to another. I am not a leader, you understand. But leaders cannot seize and occupy buildings. It takes great numbers of people to do that. I am one of those great numbers. What follows is the chronicle of a single revolutionary digit.

Monday, April 22: A mimeograph has appeared around the campus charging SDS with using coercion to gain its political ends. SDS is for free speech for itself only, it is charged. SDS physically threatens the administration. SDS breaks rules with impunity while we (undefined) are subject to dismissal for tossing a paper airplane out a dorm window. Aren't you TIRED, TIRED, TIRED of this? Will Mark Rudd be our next dean? Do something about it. Come to the SDS rally tomorrow and *be prepared.* At first anonymous, the leaflet reappears in a second edition signed Students for a Free Campus. The jocks have done it again. As with the demonstrations against Marine campus recruiting in the spring of '67, threats of violence from the right will bring hundreds of the usually moderate to the SDS ranks just to align themselves against jock violence. I personally plan to be there, but I'm not up tight about it. At the boat house, a guy says he's for the jock position. Don't get me wrong, I say, I'm not against beating up on a few pukes, I just don't think you should stoop to their level by mimeographing stuff. We both go out and kill ourselves trying to row a boat faster than eight students from MIT will be able to.

Tuesday, April 23: Noon. At the sundial are 500 people ready to follow Mark Rudd (whom they don't particularly like because he always refers to President Kirk as "that shithead") into the Low Library administration building to demand severance from IDA, an end to gym construction, and to defy Kirk's recent edict prohibiting indoor demonstrations. There are around 100 counter-demonstrators. They are what Trustee Arthur Ochs Sulzberger's newspaper refers to as "burly white youths" or "students of considerable athletic attainment"—jocks. Various deans and other father surrogates separate the two factions. Low Library is locked. For lack of a better place to go we head for the site of the gym in Morningside Park, chanting "Gym Crow must go." I do not chant because I don't like chanting.

I have been noncommittal to vaguely against the gym, but now I see the site for the first time. There is excavation cutting across the whole park. It's really ugly. And there's a chain link fence all around the hole. I don't like fences anyway so I am one of the first to jump on it and tear it down. Enter the New York Police Department. One of them grabs the fence gate and tries to shut it. Some demonstrators grab him. I yell "Let that cop go," partly because I feel sorry for the cop and partly because I know that the night sticks will start to flagellate on our heads, which they proceed to do. One of my friends goes down and I pull him out. He's on adrenaline now and tries to get back at the cops but I hold him, because I hit a cop at Whitehall and I wished I hadn't very shortly thereafter. After the usual hassle, order is restored and the cops let Rudd mount a dirt pile to address us. As soon as he starts to talk he is drowned out by jackhammers but, at the request of the police, they are turned off. Rudd suggests we go back to the sundial and join with 300 demonstrators there, but we know that he couldn't possibly know whether there are 300 demonstrators there and we don't want to leave. He persists and we defer.

Back at the sundial there is a large crowd. It's clear we've got something going. An offer comes from Vice-President Truman to talk with us in McMillin Theatre but Rudd, after some indecision, refuses. It seems we have the initiative and Truman just wants to get us in some room and bull-shit till we all go back to sleep. Someone suggests we go sit down for awhile in Hamilton, the main college classroom building, and we go there. Sitting down turns to sitting-in, although we do not block classes. Rudd asks, "Is this a demonstration?" "Yes!" we answer, all together. "Is it indoors?" "Yes!"

An immediate demand is the release of the one student arrested at the park, Mike Smith, who might as well be named John Everyman, because nobody knows him. To reciprocate for Mike's detention, Dean Coleman is detained.

At four o'clock, like Pavlov's dog, I go to crew, assuring a longhair at the door that I'll be back. At practice it is pointed out to me that the crew does not have as many WASPS as it should have according to the population per-centage of WASPS in the nation, so don't I think that crew should be shut down? I answer no, I don't think crew should be shut down.

Back at school at eight I prepared to spend the night at Hamilton. My friend Rock is there. We decide that we are absolutely bound to meet some girls or at least boys since there are 300 of them in the lobby. Every ten min-utes he yells to me, "Hey, did you make any friends yet?" I say no each time, and he says that he hasn't either, but he's bound to soon.

I go upstairs to reconnoiter and there is none other than Peter Behr of Linda LeClair fame chalking on the wall, "'Up against the wall, mother-fucker, . . ' from a poem by LeRoi Jones." I get some chalk and write "I am sorry about defacing the walls, but babies are being burned and men are dying, and this University is at fault quite directly." Also I draw some SANE symbols and then at 2:30 A.M. go to sleep.

Wednesday, April 24, 5:30 A.M. Someone just won't stop yelling that we've got to get up, that we're leaving, that the blacks occupying Hamilton with us have asked us to leave. I get up and leave. The column of evicted whites shuffles over to Low Library. A guy in front rams a wooden sign through the security office side doors and about 200 of us rush in. Another 150 hang around outside because the breaking glass was such a bad sound. They become the first "sundial people." Inside we rush up to Kirk's office and someone breaks the lock. I am not at all enthusiastic about this and suggest that perhaps we ought to break up all the Ming Dynasty art that's on display while we're at it. A kid turns on me and says in a really ugly way that the exit is right over there. I reply that I am staying, but that I am not a sheep and he is.

Rudd calls us all together. He looks very strained. He elicits promises from the *Spectator* reporters in the crowd not to report what he is about to say. Then he says that the blacks told us to leave Hamilton because they do not feel that we are willing to make the sacrifices they are willing to make. He says that they have carbines and grenades and that they're not leaving. I think that's really quite amazing.

We all go into Kirk's office and divide into three groups, one in each room. We expect the cops to come any moment. After an hour's discussion my room votes 29–16 to refuse to leave, to make the cops carry us out. The losing alternative is to escape through the windows and then go organize a strike. The feeling is that if we get busted, *then* there will be something to organize a strike about. The man chairing the discussion is standing on a small wooden table and I am very concerned lest he break it. We collect water in wastebaskets in case of tear gas. Some of it gets spilled and I spend my time trying to wipe it up. I don't want to leave somebody else's office all messy.

We check to see what other rooms have decided. One room is embroiled in a political discussion, and in the other everyone is busy playing with the office machines.

At about 8:30 A.M. we hear that the cops are coming. One hundred seventy-three people jump out the window. (I don't jump because I've been reading *Lord Jim.*) That leaves twenty-seven of us sitting on the floor, waiting to be arrested. In stroll an inspector and two cops. We link arms and grit our teeth. After about five minutes of gritting our teeth it dawns on us that the cops aren't doing anything. We relax a little and they tell us they have neither the desire nor the orders to arrest us. In answer to a question they say they haven't got MACE, either.

In through the window like Batman climbs Professor Orest Ranum, liberal, his academic robes billowing in the wind. We laugh at his appearance. He tells us that our action will precipitate a massive right-wing reaction in the faculty. He confides that the faculty had been nudging Kirk toward resignation, but now we've blown everything; the faculty will flock to support the President. We'll all be arrested, he says, and we'll all be expelled. He urges us to leave. We say no. One of us points out that Sorel said only violent action changes things. Ranum says that Sorel is dead. He gets on the phone to Truman and offers us trial by a tripartite committee if we'll leave. We discuss it and vote no. Enter Mark Rudd, through the window. He says that twenty-seven people can't exert any pressure, and the best thing we could do would be to leave and join a big sit-in in front of Hamilton. We say no, we're not leaving until our demands on the gym, IDA, and amnesty for demonstrators are met. Rudd goes out and comes back and asks·us to leave again, and we say no again. He leaves to get reinforcements. Ranum leaves. Someone comes in to take pictures. We all cover our faces with different photographs of Grayson Kirk.

It's raining out, and the people who are climbing back in are marked by their wetness. Offered a towel by one of the new people, a girl pointedly says "No, thank you, I haven't been out." Rationally, we twenty-seven are glad that there are now 150 people in the office, but emotionally we resent them. As people dry out, the old and new become less easily differentiable, and I am trying for a field promotion in the movement so that I will not fade into the masses who jumped and might jump again.

The phone continues to ring and we inform the callers that we are sorry, but Dr. Kirk will not be in today because Columbia is under new management. After noon, all the phones are cut off by the administration.

At 3:45 I smoke my first cigarette in four months and wonder if Lenin smoked. I don't go to crew. I grab a typewriter and, though preoccupied by its electricness, manage to write:

The time has come to pass the time.

I am not having good times here. I do not know many people who are here, and I have doubts about why they are here. Worse, I have doubts about why I am here. (Note the frequency of the word *here*. The place I am is the salient characteristic of my situation.) It's possible that I'm here to be cool or to meet people or to meet girls (as distinct from people) or to get out of crew or to be arrested. Of course the possibility exists that I am here to precipitate some change at the University. I am willing to accept the latter as true or, rather, I am willing, even anxious, not to think about it anymore. If you think too much on the second tier (think about why you are thinking what you think) you can be paralyzed.

I really made the conflicting-imperative scene today. I have never let down the crew before, I think. Let down seven guys. I am one-eighth of the crew. I am one-fiftieth of this demonstration. And I am not even sure that this demonstration is right. But I multiplied these figures by an absolute importance constant. I hate to hamper the hobby of my friends (and maybe screw, *probably* screw, my own future in it), I am sorry about that, but death is being done by this University and I would rather fight it than row a boat.

But then I may, they say, "be causing a right-wing reaction and hurt-
ing the cause. Certainly it isn't conscionable to hold Dean Coleman
captive. But attention is being gotten. Steps will be taken in one direction or another. The polls will fluctuate and the market quiver. Our
being here is the cause of an effect. We're trying to make it good; I
don't know what else to say or do. That is, I have no further statement
to make at this time, gentlemen."

The news comes in that Avery Hall, the architecture school, has been
liberated. We mark it as such on Grayson's map. At about 8 P.M. we break
back into Kirk's inner office, which had been relocked by security when
we gathered into one room when the cops came in the morning. The
$450,000 Rembrandt and the TV have gone with the cops.

We explore. The temptation to loot is tremendous, middle-class morality
notwithstanding, but there is no looting. I am particularly attracted by a
framed diploma from American Airlines declaring Grayson Kirk a V.I.P., but
I restrict myself to a few Grayson Kirk introduction cards. Someone finds a
book on masochism behind a book on government. Someone else finds what
he claims is Grayson's draft card and preparations are made to mail it back
to the Selective Service. On his desk is an American Airlines jigsaw puzzle
which has apparently been much played with.

We have a meeting to discuss politics and defense, but I sit at the door as
a guard. A campus guard appears and, before I can do anything, surprises me
by saying, "As long as you think you're right, fuck 'em." He hopes something
good for him might come out of the whole thing. He makes eighty-six dollars
a week after twenty years at the job.

I go down to the basement of Low, where the New York City Police have set
up shop. There are approximately forty of them; there is precisely one of me. I
ask one for the score of the Red Sox game. He seems stunned that a hippie fag-
got could be interested in such things, but he looks it up for me. Rained out.

I use the pay-phone to call a girl at Sarah Lawrence. I tell her how isolated
I feel and how lonely I am and hungry and tired and she says oh. I explain
that I'll be busted any minute and she says she knows that.

I return upstairs. One of these people who knows how to do things has
reconnected a phone, but he needs someone to hold the two wires together
while he talks. I do it. I'll do anything to feel like I'm doing something.

Thursday, April 25: I get up and shave with Grayson Kirk's razor, use his
toothpaste, splash on his after-shave, grooving on it all. I need something
morale-building like this, because my revolutionary fervor takes about half
an hour longer than the rest of me to wake up.

Someone asks if anyone knows how to fix a Xerox 3000, and I say yes, lying through my teeth. Another man and I proceed to take it apart and put it back together. To test it I draw a pierced heart with "Mother" in the middle and feed it to the machine. The machine gives back three of the same. Much rejoicing. Now we can get to work on Kirk's files. My favorite documents are a gym letter which ends with the sentence "Bring on the bulldozers!" and a note to a Columbia representative to the land negotiations telling him to be careful *not* to mention to Parks Commissioner Hoving that the date for digging has been moved up. ("We don't want him to know that we decided on this over a year ago," the note explains.)

Since a bust does not seem imminent, I climb out the window and go to crew at four. I talk to the coach and we agree that I will sleep in Low but will show up for the bus to Cambridge the next morning if I'm not in jail.

When I get back from crew I have to run a police cordon and leap for the second-story ledge. A cop, much to my surprise, bothers to grab me and tries to pull me down, but some people inside grab me and pull me up.

A meeting is going on discussing defense. J.J. wants to pile art treasures on the windows so the cops will have to break them to get in. I'm for that. But he also wants to take poles and push cops off the ledge. When this is criticized he tries to make it clear that it will be done in a nonviolent way. A friend whispers to me that J.J. is SDS's answer to the jock. A guy in a red crash helmet begins to say that maybe we won't fight because we're not as manly as the blacks, but it is well known that he is loony as hell and he is shouted down in a rare violation of the democratic process. After two hours' debate it is decided to man the barricades until they start to fall, then gather in groups with locked arms and resist passively. A motion to take off all our clothes when the police arrive is passed, with most girls abstaining.

I get back to the Xerox and copy seventy-three documents, including clippings from *The New York Times*. I hear over the radio that Charles 37X Kenyatta and the Mau Maus are on campus. This does not surprise me.

J.J. is recruiting volunteers to liberate another building. He has thirty, male and female, and at 2 A.M. he's ready to move. I go out on the ledge to check for cops. There are only three, so we climb down and sprint to Mathematics Hall. There we are joined by twenty radicals who could no longer stand the Establishment-liberal atmosphere of the previously liberated Fayerweather Hall. We get inside and immediately pile up about 2000 pounds of furniture at the front door. Only then do we discover two housekeepers still in the building. They are quite scared but only say "Why didn't you tell us you were coming?" and laugh. We help them out a window and along a ledge with the aid of the just-arrived-press movie lights.

We hold the standard two-hour meeting to decide how to deal with the cops, whom we understand to be on their way. The meeting is chaired by Tom Hayden, who is an Outside Agitator. Reverend Starr, the Protestant counselor, tells us the best positions for firehoses and so on. Dean Alexander B. Platt is allowed in through the window. He looks completely dead. We consider capturing him, but no one has the energy, so we let him go after thanking him for coming. Professor Allen Westin, liberal, comes and offers us a tripartite committee which he has no authority to constitute and which we don't want. He is thanked and escorted to the window.

At 6 A.M. I go to sleep.

Friday, April 26: I wake up at 8:55 and run to the crew bus and leave for MIT. From Cambridge I call my home in Marlboro. My mother asks me, "Are you on the side of the law-breakers in this thing?" For ten minutes we exchange mother talk and revolutionary rhetoric. She points out that neither Gandhi nor Thoreau would have asked for amnesty. I admit I haven't read them. But Gandhi had no Gandhi to read and Thoreau hadn't read Thoreau. They had to reach their own conclusions and so will I.

Saturday, April 27: I row a boat race and split. That wraps up the crew season—for me. On the MTA to Logan Airport a middle-aged man starts winking and smiling and gesticulating at my right lapel. Looking down, I see that I am wearing a broken rifle pin, symbol of the War Resisters' League. I tell him that it so happens I am on my way back to Columbia right now to carry on a Revolution. He thinks that's fine.

I get back to Math around 4:30 and sit down on the public-relations ledge over Broadway. People from a peace demonstration downtown are depositing money and food in a bucket at the bottom of a rope. Each time we haul it up and re-lower it we include I.D.'s for people who want to get into the campus. A remarkable number of cars toot their support, and when a bus driver pulls over to wave us a victory sign, ten people nearly fall off the ledge.

In the evening I discover that the electricity to the kitchen is cut off. I run downstairs and almost call for "someone important" but somehow I am unwilling to accept that kind of status relation. I tell several of my peers and one of them finds the fuse box and sets things right.

I volunteer for shopping. We buy twenty dollars of food for eighteen dollars (the merchants earlier had contributed food outright) and on the way back meet a gentleman who seems to belong to Drunken Faculty to Forget the Whole Mess. Someone whom I think of as a friend threatens to punch me because I am carrying food.

As the evening wears on I feel less useful and more alienated, so I assign myself the task of keeping the mayonnaise covered. After covering it twelve times I give up and decide to write home. I wonder whether the Paris Commune was this boring.

In the letter I try to justify rebelling on my father's money. I point out that one of the dangers of going to college is that you learn things, and that my present actions are much influenced by my Contemporary Civilization (C1001y) readings. After sealing the letter I realize that my conception of the philosophy of law comes not so much from Rousseau as from Fess Parker as Davy Crockett. I remember his saying that you should decide what you think is right and then go ahead and do it. Walt Disney really bagged that one; the old fascist inadvertently created a whole generation of radicals.

I discover a phone which has not been cut off and call my brother. As I am talking someone puts a piece of paper beside me and writes "This . . . phone . . . is . . . tapped." I address myself briefly to the third party and go on talking. It feels good to talk to someone on the outside, although it is disappointing to find out that the outside world is going on as usual.

Sunday, April 28: Four hours of meetings about tactical matters, politics, and reports from Strike Central. I begin to long for a benevolent dictator. It is announced that we are spending as much money on cigarettes as food. I wonder, as I look about me, whether Lenin was as concerned with the breast size of his revolutionary cohorts as I am. It is now daylight-saving time; under all the clocks are signs saying "It's later than you think."

I spend the day sunning and reading *Lord Jim* on the ledge. At 3 P.M. four fire trucks scream up and men go running onto the campus with axes. Some people think this is the bust, but it seems like the wrong public agency to me. It turns out to be a false alarm.

The neighborhood little kids are anxious and able to squeeze through the fences. I talk to some of them and they are all conversant with the issues and on our side. I conduct an informal class in peace graffiti and distribute chalk.

The older brothers of these same kids are in the middle of Broadway throwing eggs at us. This action—one of them tells me later—is completely apolitical.

We have red flags flying from the roof. I explain to a cop on the sidewalk below that these stand for revolution, not for communism. He says yes, he remembers reading something about that. I hope he is not referring to the *Daily News*. The *News* charges us with vandalism and alcoholism. (Actually we voted to bar both grass and liquor, and there was only one dissident, named Melvin.) One cartoon, titled "Dancing to the Red Tune," shows a beatnik and some sort of cave girl dancing as a band sings "Louse up the campuses, yeah, yeah, yeah."

In the evening I walk into a room where there is a poetry reading. I don't want to be rude so I stay. A med student who looks like Dr. Kildare reads a poem entitled "Ode to Mickey Mantle's Five-hundredth HR."

Mutiny on the Bounty (Gable) is on TV and I find it inspirational, or at least amusing.

The student radio station, WKCR, announces that a clergyman is wanted in Fayerweather; a couple wants to get married. This does not surprise me. Reverend Starr performs the ceremony and says, "I pronounce you children of the new age." Shortly after we hear it, we see a candlelight procession approaching. The bride is carrying roses. She hands them to me and I pass them inside. The demonstration peaks for me as I touch the roses—I am stoned on revolutionary zeal. The newlyweds call themselves Mr. and Mrs. Fayerweather.

I volunteer for jock-watch from 2:00 to 3:00 but do not wake up the next man and stay out on the entrance window ledge until five. I am to let no one in as we now have a population of 150 and we want a stable commune—no tourists. We even consider a Stalinist purge to reduce the mouths to feed. Only tonight does my roommate decide to occupy a building. I have about seven degrees of disdain and contempt for him, but he got in before my watch. I stamp "Rush" on the hand of anyone who leaves. This allows them to get back in.

During my watch five guys in black cowls come by dragging a coffin and murmuring in Latin.

Monday, April 29: The Majority Coalition (read: jocks) have cordoned off Low and are trying to starve the demonstrators out. We decide to break the blockade. We plan tactics on a blackboard and go, shaking hands with those staying behind as though we might not be back. There are thirty of us with three cartons of food. We march around Low, making our presence known. Spontaneously, and at the wrong tactical place, the blacks in front jump into the jock line. I go charging through the gap with my box of grapefruit and quickly become upon the ground or, more accurately, on top of two layers of people and beneath two. I manage to throw three grapefruit, two of which make it. Then I become back where I started. Some blood is visible on both sides. Back at Math, some of our people say that the jocks they were fighting had handcuffs on their belts. Band-Aided noses abound and are a mark of distinction. We discuss alternative plans for feeding Low and someone suggests blockading the jocks—"If they run out of beer they're through." In the meantime, we can see hundreds of green armbands (for amnesty) throwing food up to the Low windows. We decide on a rope-and-pulley system between a tree and the Low windows, but there is some question about how to get the line up to the people in Low without the jocks grabbing it. When one kid suggests tying an end to a broom handle and throwing it like a harpoon, John (Outside Agitator) suggests we train a bird. A helicopter has already been looked into by Strike Central, but the FAA won't allow it. Finally we agree on shooting in a leader line with a bow and arrow.

A girl and myself are dispatched to get a bow. We go to the roof of the Barnard Library where the phys. ed. archery range is. We are in the midst of discovering how incredibly locked the cabinet is when a guard comes out on the roof. We crouch. He walks right past us. It would be just like TV were I not so preoccupied with it being just like TV. After ten minutes he finds us. The girl laughs coyly and alleges that oh, we just came up to spend the night. I am rather taken with the idea, but the guard is unmoved and demands our I.D.'s. This is our first bust.

Our second bust, the real one, begins to take shape at 2:30 A.M. We hear over WBAI that there are busloads of TPF (Tactical Police Force, Gestapo) at 156th and at 125th and that patrol cars are arriving from all precincts with four helmeted cops per auto. I am unimpressed. So many times now we've been going to be busted. It just doesn't touch me anymore. I assume that the cops are there to keep the Mau Maus out.

A girl comes up to me with some paper towels. Take these, she says, so you can wipe the vaseline (slows tear-gas penetration) off your face when you're in jail. I haven't got vaseline on my face. I am thinking that vaseline is a big petroleum interest, probably makes napalm, and anyway it's too greasy. I hear over the walky-talky that Hamilton has been busted and that the sundial people are moving to Low and Fayerweather to obstruct the police. I put vaseline on my face. I also put vaseline on my hands and arms and legs above the socks and a cigarette filter in each nostril and carefully refold my plastic-bag gas mask so I'll be able to put it on quickly with the holes at the back of my head so my hair will absorb the gas and I'll be able to breathe long enough to cool the cannister with a CO_2 fire extinguisher and pick it up with my asbestos gloves and throw it back at the cops. Someone tells me that he can't get busted or he'll miss his shrink again.

I take my place with seven others at the front barricade. All along the stairs our people are lined up, ready to hole up in the many lockable-from-within rooms on the three floors above me. We sing "We Shall Not Be Moved" and realize that something is ending. The cops arrive. The officer bullhorns us: "On behalf of the Trustees of Columbia University and with the authority vested in me . . ." That's as far as he is able to get, as we answer his question and all others with our commune motto—"Up against the wall, motherfuckers." We can't hold the barricade because the doors open out and the cops simply pull the stuff out. They have to cut through ropes and hoses and it takes them fifteen minutes before they can come through. All the while they're not more than thirty feet from me, but all I can do is watch their green-helmeted heads working. I shine a light in their eyes but Tom tells me not to and he's head of the defense committee so I stop.

At 4:00 A.M. the cops come in. The eight of us sit down on the stairs (which we've made slippery with green soap and water) and lock arms. The big cop says "Don't make it hard for us or you're gonna get hurt." We do not move. We want to make it clear that the police have to step over more than chairs to get our people out. They pull us apart and carry us out, stacking us like cord wood under a tree. The press is here so we are not beaten. As I sit under the tree I can see kids looking down at us from every window in the building. We exchange the "V" sign. The police will have to ax every door to get them out of those offices. They do. Tom Hayden is out now. He yells "Keep the radio on! Peking will instruct you!" When they have sixty of us out they take us to the paddy wagons at mid-campus. I want to make them carry us, but the consensus is that it's a long, dark walk and we'll be killed if we don't cooperate, so I walk. At the paddy wagons there are at least a thousand people cheering us and chanting "Strike! Strike! Strike!" We are loaded in a wagon and the doors shut. John tells a story about how a cop grabbed the cop that grabbed him and then said "Excuse me." We all laugh raucously to show an indomitable spirit and freak out the cops outside.

We are taken to the 24th precinct to be booked. "Up against the wall," we are told. I can't get over how they really do use the term. We turn and lean on the wall with our hands high, because that's what we've seen in the movies. We are told to can that shit and sit down. Booking takes two hours. Lieutenant Dave Bender is the plainclothesman in charge. He seems sternly unhappy that college turns out people like us. He asks John if he thinks he could be a policeman and John says no; he doesn't think he's cut out for it.

We are allowed three calls each. A fat officer makes them for us and he is a really funny and good man. He is only mildly displeased when he is duped into calling Dial-a-Demonstration. He expresses interest in meeting a girl named Janice when three of us give him her number, one as his sister, one as his girl friend, and one as his ex-wife.

We go downstairs to await transportation to court. A TPF man comes in escorting Angus Davis, who was on the sixth floor of Math and refused to walk down. He has been dragged down four flights of marble stairs and kicked and clubbed all the way. A two-inch square patch of his hair has been pulled out. Ben, Outside Agitator, yells, "You're pretty brave when you've got that club." The officer comes over and dares him to say that again. He says it again. The cop kicks for Ben's groin, but Ben knows karate and blocks it. John says to the cop, "Thank you, you have just proved Ben's point." This is sufficiently subtle not to further arouse the cop, and he leaves. A caged bus takes us all the way downtown to the tombs (the courthouse). The kid beside me keeps asking me what bridge is this and what building is that. Finally he recognizes something and declares that we are going to pass his grandmother's house. I am busy trying to work a cigarette butt through the window grate so that I can litter from a police bus. Arriving, we drive right into the building; a garage door clamps down behind us.

Our combs and keys are confiscated so that we won't be able to commit suicide. In the elevator to the cells a white cop tells us we look like a fine bunch of men—we ought to be put on the front lines in Vietnam. Someone says that Vietnam is here, now. As we get out I look at the black cop running the elevator for some sort of reaction. He says "Keep the faith."

He said "Keep the faith," I say, and everyone is pleased. We walk by five empty cells and then are jammed into one, thirty-four of us in a 12x15 room. We haven't slept in twenty-four hours and there isn't even space for all of us to sit down at one time.

Some of our cellmates are from Avery. They tell us how they were handcuffed and dragged downstairs on their stomachs. Their shirts are bloody.

After a couple of hours we start to perk up. We bang and shout until a guard comes, and then tell him that the door seems to be stuck. Someone screams "All right, all right, I'll talk." It is pointed out that you don't need tickets to get to policemen's balls. We sing folk songs and "The Star-Spangled Banner." They allowed one of us to bring in a recorder and he plays Israeli folk music.

A court officer comes and calls a name. "He left," we say. Finally he finds the right list. We are arraigned before a judge. The Outsiders are afraid they will be held for bail, but they are released on their own recognizance, like the rest of us, except they have some form of loitering charge tacked on to the standard second-degree criminal trespassing.

Back at school I eat in a restaurant full of police. As audibly as possible I compose a poem entitled "Ode to the TPF." It extolls the beauty of rich wood billies, the sheen of handcuffs, the feel of a boot on your face.

Meeting a cellmate, I extend my hand to him and he slaps it. I have to remember that—handslaps, not shakes, in the Revolution.

Tom Hayden is in Chicago now. As an Outside Agitator, he has a lot of outsides to agitate in. Like the Lone Ranger, he didn't even wave good-bye, but quietly slipped away, taking his silver protest buttons to another beleaguered campus.

Everyone is organizing now—moderates, independent radicals, Liberated Artists, librarians. And the Yippies are trying to sue the University, for evicting us from our homes which we owned by virtue of squatters' rights. You can hardly move for the leaflets here. Except at Barnard. The Barnard girls are typing their papers and getting ready to go to Yale for the weekend.

We are on strike, of course. There are "liberation classes" but the scene is essentially no more pencils, no more books.

I saw a cellist math major in Chock Full O' Nuts looking alone. Liberation classes won't help him. He is screwed. Every Revolution leaves a trail of screwed drifting in its wake.

The campus is still locked, although I think you could get in with a Raleigh coupon as an I.D. today. That's our latest issue; a liberated campus should be open. We want free access by June so we can open the summer school under our own aegis.

A particularly thick swatch of air pollution drifted by today and a lot of people thought the gym site was burning. That did not surprise me. Nothing surprises me any more.

Darryl Pinckney

'75 COLUMBIA COLLEGE

The writer and critic Darryl Pinckney is a longtime contributor to the New York Review of Books, *among other publications, and author of the recent* Out There: Mavericks of Black Literature *(2002),* Sold and Gone: African American Literature and U.S. Society *(2001), and the 1992 novel* High Cotton, *a commentary on the struggle for civil rights and black political and cultural movements. Many critics saw in* High Cotton *a reflection of Pinckney's own upbringing in a well-educated, middle-class black family; it provides this selection.*

I t was over. Firecrackers and sparklers went off all over campus, from South Field to the law school terrace. Around the Sundial, the setting of many historic harangues, up and down College Walk, on the steps in front of the notorious administration building known as Low Library, the twang of guitars, the crackle of radios, the putter of three-wheeled security vans, the eruptions of voices, and the flags of the NLF said it again and again. Even the jocks were out drinking, throwing footballs in the twilight, crashing into hedges, showing off for the Ophelias of the peace movement, who straddled the windowsills of the Student Mobilization Committee.

I squinted from my dormitory's entrance across the nappy lawn to the Quad, the courtyard on the other side of campus, where student-leader types were trying to hook a pair of Harpo Marx glasses on the statue of the young Alexander Hamilton, so available to militant decoration after his shoes were painted red in the golden days of '68. No matter that since then demonstrations and sit-ins degenerated into farce; "living theater" we called it. I remained in the doorway for some time, afraid to take a step. It was the end of spring according to our psychological calendars, study period, the week before final exams, after which you would have either blown it or not blown it, but in the joyous and idle meantime Saigon had fallen.

I backed up the steps into Furnald Hall. The lobby was busy and unexpectedly cool, like a church on a travel itinerary. The guard, Jesse, union member, moonlighter, and taker of beer bribes, already snored at his post. His head rolled against the back of the chair. His bald spot matched the leather, like expensive luggage. "You ain't holdin' no air," he said, if he was awake, when I flashed my ID card in the small hours of the night. "Mess with me, boy, and I'll have to jump down your throat and swing on your liver." He was conspiratorial with black students who flouted the rules, such as they were, and distanced the white ones with a grunt, hardly condescending to hear them out. White students who knew how to give a driver the Black Power salute, or who had raised their consciousness, as the expression went, to the point where they said more than thank you to the doorman back home were intimidated by the political correctness in Jesse's glance. He was nicer to the jocks who didn't care to know even his name.

"Boy, does your daddy know you're up here running the streets?" That was the night I passed out on the subway, bolted at the 116th Street stop so as not to end up in Harlem, and turned to see the graffiti of the doors close on my glasses left rattling in the seat. But Jesse had got it right. It was as necessary to self-conscious living as the Fourteenth Amendment: your parents sent you out into the world; that is, they sadly waved you off with a cashier's check and had no idea what you were up to, apart from the information that could be extrapolated from computer printouts at the bottom of the semester or from how often you called home to beg.

My mother called every Sunday. If I had to, I would have taken a plane or an all-night train from the scene of the crime, experience, to be in my room in time to get my script together. Once she called in the middle of the week. "Are you still in school? The FBI was here to question you about Patty Hearst." Two of the heiress snatchers were from my home state, Indiana, and had lurked about the local Committee to Free Angela Davis. I rushed all over the place with the news that the FBI was looking for me, careful to wipe the smile off my face before I knocked.

My parents were not reconciled to my being in New York, so far away. One learned things in Indiana, too, they argued. From time to time I received clippings about the harm marijuana and LSD could do to chromosomes. But jurisdiction was precisely the point. What I wanted was the veil of miles, the freedom to stay up all night, to waste my time, their money, you name it. In those days, when months were like years, when students thought of themselves as bravely parasitic and "I miss you" wasn't just another lie—in those days when we had more appetite than good sense, the punishment for mistaking white clouds for distant mountains was not loss of life.

I saw a Frisbee bang through a chandelier. I saw Jesse straighten up. "You look like you about to throw up a Buick again," he said, and closed his filmy right eye, one of his many disconcerting tricks. "Don't cry Hughie 'round me." The left eye shut like a ticket window.

Upstairs was the ragged, dicey atmosphere of an inner-city bus station. People I had never seen before, many elites of one, came out of the plaster to mass in the lounge in front of the television, which was a 26-inch color job, as a result of a Cox Commission recommendation, so the rumor went, that the quality of everyday life be improved to appease some of the discontent that had helped to make all-male Columbia the most unattractive, volatile, and abandoned member of the Ivy League.

Girls—students at Barnard across the street—descended on armrests. They made O's with their mouths around bottles of Tab or Miller Lite. Coed floors were also a post-'68 improvement, but my floor, Furnald 6, was not officially one of them. "Holy shit" was the general comment as we watched, with the sound turned off, replays of film that showed people in a melee twelve time zones away. They scrambled over rooftops, clung to helicopters, accomplished gravity-defying feats of locomotion.

Was it possible, was it so? A young girl, an escapee from small-town New Hampshire, a sort of mascot to the hippies on the floor, started to hum "Kumbaya." She rocked on her haunches, a beer between her sandals, and fixed her watery, puppy stare on the Jim Morrison cultists, who snickered, and then on the bra-less Barnard women, who declined to acknowledge her. Someone handed her a joint to shut her up. She turned it over, threaded it through her grubby fingers. "Are you going to worship it or smoke it?" her old-man-of-the-week barked. The lounge was thick with the aroma of Acapulco Gold, Thai sticks, patchouli oil, leftover anchovies, squashed Marlboros, Budweiser breath, and slept-in Grateful Dead T-shirts. Through our 26-inch color window on the world we saw a Marine ball his fist. It went up and down on the mob. His brow was knitted but calm, like St. George having his vision.

Boredom is not out of the question even when worlds collapse. The party broke apart. Each to his quarters, his ardent nonchalance. I had no more connection with my fellow cellmates on Furnald 6 than spectators do after the ambulance has turned the corner. They took me for a black separatist. I knew no one on that floor, an isolation which, at that moment, was no longer as hip as I had thought. All day I had been calling people without success. I worried that my friends were hiding from me. However, loneliness was swept aside by another big emotion, one maybe common to seniors who

have not begun their term papers and who have no marketable skills: some
awful mix of love and pity for mankind.

I stood in the dim corridor dumb and, so I believed, invisible in a seizure
of oneness. An overweight girl, so important in radical circles that she always
wore a shroud-of-Leningrad expression, pounded on the wall near the
elevator to affix a leaflet crammed with fine print that announced a demonstration against—she was never not in the vanguard—the Shah. Her faded
corduroy trousers dragged on the carpet, drooped so that they revealed to
the comprador-bourgeois onlookers the crack of her rear end. I was with her
and with the onlookers. I was at one with the floor's would-be dealer on his
water bed, a longhair from Arizona whom no one trusted, whose door stood
wide open hour after futile hour, and who seemed forever stuck on the same
brown page of an old paperback edition of Kerouac.

I was also with the congressman's son in whom philosophy had gotten the
upper hand, with the pompous slogans on his door like "Relinquish no part of
me to the state" or "Hell is badly done." I was at one with the stoop-
shouldered souls on what was called Grind Row, where no posters or stickers
of any kind distinguished their cheders, where there was only the sickening
smell of a can of Chef Boyardee heating up on a hot plate. In my mind's eye
I was at one with the stupidities scrawled above the urinals and, with the
Magic Marker that was made to write yet again "Eat the Rich," I was there.
The lichen on the ledge, Jesse in his dream of Jones Beach, the shadows on
the Ho Chi Minh Trail—I was with it all, at every festival, until someone
passed by and handed me a look like a traffic violation. "Man, everybody's
stoned out of their gourds today." Down as a result of contact, as they say in
football.

My room was one of the coveted singles, which meant that I was spared
a stranger's socks and nightmares. The sink, the chest of drawers, the cot
with the plastic hospital mattress, and the desk that was unusable because of
the number of black candles I had melted on it left a bit of floor space the
size of an aisle in tourist class. I heard a blast of music—Suicidio!—from a
monster stereo system, the property of my neighbors, two guys who had
grown up drinking from the same glass but who had lately come to the fork
that led one downstairs to sleep in study hall, the Grub Room, and the other
to lavish on the walls of their room his masterpiece in oil, an endeavor
encouraged by the speed and peyote he swallowed in lieu of macaroni in the
cafeteria. At any hour he shouted to himself of his inspiration: "Well, all right
now." In everyone's face except your own a map was visible.

My inner composure depended on the lone window in my room. It looked
out on Broadway, on Chock Full o'Nuts, trucks, taxis, delis, abused chestnut
trees, panhandlers with fringed cowboy jackets slung over their shoulders,

tables of textbooks and SWAPO pamphlets at the college gates. I saw two dedicated teachers, one huge, one thin, both in the throes of tenure battles, scrape gum or shit from their soles. "Don't they know I'm the greatest poet since Dante?" Mr. Huge once demanded of a seminar. "Trotsky, who was in love with my grandmother," Mr. Thin had begun a lecture. Furious student petitions were circulated in their behalf. The pair headed toward the West End Café, the hangout of the unappreciated, the persecuted, and the fired.

Broadway was so crowded with vegetable buyers and buildings streaked with weather that I hadn't noticed the dark. Of all the things to witness in the street—flyers and newspapers that tumbled waist-high above the pavement in warm gusts; blue, lemon, red, and green lights in a diaphanous blur of gases; grit that miraculously retained the day's heat as it flew to my teeth— nothing was more consoling than the sight of people caught by nightfall in their shorts, their muscular tank tops and bobbing stripes.

Summer was coming in as fast as what we thought was the liberation of the people of Indochina. Summer, that season of disappointed travel plans and joke reading lists, that slowing down into which your classmates disappeared and from which they returned russet and altered, made the hairs of my Afro stand on end, as if life itself had been invented by my generation the day before yesterday.

The time had come. Summer had always meant no school, but it had not meant, until then, with the tanks rolling down Tu Do Street, with the Chekhovian solution imminent—either hand in those term papers or shoot yourself—no school ever again. I saw summer whistling in over the water towers of Broadway as a great postponement of the Next Move, a beautiful ellipsis limited only by my cowardice, by insufficient wantonness of mind.

My parents had never allowed me to spend the summer in New York. Their policy against dancing in the street began the August before my freshman career, when I zoomed back from my first solo moon flight with one dime. I used it to call collect, to wonder how I was going to get from JFK to the Hoosier-bound plane at LaGuardia, and then I plugged the coin into a pay toilet. After that my parents enforced between semesters the uplift principle, which I interpreted as surveillance, wing clipping, Indiana arrest.

How I'd spent my summer vacations: the uplift principle put me to work as a counselor at a "student leadership" camp where the teenagers believed down to their tan lines in nonsmoking, Our Lord Jesus Christ, "role-playing," Karen Carpenter, and the war on apathy. The uplift principle also permitted me to haunt my room back home or, sulker that I was, to teach my wounded parents that nine-dollar scoops of chicken salad and debate about busing at NAACP convention were not fun. But all of that was over. Go ahead, the lights in the wild air said, throw your heart over the fence.

Diana Trilling

The writer and critic Diana Trilling served as fiction reviewer for The Nation *from 1941 to 1949 and wrote extensively in a variety of publications for years afterward. A member of the Columbia community for decades, she edited twelve volumes of the work of her husband, Lionel Trilling, after his death in 1975. Excerpted here is an essay from one of her own collections,* We Must March My Darlings *(1975).*

The personal, moral, and intellectual offense suffered by the Columbia faculty in the uprising was indeed momentous. It is to be thought of only with pain. If Columbia has pioneered the future of the universities of this country and there are to be other insurrectionary uprisings on our campuses, it is logical to suppose that the loneliness consequent upon the rejection of our university teachers by the students to whom they have given their devotion is bound to be dispelled by multiplication, much as has happened in the instance of the rejected parents of our time. Of course it was not only the Columbia faculty that experienced insult; everyone not of the revolutionary faction suffered offense, even the nonrevolutionary students. One of the lessons taught in the uprising—it bears on the old question of why the center cannot hold—is the speed with which whatever makes its appeal to direct action achieves emotional advantage over whatever is committed to the slower and more passive (as it would appear) process of reasonableness; how to activate decency and teach it to stop feeling deficient because of its low quotient of drama is obviously one of the urgent problems of modern society. What makes the terrible near-endemic ache of contemporary parenthood, especially in enlightened homes where parental love and hope are so regularly, casually, and, in most part, inexplicably flouted by children grown to a sudden harsh scornfulness of which their parents could have no expectation, was now suddenly the experience of university professors who also had no reason to expect such an unprecedented violation of natural feeling and who in fact had supposed that they were perhaps the single remaining bridge between the dissident young and their elders. And what had built this bridge, what had made the special tenderness of the teacher for the young if not the teacher's commitment to social continuity, social improvement, to all the vaults of imagination and feeling that have traditionally defined the liberal enterprise? There were emotional breakdowns among the faculty due to the uprising, and several car accidents attributed to exhaustion. It is a fair guess that had the administration shown more sensitivity, if not to the demonstrators, at least to the student population in general and thus left the faculty with nothing to be angry at, nowhere to stand except at the administration's side, looking together at the chasm that had opened up between themselves and a generation in such newly bitter revolt against them, the toll for the faculty might have been even more severe.

But I speak of senior faculty. Junior nontenure faculty are usually still of an age to depart their elders rather than to be departed from, to reject rather than be rejected, to ask rather than give tenderness, to demand rather than share or cede power. Not that they had been demanding power at Columbia before the uprising and been refused; the possibility of improving their status came to them only by student example. There is irony in the failure of political forethought involved in the welcome of junior teaching staff into the shaky councils of the Ad Hoc Faculty Group during the sit-in. Anyone had a vote in these loosely organized meetings, anyone could tie a white handkerchief around his sleeve and join the faculty cordons at the occupied buildings: the younger, the sturdier. In this sudden heady alteration of status, the nontenure staff decided that if it was deemed equal to faculty emergency, it merited equality on all scores—one form (but perhaps it is not to be generalized from) in which this particular "radicalization" announced itself was in the unsmiling question put to a senior professor by a much-junior colleague: there being a scarcity of chairs at a meeting, must the junior rise for his senior? As I write, the junior staff is busily formulating its corporate right, equal with that of senior professors, in the shaping of departmental policy and in decisions on appointments and promotions in a University to whose future they bring only such sense of responsibility as they may have as individual persons.

And yet how are we to know—the question bears in on one with an always-increasing weight—the proper character in which responsibility now announces itself, or should announce itself? How do we even know that we will recognize it when we see it, since it may show a wholly unfamiliar face? For many among the educated classes, the right aspect of responsibility has for long been centrist moderation, a cautious mature deliberation in the implementing of social ideals; it has been difficult to envisage responsibility in any other way than this, which is the liberal way. But an inescapably more pressing sense of our public dilemmas and of the extreme inequities which exist in what we call our liberal democracy makes it always less possible for us to be content with our habitual knowledge of what responsibility looks like. Almost with each passing day it becomes harder for liberalism to claim that it has been adequate to the tasks it undertook. We caution against capitulation to the revolution designed by the New Left, point to its ugly violence, warn whoever deceives himself into supposing that it represents a movement of progress that it has no program to which people committed to the reconstruction of democracy can pledge themselves, underscore its clearly announced goal of destructiveness and the methods it employs to achieve this goal, methods that inevitably give aid solely to the forces of reaction. But must we not also caution against the comfortable assumption that liberalism has only to shine up its old medals and resurrect its old rhetoric of responsibility to be equal to the responsibility that now devolves upon it? To deal only with campus problems: Would the useful changes now being instituted at Columbia, would even the change in administration, have been this quickly accomplished without the violent disruptions of the uprising? No one, I think, can honestly answer this in the affirmative; there wasn't that much quiet will for change. And here liberalism must take its share of blame for the disorders. By confusing quiet with quietism, by buttressing legality with inertia, liberalism has earned at least some part of its present poor reputation on the campus. Yet it will suffer more than disrepute, destruction, if in admitting its deficiencies it either rests with these as its cozy guilt or, in its desire for revitalization, takes the revolution as its alternative.

And so through the month of May, in dissension and anxiety and confusion, with no resolution of these terrible conflicts of the modern world which suddenly were being acted out on the campus, the University struggled to maintain a semblance of its accustomed life. But resolution of a kind— temporary, unreliable, uneasy—was of course approaching with the end of the term and graduation: Commencement was scheduled for June 4. There had been no regular classes in the college or even in some of the graduate schools since April 23—how were students to take examinations and be graded? This problem was resolved by the decision to call off final examinations and to give all students a grade of either Pass or Fail according to the work they had done before the disruptions; should a student desire a more precise grade he could arrange with his instructor for a private examination. Less encompassable was the problem of discipline. The newly formed Joint Committee on Disciplinary Affairs had had little time to construct a body of law. It was May 9 before it could make known its new rules for student government: a first student offense was punishable by probation, a second by more severe penalties—suspension or expulsion; whoever was charged with offense would be summoned to appear before the dean of his school to learn the charge that had been made against him and the punishment that the committee had assigned to it, and if the charged student denied his guilt or even stood mute before his dean, the dean could bring the case, if he had enough evidence to support it, before a tribunal of his school, composed, like the Joint Committee, of representatives from the student body, the faculty, and the administration. From the decision of this tribunal the student might again appeal to the Joint Committee itself.

There were hundreds of summonses arising from the disturbances; they could not all go out at the same time. The first of them went (unstrategically) to the leaders of the insurrection and (sensibly) to the offenders in the senior class whose graduation depended on disciplinary clearance—it had been arranged that no offender would be denied graduation; if he answered his summons he would be put on probation or suspended for the few remaining days of the term. But a great many of these students were also awaiting action against them in the police courts on charges that arose from trespass and resistance to arrest. Legal assistance and money for bail was abundantly available to the demonstrators, and for the most part they refused their disciplinary summonses. The Columbia air was suddenly thick with talk of due process, double jeopardy, indictments unsupported by evidence, although none of the students with whom I spoke had troubled to read the body of law constructed on their own demand for participation in their governance. And this agitation would continue and increase throughout the summer, abate in fact only partially when the new acting president would call on the district attorney to dismiss such charges as arose from simple trespass and grant clemency to a good proportion of the demonstrators, those charged with only a single offense. The SDS, still led by the now suspended Mark Rudd, would settle for no less than total amnesty.

Such was the heavily laden atmosphere into which the University moved with its plans for Commencement. Usually, if the weather permits, graduation exercises are held on the steps and the plaza of Low Library. The administration decided that this year it would be unwise to have the ceremonies outdoors where they might be interfered with by the same people who had given the police all they could handle on the morning of May 22, when the second move had been made on Hamilton Hall in protest of the disciplinary actions stemming from the sit-in and had provoked another fierce confrontation with the police, with even greater brutality on the part both of the students and the police. Instead, they transferred the graduation ceremonies to the Cathedral of St. John the Divine, four blocks away, where in the past they have been held only in case of rain.

Rumors at once began to fly through the neighborhood of new and extraordinary measures being planned by the SDS to disrupt the exercises in the cathedral: tear gas, stink bombs, secret torments being prepared in secret basement laboratories. A group of campus militants, Students for a Restructured University, who had broken with the SDS leadership in the strike because they felt that the SDS was more concerned with off-campus than campus affairs, announced their boycott of Commencement in the cathedral; they would hold their own counter-Commencement in front of Low Library, its traditional location. Various members of the faculty, speaking for general faculty sentiment, pleaded with the administration to call off the exercises altogether—the University was in disruption, why ask for further disorder, why not simply announce the uncelebrated end of a miserable year? But the administration refused; letters were by now pouring in from "loyal" alumni, demanding that the administration stand firm, and the administration reassured alumni that it would no longer yield to illegal pressure. However, Class Day, the most intimate ceremony of College graduation, was called off when the marshals of the senior class informed the dean that they did not wish it to be held. And in recognition of the hostility directed to him as symbol of the hated authority, President Kirk yielded his traditional role as Commencement speaker to a member of the faculty, Professor Richard Hofstadter, the distinguished historian, whose acceptance of the assignment required, in the circumstances, a not inconsiderable courage.

One prayed for the rain one had always prayed against on other Commencements. The day was beautiful and full of promise. Or could it be threat? There was threat, surely, in the tight clusters of students one saw at various points of the campus that early afternoon, talking to each other all too earnestly, all too conspiratorially. And what except protection against threat could be implied by the big unfamiliar buses waiting on 114th Street at the entrance to Ferris Booth Hall and again on Morningside Drive at the entrance to the Faculty Club? The honored guests of the University, including those who were to receive honorary degrees, were lunching in Ferris Booth, their wives in the Faculty Club—the buses would transport them the few short sunny streets to the cathedral. Everywhere there were police; the control van that had been set up near the Amsterdam Avenue gates to the campus was well staffed. A faculty wife had urged on her reluctant husband

and his friends their own protection in the cathedral: little pocket flasks of water in which to soak their handkerchiefs should tear gas be used. The offer was made as if in joke but the situation was no more one of fun than of morbid fantasy: one doubts there were many of the faculty who marched into the cathedral that afternoon who expected the exercises to go off without incident or even actual physical assault. I can suppose that most of them, like Mailer marching on the Pentagon, marched in fear—but here, of course, they had not themselves provoked the danger. They marched nevertheless, in what must have been larger number than ever before at a Columbia Commencement. A university lived, badly weakened: they wished to be present at the ceremony of its continuing life. For this day differences of opinion about what should or should not have been done in the previous weeks must be buried, wounds must seem to be healed, rifts closed. If one had sufficient dissent from the living University, one stayed away or even went to the counter-Commencement—some few professors made this latter choice but they were not many, nor did anyone I know go out of his way to discover who they were. The division had dignity.

Mailer, too, sees life in ceremony. He contrives ceremony out of each existential moment of his experience, his art out of their sum. But much of the ambiguousness of *The Armies of the Night* stems from the strange compound of innocence and non-innocence he took with him to the ceremonies at the Pentagon or, at any rate, brings to their report. There is innocence, one feels, in his love for America and much boldness in its statement; it is no longer easy to state one's love of country. But surely there is no innocence in his flamboyant invention—it makes a rousing little chapter in the book—of the "grandmother with the orange hair," gone mad with lust and greed who is made to represent an America gone mad with greed, feeding dead Vietnamese babies into the slot machine of its imperial gamble. This is uncommonly gifted radical propaganda but too little complex for truth and therefore less than truth, a subversion, really, of truth. There is innocence in his love for the God of the Christian ethic, and its statement too takes courage, for it is also no longer easy to speak of one's imagination of God. But there is no innocence in suggesting a connection in the life of spirit between the Christian effort to improve the condition of man on earth and the hippie effort—Mailer describes it marvelously—to levitate the Pentagon, between Christ risen and the Pentagon raised. This is befuddling literary ecumenicism. And although there is innocence in Mailer's hope of rest and peace for mankind and an end to irrational violence, there is no innocence—how can there be in so conscious an intelligence as his?—in proposing this hope in circumstances where reasonableness is flouted and impulse sanctioned. The same ambiguousness, or defect in thought of course exists in whoever was witness to the disturbances at Columbia but could still propose that the insurrectionary undertaking was a good thing, necessary in order to shove our society toward greater reasonableness and peace.

I had no ticket to St. John the Divine but as the Commencement procession began to form I stood for a moment at the University gate on Amsterdam Avenue, listening for sounds of assault upon the march just as, six weeks earlier, I had listened for the sound of Harlem rushing upon our white island. Then I moved homeward across the campus, pausing briefly at the counter-Commencement gathering at the feet of the statue Alma Mater on the steps of Low Library. Here the crowd was not large, smaller than I had foreseen, and it was entirely pacific, unduly quiet, in fact; not depressed exactly, or sober, but dispirited. The students looked lost or deprived, as if left over from a festivity which even at its height had been disappointing. But this festivity had not yet begun; perhaps later it would be livelier. I tried to see the notables of this occasion of protest—the counterspeakers were to be Dwight Macdonald, critic; Dr. Erich Fromm, psychoanalyst; and Harold Taylor, former president of Sarah Lawrence. I especially wanted to see Macdonald and if possible exchange a friendly word because we had had an unhappy correspondence and telephone conversation as a result of his appeal for funds for the SDS. He was not in sight—later I was to hear that he, like Chomsky at one of the panel discussions, had been booed for certain portions of his speech: perhaps he had introduced a modification of the SDS position and thus breached the solidarity that the revolution demands of its sympathizers. I decided to go home to my good old standby, WKCR.

But my radio knew the time of day better than I did. It had done its full stint and would be pushed no further: I could coax no sound from it.

Too restless to stay indoors, I walked to the Riverside Church where the overflow from the cathedral was to assemble. I don't know what I had supposed would constitute an overflow from St. John the Divine but certainly I was not prepared for a big church filled, every seat taken in row after sober row—here indeed were the faces of sobriety and even pain, the faces of mothers and fathers separated (by what distance? only the distance of a half-dozen city blocks?) from their graduating young, having their parental epiphany, the ceremony of their accomplished motherhood and fatherhood, by closed-circuit radio. The loudspeaker was very clear, at moments it ebbed in volume, then again swelled, but it was never loud or brash: it was as if the mechanics of the occasion were sensible of moderation, gravity. I stood at the back of the nave and heard report of the last of the faculty and student procession filing into St. John the Divine—what a long line it must have been and with what measured pace it must have moved! Then there was the invocation.

The presentation of degrees. The speech of Richard Hofstadter. He spoke with a luminous simplicity of the meaning and purpose of a university and of how change must come to it by means which would preserve, not destroy, the good it stood for in our world—it might be that the good the university stood for was the best we knew in our faulty world. And these parents who listened to him without seeing him, these mothers in their nicest summer dresses, these fathers who had taken off the day so that they might see their children in this moment of fulfillment (had it been awkward for them at their work, had there been laughter as they explained that they must be free to see their sons graduate from Columbia? What Columbia?) listened to his speech as one must doubt they had ever before listened in a church. The pulpit was empty, the ceremony was an achievement of technology in our despised tech-nological society, but education was addressing the congregation. And for most of us education is still sacred, for where else in this modern universe of ours, unless to education, are we to look for our continuing civilization, where else do we issue our passports to enlightenment? Nothing interrupted the speech these parents wanted to hear. When I learned, later, that just before the Commencement address some of the graduating students and a dozen or more of the faculty had risen in their places and walked out of St. John the Divine, away from their "illegitimate" ceremonies, I was surprised. From the broadcast in the Riverside Church one knew of no disturbance of even this token kind; there had been only silence and the calm voice of reason. The emotions of the long spring weeks finally overcame me and I began to cry.

Ron Padgett

'64 COLUMBIA COLLEGE

Poet, translator, and editor Ron Padgett served for many years as publications director for the Teachers and Writers Collaborative in New York City. "A champion of the American language and experience" in the words of The New York Times Book Review, *Padgett has written or co-written more than two dozen poetry collections, including 2002's* You Never Know. *He was editor-in-chief of the three-volume set* World Poets *(2000). Here he remembers the late Kenneth Koch, a longtime Columbia professor.*

GOETHE

When Kenneth Koch
picked up a black camel
so neatly with his fingertips
and held it to the light—
yellow and red plaid,
and several dozen of those jackets please—
the face of the earth
had shadowy clouds over it,
tall hay waving in the wind
and pleasant adjectives alongside the brook.
Some airplanes appeared
but they were only one inch long
and so far away you have to smile
because some yellow triangles
have entered the air,
sent by the goddess of Geometry,
and whose figures are transparent
like our souls, sort of existing
and not existing at the same time.

Edward Koren

'57 COLUMBIA COLLEGE

The distinctive, fuzzy characters of artist Edward Koren have appeared in The New Yorker *for many years. An art professor at Brown University since 1977, Koren is also a writer, sculptor, and painter. This drawing first appeared in the Fall 2003 issue of* Columbia *magazine.*

The Arts at Columbia: Questions Learned

Acknowledgments

Auster: Excerpt from *Moon Palace*. Copyright © 1989 by Paul Auster. Reprinted by permission of Viking Penguin, a division of Penguin Group (USA) Inc.

Barzun: Excerpt from *Teacher in America*. Copyright 1944, 1945 by Jacques Barzun. Reprinted by permission of Writers' Representatives, LLC, New York, NY. All rights reserved.

Berryman: "In and Out" from *Collected Poems 1937–1971*, edited by Charles Thornbury. Copyright © 1989 by Kate Douglas Berryman. Reprinted by permission of Farrar, Strauss & Giroux, LLC, and Faber and Faber, Ltd.

Brown: Excerpt from *The Dean Meant Business*. Copyright © 1983 by Courtney C. Brown. Reprinted by permission of Columbia University.

Buchanan: Excerpt from *Right from the Beginning*. Copyright © 1988 by Patrick Buchanan. Reprinted by permission of Little, Brown and Company (Inc.).

Butler: Excerpt from *Across the Busy Years: Recollections and Reflections I*. Copyright 1935, 1936, 1939 by Nicholas Murray Butler. Reprinted by permission of Scribner, a division of Simon & Schuster Adult Publishing Group.

Cerf: Excerpt from *At Random: The Reminiscences of Bennett Cerf*. Copyright © 1977 by Random House, Inc. Reprinted by permission of Random House, Inc.

Chambers: Excerpt from *Witness*. Copyright © 1952 by Whittaker Chambers. Reprinted by permission of Random House, Inc. and John Chambers.

Chargaff: Excerpt from *Heraclitean Fire: Sketches from a Life before Nature*, pp. 64–82. Copyright © 1978 by Erwin Chargaff. Reprinted by permission of The Rockefeller University Press.

Douglas: Excerpt from *Go East, Young Man: The Early Years: The Autobiography of William O. Douglas*. Copyright © 1974 by William O. Douglas. Reprinted by permission of Random House, Inc. and The Joy Harris Literary Agency.

Edman: Excerpt from *Philosopher's Holiday*. Copyright 1938 by Irwin Edman. Reprinted by permission of Viking Penguin, a division of Penguin Group (USA) Inc.

Eisenhower: Excerpt from *At Ease: Stories I Tell My Friends*. Copyright © 1967 by Dwight D. Eisenhower. Reprinted by permission of Doubleday, a division of Random House, Inc.

Erskine: Excerpt from *The Memory of Certain Persons*. Copyright 1947 by John Erskine. Reprinted by permission of HarperCollins Publishers, Inc.

Frankel: Excerpts from *The Times of My Life and My Life with The Times*. Copyright © 1999 by Max Frankel. Reprinted by permission of Random House, Inc. and Gelfman Schneider Literary Agents, Inc. This work is available in paperback from Delta/Random House, Inc.

Gildersleeve: Excerpts from *Many a Good Crusade: Memoirs of Virginia Crocheron Gildersleeve.* Copyright 1954 by Virginia C. Gildersleeve. Reprinted by permission of Simon & Schuster Adult Publishing.

Gordon: Excerpts from *Seeing Through Places: Reflections on Geography and Identity.* Copyright © 2000 by Mary Gordon. Reprinted by permission of Scribner, a division of Simon & Schuster Adult Publishing.

Heilbrun: Excerpt from *When Men Were the Only Models We Had: My Teachers Barzun, Fadiman, Trilling.* Copyright © 2002 by Carolyn G. Heilbrun. Reprinted by permission of the University of Pennsylvania Press.

Hollander: "West End Blues" from *Selected Poetry.* Copyright © 1993 by John Hollander. Reprinted by permission of Alfred A. Knopf, a division of Random House, Inc.

Hook: Excerpt from *Out of Step: An Unquiet Life in the 20th Century* (New York: Harper & Row, 1987). Copyright © 1987 by Sidney Hook. Reprinted by permission of Writers' Representatives, LLC, New York, NY. All rights reserved.

Hurston: *Letters from Zora Neale Hurston: A Life in Letters,* edited by Carla Kaplan. Copyright © 2002 by Carla Kaplan. Letters copyright © by The Estate of Zora Neale Hurston via the Victoria Sanders Literary Agency.

Kerouac: Excerpt from *Vanity of Duluoz: An Adventurous Education,* 1935–46 (New York: Putnam, 1979). Copyright © 1968 by Jack Kerouac. Reprinted by permission of SLL/Sterling Lord Literistic, Inc.

Koren: Cartoon from *Columbia* magazine (Fall 2003). Copyright © 2003 by Edward Koren. Reprinted with the permission of Edward Koren. All rights reserved.

Kunen: Excerpt from *The Strawberry Statement: Notes of a College Revolutionary* (New York: Random House, 1969). Copyright © 1968 by James Simon Kunen. Reprinted by permission of SLL/Sterling Lord Literistic, Inc.

Lapidus: Excerpt from *Too Much is Never Enough.* Copyright © 1996 by Morris Lapidus. Reprinted by permission of Rizzoli International Publications, Inc.

Lehman: "April 2" and "June 8" from *The Daily Mirror.* Copyright © 2000 by David Lehman. Reprinted by permission of Scribner, a division of Simon & Schuster Adult Publishing.

Luening: Excerpts from *The Odyssey of an American Composer: The Autobiography of Otto Luening.* Copyright © 1980 by Otto Luening. Reprinted by permission of the Otto Luening Trust.

Mead: Excerpt from *Blackberry Winter: My Earlier Years.* Copyright © 1972 by Margaret Mead. Reprinted by permission of HarperCollins Publishers, Inc. This excerpt includes Edna St. Vincent Millay: Excerpt from "Second Fig" from *Collected Poems.* Copyright 1928, © 1955 by Edna St. Vincent Millay and Norma Millay Ellis. Reprinted by permission of Elizabeth Barnett, literary executor.

Merton: Excerpt from *The Seven Storey Mountain.* Copyright 1948 by Harcourt, Inc. Reprinted by permission of Harcourt, Inc., and Curtis Brown, Ltd.

Meyer: Excerpt from *Barnard Beginnings.* Copyright 1935 by Annie Nathan Meyer. Reprinted by permission of Houghton Mifflin Company. All rights reserved.

Morris: Excerpts from *A Threshold in the Sun* (New York: Harper & Brothers, 1943). Copyright 1943 by Lloyd R. Morris. Reprinted by permission.

Padgett: "Goethe" from *The Big Something (Great Barrington: The Figures, 1990).* Copyright © 1990 by Ron Padgett. Reprinted by permission of the author.

About the Editor

Ashbel Green is vice president and senior editor at Alfred A. Knopf, where he has worked since 1964. He is a 1950 graduate of Columbia College and also holds an M.A. in Eastern European History from the University. Green has edited books by George Bush, Walter Cronkite, Andrei Sakharov, and Gabriel García Márquez, among many others.